A Monetary and Political History of the Phoenician City of Byblos

HISTORY, ARCHAEOLOGY, AND CULTURE OF THE LEVANT

Edited by

JEFFREY A. BLAKELY *University of Wisconsin, Madison*
K. LAWSON YOUNGER *Trinity Evangelical Divinity School*

1. *The Horsemen of Israel: Horses and Chariotry in Monarchic Israel (Ninth–Eighth Centuries* B.C.E.*)*, by Deborah O'Daniel Cantrell
2. *Donkeys in the Biblical World: Ceremony and Symbol*, by Kenneth C. Way
3. *The Wilderness Itineraries: Genre, Geography, and the Growth of Torah*, by Angela R. Roskop
4. *Temples and Sanctuaries from the Early Iron Age Levant: Recovery after Collapse*, by William E. Mierse
5. *Poetic Astronomy in the Ancient Near East: The Reflexes of Celestial Science in the Literature of Ancient Mesopotamia, Ugarit, and Israel*, by Jeffrey L. Cooley.
6. *A Monetary and Political History of the Phoenician City of Byblos in the Fifth and Fourth Centuries* B.C.E., by J. Elayi and A. G. Elayi

A Monetary and Political History of the Phoenician City of Byblos

in the Fifth and Fourth Centuries B.C.E.

J. Elayi and A. G. Elayi

Winona Lake, Indiana
Eisenbrauns
2014

www.eisenbrauns.com

Library of Congress Cataloging-in-Publication Data

Elayi, Josette.
A monetary and political history of the Phoenician city of Byblos in the fifth–fourth centuries B.C.E. / J. Elayi and A. G. Elayi.
pages cm.—(History, archaeology, and culture of the Levant ; 6)
Includes bibliographical references and indexes.
ISBN 978-1-57506-304-1 (hardback : alkaline paper)
1. Byblos (Extinct city)—History. 2. Byblos (Extinct city)—Economic conditions. 3. Byblos (Extinct city)—Politics and government. 4. Money—Lebanon—Byblos (Extinct city)—History. 5. Coins, Phoenician—Lebanon—Byblos (Extinct city)—Catalogs. 6. Numismatics, Phoenician. 7. Inscriptions, Phoenician. 8. Art, Phoenician. 9. Byblos (Extinct city)—History, Military. I. Elayi, A. G. II. Title.
DS89.B9E53 2014
939.4′4—dc23

2014011325

The paper used in this publication meets the minimum requirements of the American National Standard for Information Sciences—Permanence of Paper for Printed Library Materials, ANSI Z39.48-1984.♾™

Contents

Acknowledgments

As usual when we compile a body of work on coins (the corpus), we contacted all the curators of public numismatic collections who were likely to have coins from Byblos. We received four sorts of answers: positive answers, negative answers about the Byblian coins, no answer at all, and one answer refusing access to the collection, which was especially difficult to understand because it was the collection of the National Museum of Beirut. On the other hand, some curators had to be omitted here because we were unable to read their signature and, in some cases, we could not order their photographs because we had no grant.

Our thanks go to the numerous persons all over the world during the last 25 years who helped us to expand this corpus of coins—all in different ways: our colleagues who gave us photographs and information, the curators of public collections who sent us casts and photographs, the private collectors and professional numismatists who allowed us to study their coins and provided us with information.

We are especially indebted to M. Amandry (Cabinet des Médailles, Bibliothèque de France, Paris), M. Kampmann (formerly of the Maison Platt, Paris), A. Lemaire (École Pratique des Hautes Études, IVe section, Paris), G. Le Rider (Institut de France, Paris) and P. Naster (Université Catholique, Louvain-la-Neuve).

Valuable assistance was also offered by: H. Bartlett Wells (Lexington, Massachusetts), A. Davesne (CNRS, Paris), A. Destrooper-Georgiades (École Française d'Athènes), D. Gedalje (La monnaie de Paris), H. Gitler (Israel Museum, Jerusalem), B. Gouyon (La monnaie de Paris), É. Gubel (Musées Royaux d'Art et d'Histoire, Brussels), F. L. Kovacs (San Mateo, CA), B. Métivier (Muséum National d'Histoire Naturelle, Paris), L. Mildenberg (Leu Numismatik, Zurich), M. Prieur (Paris), S. Qedar (Jerusalem), N. Shahaf (Haifa), H. Voegtli (Basel), J.-F. Voisin (Muséum National d'Histoire Naturelle, Paris), and C. Walker (British Museum, London).

Finally, we thank the curators of public collections of museums and institutions, without whose help our work could not have been completed:

Those who replied positively and gave us access to their collections:

- Athens, Greece: Nomismatico Mouseio (M. Oeconomides)
- Beirut, Lebanon: American University of Beirut Museum (L. Badre)
- Berlin, Germany: Staatliche Museum (H.-D. Schultz, S. Schultz, and B. Weisser)
- Bologna, Italy: Museo Civico Archeologico (L. Canali)
- Boston, Massachusetts: Museum of Fine Arts (M. B. Comstock)
- Brussels, Belgium: Bibliothèque Royale Albert Ier, Cabinet des Médailles (J. Lallemand and F. de Callataÿ)
- Cambridge, England: Fitzwilliam Museum (T. Volk)
- Copenhagen, Denmark: Nationalmuset (A. Kromann and J. Zahle)
- Leiden, Netherlands: Rijksmuseum, Het Koninklijk Penningkabinet (J. P. A. van der Vin)
- London, England: British Museum, Department of Coins (M. J. Price and U. Wartenberg)
- Munich, Germany: Staatliche Münzsammlung (D. Klose)
- New York, New York: American Numismatic Society (C. Arnold-Biucchi and N. Waggoner)
- Oxford, England: Ashmolean Museum, Heberden Coin Room (C. J. Howgego)
- Paris, France: Bibliothèque de France, Cabinet des Médailles (M. Amandry, D. Gérin, and H. Nicolet-Pierre)
- Rome, Italy: Bibliotheca Apostolica Vaticana, Medagliere Vaticano (G. Alteri)
- Stockholm, Sweden: Royal Coin Cabinet, National Museum of Monetary History (U. Westermark)
- Tel Aviv, Israel: Kadman Numismatic Museum (A. Kindler)
- Vienna, Austria: Kunsthistorisches Museum, Sammlung von Medaillen, Münzen und Geldzeichen (G. Dembski)

Those who gave negative answers because their collections did not contain Byblian coins:

- Aachen, Germany: Museen der Stadt (E. G. Grimme)
- Aberdeen, Scotland: Anthropological Museum, Marischal College (C. Hunt)
- Amman, Jordan: Archaeological Museum (F. Zayadine)
- Amorbach, Germany: Fürstlich Leiningensche Verwaltung (D. Oswald)
- Ann Arbor, Michigan: University of Michigan, Kelsey Museum of Ancient and Mediaeval Archaeology (M. Cool Root)
- Antioch, Turkey: Archaeological Museum (through A. Davesne)
- Avellino, Italy: Museo Irpino (C. Grella)
- Baltimore, Maryland: Johns Hopkins University (S. Tripp)
- Barcelona, Spain: Gabinet Numismàtic de Catalunya (M. Campo)
- Basel, Switzerland: Historiches Museum (B. Schärli)
- Beirut, Lebanon: Museum of University Saint Joseph (L. Nordiguian)
- Berkeley, England: Lowie Museum of Anthropology (T. Babineau and F. A. Norick)
- Bienne, Switzerland: Museum Schwab (M. Bourquin)
- Birmingham, England: Museum and Art Gallery (D. Simons)
- Bonn, Germany: Akademisches Kunstmuseum der Universität (C. Grunwald)

- Bratislava, Slovakia: Slovenské Národné Múseum (E. Minarovičová)
- Brescia, Italy: Civici Musei d'arte e storia (B. Passamani)
- Brindisi, Italy: Museo Archeologico Provinciale (B. Sciarra)
- Bristol, England: Museum and Art Gallery (J. Steward)
- Bryn Mawr, Pennsylvania: Bryn Mawr College (L. Houghtalin)
- Budapest, Hungary: Magyar Nemzeti Múzeum (M. Torbágyi)
- Cambridge, Massachusetts: Harvard University, Sackler Museum (A. Kromann and J. Zalhe)
- Cardiff, Wales: National Museum of Wales (E. M. Besly and G. B. Boon)
- Cleveland, Ohio: Cleveland Museum of Art (A. P. Kozloff)
- Copenhagen, Denmark: Ny Carlsberg Glyptotek (F. Johansen)
- Detroit, Michigan: National Bank of Detroit (L. M. Stark)
- Dresden, Germany: Staatliche Kunstsammlungen, Münzkabinett (P. Arnold)
- Dublin, Ireland: University of Dublin, Weingreen Museum of Biblical Antiquities (J. R. Bartlett)
- Dunedin, New Zealand: University of Otago (C. Ehrhardt)
- Frankfurt/Main, Germany: Historisches Museum (M. Caspers and G. Förschner)
- Frankfurt/Main: Johann Wolfgang Goethe-Universität (H. Schubert)
- Frankfurt/Main: Museum für Vor- und Frühgeschichte, Archäologisches Museum (D. Antzinger)
- Geneva, Switzerland: University of Geneva (R. F. Stucky)
- Gent, Belgium: Rijkuniversiteit, Centrale Bibliotheek (G. Milis-Proost)
- Gotha, Germany: Museen der Stadt Gotha, Schlossmuseum, Münzkabinett (W. Steguweit and U. Wallenstein)
- Graz, Austria: Landes-Museum Joanneum Graz (O. Burböck)
- Haifa, Israel: Dagon Museum (R. Hecht)
- Haifa, Israel: National Maritime Museum (N. Kashtan)
- Hanover, Germany: Kestner-Museum (F. Berger)
- Helsinki, Finland: Coin Cabinet, Museovirasto (T. Talvio)
- Istanbul, Turkey: Istanbul Arkeoloji Müzeleri Müdürlüğü, Kültür ve Turizm Bakanliği (N. Olcay and A. Pasinli)
- Jerusalem, Israel: Hebrew University, Institute of Archaeology (D. P. Barag)
- Jerusalem: Israel Museum, Department of Coins (Y. Meshorer and H. Gitler)
- Jerusalem: Rockefeller Museum (A. Sussmann)
- Karlsruhe, Germany: Badisches Landesmuseum (P.-H. Martin)
- Kassel, Germany: Staatliche Kunstsammlungen (P. Geroki)
- Kibbutz Hanita Museum, Israel (through A. Lemaire)
- Klagenfurt, Germany: Landesmuseum für Kärnten (F. Glazer)
- Koblenz, Germany: Mittlerhein-Museum
- Cologne, Germany: Römisch-Germanisches Museum (F. Naumann)
- Krakow, Poland: Muzeum Naradowe, Gabinet Numizmatyczny (J. Bezwinska and J. Bodzek)
- Lausanne, Switzerland: Cabinet des Médailles du canton de Vaud (A. Geiser)
- Leipzig, Germany: Karl-Marx-Universität Universitätsbibliothek (R. Jäger)
- Liège, Belgium: Musée Curtius (L. Engen)
- Lisbon, Portugal: Museum of the Foundation Calouste Gulbenkian (M. C. Hipolito)

- Liverpool, England: Liverpool Museum (C. Longworth and A. R. Millard)
- Lund, Sweden: Lunds Universitets, Historika Museum
- Luxembourg: Musée d'état, Cabinet des Médailles (R. Weiller)
- Madrid, Spain: Museo Arqueológico Nacional, Departamento de Numismática y Medallistica (C. Alfaro Asins)
- Mainz, Germany: Städtisches Münzkabinett (Dr. Falck)
- Manchester, England: University, Manchester Museum (K. Sugden)
- Milan, Italy: Castello Sforzesco, Gabinetto Numismatico (R. Martini)
- Munster, Germany: Westfälisches Landesmuseum für Kunst und Kulturgeschichte (P. Ilisch)
- Naples, Italy: Medagliere del Museo Nazionale (E. Pozzi)
- Newcastle, England: University of Newcastle upon Tyne (D. A. Spawforth)
- Nicosia, Cyprus: Archaeological Museum (I. Nicolaou)
- North Terrace, Australia: Art Gallery of South Australia (B. Fargher)
- Oslo, Norway: Universitetet, Myntkabinettet (H. Ingvaldsen and J. H. Nordbø)
- Padua, Italy: Museo Bottacin (A. Saccocci)
- Palermo, Italy: Museo Archeologico Regionale (C. A. di Stefano)
- Paris: Institut Catholique, Musée Bible et Terre Sainte (J. Briend)
- Perpignan, France: Musée de Numismatique J. Puig (J. Joussemet)
- Philadelphia, Pennsylvania: University Museum of Archaeology/Anthropology (J. B. Klein and D. G. Romano)
- Prague, Czech Republic: Narodni Muzeum (J. Haskova and K. Kurz)
- Princeton, New Jersey: Princeton University Libraries (B. E. Levy)
- Providence, Rhode Island: Brown University, Center for Old World Archaeology and Art (R. Holloway)
- Ravenna, Italy: Museo Nazionale, Medagliere (F. Zurli)
- Rome, Italy: Medagliere dei Musei Capitolini (L. Travaini)
- Rome: Museo di Villa Giulia (P. Pelagatti)
- Rome: Museo Nazionale Romano (S. Balbi de Caro)
- Saint Louis, Missouri: Saint Louis Art Museum (S. M. Goldstein)
- São Paulo, Brazil: Museu de Arqueologia e Etnologia da Universidade de São Paulo (M. B. Borba Florenzano)
- Sassari, Italy: Medagliere del Museo Nazionale G. A. Sanna (F. Lo Schiavo)
- Seville, Spain: Museo de l'Ayuntamiento
- Sofia, Bulgaria: Archaeological Institut (K. Dimitrov)
- Szczecin, Poland: Muzeum Naradowe (W. Filipowiak)
- Toronto, Canada: Royal Ontario Museum (A. H. Easson)
- Turin, Italy: Museo Civico (A. S. Fava and S. Pennestri)
- Vienna, Austria: Universität Wien, Institut für Numismatik (W. Szaivert)
- Wageningen, Netherlands: Gelderse Archaelogische Stichting
- Washington, D.C.: Smithsonian Institution, National Museum of History and Technology, Numismatic Department (D. G. Mitten and E. Clain-Stefanelli)
- Warsaw, Poland: Museum Narodowe (A. Krzyzanowska)
- Winterthur, Switzerland: Münzkabinett der Stadt Winterthur (C. Zindel)
- York, England: Yorkshire Museum (M. Mays)
- Zagreb, Republic of Croatia: Arkheološki Muzej (I. Mirnik)
- Zurich, Switzerland: Musée National Suisse (H.-U. Geiger)

We did not receive an answer from the following museums and institutions:

- Alexandria, Egypt: Greek-Roman Museum, Department of Coins and Medals
- Charleville-Mézières, France: Musée de l'Ardenne
- Damascus, Syria: National Archaeological Museum
- Geneva, Switzerland: Art Museum, Department of Coins
- Stuttgart, Germany: Württembergisches Landesmuseum
- Tehran, Iran: National Museum
- Valetta, Malta: Archaeological Museum

We were not allowed to consult the following collection:

- Beirut, Lebanon: Beirut National Museum

Abbreviations

Note: The abbreviations used for journals and books are from the standard lists of the *SBL Handbook of Style* (ed. P. H. Alexander et al.; Peabody, MA, 1999); other abbreviations used in this volume are spelled out here.

General

AM	Ashmolean Museum
ANS	American Numismatic Society
ArchM	Archaeological Museum
AUB	American University of Beirut
BM	British Museum
BNF	Bibliothèque Nationale de France
cent.	century
CH	Coin Hoards
chap(s).	chapter(s)
cm	centimeter(s)
col(s).	column(s)
coll.	collection
ed(s).	editor(s), edited by
fig(s).	figure(s)
FM	Fitzwilliam Museum
F.O.T.	fractions of a 12th-shekel (see p. 78 for precise definitions)
g	gram(s)
h	hour(s) of arc
IDAM	Israel Department of Antiquities and Museums
KHM	Kunst Historisches Museum
KNM	Kadman Numismatic Museum
m	meter(s)
MFA	Museum of Fine Art
mm	millimeter(s)
n(n).	note(s)
NatMus	Nationalmuset
NM	National Museum
no(s).	number(s)
NomM	Nomismatiko Mouseio
n.s.	new series
O	obverse side of coin
p(p).	page(s)
pl(s).	plate(s)
R	reverse side of coin
RCC	Royal Coin Cabinet
RM	Rijksmuseum, het Koninklijk Penningkabinet
SM	Staatliche Museum

SMS	Staatliche Münzsammlung
TX	identification number of the oldest Byblian hoard found to date
VM	Vatican Museum
vol(s).	volume(s)
ACFP	*Atti del Congresso Internazionale di Studi Fenici e Punici*

Reference Works

AHB	*Ancient History Bulletin*
AIIN	*Annali dell'Istituto Italiano di Numismatica*
AJN	*American Journal of Numismatics*
AncSoc	*Ancient Society*
ANSMN	*American Numismatic Society Museum Notes*
Babelon, *Perses*	E. Babelon. *Catalogue des monnaies grecques de la Bibliothèque Nationale: Les Perses achéménides*. Paris, 1893
Babelon, *Traité*	E. Babelon. *Traité des monnaies grecques et romaines*, part 2/2. Paris, 1910
Baramki, *Coins AUB*	D. Baramki. *The Coins Exhibited in the Archaeological Museum of the American University of Beirut*. Beirut, 1966
BCEN	*Bulletin du Cercle d'Études Numismatiques*
BCH	*Bulletin de Correspondance Hellénique*
BES	*Bulletin of the Egyptological Seminar*
Betlyon, *Coinage of Phoenicia*	J. W. Betlyon. *The Coinage and Mints of Phoenicia: The Pre-Alexandrine Period*. Chico, CA, 1982
BICSSup	Bulletin of the Institute of Classical Studies: Supplement
BMB	*Bulletin du Musée de Beyrouth*
BMC Alexandria	G. F. Hill. *A Catalogue of the Greek Coins in the British Museum: Greek Coins of Alexandria*. London, 1892
BMC Attica, Megaris, Aegina	G. F. Hill. *A Catalogue of the Greek Coins in the British Museum: Greek Coins of Attica, etc.* London, 1888
BMC Caria and Islands	G. F. Hill. *A Catalogue of the Greek Coins in the British Museum: Greek Coins of Caria and Islands*. London, 1897
BMC Cyprus	G. F. Hill. *A Catalogue of the Greek Coins in the British Museum: Greek Coins of Cyprus*. London, 1904
BMC Galatia, Cappadocia and Syria	G. F. Hill. *A Catalogue of the Greek Coins in the British Museum: Greek Coins of Galatia, Cappadocia and Syria*. London, 1899
BMC Ionia	G. F. Hill. *A Catalogue of the Greek Coins in the British Museum: Greek Coins of Ionia*. London, 1892
BMC Lycaonia, Isauria, Cilicia	G. F. Hill. *A Catalogue of the Greek Coins in the British Museum: Greek Coins of Lycaonia, Isauria, Cilicia*. London, 1900
BMC Lydia	G. F. Hill. *A Catalogue of the Greek Coins in the British Museum: Greek Coins of Lydia*. London, 1902
BMC Macedonia, etc.	G. F. Hill. *A Catalogue of the Greek Coins in the British Museum: Greek Coins of Macedonia, etc.* London, 1879
BMC Mysia	G. F. Hill. *A Catalogue of the Greek Coins in the British Museum: Greek Coins of Mysia*. London, 1892

BMC Palestine — G. F. Hill. *A Catalogue of the Greek Coins in the British Museum: Greek Coins of Palestine*. London, 1914

BMC Phoenicia — G. F. Hill. *A Catalogue of the Greek Coins in the British Museum: Greek Coins of Phoenicia*. London, 1910

BMC Troas, Aeolis and Lesbos — G. F. Hill. *A Catalogue of the Greek Coins in the British Museum: Greek Coins of Troas, Aeolis and Lesbos*. London, 1894

BSFN — *Bulletin de la Société Française de Numismatique*

Catalogue De Luynes — J. Babelon. *Catalogue de la Collection de Luynes, Monnaies grecques*, vol. 3: *Asie Mineure et Phénicie*. Paris, 1930

Chéhab, *Monnaies* — M. Chéhab. *Monnaies gréco-romaines et phéniciennes du Musée national, Beyrouth, Liban*. Paris, 1977

CRIPEL — *Cahiers de Recherches de l'Institut de Papyrologie et d'Égyptologie de Lille*

DAGR — C. Daremberg and E. Saglio. *Dictionnaire des Antiquités Grecques et Romaines*. 6 vols. Graz, 1962–63

DArch — *Dossiers de l'Archéologie*

Dunand, *Byblos I* — M. Dunand. *Fouilles de Byblos I: 1926–1932*. Paris, 1937

Dunand, *Byblos II* — M. Dunand. *Fouilles de Byblos II: 1933–1938*. Paris, 1958

Elayi, *Byblos* — J. Elayi. *Byblos, cité sacrée (8*^{e}*–4*^{e} *s. av. J.-C.)*. Paris, 2009

Elayi, *Économie* — J. Elayi. *Économie des cités phéniciennes sous l'Empire perse*. Naples, 1990

Elayi, "Phénomène monétaire" — J. Elayi. "Le phénomène monétaire dans les cités phéniciennes à l'époque perse." Pp. 59–76 in *Numismatique et Histoire économiques dans le monde phénico-punique*, ed. T. Hackens and G. Moucharte. Louvain-la-Neuve, 1992

Elayi, *Sidon* — J. Elayi. *Sidon: Cité autonome de l'Empire perse*. 2nd ed. Paris, 1990

Elayi-Elayi, *Coinage of Tyre* — J. Elayi and A. G. Elayi. *The Coinage of the Phoenician City of Tyre in the Persian Period (5th–4th Cent.* BCE*)*. Leuven, 2009

Elayi-Elayi, *Monnayage de Sidon* — J. Elayi and A. G. Elayi. *Le monnayage de la cité phénicienne de Sidon à l'époque perse (V*^{e}*–IV*^{e} *s. av. J.-C.)*. 2 vols. Paris, 2004

Elayi-Elayi, *Poids phéniciens* — J. Elayi and A. G. Elayi. *Recherches sur les poids phéniciens*. Paris, 1997

Elayi-Elayi, *Trésors* — J. Elayi and A. G. Elayi. *Trésors de monnaies phéniciennes et circulation monétaire (V*^{e}*–IV*^{e} *siècles avant J.-C.)*. Paris, 1993

Elayi-Lemaire, *Graffiti* — J. Elayi and A. Lemaire. *Graffiti et contremarques ouest-sémitiques sur les monnaies grecques et proche-orientales*. Milan, 1998

EMC — *Échos du Monde Classique*

Forrer, *Weber Collection* — L. Forrer. *The Weber Collection*. London, 1929

GöMisz — *Göttinger Miszellen*

Head, *A Guide* — B. V. Head. *A Guide to the Principal Coins of the Greeks*. London, 1959

Head, *Historia Numorum* — B. V. Head. *Historia Numorum*. Chicago, 1967 [1st ed.: Oxford, 1887]

ID — *Inscriptions de Délos*

IGCH — M. Thompson et al. *An Inventory of Greek Coin Hoards*. New York, 1973

Imhoof-Blumer, *Choix*	F. Imhoof-Blumer. *Choix de monnaies grecques de la collection de F. Imhoof-Blumer*. 2nd ed. Paris, 1883
Jenkins, *Greek Coins*	G. K. Jenkins. *Ancient Greek Coins*. London, 1972
JIAN	*Journal International d'Archéologie Numismatique*
Jidejian, *Lebanon*	N. Jidejian. *Lebanon and the Greek World*. Beirut, 1988
Jidejian, *Lebanon, Its Gods*	N. Jidejian. *Lebanon: Its Gods, Legends and Myths Illustrated by Coins*. Beirut, 1985
JNG	*Jahrbuch für Numismatik und Geldgeschichte*
JSav	*Journal des Savants*
KAI	H. Donner and W. Röllig. *Kanaanäische und aramäische Inschriften*. Vols. 1–3. Wiesbaden, 1966–69
Klein, *Sammlung*	D. Klein. *Sammlung von Griechischen Kleinsilbermünzen und Bronzen*. Milan, 1999
Kraay, *Greek Coins*	C. M. Kraay. *Archaic and Classical Greek Coins*. London, 1975
Kraay-Hirmer, *Greek Coins*	C. M. Kraay and M. Hirmer. *Greek Coins*. London, 1966
LÄ	W. Helck, E. Otto, and W. Westendorf, eds. *Lexikon der Ägyptologie*. 7 vols. Wiesbaden, 1972–92
MÄS	*Münchner Ägyptologische Studien*
MdI	*Mitteilungen des deutschen archäologische Instituts*
Mildenberg-Hurter, *Dewing Collection*	L. Mildenberg and S. Hurter. *The Arthur S. Dewing Collection of Greek Coins*. New York, 1985
NAC	*Numismatica e Antichità Classiche*
Naster, *Collection de Hirsch*	P. Naster. *La Collection Lucien de Hirsch*. Brussels, 1959
NC	*Numismatic Chronicle*
NNM	*Numismatic Notes and Monographs*
NZ	*Numismatische Zeitschrift*
RAHAL	*Revue des Archéologues et Historiens d'Art de Louvain*
RB	*Revue Biblique*
RBN	*Revue Belge de Numismatique*
RdE	*Revue d'Égyptologie*
RIN	*Rivista Italiana di Numismatica e scienze affini*
RN	*Revue Numismatique*
RSF	*Rivista di studi fenici*
SEAP	*Studi di Egittologia e di Antichità Puniche*
SNG ANS	*Sylloge Nummorum Graecorum ANS: The Burton Y. Berry Collection*. New York, 1961–62
SNG Cambridge	*Sylloge Nummorum Graecorum*, vol. 4: *Fitzwilliam Museum*. Oxford, 1940
SNG Copenhagen	*Sylloge Nummorum Graecorum: The Royal Danish Collection*. 43 vols. Copenhagen, 1942–77
Syr	*Syria*
Trans	*Transeuphratène*
Troxell, *Davis Collection*	H. A. Troxell. *The Norman Davis Collection*. New York, 1969
VDI	*Vestnik Drevnej Istorii*

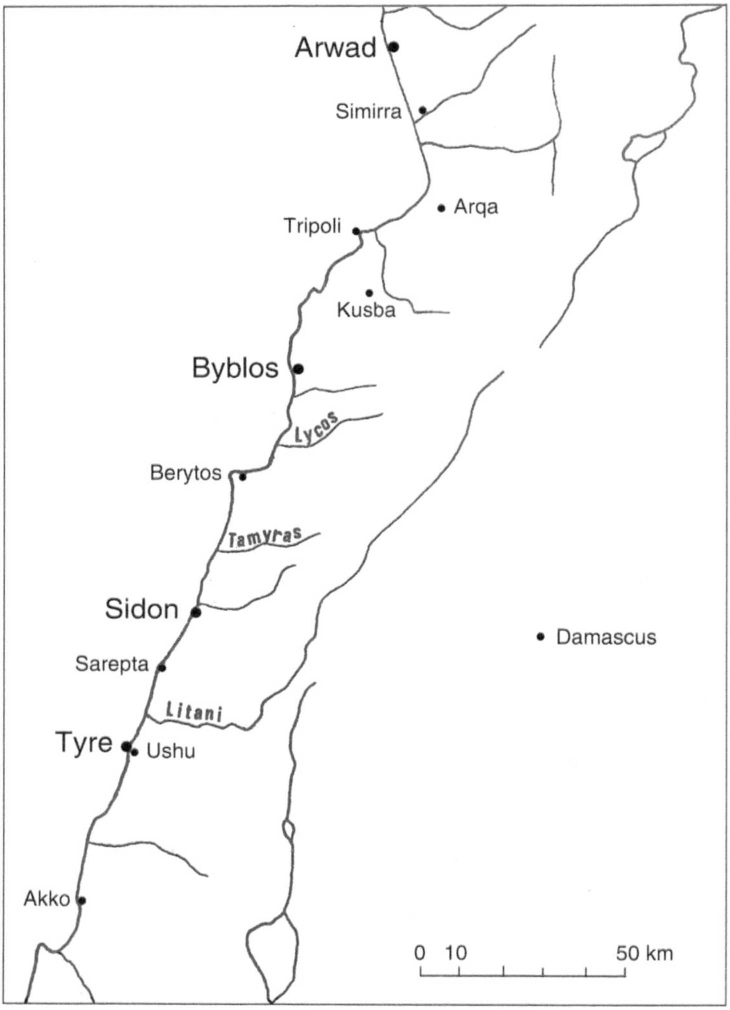

Map. *Byblos in Phoenicia in the Persian period.*

Introduction

There were four main Phoenician mints in the Persian period (map 1): from north to south, the mint at Arwad/*ʾRWD* (now ʾArwād in Syria), Byblos/*GBL* (now Jbeil in Lebanon), Sidon/*ṢDN* (Saida in Lebanon) and Tyre/ṢR (Sour in Lebanon).[1] This book is the third of our four projected monetary and political histories of Phoenician cities under Persian rule[2] before Alexander's conquest of these cities in 333/332 B.C.E. The city-state of Byblos had a territory smaller than that of the other Phoenician cities, bounded as it was to the east by the Lebanon range and to the south by the promontory of the Nahr el-Kelb, and ending as it did in the north before reaching Batroun.[3] The main part of the city was situated on a rocky promontory that reached 28.30 meters at its highest point, and sloped down to mediocre harbors: the small northern harbor (still in use today), Chamiye Bay (a mooring for small boats), and El Skhiny Bay (used mainly by lumber traders).[4]

This book represents a new step of our research on the history of the Phoenician cities in the Persian period before Alexander's conquest of these cities in 333/332 B.C.E. In the first stage of research, in 1990, we provided an overview of their economy under Persian rule.[5] The second stage, in 1993, provided an analysis of all hoards, which included Phoenician coins dating to the Persian period, as well as of coins found in excavations.[6] The third stage, in 1997, was an investigation of Phoenician weights, in which we used an original method that is also suited to numismatic studies: we adapted statistical models to these weights that enabled us to establish cautious but solid foundations for Phoenician metrology.[7] The fourth stage concerns

1. Other Phoenician cities had minted coins during this period, but these mints are not well known: cf. Elayi-Elayi, *Coinage of Tyre*, 7–9.

2. Cf. J. Elayi, "Les cités phéniciennes entre liberté et sujétion," *DHA* 16 (1990) 93–113; idem, "La domination perse sur les cités phéniciennes," in *ACFP* (Rome, 1991) 2:77–85.

3. Idem, *Byblos*, 31–41.

4. Ibid., 41–49. See the project of exploring El Skhiny Bay, following our hypothesis: "À la recherche du port antique de Byblos," *L'Orient-Le Jour*, April 2, 2011 (Lebanese newspaper).

5. Elayi, *Économie*.

6. Elayi-Elayi, *Trésors*.

7. Idem, *Poids phéniciens*.

the monetary and political histories of the four Phoenician cities. The first book, which covered Sidon, was published in 2004;[8] its coinage is the best known and therefore provides chronological benchmarks that can be used for the study of other coinages. The second book, which is about Tyre, was published in 2009;[9] its coinage also provides a number of chronological benchmarks. This (the third) book, on Byblos, lacks such benchmarks. We have selected only the Persian period instead of studying a more complete history of the Byblian mint, because it corresponds to the chronological limits of our research program. Moreover, it is already a major task because 1,662 coins have been assembled in the catalog. Preliminary to the fourth stage of our program, we have devoted many articles to specific numismatic problems, several of them on the Byblian mint: the inauguration date of its coinage,[10] a series of coins with sphinxes and hawks,[11] a series of minute coins,[12] the methodology of iconographic and epigraphic monetary studies,[13] the system of abbreviations,[14] specific problems with regard to the coinage of Byblos,[15] the military symbols represented on these coins,[16] the order of succession of the last three kings of Byblos,[17] and new hoards containing Byblian coins.[18] Thus, our research on the Phoenician cities is part of a larger program on Transeuphratene (the Transeuphrates

8. Elayi-Elayi, *Monnayage de Sidon.*

9. Idem, *Coinage of Tyre.*

10. Elayi, "Phénomène monétaire," 59–76; idem, "L'ouverture du premier atelier monétaire phénicien," *BCEN* 32 (1995) 73–78.

11. Idem, "Les monnaies de Byblos au sphinx et au faucon," *RSF* 11 (1983) 5–17; A. Lemaire and J. Elayi, "Les monnaies de Byblos au sphinx et au faucon: Nouveaux documents et essai de classement," *RBN* 137 (1991) 29–36.

12. J. Elayi, "Une monnaie phénicienne de 0,05g," *RSF* 12 (1985) 1–4.

13. Idem, "Remarques méthodologiques sur l'étude iconographique des monnaies phéniciennes," *MUSJ* 5 (*Mélanges J.-P. Rey-Coquais*; 2006) 47–54; idem, "Étude paléographique des légendes monétaires phéniciennes d'époque perse," *Trans* 5 (1992) 22–24 and 37, table I.

14. J. Elayi and A. G. Elayi, "Systems of Abbreviations Used by Byblos, Tyre and Arwad in Their Pre-Alexandrine Coinages," *JNG* 37–38 (1987–88) 14–18.

15. J. Elayi, "Le monnayage de Byblos avant Alexandre: problèmes et perspectives," *Trans* 1 (1989) 9–20.

16. Idem, "Les symboles de la puissance militaire sur les monnaies de Byblos," *RN* 26 (1984) 40–47.

17. J. Elayi and A. G. Elayi, "L'ordre de succession des derniers rois de Byblos," *Syr* 70 (1993) 109–15.

18. Idem, "Nouveau trésor de monnaies de Byblos (1992)," *RBN* 139 (1993) 17–30; idem, "Nouveaux trésors de monnaies phéniciennes (*CH* VIII)," *Trans* 11 (1996) 95–114; idem, "Nouveaux trésors de monnaies phéniciennes (*CH* IX)," *Trans* 26 (2003) 105–17; idem, "Nouveau trésor de Byblos d'après les archives de H. Seyrig (TLXXXIII)," *Trans* 38 (2009) 65–76; J. Elayi and A. Lemaire, "Le trésor de Byblos TIX," *Trans* 38 (2009) 77–98.

region) during the Persian period[19] and is an indispensable reference for understanding, for example, monetary circulation and trading exchanges in the whole area.

Although they are not as spectacular as the Sidonian double-shekels (28.02 g and 30–35 mm in diameter until 366 B.C.E.), the Byblian shekels of Phoenician standard (13.66–14.21 g and 23–30 mm in diameter) have always interested numismatists, perhaps because of their skillful carving and because they are not very common. Until today, they have almost always been included in Greek numismatics, in spite of their long Phoenician inscriptions.[20] Following the works of J. P. Six,[21] J. Rouvier established the first catalog of Byblian coins, mainly based on his large personal collection.[22] He was a connoisseur of these coins, but the photographs of his publication were not of a good quality, and his collection was scattered. Part of his collection was acquired by the American Numismatic Society in New York through the Newell collection. The Cabinet des Médailles of the Bibliothèque de France in Paris contains several collections of Byblian coins: most of them were listed in the catalogs of E. Babelon in 1893 and 1910, and of J. Babelon in 1930.[23] However, the coins that were acquired on several occasions later on, mainly from the Seyrig collection, are not listed in any catalog. The collection of Byblian coins in the British Museum in London was published by G. F. Hill in 1910.[24] Other museum collections were partially published between 1961 and 1982, such as those of the Nationalmuset in Copenhagen, the American University and National Museum in Beirut, and the American Numismatic Society in New York.[25] However, these books are quite concise compared with the Babelon and Hill catalogs, which remain the primary reference in the absence of a

19. On the Transeuphratene program, cf. J. Elayi and J. Sapin, *Nouveaux regards sur la Transeuphratène* (Brepols, 1991) [*Beyond the River: New Perspectives on Transeuphratene* (JSOTSup 250; Sheffield, 1998)]; idem, *Quinze ans de recherches (1985–2000) sur la Transeuphratène à l'époque perse* (Paris, 2000) 169–70.

20. See, for example, Kraay, *Greek Coins*; C. Morrisson and B. Kluge, eds., *A Survey of Numismatic Research 1990–1995* (Berlin, 1997) 101–2; C. Alfaro and A. Burnett, *A Survey of Numismatic Research 1996–2001* (Madrid, 2003) 151–52.

21. J. P. Six, "Observations sur les monnaies phéniciennes," *NC* n.s. 17 (1877) 127–241.

22. J. Rouvier, "Numismatique des villes de la Phénicie: Gebal-Byblos," *JIAN* 4 (1901) 39–42.

23. E. Babelon, *Perses*; idem, *Traité*; J. Babelon, *Collection de Luynes* (the reader is directed to the list of abbreviations for the complete publication information for these and other abbreviated references in the footnotes of this book). All the other collections are listed in the "Index of Public and Private Collections" at the end of this volume.

24. *BMC Phoenicia*.

25. *SNG Copenhagen* 37 (1961); D. Baramki, *The Coin Collection of the American University of Beirut Museum* (Beirut, 1974); idem, *Coins AUB*; Chéhab, *Monnaies*; Betlyon, *Coinage of Phoenicia*.

corpus of the Byblian coinage. There was an initial wave of specific publications partly related to the coinage of Byblos during the second half of the 19th century, such as those by H. de Luynes, J. Brandis, O. Blau, J. P. Six, and J. Rouvier.[26] The second wave of publication occurred mainly after 1950, including those of P. Naster, W. W. Sheridan, É. Puech, L. Sole, A. Destrooper-Georgiades, H. Gitler, A. Ronde,[27] and us.[28] As for the publications of coins from excavations and sale catalogs, we refer to the six bulletins entitled "Numismatique" by J. Elayi and A. Lemaire, published in the *Transeuphratène* journal, and to the book by J. Elayi and J. Sapin, which includes an analysis of numismatic research and discoveries, especially Byblian coins.[29]

26. H. de Luynes, *Essai sur la numismatique des Satrapes de la Phénicie* (Paris, 1846) 88–92, and pls. 15:41–45; 16:46–48; J. Brandis, *Das Münz-, Mass- und Gewichtswesen in Vorderasien bis auf Alexander den Grossen* (Berlin, 1866) 116–17, 234, 511–12; O. Blau, "ʾAzubal König von Byblos," *NZ* 8 (1876) 231; Six, "Observations sur les monnaies phéniciennes"; Rouvier, "Numismatique des villes de la Phénicie." See also the Byblian coins in general books: Head, *Historia Numorum*, 791; F. Imhoof-Blumer, *Monnaies grecques* (Paris, 1883) 440–41; R. Pietschmann, *Geschichte der Phönizier* (Berlin, 1889) 173; E. Babelon, *Les monnaies grecques: Aperçu historique* (Paris, 1921) 52–53; P. R. Franke and M. Hirmer, *Die Griechische Münzen* (Munich, 1964) pl. 195; Kraay, *Greek Greek Coins*, 289–90.

27. See, however, E. T. Newell, *Some Unpublished Coins of Eastern Dynasts* (NNM 30; New York, 1926) 9–12; P. Naster, "La technique des revers partiellement incus des monnaies phéniciennes," in *Centennial Publications of the American Numismatic Society* (New York, 1958) 503–11; idem, *La Collection Lucien de Hirsch* (Brussels, 1959); idem, "L'ordre de succession des rois de Byblos d'après leurs monnaies," *BSFN* 20 (1965) 478; idem, "Le développement des monnayages phéniciens avant Alexandre, d'après les trésors," in *The Patterns of the Monetary Development in Phoenicia and Palestine in Antiquity—International Numismatic Convention: Jerusalem 1963* (ed. A. Kindler; Jerusalem, 1967) 3–24 [= P. Naster, *Scripta Nummaria: Contributions à la méthodologie numismatique* (Louvain-la-Neuve, 1983) 178–96]; idem, "Trésors de monnaies de Byblos du IVᵉ s. av. J.-C. trouvés à Byblos," in *Numismatique et histoire économique phéniciennes et puniques* (ed. T. Hackens and G. Moucharte; Studia Phoenicia 9; Louvain-la-Neuve, 1992) 41–49; W. W. Sheridan, "From Cyzicus to Tyre: Numismatic Evidence of an Ancient Ship's Trip, circa 400 B.C.," *Numismatist* 8 (1971) 1127–33; É. Puech, "Les premières émissions byblites et les rois de Byblos à la fin du Vᵉ siècle av. J.-C.," in *ACFP* (Rome, 1991) 2:287–98; L. Solé, "Le emissioni monetali della Fenicia prima di Alessandro-I," *SEAP* 16 (1997) 75–125; idem, "Le emissioni monetali della Fenicia prima di Alessandro-II," *SEAP* 18 (1998) 81–147; idem, "Nuove considerazioni sull'unità ponderale della prima serie monetale di Biblo," *Trans* 20 (2000) 61–72; A. Destrooper-Georgiades, in *La civilisation phénicienne et punique. Manuel de recherche* (ed. V. Krings; Leiden, 1995) 150–51; C. Alfaro and A. Burnett, eds., *A Survey of Numismatic Research 1996–2001* (Madrid, 2003) 151–55; A. Ronde, "Étude sommaire de trois 'trésors' proche-orientaux de provenance incertaine," *BSFN* 57/4 (2002) 57–62.

28. See above, nn. 10–18; Elayi, *Byblos*.

29. J. Elayi and A. Lemaire, "Numismatique," *Trans* 1 (1989) 155–59; *Trans* 4 (1991) 119–376; *Trans* 10 (1995) 151–77; *Trans* 17 (1999) 117–41; *Trans* 25 (2003) 65–87; *Trans* 33 (2007) 21–25; Elayi-Sapin, *Nouveaux regards sur la Transeuphratène*, 155–56.

Contrary to the other Phoenician coinages, which are usually anepigraphic or inscribed with abbreviations, most of the coins of Byblos bear the full names of the city and the king. In this respect, P. Naster used to say: "Only the attribution to Gebal/Byblos is certain thanks to the explicit monetary legend which does not need to be interpreted, but just read."[30] However the anepigraphic coins were not easy to attribute to the mint of Byblos. J. Rouvier was the first to suggest that the coins of Group I with the crouched sphinx were struck at Byblos due to their provenance.[31] Yet G. F. Hill and E. Babelon did not include this group in the catalog of Byblian coinage.[32] The attribution of Group I to Byblos is confirmed by the discovery of most of these coins in the territory of Byblos, for example, in hoards TX, TXIII, TXIV, TXV (?), and on the beach by H. Seyrig.[33] The seated sphinx and the lotus flower of Group II seem to be motifs that are similar to Group I's. Other minute, fractional coins are more difficult to attribute to the Byblian mint: the series bearing two heads, one of them wearing a *kausia*, was more likely struck in Byblos than in Arwad because it was discovered on the beach of Byblos.[34] Other attributions to the mint of Byblos are erroneous: for example, that of the coin with a winged lion in hoard TX by J. W. Betlyon, which is a Lycian stater of Tenegures.[35] There was also confusion between the coins of ʿOzbaʿal of Byblos and ʿOzbaʿal of Kition.[36]

This book on the coinage of Byblos is not just a traditional numismatic study; it is also a study of all the other fields of research enlightened by numismatic studies—in particular, epigraphy, iconography, technology, metrology, political and economic history, history of religions, and so on. It allows us to update our book on Phoenician hoards and to establish with greater precision the relations between the metrology of weights and that of coins. It benefits from the first corpus on Sidon and the second corpus on Tyre, and in return will complete the conclusions of those two books.

As usual, an introduction to a corpus of coins must inform the readers about its genesis. We have encountered the same difficulties here as in the

30. Naster, "La technique," 510–11 [= idem, *Scripta Nummaria*, 29]; idem, "Le développement," 3–4 [= idem, *Scripta Nummaria*, 178–179].

31. Rouvier, "Numismatique des villes de la Phénicie," 38, no. 629; Newell, *Some Unpublished Coins*, 9–10; G. K. Jenkins, "Recent Acquisitions of Greek Coins by B.M.," *NC* 19 (1959) 41–42.

32. G. F. Hill (*BMC Phoenicia*, lxv) only quoted Rouvier's suggestion without any comment.

33. Elayi-Elayi, *Trésors*, 87–90, 92–114.

34. Elayi, "Une monnaie phénicienne de 0,05g," 1–4.

35. Betlyon, *Coinage of Phoenicia*, 127 n. 23; Elayi-Elayi, *Trésors*, 88, no. 12; Elayi, *Byblos*, 140.

36. Blau, "ʾAzubal König von Byblos," 230–31.

preceding two works: the wide scattering of the coins in public and private collections all around the world, the bad quality of photographs in many sale catalogs, the sale of the majority of the coins on the antiquities market, the problem of forgeries, the insufficiency of the financial aid provided by the CNRS, and the unjustified refusal of access to the Museum of Beirut's collection.[37] However, some difficulties are specific to Byblos. Unlike the situation at the sites of Sidon and Tyre, the Persian levels in Byblos were largely excavated by M. Dunand between 1926 and 1965.[38] However, these excavations raised several problems: most of them remain unpublished, and the published excavations are difficult to use because of the Dunand method, which was nonstratigraphic.[39] The mentions of coins are rare and scanty. As a matter of fact, M. Dunand was obviously not interested in the discovery of coins. He systematically avoided fractional coins and isolated shekels. He found at least four shekel hoards, which he stored at the National Museum and never published (TIX, TX, TXI, TXX).[40] Byblian hoards from other provenances are also stored in the museum. Although we have been refused access to its collections, we have nonetheless succeeded in publishing two of these hoards (TIX and TLXXXIII) by using Seyrig's archives and photographs provided by other colleagues, with the authorization of R. Doncel, P. Naster, M. Amandry, and A. Lemaire.[41] Another difficulty arose with the plundering of this site during the Lebanese war of 1975–85. Many hoards and coins were unearthed due to the large-scale illicit excavations: "The ruins of Gbayl are the prey of a regular plundering from a few years, with the help of cranes, metal detectors and weapons when necessary."[42] We have tried to study as many as possible of the many coins that are scattered everywhere on the antiquities markets and in public and private collections in Great Britain, the United States, Switzerland, France, Israel, and Belgium. We have succeeded in publishing 20 lots that probably belonged to three different hoards (TXIII, TXIV, TXV?), together with a fourth one.[43] Once again, we have tried to overcome these difficulties as much as possible. We apologize in advance for the deficien-

37. See in detail all these difficulties in Elayi-Elayi, *Coinage of Tyre*, 14–19.

38. Dunand, *Byblos I*; idem, *Byblos II*; and numerous articles published in *BMB*.

39. Cf. P. Leriche, "La méthode de fouille de Maurice Dunand à Byblos, I: M. Dunand et l'archéologie au Proche-Orient au début du XXe siècle," *Topoi* 5 (1995) 439–52; J. Lauffray, "La méthode de fouille de Maurice Dunand à Byblos, II: Introduction à la méthode M. Dunand," ibid., 453–68.

40. Elayi-Elayi, *Trésors*, 83–92.

41. Elayi-Lemaire, "Le trésor de Byblos TIX," 77–98; Elayi-Elayi, *Trésors*, 65–76.

42. *Al-Masira*, January 30, 1988, 62–63 (Lebanese newspaper), quoted by S. Hakimian, "Une archéologie parallèle: Les découvertes clandestines et fortuites au Liban," *Ber* 35 (1987) 201.

43. Elayi-Elayi, *Trésors*, 92–114; idem, "Nouveau trésor de monnaies de Byblos (1992)."

cies caused by concealed documents and information, the impossibility of checking all the coins published in this book, and for any imperfections in presentation due to the lack of financial support. We assume responsibility for any other imperfections that may be present herein.

Chapter 1 begins with the analysis of monetary inscriptions from the point of view of their reading, meaning, and writing. Chapter 2 focuses on iconography in regard to the personal interpretation of the engravers and the minting authority's messages. The aim of chap. 3 is to study the various manufacturing techniques and the functioning of the workshop. In chap. 4, we deal with the metrology of the Byblian coins, its relation to that of the Sidonian and Tyrian coins, to weights, and the place of Byblian metrology in relation to contemporary metrological systems of the ancient Near East. Chapter 5 presents historical conclusions about the city of Byblos drawn from its coinage and other available sources. Four appendixes cover technical topics that had no place in the exposition of the book: a catalog of the coins of Byblos, with directions for use to make it easier to consult (appendix 1); counterfeit or dubious coins (appendix 2); a study of dies and relative chronology (appendix 3); hoards containing Byblian coins (appendix 4).

Chapter 1

Analysis of the Monetary Inscriptions

Incriptions appear more frequently on Byblian coins than on other Phoenician coins, but their appearance is not systematic. As in the Sidonian coinage,[1] the first series of Group I were all anepigraphic. In Group II—which is characterized by an absence of shekels and by four series of denominations—only one (II.2.2) bore an inscription. Group III was again entirely anepigraphic. Then, almost all of the series of Group IV bore one or two inscriptions, except for Series IV.4.7. The alternation of anepigraphic and inscribed series also occurs in the Tyrian coinage.[2] Byblos was the first Phoenician city to mint coins but the second after Tyre to put inscriptions on its coins. Both early Tyrian and Byblian monetary inscriptions are difficult to interpret. The early Tyrian inscriptions seem to be weight indications,[3] but the system is different for the monetary inscriptions of Byblos. In the Tyrian and Sidonian coinages, just as on Aradian coins, two other categories of inscription are found: graffiti and countermarks,[4] which are virtually absent in the coinage of Byblos.

The coinage of Byblos, just as other Phoenician coinages, has always been considered Greek and has been studied using two different approaches. Either the iconography was studied without taking into account the Phoenician inscription (numismatists being ignorant of Semitic languages), or the inscription was studied alone without taking into account the numismatic aspect of the coin (by specialists of West-Semitic scripts). However, even for them, monetary inscriptions have never been considered real epigraphic documents that may be as significant as other sorts of documents that were considered important in their own right.[5] We consider the most scientific approach to entail considering each coin

1. Elayi-Elayi, *Monnayage de Sidon*, 35–55, 437.
2. Idem, *Coinage of Tyre*, 221.
3. Ibid., 225–31.
4. Ibid., 222–24, 238–41; idem, *Monnayage de Sidon*, 453–56; Elayi-Lemaire, *Graffiti.*
5. See, for example, V. Krings, ed., *La civilisation phénicienne et punique: Manuel de recherche* (Leiden, 1990) 205–14 (epigraphic category not considered); compare Elayi, *Sidon*, 49.

as a whole, in all its aspects: first the iconographic, epigraphic (inscription, countermark, and graffito, if any), metrological, and technical aspects; and then the coin's meaning and function. The first study of Byblian monetary inscriptions at the beginning of the 20th century was made by G. F. Hill, who compiled in a table the different written forms found on the coins of the British Museum.[6] More recently, J. B. Peckham studied them, based on Hill's table, as well as the old catalog of E. Babelon and an incomplete publication of a Byblian hoard.[7] Several recent numismatic publications include the study of Semitic monetary inscriptions, and other publications study some specific inscriptions.[8] After a preliminary study of Phoenician monetary inscriptions, including the Byblian inscriptions,[9] we have made basic studies of the Sidonian and Tyrian inscriptions, taking into account a very large number of them, an updated chronology, and the specific context of the script.[10]

1. *The Monetary Inscriptions*

Although the specialists of West-Semitic epigraphy in general do not cover monetary inscriptions, these inscriptions are essential to one's knowledge of Phoenician scripts in the Persian period and their sociocultural contexts. It is all the more necessary because the corpora of Phoenician inscriptions dated to this period are all limited to some extent. The corpus of Byblos for this period is especially small—consisting of about ten inscriptions.[11] Compared with other sorts of inscriptions, a monetary

6. *BMC Phoenicia*, cxlvi.

7. J. B. Peckham, *The Development of the Late Phoenician Scripts* (Cambridge, MA, 1968), esp. pp. 47–50, 71–75; *BMC Phoenicia*; Babelon, *Perses*; Dunand, *Byblos I*, 407–9.

8. For additional sources, see J. Elayi and A. Lemaire, "Numismatique," *Trans* 1 (1989) 155–64; 4 (1991) 119–32; 10 (1995) 151–87; 17 (1999) 117–53; 25 (2003) 63–105; 33 (2007) 23–55; A. Lemaire, in *A Survey of Numismatic Research 1985–1990* (ed. T. Hackens et al.; Brussels, 1991) 151–87; H. Gitler, in *A Survey of Numismatic Research 1990–1995* (ed. A. Burnett et al.; Berlin, 1997) 101–5; idem, in *A Survey of Numismatic Research 1996–2001* (ed. C. Alfaro and A. Burnett; Madrid, 2003) 151–55; P. Naster, "Toponymes en caractères araméens sur les monnaies anatoliennes," *RBN* 134 (1998) 5–17.

9. J. Elayi, "Étude paléographique des légendes monétaires phéniciennes d'époque perse," *Trans* 5 (1992) 24–25; idem, "Remarques méthodologiques sur l'étude paléographique des légendes monétaires phéniciennes," in *Phoinikeia Grammata: Lire et écrire en Méditerranée* (ed. C. Baurain et al.; Namur, 1991) 187–200.

10. Elayi-Elayi, *Monnayage de Sidon*, 437–70; idem, *Coinage of Tyre*, 221–52.

11. For the corpus of Byblian monetary inscriptions, see Elayi, *Byblos*, 13–23, 223–28, 230–33: inscription nos. 1–3, 19, 22 (?), 23–27 (with bibliography). However, about 50 Byblian inscriptions, between one letter and several lines, are scattered in the volumes of excavations published by M. Dunand. Most of them are presented without sufficient elements for dating them. Two other Byblian inscriptions are doubtful: P. Bordreuil, "Artarté, la dame

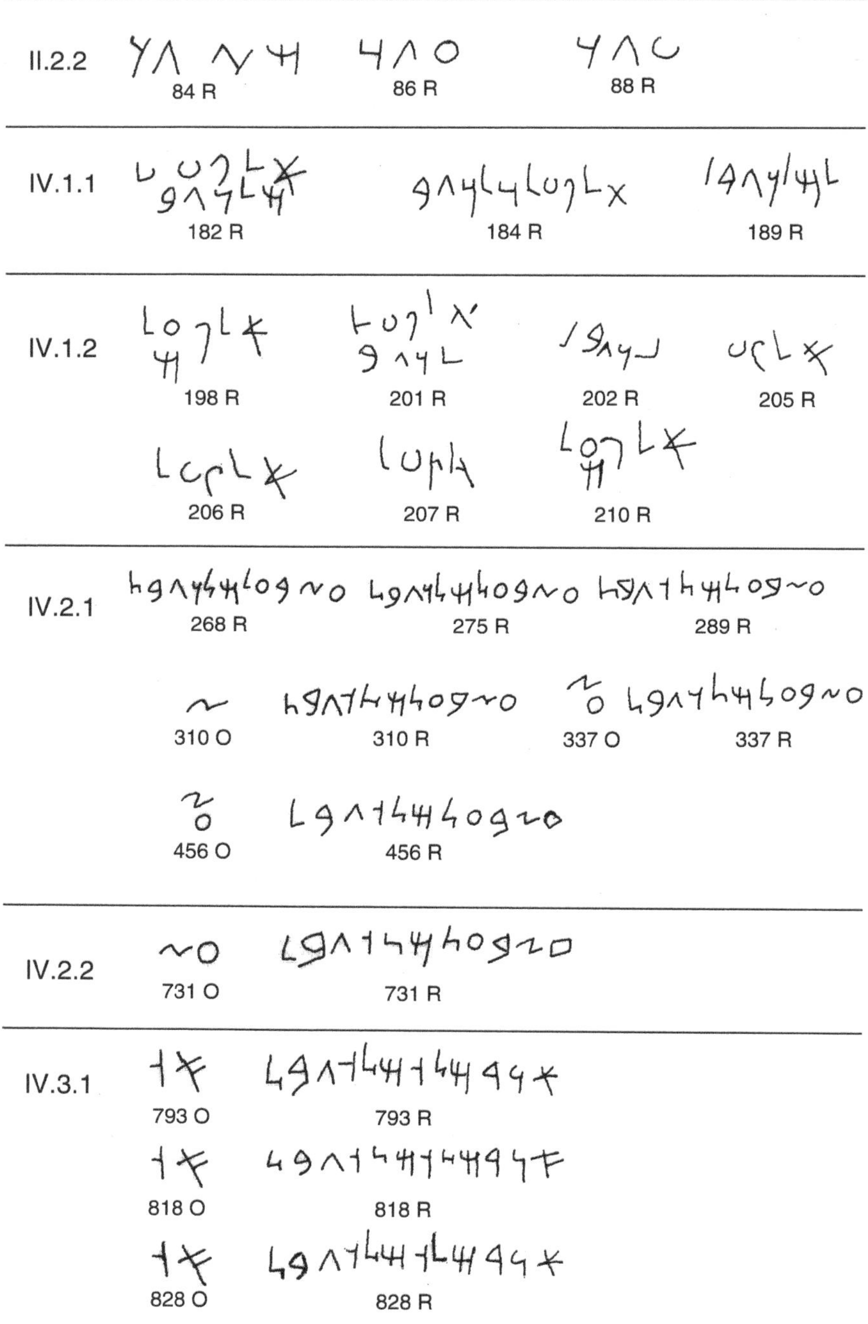

Fig. 1.1. *Monetary inscriptions of Byblos.*

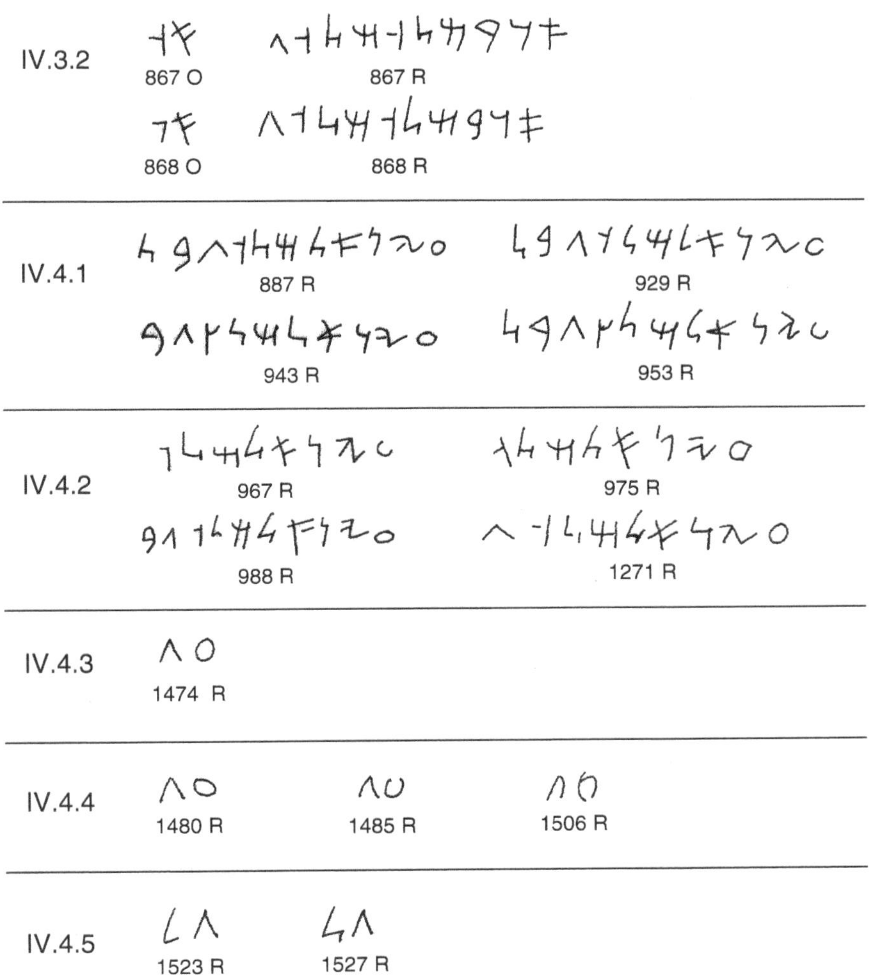

Fig. 1.1 (*cont.*). *Monetary inscriptions of Byblos.*

inscription has the considerable advantage of existing in several, sometimes many specimens. By examining them, one can carefully check the

de Byblos," *CRAIBL* (1998) 1153, 1164; idem and É. Gubel, "BAALIM," *Syr* 62 (1985) 182–83; C. Bonnet, *Astarté: Dossier documentaire et perspectives historiques* (Rome, 1996) 19–30; J. Elayi, "La présence grecque dans les cités phéniciennes sous l'Empire achéménide," *REG* 105 (1992) 320 and n. 52; idem, in *Trans* 17 (1999) 180.

forms of letters and identify the variants made by only one engraver or by various contemporary engravers.

Our first list of Byblian monetary inscriptions with some remarks and translations was presented in the book *Byblos*.[12] First, we noticed that the monetary inscriptions of Byblos almost always appear on the reverse, except for the second abbreviated inscription appearing on the obverse (see appendix 1; Series IV.2.1, IV.2.2, IV.3.1, IV.3.2). The positioning of the inscription is different in the various series of Tyrian and Sidonian coinages. One would normally think that the obverse is more important than the reverse. Therefore, why was the obverse not chosen for the inscription, especially when it contained the name and title of the king? Was it a question of space? In Group II, there is no less space on the obverse around the seated sphinx than on the reverse around the hawk with the lotus flower. This could mean that the inscription was related to the motif, that is, the hawk with crook and flail, which are symbols of kingship. In Group IV, it could be a matter of space. There is no more space on the obverse, where the galley, warriors, seahorse, and shell occupy the entire field. The engraver found only a small space between the line of waves and the back of the seahorse on which to put a secondary inscription of one or two letters. On the reverse, there was not much space either, but the engraver managed to squeeze in a 12-letter inscription above the lion and bull by reducing the size of the letters. In all the series of ʿAynel (IV.4.1 to IV.4.7), there was only one inscription, always on the reverse, even when it was an abbreviation of only 2 letters. As far as the arrangement of the inscription is concerned, it may have depended on the space available (probably in most cases) or simply on the engraver's fancy. It is also possible that the long upper or lower shafts of some letters partly "fell off" the field when there was not enough space for them: this possibility must not be confused with the shape of the letters.

We present here an epigraphic analysis of Byblian monetary inscriptions (reading and interpretation) by following, as much as possible, the chronological order established in our corpus (fig. 1.1). From a methodological point of view, it is necessary to analyze the inscriptions not in themselves but as integrated into a specific context and a particular system. We propose explaining first what can be said of the minting authority's logic in choosing the monetary inscriptions. These inscriptions were official inscriptions because they were selected by the political power to represent itself on coins. In the presentation of each inscription, after our

12. J. Elayi, *Byblos*, 17–20 and 228–30, nos. 5–18.

epigraphic study, we first examine the various interpretations, and then we try to find the interpretation that best fits the Byblian logic.

In Series II.2.2, the inscription is very difficult to read (fig. 1.1). It is not clear whether the letters behind the hawk and those in front of it belong to the same inscription or whether there are two inscriptions. In 1991, É. Puech proposed reading *ʿGK* behind the hawk and interpreting it as an abbreviation for *G(RML)K* *ʿ(ŚR[Y]T)* or *ʿ(ŚRN)*—that is, the name of the king and the weight: one-tenth of a half-shekel or one-twentieth of a shekel; and in front of the hawk, he read *MLK GB[L*, 'king of Byblos'.[13] As we have shown, the reading *MLK GB[L* is impossible, except for *M*; *GK* cannot be an abbreviation for *GRMLK*, a ghost king, and *ʿ* cannot be an abbreviation for a fraction of a shekel because it does not tie in with the weight and standard of this series.[14] Moreover, the weight would be placed between the royal title and the name of the king. The first letter behind the hawk is clearly *M* with a moderate shaft, tilted slightly right, with a curved open head; the central line is vertical, not very long, but it crosses the baseline (coin no. 84R). The second letter is not easy to read; on coin no. 84, it could be *Y* or *Z*, with an angular shape and a rotated stance to the left; the line on the right crosses the oblique line as for *Y*, but the central cross-line is missing.[15] There are traces of letters or of a motif (olive twig?) after this letter; according to A. Lemaire, it could be part of the curved shaft of *B*.[16] In front of the hawk, three letters are visible. The first one is *ʿ*, with a circular shape (see appendix 1: no. 86R). The second is the letter *G* reverted, with unequal legs, the left being slightly longer (no. 86R). The third seems to be *K*, with a short vertical shaft (no. 86R) or longer and tilted slightly right (coin no. 84R). The head is angular, with the baseline oblique. Thus, what is the meaning of this inscription or of these two inscriptions: *MY/Z ʿGK*? Among other hypotheses, if the reading is *MY*, it could be the abbreviation *M(LK) Y(ḤMLK)*, 'K(ing) Ye(ḥawmilk)', who was king of Byblos in the middle of the 5th century B.C.E.[17] *ʿGK* is probably an abbreviation because the root *ʿgk* is unknown in West Semitic, and we see no connection with the letters behind the hawk. As we shall see, *ʿG* exists as an abbreviation in

13. É. Puech, "Les premières émissions byblites et les rois de Byblos à la fin du Ve siècle avant J.C.," in *ACFP* (Rome, 1991) 2/1:288, 294–96.

14. A. Lemaire and J. Elayi, "Les monnaies de Byblos au sphinx et au faucon: Nouveaux documents et essai de classement," *RBN* 137 (1991) 34–35. See also below, chap. 4.

15. A. Lemaire does not exclude *L* on coin no. 87: Lemaire-Elayi, "Les monnaies de Byblos au sphinx et au faucon," 35.

16. Ibid., 31, no. 8.

17. Ibid., 34 n. 19; Elayi, *Byblos*, 18, 142, 273.

Series IV.4.5, but it probably has another meaning and, furthermore, how is the *K* to be interpreted?

The monetary inscriptions of Group IV are explicit royal inscriptions with the name of the king followed by the royal title (fig. 1.1). The shekels of ʾElpaʿal (Series IV.1.1) bear a horizontal inscription of one or two lines on the reverse: *ʾLPʿL/MLK GBL*, ʻʾElpaʿal, King of Byblos' (no. 181R, 182R), *ʾLPʿL MLK GB*[no. 184R]*ʿL MLK GBL* (no. 189R). The name ʾElpaʿal means 'El has done'.[18] The letter *ʾ* has a long straight shaft that is more or less tilted left; its head is large, with cross-lines converging to the left of the shaft (no. 181R), or parallel (no. 205R); the cursive form also exists with one line crossing the shaft (no. 212R). The letter *L* has a vertical stance, or is slightly slanting rightward or leftward; its shaft is straight but is interrupted by the border of dots; its foot is horizontal (no. 182R), slightly oblique (no. 184R), or nonexistent when the space is very limited (no. 189R). The letter *P* has a shaft dropping vertically (no. 184R) or slightly curved (no. 181R) before veering to the left in a slightly curved stroke. The letter *ʿ* has an open circular shape. The letter *M* has the same shape as in Series II.2.2 (no. 182R); sometimes its shaft is longer and slightly curved leftward, just as is the central line (no. 189R). The letter *K* has various shapes: a moderate, straight, vertical shaft and a head consisting of a line drawn horizontally into the shaft, its left tip slightly curved upward (no. 182R); a similar shaft with a square open head (no. 184R); a long, straight shaft, slightly tilted left, and a curved open head (no. 189R). The letter *G* has equilateral legs (no. 184R) or unequal legs, the right being longer (nos. 182R, 189R). The letter *B* is tilted slightly right or vertical; its shaft is tilted left; the tail breaks off sharply, is long, and is slanted downward; the head is triangular (nos. 182R, 184R, 189R). In order to avoid the horn of the bull, the stance of the letter is not vertical but tilted right (nos. 181R, 182R). The writing on shekels is not very skillful; it is even less skillful on the quarter-shekels (Series IV.1.2) where there was even less space. The arrangement of the letters is not always the same: *ʾLPʿL/M* on two lines (nos. 193R, 198R), *ʾLPʿL/*[*M*]*LK GB*[on two lines (no. 201R), *ʾLPʿL* on one line (no. 206R). The letter *ʾ* does not have an angular head on coin no. 205 but two parallel lines crossing the shaft, the upper one being shorter. The letter *L* has its shaft tilted left on coin nos. 205 and 206. The letter *ʿ* is circular, either open (nos. 201R, 206R) or closed (nos. 198R, 210R). *G* is much smaller than the next letter, *B*, on coin no. 202. *P* is reversed on coin nos. 205, 206, and 207.

18. F. L. Benz, *Personal Names in the Phoenician and Punic Inscriptions* (Rome, 1972) s.v.

The inscription on the reverse of the following series of shekels (IV.2.1) is carefully written, either on a horizontal line (no. 280R) as in the preceding series, III.1, or on a curved line following the circular border of dots (no. 337R). The inscription on the obverse is the letter *Z* alone or letters *ʿZ* written vertically from the base upward. The *ʿ* has the usual circular form, always closed. The letter *Z* has an angular form with a stance that is vertical or rotated to the left. The join-line is still vertical (no. 456R) or moves leftward (no. 275R, 289R). The upper line and diagonal are sometimes slightly curved (no. 310O). The letter *B* has different forms: the head is triangular (no. 289R) or almost rounded (no. 268R); the shaft is tilted left; and the tail breaks off sharply (no. 456R) or is curved (no. 275R). The stance of this letter is vertical (no. 456R) or is more or less tilted right (no. 289R). The letter *L* has a vertical shaft as in Series IV.1.1 (no. 275R), or it tilts slightly to the right (no. 310R); its baseline is horizontal and, in most cases, a short dropline is added at the right tip (no. 337R). The letter *M* has the same form as in Series IV.1.7 (no. 275R), but the left shoulder of its head is sometimes straight (no. 456R). The letter *K* has the same forms as in the preceding series, but it has a shorter shaft (no. 456R). The letter *G* has an equilateral form (no. 310R), but sometimes the right leg is longer (no. 268R). In the 16th-shekels (Series IV.2.2) (fig. 1.1), the inscription of the obverse *ʿZ* is on the same line; *ʿ* is bigger than *Z*, which tends to flatten in a more continuous form (no. 731O). *ʿZ* is an abbreviation for *ʿZBʿL*, 'ʿOzbaʿal', which means '(my) strength is Baʿal'.[19] The letter *Z* alone (or number 20, which is the same sign) is difficult to explain. J. B. Peckham proposed reading *Z*[*KR*],[20] but Zakur is a ghost king. For the moment, we have no explanation for *Z*.

The 12-letter inscription on the reverse of the shekels in Series IV.3.1 has always been read *ʾDRMLK MLK GBL*, 'ʾAddirmilk, King of Byblos'. *ʾDRMLK* means 'Milk is mighty'.[21] The two letters, *ʾK*, on the obverse were thought to be an abbreviation for *ʾDRMLK*, based on the first and last letters of his name.[22] There is a problem with the king's name, however, that we are now going to examine: first of all, it is necessary to establish the reading. The first letter is *ʾ*; it has a straight shaft slanting leftward; the two cross-lines are parallel, but the upper line breaks through farther to the left (no. 818R). Sometimes the shaft is vertical (no. 818R). In some coins, the crossbars are drawn down at an angle from the right (no. 828R). We shall

19. Ibid. On the Phoenician abbreviations, see J. Elayi and A. G. Elayi, "Systems of Abbreviations used by Byblos, Tyre and Arados in Their Pre-Alexandrine Coinages," *JNG* 37–38 (1987–88) 11–22.

20. Peckham, *Development of the Late Phoenician Scripts*, 50 n. 21.

21. Benz, *Personal Names*, s.v.

22. Elayi-Elayi, "Systems of Abbreviations," 11–22.

examine the second letter later below. The third letter is an *R* rather than a *D* because its shaft is not short; the stance is vertical (no. 818R); the head is triangular (no. 828R). The letter *M* has a moderate, vertical shaft, a square head, and a long center line crossing the baseline (no. 793R). The letter *L* is vertical; it has a long, straight shaft limited by the border of dots; its baseline is horizontal and has a short dropline at the right tip (no. 793R). The letter *K* has a moderate, vertical, straight shaft, with a single stroke head (no. 818O). The letter *G* has an equilateral form (no. 793R). The letter *B* has a shaft tilted left, with the tail breaking off sharply; its head is triangular, with a horizontal baseline (no. 828R). In the 16th-shekels of Series IV.3.2, the shapes of the letters are the same, but there are some differences: a vertical ʾ (no. 867R); an *M* with a rounded shoulder (no. 868R), with a slightly curved shaft and cross-line (no. 867R); a *G* with unequal legs, the right one being longer (no. 867R).

Let us now examine the shape of the second letter in Series IV.3.1 and IV.3.2, in order to determine whether it is a *D* or another letter. The letter is vertical; it has a straight shaft of moderate length; its head is angular (nos. 818R, 863R) or curved (nos. 815R, 867R); it is open, but in a few cases, it gives the impression that it is closed or almost closed (nos. 789R, 796R, 827R, 833R). The left shoulder can be sharp (no. 830R); the baseline can be horizontal (nos. 830R, 863R), or it tends to be drawn upward toward the top of the shaft (nos. 772R, 881R). Therefore, we must conclude that this letter is not a *D* in spite of a few cases where the head seems to be closed; it could be an *N*, but the name *ʾNRMLK* is unknown; it looks more like a *W*, and the name would be *ʾWRMLK*. This proposition was made for the first time by A. Lemaire in 2009,[23] and we were waiting to check all the coinage of this king in our corpus before adopting it. In the meantime, we used the two alternative names ʾAddirmilk/ʾUrimilk.[24] Now it must be said that the name of this king, unknown from other sources, was probably ʾUrimilk. However, there remain some difficulties: first, two other kings of Byblos bore the name ʾUrimilk: ʾUrimilk I (*U-ru-mil-ki*) was a local king under the domination of Sennacherib (704–681), and ʾUrimilk II was a local king who ruled under Xerxes I (486–465). But the writing of the name was different: *ʾRMLK* instead of *ʾWRMLK*. A. Lemaire explains this as being due to the use of *matres lectionis* at this early date.[25]

---

23. J. Elayi and A. Lemaire, "Le trésor de Byblos TIX," *Trans* 38 (2009) 92.

24. Elayi, *Byblos*, 173, 273.

25. A. Lemaire, "Le problème de l'emploi des matres lectionis en épigraphie phénicienne reconsidéré," in *VII*[e] *Congrès international des études phéniciennes et puniques*, Hammamet, Tunisia, November 10–14, 2009.

The shekels of ʿAynel (Series IV.4.1) (fig. 1.1) have no inscription on the obverse but a long, 11-letter inscription on the reverse: *ʿYNʾL MLK GBL*, 'ʿAynel, King of Byblos'. The head of a lion that was added to some coins sometimes obliterates part of the name of the city, whether this was deliberate or not. The name ʿAynel means 'El is my eye'.[26] The letter ʿ is circular (no. 887R) or oval (no. 943R). The letter *Y* has a vertical stance (no. 953R) or has rotated to the left (no. 929R); the top line is horizontal (no. 887R) or raised upward; the tail is long and straight (no. 943R) or slightly curved (no. 887R); the center line is short, horizontal (no. 943R), or downward (no. 929R). The letter *N* has a straight shaft, slanted a little to the right (no. 929R) or slightly curved (no. 953R); the left side of the head is fairly vertical, and a right shoulder has developed. The letter ʾ has the two forms attested in the preceding series: a straight shaft slanting leftward, with an angular head (no. 953R) or two parallel cross-lines (no. 929R); the shaft can be slightly curved (no. 943R). The letter *L* slants toward the right, with a horizontal baseline and a short dropline at the right tip (no. 953R). The letter *M* slants slightly to the right, with a short shaft and a large square head (no. 929R). The letter *K* is vertical (no. 887R) or slants slightly to the right (no. 929R), with a single-stroke head (no. 887R); it is sometimes reversed (nos. 943R, 953R). The letter *G* has an equilateral form (no. 887R). The letter *B* has a shaft tilted left, with the tail breaking off sharply (no. 887R) or rounded (no. 953R); its head is triangular, with a horizontal baseline. In the 16th-shekels (Series IV.4.2, IV.4.4, IV.4.5), the shapes of the letters are the same, albeit with a few differences: an open ʿ (nos. 967R, 1480R), *M* with rounded head and a central line as long as the shaft (no. 988R), *L* without the short dropline at the right tip (no. 1527R), *G* with a curved right leg (no. 1560R). Letters *ʿG* in Series IV.4.3 and IV.4.4 are abbreviations of *ʿ(YNʾL) G(BL)*, 'ʿA(ynel) of By(blos)', or of *ʿ(M) G(BL)*, 'Peo(ple) (that is, assembly of people) of By(blos)'.[27] Letters *GL* in Series IV.4.6 are an abbreviation of *G(B)L*, 'Byblos'. Letters *ʿMG*(?) in Series IV.4.4 may be an abbreviation for *ʿ(YNʾL) M(LK) G(BL)*, 'ʿA(ynel), K(ing) of By(blos)' or of *ʿM G(BL)*, 'people of By(blos)'. The political representation of the citizens of Byblos is attested on the coins bearing the name of the city alone. Moreover, the existence of an 'assembly of the people' (*ʿM ʾRṢ*),[28] literally, 'people

26. Benz, *Personal Names*, s.v.

27. Elayi, *Byblos*, 19, 175–76 (with bibliography).

28. Well known: see, for example, R. de Vaux, "Le sens de l'expression 'peuple du pays' dans l'Ancien Testament et le rôle politique du peuple en Israël," *RA* 58 (1964) 167–72; J. Elayi, *Recherches sur les cités phéniciennes à l'époque perse* (Naples, 1987) 42–43 (with bibliography).

228 R 1486 0

Fig. 1.2. *Countermarks on Byblian coins.*

of the land', is probably mentioned in the inscription of Yeḥawmilk.[29] The word *ʿM* followed by the name of the city is well attested in the Hellenistic period to refer to the official era of the Phoenician cities: for example, *ŠLŠ ḤMŠM ŠT LʿM* (*ṢR*), 'the fifty-third year of the people (of Tyre)'.[30]

2. *Monetary Countermarks*

There is no graffito on the 1,662 coins of Byblos that we have assembled in this corpus, unlike the corpus of Sidon (15 graffiti) and the corpus of Tyre (7 graffiti). There are only 2 countermarks, which is less than in the corpus of Sidon (4) and in the corpus of Tyre (7). A countermark can be stamped anywhere on the coin because it obliterates the previous impression and is always legible. The first countermark is stamped on the reverse of a 16th-shekel, no. 228 (Series IV.1.3.a), above the lion (fig. 1.2). It has an approximately circular, hollow form with one Phoenician letter in relief: *G*, with equilateral form. Other hypotheses are that it could be an abbreviation for *G*(*BL*), 'By(blos)'. The second countermark is stamped on the obverse of 16th-shekel no. 1486 (Series IV.4.5), between the galley and the seahorse. It has a hollow, irregular form, with one (or more) Phoenician letter(s) in relief: possibly *T*, with a straight shaft tilted right; the crossbar is drawn upward to the right, and the tick makes a slightly leftward curve. We have no idea of the meaning.

3. *Paleographical Analysis of Byblian Monetary Inscriptions*

Before proceding to a paleographical analysis of the Byblian monetary inscriptions, we need to analyze possible physical reasons that the script was modified. The forms of letters are explained first by the sort of object or tool that was used. The engraver was working against the particular hardness of the die, which was made of iron and was sometimes hardened, or of bronze; and also he had to deal with the difficulty in drawing curved lines with a burin—for example, the circular letter ʿ, the head of *B*, or the

29. *KAI* 10; Elayi, *Byblos*, 176 (with bibliography).

30. Elayi, *Recherches sur les cités phéniciennes*, 43; *KAI* 19, line 8.

curved letter *P*.[31] This could explain, at least partly, some of the triangular heads and angular shoulders, such as, for example, those of *B*, *M*, and *N*. This could also explain the "broken writing" of one of the engravers who worked on ʿAynel's coinage; he systematically engraved letters by means of a succession of straight short strokes (nos. 975R, 1271R, 1506R).[32] The need to engrave in reverse order could explain why some letters are tilted in the wrong direction (*L* in no. 206R, for example), or even completely reversed—for example, the *L* and *P* in some inscriptions of ʾElpaʿal (nos. 202R, 205R, 206R, 207R). Two other difficulties for the engraver were the very small size of some dies and the restricted amount of space available in the field. This could explain why the letters were quite small and the upper and lower shafts sometimes shorter and slanting, especially in the 16th-shekels (Series IV.2.2, IV.3.2, IV.4.2). We also want to point out that vertical letters take up less space in width than tilted letters, which is important for long inscriptions—for example, in Series IV.3.1 and IV.3.2. Another solution was to write the long inscription on two lines (IV.1.1, IV.1.2) or to cut it into several sections placed behind and in front of the bull's head and forelegs (for example, coin nos. 731R, 988R, 1271R). These sorts of details that were caused by physical limitations must not be confused with the local characteristics of the script. The above-mentioned difficulties encountered by engravers of coin dies were the same for engravers of countermark dies.[33] The constraints encountered by engravers could also come from the minting authority. Even though we have no information on Phoenician mints about this point, it is likely that the mint's die engravers had models at their disposal. These models represented an official order and were highly symbolic due to the fact that civic coinages conveyed the symbols of the minting authority of Byblos. The engravers of Byblian dies were probably given specifications and had to conform to them as much as possible. They were probably given a memorandum about the respective importance and place of the various inscriptions on the obverse or reverse (name and title of the king) and the abbreviations to be used.

Even if the rules in use in the mint of Byblos were strict, the engravers had some freedom in the arrangement of items in the space on the dies. They probably were not obligated to reproduce the forms of the letters inscribed on the memorandum exactly. However, any illiterate engravers would have had to draw the letters without using creative initiative in

31. For the technical aspects of engraving dies, see chap. 3.

32. J. Elayi, "Remarques méthodologiques sur l'étude paléographique des légendes monétaires phéniciennes," in *Phoinikeia Grammata: Lire et écrire en Méditerranée* (ed. C. Baurain et al.; Namur, 1991) 198.

33. Cf. Elayi-Lemaire, *Graffiti*, 157–59.

order to avoid mistakes. No doubt the engravers themselves chose the kind of script: archaistic, cursive or semicursive; however, they needed to take into account the tradition of monetary script in the Byblian workshop, which was rather conservative.[34] When they had enough space, they could change the size of the letters; in general, Byblian monetary inscriptions were smaller than the Sidonian and Tyrian. Graphic variants sometimes appear in the same inscription, depending on the engraver's preference: for example, the two or three *L* letters in the inscriptions of Series IV.1.1 and IV.1.2 have different forms. This is very important for a paleographical study because it means that any given letter might not have just one form at a particular time or place but might have several. The engravers could choose their tools: some letters were engraved by two burins of different sizes, which produced a combination of thin and thick strokes as in ink writing—for example, on coin no. 280. Finally, the style of writing was unique to each engraver, whether careful (no. 793) or careless (no. 1506). The analysis of monetary scripts reveals different hands; for example, in the coinage of ʾElpaʿal (Series IV.1.1), the incriptions on coin nos. 198R and 206R were made by two different engravers.

The monetary inscriptions provide important complementary information for the study of the Byblian script, all the more so because there are few nonmonetary inscriptions. Until now, most epigraphists, who have mainly been interested in monumental inscriptions, have ignored them. However, these scholars should be all the more cautious in theorizing about the characteristics of a given letter when they have only a few examples (or even only one).[35] As far as Byblos is concerned, the monetary inscriptions are valuable because they offer several occurrences of letters and therefore provide a solid basis for epigraphic study. It is now possible to know the characteristics of the Byblian script from about 450 to 333 B.C.E. by using monetary inscriptions, to describe its evolution, and to compare the script tradition of the Byblos mint with other Phoenician mints.[36] In the Byblian monetary inscriptions, as in those of Tyre, 13 different letters have been used (only 6 in the Sidonian).[37] We have divided the forms of letters into five periods: Group II (3rd quarter of the 5th century), Group IV.1 (end of the 5th century), Group IV.2 (1st third of the 4th century), Group IV.3

34. Elayi, "Remarques méthodologiques sur l'étude paléographique," 196.

35. Ibid.

36. The analysis of monetary inscriptions by J. B. Peckham (*Development of the Late Phoenician Scripts*, 71–72) is useless because it is based on a small number of coins and a mostly outdated bibliography.

37. Elayi-Elayi, *Coinage of Tyre*, 244–49; idem, *Monnayage de Sidon*, 459–61.

(shortly before 350 B.C.E.), and Group IV.4 (around 350–333 B.C.E.) in order to show the possible evolution (fig. 1.2).

The letter ʾ is represented in Groups IV.1, IV.3, and IV.4. In the inscriptions of ʾElpaʿal (IV.1), ʾ has a long, straight shaft that is tilted left; its head is large, with cross-lines that converge to the left of the shaft and, less frequently, are parallel. It is sometimes cursive, with only one long cross-line, and sometimes curved downward. In the inscriptions of ʾUrimilk (IV.3), the shaft of ʾ is tilted slightly left or vertical, but it seems to be the tendency of the engravers to draw the shafts of all letters vertically. Most of the time, the cross-lines of the head are parallel, and only in some cases do they converge to the left of the shaft. In the inscriptions of ʿAynel (IV.4), the shaft is slanted more to the left, most of the time straight, but sometimes slightly curved. The head has two parallel lines, the upper one only crossing the shaft; the converging cross-lines have almost disappeared.

The letter *B* is represented in Groups IV.1, IV.2, IV.3 and IV.4. It always has quite a small head, approximately triangular, rarely rounded. Its shaft is tilted left, with a tail breaking off sharply, long and slanted downward; the shaft is more and more curved, possibly under the influence of cursive writing (IV.3, IV.4). The stance of *B* had a developmental tendency to tilt from right to left: tilted to the right (IV.1), then roughly vertical (IV.2), and finally tilted leftward (IV.3, IV.4).

The letter *G* is represented in all groups. Initially it had unequal legs, the right one being longer and less oblique, sometimes slightly curved; the equilateral form is rare (II.2.2, IV.1). More and more in the following groups (IV.2, IV.3, IV.4), it had only the equilateral form. This became its only form in the Byblos coinage after the Persian period.

The letter *W* is now identified in Group IV.3 instead of *D*. Perhaps somewhat influenced by cursive writing, it is vertical, with a straight shaft of moderate length; its head is angular or curved, with the left shoulder sharp or rounded.

The letter *Z* is not clearly identified in Group II and is only represented in the coinage of ʿOzbaʿal (IV.2). It has an angular form with a stance that is vertical or rotated to the left. Most of the time, the join-line is vertical, but it also moves leftward. The upper line and the diagonal are sometimes slightly curved.

The letter *Y* is only represented in the coinage of ʿAynel (IV.4). It has a vertical stance or has rotated to the left. The top headline is horizontal or raised upward; the tail is long, straight, or slightly curved, sometimes passing beyond the shaft.

To begin with, the letter *K* had a more-or-less long vertical shaft, or tilted slightly right, with an angular open head. Then it had a curved open

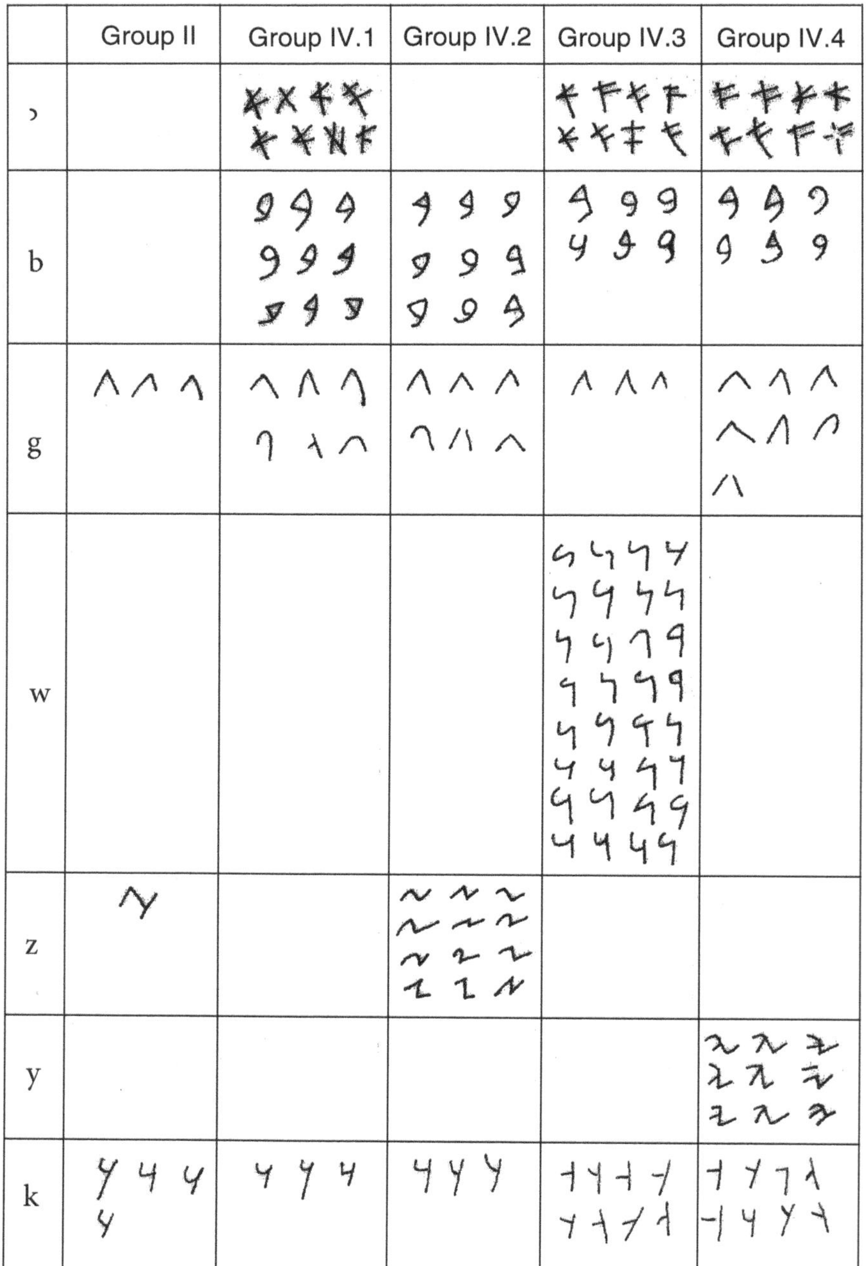

Fig. 1.3. *Paleographical chart of the Byblian monetary inscriptions.*

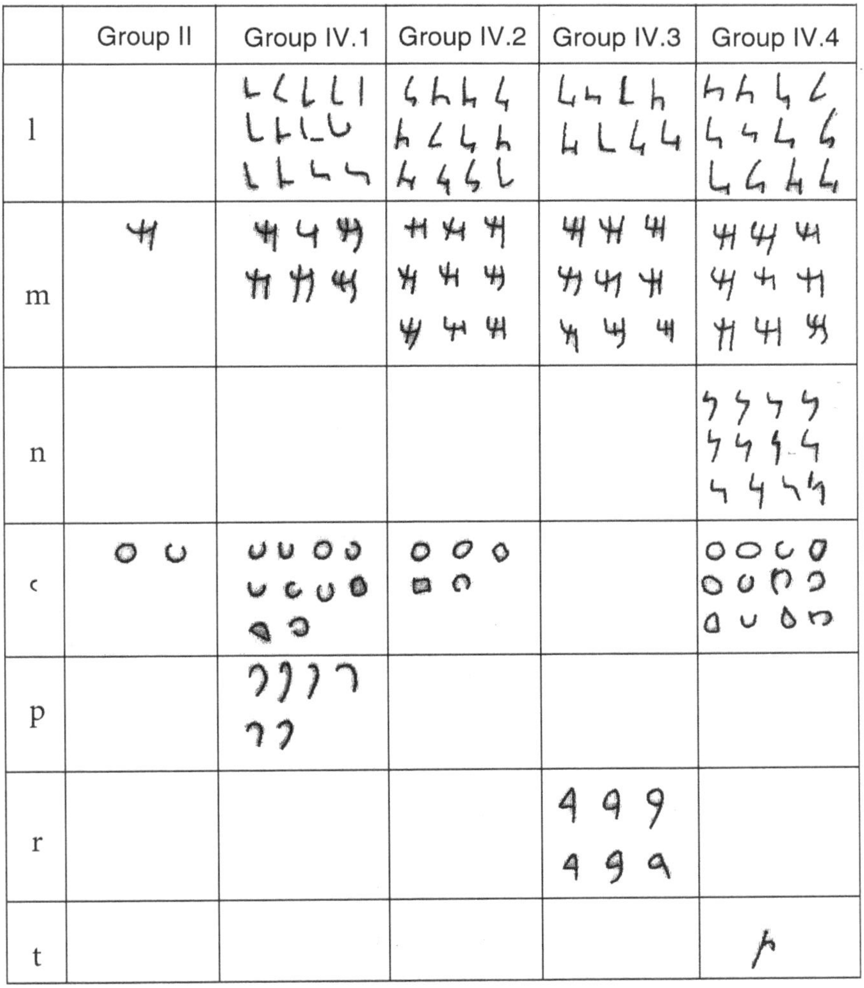

Fig. 1.3 (*cont.*). *Paleographical chart of the Byblian monetary inscriptions.*

head or a head with a horizontal line, with its left tip slightly curved upward. Finally, it had a vertical, straight shaft, with a single-stroke head.

The letter *L* has a long straight shaft limited by the border of dots, sometimes slightly curved; it is vertical or slanting slightly rightward, rarely leftward; its foot is horizontal or slightly oblique, with or without a short dropline at the right tip.

The development of the letter *M* can be seen throughout all the Byblian coinage. Initially it had a moderate, vertical shaft, with a fairly deep, curved shoulder and a short central line. Then the shaft and central line lengthened; they were straight or slightly curved; the shoulder is always deep but curved or square. The most evident characteristic of development is the progressively longer breakthrough of the center line.

The letter *N* is rarely represented; it has a straight shaft, slanted a little to the right or slightly curved; the left side of the head is fairly vertical, and a right shoulder developed. The letter ʿ is circular or oval, sometimes open. The letter *P* is rarely represented; it has its shaft dropping vertically or slightly curved, before veering to the left in a slightly curved stroke. The letter *R* is rarely represented; it has a moderate vertical shaft, with a triangular head, sometimes rounded.

If we now compare the script of the Byblian monetary inscriptions with that of the other three Phoenician mints, it will be possible to characterize its peculiarities. The comparison can be made with the letters attested in the other mints: 10 of the 13 Byblian letters are attested in the Aradian monetary inscriptions, 9 in the Tyrian, and only 3 in the Sidonian. The Byblian ʾ is very different from the Tyrian and the Sidonian, which are rarely attested; its cursive form is closer to the Aradian.

The Byblian *B* is comparable with the Tyrian *B* but different from the Sidonian and Aradian letter (which is rarely attested). The Byblian *G* is different from the Aradian and is not attested in the monetary inscriptions of Sidon and Tyre. The letter *W* is not attested in the other three Phoenician mints. The Byblian *Z* is similar to the Tyrian *Z*; it can be compared with the Sidonian letter, but not in Mazday's monetary inscriptions because of the Aramaic influence on this script. The *Y* is different from the Aradian *Y*, which is rarely attested.

The letter *K*, in its initial form, is similar to the Aradian *K*. The *L* is only attested on Tyrian coins: the forms with a vertical stance are similar, but the tendency of the shaft to tilt to the right appears in the mid-5th century in Tyre and only in the first half of the 4th century at Byblos. The letter *M*, attested in all four mints, has some similar characteristics in the second half of the 5th century: the vertical stance, the short straight shaft, and the rather long central line crossing the baseline; but the shoulder is rounded at Byblos but mostly square at Sidon and Arwad—with both forms represented at Tyre. The evolution of this letter in the 4th century was completely different at the other mints: in Byblos, the central line lengthens while in Tyre the shaft is longer, the shoulder is mostly square, and the central line rarely crosses the baseline; in Arwad, the letter tilts to the right, and the shaft becomes longer and curved; it is not attested at Sidon during this period.

The Byblian *N* of the 4th century is close to the Tyrian *N* of the 5th century and different from the Aradian; it is not attested at Sidon. The letter ʿ is represented in the four mints: it is mostly circular, but other forms are also attested: the open form is more frequent at Byblos. The letter *P* is close to the Aradian *P* but less curved and less tilted to the right. The Byblian *R* is similar to the different forms of the Tyrian letter, except that its shaft always seems to be vertical and not tilted to the left.

The comparison of the monetary scripts of the four Phoenician mints is somewhat biased because it is based on a systematic analysis of the Byblian, Tyrian, and Sidonian coins, not of the Aradian, and because not all the letters of the Byblian coinage are attested in the other coinages.[38] However, each monetary script seems to have its own features. There is some similarity among the Byblian, Tyrian, and Sidonian monetary scripts but less with the Aradian. However, the monetary scripts seem to be less formal and conservative in their development in Byblos and Arwad than in Tyre and Sidon. It is possible to compare them for the letters attested at different periods in the different mints. The lack of contemporary cursive scripts for Byblos and the other Phoenician cities during this period makes the study of the cursive influence on the monetary scripts difficult. However, it is possible to detect a cursive influence on the Byblian letters ʾ, *K*, *L*, and ʿ.

4. *Sociocultural Aspects of the Byblian Monetary Script*

The sociocultural aspects of scripts, such as the different points of view of those who ordered, wrote, and read the inscription, especially monetary inscriptions, is rarely of interest to epigraphers.[39] Did the engravers of Byblian dies know how to write or not?[40] In theory, it was not necessary since they had to reproduce a model, and the example of the El-Hofra inscription shows that its engravers were illiterate.[41] However, two arguments tend to prove that they were usually literate. The first argument is the graphic variants that can be observed on the dies made by the same engravers, or in the reengraved dies (more difficult to observe): for example, in the inscriptions of ʾElpaʿal, the letter *L* is written several times and often

38. The comparison of monetary scripts by J. B. Peckham is not documented or argued well enough: *Development of the Late Phoenician Scripts*, 54–63.

39. Cf. Elayi, "Étude paléographique des légendes," 32–34; idem, "Remarques méthodologiques," 190–191.

40. We posed this question for the die engravers and molds-makers of weights: Elayi-Elayi, *Poids phéniciens*, 258–60.

41. *RES* 1543; cf. Elayi-Elayi, *Coinage of Tyre*, 242.

with different shapes (nos. 182R, 184R, 206R). Illiterate engravers would not have risked graphic variants, which means that the Byblian engravers mastered the writing. The second argument is the phenomenon of reversed letters, for example, the letter *P* in some inscriptions of ʾElpaʿal (nos. 205R, 206R) or the letter *K* in some inscriptions of ʿAynel (nos. 943R, 954R). These errors are due to the fact that the engravers were in the habit of writing from right to left and consequently sometimes engraved backward on the dies. However, we do not know whether they were just barely literate or were really educated.

What was the function of the monetary inscriptions? Just like the motifs on the coins, they were intended to represent the minting authority but with much more precision: the name of the king and his title. The Byblian coins were not exported as merchandise coins as were the other Phoenician coins.[42] In their local circulation within the territory of Byblos, Byblian coins could be read by the literate inhabitants of the city. However, they were not read by the illiterate inhabitants, by other Phoenicians who were illiterate, or by foreigners staying in or just passing by the city who were ignorant of the Phoenician script. If these people had to use Byblian coins, they probably identified them by the typology, weight, or denomination. The purpose of propaganda is obvious due to the writing of the complete inscription with the name of the king and his title, which is unlike the other Phoenician coinages, which used only abbreviations. In the Byblian coinage, the abbreviations were used in the first inscribed series (II.2), the last inscribed series (IV.4.3, IV.4.4, IV.4.5, IV.4.6), and on the obverse of ʿOzbaʿal's and ʾUrimilk's inscriptions (IV.2, IV.3). The first inscribed Byblian series (II.2) dates approximately to the third quarter of the 5th century, which was after Tyre (I.1) and before the first inscribed Sidonian series (III.1).[43] In addition to other possible reasons, the minting authority of Byblos probably intended the monetary inscriptions to be read by some of the local users. We know they were able to read them because the high percentage of literacy is well documented for the Persian period.[44] Unlike the other three Phoenician mints, the Byblos coins attest no graffiti and only two countermarks. We have shown that there was a relationship between the small countermarks and the monetary graffiti and that both seem to be linked to the circulation of coins out of their minting area.[45] Therefore, their quasi-absence on the Byblian coins can be explained by the fact that they were not exported out of the city.

42. Elayi-Elayi, *Trésors*, 341–42 and fig. 22.

43. Idem, *Coinage of* Tyre, 28; idem, *Monnayage de Sidon*, 54–89.

44. Cf. idem, *Coinage of Tyre*, 250–51.

45. Ibid., 251–52 (with bibliography).

Chapter 2

Analysis of Iconography

The iconography on the Byblian coins of the Persian period was slightly less conservative than on Sidonian and Tyrian coins[1] because the Byblian coins had 13 different motifs, instead of 8 and were represented as either primary or secondary motifs or both. All the Byblian motifs are turned to left. The galley, seahorse, sphinx, lion, vulture, ram, bull, griffin, hawk, helmet, and two different bearded heads were only used as primary designs. The lotus flower was alternately used as a main and a secondary motif. The shell was only used as a secondary motif. The sea, symbolized by a zigzag line of waves was usually positioned under the galley. One-, two-, or three-pronged ankhs appear on some late shekels of ʿAynel. Some types are complex, such as a galley above waves, a seahorse, and a shell. In these cases, it is difficult to see all the details because many coins are more or less worn or damaged. As for the inscriptions analyzed in chap. 1, it is necessary to give as accurate a description as possible of the motifs represented with them on the coins before moving on to their interpretation. We shall study them by order of frequency and importance: primary or secondary use, obverse or reverse, shekels or small denominations. We shall also consider the possible evolution of these motifs, their relation to the monetary inscriptions, and the relation between obverse and reverse types. The details of the motifs are easier to observe on shekels, but their representations on small denominations are also taken into account.

1. *The Galley*

The galley is the most frequently used motif in the coinage of Byblos, except for Groups I and II and a few series of Group V. It is always represented on the obverse on a line of waves. It appears for the first time in the coinage of the anonymous king, on the shekels of Series III.1, without a line of waves. It is represented in a stylized but fine manner, without sails, oars, or rudder. It is shown from the port side, as it also appeared on Sidonian coins. The prow ends with a ram (*embolon*), which is long as in the case of

1. Elayi-Elayi, *Monnayage de Sidon*, 471–539; idem, *Coinage of Tyre*, 253–80.

all Phoenician galleys (here maybe one-fifth of the total length) and with two prongs (no. 102). A line of holes is represented on the hull: these are probably not reinforcing wales but holes for oars, without space enough to represent more than one row.[2] There is a row of portholes separated by stanchions and, hanging along the bulwark, a line of shields that ends at the stern and bow. The number of portholes corresponds only approximately to the number of shields because they are not hung exactly above the portholes but somewhat randomly. The number of shields (16 on coin no. 102) is low in contrast to some coins of the following series (for example, 28 on coin no. 779). It may be that the small size of the coin and the skillfulness of the engraver limited the number of shields that could be depicted, and therefore it is difficult to estimate the exact size of the galley. The heads of the oarsmen are not represented here in the portholes as on some Sidonian double shekels.[3] The diameter of a shield was about 90 cm; when there were as many shields as oarsmen, the galley would correspond to a classical *interscalmium*. If the representation of the Byblian galley is relatively accurate and if it was a trireme (in spite of the single row of holes for oars), the galley represented on coin no. 102, which has 16 portholes, would have carried 48 oarsmen (16 by row of oars), plus the crew, and would have measured about 15 m long (0.90 m × 16 shields + the length of the ram). The galley of coin no. 779, which has 28 portholes, would have carried 84 oarsmen (28 per row of oars), plus the crew, and would have measured more than 25 m long (0.90 m × 28 shields + the length of the ram). This is much less than the Athenian trireme in the 4th century, which carried 170 oarsmen and measured 36 or 37 m.[4] The best reference we have is the contemporary hangars for Phoenician galleys in the Phoenician harbor of Kition in Cyprus: the galleys of Kition measured at least 30 m long and at the most 5.20 m wide (out of 6 m).[5] Therefore the engravers of Byblian

2. For the wales, see L. Basch, "Phoenician Oared Ship. Part II," *The Mariner's Mirror* 55 (1969) 156; J. Elayi and A. G. Elayi, "A Treasure of Coins from Arwad," *JANES* 18 (1986) 8.

3. Cf. Elayi-Elayi, *Monnayage de Sidon*, 477 and pl. 2:26.

4. Cf. Basch, "Phoenician Oared Ship. Part II," 160. See the trireme built by J. Morrison, "Olympias, une trière athénienne," *DArch* 183 (1993) 22, based on all the available data.

5. Y. Calvet, "Kition, French Expedition," in *Kinyras: L'archéologie française à Chypre* (ed. M. Yon; Paris, 1993) 107–38; M. Yon, "Le port de guerre de Kition (Chypre)," *DArch* 183 (1993) 40–41; idem, "Kition in the Tenth to Fourth Centuries B.C.," *BASOR* 308 (1997) 14–15; D. Christou, "Chronique des fouilles et découvertes archéologiques à Chypre en 1995. 13. Kition-Bamboula (Mission française)," *BCH* 120 (1996) 1084–86; O. Callot, "Les Hangars du Port de Kition," in *Res Maritimae: Cyprus and the Eastern Mediterranean from Prehistory to Late Antiquity* (ed. S. Swiny et al.; Atlanta, 1997) 71–82; M. Yon, "Les hangars du port de Kition (Larnaca, Chypre), Mission française de Kition-Baboula 1998," *Orient-Express* (1999) 39–41.

coins were probably not representing the precise number of shields and portholes but only what could be contained in the meager space.

There is an eye on the prow, smaller than the huge eye of Aradian galleys,[6] and it was on the same level as the portholes. A huge horsehead turned to the left is represented on the prow; it is harnessed, with a forelock on its head,[7] and bent as though somebody is pulling the reins. The design represented above the stern seems to be a griffin's head, also turned to the left. Both animals have open mouths. The presence of these animals, the prophylactic eye, and the warriors served the purpose of protecting the war-galley.[8] Three huge warriors are represented on the deck, enlarged as though the engraver had taken a closeup shot on the stern of the galley. On coin no. 102, the bearded faces and neck and shoulders of the warriors are represented with their helmets raised above their heads. On other coins (no. 209), only pulled-on helmets are represented, showing that the heads are being protected. The helmet (κυνῆ) is of the so-called Corinthian type, which was not only represented on Corinthian coins but also widely used in northern Greece, on the islands, and in the Greek territories of Asia. The Corinthian helmet was frequently represented on Greek coins—for example, in Lesbos, Neandria, Elaea Troad, Kalymna and Epiphaneia, and also in Lapethus (Cyprus).[9] On some Thracian-Macedonian coins from the end of the 6th century, it is represented in a field above a team of oxen.[10] It could be a motif borrowed from Thracian-Macedonian coins that were imported as merchandise coins in Phoenician cities. However, when Herodotus described the weapons of Phoenician warriors in the navy of Xerxes, he wrote: they had 'helmets approximately similar to the type of Greek helmets' (κυνέας εἶχον ἀγχοτάτω πεποιημένας τρόπον τὸν Ἑλλενικόν).[11] Even if this passage did not specifically concern the warriors of the war-galleys of Byblos, it is likely that they too wore Corinthian helmets and that their representation on the coins was not a simple iconographic borrowing. It seems that the cheek guard is pointed (coin no. 102)

6. Cf. Elayi-Elayi, "A Treasure of Coins from Arwad," 8 and n. 17.

7. This forelock is an element of equestrian tradition in the whole Achaemenid Empire: cf. N. Vismara, "Un particolare nell'iconografia del cavallo nelle terre di confine nell'Asia Minore: Elemento decorativo diffuso od indizio culturale? Alcuni spunti per una riflessione," *Trans* 37 (2009) 155–67.

8. Cf. J. Elayi, "Les symboles de la puissance militaire sur les monnaies de Byblos," *RN* 26 (1984) 40–47.

9. *BMC Troas, Aeolis and Lesbos*, pl. 33.19 (Lesbos); 14.3 (Neandria); 25.5–8 (Elaea); *BMC Caria and Islands*, pl. 29.8; *BMC Galatia, Cappadocia and Syria*, pl. 28.4; *BMC Cyprus*, pl. 6.3, 4; 20.1 (the helmet is raised, with or without crest).

10. *BMC Macedonia, etc.*, 150, no. 1.

11. Hdt. 7.89.

and sometimes rounded (coin no. 779). The nape cover is long. There is, apparently, a combination chenille helmet and panache, because the crest is first made of hairs or short, rigid strips, then ends in a long flowing tail that apparently is fixed at the back of the crest.

The shields are rounded and surrounded by an 'edge' (ἴτυς). If the size of the shields is proportional to that of the helmets, then apparently these warriors had small shields that protected them only from the shoulder to the hip. The Byblian shield could therefore be compared with the Greek ἀσπίς because of its rounded form and the presence of an ἴτυς, and to the πέλτη because of its small size.[12] Herodotus wrote that the Phoenicians 'had shields without borders' (ἀσπίδας δὲ ἴτυς οὐκ ἐχούσας εἶχον).[13] Neither the great size of the ἀσπίς nor the absence of ἴτυς seems to fit with the shields represented on Byblian coins. If Herodotus was inspired by his own experience of Phoenician warriors, he was describing Tyrian warriors, because the only Phoenician city he had visited was Tyre. If he relied on evidence contemporary with the Persian Wars, the Phoenician warriors used in the Persian fleet were not Byblian, since Byblos had no fleet at that time.[14] The Greek word 'hoplites' that is traditionally used is not appropriate for the Byblian warriors because they have no javeline, and their shield does not correspond exactly to the ἀσπίς. On fractional coins, three warriors are still represented on the quarter-shekels of Series III.2 (coin no. 149) and only one on 16-shekels and half-16ths (nos. 163, 174). Only the helmets are represented, minus the heads, probably because of the lack of available space. For the same reason, no more than 10 shields are represented along the bulwark.

The war-galley represented on the ʾElpaʿal shekels is slightly different from the previous one. There is a line of waves under the hull. The large figurehead at the prow is no longer a horse but a roaring lion. The small head at the stern is not very clear; it could still be a griffin (no. 181). The shields hung along the bulwark are smaller and more numerous (20 on coin no. 181). The stanchions are taller and the portholes less numerous than the shields (18 on coin no. 181). On fractional coins: 3 warriors are represented on the quarter-shekels of Series IV.1.2 (coin no. 210) and only one on 16th-shekels and half-16ths (no. 221, 261). Only the helmets are represented, minus the heads—no more than 12 shields on the quarters (no. 210) and less on the small fractions (6 on coin no. 221); most of the time, the motif is stylized (coin no. 221).

---

12. For the weapons of Greek warriors, see A. M. Snodgrass, *Arms and Armour of the Greeks* (London, 1967) 50–55.

13. Hdt. 7.89 (translations of Classical quotations are our own).

14. J. Elayi, "The Role of the Phoenician Kings at the Battle of Salamis (480 B.C.E.)," *JAOS* 126 (2006) 411–18; Elayi, *Byblos*, 129–31.

The representation of the galley continues to evolve in the coinages of successive kings. On ʿOzbaʿal's coins, the rudder was represented by two large oars at the stern.[15] The small head on the stern disappeared, and the stern ends in an ornament that curves to a point, similar to the Greek *aphlaston.*[16] The line of holes on the hull is replaced by wales: the forked tip of the *aphlaston* on some coins (nos. 280, 308) could confirm the presence of wales (2?). The shields are even smaller and are numerous (25 on coin no. 296); the portholes have shorter stanchions, they are interrupted in the front by the presence of the eye, and are less numerous than the shields (18 on coin no. 296). On some coins of series IV.2.1.a, the front of the galley is slightly different: the ram is quite thin, and the proembolon above it is thicker (coin no. 280). In the rest of this series, it is the reverse: the ram is thicker, with 3 prongs, and the proembolon above it is much thinner (coin no. 308). Series IV.2.1.b and IV.2.1.c have the same representation (coin nos. 308, 326). The 16th-shekels have only 2 stylized warriors, with helmets but minus the heads. The number of shields is smaller (9 on coin no. 738). The line of waves under the galley that is present on the shekels does not figure on the 16ths. On the shekels of ʾUrimilk, the ram has 3 prongs; one or 2 large oars are represented at the stern (coin nos. 779, 793). The shields of the bulwark are smaller yet and more numerous (28 on coin no. 779). The helmets of the 3 warriors appear without heads (coin no. 779). The galley of the 16ths is the same as on those of ʿOzbaʿal (coin no. 975). The galley represented in ʿAynel's coinage is similar to the preceding one, but the heads of the warriors are represented under the helmets on the shekels (coin nos. 931, 937); not, however, on the 16ths (coin nos. 975, 1047). In the unclassified Series V.1 with the seated griffin on the reverse, the galley is represented without a line of waves and without oars at the stern. Its figurehead is a roaring lion, and it carries 2 warriors without heads. There are 8 shields along the bulwark on coin no. 1544.

2. *The Seahorse*

The seahorse is, after the galley, the most frequently used motif in Byblian coinage. With the galley, it shared the obverse field on shekels and smaller denominations in Groups III and IV, except in Series III.4 and IV.1.4.

15. On the rudder, see J. Thurneyssen, "Le gouvernail antique," *DArch* 29 (1978) 74–80.

16. Cf. J. N. Svoronos, "Stylides, ancres, hierae, aphlasta, stoloi, akrostolia, embola, proembola et totems marins," *JIAN* 16 (1914) 81–152; and Betlyon (*Coinage of Phoenicia*, 81, 86–87, 105), who considered this ornament to be a sort of *aphlaston*. However, see G. F. Hill, *BMC Phoenicia*, xxii and c ('curved ornament [afterwards developed into an aphlaston]'); and L. Casson, *Ships and Seamanship in the Ancient World* (Princeton, 1971) 96.

The seahorse of the Byblian coinage is an entirely mythical animal, just like the sphinx and the griffin, but unlike the other animals represented on these coins (lion, bull, vulture, ram, hawk). Even if the starting point for the image was the marine animal known as the seahorse (*syngnathus hippocampus*), which the engravers of Byblos were probably familiar with, this mythical seahorse is quite different. It has the head, forelock, and forelegs of a horse that is galloping but is not harnessed, except for the forelock.[17] It is similar to the Tyrian seahorse of Group II, beginning in the last quarter of the 5th century and then contemporary with Group II.[18] It has the same tail and fins, and its wing is reminiscent of that of the sphinx and of the vulture in other series. It is shorter than the wing of the Tyrian seahorse and is vertical; it faces left, unlike the Tyrian and Aradian seahorses, which are turned toward the right.[19] Since it is a mythical animal, the representations rely partly on a conventional stereotype and partly on the imagination of each engraver.

In the carefully worked representations of Series III.1 and III.2, the forepart of the seahorse is realistic and even expresses the effort being expended by the galloping animal, with the curved neck and open mouth. All the details of the head—the short mane, prominent neck, cheek, eye, nose, and chin—together with the jointed legs and hoofs are indicated (no. 102). The tail of the seahorse is curved upward, ending with a bifurcated caudal fin. In addition, it has one ventral fin (no. 102), which shows grooves made with several short, oblique strokes. The wing is curled and is generally composed of two sets of long, parallel, curled feathers that cover a third, identical set of feathers but that are much longer and curled upward. The differences in detail, thickness, number of feathers, orientation of the wing, and care or clumsiness depend on the style of the individual engravers.

In the following Series of Group IV, the evolution of the representation of the seahorse is slight. A second ventral fin appears on ʿOzbaʿal's coins (no. 296). Only one foreleg is represented on ʾUrimilk's shekels (no. 779). The representations of the seahorse on the coins of smaller denominations corresponding to the shekels are the same, but in most cases they are stylized (no. 221).

The seahorse appears in Phoenician iconography and, more frequently, in Greco-Roman iconography. For example, in the Aradian coinage, there is a seahorse under the war-galley of the more-or-less contemporary sec-

17. See above, n. 7.

18. Elayi-Elayi, *Coinage of Tyre*, 262–265. There is a misunderstanding about this motif ("incuse ibex") in F. Imhoof-Blumer, *Monnaies grecques* (Amsterdam, 1883) 440, no. 9.

19. Elayi-Elayi, ibid., pl. 34:1061 (Tyre); *BMC Phoenicia*, pl. 1:4–7, 11 (Arwad).

ond Aradian series, but it has a thinner, smaller wing and a more sinuous tail, and it is represented together with a dolphin on a Phoenician seal dated to the 6th or 5th century.[20] It is frequent in Tyrian coinage, in the series with the deity riding on it (Group II) and as the main motif on several silver and bronze smaller denominations (Series II.1.1.3, II.1.2.2, II.2.1, III.1.1, III.2.1).[21] A series from Tarsus bears the protome of an animal with the head and forelegs of a horse and a wing on the obverse. This could be either the seahorse or the winged horse Pegasus, which is another type from the same mint.[22] In Delos, the Berytians and Ascalonites worshiped the god Poseidon, who was carried on a chariot driven by seahorses, which are also represented on the Hellenistic coins of Berytus.[23] The same scene is also attested in the Punic world—for example, in a mosaic of Sousse, now in the Bardo Museum, in Tunis.[24] The seahorse alone or as a divine mount driven mostly by Poseidon/Neptune is frequently found in the Greek world.[25] However, most of the time, the seahorse is not winged as on the Phoenician coins.

The symbolic meaning of the seahorse is difficult to interpret, because Byblian mythology is not well known, and the minting authority's purpose in using this symbol not clearly understood. However, what can be said is that the seahorse represented an excellent mount for traveling, since it was a combination of three animals, each of them living in a different element: the horse on earth, the bird in the air, and the dolphin in the sea. Moreover, all these animals are renowned for their speed. Therefore, the seahorse represented the divine mount *par excellence*, as can be seen from the fact that the Tyrian deity rode the seahorse,[26] which has been compared with the Cherub (*kĕrūb*) in Ezekiel's biblical prophecy.[27] The writer, at

20. *BMC Phoenicia*, pls. 11:9–15; 12:1–4; É. Gubel, ed., *Les Phéniciens et le monde méditerranéen*, Catalogue de l'Exposition de Bruxelles, May 21–July 6, 1986, no. 256.

21. Cf. Elayi-Elayi, *Coinage of Tyre*, 264.

22. Kraay, *Greek Coins*, no. 1034; Babelon, *Traité*, part 2/2, nos. 522, 524, 525, 530; P. Chuvin, "Apollon au trident et les dieux de Tarse," *JSav* (1981) 305–26; C. Bonnet, *Melqart: Cultes et mythes de l'Héraclès tyrien en Méditerranée* (Leuven, 1988) 153–155.

23. P. Roussel and M. Launey, *Inscriptions de Délos (N°s 1497–2879)* (Paris, 1937) 1519:37–39; 1720; 2325; *BMC Phoenicia*, pl. 7:1–12.

24. Cf. M. Fantar, "Le cavalier marin de Kerkouane," *Africa* (1966) 31–42, pl. 1:2 (with refs.).

25. *DAGR*, s.v. "hippocampus"; G. M. A. Richter, *Engraved Gems of the Greeks and the Etruscans* (London, 1968) no. 332; P. Gauckler, *Inventaire des mosaïques de la Gaule et de l'Afrique*, vol. 3: *Afrique Proconsulaire* (Paris, 1910) nos. 421, 433; E. Lipiński, *Itineraria Phoenicia* (Leuven, 2004) 428–29.

26. Elayi-Elayi, *Coinage of Tyre*, 262–65.

27. Ezek 28:14, 16; cf. P.-M. Bogaert, "Le Chérub de Tyr (Ez 28, 14.16) et l'hippocampe de ses monnaies," in *Prophetie und geschichtliche Wirklichkeit in alter Israel: Festschrift für*

the draft stage, might have intended his reference to the Cherub to evoke the Tyrian seahorse, but this hypothesis needs to be confirmed.[28]

3. *The Sphinx*

The sphinx is used as a primary motif on the obverse side in Groups I and II, both on shekels and on smaller denominations. The sphinx is absent from other Phoenician coinages, but it appears frequently on contemporary Greek coins.[29] However, its representation on the coins of Byblos is very different from the Greek and is not a "combination of local types with some imitation of Greek or East Greek types," as stated by J. W. Betlyon.[30] Here, there are two different types: the crouched sphinx and the seated sphinx.

The crouched sphinx is depicted on the obverse of all the coins of the series of Group I. It is crouched to the left, with a male human head, it wears an Egyptian *klaft* and double crown with the *uraeus* (no. 1). This type of sphinx is the traditional Egyptian type of the New Kingdom, which is represented, for example, on the stelae of Yukh or Tw-Tw-Ia.[31] J. W. Betlyon notes slight differences between the engraving of the shekels' dies and that of the smaller coins: in this case, it is "crouched rather than truly seated."[32] As a matter of fact, the type is always a crouched sphinx but is less carefully engraved in the cramped space. As said above, this type of sphinx is rare in Phoenician iconography; one example is the sphinx of Cagliari, but it is without the double crown and is dated to the 2nd–1st centuries B.C.E.[33] The closest parallels can be found on two scarabs from

S. Herrmann (ed. R. Liwak and S. Wagner; Stuttgart, 1991) 29–38; P. Bordreuil, "*parōket* et *kappōret*: À propos du saint des saints en Canaan et en Judée," in *Les espaces syro-mésopotamiens: Volume d'hommage offert à Jean-Claude Margueron* (ed. P. Butterlin et al.; Subartu 17; Turnhout, 2000) 164–65.

28. See our interpretation: Elayi-Elayi, *Coinage of Tyre*, 264–65.

29. In Idalium (*BMC Cyprus*, pl. 5:1–16), Lesbos (*BMC Troas, Aeolis and Lesbos*, pl. 10:14–15), Cyzicus (*BMC Mysia*, pls. 17–18, 35–36), Chios (*BMC Ionia*, pls. 1:19; 3:19; 32:1), Samothrace (G. K. Jenkins, *Monnaies Grecques* [Paris, 1972] nos. 96, etc.) The seated sphinx represented on the obverse of a "Philistine" coin (*BMC Palestine*, 181, no. 31 and pl. 19:31) is closely related to that of Byblos.

30. Betlyon, *Coinage of Phoenicia*, 112 n. 13.

31. S. Hassan, *The Sphinx: Its History in the Light of Recent Excavations* (Cairo, 1949) figs. 13, 35; idem, *Excavations at Giza, 1936–1937*, vol. 7 (Oxford, 1953) 84, fig. 67; and p. 85, fig. 68; A. Dessenne, *Le Sphinx: Étude iconographique* (Paris, 1957) 38, 99; C. M. Kraay, *Greek Coins*, 291, probably means the crouched sphinx.

32. Betlyon, *Coinage of Phoenicia*, 112 (there is no lion on the reverse of coin no. 3).

33. S. Moscati, ed., *I Fenici* (Milan, 1988) 288.

Tharros, the first of which is dated to the second quarter of the 6th century B.C.E., and the second to the 8th–7th centuries.[34] Another parallel is a seal dated to the 5th century, but its sphinx is raising its left foreleg.[35] The type in Egypt originally signified a combined head of Pharaoh and body of a lion, giving the idea of strength, capacity for fighting, and domination.[36] On the coins of Byblos, the significance of the type is not clear: perhaps it is only decorative, but it is possible that it also represents the city's kingship. We must bear in mind that this type was chosen by the minting authority as the main symbol of the first series of Byblian coins, which was the first Phoenician coinage to be struck.

The seated sphinx is only depicted on the obverse of Series II.1, II.2, II.3, and II.4. It is also turned to the left, with a male human head, wearing the *klaft* and the double crown of Egypt with the *uraeus*. In addition, it is wearing an apron that may be borrowed from Egyptian iconography (no. 67). All its other characteristics, however, derive from the Syrian iconography of the 2nd millennium, which was only partially influenced by Egypt.[37] It is seated, winged (one or two wings visible), and its tail is *S*-shaped. This type of sphinx was widespread at the beginning of the 1st millennium in Phoenicia and neighboring areas and mainly appeared on ivories and seals—for example, on ivories at Nimrud, Samaria, and Arslan-Tash, but it is walking instead of being seated; on ivories from Megiddo, it is seated but does not wear either the double crown or the apron.[38] The relief at Arwad and the Phoenician seal from *YZBL* has the same type of sphinx, but it is crouched

---

34. J. Boardman, "Scarabs and Seals: Greek, Punic and Related Types," in *A Catalogue of Material in the British Museum and Other Tombs at Tharros, Sardinia* (ed. R. D. Barnett and C. Mendleson; London, 1987) 100–101 n. 3/22; p. 136, pl. 55; G. Pisano, "Una sfinge in osso da Cadice," *RSF* 21 (1993; supplement) 73 and pl. 7:6; N. Avigad and B. Sass, *Corpus of West Semitic Stamps* (Jerusalem, 1997) 277, no. 745.

35. É. Gubel, "La glyptique et la genèse de l'iconographie monétaire phénicienne," in *Numismatique et histoire économique phéniciennes et puniques* (ed. T. Hackens and G. Moucharte; Studia Phoenicia 9; Louvain-la-Neuve, 1992) 4–5 and pl. 2:6; idem, "Byblos: l'Art de la métropole phénicienne," in *Biblo una città e la sua cultura* (Rome, 1994) 73–96.

36. C. Zivie-Coche, *Sphinx! Le Père de la terreur: Histoire d'une statue* (Paris, 1977); E. Lipiński, ed., *Dictionnaire de la civilisation phénicienne et punique* (Turnhout, 1992), s.v. "sphinx."

37. Dessenne, *Le Sphinx*, 27–28, 41; H. Frankfort, *Cylinder Seals* (London, 1939) 256 and pl. 41:o; pp. 266, 269, 285 and pl. 44:n.

38. R. D. Barnett, *A Catalogue of the Nimrud Ivories* (London, 1957) pl. 1:A4; M. E. L. Mallowan, *Nimrud and Its Remains* (London, 1966) 569, fig. 519; p. 565, fig. 506 (however, the tail has a semicircular shape); J. W. Crowfoot and G. M. Crowfoot, *Early Ivories* (London, 1938) and pl. 5:1; p. 21 and pl. 7:7; F. Thureau-Dangin et al., *Arslan-Tash* (Paris, 1931) 104 and pls. 30–31; G. Loud, *The Megiddo Ivories* (Chicago, 1939) pl. 11 h:44.

and without an apron.[39] The Phoenician seal of *BʿLNTN* has the same type but walking and without a double crown.[40] The coins of Idalium on Cyprus have a winged sphinx on the obverse, with no apron or headdress, seated on a floral ornament, and on the reverse a lotus flower on two spiral tendrils.[41] The closest parallel is on a Phoenician seal dated to the end of the 8th century B.C.E. (?), but it has no double crown, and it faces right.[42] This type of sphinx, with some variation, is also represented on Phoenician sculpture of the 1st millennium—for example, at Byblos, Sidon, and Umm el-ʿAmed.[43] Because of the success of this type in Phoenicia, it probably had not only a decorative function but also a symbolic meaning. Like the crouched sphinx of the first type, it probably represented the kingship of the city. It has sometimes been related to the *kĕrūb* of the Bible and to the Akkadian verb *karābu*, 'to intercede'.[44] This is another hypothesis yet to be confirmed.[45]

In spite of some common points, the two types of sphinx represented on the Byblian coins expressed two different sorts of vision. If they were considered decorative, the first one was borrowed from Egyptian iconography; the second was expressing local Phoenician art, which originated earlier in the Syro-Phoenician area. If they had political or religious meanings, the first one would have had an Egyptian meaning, and the second would have had an easily understood Phoenician meaning. These different aspects could be combined, thus giving a more complex interpretation. On

39. H. Bossert, *Altsyrien* (Tübingen, 1951) 157, no. 510; É. Gubel, ed., *Art phénicien: La sculpture de tradition phénicienne* (Paris, 2002) 29–30, no. 3 (850–750 B.C.E.); Moscati, ed., *I Fenici*, 300 (6th–5th cent. B.C.E.); Avigad-Sass, *Corpus of West Semitic Stamps*, 275, no. 740.

40. R. Hestrin and M. Dayagi-Mendels, *Inscribed Seals* (Jerusalem, 1979) 154, no. 120.

41. Babelon, *Perses*, 104, no. 726 and pl. 19:19; cf. T. Petit, *Œdipe et le chérubin: Les sphinx levantins, chypriotes et grecs comme gardiens d'immortalité* (Fribourg-Göttingen, 2011) 56.

42. K. Galling, "Beschriftete Bildsiegel des ersten Jahrtausends v. Chr. vornehmlich aus Syrien und Palästina," *ZDPV* 64 (1941) 135 and pl. 5:14.

43. On thrones, sarcophagi, and other sculptures: M. Dunand and R. Duru, *Oumm el-ʿAmed* (Paris, 1962) 167 and pls. 34, 67; A. Parrot et al., *Les Phéniciens* (Paris, 1975) figs. 114, 116; Dunand, *Byblos II*, pl. 152; M. Jaber, *Recherches sur quelques aspects religieux à Byblos aux IIIe et Ier millénaires* (Paris, 1982), thèse de 3e cycle (unpublished). Cf. also Gubel, ed., *Art phénicien*, 121, no. 118; Lipiński, ed., *Dictionnaire*, s.v. "Ahiram"; Moscati, *I Fenici*, 36, 127, 148, 158, 347, 406, 407.

44. See above, n. 27; Petit, *Œdipe et le chérubin*, 19–36 (with bibliography).

45. On the difficulty in understanding monetary symbols, see L. Lacroix, "Les types des monnaies grecques," in *Numismatique antique, problèmes et méthodes* (Nancy, 1975); E. W. Klimowsky, *On Ancient Palestinian and Other Coins: Their Symbolism and Metrology* (Tel Aviv, 1974) 44; J. Elayi, "Remarques méthodologiques sur l'étude iconographique des monnaies phéniciennes," *MUSJ* 59 (2007) 47–54.

one-third-shekels (Series II.1), the sphinx is represented with one wing visible and a circle of dots (nos. 67, 68). On one-twelfth-shekels, there are two variants in the representation of the sphinx: in the anepigraphic Series II.2.1, it has one wing visible and a circle of dots (for example no. 81); in the inscribed Series II.2.2, it is represented with two wings visible and a double circle of dots (no. 84). These variants in representation were probably intended to provide help in distinguishing different series or different issues of the same denomination. It is impossible to know whether they were issued contemporaneously or successively. Nor do we know the meaning of the change from the crouched sphinx of Group I to the winged seated sphinx of Group II. The minting authority decided to keep the same symbol of the sphinx; however, its representation was no longer borrowed from the Egyptian model but from the Syrian model. It could simply be a change of artistic influence, or maybe not. Nevertheless, the conception of the Byblian coinage by the minting authority had changed significantly: from a unique type for the shekel and all the denominations in Group I to several types in the denominations of Group II.

4. *The Lion*

The lion appears in four different aspects in the Byblian coinage: attacking a bull, seated, as the figurehead on the prow, and as a head *en face*. The lion attacking a bull is represented on the reverse of all the series of Group IV. It is very carefully engraved in most of the series of ʿOzbaʿal, ʾUrimilk, and ʿAynel (IV.2, IV.3, and IV.4), but it is sometimes more-or-less stylized (coin no. 528). The attitude of the lion is that of a strong predator bringing down its prey, which it holds with its forepaws and jaws. The head is seen from above with the eyes represented by dots and eyebrows, the ears by a crescent-shape; the nose, cheeks, and musculature of the body are also represented. The mane is represented by short parallel strokes on each side of the head and dots on the forehead and the back of the head, between the shoulders. Therefore, it was a lion with a short mane as on Sidonian coins, and not a lion with a long mane covering the shoulders, flanks, and part of the stomach as in Assyrian and Persian representations.[46] The lion with a long mane was attested in Syria–Phoenicia as early as the 4th millennium B.C.E.: it is the so-called

46. Elayi-Elayi, *Monnayage de Sidon*, 484–85. For Persian lions, see, for example, A. Farkas, *Achaemenid Sculpture* (Istanbul, 1974) pl. 15, fig. 32; pl. 19, fig. 36; M. C. Root, *The King and Kingship in Achaemenid Art* (Leiden, 1979) pl. 16, fig. 16b; pl. 28, fig. 28a–b (with bibliography). For Neo-Assyrian lions, see, for example, P. Albenda, "Lions on Assyrian Wall Reliefs," *JANES* 2 (1974) 9 and 24, fig. 19; C. E. Watanabe, "Symbolism of the Royal Lion Hunt in Assyria," in *Intellectual Life of the Ancient Near East* (ed. J. Prosecky; Prague, 1998) 439–50.

Indian or Asian lion (family: *Panthera*; species: *leo*; genus: *Persicus*).[47] It is impossible to check the length of the mane from the bones found in the excavations, of course, and there are no longer any lions today in the whole of the Near East. However, one can still note the same difference between the lions of North Africa, which have a long, abundant mane; and those on the Indian reserve of the Gir Forest, which have a short mane. Such a difference in representation between Byblian, Sidonian, (and Tyrian?) lions, and Assyrian and Persian lions may correspond to a geographical distribution of short- and long-mane lions—something that unfortunately cannot be checked;[48] or it may be explained by different artistic representations. In addition, it should be noticed that the Byblian lion has a somewhat human appearance due to the shape of its forehead, and the appearance of its eyes with eyebrows: this may have been the engraver's choice or may have been based on some mythical aspect of lions.

The seated lion represented on the reverse of Series IV.1.4 is a resting lion, its body in profile and its head *en face*, with an S-shaped tail, like the seated winged sphinx. The length of the mane is not visible, and it has a somewhat human appearance. As a secondary motif, the lion's head replaced the horse's head as the figurehead on the war-galley, from the coinage of King ʾElpaʿal on, until the end of the Persian period. It is represented in profile and is roaring.

The Byblian lion's head in profile is quite similar to the lion's head in Tyrian and Sidonian coinages—in the scene of the man (Sidonian deity) slaying the lion, which is standing in front of him on its hind legs.[49] The lion motif is quite common in Phoenician iconography; for example, in the *maʿabed* and in the *meghazil* of Amrit, on the so-called Stele of Amrit, on the Stele of Qadbun, on the Aḥiram sarcophagus, on low reliefs and statues from Byblos and Umm el-ʿAmed, on two Sidonian sculptures, and on a late Tyrian sarcophagus.[50] The main function of lions was to protect

47. See, for example, J.-O. Gransard-Desmond, "Le lion dans la Syrie antique: Confrontation des textes au matériel archéologique," *Orient-Express* (2001/2) 16–18. We thank F. Petter, Prof. at the Muséum National d'Histoire Naturelle of Paris, Department "Mammifères et Oiseaux," who gave us information on this subject.

48. According to F. Petter, Indian lions would be differentiated by a smaller brain and a more elongated head. This observation ought to be taken into account in analyses of ancient lions' bones.

49. Elayi-Elayi, *Coinage of Tyre*, 273–76; idem, *Monnayage de Sidon*, pl. 12:320.

50. See, for example, E. Renan, *Mission de Phénicie* (Paris, 1864) pls. 12, 13, 15; Gubel, ed., *Art phénicien*, 18, fig. 17; p. 51, no. 38; p. 53, fig. 9; p. 64, no. 49; p. 67, nos. 51–52; p. 71, no. 59; p. 87, no. 79; Lipiński, ed., *Dictionnaire*, 10–11 and fig. 7, s.v. "Ahiram/Ahirôm" (with bibliography); N. Jidejian, *Tyre through the Ages* (Beirut, 1969), fig. 74; M. Dunand and

doors, palaces, temples, or tombs, the purpose of which was expressed in the powerful, aggressive, and impressive presentation.[51] This function is well illustrated by the inscriptions of the two lions that guard a door in Til-Barsip: the eastern lion is called "the impetuous hurricane, powerful attacker, which fells the rebels, which provides the heart with satisfaction"; and the western lion, "the one which charges at rebels and devastates enemy country, which ejects the bad and welcomes the good people."[52] This type of lion first appeared in the Byblian coinage during the reign of King ʾElpaʿal, who chose it for unknown reasons. We do know that the powerful, aggressive, and impressive image of the lion was adapted to the new war fleet inaugurated by his predecessor, the anonymous king. Perhaps the lion was also a religious symbol connected with one of the deities of Byblos. In Tyre, particularly on coins, the lion was probably connected with the Heracles Myth involving the Tyrian deity Milqart,[53] who was possibly the deity riding on a seahorse on the shekels. The Milqart-Heracles assimilation, attested by Herodotus in the middle of the 5th century, may have appeared earlier, but it clearly existed at the beginning of Tyrian coinage. The Heraclean type, wearing the *leonte*, had been known in Phoenicia since the 6th century B.C.E.; it also inherited Near Eastern traditions such as the function of master of lions, which symbolized domination over evil forces.[54] The motif of the lion can therefore be understood as being connected with the deity riding on a seahorse, possibly Milqart. In Byblos, the connexion of the lion with a local deity, such as Baʿalat Gubal, is not impossible but is difficult to establish.[55] A lion head *en face* was added on the reverse of some shekels of ʿAynel, at the end of the inscription or on the last letter; the lion seems to have an open mouth (no. 886).

N. Saliby, *Le temple d'Amrit dans la pérée d'Aradus* (Paris, 1985) 20–21, figs. 6–7; Dunand, *Byblos II*, no. 7167 and pl. 152.

51. See, for example, Gransard-Desmond, "Le lion dans la Syrie antique," 16–18; I. Cornelius, "The Lion in the Art of the Ancient Near East: A Study of Selected Motifs," *JNSL* 15 (1989) 63.

52. F. Thureau-Dangin and M. Dunand, *Til-Barsib* (Paris, 1936) 148–50 ; cf. also N. Avigad and B. Sass, *Corpus of West Semitic Stamp Seals* (Jerusalem, 1997) 274, no. 738 (seal).

53. *BMC Phoenicia*, cxxiv–cxxvii n. 2; cf. C. Bonnet, *Melqart: Cultes et mythes de l'Héraclès tyrien en Méditerranée* (Leuven, 1988) 399–415.

54. See Bonnet, ibid., 409–15 (with bibliography).

55. See, for example, Betlyon, *Coinage of Phoenicia*, 113–15, 130 (with bibliography). He related the lion to ʾAšerah, identifying her with Baʿalat Gubal, which cannot be proved.

5. *The Vulture*

The vulture is only represented in three series of the coinage of the anonymous king: on the reverse of shekels, quarter-, and 16th-shekels, above a ram (Series III.1; III.2 and III.3) and alone on the reverse of Series III.4. In series III.2, 3, and 4, one closed wing is visible (no. 166); in Series III.1, the left wing is closed, and the right wing is spread over the head of the ram (no. 107). It is interesting to note that the vulture of Series III.4 bears the crook and flail on its shoulder, just like the hawk of Group II. The vulture is not represented on other Phoenician coins and is unusual in Phoenician iconography. The meaning of the scene of the vulture above the ram remains obscure. E. Babelon interpreted it as an allusion to Evagoras I of Salamis who used the symbol of the ram on his coins.[56] However, the meaning of the ram is not clear, and the Byblian series probably preceded Evagoras I's reign. R. Pietschmann proposed interpreting the vulture as some destructive deity, which is not provable.[57] There could be some correlation between this scene and the following scene, in the ʾElpaʿal coinage, where a lion is attacking a bull, in what is clearly an animal fighting scene. The image of a vulture and ram fighting was not as common as a lion and bull fighting. The parallel proposed by J. W. Betlyon is not relevant: a scaraboid from Aleppo dated to the 9th or 8th century B.C.E. represents an eagle rather than a vulture above a deer, ibex, or stag, not a ram.[58] In the Byblian scene, it must be pointed out that the attitude of the vulture is not necessarily threatening to the ram. Anyway, the vulture never attacks its prey because it is a carrion feeder: if a ram is wounded, it waits nearby until it is dead.[59] It is possible that the engravers of these coins had observed this kind of scene in the high mountains of the territory of Byblos, where there were vultures—for example, in the area of Afqa. The Egyptian goddess Nekhbet, who was revered in El-Kab, in front of the Hierakonpolis, was represented iconographically by a vulture. She was the protector of the Egyptian kingship as early as Narmer's reign; in El-Kab, she was associated with Hathor and Sobek.[60] Because of the traditional connection between Byblos and Egypt and the presence of a crook and flail in Series III.4, the symbol of the vulture in the coinage of Byblos may be a reference to the

56. Babelon, *Perses*, clxvi.

57. R. Pietschmann, *Geschichte der Phönizier* (Berlin, 1889) 173.

58. Betlyon, *Coinage of Phoenicia*, 114–15, 129–31; D. Harden, *The Phoenicians* (London, 1962) 317, no. 108a.

59. We thank J.-F. Voisin (Muséum National d'Histoire Naturelle, Paris) for this information.

60. M. H. von Voss, "Nechbet," in *LÄ* (Wiesbaden 1980) vol. 4, cols. 366–67; J. Leclant, ed., *Dictionnaire de l'Antiquité* (Paris, 2005), s.v. "Nekhbet."

idea of protecting the kingship and may have a correlation with Baʿalat Gubal through Hathor, "Lady of Byblos."

6. *The Ram*

The ram is only represented in the coinage of the anonymous king in association with the vulture, in three series, on the reverse of the shekels and 16th-shekels (Series III.1, III.2, and III.3). The motif is somewhat difficult to see in detail because it is incuse. It is located under the vulture and is generally larger. It is recumbent, facing left, with head reverted, forelegs folded, and hindlegs stretched. Its position is different from the dancing incuse goat in Sidonian coinage,[61] but there is uncertainty about whether it is being attacked by the vulture or resting.

The identification of the ram is quite clear on some coins (nos. 107, 163), with the characteristic head shape in profile and the dotted semicircular horn, turned to the left. The horn is a little less clear on coin no. 166; however, engraving such details on small coins is not easy.

This domestic sheep (male ram) was widespread in Syria–Phoenicia at that time (family: *Bovidae*; subfamily: *Caprinae*; genus: *Ovis*; species: *Aries*, Linné 1758).[62] The motif of the ram is well attested in Phoenician iconography, although not as common as the lion motif: for example, on Tyrian, Sidonian, and Salaminian coins, on steles, bowls, amulet cases, and scepters. On Sidonian coins, the king, who is represented in a religious function, follows the deity, who is carried on a chariot. The king holds a scepter with a ram's head surmounted by the Hathoric symbol: this royal scepter has its origin in the liturgical Egyptian scepter of Khnum, borrowed by the Phoenicians, via Ugarit.[63] The original Egyptian motif of a ram was a representation of Amon with a ram's head; it symbolized protection.[64] The head of this animal is also represented on a silver rhyton bearing a Neo-Elamite inscription under its chin.[65] The Tyrian coin motif seems to be indicative of a non-marine animal (such as an owl) that was

---

61. Elayi-Elayi, *Monnayage de Sidon*, pl. 7:219.

62. We thank F. Poplin, Department "Anatomie comparée" (Muséum National d'Histoire Naturelle, Paris), for his comments.

63. *BMC Phoenicia*, 94, no. 1 and pl. 11:9; L. Mildenberg, *Vestigia Leonis* (Freiburg-Göttingen, 1998) pl. 6:56; É. Gubel, *Phoenician Furniture* (Studia Phoenicia 7; Leuven, 1987) pl. 10:29; Moscati, ed., *I Fenici*, 311, 388, 437; P. Naster, *Scripta Nummaria: Contributions à la méthodologie numismatique* (Louvain-la-Neuve, 1983) pl. 10:5a–b.

64. See, for example, C. Aldred et al., *L'Égypte du crépuscule* (Paris, 1980) 179, fig. 158; 229, fig. 223; 252–53, figs. 249–50.

65. F. Vallat, "Une inscription élamite sur un rhyton en argent à tête de bélier," *Akkadica* 116 (2000) 585–39.

especially revered in the Tyrian cult, and that possibly symbolized religious protection over the city.[66] Because of the lack of documentation, we cannot interpret the Byblian scene of the vulture above the ram; an animal confrontation is a hypothesis that has yet to be confirmed.

7. *The Bull*

The bull replaced the ram while the lion replaced the vulture from the coinage of ʾElpaʿal onward. The type was continued by ʿOzbaʿal, ʾUrimilk, and ʿAynel. It appeared in three series of ʾElpaʿal: on shekels (Series IV.1.1), quarter-shekels (Series IV.1.2), and 16th-shekels (Series IV.1.3). The body of the bull is incuse but not the facing head. Here the lion is clearly bringing down the bull. Its left foreleg is folded, and its hindlegs are stretched. The engraving of the semiincuse bull is difficult and rather unskillful; it is more-or-less stylized on the small coins (for example, no. 221). The bull is represented as being larger than the lion, as it is in reality. An incuse bull passing, with head reverted, was represented on the archaic coins of Sybaris.[67] In the coinages of Kings ʿOzbaʿal, ʾUrimilk, and ʿAynel, the incuse method, which partially involved a side in relief and partially involved a side that was hollowed-out, was not used anymore. A bull was much easier to engrave, and its representation was skillful and fairly realistic: its head was lifted, its body was half-collapsed, and its hindlegs were still standing. This lion-and-bull fighting scene was represented on all the series of shekels, quarters, and 16th-shekels of the last three kings of Byblos (Series IV.2.1, IV.2.2, IV.3.1, IV.3.2, IV.4.1, IV.4.2, IV.4.4, IV.4.5, IV.4.6, IV.4.7).

The bull does not appear in other Phoenician coinages, but was used in Phoenician iconography and in Sidonian sculpture, for example.[68] The scene in which a lion kills a bull is common in the Levant: according to E. Porada, it is "one of the stock motifs of Mesopotamian art; the theme became stereotyped after the Middle Assyrian period."[69] The reverse of the coins struck by Mazday/Mazaios in Tarsus also bears an animal combat,

66. Elayi-Elayi, *Coinage of Tyre*, 276–77.

67. Head, *Historia Numorum*, 84, fig. 44.

68. Gubel, ed., *Art phénicien*, 125, no. 122; R. Stucky, *Das Eschmun-Heiligtum von Sidon: Architektur und Inschriften* (Basel 2005) pls. 16–18.

69. E. Porada, *The Collection of the Pierpont Morgan Library* (New York, 1968) 105 and nos. 842–43. See also G. Perrot and C. Chipiez, *History of Art in Phoenicia and Its Dependencies* (2 vols.; London, 1885) 2:405, 421, and figs. 348–49; G. M. A. Richter, *Engraved Gems of the Greeks and Etruscans* (London, 1968) nos. 16–17, 194–97, 379–80; A. D. H. Bivar, "A Persian Monument at Athens and Its Connections with the Achaemenid State Seals," in *W. B. Henning, Memorial Volume* (London, 1970) 43–61.

with a lion killing a stag, not a bull.[70] The beginning of the animal combat scene in ʾElpaʿal's coinage was probably earlier than this Mazday coinage. The same scene, with a lion and a stag, is also found on the reverse of the coins of several kings of Kition in the second half of the 5th century B.C.E. and at the beginning of the 4th.[71] Be that as it may, as J. W. Betlyon stated, "Borrowing becomes a most imprecise concept, especially when dealing with cross-cultural, iconographic motifs."[72] In Byblian coinage, the scene of a fighting lion and bull seems to have a religious meaning, but it is impossible to know what meaning. Byblos was a holy city,[73] and it was probably just as important for the minting authority to represent a religious symbolic scene on the reverse as to print a symbol of power on the obverse.

8. *The Hawk*

The hawk is represented on the reverse of the series bearing a seated winged sphinx on the obverse. These are anepigraphic, inscribed 3rd-shekels (Series II.1) and 16th-shekels (Series II.2.1 and II.2.2). The hawk is standing to the left, wearing the double crown of Egypt with the *uraeus*, and with a crook and flail on its shoulder; it is inside a slight or shallow incuse impression. This bird was first identified as an eagle, which is represented on the Paphos coins.[74] The identification of the hawk on the Byblian coins is clear, however, especially since its crown and attributes are borrowings from Egypt. Some of the Egyptian gifts from pharaohs that were found in Byblos were decorated with hawks.[75] The hawk with flail is the hieroglyph bịk; the hawk wearing the double crown, with or without *uraeus* and with or without flail, is usually interpreted as the symbol of Horus.[76] However, the hawk of Byblos can be distinguished from the Egyptian hawk by its two attributes: flail and crook. It is well known that these two attributes were

---

70. Head, *Historia Numorum*, 731 and fig. 323; *BMC Lycaonia, Isauria, and Cilicia*, 170.

71. Babelon, *Perses*, 97–100; cf. Gubel, "La glyptique," 3 and pl. 1:2a. See also a seal bought in Aleppo: Avigad and Sass, *Corpus of West Semitic Stamp Seals*, 268–69, no. 721.

72. Betlyon, *Coinage of Phoenicia*, 132 n. 47.

73. Elayi, *Byblos*, 196–202.

74. *BMC Cyprus*, pl. 7:10–21; Babelon, *Perses*, pl. 20:17–20.

75. Dunand, *Byblos I*, 329, no. 4909 (hawk with double crown on a fragment of alabaster vase); Moscati, ed., *I Fenici*, 525 (hawk and two hawk heads on a gold pectoral).

76. P. Montet, *Byblos et l'Égypte* (Paris, 1928–29) 113, no. 396 and pl. 61; S. Mercer, *Horus Royal God of Egypt* (Grafton, 1942) 56, 113; A. Altenmüller, "Falke," *LÄ* 2:94–97; D. Wildung, "Falkenkleid," *LÄ* 2:97–99); D. Valbelle, "Le faucon et le roi," in *L'imperio ramesside* (Rome, 1997) 205–20.

the symbol of kingship worn by Osiris.[77] There is a combination of Osiris and his attributes with the hawk Horus on a stela.[78] The hawk wearing the double crown and the flail is represented on Phoenician seals dated from the late 9th to 7th centuries: for example, the seal of *YZBL* wearing in the upper register a crouched winged sphinx with a double crown and above a hawk with a flail; and the seal of *YḤZBʿL*.[79] A seal from Kition, which we've only been able to see on a facsimile, could represent a hawk with the name *ḤR*.[80] In the Roman period, the Horus-hawk appears frequently in the coinage of Alexandria but without a flail and crook, or with a crook only.[81] All these incomplete parallels mean that, even if the iconography of the seals partly influenced the monetary iconography,[82] the hawk of the Byblian coinage (wearing the double crown, crook, and flail) was a local re-interpretation of the Egyptian hawk. The only precise parallel to the hawk of the Byblian coins is a contemporary seal in the Virolleaud collection.[83] A relation between the sphinx on the obverse and the hawk on the reverse of the coins is likely.[84] However, the older parallels of sphinx and hawk (?) presented by É. Gubel do not have the same attributes and could have a different meaning.[85] Interpreting the hawk of Byblos is difficult because it could be an iconographic, religious, or linguistic borrowing from Egypt, or a combination of these—directly or through older Phoenician borrowings. The existence in Byblos of a cult of Hathor, whose relations with Horus are

77. Cf. *LÄ*, s.v. "Herrschaftembleme"; A. Hassan, "Stöcke und Stäbe im Pharaonischen Ägypten," *MÄS* 33 (1976) 104 and fig. 32.

78. E. Bresciani, "La Stele Cat. 1908 del Museo Civico di Bologna," *MdI* 37 (1981) 85 and pl. 12.

79. N. Avigad, "The Seal of Jezebel," *IEJ* 14 (1964) 274–76; Avigad and Sass, *Corpus of West Semitic Stamp Seals*, 275, no. 740; idem, "Note on Some Inscribed Syro-Phoenician Seals," *BASOR* 189 (1968) 49. See also the sphinx and hawk on a throne of the Theban grave no. 16 in Medamoud: F. Bisson de la Roque, "Rapport sur les fouilles de Médamoud (1925)," *BIFAO* 3 (1926) 51, fig. 35. The hawk with crook and flail also appears on a seal from Ibiza: A. Vives y Escudero, *Estudio de Arqueología Cartaginesa: La Necropólis de Ibiza* (Madrid, 1917) pl. 24:17.

80. M. G. Amadasi Guzzo and V. Karageorghis, *Fouilles de Kition, III: Inscriptions phéniciennes* (Nicosia, 1977) 129–30, no. D1 and fig. 18.

81. *BMC Alexandria*, 33, nos. 275–76; p. 40, nos. 328–32; p. 97, nos. 826–29; p. 141, no. 1182; p. 150, nos. 1245–47 (with a crook only); p. 165, no. 1343.

82. Gubel, "La glyptique," 2–11.

83. Ibid., 4 and pl. 2:5.

84. On this relation in general, see L. Lacroix, "La typologie du bronze par rapport à celle de l'argent," *AIINSup* 25 (1980) 265–86.

85. Gubel, "La glyptique," 5 and pl. 2:6–7.

well known, and the Byblian legend of Isis[86] could indicate a religious borrowing. However, the addition of a scepter shows a local reinterpretation of the borrowing—possibly, for example, to symbolize the Byblian kingship and its religious function (as for the sphinx on the obverse).

9. *The Griffin*

The seated griffin is the reverse type of the halves of 16th-shekels in the unidentified Series V.1, and a griffin head is represented on the reverse of the small-denomination coins of Series V.2. E. Babelon described the seahorse head on some shekels of Series III.1 as a horned griffin head.[87] Considering all the coins of this series, the seahorse seems to have something of a horse's head, with a forelock, not a horn. G. F. Hill was wondering whether the figurehead of the galley in Series IV.1 of ʾElpaʿal is a griffin's head,[88] but it looks more like a horse's head. The griffin image here is seated with its right foreleg raised. It is winged, with an S-shaped tail; it has a short mane and a slightly open beak. The representation of the animal head on the minute coins is stylized but seems to be a griffin's head.

The griffin was a mythical animal that was common in Phoenician iconography—for example, in the Sidonian sarcophagus "of the Lycian" and in an Aradian relief.[89] It also appears on several bullae from Wadi ed-Daliyeh that are dated to the middle of the 4th century B.C.E.[90] The griffin was a very common motif in Mesopotamian and Syrian art, for example, in the Megiddo ivories, in Phoenician and Hebrew seals of the 8th century, and in the Cypro-Phoenician seals of the 9th–7th centuries.[91] Griffins were represented in the coinage of Abdera, which is considered by some scholars to have been a Phoenician trading station or factory.[92] The symbolic meaning

86. Isis took his son Horus to Byblos after the murder of Osiris: see, for example, J. G. Griffiths, *The Conflict of Horus and Seth* (Liverpool, 1960) 113.

87. Babelon, *Perses*, 192, no. 1342.

88. *BMC Phoenicia*, 94, no. 2.

89. T. Macridy, "Le temple d'Echmoun à Sidon: Fouilles exécutées par le Musée Impérial ottoman (suite)," *RB* (1904) 396, pl. 11:1–2; B. Schmidt-Dounas, *Der Lykische Sarkophag aus Sidon* (Tübingen, 1985); Gubel, ed., *Art phénicien*, 27–28, no. 2.

90. P. W. Lapp and N. L. Lapp, eds., *Discoveries in the Wâdī ed-Dâliyeh* (Cambridge, 1974) 28–29 and pls. 62–63.

91. Moscati, ed., *I Fenici*, 406, 515; Avigad and Sass, *Corpus of West Semitic Stamp Seals*, 278, no. 747; 77, no. 85; É. Gubel, "'Syro-Cypriote' Cubical Stamp: The Phoenician Connection," in *Phoenicia and the East Mediterranean in the First Millennium* B.C. (ed. E. Lipiński; Leuven, 1987) 214–15, fig. 13:1.

92. Head, *Historia Numorum*, 253; D. Raymond, *Macedonian Regal Coinage* (New York, 1953) 22, 25; J. M.F. May, *The Coinage of Abdera* (London, 1966) 8.

of the griffin is unknown, except its decorative value in some cases;[93] in Byblos, whatever religious function it may have played is unknown, if indeed there was such a function.

10. *The Shell*

The shell is a secondary motif that is engraved under the seahorse in Series IV.1.1 of ʾElpaʿal and in Series IV.2.1, IV.3.1, and IV.4.1. The scene represented on the obverse of the shekel is complex, and it was difficult to put a wavy line, seahorse, and shell in the field under the galley; thus the shell is often, at least partly, off the flan (for example, no. 659). The difficulty increased in the case of fractional denominations, and so, due to lack of space, the shell is not represented, except in Series IV.4.3. The shell is also a motif used in Tyrian coinage.[94] This shell was misinterpreted as a murex representing the role of the city in the production of purple dye, until our article of 1991 in which, based on scientific arguments, we showed that it was definitely not a murex.[95] However, the older misinterpretation has not disappeared entirely.[96] We shall demonstrate again why this shell cannot be a murex and what it is precisely. M. Dunand had already questioned the suggestion that the shell represented on Byblian coins was a murex and identified it as a conch; P. Naster cautiously called it a shell.[97] Later imperial Tyrian coins have a murex, which sometimes represents the legend of the dog finding a murex.[98] The shell discovered by the dog is clearly a *Murex brandaris*, which has a spiral body with spikes and an elongated, siphon-shaped canal; the dot on the opening could represent the hypobranchial, purple-producing gland.[99] The shell represented on

93. A. M. Bisi, *Il grifone* (Rome, 1965); J. Flagge, *Untersuchungen zur Bedeutung des Greifen* (Sankt Augustin, 1975); C. Delplace, *Le griffon de l'archaïsme à l'époque impériale* (Brussels, 1980); Lipiński, ed., *Dictionnaire*, s.v. "griffon."

94. Elayi-Elayi, *Coinage of Tyre*, 272–73.

95. J. Elayi, "Étude typologique des sicles de Tyr au dauphin," *Cahiers Numismatiques* 108 (1991) 13–17 (with bibliography).

96. L. Sole, "Le emissioni monetali della Fenicia prima di Alessandro-II," *SEAP* 18 (1998) 93–94; C. Mazzucato, "Il murice nelle monete fenicie e puniche," *Byrsa* 2 (2003) 121–30.

97. Dunand, *Byblos I*, 407–8; P. Naster, "Trésors de monnaies de Byblos du IVe s. av. J.-C. trouvés à Byblos," in *Numismatique et histoire économique phéniciennes et puniques* (ed. T. Hackens and G. Moucharte; Studia Phoenicia 9; Louvain-la-Neuve, 1992) 42.

98. *BMC Phoenicia*, 291, no. 473; P. Naster, "Le chien et le murex des monnaies impériales de Tyr," *NAC* 14 (1985) 257–60.

99. *Traité de zoologie* 5/3 (Paris, 1968) 59, 306. Cf. A. Gruvel, *Les états de Syrie: Richesses marines et fluviales – Exploitation actuelle – Avenir* (Paris, 1931) 441; L. B. Jensen, "Royal Purple of Tyre," *JNES* 22 (1963) 104–18; Lipiński, ed., *Dictionnaire*, s.v. "pourpre"

Byblian, pre-Alexandrine coins, however, is not a muricid but a *Charonia variegata* (Lamarck 1816; *Charonia seguenza* is a junior synonym), a marine gastropod of the Ranellidae family, commonly known as the Atlantic Trumpet Triton which is widespread in the eastern Mediterranean.[100] The shape of the shell is characterized by a long spiral that is more or less smooth (no. 308) or patterned (nos. 326, 779); its opening is quite wide, with a siphon-shaped canal turned upward, as in the bronze Tyrian Series III.2.3.[101] The representation of a conch is quite clear and realistic. The Atlantic Trumpet Triton was a well-known shell in Antiquity that was used as a trumpet, for example, when the end was broken off; it was used in a funeral context in several Near Eastern cultures.[102] Several conchs were found by M. Dunand in Byblos near offering deposits and may have been used as drinking vases.[103] The meaning of this shell on Byblian coins is not clear, but it was definitely not economic, as in the case of the murex, and it was probably a religious marine motif, related to the seahorse. It may have been used in a local ritual from the reign of ʾElpaʿal right through to the end of the Byblian coinage of the Persian period.

11. *The Lotus Flower*

The lotus flower was used as a main motif on the reverse side of all the series of Group I and as a secondary motif in Series II.2.2. In this last series, the lotus flower is positioned in the bottom left corner of the incuse square, before the legs of the hawk and under the vertical inscription. It has an easily identifiable form, with a short stem, two petals, and a central triangular bud—which is different from the lily on Judean coins, which has longer petals and bud, and the calyx is represented by a ring.[104]

The identification of the lotus flower in the series of Group I is not easy. It is a double motif, composed of two opposing motifs that are lotus flower-shaped. It was first interpreted as a thunderbolt or lightening

(with bibliography). A *Murex brandaris* is also represented on the Sidonian coins of Severus Alexander: Babelon, *Perses*, 269, no. 1849.

100. See, for example, G. d'Angelo and S. Gargiullo, *Guida alle Conchiglie Mediterranee* (Milan, 1979) 132. We thank B. Métivier from the Department of the "Milieux et Peuplements Aquatiques," Muséum National d'Histoire Naturelle, Paris, for helping us to identify this shell and giving his comments.

101. Elayi-Elayi, *Coinage of Tyre*, 273: however, in other Tyrian series, the siphon-shaped canal was erroneously represented reversed.

102. Cf. Dunand, *Byblos I*, 407–8 (with bibliography).

103. Ibid.

104. See, for example, *BMC Palestine*, 199, no. 9 and pl. 20:13 (?); T. Fischer, *Silber aus dem Grab Davids* (Buchum, 1983) 13, fig. 7.

bolt,[105] which is a common motif encountered, for example, on Greek and Ascalonite coins.[106] J. W. Betlyon followed this hypothesis, connecting the thunderbolt with Baʿal Šamim and Baʿal Hadad.[107] G. K. Jenkins hesitantly proposed interpreting it as a stylized double-lotus,[108] and his hypothesis has been followed by most scholars.[109] É. Gubel recently proposed a new hypothesis: "a double palmette extremely stylized" resulting from an evolution leading to a similarity with the double lotus.[110] Although interesting, this last hypothesis does not fit exactly with the features of the motif on the Byblian coins. Second, the presence of a lotus flower in the next unquestionable series, Series II.2.2, together with the sphinx on the obverse is a strong argument in favor of the double-lotus. Third, an identical lotus flower was stamped on the handle of an amphora found by M. Dunand in the excavations of Byblos.[111] The lotus and double-lotus motifs are used for their decorative value, for example, in the frieze of Aḥiram's sarcophagus and in the frieze of a silver bowl dated to the 5th century.[112] The local meaning of the lotus flower is unknown, but it accompanied the hawk, the symbol of Horus, so perhaps it was related to the child Horus, who sits on a lotus flower.[113]

12. *The Helmet*

The helmet is often represented, as seen above, as part of the equipment of the warriors on the war-galley. It is a primary motif on the obverse of small denominations of Series II.3. In spite of the size of these coins,

105. E. T. Newell, *Some Unpublished Coins of Eastern Dynasts* (NNM 30; New York, 1926) 9; P. Naster, "Le développement des monnayages phéniciens avant Alexandre, d'après les trésors," in *The Patterns of Monetary Development in Phoenicia and Palestine in Antiquity* (Jerusalem, 1967) 13; D. Baramki, *The Coin Collection of the American University of Beirut Museum: Palestine and Phoenicia* (Beirut, 1974) 149, no. 1.

106. L. Anson, *Numismata Graeca* (London, 1910) pls. 9–13; *BMC Palestine*, 138, no. 242 and pl. 14:13.

107. Betlyon, *Coinage of Phoenicia*, 112–13.

108. G. K. Jenkins, "Recent Acquisitions of Greek Coins by British Museum," *NC* 19 (1959) 41.

109. Kraay, *Greek Coins*, 288; D. R. Sear, *Greek Coins and Their Values* (London, 1975) 551; J. Elayi, "Les monnaies de Byblos au sphinx et au faucon," *RSF* 11 (1983) 5–7; A. Lemaire and J. Elayi, "Les monnaies de Byblos au sphinx et au faucon: Nouveaux documents et essai de classement," *RBN* 137 (1991) 34.

110. Gubel, "Syro-Cypriote," 5–7 and pl. 3:a–j.

111. Dunand, *Byblos II*, no. 17630; see. also pp. 79–80, no. 7225.

112. E. Porada, "Notes on the Sarcophagus of Ahiram," *JANES* 5 (1973) 355–72 (with bibliography); I. Rabinowitz, "Aramaic Inscriptions of the Fifth Century B.C.E. from a North-Arab Shrine in Egypt," *JANES* 15 (1956), pls. 6–7.

113. Lipiński, ed., *Dictionnaire*, s.v. "Horus" and "Harpocrate" (with bibliography).

the details of the helmet can be seen more easily than on the warriors represented on the shekels. Although this helmet is also of Corinthian type, there are slight differences. The nasal is visible and is very long, which is an archaic feature because we know that the nasal, or nosepiece, of the Corinthian helmet tended to become shorter and even to disappear.[114] Apparently, there is no opening for the ears. The shape of the cheek guard is also archaic because it is long and very pointed, unlike its representation in ʿAynel's coins where it is short and rounded. This evolution provides help in establishing the chronology of Byblian coins. The helmet is a true face mask, with openings for the eyes, which were another archaic feature. The nape cover is rather long, contrary to how it usually is on Corinthian helmets. The crest consists of short, rigid strips just like the chenille helmet; a long flowing panache seems to be fixed at the end of the crest. The slight differences between the various helmets of Byblian coins were probably related to different stages in the evolution of the Corinthian helmet, but it always seems to be represented with the same category of warriors. However, this type of helmet was not the only type used in Byblos, as can be seen from the statuette of a bowman rider dated to the 8th–6th centuries,[115] and from Series II.3, as we shall see.

13. *The Bearded Heads*

Bearded heads turned to the right are represented both on the obverse and the reverse of the minute coins of Series V.3. Some of them were discovered by H. Seyrig and J. Rouvier on the beach at Byblos.[116] The attribution to Byblos is therefore likely. These coins weigh less than 0.10 g, and they are all somewhat damaged, so it is difficult to see the details of the types.[117]

One of the bearded heads is better preserved: it is wearing a headdress. It is a kind of καυσία, well adjusted, with the brims lifted, mainly on the nape of the neck. This headgear looks like the felt hat of the Macedonians, but it is more similar to the leather helmet derived from the καυσία, which is represented in the Bactrian coinage, in particular on the coins of Eucratides.[118] This headgear is clear on coin no. 1570.[119] The minting authority of Byblos seems to have represented another category of warrior

114. *DAGR*, s.v. "galea."

115. Moscati, ed., *I Fenici*, 133.

116. Cf. Elayi, *Byblos*, 47–48.

117. On these difficuties, see J. Elayi, "Une monnaie phénicienne de 0.05 g," *RSF* 13 (1985) 1–4.

118. *DAGR*, s.v. "causia." Cf. *BMC Macedonia, etc.*, 141, no. 5; 142, no. 6; and 158, no. 15.

119. Cf. Elayi, "Les symboles de la puissance militaire," 45 and pl. 2:7.

than the category with the Corinthian helmet that adorns almost all the series from Group III onward. This category, with καυσία, was probably much less important than the other one since it is only represented on some minute coins.

14. *The Olive Twig*

The olive twig is represented on the reverse side, as a secondary motif, only in Series II.1 and II.2.1 (nos. 73, 75), but most of the time it is off the flan. It is located to the right of the hawk, above the crook and flail. It seems to be a borrowing from the reverse of Athenian tetradrachms, with an olive between two leaves (the archaic tetradrachms where the owl is turned left, not the later tetradrachms where the owl is turned right and the olive bough is on the left).[120]

Thus, it appears that the Byblian coins display symbols that were chosen by the minting authority to represent the city. The selected motifs were more numerous and less organized than in Sidonian and Tyrian coinages. No single motif is used in all groups of Byblian coinage. Groups I and II are distinct from Groups III and IV. The sphinx was the main motif on the obverse of Group I; it continues, with some changes, in Group II. The double-lotus, which was the main motif in Group I, became a secondary motif in Group II, replaced on the obverse by the hawk or the helmet. In Groups III and IV, the motifs are firmly organized in a hierarchy. There were two main motifs on the obverse: the war-galley and the seahorse. The vulture and the ram were the main motifs of the reverse only in Group III. In Group IV, these two animals were replaced by the lion and bull. A secondary motif appeared in Group IV: the shell under the seahorse. The relationship between the obverse and reverse motifs is worth analyzing because it provides a better understanding of the message conveyed by the minting authority. The first key idea was the religious protection of the city, symbolized by protective animals (hawk, vulture, ram, lion, bull, seahorse, griffin) and objects (double-lotus, lotus, shell). The second idea, also expressed through certain religious symbols and connected with them, was that of the city's sovereignty and power. It was expressed first through the sphinx, the crook and flail on the hawk's and vulture's shoulders, and the helmet. Then it was expressed through the galley, warriors, and figureheads. Even though the representation of the galley, warriors, shell, and animals was based on observation, the mythical aspect is more present than in Sidonian coinage but less than in Tyrian coinage (sphinx, seahorse, griffin). Consequently, the Byblian motifs provide, for one thing, a great deal of information—for

120. *BMC Attica, Megaris, Aegina*, pls. 4–5.

example, on the Byblian galley equipment and the warriors' weapons, on the species of animals, and on borrowings from Egypt, Syria, and Greece. For another thing, they provide some information on Byblian mythology—its relationship to Egyptian myths; the seahorse with its triple functions on sea, earth and air; animal symbols; and the symbol of the shell.

Chapter 3

The Monetary Workshop of Byblos

A coin must be studied as a whole: besides the inscription, the iconography, the weight and the style, which are usually considered, it is also necessary to consider the metal used, manufacturing techniques, and possible alterations of the coins. What is also important is to think about the monetary workshop: the craftmen involved, organization of the manufacturing process, volume of production, and counterfeiting. Although explicit Phoenician inscriptions related to this subject and discoveries of a workshop or monetary tools are lacking, valuable information is provided by the technical details and defects of the coins, what we know from other mints, the engraving of seals, and the experience of modern engravers. We have already studied the monetary workshops of Sidon and Tyre[1] and will focus here on the characteristics of the Byblian workshop.

1. *The Monetary Metal*

The Byblian workshop only used silver for coins in the Persian period, unlike the Sidonian, Tyrian, and Aradian workshops, which also used bronze in the 4th century B.C.E. The Phoenician cities did not possess silver mines (*KSP*)[2] within their territories, and Byblos, just like the other Phoenician cities, may have obtained its supplies of silver from Anatolia (Taurus) and Iberia, which had numerous lodes of silver-bearing lead (areas of Huelva, Upper Andalusia, and Ibiza).[3] Another important source

1. Elayi-Elayi, *Monnayage de Sidon*, 541–80; idem, *Coinage of Tyre*, 281–321; see also P. Naster, "La technique des revers partiellement incus des monnaies phéniciennes," in *Centennial Publication of the American Numismatic Society* (New York, 1958) 503–11 (= *Scripta Nummaria: Contributions à la méthodologie numismatique* [Louvain-la-Neuve, 1983]) 22–29; J. Elayi, "Remarques méthodologiques sur l'étude paléographique des légendes monétaires phéniciennes," in *Phoinikeia Grammata: Lire et écrire en Méditerranée* (ed. C. Baurain et al.; Namur, 1991) 187–98; Elayi-Elayi, *Poids phéniciens*, 207–63.

2. *KAI* 13, line 4 ; cf. *DISO*, s.v. "KSP"; J. Hoftijzer and K. Jongeling, *Dictionary of the North-West Semitic Inscriptions* (Leiden, 1995), s.v. "ksp_2."

3. Cf. K. A. Yener, "The Archaeometry of Silver in Anatolia: The Bolkardağ Mining District," *AJA* 90 (1986) 469–72; V. Kassianidou, "May He Send Me Silver in Very Great Quantities: EA 35," in *Proceedings of the International Conference: Egypt and Cyprus in An-*

for the silver of Byblian coins was probably the import of Athenian tetradrachms which were found in large quantities in the ancient Near East.[4] They could not be overstruck, because their weight was different from the Byblian shekels, so they were probably melted. However, we have noticed some traces of overstriking on Byblian coins of previous series of the same weight and diameter, probably because overstriking was easier and more economic. The phenomenon of overstriking seems to be restricted in Byblos (about 13 cases),[5] as in Tyre (about 10 cases), but unlike Sidon (about 100 cases). After having analyzed the metallic composition of Sidonian and Tyrian coins,[6] we have also analyzed a sample of Byblian coins.[7] When the Byblians set up their monetary workshop, they drew on a long Phoenician tradition of metalworking, mainly developed during the first half of the 1st millennium, and attested, for example, in the inscription of King Yeḥawmilk.[8] They knew the process of producing silver from lead ores by smelting these ores, especially galena, and by cupellation; ore was probably processed in the mining districts.[9]

---

tiquity (ed. D. Michaelides; Oxford, 2009) 48–57; F. Liard, "Les sources d'argent pour la frappe des monnaies grecques aux époques archaïque et classique: Aperçu des dernières découvertes scientifiques et archéologiques," *RBN* 155 (2009) 159–76; A. Blanco Freijeiro et al., *Excavaciones arqueológicas en el Cerro Salomón (Riotinto, Huelva)* (Seville, 1970); idem, *Ancient Mining and Metallurgy in South-West Spain* (London, 1982); D. Ruíz Mata and J. Fernández Jurado, *El yacimiento metalúrgico tartésico de San Bartolomé de Almonte* (Huelva Arqueológica 8; Huelva, 1986; C. Domergue, *Les mines de la Péninsule Ibérique dans l'Antiquité romaine* (Rome, 1989) 141–54; J. Elayi and A. Planas Palau, *Les pointes de flèches en bronze d'Ibiza dans le cadre de la colonisation phénico-punique* (Paris, 1995) 223–60 (with bibliography).

4. Cf. Elayi, "Phénomène monétaire," 26; J. Elayi and J. Sapin, *Quinze ans de recherche (1985–2000) sur la Transeuphratène à l'époque perse* (Paris, 2000) 175–78 (with bibliography).

5. Nos. 164, 190, 459, 549, 786, 790, 834, 906, 930, 1077, 1444, 1481, 1482, 1487, 1491.

6. Cf., in general, J.-N. Barrandon and M. F. Guerra, "Méthodes d'analyse appliquées à la numismatique," in *A Survey of Numismatic Research 1990–1995* (ed. C. Morrisson and B. Kluge; Berlin, 1997) 825–30 (with bibliography); B. Bouyon et al., *Systèmes et technologie des monnaies de bronze (4e s. avant J.-C.–3e s. après J.-C.)* (Wetteren, 2000) 92–197 (with bibliography); M. R. Cowell, "A Short Review of the Application of Scientific Analysis Techniques to Coinage," in C. Alfaro and A. Burnett, eds., *A Survey of Numismatic Research, 1996–2001* (Madrid, 2003) 929–33 (with bibliography). For Sidon, cf. A. G. Elayi, J. N. Barrandon, and J. Elayi, "The Devaluation of Sidonian Coins in 365 B.C.E. as Determined by Fast Neutron Activation Analysis and First Bronze Issues," *AJN* 17 (2007) 1–8. For Tyre, cf. A. G. Elayi, J. N. Barrandon, and J. Elayi, "The Change of Standard of Tyrian Silver Coinage about 357 BCE as Determined by Fast Neutron Activation Analysis," *NC* (2008) 15–20.

7. A. G. Elayi, M. Blet-Lemarquand, and J. Elayi, "Silver Coinage Fluctuations at Byblos (5th–4th cent. BCE) as Determined by LA-ICP-MS and FNAA," *AJN* (2012) 1–10.

8. *KAI* 10.

9. Cf. Elayi-Elayi, *Coinage of Tyre*, 283–84 (with bibliography).

2. The Flans

The Byblian monetary workshop, having obtained the silver probably by buying the refined metal processed in the mining district, began manufacturing the flans. Since no Byblian flans have been discovered, the only information we have available on this manufacturing process is the evidence on the coins themselves. If we disregard alterations produced later by the striking—such as flattening, increasing of the thickness at the periphery, distortions, cracks, splits, etc.—we can obtain some precise information about the flans. The shapes of the flans vary from very irregular to almost perfectly circular. The very irregular forms occurred mainly in the first phase of the Byblian coinage (first standard) and the circular forms in the second phase (Phoenician standard). Several flans are relatively oval (nos. 5, 27, 38, 103, 187, 196, 427, 752, 915, 1066, 1152, 1363, 1413, 1427, and 1502),[10] rarely square (nos. 181 and 955), and most of them have no special shape. A few flans are very irregular (nos. 112, 198, 590, 661, and 896), most of them being only slightly irregular (nos. 6, 88, 151, 178, 182, 200, 206, 210, 272, 291, 342, 352, 422, 465, 505, 749, 913, 1313, 1468, and 1516). Some flans are almost perfectly circular (no. 68, 95, 105, 113, 331, 364, 580, 737, and 774), most of them being roughly circular (no. 1, 39, 56, 67, 76, 102, 334, 758, and 828). Some flans bear one sprue (nos. 2, 211, 504, 599, 600, 818, and 1391). Some flans are relatively thick—mainly in the first phase up to Group IV.1 (nos. 4 and 189); some others, mainly in the next phase, are relatively thin (nos. 671 and 886). A few flans may have been recut (nos. 81, 181, and 955).

How can these observations be interpreted? The irregularly shaped flans were probably not made in a mold with circular alveoli. We have proposed the following hypothesis: small silver ingots of no particular shape were poured onto a stone slab, taken from the melted metal using a measure (kind of spoon?) in order always to have the same weight.[11] It is difficult to know how the flans that have a kind of geometrical shape (oval or square) were made. The flans that may have been recut were probably not made by cutting a silver slab or metallic bar into sections, because they are only partly recut. Their weight is normal (0.69 g, 14.85 g, and 13 g, respectively): therefore, some metal was removed, not fraudulently, but weights that were too high after the flans had been struck were quite possibly adjusted. The process of manufacturing flans with one casting sprue is easy to explain. During manufacturing, the flans were made using mo-

10. We are providing some examples of each feature described only in this chapter; for a complete view of the examples, see appendix 1.

11. Cf. Elayi-Elayi, *Coinage of Tyre*, 285.

novalve or bivalve molds containing circular alveoli arranged in strings. Some sprues may have been forgotten by the workers making the flans, but this doesn't seem to be the answer since the weights of the coins with sprues are correct. It is more likely that the flans were weighed before being struck and that one or two sprues were kept in order to make up for any weight shortage. There may also be one sprue on a flan that was placed on the lower side of the mold. The flans are rarely perfectly circular, which could be explained either by the unequal cooling of the metal poured[12] or by the deformations produced by the striking; even today this can happen, for example, on metals that are not surrounded by a protective collar.[13]

As is well known, in Antiquity, mainly in the Near East, monetary flans were made by casting metal into molds and then striking them.[14] There is no evidence for determining whether the Byblian molds used for flans in strings were made from one, two, or three slabs. Adjusting the weights was one of the most delicate steps in the flan manufacturing process. The quantity of silver had to be measured out as carefully as possible before making the flans. In principle, the use of molds with alveoli ought to have made it easier to adjust the weights, thereby minimizing the need to weigh the flans. In reality, observation of some recut edges shows that weighing was still in use. However, the use of overstriking saved a good deal of time because there was no need to weigh flans or manufacture them. But now the accuracy of the weight depended on the weight and composition of the previously used coin. The erroneous weights of some Byblian coins that show no visible alteration[15] are difficult to explain: an error in adjusting the weight in Antiquity or an error of modern weighing?

Some coins reveal errors at the metal preparation stage. For example, the edges of several coins have cracks or splits (nos. 35, 41, 58, 848, 911, 985, 1028, 1125, 1185, 1201, and 1459): according to D. R. Cooper, they were caused by the metal cooling more rapidly toward the exterior than in the center but, as we shall see below, most of them are probably explained by the phenomenon of striction during the striking.[16] Some coins are a bit riddled with small holes on the surface (nos. 101, 292, 308, 421, 511, 651, 685, 782, and 838). If there were bubbles caused by humidity inside the alveoli,

12. Bouyon et al., *Systèmes et technologie*, 7.

13. We thank D. Gedalje, engraver at the Monnaie de Paris, for his explanations.

14. On monetary molds and other molds, cf. Elayi-Elayi, *Coinage of Tyre*, 286–89 (with bibliography).

15. For example, coin no. 726.

16. D. R. Cooper, *The Art and Craft of Coinmaking: A History of Minting Technology* (London, 1988) 9, fig. 4. We thank P. Andrieux for his explanations on this subject.

Table 3.1. *Diameter of the Shekels Compared*

Diameter in mm	*Series I.1*	*Series III.1*	*Series IV.1.1*	*Series IV.2.1*	*Series IV.3.1*	*Series IV.4.1*
30		1		1		
29			1			
28		1	1			1
27		2	1	4		1
26		1	1	4	2	4
25		1	2	17	1	4
24		3	4	2	1	
23						1
22	1					
21	1	1				
20	1					1
19	3					

Table 3.2. *Diameter of the Quarter-Shekels Compared*

Diameter in mm	*Series III.2*	*Series IV.1.2*
19		1
18		3
17	1	4
16	3	7
15	2	6
14	2	2
13		
12		1

Table 3.3. *Diameter of the Sixteenth-Shekels Compared*

Diameter in mm	*Series III.3*	*Series IV.1.3*	*Series IV.2.2*	*Series IV.3.2*	*Series IV.4.2*
12	1				3
11	2		5	7	136
10	6	12	5	2	43
9		3		1	1

the bubbles would have been crushed by the striking: unfortunately, we could not check this interpretation because we were unable to examine any of the coins that display these small holes.

The flan manufacturing process in the Byblian workshop went through several stages and evolved during the Persian period, just as it did in the Sidonian and Tyrian workshops. As in the Tyrian workshop, the flans of Byblian coins were somewhat circular at the beginning (Groups I and II), meaning that molds with alveoli were already used for different denominations. Yet at the same time, irregular flans show that molds were not systematically used. In Groups III and IV.1, both techniques were also used simultaneously. It seems that, from the beginning of Group IV.2, the flans were made mainly by using molds with circular alveoli. This was apparently more systematic for 16th-shekels than for shekels. However, the other technique, without the mold, had never disappeared, even in the coinage of the last king, ʿAynel. The change at Byblos, with the extensive use of molds, was not as obvious as at Sidon and Tyre, and it occurred earlier: around 400 B.C.E. instead of 365 in Sidon and around 357 in Tyre.

The diameter of the flans corresponds in principle to the diameter of the coins, except for some minor differences due to the crushing of the striking, for example. Just as in Sidonian and Tyrian coinages, the flan diameter evolved during the Persian period but differently, depending on the denomination. However, the diameters are not known for many of the Byblian coins that come from hoards, and our analysis is based on a relatively small amount of data in some of the series. If we consider the diameter of the shekels, to begin with it was (Group I.1) about 20 mm, with a small variation between 19 and 22 mm (table 3.1). After the change of standard, it increased to about 25 mm in Groups III and IV, with an increased variation: 21–30 mm (Group III.1), 24–29 mm (Group IV.1), 24–30 mm (Group IV.2), 20–28 mm (Group IV.4); however, it was small in Group IV.3: 24–26 mm. The variations in diameter depended on the systematic use of molds and also the thickness of the flans. The quarter-shekels, of which we have fewer examples, have the same diameter (16 mm) and followed a similar increase in regard to variation (table 3.2): 14–17 mm (Group III.2) and 12–19 mm (Group IV.1.2). The 16th-shekels (table 3.3) have a diameter of 10 mm (Groups III.3 and IV.1.3), then increase slightly to 11 mm (Groups IV.2.2, IV. 3.2, and IV.4.2) but always with quite small variations: 10–12 mm (Group III.3), 9–10 mm (Group IV.1.3), 10–11 mm (Group IV.2.2), 9–11 mm (Group IV.3.2), and 9–12 mm (Group IV.4.2). The half-16ths have a diameter of 8 mm with small variations: 7–8 mm (Group III.4), 7–9 mm (Group IV.1.4), and 7–8 mm (Group V.1).

3. The Dies

We have already studied, for the Sidonian and Tyrian workshops, the die-making operation.[17] Analysis of the Byblian coins gives us an idea of the diameter and shape of the dies that have been used. Normally, only the engraved part of the die needed to be visible on the coin; however, the substantially off-centered motif on the obverse of some coins reveals the minimum diameter of the dies. Even if the obverse die was securely fixed in the anvil, it would be possible, with a strong magnifying glass, to distinguish the trace of the edge of the die on the coins. Byblian shekels are rarely very off-center, probably because the striking operation was more carefully done, but some cases that are off-centered do give an idea of the minimum diameter of the obverse dies. For example, the obverse die of coin no. 280 had a diameter of at least 31 mm (4 mm visible because it's off-centered on both sides +23 mm for the diameter of the circular border).

Similar observations can be made on small denominations: for example, the obverse die of quarter-shekel no. 144 had a diameter of at least 22 mm (3 mm × 2 + 16 mm). The obverse die of coin no. 98 (small denomination) had a diameter of at least 12 mm (3 mm × 2 + 6 mm). The obverse die of coin no. 1296 (16th-shekel) had a diameter of at least 21 mm (5 mm × 2 + 11 mm). The reverse die had a much smaller diameter than the obverse die, which hardly goes beyond the border (1 or 2 mm): therefore, in contrast to the obverse dies, it is easier to know the precise diameter of the reverse dies. For example, the reverse die of coin no. 280 (shekel) had a diameter of 26 mm (1.5 mm × 2 + 23 mm), the same diameter as the flan. Sometimes there is no space between the circle and the edge of the die (no. 327R).

Two kinds of reverse dies were used: square section dies for incuse squares and circular section dies for circular reverse types. The square reverse die of shekel no. 2 had 13 mm on one side. Different square reverse dies were used for the different denominations of Group I: the reverse die of coin no. 25 had 8 mm (3.28 g); of coin no. 28, 6 mm (1.51 g); of coin no. 37, 5 mm (0.66 g); of coin no. 56, 4 mm (0.30 g); of coin no. 63, 4 mm (0.22 g); and of coin no. 64, 3 mm (0.10 g). The use of reverse square dies having different side lengths could provide some help in differentiating the denominations. The reverse dies used for making incuse squares were not entirely square: their angles were sometimes slightly rounded, maybe by wear (nos. 2 and 37). For Group II, the square reverse die of coin no. 77

17. Elayi-Elayi, *Monnayage de Sidon*, 551–60; idem, *Coinage of Tyre*, 289–97 (with bibliography).

had 6 mm on one side, and that of coin no. 94 had 4 mm. Circular section dies for circular reverse types are mainly used in Groups III and IV: for example, on shekel no. 280, it had a diameter of 26 mm. However, the section of some reverse dies is more oval than circular—for example, on the quarter-shekels of ʾElpaʿal, nos. 206 and 207. The method of the incuse square on the reverse of some Byblian coins has nothing to do with the "primitive incuse squares" frequently used on the reverse of archaic Greek and Persian coins, but they are "evolved type squares."[18] In the Byblian coinage, the incuse square was not systematically used on the reverse, and it can be found on all denominations: for example, no. 2 (shekel), no. 25 (3rd-shekel), no. 28 (1.51 g), no. 37 (0.66 g), no. 56 (0.30 g), no. 64 (0.10 g).

Contrary to the similar technique of engraving seals where the motif and the inscription could be done by different engravers, the motif and inscription on the same side of Byblian coins were executed by the same engraver, as we have observed. It is logical since both represented the symbol chosen by the minting authority for the issue. However, it occasionally happened that the engraver of the obverse die was different from the engraver of the reverse die, which can be explained by a different life-span for the two dies:[19] the reverse die wore out more quickly because of its movement. While the obverse die was still in use, a new reverse die could have been made by another engraver.

Some Byblian coins have retained traces of the preliminary work performed by the engraver on the die before the engraving. The use of a compass for tracing a circle is attested by several details: traces of the circle in relief on the coins, visible between the dots of the border (nos. 107R, 205R, 276R, 307R, 738O and R), circle not closed (nos. 20R and 775O), dot in the center of the circle produced by the hole of the point of the compass in the die (nos. 399R, 405R, 430R, 516R, 616R, 622R, and 741O).[20] This dot is much more frequently observed on Sidonian coins.[21] On Tyrian coins,

18. Elayi-Elayi, *Coinage of Tyre*, 292–93.

19. Cf., for example, L. Robert, "Monnaies dans les inscriptions grecques," *RN* 6 (1962) 18–24; *ID*, no. 1450, side A, line 198; and no. 1430, line 30 (5 obverse and 18 reverse dies); Bouyon et al., *Systèmes et technologie*, 61 (on average, in the Hellenistic period, 1 obverse die was used with 3.6 reverse dies).

20. The interpretation of this central dot is accepted in other coinages such as ancient Greek coinages: G. F. Hill, "Ancient Methods of Coining," *NC* 5 (1922) 23; G. Le Rider, "Sur la fabrication des coins monétaires dans l'antiquité grecque," *Schweizer Münzblätter* 29 (1958) 4–5 (with bibliography); M. Dhénin, "Quelques remarques sur le travail des graveurs de coins," in *Rythmes de la production monétaire, de l'Antiquité à nos jours* (ed. G. Depeyrot et al.; Louvain-la-Neuve, 1987) 453–57.

21. Cf. Elayi-Elayi, *Monnayage de Sidon*, 554–55.

either it is not visible because of the high relief of the motif at this position or, less likely, because it has been carefully rubbed away on the coins.[22] The use of compasses is as well attested on shekels as it is on small denominations. However, it became increasingly difficult to use on small coins, such as no. 56R, where the well-drawn circle was probably done without a compass. Several borders were also drawn without compasses, for example, on no. 56R which reveals no trace of a circle between the spaced dots, no. 107R with no traces of a circle when the border is interrupted, and several coins with an irregular border (nos. 41R, 102R, 112R, and 114R).

The incuse method, which partly produced some elements in relief and some concave, was used on the reverse dies of Aradian, Sidonian and Tyrian coinages just like the incuse square method, but less frequently and only during a limited period. It was only used in Byblos for the series of Groups III and IV.1. Here it is different from other Phoenician coinages: in Group III, the ram with its head looking back to the right is entirely incuse. This method of engraving was misunderstood by E. Babelon who wrote, for example, that Byblos coins had a "ram engraved in hollow" and for Sidon, a "goat engraved in hollow,"[23] whereas they were actually engraved in relief on the dies. J. P. Six also misunderstood the method, using the term "countermark."[24] P. Naster wondered whether the hollow elements were added using punches after the striking.[25] He gave several reasons to prove that punches were not used, such as the absence of deformation on the other side of the coins, and an analysis of the process: the engraver first prepared the field level, keeping the elements that were to be debossed on the coin in relief, then he engraved these elements in hollow, and finally the details of the remaining surface. This incuse method was very difficult to execute: for example, the relief of the body of the ram and the details of the head were rarely well represented—most of the time in a hasty and clumsy way (nos. 106, 108, and 113). According to P. Naster, the semi-incuse method "used by the cities of Tyre, Arados and Byblos was in fact always the same and is a simple variant of the usual method or, in a way, it is the sum of the usual hollow engraving and the incuse engraving of coins as it was practiced in Magna Graecia."[26] What he means is the method of

22. Idem, *Coinage of Tyre*, 292.

23. Babelon, *Perses*, 192, no. 1342; p. 229, no. 1565.

24. J. P. Six, "Observations sur les monnaies phéniciennes," *NC* 17 (1877) 177–241.

25. P. Naster, "Le carré creux en numismatique grecque," in *Numismatique antique: Problèmes et méthodes* (Annales de l'Est; Nancy, 1975) 25–28 (= idem, *Scripta Nummaria*, 45–50).

26. Ibid., 28.

engraving the same motif on both sides of the coin in relief on the obverse and in hollow on the reverse, a method that was in use at the end of the 6th century in some mints in Magna Graecia (Tarentum, Poseidonia, Caulonia, Sybaris, Sirinos, Metapontum and Croton).[27]

In fact, the Phoenician incuse method seems to have an origin other than these coinages: the engravers of the incuse Tyrian coins, who probably inaugurated this method before Sidon, Byblos, and finally Arwad, may have been inspired by a method of sculpture used in Egyptian bas-reliefs. It is the so-called relief in hollow, which is obtained by surrounding all the low relief motifs with an incuse impression. The incuse impression surrounding the owl of the Tyrian coins could be a derivative of the Egyptian method, frequently used over several centuries.[28] We must also mention the possible influence of the earlier coins of Kalymna of Caria, minted in about 520: they depict a lyre surrounded by an incuse impression, unique among all the Greek coinages and that could itself have been borrowed from Egypt bas-reliefs.[29] Following Tyre, the other Phoenician monetary workshops used the same incuse method, but each of them in a different and original way: an incuse ram and a bull's head on the Byblian coins, the heads of Bes and a goat on the Sidonian coins, and a crescent on the Aradian coins. In conclusion, the incuse method was a Tyrian innovation, used in the second stage of the Tyrian coinage, and followed by Byblos and other Phoenician mints. It was only in use for a short time, probably because it was a difficult method and perhaps also because it was not very attractive. As in the Sidonian and Tyrian coinages, it was used in Byblos during the last third of the 5th century.

The Byblian engravers used to surround the coin design on both the obverse and the reverse with a border of dots. Some obverse or reverse dies had no borders: for example, coin no. 1O and no. 88R. The dots of the border can be very small (nos. 666O and R, 932O) or larger (coin no. 113 O and R); they are more-or-less closed or spaced. Series II.2.2 has a double border of dots on the obverse, not because the coins were restruck (nos. 84, 88).

It sometimes happened that the size of the dies was not adapted to the size of the flans. For example, several dies are too small: nos. 25R, 1485R,

27. Idem, "La technique des monnaies incuses de Grande Grèce," *RNB* 93 (1947) 5–17 (= idem, *Scripta Nummaria*, 8–17).

28. Cf., for example, E. Naville, *The XIth Dynasty Temple at Deir el-Bahari* I (London, 1907), pl. 18; II (London, 1910) pl. 9G and (4b); C. Aldred et al., *L'Égypte du crépuscule* (Paris, 1980) 81, fig. 62 and p. 82, fig. 63; J. Elayi, "Les sicles de Tyr au dauphin," *NAC* 21 (1992) 42; idem, "La place de l'Égypte dans la recherche sur les Phéniciens," *Trans* 9 (1995) 22.

29. Cf., for example, G. K. Jenkins, *Monnaies grecques* (Fribourg, 1972) pls. 30–31.

1494–95R, 1504–7R, 1510R, 1514R, 1516–17R; less often they are too large: no. 640.[30] This could be explained by a lack of synchronization between the person making the flans and the die engraver, or by a mistake on the part of the hammerer, who used dies of smaller or larger denominations. On several hundred coins, we have observed one or several defects that are relatively visible, but the damaged dies continued to be used (for example, nos. 2R, 35R, 104O, 143O, 242O, 468R, 554O, 779R, 801R, 1181O, 1237R, 1325O, 1488R, and 1522R). It was the same for dies that were split (for example, nos. 195, 200, 216, 391, 610, 729, 732, 1019–23, 1092–1122, 1123–1777, 1189–1203, 1278–1308, 1544), because they were probably used until they were totally broken. The most damaged was an obverse die of ʿAynel (nos. 931–60). When dies were worn, especially reverse dies, which wore out more quickly, the engravers could reengrave them, as can be seen in other coinages,[31] but reengraving of this nature is difficult to detect: for example, a lion's head is engraved on the last letter of the inscription of ʿAynel (nos. 888R, 894R, 898R). The mint of Byblos reused obverse dies of ʿOzbaʿal for ʾUrimilk (nos. 846–50) and obverse dies of ʾUrimilk for ʿAynel, after having obliterated—or not—the letters (nos. 966–1088). Therefore, just like the Sidonian and Tyrian mints,[32] the Byblian mint decreased its workload significantly during this whole period, especially in regard to Group IV.

None of the tools used by the Byblian engravers has been discovered; however, it is possible to infer some of them from their indirect traces on the coins, by means of the dies. The engravers had compasses, probably of different sizes for the different denominations, because it would not have been easy to draw circles of 27 mm (no. 307R) and 10 mm (no. 738O), for example, with the same tool; at least the points were probably thinner. They also had at their disposal different-sized burins for motifs and inscriptions (even in the same inscription: no. 189), and hammers adapted to the burins. In addition, they needed a type of vice in which the dies could be held during the engraving process. We still do not know whether a magnifying process was used for engraving the dies of minute coins, since to date, no tool resembling a magnifying glass has ever been discovered, even though this is quite conceivable.

30. Sometimes one die, sometimes the pair of dies has an inadequate size.

31. Cf., for example, G. Le Rider, *Antioche de Syrie sous les Séleucides: Corpus des monnaies d'or et d'argent I. De Séleucos I à Antiochos V c. 300–161* (Paris, 1999) 61, no. 15; p. 64, nos. 54–55; p. 65, no. 76; p. 77, no. 3; pp. 97–98, no. 13; p. 100, no. 79, etc.; cf. F. de Callataÿ, "Étude de technique monétaire: le rapport 'nombre de coins de revers/nombre de coins de droit' à l'époque hellénistique," *RAHAL* 32 (1999) 91–102.

32. Cf. Elayi-Elayi, *Monnayage de Sidon*, 558–60; idem, *Coinage of Tyre*, 295–96.

Concerning the much-debated question of the existence of standard punches for Greek dies[33]—based on our observations, neither Byblos nor any other Phoenician workshop seems to have used a complete punch to make dies in the Persian period. However, the use of partial punches seems likely but was probably limited to the dot-shaped element, of different sizes, used for the border and sometimes for other motifs, such as the manes and legs of lions and legs of bulls (nos. 220R, 784R). There are also some isolated dots (one on coin nos. 757O and 149R, and two on no. 934R). The more extensive use of these dot-shaped punches in some series (IV.4) was probably due to hurried, clumsy, or careless engravers. When such a punch was used for the border of dots, its position was not always vertical but sometimes oblique, and the circular shape of the dots became oval (no. 37R). The tools still used today by the traditional engravers of the *Monnaie de Paris*, because they correspond to the same needs, probably differ very little from those of the Byblian engravers:[34] compasses, burins, gravers, and hammers—all of them in different sizes for specific uses, often made by the engravers themselves in order to suit their precise needs. For example, they often use partial punches that they make; some of them bear a double or triple motif (one, two, or three juxtaposed dots) in order to save time. They need magnifying glasses, for engraving letters of 2–3 mm, for example, and use very thin burins. As we have seen in this chapter, the engravers probably followed a pattern provided by the minting authority, but they could arrange the field to be engraved, depending on material restraints as well as their own fancy.

4. *Striking*

After the monetary flans and dies had been made, the striking was performed. The Byblian workshop is only known from its coinage. At first, the obverse die had to be fixed in the anvil; the flan was then placed over this die and the reverse die over the flan before it was struck with a hammer (or by some other means?). The reverse Byblian die had a maximum diameter of about 26 mm for shekels: it was therefore possible to hold it firmly in one's hand, holding the coin between the thumb and the index and second

33. The theory of complete punches was mainly supported by G. F. Hill, O. Ravel, C. Seltman, and W. Schwabacher but was fought by L. Naville, S. P. Noe, and G. Le Rider. H. A. Cahn and G. K. Jenkins found no traces of punches in the coinages that they examined: see bibliography in Le Rider, "Sur la fabrication des coins monétaires," 1–5; and T. Hackens, "Terminologie et techniques de fabrication," in *Numismatique antique: Problèmes et méthodes* (Annales de l'Est; Nancy, 1975) 11–12 ; Elayi, "Remarques méthodologiques," 192–94; cf. Elayi-Elayi, *Coinage of Tyre*, 196–97

34. All this information was provided by D. Gedalje.

finger.[35] For the sake of convenience, the person in charge of the striking is called "the hammerer" (Roman *malleator*). The Byblian shekels of the Phoenician standard were large coins (not as large as the Sidonian double-shekels, however). The engraving was in high relief, especially in the case of an incuse impression, in which the thickness of the motif in hollow was added to that of the motif in relief.[36] The strength required for striking was so great that it was probably impossible to hold the reverse die at the same time in one hand and the hammer in the other hand. There were probably two people: one person who held the die, perhaps with tongs for safety, and one who struck with the hammer.[37]

The off-centered motifs on the coins provide us with indirect information about the striking process. Our observations of Byblian coins are almost identical to our observations of Sidonian and Tyrian coins.[38] First, off-centered elements occurred at Byblos much more often on the obverse side than on the reverse[39] (obverse: nos. 9, 32, 340, 466, 540, 659, 727, 857, 954, 1068, 1123, 1225, 1351, 1385; reverse: 77, 79, 118). Off-centering on the reverse implies that the reverse die was not correctly placed over the flan. The off-centered obverse can be explained by the fact that the flan was not correctly placed over the fixed obverse die, but it may also mean that the hammerer did not hold his reverse die perpendicular to the plane of striking. In this case, the reverse die was pushed to the side by the stroke of the hammer, producing an off-centered flan on the obverse.[40] In most cases, the instances of off-centering appear to follow the same direction and were between 12 h and 13 h, depending on the nomenclature used for die axes. This observation was already made by F. de Callataÿ for the Seleucid tetradrachms.[41] According to him, this is normal because it confirms a clear preponderance, both in Antiquity as well as today, of right-handed people in the population: as a matter of fact, the hammer stroke made by the right hand pushes the metal in the 9–12 h direction with respect to the obverse

35. According to F. de Callataÿ ("La dimension des coins monétaires de tétradrachmes hellénistiques d'après l'étude des monnaies décentrées," in *XII. Internationaler Numismatischer Kongress, Berlin 1997, Akten I* [ed. B. Kluge and B. Weisser; Berlin, 2000] 250), the limit is a diameter of 35 mm.

36. Some authors question whether human strength was sufficient for striking the largest denominations such as Syracusan decadrachms: cf., for example, L. Mildenberg, *The Coinage of the Bar Kokhba War* (Aarau, 1984) 18 and n. 28.

37. The use of tongs for holding the dies is attested during the Roman period; cf. Elayi-Elayi, *Coinage of Tyre*, 297–98.

38. Cf. idem, *Monnayage de Sidon*, 562–63; idem, *Coinage of Tyre*, 297–302.

39. We only take into consideration the coins that are most off-center.

40. Cf. de Callataÿ, "La dimension des coins," 246.

41. Ibid., 247 (with bibliography).

die, which appears as 12–3 h on the coin. This also means that the obverse die fixed in the anvil was positioned vertically in relation to the hammerer, which was logical. It can also be noticed that off-centering generally occurred much more often on small denominations than on shekels, possibly because the shekels were struck more easily and more carefully than the smaller denominations.

The orientation of die axes had already been used, at the end of the 6th century, by several cities of Magna Graecia for their incuse series, but it was a technical necessity for a short period because the obverse motif had to fit in exactly with the identical incuse motif on the reverse. The systemization of this process in all Sidonian coinage, shortly after 450, was understood as being a technical innovation and was progressively followed.[42] The other Phoenician cities only adopted die orientation in the 4th century: Tyre, then Arwad, then Byblos, according to F. De Callataÿ.[43] This was true for Tyre, Group II, after the change of Phoenician standard to "Attic" standard.[44] It is impossible to confirm this die orientation for Arwad before having finished our corpus on Aradian coinage. But we can say now that Byblos had not adopted the Sidonian orientation of die axes at 12 h in the Persian period. In the Byblian Group I, there are not many coins, but there is no fixed orientation, either at 12 h or at another hour: 5 coins at 12 h, 3 (11 h), 2 (2 h), 1 (10 h), and 1 (3 h). In Group II, the situation had not changed: 7 coins (6 h), 4 (12 h and 5 h), 3 (3 h and 9 h), 2 (7 h), and 1 (4 h, 8 h, 11 h). In Group III, there are: 7 coins (6 h), 6 (6 h and 7 h), 4 (1, 3, 8, and 9 h), 3 (12 h), 2 (4, 5, and 10 h), and 1 (2 h). In Group IV.1, there are: 7 coins (1 h and 9 h), 6 (6 h and 12 h), 5 (5 h), 4 (2 h and 11 h), and 2 (3 h, 4 h, 7 h, and 10 h). In Group IV.2, there are: 22 coins (4 h), 21 (3 h and 10 h), 19 (11 h), 17 (5 h), 13 (6 h), 12 (7 h), 10 (1 h, 9 h, and 12 h), 9 (2 h), and 2 (8 h). In Group IV.3, there are: 9 coins (6 h), 7 (9 h), 5 (7 h), 4 (11 h), 2 (1 h, 3 h, 4 h, and 12 h), and 1 (2 h and 10 h). In Group IV.4, there are: 40 coins (6 h), 31 (5 h), 30 (7 h), 23 (3 h), 20 (12 h), 19 (4 h), 15 (11 h), 12 (9 h), 10 (1 h), 9 (2 h), 7 (8 h), and 6 (10 h). In the last series of the Persian period (IV.4.3, IV.4.4, IV.4.5, IV.4.6, IV.4.7), there are: 8 coins (1 h), 6 (12 h), 5 (9 h), 4 (11 h and 6 h), 3 (3 h), 2 (4 h), and 1 (2 h, 5 h, 7 h, 8 h, and 10 h). In these last series, even if 18 coins are oriented at 11 h–12 h–1 h, 19 have another orientation; therefore, it is difficult even to see a tendency at 12 h.

42. On the question of the orientation of die axes, cf. Elayi-Elayi, *Monnayage de Sidon*, 563–68; idem, *Coinage of Tyre*, 298–301.

43. According to F. de Callataÿ, "La dimension des coins," 83–85 (with bibliography); pp. 102–19: maps showing the spread of the adjustment at 12 h in the whole Mediterranean world.

44. Elayi-Elayi, *Coinage of Tyre*, 299–301.

Some defects noticed on the coins also provide indirect information on the process of striking. The question of the temperature of the flan when it was struck remains unsolved: however, the traces of overstriking on several coins could mean that the flan was not hot. Overstriking on previous series that were no longer in circulation was used in the Byblian workshop, in Group III: no. 1640; but mainly in Group IV: nos. 190O, 459R, 549O, 786O, 790O, 834O, 1077O, 1444O, 1481R, 1482R, 1487R, and 1491O. Either it was not in current use (as in the Sidonian workshop),[45] or the traces of overstriking were deleted (by heating the flan before striking?). Finally, we have observed traces of poor striking (nos. 474R, 512O) and traces of restriking when the outline of the motif is double, due to a second hammer stroke, which could be an error or may have been intentional in order to correct a first, badly aimed stroke. They appear only in Group IV: 268O, 333R, 358R, 457R, 514R, 567R, 597R, 611O, 783R, 1206R, and 1380O.

5. *Alterations Not Related to the Manufacturing Process*

Coin defects related to the manufacturing process must not be confused with alterations of various sorts related to the circulation of the coins from the time they were minted until they were discovered. These alterations can be classified in two categories: casual and deliberate. As casual alterations, note, for example, flaws and scratches (nos. 80O, 285O, 347O, 526R, 637O, 783O, 819O, and 1389O), traces of grazing and scrapes mainly caused by cleaning (nos. 671O, 684O, and 722O), traces of corrosion (nos. 8, 50, 165, 222, 263, and 1391) due to a long period in a damaging environment, and frequent breaking of the edges, mainly due to the brittleness of the metal (for example, nos. 65, 101, 111, 147, 157, 158, 208, 255, 302, 770, 916, 1400, 1359, 1523, and 1565). The most frequent casual alterations are, by far, the traces of wear, because most of the coins listed in the catalog of our corpus came from the mass coinage in circulation and are consequently quite worn. The different stages of wear are indicated in the catalog in chap. 1; some of them are very worn (nos. 246, 588, 706, and 715), but the most worn coins were not listed because their types are not recognizable. Among the hoards of Byblian coins that we have listed (appendix 4), most of the coins hoarded are relatively worn because they were taken from the monetary mass in circulation (for example, TXIII, TXIV, TXV?). Interesting research has been conducted to calculate the amount of wear on coins by year, but it is not relevant to Byblian coins because, unlike Sidonian and Tyrian coins, they are not dated.

45. Idem, *Monnayage de Sidon*, 568.

Deliberate alterations are of different sorts in the Byblian coinage of the Persian period. We have recorded only two countermarks made with a punch (nos. 228R and 1486R). Seven coins are broken (nos. 111, 770, 771, 1470, 1471, 1472, and 1523). Only 4 coins have one chisel cut: nos. 183 (IV.1.1), 416, 418 (IV.2.1c), and 1372 (IV.4.2), the first being dated to the end of the 5th century B.C.E., and the others to the 4th century. Conversely, there are many in the Sidonian coinage (66 coins) and Tyrian coinage (56 coins), and they are mainly dated to the 5th century.[46] Fragments of coins can be explained in a context of weighed metal: in order to obtain a certain weight of silver, the coins were divided, when necessary, into fragments, just like ingots, jewels, or other silver fragments. Coins could also be cut in order to reveal whether they were plated. This was frequently done to check whether the coin was genuine or not.[47] It was a phenomenon linked to the circulation of coins, but since the coins of Byblos were not exported, inside the territory of the city they were known, so the inhabitants did not need to check their composition by making chisel cuts. Among other deliberate alterations, we should also mention two cases of edge clipping (nos. 2 and 793) that could be interpreted as the fraudulent theft of metal, and one pierced coin (no. 732) that may have been used as an piece of jewelry.

6. *Workshop Operations*

How did the Byblian monetary workshop operate? Just like the Sidonian and Tyrian workshops that we have studied, it was probably under the direct control of the minting authority of Byblos, since it printed the symbols of the city. Byblos had been allowed to mint money by the Persian king just as the other autonomous Phoenician cities had, and could control everything in the minting process: choice of symbols, standard, types of denomination, quality of manufacturing, volume of production, and function of this civic coinage. We have already discussed the craftmen involved in the coin-manufacturing process, control over production, and equipment in the monetary workshop.[48] The phenomenon of ancient forgery,[49] evidenced by counterfeit coins, was not developed in Byblos but mainly occurred in Tyre. There is one plated coin (no. 203), revealed by metallic

46. Ibid., 569; idem, *Coinage of Tyre*, 303. They are also numerous in the coinages of Cyprus: cf. A. Destrooper-Georgiades, "Le reflet des crises de l'époque achéménide dans le monnayage chypriote," *Trans* 40 (2011) 57–59.

47. Cf. Elayi, "Remarques méthodologiques," 189.

48. Elayi-Elayi, *Coinage of Tyre*, 303–6.

49. For modern counterfeits, cf. appendix 2.

Table 3.4. *Number of Coins Preserved, by Group and Denomination*

	Shekels	*Thirds*	*Quarters*	*Sixths*	*Twelfths*	*Sixteenths*	*F.O.T.1*	*Half-Sixteenths*	*F.O.T.2*	*F.O.T.3*	*Total by Group*
Group I	18	9		6	22		7		1	3	66
Group II		6			21		6		1		34
Group III	41		17			15		7			80
Group IV.1	12		27			31		17			87
Group IV.2	459					45					504
Group IV.3	74					40					114
Group IV.4	80		4			574					658
Group V							20			7	27
Total	684	15	48	6	43	705	33	24	2	10	1,570

Table 3.5. *Proportion of Coins by Denomination*

	Number of coins	*%*
Shekels	684	43.56
Third-shekels	15	0.96
Quarter-shekels	48	3.06
Sixth-shekels	6	0.38
Twelfth-shekels	43	2.74
Sixteenth-shekels	705	44.90
F.O.T.1	33	2.10
Half-sixteenths	24	1.53
F.O.T.2	2	0.13
F.O.T.3	7	0.45
Total	1,570	

analysis;[50] shekel no. 726 could be a forgery because of its erroneous weight (15.58 g), but it could also be an error of modern weighing. Coin no. 809 was clipped in order to remove some of the silver. It is difficult to know why there was practically no ancient forgery in the Byblian coinage; it may have been because it was easier to control a smaller monetary workshop, with less production, and a coinage minted exclusively for the city's internal use.

50. Cf. Elayi, Blet-Lemarquand, and Elayi, "Silver Coinage Fluctuations at Byblos."

Finally, we shall consider the Byblian workshop's production from the point of view of quality and quantity. Even though Byblos was the first Phoenician city to inaugurate a civic coinage, it was less innovative than the Tyrian and (especially) the Sidonian workshops:[51] it had no dating, no bronze coins, and no orientation of the axes at 12 h. It followed Tyre and Sidon regarding the incusion technique. The Byblian types were in general less complex than the Sidonian, but at the beginning of its coinage, Byblos used skillful die engravers just as Sidon and Tyre did. The Byblians also displayed a concern for quality in the first stage of their coinage; they were apparently less intent than Sidon on performing technical feats. The Byblian workshop worked cheaper, at least in some periods, as the Sidonian and Tyrian workshops did, by lowering the quality of their production: some use of overstriking (less than Sidon), reengraving worn dies, using damaged coins over long periods, putting into circulation restruck and **off-center** coins or coins with various defects, or recruiting some clumsy die engravers (the engraver with "broken" style). However, the Byblian workshop craftsmen do not seem to have had to work under as much pressure as those in Tyre and Sidon did, except in the last part of ʿAynel's coinage. In part of ʾElpaʿal's coinage, clumsy engravers worked in the workshop, both on inscriptions and on motifs. The Byblian coins are original: in terms of type, explicit inscriptions, different denominations, a particular treatment of incusion, and borrowings from Egypt, Syria, and Greece.

We shall now examine the Byblian production of coins from a quantitative point of view and try to understand its evolution. We shall first consider the number of coins that have been preserved (table 3.4). The 1,662 silver coins can be broken down as follows: 66 coins (Group I), 34 coins (Group II), 80 coins (Group III), 1363 coins (Group IV), and 27 coins (Group V). The two most abundant series by far are Series IV.2.1, with 459 shekels minted by ʿOzbaʿal; and Series IV.4.2, with 508 16th-shekels minted by ʿAynel. The number of coins decreased between Group I and Group II, then increased significantly from one group to another. By far the most numerous denominations are the 16th-shekels (705 coins, representing 44.90% of the total amount), followed by the shekels (684, that is, 43.56%; see table 3.5). The other denominations are far less numerous: the quarter-shekels (48, that is, 3.06%), then the 12ths (43, that is, 2.74%), then the F.O.T.1 (33, that is, 2.10%), then the half-16ths (24, that is, 1.53%), then the 3rds (15, that is, 0.96%), then the F.O.T.3 (7, that is, 0.45%), then the 6ths (6, that is, 0.38%), followed by the F.O.T.2 (2, that is, 0.13%). In reality,

51. Elayi-Elayi, *Monnayage de Sidon*, 574–75; idem, *Coinage of Tyre*, 305–6.

Table 3.6. *Number of Obverse Dies by Group and Denomination*

	Shekels	*Thirds*	*Quarters*	*Sixths*	*Twelfths*	*Sixteenths*	*F.O.T.1*	*Half-Sixteenths*	*F.O.T.2*	*F.O.T.3*	*Total by Group*
Group I	5	4		3	5		2				19
Group II		2			10				3		15
Group III	7		4			3		3			17
Group IV.1	3		7			7		5			22
Group IV.2	17					14					31
Group IV.3	3					10					13
Group IV.4	4		3			48					55
Group V.1-3								5		4	9
Total	39	6	14	3	15	82	2	13	3	4	181

Table 3.7. *Proportion of Obverse Dies by Denomination*

	Number of Obverse Dies	%
Shekels	39	21.57
Third-shekels	6	3.31
Quarter-shekels	14	7.73
Sixth-shekels	3	1.66
Twelfth-shekels	15	8.29
Sixteenth-shekels	82	45.30
F.O.T.1	2	1.10
Half-sixteenths	13	7.18
F.O.T.2	3	1.66
F.O.T.3	4	2.21
Total	181	

the small number of small denominations preserved is probably due to the difficulty in finding them. The quarter-shekels were minted in Groups III and IV.1, not in Groups IV.2 and IV.3, then again in Group IV.4. The minute coins are identified in Groups I, II, and III because of their specific types (I.4, I.5, I.6, I.7, II.3, II.4, III.4, and IV.1.4). Other minute coins listed in the unclassified series of Group V (V.1, V.2, V.3) could belong to Groups IV.2, IV.3, or IV.4.

The preceding statistical procedure can be applied to the number of obverse dies (table 3.6). We consider only the obverse dies that are related to reverse dies, not isolated obverse dies; 15 other obverse dies are isolated

Table 3.8. *Number of Reverse Dies by Group and Denomination*

	Shekels	*Thirds*	*Quarters*	*Sixths*	*Twelfths*	*Sixteenths*	*F.O.T.1*	*Half-Sixteenths*	*F.O.T.2*	*F.O.T.3*	*Total by Group*
Group I	4	4		3	4		3				18
Group II		2			13				3		18
Group III	8		5			4		3			20
Group IV.1	5		11			8		8			32
Group IV.2	36					20					56
Group IV.3	14					15					29
Group IV.4	30		3			75					108
Group V.1-3								5		4	9
Total	97	6	19	3	17	122	3	16	3	4	290

Table 3.9. *Proportion of Reverse Dies by Denomination*

	Number of Reverse Dies	%
Shekels	97	33.45
Third-shekels	6	2.07
Quarter-shekels	19	6.55
Sixth-shekels	3	1.03
Twelfth-shekels	17	5.86
Sixteenth-shekels	122	42.07
F.O.T.1	3	1.03
Half-sixteenths	16	5.52
F.O.T.2	3	1.03
F.O.T.3	4	1.38
Total	290	

because the reverse was damaged and therefore unidentifiable. The 181 obverse dies that we have identified are distributed as follows: 19 obverse dies (Group I), 15 (Group II), 17 (Group III), 121 (Group IV), plus 9 obverse dies in unclassified Group V. The highest number is in Series IV.4.2 minted by King ʿAynel, with 48 obverse dies. The proportion of obverse dies by denomination is the following: the most numerous by far are the 16th-shekels (82 obverse dies, that is, 45.30% of the total amount), followed by the shekels (39O, that is, 21.57%; table 3.7). The number of obverse dies for the other denominations is much smaller: the 12th-shekels (15O, that is, 8.29%), then the quarter-shekels (14O, that is, 7.73%), then the half-16ths (13O, that is,

7.18%), then the 3rd-shekels (6O, that is, 3.31%), then the F.O.T.3 (4O, that is, 2.21%), then the F.O.T.2 and the 6ths (3O, that is, 1.66%) and then the F.O.T.1 (2O, that is, 1.10%).

Turning now to the reverse dies (table 3.8)—we consider only those related to obverse dies, not isolated reverse dies; 36 other reverse dies are isolated because the obverse was damaged and therefore unidentifiable. The reverse dies are in general more numerous than obverse dies: 290 versus 181. They are distributed as follows: 18 reverse dies (Group I), which are fewer in number than obverse dies; 18 (Group II); 20 (Group III), which are fewer than obverse dies; 225 (Group IV); plus 9 for Group V. The highest number is in Series IV.4.2 minted by King ʿAynel, with 75 reverse dies. The proportion of obverse dies by denomination is the following: the most numerous by far are the 16th-shekels (122R reverse dies, that is, 42.07% of the total amount), followed by the shekels (97O, that is, 33.45%; table 3.9). The number of reverse dies for the other denominations is much smaller: the quarter-shekels (19O, that is, 6.55%), then the half-16ths (16O, that is, 5.52%), then the 3rds (6O, that is, 2.07%), then the 12ths (17O, that is, 5.86%), then the 6ths, the F.O.T.1 and F.O.T.2 (3O, that is, 1.03%), and then F.O.T.3 (4O, that is, 1.38%).

Let us now compare the obverse dies minted by the various kings of Byblos during their entire reign, because we do not know the yearly production: ʿAynel was the first with 55 obverse dies, then comes ʿOzbaʿal with 31 obverse dies, then ʾElpaʿal with 22 obverse dies, then the anonymous king (vulture and ram) with 17 obverse dies, and finally ʾUrimilk with 13 obverse dies. If we compare these numbers with other Phoenician kings, the total obverse dies for the Tyrian king ʿOzmilk (17 years of reign) was 102; for the Sidonian king Baʿalšillem II (36 years of reign) 176, for ʿAbdʿaštart I (14 years of reign) 74, and for Evagoras (4 years of reign) 38.[52]

Numerous publications are still being devoted to evaluating the number of coins issued.[53] Quantifying the number of minted coins must be

52. Idem, *Coinage of Tyre*, 307–8.

53. Cf., for example, F. J. Mora Màs, "El coeficiente entre al número de ejemplares y al número de cuños; alcance de su contenido de informaciòn estadistica," in *Symposium numismático de Barcelona, 27–28 febrero de 1979*, vol. 1 (Barcelona, 1980) 514; J. W. Müller, "Estimation du nombre originel de coins," in *PACT* 5 (1981) 157–72; F. de Callataÿ, "À propos du volume des émissions monétaires dans l'Antiquité," *RBN* 130 (1984) 37–48; W. W. Esty, "Estimating the Size of a Coinage," *NC* 144 (1984) 180–83; idem, "Estimation of the Size of a Coinage: A Survey and Comparison of Methods," *NC* 146 (1986) 185–215; L. Villaronga, "De nuevo la estimación del número original de cuños de una emisión monetaria," *Gacetta Numismática* 85 (1987) 31–36; T. V. Buttrey, "Calculating Ancient Coin Production: Facts and Fantasies," *NC* 153 (1993) 335–51; F. de Callataÿ, G. Depeyrot, and L. Villaronga, *L'argent monnayé d'Alexandre le Grand à Auguste* (Brussels, 1993) with bibliography; F. de

Table 3.10. *Ratios of the Various Groups and Denominations*

Group	*Shekels*	*Thirds*	*Quarters*	*Sixths*	*Twelfths*	*Sixteenths*	*F.O.T.1*	*Half-Sixteenths*
I.1	1.20							
I.4					1.60			
I.5							1.50	
II.2.1					1.29			
II.2.2					1.67			
III.1	2.29							
III.2			2.50					
III.3						1.33		
III.4								1.33
IV.1.1	2							
IV.1.2			2.57					
IV.1.3						1.29		
IV.1.4								2.20
IV.2.1	17.29							
IV.2.2						2.50		
IV.3.1	21							
IV.3.2						2.30		
IV.4.1	19.25							
IV.4.2						9.39		
IV.4.5						1.31		
IV.4.6						9		
IV.4.7						3		
V.1								2.40

Callataÿ, "L'estimation du nombre originel de coins: En augmentant l'échantillon," *Acta Numismatica* 21–23 (1991–93; *Homenatge al Dr. Leandre Villaronga*) 31–48; idem, "Calculating Ancient Coin Production: Seeking a Balance," *NC* 155 (1995) 289–311; idem, "Le volume des émissions monétaires dans l'antiquité," *AIIN* 44 (1997) 53–62; idem, "Les taux de survie des émissions monétaires antiques, médiévales et modernes: Essai de mise en perspective et conséquences quant à la productivité des coins dans l'Antiquité," *RN* (2000) 87–109; S. Buttrey and T. Buttrey, "Calculating Ancient Coin Production, Again," *AJN* 9 (1997) 113–35; A. Savio, "La numismatica e i problemi quantitativi: Intorno al calcolo del volume delle emissioni," *RIN* 98 (1997) 11–48; idem, "Ancora sulla numismatica e i problemi quantitativi," *AIIN* (1997) 45–52; K. Lockyear, "Hoard Structure and Coin Production in Antiquity: An Empirical Investigation," *NC* 159 (1999) 215–43; F. de Callataÿ, "A Quantitative Survey of Hellenistic Coinages: Recent Achievements," in *Making, Moving and Managing: The New*

performed in two steps: (1) estimate the original number of obverse dies produced by using a statistical method; (2) multiply this estimate by the average number of coins that each die was able to strike. This number is estimated by using written sources, results of numismatic studies, and experimental simulations. It is very tempting, from the perspective of economic history, to attempt to determine the volume of issues. What results can reasonably be reached for the Byblian monetary workshop during the Persian period? The ratio (table 3.10) is very good for the five series that have a sufficient number of coins: n:o[54] = 21:1 for Series IV.3.1 (shekels), n:o = 19.25:1 for Series IV.4.1 (shekels), n:o = 17.29:1 for Series IV.2.1 (shekels), n:o = 9.39:1 for Series IV.4.2 (16th-shekels) and n:o = 9:1 for Series IV.4.6 (16th-shekels). The ratio is relatively good for the nine succeeding series: n:o = 3:1 for Series IV.4.7 (16ths), n:o = 2.57:1 for Series IV.1.2 (quarters), n:o = 2.50:1 for Series III.2 (quarters), n:o = 2.50:1 for Series IV.2.2 (16ths), n:o = 2.40:1 for Series V.1 (half-16ths), n:o = 2.30:1 for Series IV.3.2 (16ths), n:o = 2.29:1 for Series III.1 (shekels), n:o = 2.20:1 for Series IV.1.4 (half-16ths), and n:o = 2:1 for Series IV.1.1 (shekels). The ratio is not good for the next nine series: shekels: n:o = 1.20:1 (I.1); 12th-shekels: n:o = 1.67:1 (II.2.2), 1.60:1 (I.4), 1.29:1 (II.2.1); 16ths: n:o = 1.33:1 (III.3), 1.31:1 (IV.4.5), and 1.29:1 (IV.1.3); half-16ths: 1.33:1 (III.4); or F.O.T.1: n:o = 1.50:1 (I.5).

We shall apply the so-called Carter method[55] to the series for which the ratio of n:o is relatively good and the number of preserved coins sufficient. In this way, it will be possible to derive an approximate comparison of the number of coins issued for four series, for shekels and 16th-shekels: those of King ʿOzbaʿal (IV.2.1), King ʾUrimilk (IV.3.1), and King ʿAynel (IV.4.1 and IV.4.2). As far as the average number of coins struck with a single obverse die is concerned, several divergent hypotheses have been proposed (between 4,000 and 50,000).[56] However, the coinages and periods must not be confused. It is also important to take into account the specific conditions of each issue, in particular the workshop's policy re-

World of Ancient Economies, 323–31 BC (ed. Z. H. Archibald et al.; Oxford, 2005) 73–91; idem, ed., *Quantifying Monetary Supplies in Greco-Roman Times* (Bari, 2011).

54. n = number of coins studied; o = number of obverse dies.

55. G. F. Carter, "Simplified Method for Calculating the Original Number of Dies from Die-Link Statistics," *ANSMN* 28 (1983) 195–206; on the other methods, cf., for example, De Callataÿ, "À propos du volume des émissions monétaires," 37–48; idem, "L'utilisation des statistiques en numismatique (métrologie, estimation du nombre de monnaies émises)," *Les nouvelles de l'archéologie* 39 (1988) 8–10 (with bibliography); W. W. Esty, "How to Estimate Original of Dies and the Coinage of a Sample," *NC* 166 (2006) 359–64.

56. Cf., for example, De Callataÿ, "L'estimation du nombre originel de coins," 46–48; Buttrey, "Calculating Ancient Coin Production," 335–51; De Callataÿ et al., *L'argent monnayé d'Alexandre le Grand à Auguste*, 8–11 (with bibliography).

garding the useful life of the dies. As we have shown, in the Byblian workshop, a high tolerance level was set in relation to die defects, just as in the Tyrian and Sidonian workshops. It is possible to use the estimate for an obverse die engraved in Delphi by the Amphictionic league in the 4th century B.C.E.: based on the written sources and on numismatic analysis, P. Kinns concluded that this die was used for striking between 23,333 and 47,250 coins.[57] According to F. de Callataÿ, in this case, the real figure would have been closer to 47,250.[58] All things considered, we shall use the lower limit of around 20,000, which was agreed on by F. de Callataÿ, G. Depeyrot, and L. Villaronga in 1993.[59] What results can be obtained in this way? We shall only consider the four best-documented cases. King ʿOzbaʿal of Group IV.2.1 minted 340,000 shekels (of around 14 g) during an unknown lapse of time—that is, around 4.76 tons of silver, plus the series of small denominations. King ʾUrimilk of Group IV.3.1 minted 40,000 shekels during an unknown period of time—that is, around 0.56 tons of silver, plus the series of small denominations. King ʿAynel of Group IV.4.1 minted 80,000 shekels during an unknown period of time—that is, around 1.12 tons of silver. The volume of production for the shekels of these three successive kings was very different: for ʿOzbaʿal, it was eight times greater than for ʾUrimilk and four times greater than ʿAynel. However, the comparison is problematic due to the fact that the lengths of the three reigns are unknown; however, it seems that ʾUrimilk's reign was shorter than his predecessor's. If we compare this with the volume of production of other Phoenician kings, King ʿOzmilk of Tyre used 16.32 tons of silver for minting shekels during a reign of 17 years. The volume of production of Byblian kings is closer to that of some Sidonian kings: 1.53 tons for ʿAbdʿaštart I (during 14 years), 1.7 tons for Tennes (5 years), 2.7 tons for Evagoras? (4 years), and 1.5 tons for ʿAbdʿaštart II (10 years).[60]

57. P. Kinns, "The Amphictionic Coinage reconsidered," *NC* 143 (1983) 19.

58. De Callataÿ, "L'estimation du nombre originel de coins," 47 n. 10.

59. De Callataÿ et al., *L'argent monnayé d'Alexandre le Grand à Auguste*; T. Faucher recently conducted experiments and arrived at a figure of 15,000 as a minimal number (*L'atelier monétaire d'Alexandrie sous les Lagides: problèmes techniques et stylistiques* (Ph.D. diss., Paris, 2006).

60. Elayi-Elayi, *Monnayage de Sidon*, 580; idem, *Coinage of Tyre*, 309–10.

Chapter 4
Metrological Study

Compared with Sidonian and Tyrian coinages,[1] the evolution of the weight and metallic composition of Byblian coinage appears to have been more complex. This complexity was due to several monetary changes, which have now been identified thanks to metrological and metallic analyses. These changes were probably linked to political events and economic evolutions, some of which we know about, as we shall see in chap. 5.

1. *Metrological Method*

In this chapter, we shall follow the metrological method that we have developed elsewhere.[2] This method proved to be extremely effective in avoiding the primary difficulties that are encountered during a metrological study of ancient coins: for example, wear and tear, imprecise weighing, etc., and even devaluation by adding copper or other metals to silver coins. The greatest difficulty in applying it is developing software that is able to extract the right information from the rough data and handle it carefully. This is only possible if one is aware of what information can be extracted and what cannot. Chapter 6, "Metrological Study," in our book *Coinage of Tyre* addresses this method in considerable detail. Thus, there is no need to develop the basis of this method again here.[3] We simply reiterate that the data cannot give us access to the value of the original standard but can give us the value of a new standard that is more or less modified from its original value by a relatively large number of parameters. This modification is minimized by the method used here, however.

2. *Metrological Analysis of the Byblian Silver Coinage*

As in other Phoenician coinages, two categories of denominations were minted in Byblos: the first category contained a large amount of silver

1. Elayi-Elayi, *Monnayage de Sidon*; idem, *Coinage of Tyre*.
2. Idem, *Monnayage de Sidon*, 581–86; idem, *Coinage of Tyre*, 311–19.
3. Ibid., *Coinage of Tyre*.

and was used for important transactions; the second was used for daily transactions. Byblian shekels were in the first category, just like Tyrian shekels and Sidonian double-shekels. Their use in transactions was quite limited compared with the second category of coins. Byblian 3rd- and quarter-shekels complemented the sizable transactions and were therefore rare. The denomination of the second category, used in daily transactions, was a large, one-gram fraction. These coins can be found in Byblos as in all Phoenician coinages (16th-shekels or similar): 0.57 g for the first standard (Groups I and II) and 0.71 g for the second standard (Groups III and IV). This denomination corresponded to the Sidonian: 0.76 g before devaluation and 0.72 g after devaluation,[4] and to the Tyrian: 0.63 g before the change of standard and 0.53 g after the change of standard.[5] As far as its trade function is concerned, it was probably the denomination equivalent to the approximately 0.72 g obol in Greek coinages.[6] Like the Greek obol, this denomination was complemented by smaller denominations to facilitate everyday transactions. Parallel with the metrological study of Sidonian and Tyrian coins, we conducted a series of analyses to determine their metallic composition.[7] Because these analyses showed interesting results, we decided to perform a similar analysis of the metallic composition of Byblian coins. A series of 10 coins were first analyzed to make a general exploration of the coins, followed by another series of 17 coins to complement the study and by another series of 13 coins to confirm and complement the first results.[8]

a. *The First Standard of Byblian Coinage*

Even though the first Byblian group did not have the same value as the initial Tyrian and Sidonian groups, the coins of this group followed (albeit not exactly the same) at least a similar evolution. They were quite regular, relatively flat with fine engraving, displayed a good striking technique, and constituted a complete system of probably 8 denominations. This is true for Group I, but only partly true for Group II, which had no shekel and possibly 4 denominations.

4. Idem, *Monnayage de Sidon*, 588–89.

5. Idem, *Coinage of Tyre*, 320–21.

6. On the Greek obol, cf., for example, S. Psoma, "Le nombre de chalques dans l'obole dans le monde grec," *RN* 154 (1998) 12–24.

7. A. G. Elayi, J.-N. Barrandon, and J. Elayi, "The Devaluation of Sidonian Silver Coinage in 365 BCE and the First Bronze Issues," *AJN* n.s. 19 (2007) 1–8; idem, "The Change of Standard of Tyrian Silver Coinage about 357 BCE as Determined by Fast Neutron Activation Analysis," *NC* (2008) 15–20.

8. Cf. A. G. Elayi, M. Blet-Lemarquand, and J. Elayi, "Silver Coinage Fluctuations at Byblos (5th–6th Cent. BCE) as Determined by LA-ICP-MS and FNAA," *AJN* (2012) 1–10.

Only 8 shekels with known weights have been preserved for the first series (I.1): the value of their modified standard is 9.42 g. With regard to what we call the 3rd-shekel (Series I.2), the data show 2.75 g for the modified standard. Its value is less than what can be expected from the shekel (as is usually the case for fractional Phoenician coins). In this first group, the political authority seems to have chosen to strike a large number of denominations in order to implement a real policy of monetary economy. Possibly 7 denominations range from the shekel down to approximately 0.11 g: about 9.42 g (shekel), 2.75 g (3rd-shekel), 1.40 g (6th-), and 0.70 g (12th-shekel). Since this series had the same iconography, it was difficult to differentiate the smallest denominations from each other, given the tiny differences in size and weight. Because the 12th-shekel in the first Byblian standard and the 16th-shekel in the second standard played the role of the Greek obol, we expect their fractions to follow a similar sort of pattern. We know that the fractions of the obol followed a complicated system in the same way as the trihemitetartemorion (3 times the half quarter-obol). The small denominations of the Attic monetary system were identified from the Greek texts. No similar Phoenician texts have been discovered, and even the name of the Phoenician equivalent of the Greek obol remains unknown. Given these conditions, it is clear that it is impossible to identify the fractions of the 12th or the 16th, for at least three reasons: the very small number of coins preserved in each denomination, the wear, and the insufficient precision of weighing, which ought to be made to one-hundredth of a gram. Therefore, we shall adopt the following names for the fractions of a 12th: F.O.T.1 (about 0.35 g), F.O.T.2 (about 0.20 g), and F.O.T.3 (about 0.10 g).

There were 4 or 5 denominations that proved to be easy to identify: 1 or 2 for large transactions and 2 or 3 for small transactions; shekels, on the one hand, and 12th-shekels for Groups I and II and 16th-shekels for Groups III and IV, on the other hand, were in each group the 2 master denominations. The use of bronze coins in the other Phoenician coinages solved the difficulty of handling and identifying coins of about 0.10 or 0.20 g, but the Byblian coinage workshop did not mint bronze coins during the Persian period.

Only 4 denominations, perhaps, and a relatively small number of coins have been identified for Group II. The main features of this group are:

1. it follows the same standard as Group I, essentially because Series II.2 (12th-shekel) is clearly different from Series III.3 and IV.1.3 (16th-shekels),
2. no shekel is known in this group,

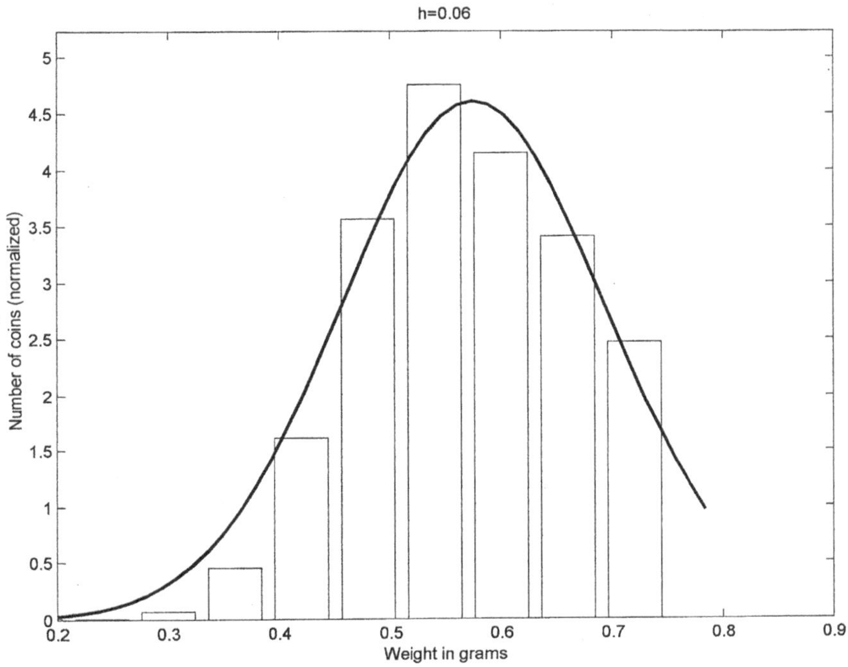

Fig. 4.1. *Byblian 16th-shekels (II.2).*

3. its metallic composition began to be debased slightly by the addition of copper and lead.[9]

Few 3rd-shekels have been found, and they do not provide any significant weight statistically (2.37–3.30 g). The 12th-shekel (with its iconographical variants) is the only denomination to give a statistically significant value: 0.57 g with 21 coins preserved (fig. 4.1). Another series with a helmet on the reverse (6 coins preserved) has a weight ranging from 0.36 g to 0.13 g. And last, the series with a griffin's head on the reverse (1 coin preserved) has a weight of 0.28 g. It seems that the reduction in the number of different denominations began with this series.

What was the origin of the first Byblian standard? It was not similar to the Attic standard (didrachms of 8.66 g at the time of Philip II of Macedonia);[10] it had some proximity to the second Aradian standard

9. Cf. ibid.

10. Cf. G. Le Rider, *Le monnayage d'argent et d'or de Philippe II frappé en Macédoine de 359 à 294 avant J.-C.* (Paris, 1977) 408; idem, *Monnayage et finances de Philippe II: Un état*

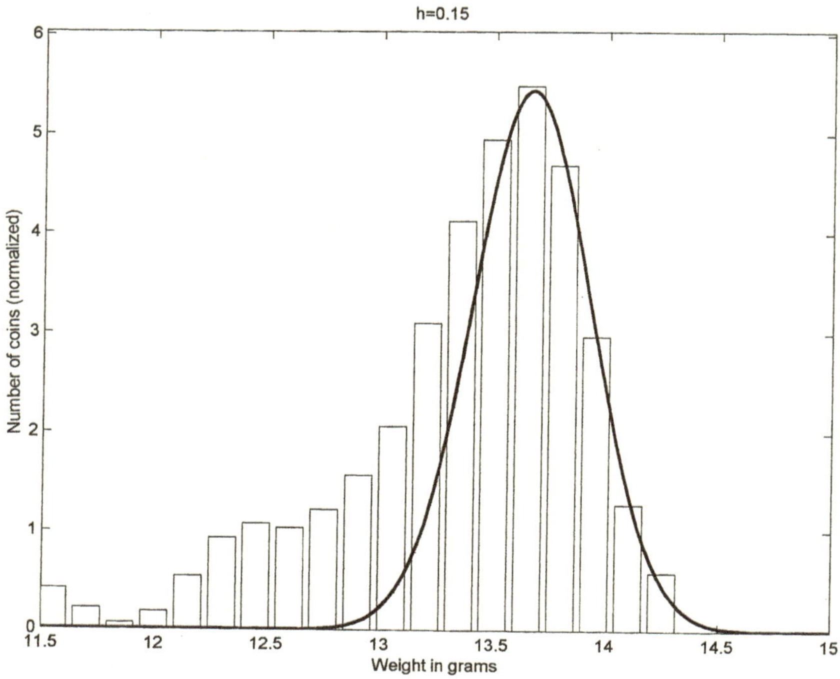

Fig. 4.2. *Byblian shekels (III.1).*

(about 9.50 g), but it was more than half a century earlier, and the contemporary Aradian standard that weighed about 11.50 g.[11] It was different from the kite value in the Egyptian system of weights; at that time, Egypt had no coinage.[12] The closest parallel to the first Byblian standard was the Lycian standard; unfortunately, neither the Lycian metrology nor the

de la question (Athens, 1996) 50: the Attic standard chosen by Philippus II was retained by Alexander for gold coinage. The value of this standard decreased in silver tetradrachms for the Aradian mint after ca. 320 and for the Tyrian mint after ca. 320: cf. F. Duyrat, *Arados hellénistique: Étude historique et monétaire* (Beirut, 2005) 127; O. Mørkholm, "The Attic Coin Standard in the Levant during the Hellenistic Period," in *Studia Paulo Naster Oblata I: Numismatique antique* (ed. S. Scheers;Leuven, 1982) 143, 146.

11. Cf. Elayi-Elayi, *Trésors*, 24–82.

12. D. Valbelle, *Catalogue des poids à inscriptions hiératiques de Deir el-Médineh n° 5001–5423* (Cairo, 1977); M.-A. Cour-Marty, "Une norme pondérale dominante en Égypte pharaonique," *GöMisz* 69 (1983) 27–30; idem, "La collection de poids du Musée du Caire revisitée," *RdE* 36 (1985) 189–200; idem, "Les poids égyptiens, de précieux jalons archéologiques," *CRIPEL* 12 (1990) 17–55.

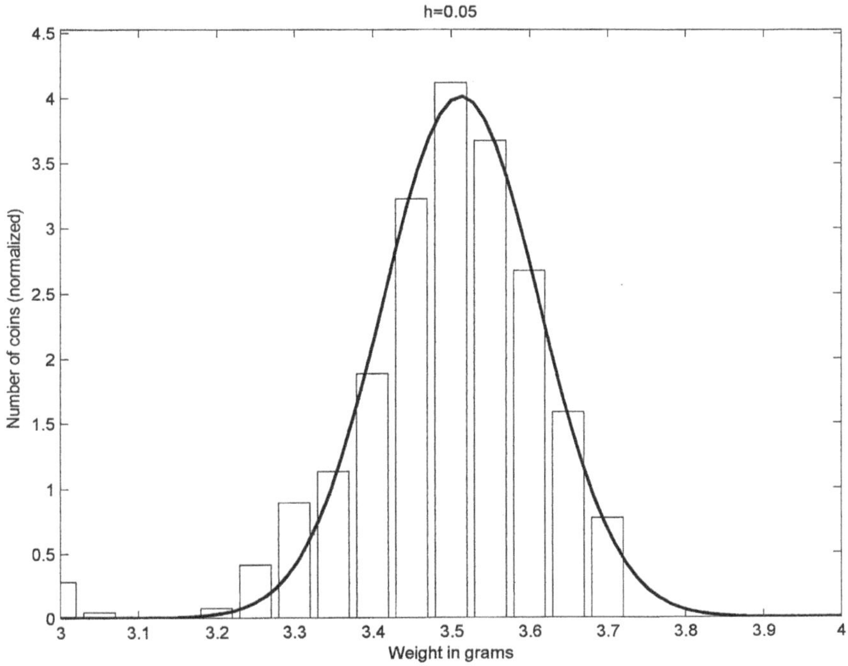

Fig. 4.3. *Byblian quarter-shekels of ʾElpaʿal (IV.1.2).*

chronology of the Lycian coinage was studied in detail.[13] However, a stater minted by King Tenegures was found in the oldest Byblian hoard (TX) containing Byblian coins of Group I.[14] Therefore, Tenegures' coinage was contemporary with Byblian Group I; the weight of his staters ranges from about 8.50 g to 9.50 g.[15] The motifs of these Lycian coins are parallel to the motifs of the first Byblian coins: on the obverse, a mythical animal (winged horse and crouched sphinx); and on the reverse, a symbol (triskeles and double lotus flower). Therefore, in the present state of research, the Lycian

13. Cf., for example, O. Mørkholm, "The Classification of Lycian Coins before Alexander the Great," *JNG* 14 (1964) 65–76; N. Cau, "La classificacione delle monetazioni licie in età achemenide: storia e problemi," *Annali* 44 (1997) 241–279; N. Vismara, *Monetazione arcaica della Licia III* (Milan, 1996); idem, "Monetazione arcaica della Lycia: Prime rilevanze circa l'approvvigionamento metallico," *REA* 103 (2001) 343–67.

14. Elayi-Elayi, *Trésors*, 87–90.

15. *BMC Lycia, Pamphylia and Pisidia*, 18, no. 82 and pl. 5:1; Babelon, *Traité* 2/2:206 and pl. 93:23.

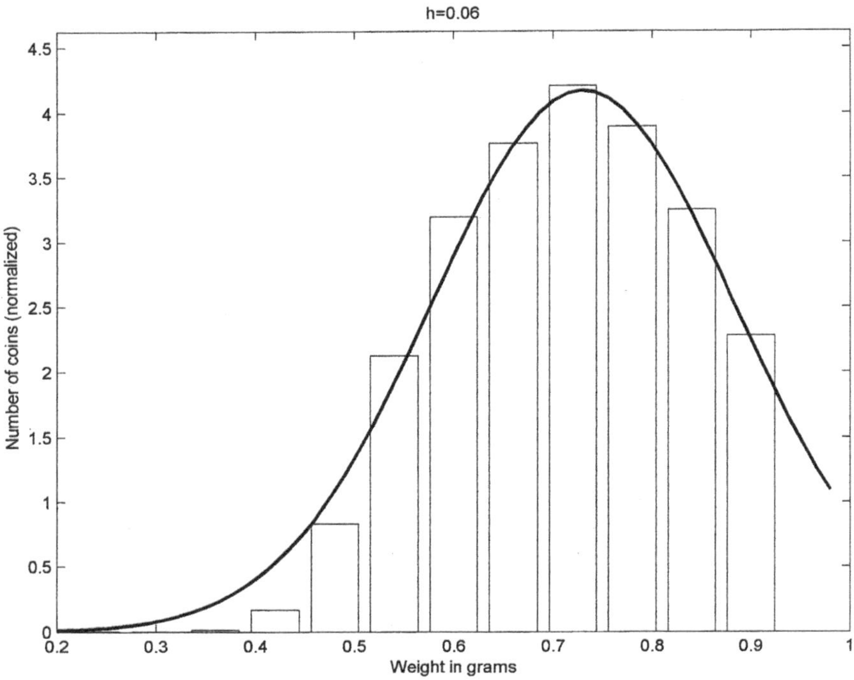

Fig. 4.4. *Byblian 16th-shekel of ʾElpaʿal (IV.1.3).*

coinage of Tenegures is the most likely model for the Byblian Group I, both for standard and for motifs.

b. *The Second Standard of Byblian Coinage*

At the end of the issue of Group II, major political and economic changes occurred in Byblos[16] that produced significant changes in the characteristics of the Group III coins that were minted by the so-called anonymous king. First, the standard was revalued from 9.42 g to 13.66 g. Second, the new denominations were a shekel, a quarter-shekel instead of the 3rd, a 16th instead of the 12th, and a half-16th. Third, the percentage of silver again reached about 98.5%, as in Group I.[17] Fourth, the motifs changed: the war-galley and seahorse replaced the sphinx on the obverse, and the vulture and ram replaced the hawk on the reverse. Fifth, the engravers used the incuse method for engraving on the reverse. As far as the metrological

16. See further, chap. 5.
17. Cf. here above, n. 8.

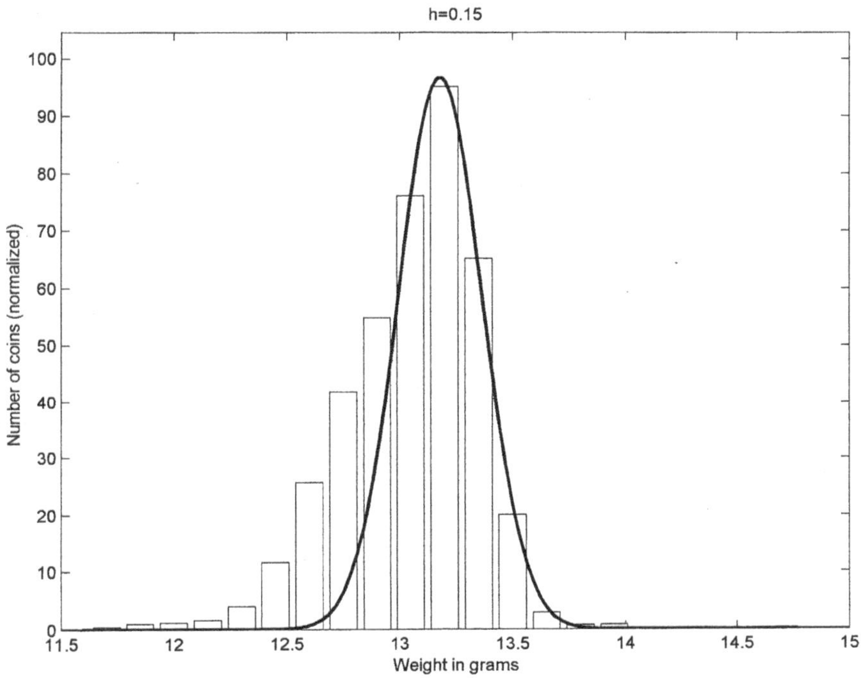

Fig. 4.5. *Byblian shekels of ʿOzbaʿal (IV.2.1).*

aspect is concerned, during this period there was a succession of five kings, and we shall try to analyze the distinctives of their five successive issues. In general, the number of shekels preserved[18] is relatively small for these five issues except for the 414 shekels of King ʿOzbaʿal: 42 for the anonymous king, 12 for ʾElpaʿal, 54 for ʾUrimilk, and 79 for ʿAynel.

The well-being of the city is visible at the beginning of the inauguration of Group III through the change of the standard from 9.42 g to 13.66 g and the recovery of the silver percentage to its normal, approximately 98.5% value. Four denominations are clearly identified for this group: 42 shekels with a 13.66 g modified standard (fig. 4.2), 14 quarter-shekels with a 3.36 g modified standard, 12 16th-shekels with a 0.84 g modified standard, and the one-half 16ths weighing 0.31 g. These values must be considered with some caution because of the relatively small number of coins for each denomination. The 16th-shekel of this group seems to be heavier than would be expected from our overall knowledge of the relationship between the

18. Only coins with a known weight are taken into account here.

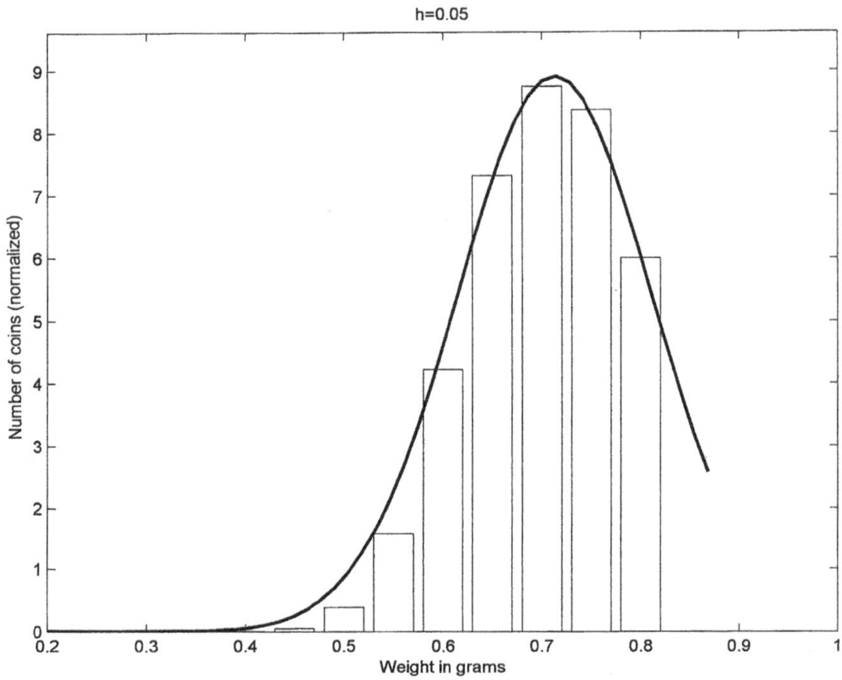

Fig. 4.6. *Byblian 16th-shekels of ʿOzbaʿal (IV.2.2).*

shekel and the 16th-shekel in Phoenician coinages; however, the number of coins on hand is only 12.

Only 12 shekels have been preserved in Group IV.1, which was minted by King ʾElpaʿal. He increased the weight of the shekel to a 14.21 g modified standard but increasingly added other metals, especially copper. The percentage of silver dropped to 91.6% in the coins that we have analyzed. Twenty-five quarter-shekels have been identified with a 3.51 g modified standard (fig. 4.3); 24 16th-shekels have given a 0.73 g modified standard (fig. 4.4); 18 half-16ths have a 0.32 g modified standard. If the reference for the smallest denominations was not the shekel but the 16th-shekel, as it was for the Greek divisions of the obol, for example, there would have been a denomination of a half-16th. Since the Phoenician name of this denomination is unknown, for the moment we shall refer to it as a "half-16th." What characterizes these issues is the increasing amount of copper that has been added to the silver. A small percentage of copper does not significantly change the color of the coins. However a large percentage gives a clear yellowish color. The flan makers of the Byblian monetary workshop

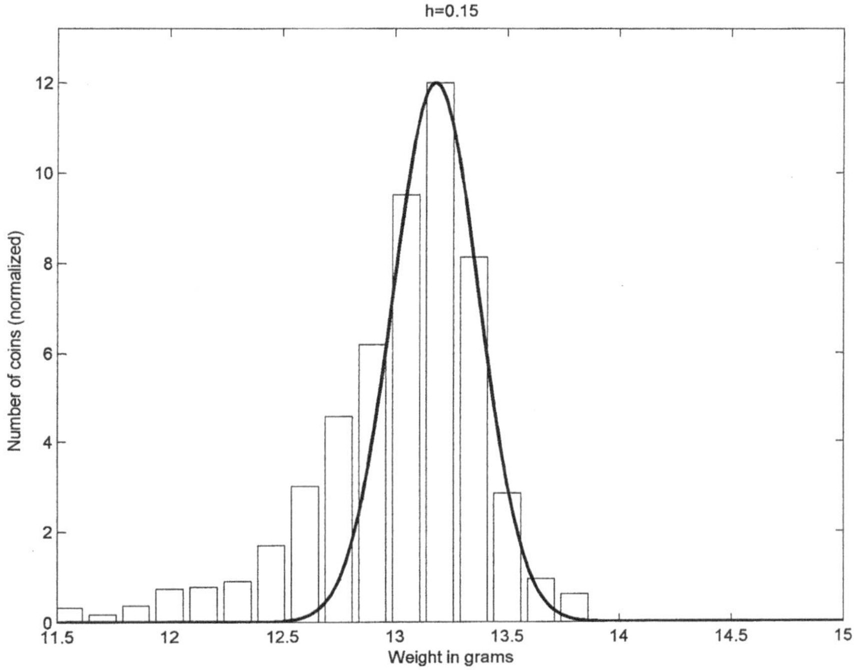

Fig. 4.7. *Byblian shekels of ʾUrimilk (IV.3.1).*

seem to have been aware of this problem. Therefore, they probably also added some lead in order to avoid the yellowish coloring.

Another important political change occurred with the reign of King ʿOzbaʿal. It resulted in the recovery of the 98–99% amount of silver in the coins, but this was compensated by a loss in weight, from 14.21 g to 13.18 g, for the shekels. It recalls a similar loss of weight that occurred in Sidonian coinage. Another peculiarity of the coinages of King ʿOzbaʿal and of his two successors, ʾUrimilk and ʿAynel, is the absence of identified denominations smaller than the 16th-shekels. Since it is inconceivable that there could only have been one denomination (16th-shekel) for commercial usage, this means that smaller denominations must partly figure into the unidentified Group V, but partly it means that some have not yet been discovered, as is frequently the case for minute coins. Another problem concerning these three kings arises in relation to hoard TIX, for which we have performed a metrological analysis.[19] It contained 139 shekels of ʿOzbaʿal, 13 of ʾUrimilk,

19. J. Elayi and A. Lemaire, "Le trésor de Byblos TIX," *Trans* 38 (2009) 77–98.

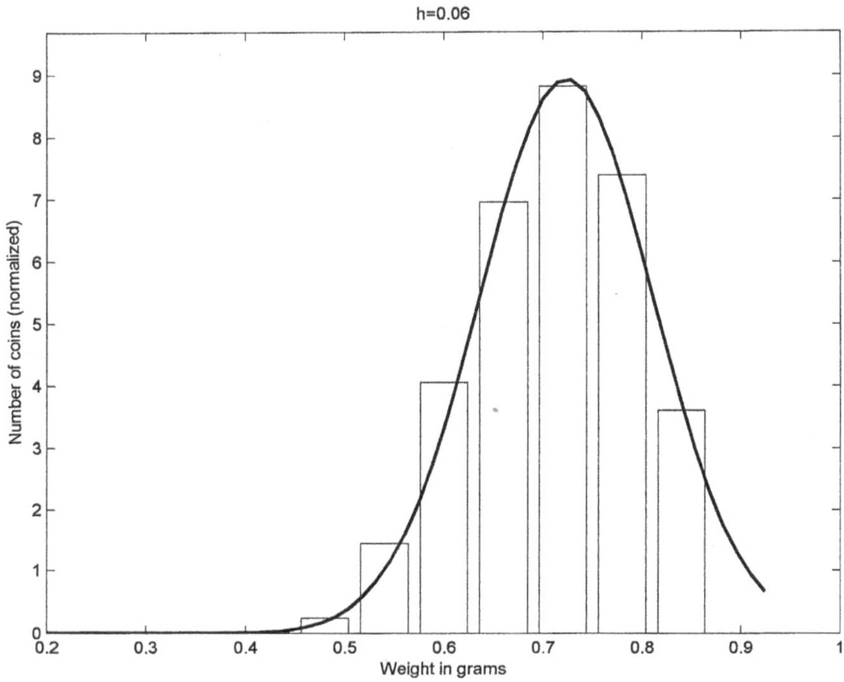

Fig. 4.8. *Byblian 16th-shekels of ʾUrimilk (IV.3.2).*

and 49 of ʿAynel. The modified standards of the shekels from this hoard are 12.87, 12.78, and 12.71 g, respectively. The first two values are in conflict with the modified standards extracted from the whole coinage of ʿOzbaʿal and ʾUrimilk (13.18 g), while the third value, of ʿAynel, is not (12.81 g).

Our statistical method must help us to understand this abnormal result. We repeated the analyses of the data without the coins of hoard TIX. The three modified standards became consistent, all together, at about 13.15 g. Why are the coins of hoard TIX statistically lighter than the other coins of these three kings? This is due either to a systematic error in the weighing of this hoard (for example, the zero of the scale was not adjusted) or, less likely, to the fact that this hoard is especially worn. Why did our method give correct modified standards for the shekels of Kings ʿOzbaʿal and ʾUrimilk, as it should, and not for those of King ʿAynel? In the case of ʿAynel, the total number of shekels is 76, 49 of which come from hoard TIX and only 27 of which do not. The modified standard takes into account the majority of the coins as expected. The proportion of coins from hoard TIX is smaller for the other two kings than for ʿAynel, and this is why they do

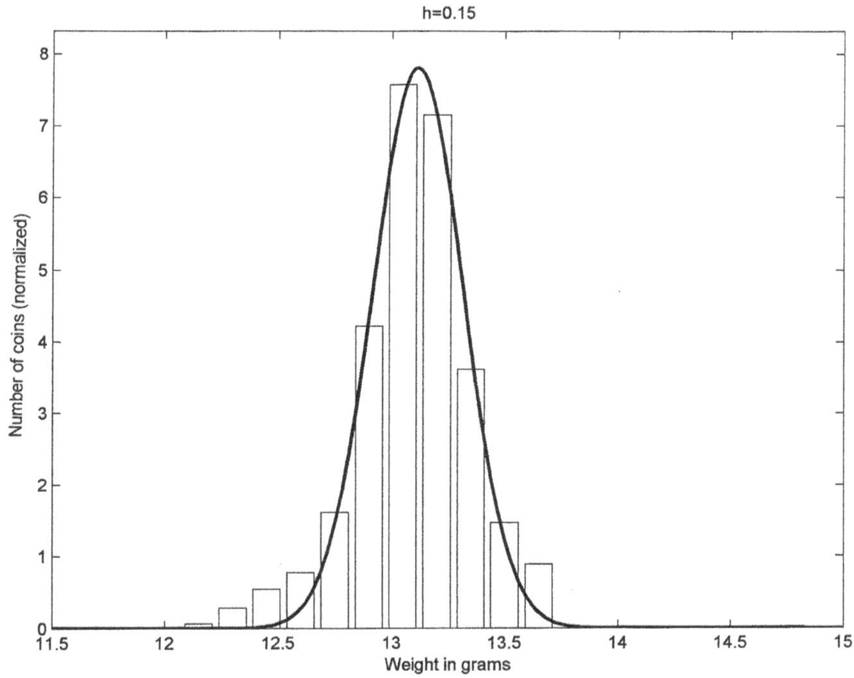

Fig. 4.9. *Byblian shekels of ʿAynel (IV.4.1).*

not affect the result of the modified standard. This proves again how efficient this statistical approach is. The weights of hoard TIX were known by P. Naster and biased his conclusions concerning the weights of ʾUrimilk's and ʿAynel's coins. In fact, the modified standard value of 13.12 g (fig. 4.9) is in line with those of his two predecessors. Therefore, there was no devaluation, as proposed by P. Naster.[20]

The 414 shekels that have been identified for King ʿOzbaʿal have a 13.18 g modified standard (fig. 4.5). Only 38 16th-shekels have been identified with a 0.71 g modified standard (fig. 4.6). This value of the 16th is more in line with the usual value of the shekel than the value of the shekel in Group III. We note the absence of quarter-shekels in the coinages of ʿOzbaʿal and ʾUrimilk. The small number of 16ths minted by ʿOzbaʿal compared with the large number of shekels can at least partly be explained by the fact that the excavator of Byblos, M. Dunand, was not interested in

20. P. Naster, "Trésors de monnaies de Byblos du IVe s. av. J.-C. trouvés à Byblos," in *Numismatique et histoire économique phéniciennes et puniques* (ed. T. Hackens and G. Moucharte; Studia Phoenicia 9; Louvain-la-Neuve, 1992) 17.

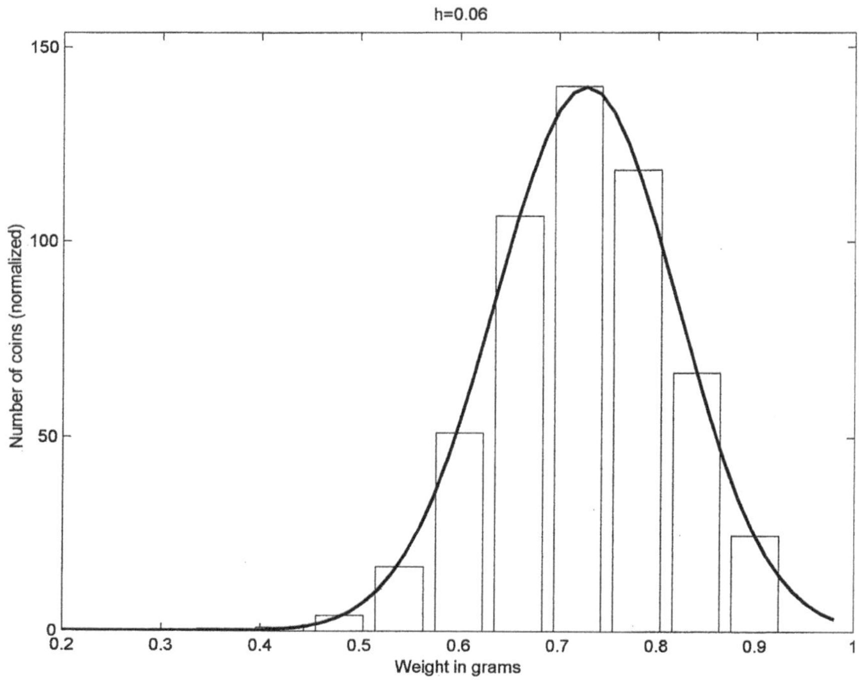

Fig. 4.10. *Byblian 16th-shekels of ʿAynel (IV.4.2).*

small denominations and collected only shekels. Moreover, the number of preserved 16ths for Series IV.2.2 is not representative of the number of coins minted, contrary to the number of preserved shekels for Series IV.2.1, which is representative, as shown by the ratios calculated for the two series.[21] King ʾUrimilk, ʿOzbaʿal's successor, minted a much smaller number of shekels: 54 with a 13.18 g modified standard (fig. 4.7). His 32 16th-shekels have a 0.73 g modified standard (fig. 4.8).

King ʿAynel minted a large quantity of 16th-shekels (586) with the complete inscription (Series IV.4.2), with a 0.73 g modified standard (fig. 4.10). At the end of his reign, he minted a small series of quarter-shekels (IV.4.3), of which 4 coins have been preserved (3.65–2.97 g). He also minted a series of 16ths bearing the inscription *ʿG* (Series IV.4.5), with a 0.72 g modified standard (fig. 4.11). The number of coins of two other series of 16ths, one of which bears the inscription *GL* (Series IV.4.6) and one of which is anepigraphic (Series IV.4.7), is insufficient for calculating statistically significant values. Contrary to the coinage of ʿOzbaʿal, the proportion of

21. Cf. further, appendix 3.

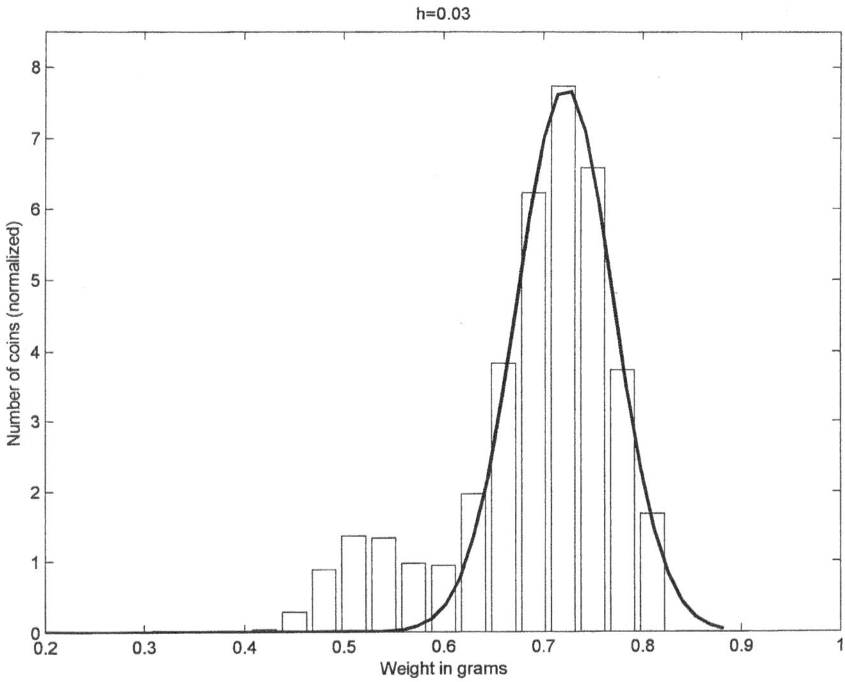

Fig. 4.11. *Byblian 16ths-shekels with ʿG (IV.4.4).*

shekels minted by ʿAynel is relatively small (Series IV.4.1: 76 coins preserved); meanwhile, the 16th-shekel was the most abundant of the Byblian coinage series (Series IV.4.2: 586 coins preserved). In this case, the number of preserved coins in both series is representative of the number of coins minted, as shown from the calculated ratios,[22] which means that this proportion of shekels and 16th-shekels is meaningful. How can we interpret this large quantity of 16th-shekels minted by ʿAynel compared with the relatively small number of shekels? It was probably due to a large need for this small denomination, possibly in relation to the need to pay craftsmen, such as those who built and repaired war-galleys during this very troubled period.[23]

The unclassified half-shekels (V.1) were probably minted by one of the last three kings whose half-shekels have not been identified; they have a 0.31 g modified standard (fig. 4.12).

22. Cf. ibid.

23. See further, chap. 5.

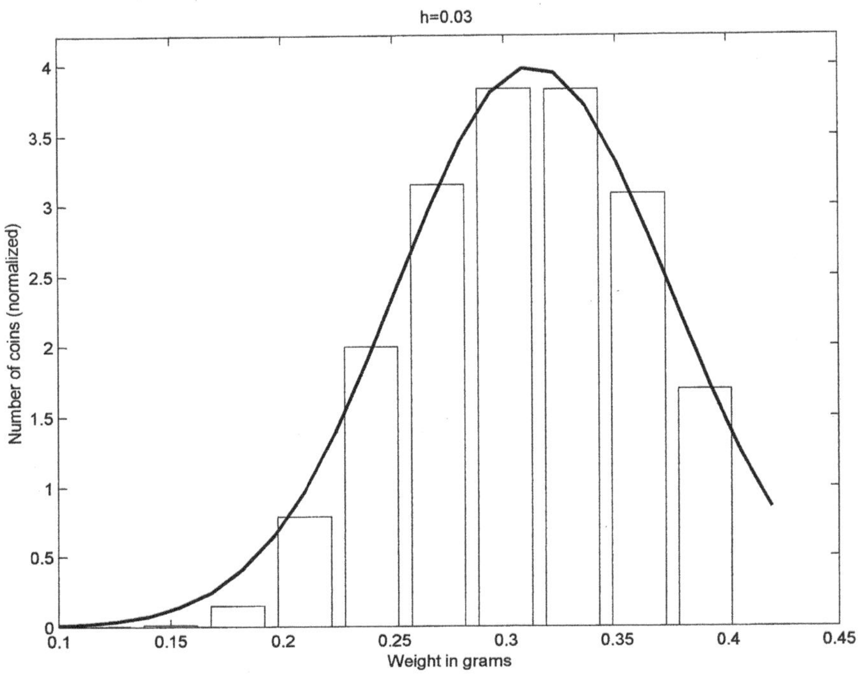

Fig. 4.12. *Byblian half-16th shekels (V.1).*

This metrological study of the coinage of Byblos shows some similarities with the coinages of Tyre and Sidon. The three workshops tried a number of experiments, the first consisting of the addition of some lead and copper to the silver metal: however, this addition was limited in percentage and time and was followed by a return to almost pure silver coins, as was the case for Tyre and Sidon. Another common experiment was to increase the weight in order to compensate for the decrease in the percentage of silver. All three cities used, for a large proportion of their coinages, the Phoenician standard of about 14 g. However, the coinage of Byblos shows several peculiarities. A large increase in weight was associated with the change of standard (from 9.42 g to 13.66 g). Two major local events influenced this coinage: the building of a war fleet and the usurpation of the throne by ʿOzbaʿal, the son of a priest. The Byblian workshop, unlike those of Sidon, Tyre, and Arwad never minted bronze coins. Nor did Byblos export its shekels. Finally, because of not having been circulated outside the territory of the city, the Byblos coins do not bear graffiti or countermarks.

Chapter 5

The Coinage of Byblos and the History of the City

Unlike the previously published study of the history of Byblos from the 8th to the 4th centuries B.C.E.,[1] this chapter focuses on the period of Byblian coinage, from the end of the second quarter of the 5th century to 333 B.C.E. Its aim is to propose a historical and socioeconomic interpretation of the coinage with reference to its context and all other available sources. This interpretation is enlightened by our knowledge of the history of the other Phoenician cities. We shall follow the chronological order of the various Byblian monetary groups in order to underscore their particular contexts and the light that they can shed.

1. *Byblos before the Inauguration of Its First Coinage*

As we have already pointed out,[2] it is important to understand how the Byblians operated before they began to issue coins. In brief, Byblos, like the other Phoenician cities, knew Greek coinages, which had appeared at least one and a half centuries earlier. We know this because numerous imported coins have been discovered from the ancient Near East. However, the Byblians continued to use systems that had been working well for a long time. What system they used depended on the trading partners, goods, or periods involved—whether it was bartering, weighed metals, or counted metals. These "premonetary" systems (meaning that coins were not used as such) worked perfectly and were suited to all sorts of operations, even the most complex; everyone was completely satisfied.[3] Payments in weighed metal were probably the most frequently used in Byblian trade because this was the common system throughout the ancient Near East before the

1. Elayi, *Byblos*.

2. For this question in general and Tyre in particular, see Elayi-Elayi, *Coinage of Tyre*, 323–28.

3. Cf. already G. Perrot and C. Chipiez, *Histoire de l'art dans l'Antiquité, III: Phénicie-Chypre* (Paris, 1885) 893–94: "[L]es Phéniciens n'ont pas inventé la monnaie parce qu'ils pouvaient s'en passer."

commercial use of coins, and it was still in use after the diffusion of Greek and Persian coins, for example, in Babylonia, where it was the only currency until the Seleucid period.[4] The use of gold for payments was unique to Egypt.[5] The Byblian hoard TX (appendix 4) contains coins and fragments of silver coins, a gold coin and a gold flan, fragments of silver coins and jewels, and casting waste. This sort of treasure is traditionally called a "silversmith's hoard," because of the fragments of metal and casting waste. It did not necessarily belong to a silversmith, but it was used in the context of weighed metal: either silver and gold were intended to make new jewels, or these two metals were uniquely used for payments, as in Egypt. Because of Persian dominion during the Persian period, the Byblian economy was necessarily integrated with the Persian economy. In the same way as the other Phoenician cities, Byblos was apparently allowed to retain its political and economic autonomy, on condition that it payed the tribute and various taxes, had a compliant foreign policy, and accepted Persian control.[6] It is uncertain whether Rikiš-kalāmu-Bēl, who was appointed by Darius I as governor of a Phoenician city, was over Byblos or another city, such as Gabala.[7] If this governor was over Byblos, this would have changed the political and economic situation of the city under the reign of Darius I (522–486; see table 5.1).

2. *The Inauguration of Byblian Coinage Group I: End of the Second Quarter of the 5th Century*

The question of the inauguration of Byblian coinage Group I must be considered in comparison with that of other Phoenician coinages since they were closely connected. Several proposals have been made for dating this inauguration to between the beginning of the 5th century and the beginning of the 4th, but the arguments were without foundation. For example, E. T. Newell and G. K. Jenkins proposed the beginning of the 5th

4. See, for example, F. Joannès, "Métaux précieux et moyens de paiement en Babylonie achéménide et hellénistique," *Trans* 8 (1994) 137–44; P. Vargyas, "Silver and Money in Achaemenid and Hellenistic Babylonia," in *Assyrologia et Semitica: Festschrift für J. Oelsner* (AOAT 252; Neukirchen-Vluyn, 2000) 513–21: even during the Seleucid period, when coins were in currency, silver was still weighed, at least in strictly "Babylonian" milieus.

5. P. Briant and R. Descat, "Un registre douanier de la satrapie d'Égypte à l'époque achéménide (*TAD* C3, 7)," in *Le commerce en Égypte ancienne* (ed. N. Grimal and B. Menu; Cairo, 1996) 75–78.

6. Cf. Elayi, *Byblos*, 119–38 (with bibliography).

7. M. Dandamayev, "A Governor of Byblos in Sippar," in *Immigration and Emigration within the Ancient Near East, Festschrift E. Lipiński* (ed. K. van Lerberghe and A. Schoors; Leuven, 1995) 29–31; Elayi, *Byblos*, 24–26, 129.

century, J. W. Betlyon proposed ca. 425 B.C.E., E. Babelon and J. Babelon proposed 410, B. V. Head ca. 400 and G. F. Hill the early 4th century.[8] Several proposals have also been made for the order of the inauguration of the four Phoenician coinages: Tyre, Arwad, Sidon, and Byblos according to B. V. Head; Arwad, Sidon, Tyre, and Byblos according to G. F. Hill; Sidon, Tyre, Byblos, and Arwad according to E. Babelon and J. Babelon; Sidon, Tyre, Arwad, and Byblos according to J. W. Betlyon.[9] In terms of relative chronology, we have shown that the order of the initial issues of Phoenician coins seems to have been the following: Byblos, Tyre, Sidon, and Arwad.[10] As a matter of fact, the dates of inauguration cannot be established absolutely but only approximately, given the present state of our documentation.

By way of preliminary remark, the total absence of Phoenician coins in the hoards dated to the first half of the 5th century provides us with a *terminus post quem*.[11] The Byblian coins of Group I with the crouched sphinx and stylized double lotus, several of which were discovered on the beach, seem to be the oldest coins from the city, since they conform neither to the weight system nor to the motifs of the following Byblian series, and since their production technique is similar to that of the first Tyrian and Sidonian coins. Some indications suggest that they were issued slightly earlier than Tyrian coins: (1) the use of the non-Phoenician standard in the first series; (2) the composition of the Syrian hoard TXVII (appendix 4), which contains only Byblian coins from the first series; (3) and the composition of the Byblian hoard TX (appendix 4), which contains 10 similar Byblian coins and only 1 Tyrian coin from the first series, I.1.1, which are very well preserved. The date of the first Byblian coinage can be determined, approximately, from the date of the inauguration of Tyrian coinage, which was around 450 B.C.E.: there was indeed a Tyrian shekel from Series I.1.1 in Jordan hoard TLIII.[12] If, as it seems, this hoard is near-enough complete,

8. E. T. Newell, *Some Unpublished Coins of Eastern Dynasts* (NNM 30; New York, 1926) 9; G. K. Jenkins, "Recent Acquisitions of Greek Coins by the British Museum," *NC* 19 (1959) 41; Betlyon, *Coinage of Phoenicia*, 111; Babelon, *Perses*, 192; *Catalogue De Luynes*, 142; Head, *Historia Numorum*, 791; *BMC Phoenicia*, 94.

9. Head, *Historia Numorum*, 788, 794, and 799; *BMC Phoenicia*, 1, 139, and 227; Babelon, *Perses*, 123, 228, and 290; *Catalogue De Luynes*, 125, 149, and 157; Betlyon, *Coinage of Phoenicia*, 3, 39, and 78.

10. Elayi, "Phénomène monétaire," 22–24; idem, *Sidon*, 197–98. This order is now generally followed: cf., for example, L. Sole, "Le emissioni monetali della Fenicia prima di Alessandro-I," *SEAP* 16 (1997) 75–125; idem, "Le emissioni monetali della Fenicia prima di Allessandro-II," *SEAP* 18 (1998) 81–147.

11. Elayi-Elayi, *Trésors*, 363.

12. Ibid., 240–41.

Table 5.1. *Chronology of the Reigns of Byblian Kings (Persian Period)*

Periods	*Dates*	*Byblian Kings*	*Coin Series*	*Related Events*	*Persian Kings*
550–526	549				Cyrus II (549–530)
	539			Conquest of Phoenician cities by Cyrus II	
	530				Cambyses II (530–522)
	525			Cambyses' campaign in Egypt	
525–501	522				Smerdis (522)
					Darius I (522–486)
		Shipitbaal III (?) (*ŠPṬBʿL*)			
500–476	486				Xerxes I (486–465)
	480	Urimilk II (*ʾRMLK*)		Persian defeat of Salamis	
	479			Persian defeat of Mycale	
475–451	466	Yeharbaal (?) (*YḤRBʿL*)		Persian defeat of Eurymedon	
	465				Artaxerxes I (465–424)
	460/459		Series I.1	Persian defeat in Egypt	
450–426	450	Yehawmilk (*YḤWMLK*)	Series II.1	Persian defeat of Salamis (Cyprus)	
425–401	424		Series III.1		Xerxes II (424–423)
	423				Darius II (423–404)
	404	Elpaal (*ʾLPʿL*)	Series IV.1		Artaxerxes II (404–359)
400–376	394	Ozbaal (*ʿZBʿL*)	Series IV.2	Victory of Knidos	
	385–383?			Capture of Tyre by Evagoras of Salamis	
				Failure of Persian campaign in Egypt	
	381			Persian victory of Kition, capture of Salamis (Cyprus)	

Table 5.1. *Chronology of the Reigns of Byblian Kings (Persian Period)*

Periods	*Dates*	*Byblian Kings*	*Coin Series*	*Related Events*	*Persian Kings*
375–351	373			Failure of Persian campaign in Egypt	
	369			First revolt of satraps	
	359			Tachos' expedition in Syria	Artaxerxes III (359–338)
				Flight to Sidon	
				Abdashtart I's revolt	
	355			End of Abdashtart I's revolt	
	353				Mazday's governorship in Trans-euphratene (353–333)
		Urimilk III (*ʾWRMLK*)	Series IV.3		
	351			Failure of Persian campaign in Egypt	
350–326	ca. 350		Tennes' revolt		
	347			End of Tennes' revolt	
	343–342			Persian reconquest of Egypt	
		Aynel (*ʿYNʾL*, Gr. *Enylos*)	Series IV.4.1		
	338		Series IV.4.5		Arses (338–336)
	336		Series IV.4.6		Darius III (336–330)
	333–332			Alexander's conquest of Phoenician cities	

its chronological analysis is reliable. Beginning with the most-recent coins (Athenian tetradrachms from C. G. Starr's Group V, coins from Baʿalmilk I of Kition, and a Lycian coin), the different authors agreed in dating the burial to around the middle of the 5th century. C. M. Kraay and P. R. S. Moorey proposed a date of "around 445," C. G. Starr thought "450 or slightly after," and H. Mattingly proposed linking the burial of the hoard to the attack of Kition by the Athenian general Kimon in 450/449 and then more-recently dated it to 454.[13] Since the Tyrian coin of the hoard is almost *fleur-de-coin*, it was probably hoarded slightly after having been struck, which means that the date of hoarding probably took place a very short time after the inauguration of Tyrian currency. Thus, this hoard is very important because it provides a relatively reliable chronological marker for the inauguration of Tyrian coinage, and as a result, for the beginning of the Byblian coinage, which would have been around the end of the second quarter of the 5th century. The absence of Sidonian coins—which one would normally expect to be represented in the hoard because of the location of its discovery and because of its composition—is an indication of the posteriority of the Sidonian coinage; thus, it was *not* expected that either Aradian or Byblian coins would be found in this area. None of these three hoards (TX, TXVII, or TLIII), which were buried around the middle of the 5th century, contains Sidonian coins,[14] which means that the city of Sidon had no mint at that time. We have shown that the first Sidonian coinage was issued quite some time before 425 B.C.E., during the third quarter of the 5th century, probably a short time after Tyre's, which was inaugurated around 450.[15] The Aradian coinage was the last of the four Phoenician coinages because Aradian coins are even later than the Sidonian coins represented in hoards: it was probably inaugurated around the end of the third quarter of the 5th century.[16]

How is it possible that Byblos, which at that time was the least powerful city because it was apparently the only one not to have a fleet,[17] began to produce a currency before Sidon, the first Phoenician city in the Persian period? Unlike during the 2nd millennium, Byblos was no longer a powerful city during the first half of the 1st millennium for several reasons that have already been published.[18] However, it did not have the same difficulties as the other Phoenician cities, Sidon, Tyre, and Arwad, which had experienced several naval defeats after 480 B.C.E., when they were fighting for the Persians.[19] Because it had no fleet at that time, Byblos did not share

13. Ibid.; C. M. Kraay and P. R. S. Moorey, "Two Fifth Century Hoards from the Near East," *RN* 10 (1968) 209–10; C. G. Starr, *Athenian Coinage 480–449 B.C.* (Oxford, 1970) 63; H. B. Mattingly, "The Jordan Hoard (IGCH 1482) and Kimon's last Expedition," in *Proceedings of the 10th International Congress of Numismatics* (London, 1986) 59–64; idem, "A New Light on the Early Coinage of Teos," *SNR* 73 (1994) 8.

14. Elayi-Elayi, *Trésors*, 87–90, 115–16 and 240–41.

15. Idem, *Coinage of Tyre*, 329–30.

16. Elayi, "Phénomène monétaire," 23–24.

17. Idem, *Byblos*, 185–94.

18. Ibid., 51–138.

19. Elayi-Elayi, *Monnayage de Sidon*, 622–23; idem, *Coinage of Tyre*, 330–35.

in their losses. The chase of Phoenician war-galleys by the Greeks as far as Phoenicia and the eventual battles on the seashore probably concerned only the cities that had fleets.[20] Even if Byblos did happen to be devastated in the process, this action would have been limited. Unlike the other Phoenician cities, Byblos was apparently going through a peaceful period, as is shown for example by the inscription of King Yeḥawmilk (probably contemporary with the first Byblian monetary series) related to prestigious works that had been produced in the temple of *BˁLT GBL*, 'Mistress of Byblos', during his reign.[21] Yeḥawmilk wrote that he was the son of Yaḥarbaˁal (or Yaḥadbaˁal) and the grandson of ʾUrimilk, king of Byblos. This would mean that, for some unknown reason, Yaḥarbaˁal did not reign. However, the dynasty was stable since Yeḥawmilk succeeded his grandfather, ʾUrimilk.[22] If it is possible to restore 'I ʾU[rimilk]' (*ʾNK ʾ*[) at the end of line 4 in the inscription of the son of Šipiṭbaˁal III (?),[23] this inscription would still be referring to the same dynasty, producing the following succession sequence: around 500, Šipiṭbaˁal III (?), then ʾUrimilk II, [Yaḥarbaˁal?], and Yeḥawmilk around 450 or slightly later—with fairly long reigns, which is another sign of stability.

What was the new context during this Byblian dynasty that made it favorable to the inauguration of struck coins? Was the value of coins perceived during the time period just before the first issue of Byblos's coinage? In other words, had the Byblians appraised just how useful Greek coins were in commercial exchanges? The traditional hypothesis about the commercial function of coins for explaining the first Greek coinages is much debated today with strong arguments.[24] As a matter of fact, from the moment that the monetary workshops minted very small denominations, their usefulness in daily exchanges was probably one of the aims. The next

20. *IG* I²; B. D. Meritt et al., *The Athenian Tribute Lists* (Princeton, 1953) 11 n. 23, and 174; R. Meiggs and D. Lewis, *A Selection of Greek Historical Inscriptions to the End of the Fifth Century* B.C. (Oxford, 1969) no. 33; C. W. Clairmont, *Patris nomos: Public Burial in Athens during the Fifth and Fourth Centuries* B.C. (Oxford, 1983) 130–35, 298–300; cf. Elayi, *Byblos*, 137–39.

21. *KAI* 10.

22. On this dynasty, cf. J. Elayi, "An Updated Chronology of the Reigns of Phoenician Kings during the Persian Period (539–33 BCE)," *Trans* 32 (2006) 26–27 (with bibliography).

23. *KAI* 9; this restoration has been proposed by J. B. Peckham, *The Development of the Late Phoenician Scripts* (Cambridge, MA, 1968) 53 n. 35; and was followed by É. Puech, "Remarques sur quelques inscriptions de Byblos," *RSF* 9 (1981) 156–57.

24. Cf., for example, C. M. Kraay, "Hoards, Small Change and the Origin of Coinage," *JHS* 84 (1964) 76–91; O. Picard, *Les Grecs devant la menace perse* (Paris, 1980) 77; J.-M. Servet, *Numismata: État et origines de la monnaie* (Lyon, 1984) 41–74; G. Le Rider, *La naissance de la monnaie: Pratiques monétaires de l'Orient ancient* (Paris, 2001) 260–66.

step, making these exchanges even easier, was the issue of bronze coins: this did not occur in Byblos during the Persian period. Let us recall that the electrum coinage of Lydian kings already had very small denominations of the stater (weighing a little more than 14 g): 24ths, 48ths and 96ths, just like the small denominations of the drachma (tritartemorions, hemiobols, trihemitartemorions, tartemorions, and hemitartemorions) minted at the end of the 6th or the beginning of the 5th century, for example in the coinage of Thebes.[25] It is possible that the merchants of Byblos had appreciated, in the Greek harbors that they visited, how useful coins were for trade. If this hypothesis is correct, could Byblos, at the beginning of its coinage, have created an operational monetary system, using its first series of coins in local commercial exchanges? The first monetary group of Byblos (Group I), with the crouched sphinx, constituted a very flexible system, with a shekel of 9.42 g (Series I.1) and five or six different denominations (Series I.2, I.3, I.4, I.5, I.6, and I.7), the smallest one weighing around 0.10 g.[26] Theoretically, this system fit in with commercial usage, even if the smallest silver series was still a little too much for the most modest purchases.[27] However, the main difficulty was probably the small volume of the issues, if we can judge from the small number of exemplars preserved, which would have hindered a broader commercial usage. Perhaps also King Yeḥawmilk (if he was the king who inaugurated the coinage)[28] wanted to benefit from the authorization given to him by the Persians to mint coins; he could thus assert his status of relative autonomy within the Empire and give a prestigious picture of his sovereignty in the city in the Egyptian manner of the New Empire: crouched sphinx with a male human head, wearing the *klaft* and the double crown of Egypt, and a lotus flower. Another reason for inaugurating a coinage may have been mimesis: the Cypriot city of Lapethus (*LPŠ*), which was related to Byblos, began minting coins in the first half of the 5th century. If at this time Byblos also had a great quantity of silver available, this may have been another reason.

When Byblos began minting its Group I, it did not choose to issue a shekel following the Phoenician standard of around 14 g but a lighter standard of 9.42 g, which may have been the Lycian standard, as we have

25. *BMC Lydia*, 4, 21, 24 and 26; cf., for example, Le Rider, *La naissance de la monnaie*, 96–100; D. Bérend, "Réflexions sur les fractions du monnayage grec," in *Studies in Honor of Leo Mildenberg* (ed. A. Houghton et al.; Wetteren, 1984) 7–30 (with bibliography).

26. See above, chap. 4.

27. This is why other cities replaced the minute silver coins with larger bronze coins.

28. *MY* could be interpreted as *M*[*LK*] *Y*[*ḤWMLK*] in Series II.2.2, among other theories: cf. above, chap. 1.

shown. It had chosen a flexible monetary system with a shekel and five or six smaller denominations; however, the total amount of coins in Group I that have come down to us (66), small in comparison with later groups, points to a limited number of issues. Perhaps at the beginning, Byblos wanted to run a test just as Tyre and Sidon did later. However, it selected its political and religious symbols (sphinx with Egyptian double crown, and double lotus flower), intended to present the best image of the city, but not identifying the king who was responsible for the issue. The purpose of giving a good image is confirmed by the fact that the first Byblian currency was carefully executed in terms of engraving and manufacturing. Even though it was probably rather costly to open a monetary workshop, the expenses incurred in producing the coins of Group I, with a restricted volume, were not very significant. What functions did these first coins have? They probably had no fiscal function since, as it seems, the city encountered no financial difficulties at that time. Their political value is almost certain. Their commercial usefulness was probably due to the flexibility of the system; however, it was restricted by the small volume of production. In any event, the coins would not have been used for all sorts of payment. Given these limitations, it follows that Group I, inaugurated around the end of the second quarter of the 5th century, probably did not last for long (until around 450 B.C.E. or somewhat later).

3. *Group II: Beginning of the Third Quarter of the 5th Century*

Group II seems to have retained only some elements of Group I: the sphinx on the obverse, the small volume of production, and the first Byblian standard. However, there were several differences between the two groups: no 1-shekel coins have been preserved, and there were only three smaller denominations: 3rd-shekels (Series II.1), 12th-shekels (Series II.2), F.O.T.1, and F.O.T.2 (Series II.3 and II.4). The format of the sphinx was no longer Egyptian but Syrian. The motifs on the reverse changed and were varied: hawk, helmet, and griffin's head. One series was inscribed (II.2.2), and the others were anepigraphic (II.1, II.2.1, II.3, and II.4). All these coins were, generally speaking, less carefully executed in terms of manufacturing. Neither Group II nor Group I can be attributed to a known king: the attribution of Group I and/or Group II to King Yeḥawmilk is merely a hypothesis that needs to be confirmed. Dating Group II precisely is difficult. On the one hand, coins in this group are represented in hoards TXIII, TXIV, TXV?, for which it is impossible to propose a burial date, and in hoard TLXXXIII, which was buried during the last quarter of the

5th century, probably a short time after 425.[29] On the other hand, Group II followed Group I, and it is dated to around the end of the second quarter of the 5th century. The correspondence of the period when the incuse method was used for the three coinages of Byblos, Tyre and Sidon and their simultaneous presence in hoard TLXXXIII give us some clues. Consequently, we propose dating Group II to the third quarter of the 5th century—perhaps only part of it (around 445–435?) since the production of this group was limited.[30] One must remember that, although the relative chronology of Byblian coins is secure, their absolute chronology is approximate.

Group II appears to have been a transitory group between the two well-structured Groups, I and III: it presents features of Group I and at the same time foreshadows Group III with the representation of a helmet, which is a military symbol. It seems to correspond to a period with some unknown difficulties for the Byblian coinage and/or its need to find its identity. Nothing is known about the history of Byblos during the third quarter of the 5th century. Our documentation is also deficient with regard to other Phoenician cities, and it is exclusively non-Phoenician (Thucydides and Diodorus). In contrast to the preceding period, the so-called Phoenician fleet (Sidonian, Tyrian and Aradian) in Persian service was never drafted for military purposes. Yet strangely enough, it did play a major role in Persian policy in the Eastern Mediterranean: sometimes it was brandished as a threat, and sometimes it was promised as an unexpected source of assistance.[31]

4. *Group III: End of the Third–Beginning of the Last Quarter of the 5th Century*

It is not possible to establish an absolute chronology for Group III either. For several reasons that will be discussed, we tentatively propose to date it from the end of the third to the beginning of the last quarter of the 5th century.[32] Group III is completely different from Groups I and II: it follows a new standard—the Phoenician standard (13.66 g); it has four denominations: shekels (Series III.1), quarter-shekels (Series III.2), 16ths (Series III.3) and half-16ths (Series III.4); the incuse method is used on the reverse. However, the main change concerns the motifs: war-galley and seahorse on the obverse, vulture and ram on the reverse. This group of

29. Elayi-Elayi, *Trésors*, 113; idem, "Nouveau trésor de Byblos d'après les archives de H. Seyrig (TLXXXIII)," *Trans* 38 (2009) 75.

30. As we have tentatively proposed in ibid., 72 and n. 17.

31. Cf. idem, *Coinage of Tyre*, 336–338 (with bibliography).

32. Idem, "Nouveau trésor de Byblos," 75; Elayi, *Byblos*, 146 (around 435–25?).

coins represents a major event that occurred in Byblos at that time: the building of a war fleet. For a city without a fleet for several centuries, a city that had begun its coinage with other motifs and retained the war-galley until the end of the Persian period, this interpretation is obvious. It is also confirmed by classical sources.[33] As we have shown,[34] an analysis of this military iconography produces a great deal of information. The symbols of the new military power of Byblos appear to be more distinctive than the symbols of Sidon and Arwad. They reveal the intention of the minting authority to express several qualities: the existence of a fleet, a body of warriors with the Corinthian helmet, and a body of warriors wearing the καυσία (which no doubt was less important). Does the fact that the warriors with a Corinthian helmet are associated with the galley in most series mean that they were naval troops? The order of appearance of the various symbols of military power on Byblian coins may furnish some information. Now, the motif of the Corinthian helmet on the reverse of Series II.3 with a seated sphinx appeared earlier than Series III.1 with its galley, vulture, and ram.[35] Moreover, the helmet alone and the helmet of the warriors on the galley belong to different stages of the evolution of the Corinthian helmet. It could mean that the warriors on the galley were not specialized in fighting at sea but that ground forces were also used for fighting at sea.[36] The series representing these new military symbols probably date from the period when Byblos was building its military power. The preeminent place of the warriors with Corinthian helmets among the monetary symbols suggests that possibly they were 'citizen-warriors' like the πολιτικοὶ στρατιῶται of Sidon that are mentioned by Diodorus.[37] It is uncertain whether the other Byblian warriors, such as those wearing the καυσία, which were given a minor place on the coins (Series V.3), belonged to the same social category; moreover, it is difficult to date this small series.[38]

Given that the first representation of a galley on Byblian coins (Group III) was probably the result of the building up of a war-fleet, it is important to date these coins. Thanks to hoard TLXXXIII, it was possible to confirm that Group III followed Group II, and we propose dating it around the end of the third to the beginning of the last quarter of the 5th century—that is, slightly before 433 but slightly after 425 B.C.E. From the moment the

33. J. Elayi, "Les symboles de la puissance militaire sur les monnaies de Byblos," *RN* 26 (1984) 40–47.

34. Cf. above, chap. 2.

35. See further in appendix 3.

36. Cf. Elayi, "Les symboles de la puissance militaire, 45.

37. Diod. 16.42.2.

38. See further in appendix 3.

decision to build a fleet was made, the operation probably lasted several years, even if the Byblian fleet was smaller than the fleets of the other Phoenician cities. It is impossible to know whether its first representation in Group III dated from the time of the decision or from the time when the construction of the fleet was finished. Who was the king who decided to build the fleet? It was probably the anonymous king of Group III, with the galley, vulture, and ram. However, the previous king, who minted the badly structured and transitory Group II, either King Yeḥawmilk or another unknown king, was the first to put a military symbol (helmet) on some of his coins. However, this king was probably not the same as the anonymous king of Group III, since there was a break between the two groups in many respects (motifs, inscriptions, standard, denominations, technique, and style). This important military change also seems to correspond with the beginning of an architectural evolution. Although interpreting M. Dunand's excavations is problematic, it seems likely that, after this military change, Byblos reinforced its system of defense: it built an impressive stronghold, of which seven towers have been unearthed (end of the 5th or beginning of the 4th century), a ramp was added to it (mid-4th century), an ancient lookout tower was reconstructed (2nd third of the 4th century), and a new ramp was built between this tower and the monumental podium.[39]

The militarization of Byblos was a major political change for the city, since it put an end to a long period of neutrality and marginalization.[40] Byblos decided to have a war-fleet like the other Phoenician cities; although it was even smaller than the Sidonian, Tyrian and Aradian fleets, it too became a constituent of the Persian fleet. Byblos also decided to have an army comprising at least two categories: the main army, the warriors with Corinthian helmet, probably used in both land and sea battles; a second, less important army, the warriors with a καυσία, who were probably used for fighting on the ground. The city fully assumed these decisions, as is shown by the representation of military symbols on its coins; in this way, it affirmed its sovereignty and will to power without any ambiguity. In which context did this change occur? At this time, Byblos was in a period of prosperity, which is apparent due to the reevaluation from the standard

39. M. Dunand, "Rapport préliminaire sur les fouilles de Byblos en 1964," *BMB* 19 (1966) 97–102; idem, "Rapport préliminaire sur les fouilles de Byblos en 1965," *BMB* 20 (1967) 22–25; idem, "La défense du front méditerranéen de l'Empire achéménide," in *The Role of the Phoenicians in the Interaction of Mediterranean Civilizations: Archaeological Symposium at the American University of Beirut* (ed. W. A. Ward; Beirut, 1968) 44–46; idem, "L'architecture à Byblos au temps des Achéménides," *BMB* 22 (1969) 93–99.

40. Elayi, *Byblos*, 185–217.

of 9.42 g (Groups I and II) to a standard of 13.66 g (Group III). Such military decisions also required a great deal of money, just as did the abovementioned monument building and architectural decoration undertaken by Yeḥawmilk in the preceding period and the building of defense works in the following period.

The militarization of Byblos doubtless had important consequences, not all of them positive. Among the positive consequences was the fact that the city came out of its isolation, marginalization, and near inexistence. Once again, it was open to the outside world and became visible on the regional and international political scene. Henceforth, its military power had to be taken into consideration by the various powers of the Levantine area, including the other Phoenician cities. Among the negative consequences was the fact that Byblos was obliged to place its strength at the disposal of the Persians, have their same foreign policy, and participate in their military campaigns, with all the constraints and expenses that they incurred, especially in the event of defeat. It could no longer retain its traditional privileged relations with Egypt, which the Persians wanted to reconquer. Taking advantage of its central position in Phoenicia, it could no longer remain neutral and was obliged to ally itself with the northern or southern Phoenician cities. Under the reign of Artaxerxes I, the anonymous king of Group III probably put his fleet at the disposal of the Persian king, together with the Sidonian, Tyrian, and Aradian fleets. Although there is no specific information available on the Byblian fleet, Byblos had followed the logic of the other three Phoenician cities under Persian domination; therefore, like them, it was obligated to be integrated into the Persian military system. Thucydides and Diodorus, our only documentation on this period, do not specify the precise role of each Phoenician fleet.[41] The so-called Phoenician fleet that was at the Persians' disposal never engaged militarily, but it did play a major role in Persian policy in the Eastern Mediterranean. The theory that, after Salamis and Mycale, "the Achaemenids had no more permanent navy" is unfounded.[42] This is clear from the Sidonian and Aradian

41. Thuc. I, 116.1,3; Diod. XII, 27.4.

42. H. Wallinga, "The Ancient Persian Navy and Its Predecessors," in *Achaemenid History I: Sources, Structures and Synthesis* (ed. H. Sancisi-Weerdenburg; Leiden, 1987) 47–78; idem, *Ships and Sea-Power before the Great Persian War: The Ancestry of the Ancient Trireme* (Leiden, 1993) 30: "Accordingly, the current belief that the Phoenician cities possessed large standing navies, which in the event they had to put at the disposal of the Persian king, is no more than adventurous speculation." This assertion is based on insufficient information, especially in numismatics, and cannot be accepted: see the comments of J. Elayi, in *Trans* 8 (1994) 177–80; see also R. Descat, "Remarques sur les rapports entre les Perses et la mer Noire à l'époque achéménide," in *Ikinci Tarih Boyunca Karadeniz Kongresi Bildileri*

coinages, in which the continuous representation of the city's war-galley means that this fleet was always at Artaxerxes I's disposal. In spite of the purported agreement known as the "Peace of Callias,"[43] Miletus came into conflict with Samos in 441 over a border issue. The Milesians were defeated and appealed to Athens to establish a democratic government in Samos. The Samian exiles appealed to Pissouthnes, the satrap of Sardis, to help them reconquer Samos; after they had expelled the Athenians, Pericles sailed toward Samos. Pissouthnes intended to send the Phoenician fleet to support the Samians against Athens.[44] It was said to have sailed toward Caria and Caunus, in violation of the second clause of the "Peace of Callias." However, both the Athenians and the Samians searched for it, for opposing reasons, but could not find it. It could be that false news was spread by the Persians as propaganda, but the most likely conclusion is that the Samos affair was a major incident for the Athenians but was probably quite minor for the Persians.[45] In any case, what needs to be stated is that Byblos probably did not participate in these events, or only did so later. And, since the Phoenician fleet did not suffer losses due to naval battles during this period, it also did not incur expenses in having to rebuild its fleet.

The volume of the coinage of Group III (80 coins preserved) is larger than that of Group II (34). Its political function is certain because of the representation of the militarization of the city. Its commercial function, limited to the territory of the city, was facilitated by the flexibility of the system but restricted by the still-small volume of production.

(Samsun, 1990) 544; P. Briant, *From Cyrus to Alexander: A History of the Persian Empire* (Winona Lake, IN, 2002) 949–50.

43. On the "Peace of Callias," see in particular E. Badian, "The Peace of Callias," *JHS* 107 (1987) 1–39 (with bibliography); idem, "The King's Peace," in *Georgica: Greek Studies in Honor of G. Cawkwell* (BICSSup 58; London, 1991) 25–48; A. B. Bosworth, "Plutarch, Callisthenes and the Peace of Callias," *JHS* 110 (1990) 1–13; V. M. Strogetsky, "The Problem of Callias' Peace and Its Significance for the Evolution of the Delian League," *VDI* (1991) 158–68; E. Bloedow, "The Peaces of Callias," *SO* 67 (1992) 41–68; G. Shrimpton, *EMC* 13 (1994) 415–18.

44. Thuc. I, 116.1, 3; Diod. XII, 27.4; cf. Elayi, *Sidon*, 171; Briant, *From Cyrus to Alexander*, 564.

45. E. Will, *Le monde grec et l'Orient* I (Paris, 1980) 282–84; A. W. Gomme (*A Historical Commentary on Thucydides* I [Oxford, 1945] 353) pointed out, without explanation, the absence of an article before Φοινίσσα νῆες (§3, contrary to §1). It could be a simple omission, or it could mean that the Persians would not use the whole Phoenician fleet in the affair of Samos if the need for support arose.

5. *The Coinage of ʾElpaʿal, Group IV.1: End of the 5th Century*

We tentatively propose dating Group IV.1 to the end of the 5th century. The successor to the anonymous king of Group III put his name and royal title on his coins for the first time: 'ʾElpaʿal, King of Byblos' (*ʾLPʿL MLK GBL*). This new official inscription, which was a clear and ostentatious affirmation of sovereignty, was retained by his successors ʿOzbaʿal, ʾUrimilk, and ʿAynel. ʾElpaʿal possibly belonged to the same dynasty as the anonymous king, who may have been his father because he retained the main characteristics of the preceding coinage. His coinage also had four denominations: shekels (Series IV.1.1), quarter-shekels (Series IV.1.2), 16ths (Series IV.1.3) and half-16ths (Series IV.1.4); the incuse method is used on the reverse. However, he wanted to distinguish himself from the anonymous king with several initiatives. First, he added an inscription and replaced the vulture and ram on the reverse with a lion and bull. The modified standard was higher (14.21 g instead of 13.66 g), while the percentage of silver was lower (down to 91.6%) than the 99–98% of Group III,[46] which may reflect some financial difficulties.

What was the political context of ʾElpaʿal's reign? After the death of Artaxerxes I (424 B.C.E.) and the murders of his legitimate son, Xerxes II, and his half-brother Sogdianos (423), another half-brother seized power under the name of Darius II (423–404). While it is uncertain whether the anonymous king of Group III and his fleet participated in the first events regarding Samos, it is likely that ʾElpaʿal and his fleet did participate in the new events on Samos in 412–409 B.C.E. The main actors were Darius II, through his satraps Tissaphernes and Pharnabazus, and the Greek cities, particularly Athens and Sparta. As before, the Phoenician fleet played an enigmatic role—that of a "ghost-fleet," which was keenly expected by some and feared by others. Thucydides and Diodorus diverge on the Persian strategy, but because of Thucydides' qualities as a historian and the fact that he was contemporary with the Peloponnesian War, his testimony seems to be more reliable.[47] The first passage of Diodorus is concerned with the summer of 412, when the first treaty of alliance was concluded between Sparta and Darius II.[48] The Phoenician fleet was sent to bring help to the

46. Cf. A. G. Elayi, M. Blet-Lemarquand, and J. Elayi, "Silver Coinage Fluctuations at Byblos (5th–4th Cent. BCE) as Determined by LA-ICP-MS and FNAA," *AJN* (2012) 1–10.

47. Diod. XIII, 36.5, 37.5; Thuc. VIII, 41.1, 5; 59. For a more detailed analysis of these events, cf. Elayi-Elayi, *Coinage of Tyre*, 338–45 (with bibliography).

48. Diod. XIII, 36.5 and 38.4; see also Thuc. VIII, 46.5. On these events and Thucydides' sources, cf. E. Lévy, "Les trois traités entre Sparte et le Roi," *BCH* 107 (1983) 221–37.

Spartans. However, it never reached its destination because, in the winter of 412–411 or at least after the summer, Alcibiades advised the satrap Tissarphernes to send back the Phoenician fleet, thinking this would facilitate his return to Athens. The second passage of Diodorus is related to the third treaty concluded between the Spartans and the Persians in the summer of 411, with a particular issue at stake: the arrival of the Phoenician fleet as promised. Tissaphernes again promised but intended to follow Alcibiades' advice. The reciprocity expressed in the terms of the treaties between the Spartans and the Persians was in reality only apparent because the Spartans had to give up Ionia in return for a Persian grant and naval support, which they never received. Thucydides did not understand that the Spartans had made a fool's deal.

He then related how, in Athens, the democracy had been replaced by the Four Hundred. The Peloponnesians of Miletus began to have doubts about the arrival of the Phoenician fleet promised by Tissaphernes. And Alcibiades changed his message in the Athenian assembly on Samos, explaining that Tissaphernes had promised him that the Phoenician fleet would support the Athenians.[49] Thucydides stated that Alcibiades invented this story and, for the first time, provided information about the position of the Phoenician fleet: it was at Aspendus, close to the Eurymedon, which was indeed a stopping point on the road to Ionia. He even specified the number of Phoenician triremes (147). Diodorus mentions this number twice (300), which is the same number as was provided by Herodotus for the battle of Salamis.[50] The lying speech of Alcibiades did not exactly fulfill his aim: Tissaphernes was completely discredited in the eyes of the Spartans, but he tried to make up for it by pretending once more to send the Phoenician fleet to their aid. On hearing this, Alcibiades also hastened toward Aspendus to bring the Phoenician fleet or, at least, to prevent it from helping the Spartans.[51]

Thucydides and Diodorus both related the events subsequent to the establishment of the Five Thousand in Athens.[52] At that time, the Spartans were more confident that the Phoenician fleet would arrive because they were sure that it was at Aspendus and that Tissaphernes had fetched it.[53] However, their hopes were again dashed by the Athenian victory over

49. Thuc. 78; 81.3; 87.1; 88.1; 99.

50. Thuc. 87.1, 3; Diod. XIII, 42.4; 46.6. Cf. Hdt. VII, 89; however, this number represented both Phoenician fleets and those of the "Syrians of Palestine"; cf. Gomme, *Historical Commentary on Thucydides*, 1:341–42.

51. Thuc. VIII, 87.1, 3, 6; 88.1; 99; cf. Lévy, "Les trois traités," 237.

52. Diod. XIII, 38.4–5, 42.4, 46.6; Thuc. VIII, 108.1, 109.1.

53. Diod. XIII, 38.4–5: this passage is parallel to that of Thuc. VIII, 99.

Tissaphernes at Cynossema: the fleet was once more sent back home. The events of the autumn of 411 are then related: the triumphal return to Samos of Alcibiades, who claimed that he had contributed to the departure of the fleet; and Tissaphernes' attempted explanation to the Spartans, especially regarding the promise of support from the fleet.[54]

It would be reasonable to infer that Darius II did not want the Phoenician fleet to neglect its surveillance of Egypt for very long; as a matter of fact, the troubles with Egypt were probably more worrisome than the conflict between the Athenians and Spartans, which was quite minor for the Persian Empire. One may well wonder why Tissaphernes always promised to send the Phoenician fleet, first to the Spartans, then to the Athenians, but never sent it. He may have been following Alcibiades' advice that the Persian king ought not allow either Athens or Sparta to become very powerful. In spite of the role played by Tissaphernes, then by Pharnabazus, one cannot speak of the weakening of the Persian Empire simply on the grounds that the Persian king did not personally intervene in these events, since he had no reason to do so. He may have been waiting for the Greeks to tire themselves out fighting each other. On the other hand, Tissaphernes' increasing embarrassment may have shown that he was not really able to send the Phoenician fleet. Since the Phoenicians were still loyal to the Persian king, they probably took orders from him and not from a satrap. The only time that they may have been obeying a direct order from the Persian king was when they assembled their ships at Cilicia.[55] However, Darius II's strategy in Asia Minor is far from clear: perhaps he thought that the satraps could gain something from an alliance with the Spartans, the military operations would be financed by the reestablishment of the tribute in the Greek cities, and competition between satraps was the best way to prevent them from becoming too powerful.[56] However, Persian policy became much more drastic after 407 B.C.E., when Darius sent his son Cyrus to Asia Minor, as κάρανος with full authority and plenty of money; Pharnabazus and Tissaphernes were probably subordinate to him.[57]

The relations between Byblos and Egypt seem to have changed, possibly because the city had to follow the foreign policy of the Persians, who

54. Thuc. VIII, 108.1, 109.1; Diod. XIII, 42.4; 46.6; cf. D. M. Lewis, "The Phoenician Fleet in 411," *Historia* 7 (1958) 392–97; Briant, *From Cyrus to Alexander*, 579–82 (with bibliography).

55. Thuc. VIII, 88.5.

56. Briant, *From Cyrus to Alexander*, 576–78.

57. In Lycia in particular, there would have been a strengthening of the Persian authority at the end of the 5th century: cf. W. A. P. Childs, "Lycian Relations with Persians and Greeks in the Fifth and Fourth Centuries Reexamined," *AS* 31 (1981) 69.

wanted to dominate Egypt. As a matter of fact, in the cultural field, the imitation of Egyptian art by Byblos had decreased considerably and was increasingly being replaced by the imitation of Greek art. For example, in the Byblian coinage, the traditional Egyptian motifs of Group I were replaced by Egyptizianing motifs in Group II, then progressively abandoned in the following groups, with some borrowings from Syrian and Greek art. As we have shown, the representation of the vulture is quite significant of this evolution within the same coinage: first there was the traditional Egyptian vulture in profile, turned toward the left, with the crook and flail on its shoulder (Series III.4); however, the Egyptian vulture only bears the flail, and the crook is a local addition. In another interpretation, the vulture no longer has the crook and flail but retains its Egyptian style (Series III.2, III.3). Finally, the vulture is represented in a realistic style, with one wing closed and one wing spread (Series III.1). The transition between borrowing from Egyptian art and borrowing from Greek art is also apparent in other fields, not just monetary iconography: terra-cotta, pottery, sculpture, and sarcophagi. In the 5th and 4th centuries B.C.E., Byblos imported terracotta and numerous Greek vases, such as Attic black-figured, red-figured, and black-glazed vases,[58] which probably inspired local production.[59] The Phoenician production of anthropoid sarcophagi had clearly evolved from the imitation of Egyptian art to the imitation of Greek art, with a transitional stage ("Egypto-Greek"), when the two sources of inspiration were mixed.[60] The transition between the "Egypto-Greek" stage and the "Hellenizing" stage seems to have taken place in the second half of the 5th century, thus corresponding to the evolution of Byblian monetary iconography. For example, in sarcophagus K44, which is said to have been found in Byblos, the Egyptian *nemes* was replaced by hair, and the features of the face were inspired by Greek art.[61] However, the funeral ritual and mummification were still inspired by Egypt.[62] The fact that only two sarcophagi

58. Cf. J. Elayi, *Pénétration grecque en Phénicie sous l'Empire perse* (Nancy, 1988) 177–78 (figs. 3–4), 189–93 (figs. 15–19), 198 (fig. 24).

59. Ibid., 110–17, 197–98 (figs. 23–24), 203 (fig. 29).

60. Cf. G. Scandone, "Testimonianze egiziane in Fenicia dal XII al IV sec. a.c.," *RSF* 12 (1984) 133–63; J. Elayi, "La place de l'Égypte dans la recherche sur les Phéniciens," *Trans* 9 (1995) 22–24; J. Elayi and M. R. Haykal, *Nouvelles découvertes sur les usages funéraires des Phéniciens d'Arwad* (Paris, 1996) 66–76 (with bibliography).

61. E. Kukahn, *Anthropoide Sarkophage in Beyrouth* (Berlin, 1955) pl. 35.4:44; C. Virolleaud, "Découverte à Byblos d'un hypogée de la douzième dynastie égyptienne," *Syr* 3 (1922) 290 n. 2.

62. Cf. J. Leclant, "Les Phéniciens et l'Égypte," in *ACFP* (Rome, 1991) 2/1:17.

were found in Byblos,[63] compared with the numerous discoveries in Sidon and Arwad (Tartous and Amrit), could be explained either by a preference for sarcophagi of the *theke* type, of Greek origin, or by our insufficient knowledge of Byblian necropolis.[64]

The volume of production of ʾElpaʿal's coinage (87 coins preserved) is roughly the same as that of Group III (80); however, its ratio is weak, which means that it was not well known. Its functions seem to have been the same: political at first; but the commercial function, if there was any, was restricted. The reasons for any eventual difficulties underlined by metallurgical analyses[65] are not clear at all, unless they were partly due to expenses incurred by King ʾElpaʿal. Even if Byblos had to spend money for the maintenance of its fleet, it did not incur any expenses for repairing or rebuilding its fleet, because as far as we know it did not suffer any naval defeat during this period.

6. *The Coinage of ʿOzbaʿal, Group IV.2: First Third of the 4th Century*

The successor to ʾElpaʿal was ʿOzbaʿal, who inscribed his name in the monetary inscription as 'ʿOzbaʿal, King of Byblos' (*ʿZBʿL MLK GBL*). He retained the same iconography but no longer used the incuse method, thus imitating the Tyrian and Sidonian mints. He modified the system of denominations somewhat, retaining only the two main denominations: shekels (Series IV.2.1) and 16th-shekels (Series IV.2.2). However, there may have been several smaller denominations that are now in the unclassified series. King ʿOzbaʿal reestablished the higher percentage of silver (99%)[66] and, at the same time, decreased the weight to 13.18 g (modified standard) from the 14.21 g of the previous king's shekels.

The major event for Byblos around the end of the 5th century was the takeover of ʾElpaʿal's Dynasty by a usurper, ʿOzbaʿal, son of Palṭibaʿal, the priest, who led the clergy in a coup. This event is evidenced by the inscription engraved on Batnoʿam's sarcophagus.[67] She was ʿOzbaʿal's mother and therefore had a royal burial; her name, Batnoʿam (*BTNʿM*),

63. Kukahn, *Anthropoide Sarkophage*, no. 44; É. Gubel, *Art phénicien: La sculpture de tradition phénicienne* (Paris, 2002) 72, no. 60; and National Museum of Damascus no. 81.

64. Cf. Elayi and Haykal, *Nouvelles découvertes*, 64–66; J.-F. Salles, "La mort à Byblos: Les nécropoles," in *Biblo: Una città e la sua cultura* (ed. E. Acquaro et al.; Rome, 1994) 59–61; cf. also E. Renan, *Mission de Phénicie* (Paris, 1864) 204–5; P. Montet, *Byblos et l'Égypte: Quatre campagnes de fouilles à Gebeil 1921, 1922, 1923, 1924* (Paris, 1928) 6.

65. Cf. above, n. 46.

66. Ibid.

67. *KAI* 11.

meant 'daughter of pleasantness'. Palṭibaʿal was not presented as her husband but as the king's father. This priest bore a theophoric name with the suffixed -*BʿL*—that is, *PLṬBʿL*, '(my) salvation (is) Baʿal'; he also chose a name with the same suffix for his son: *ʿZBʿL* (ʿOzbaʿal), '(my) strength (is) Baʿal'.[68] Thus, Palṭibaʿal was more likely to have served the god Baʿal than Baʿalat Gubal, the main deity of Byblos at that time and the dynastic deity of the previous king, ʾElpaʿal. Some of the information about the political role played by the Tyrian clergy during the Neo-Babylonian period is known to us.[69] Josephus only mentions a usurpation that occurred before the foundation of Carthage: the murder of King Phelles by Ittobaʿal, 'priest of ʿAštart', who reigned 32 years.[70] We do not know whether ʿOzbaʿal took the throne of Byblos in the same violent way, by murdering King ʾElpaʿal. ʿOzbaʿal was apparently not a priest as his father, Palṭibaʿal, was. However, Palṭibaʿal was probably not just an ordinary priest but was one of the most influential clergymen. In this sacred city where the clergy already played an important role,[71] why did he decide to seize power through ʿOzbaʿal? Possibly the clergy of Baʿal were not satisfied with the Dynasty of ʾElpaʿal, perhaps because their role in the city had decreased compared with that of the clergy of Baʿalat Gubal; maybe he also disapproved of ʾElpaʿal's policies—a prime example of which is the devaluation of his coinage. However, the retention of military symbols on the coinage of ʿOzbaʿal and the retention of the militarized Byblos meant that there was no important change in the policy orientation, except for the return to a reliable coinage. This control of political power by the clergy of Byblos was not limited but lasting, because ʿOzbaʿal's reign was probably lengthy, as shown by his abundant coinage, and because his dynasty seems to have lasted until the end of Persian period.

We propose dating ʿOzbaʿal's reign to the first third of the 4th century. This proposal is based on the classification of the Byblian coin series of the successive kings, on their probable volume of production, on the associations of coins from different mints in the hoards, and on the inscription of

68. Cf. F. L. Benz, *Personal Names in the Phoenician and Punic Inscriptions* (Rome, 1972, s.v.). According to M. Gras et al. (*L'univers phénicien* [Paris, 1989] 39), it was not a usurpation by the clergy but an agreement between the king and the clergy: this curious hypothesis is presented without argumentation and is groundless.

69. Jos., *Ag. Ap.* I, 157.

70. *Ag. Ap.* I, 123–24. On the problems involved in Josephus's chronology, see, for example, D. Henige, "Josephus and the Tyrian King List," *Trans* 38 (2009) 35–64.

71. J. Elayi, "Byblos et Sidon: Deux modèles de cités phéniciennes à l'époque perse," *Trans* 35 (2008) 100–114.

Batnoʿam. The usurpation of ʿOzbaʿal occurred around 400 B.C.E., but it is impossible to be more precise in the present state of the documentation.

What was the political context of ʿOzbaʿal's reign? At the end of the 5th century, Byblos was apparently a flourishing city with considerable military power (both defensive and offensive), even though its military was less significant than that of Sidon, Tyre, or Arwad. After Darius II's death in 404, his oldest son ascended the throne under the name Artaxerxes II and began a fratricidal struggle with Cyrus the Younger that ended in the latter's death in the Battle of Cunaxa in 401. Artaxerxes II assembled an army in Phoenicia (we do not know precisely where) under the command of a general named Abrocomas, probably slightly after his accession in 404, in order to prepare a campaign against Amyrtaeus, who had proclaimed himself pharaoh and had seized the Delta, whereas Upper Egypt was still under Persian domination; in 398, Nepherites founded the XXIXth Dynasty. However, there was no campaign against Egypt, which is difficult to understand.[72]

Artaxerxes put Pharnabazus in charge of preparing the Persian fleet and gave him the necessary funds. The satrap sailed across to Cyprus and ordered the Cypriot kings to prepare a fleet of some 100 triremes: he appointed Conon as its admiral, a man who had taken refuge at the court of Evagoras after the Athenian defeat of 405. Then Conon sailed across to Cilicia, where he began preparations for war against the Spartans.[73] He was informed of the preparation of a Persian naval force by a Syracusan trader returning from Phoenicia.[74] According to him, there were three categories of Phoenician war-galleys in a Phoenician harbor (possibly Sidon): those already fitted out (probably Sidonian), those being fitted out (probably Sidonian too), and those coming from other Phoenician cities, probably from Tyre, Arwad, and perhaps also Byblos. In the spring of 396, the Spartan king Agesilaus arrived in Ephesus with 12,000 soldiers. Tissaphernes was obliged to gain time, since he had to wait until the royal Persian army had rejoined him and until the Phoenician shipyards had finished building the war-galleys promised to Conon.[75] According to Diodorus, probably after 396, his fleet was rejoined by a Cilician contingent of 10 triremes and a Phoenician fleet of 80 triremes led by the king of Sidon.[76] Because of his

72. P. Grelot, *Documents araméens d'Égypte* (Paris, 1972) no. 7 and 105; cf. Briant, *From Cyrus to Alexander*, 615–16.

73. Diod. XIV, 39.1–4.

74. Xen., *Hell.* III, 4.1

75. Xen., *Hell.*, III, 4.1–6; Nep., *Ag.* 2.4; Diod. XIV, 79.4–8; *Hell. Oxyr.* IX, 2–3.

76. Diod. XIX, 79.7–8; *Hell. Oxyr.* 4.2.

presence and his function, it can be assumed that most of the ships were Sidonian, but there were probably other Phoenician ships too.

The Battle of Knidos was brilliantly won by the Persian fleet in 394.[77] It is well worth noting that the Phoenician fleet was relatively small at Knidos (only 80 ships): Artaxerxes had probably left the main part of the fleet to keep an eye on Egypt. The Battle of Knidos was important to the Athenians, because it stimulated Athenian imperialism. Apparently, the Phoenicians—especially the king of Sidon, Baʿalšillem II, the leader of the fleet—were always loyal to Artaxerxes II and represented his main naval support. However, the situation was very different from the situation at the time of the Persian Wars because the Phoenicians were no longer under the command of the Persian king but were under the satrap Pharnabazus, and they fought by the side of the Athenian Conon. It is uncertain whether the fleet of Byblos, or only part of it, had participated in the Battle of Knidos or had stayed in reserve to guard Egypt. After the sea Battle of Knidos, Pharnabazus and Conon took advantage of the situation to expel the Spartans from the Ionian cities and the islands.[78]

In the spring of 393, the Persian fleet went back to sea, liberated the Cyclades, seized Cythera and landed in the Isthmus of Corinth. Then Pharnabazus left a part of the fleet (80 triremes) and money to Conon to rebuild the walls of Athens and Piraeus.[79] The composition of the fleet left to Conon is unknown, but since the number was the same as the fleet of Knidos, we can assume that it was the same Phoenician fleet, possibly with some war-galleys from Byblos.

Outside the events of Asia Minor, Artaxerxes II was mainly concerned with the troubles of Cyprus and Egypt, but the reconquest of Egypt could not be achieved without first reconquering Cyprus. Evagoras I of Salamis had collaborated with the Persians against the Spartans before 394, but then he began to extend his rule over the other Cypriot cities. Diodorus and Isocrates relate that Evagoras rebelled against the Persians, took the major part of the island, and tried to extend his dominion to Asia. Diodorus insists that he conquered Tyre, without mentioning any other Phoenician cities precisely (τινων ἑτέρων, 'some others').[80] These events are presented in the same manner by Isocrates[81] but with the usual panegyric pomposity.

77. For more details, cf. Elayi-Elayi, *Coinage of Tyre*, 343–46.

78. Diod. XIV, 84.3.

79. Ibid.

80. Diod. XV, 2.4.

81. Isocr., *Paneg.* 161; *Evag.* 62; see also Theopompus, in F. Jacoby, *Die Fragmente der Griechischer Historiker* (Berlin, 1923–58) 115, F 103; cf. F. W. König, *Die Persika des Ktesias von Knidos* (Graz, 1972) 26, §63.

This insistence on Tyre is unexplainable, when the most powerful city at that time was Sidon. Did Evagoras "seize" other Phoenician cities? Certainly, he did not try to seize the powerful city of Sidon, where there was a Persian garrison. It is uncertain whether other Phoenician cities, especially Byblos, supported his action. In any case, he had sought out any possible avenue for foreign support: first, he dispatched representatives to Athens, which sent him 10 triremes in 390–389 (seized by the Spartans), then 10 triremes and 800 peltasts ordered by Chabrias in 388–387; he also sent an embassy to Pharaoh Achoris, who gave him an insufficient amount of money.[82] Xenophon draws attention to the inconsistency of these alliances: Athens, an ally of Artaxerxes, supported Evagoras to fight against him, while the Spartans, who were at war with Artaxerxes, stopped the Athenian triremes that were sailing to fight with him.[83] The date of Evagoras's campaign in Phoenicia is difficult to establish: the dating of the "seizure" of Tyre to around 385–383 is a weak theory because it is itself based on hypotheses.[84]

Evagoras's campaign in Phoenicia is far from clear. After the Battle of Knidos, there was a reversal of alliances. It is unclear whether the Phoenicians, in particular the Sidonians and Tyrians (and possibly Byblians), who probably took part in the first expedition against Egypt, interrupted their relations with Athens and Pharnabazus at that time in order to stay loyal to the Persians. Classical sources are rather ambiguous on the Phoenician cities' attitude toward Evagoras's expedition to Phoenicia: neither favorable nor hostile, they seem to have remained cautious. Why did Artaxerxes not use any of the Phoenician fleets, which had probably already made up the main part of the Persian fleet in the first campaign of Egypt? Perhaps because he reserved them for conquering Egypt. Isocrates wrote with his usual rhetorical exaggeration in the *Panegyric* published during the summer of 380: "Did not Egypt and Cyprus revolt against him (the Persian king), are not Phoenicia and Syria devastated by war, is not Tyre, the object

---

82. Lysias, *Aristophanes* XIX, 21–23, 43; Xen., *Hell.* VI, 8.24; Diod. XV, 4.3, 8.2; cf. A. Destrooper- Georgiades, "Chypre et l'Égypte à l'époque achéménide à la lumière des témoignages numismatiques," *Trans* 9 (1995) 152–54. On the dating of the reign of Psammouthis I, see D. Devauchelle, "Notes sur les inscriptions démotiques des carrières de Tourah et de Mâsarah," *ASAE* 69 (1983) 169–80; J.-Y. Carrez-Maratray, "Psammétique le tyran: Pouvoir, usurpation et alliances en Méditerranée orientale au IVe s. av. J.-C.," *Trans* 30 (2005) 39–40: according to this author, the alliance concluded between Athens and Egypt in 389, just before the performance of the *Ploutos* of Aristophanes, was not anti-Persian but was due to the fact that Athens needed corn and money.

83. Xen., *Hell.* VI, 8.24.

84. On this subject, cf. Elayi-Elayi, *Coinage of Tyre*, 347–48.

of his pride, occupied by his enemies?"[85] After the failure of the first Egyptian campaign, the Phoenician fleets and the Persian army (which was probably raised largely from the peoples of Transeuphratene) may have suffered heavy losses, and thus they could not be used in the Persian expedition against Cyprus. The Persian fleet won a naval battle at Kition while the army besieged Salamis in 383/381.[86] Afterward, Tyre probably came back under Persian control, just like the other Phoenician cities that had eventually supported Evagoras.[87] The Cypriot king himself was permitted to remain on the throne at Salamis, provided that he paid tribute and obeyed the Persian king. The Peace of Antalcidas and the end of Evagoras's uprising meant that the strenuous policy of Artaxerxes was successful.

In 373, date of the second Persian campaign against Egypt, alliances had again changed: there was a temporary reconciliation between Athens and Artaxerxes. This time, preparations for the campaign took place in the territory of Tyre, in the city of Akko, and therefore with the participation of the Tyrians and possibly other Phoenicians, including the Byblians. One reason for this participation could be the fact that, from 383 on, they had enough time to rebuild their fleets; however, we do not know whether the Phoenicians (mainly Byblians who still had relations with Egypt) took part in this expedition of their own free will. This second Persian attempt to reconquer Egypt, in 373, was a failure, just as the first had been, although Pharaoh Nectanebo was then deprived of the support of Chabrias.[88]

These repeated failures of the Phoenician fleets, which were only battling the Egyptian fleet, are quite surprising, but we know of no explanation; as far as Byblos is concerned, it was probably less motivated to fight against a traditional ally. Some authors consider the second Persian failure in Egypt as the event that launched (after 369) the first satrap revolts,[89] in which the two primary figures were Datames (Tarkumuwa?), satrap of

85. Isocr., *Paneg.* 161.

86. Diod. XV, 3.4–6; 4.1; A. J. Sachs and H. Hunger, *Astronomical Diaries and Related Texts from Babylonia, I: Diaries from 652 B.C. to 262 B.C.* (Vienna, 1988) no. 441; M. Heltzer, "The Persian Invasion to Cyprus and the Date of the Submission of Evagoras," in *Acts of the Third International Congress of Cypriot Studies* (Nicosia, 2000) 717–19.

87. Diod. XV, 8.2–3; 9.2.

88. On Iphicrates' expedition against a Phoenician town, cf. Elayi-Elayi, *Coinage of Tyre*, 351–52 (with bibliography).

89. E. Will et al., *Le monde grec et l'Orient* (Paris, 1975) 2:67–68; Childs, "Lycian Relations with Persians and Greeks," 72–77; R. A. Moysey, *Greek Relations with the Persian Satraps: 371–343 B.C.* (Princeton, 1974) 93–164. Cf. Elayi-Elayi, *Coinage of Tyre*, 351–57 (with bibliography).

Cappadocia, and Ariobarzanes, satrap of Phrygia or Dascylium.[90] However, Diodorus mentions Datames' revolt separately from the so-called Great Satraps' Revolt.[91] The chronology and the precise development of Datames' revolt are slightly uncertain, but it probably occurred much earlier than 361.[92] There is no information about the Phoenician cities at that time; they were probably still loyal to the Persian king, and it is likely that their fleets, including the Byblian fleet, took part in the Persian operations against the rebels, presumably without being affected very much by these revolts located in Asia Minor.[93]

In short, the first third of the 4th century, which probably corresponded with ʿOzbaʿal's reign, was a troubled period. All the classical authors show that Artaxerxes faced numerous revolts, which were not only concomitant but also linked by networks of alliances between rebels. For example, during Evagoras's revolt, the whole Transeuphratene would have seceded, just like Egypt. However, nothing suggests that there was a vast common front formed at the instigation of Achoris and/or Evagoras.[94] The biased accounts of classical authors can be explained by the following: Isocrates' intention was to demonstrate how weak the Persian army was and to convince the Greeks that they should launch a new offensive in Asia Minor. Other authors, such as Diodorus, for example, strove to capture spectacular events and therefore interpreted dramatically.[95] Concerning the Phoenician cities, a network of alliances probably existed between Tyre and Evagoras, but we lack information on other cities. The Phoenician fleet (including that of Byblos) was probably still part of the Persian fleet in the two campaigns against Egypt and, since both campaigns failed, they would have had to face heavy losses.

The volume of production of ʿOzbaʿal's coinage (504 coins preserved) is much more significant than ʿElpaʿal's (87). The political function was very

90. On the name of Datames, cf. A. Lemaire, "Recherche d'épigraphie araméenne en Asie Mineure et en Égypte et le problème de l'acculturation," in *Achaemenid History*, vol. 6: *Asia Minor and Egypt: Old Cultures in a New Empire* (ed. H. Sancisi-Weerdenburg and A. Kuhrt; Leiden, 1991) 203–5; Briant, *From Cyrus to Alexander*, 666–67; O. Casabonne, "Notes ciliciennes," *Anatolia Antiqua* 5 (1997) 35–38; G. Le Rider, "Le monnayage perse en Cilicie au IVe siècle," *NAC* 26 (1997) 157–59; Elayi and Lemaire, *Graffiti*, 188–89; J. Wiesehöfer, "Tarkumuwa und das Farnah," in *A Persian Perspective: Essays in Memory of Heleen Sancisi-Weerdenburg* (ed. W. Henkelman and A. Kuhrt; Leiden, 2003) 173–87.

91. Diod. XV, 91.1.

92. Cf. Briant, *From Cyrus to Alexander*, 639–43.

93. On the political context in Asia Minor, see Briant, ibid., 641–46; P. Debord, *L'Asie Mineure au IVe siècle (412–323 a.c.): Pouvoirs et jeux politiques* (Bordeaux, 1999) 346.

94. Briant, *From Cyrus to Alexander*, 632.

95. For example, Isocr., *Paneg.* 161–62; Diod. XV, 90.2–4.

important: as a usurper, ʿOzbaʿal wanted to mint an abundant number of coins. This coinage may also have had a fiscal function, to try to overcome the economic difficulties provoked by the participation of the Byblian fleet in the Persian campaigns. However, Byblos was not overwhelmed by heavy financial difficulties as Sidon and Tyre were in the 4th century B.C.E.[96] Its fleet was a small fleet that did not make serious demands on its treasury to maintain it. The coinage of ʿOzbaʿal may also have had, at least partly, a commercial function because it was abundant; however, the number of different denominations was more limited than in ʾElpaʿal's coinage.

7. The Coinage of ʾUrimilk, Group IV.3: Shortly before 350 B.C.E.

ʿOzbaʿal's successor was ʾUrimilk (rather than ʾAddirmilk). If we can judge from the relatively small number of ʾUrimilk's coins preserved (114 instead of ʿOzbaʿal's 504), his reign was probably much shorter than ʿOzbaʿal's reign. At the beginning of his reign, ʾUrimilk reused some of ʿOzbaʿal's obverse dies, perhaps for economic reasons or to maintain a legitimate link with his predecessor, who had founded the dynasty. ʾUrimilk's successor, King ʿAynel, then reused several obverse dies from ʾUrimilk's coins, after having obliterated the abbreviation *ʾK* (*ʾ*[*WRML*]*K*), which means that the dies were well preserved and had only been used for a short period. ʾUrimilk did not change the coinage of his predecessor, except for his name: 'ʾUrimilk, king of Byblos' (*ʾWRMLK MLK GBL*). This can be explained by the fact that he belonged to the illegitimate dynasty inaugurated by King ʿOzbaʿal. He had the same system of denominations: shekels (Series IV.3.1) and 16ths (Series IV.3.2); there were possibly other smaller denominations that are now in our unclassified series. We tentatively propose dating ʾUrimilk's coinage to a period just before 350 B.C.E.

What was probably the political context of ʾUrimilk's reign? During the second third of the 4th century, the troubles increased even more. The end of the long reign of Artaxerxes II (until 359 B.C.E.) seems to have been difficult for him. The question of the connection between the western revolts against the Persian king arises for this period even more acutely. The answer is always much disputed—and all the more so because the sources often have lacunae and are uncertain. The two main theories are conflicting: the first one, which could be labeled "maximalist," considers all the

96. Cf. A. G. Elayi, J.-N. Barrandon, and J. Elayi, "The Devaluation of Sidonian Silver Coinage in 345 BCE and the First Bronze Issues," *AJN* 19 (2007) 1–8; Elayi et al., "Silver Coinage Fluctuations at Byblos."

western revolts against the Persian king to be in line with a large coalition that aimed to put an end to Persian domination.[97] The second theory, which could be called "minimalist," has more recently been elaborated and tends to reduce the revolts to localized conflicts that never seriously threatened the Persian Empire.[98] These two theories are probably both excessive, and each revolt ought to be analyzed with more objectivity: however, such a sizable study goes beyond the scope of the present Byblian corpus. We shall focus here on the participation of the Phoenicians—more specifically, the Byblians—in the revolts and try to verify whether the city of Byblos fell within possible networks of alliances.

According to Diodorus, the "Great Satraps' Revolt" began in 362/361, the rebels "having made an agreement for a concerted action." Among them were Ariobarzanes, satrap of Phrygia; Mausolus, dynast of Caria; Orontes, satrap of Mysia; Autophradates, satrap of Lydia; and also Lycians, Pisidians, Pamphylians, Cilicians, Syrians, "Phoenicians and almost all the coastland peoples" (Φοίνικες καὶ σχεδὸν πάντες οἱ παραθαλάσσοι).[99] It is clear that Diodorus's spectacular presentation cannot be taken literally. He has combined revolts that did not occur at the same time—for example, Ariobarzanes' revolt, which occurred earlier. During the years 360 and (probably) slightly later, several revolts did take place, some of them being coordinated, and they provoked a degree of destabilization in the western part of the Persian Empire.

Is Diodorus reliable when he writes that the Phoenicians took part in this coordinated action? It seems unlikely that all of them rebelled, because the Persian fleet remained powerful, as mentioned above. Diodorus's restriction probably concerned some of them. The spread of Tachos's rebellion toward Syria in about 359 was probably the most likely period when Phoenician revolts would have occurred. The situation was always troubled

97. See mainly Moysey, *Greek Relations with the Persian Satraps*; idem, "IG II^2 and the Great Satraps' Revolt," *ZPE* 67 (1987) 93–100; idem, "Observations on the Numismatic Evidence relating to the Great Satrapal Revolt of 362/1 B.C.," *REA* 91 (1989) 107–39; idem, "Diodorus, the Satraps and the Decline of the Persian Empire," *AHB* 5 (1991) 113–22; idem, "Plutarch, Nepos and the Satrapal Revolt of 362/1 B.C.," *Historia* 41 (1992) 158–66.

98. M. Weiskopf, *Achaemenid System of Governing in Anatolia* (Ph.D. diss., Berkeley, 1982); idem, *The So-Called 'Great Satraps' Revolt', 366–360 B.C.* (Wiesbaden, 1989); Briant (*From Cyrus to Alexander*, esp. pp. 659, 993, and 994) follows M. Weiskopf, but with several reservations; idem, "Histoire et idéologie: Les Grecs et la 'décadence perse'," in *Mélanges P. Lévêque* (Paris, 1989) 2:33–47; J. Elayi (*Sidon* [1989] 179–84) followed R. A. Moysey, since the typed version of M. Weiskopf's dissertation was not yet available.

99. Diod. XV, 3–4. On these revolts, cf. Elayi-Elayi, *Coinage of Tyre*, 353–371 (with bibliography).

in the western part of the Persian Empire. The succession of Artaxerxes II in 359 was difficult because Artaxerxes III Ochus had unseated his two older brothers, Darius and Ariaspes, from the throne. King ʿAbdʿaštart I of Sidon had revolted against the Persians, probably around 360/359, but this revolt was repressed in about 355; we know this because of the Babylonian tablet that mentions the sending of Sidonian prisoners by Artaxerxes III to Babylon and Susa, which is dated to year 4 (355) rather than year 14 (345).[100] After the suppression of ʿAbdʿaštart's revolt, Artaxerxes III did, however, allow him to remain on the throne, just as Artaxerxes II permitted Evagoras to remain on the throne of Salamis after his revolt. In spite of Diodorus's assertion about the participation of the Phoenicians in a revolt around 362/1,[101] there is no confirmation of the participation of Byblos. From 355 on, Transeuphratene was clearly under the control of Mazday/Mazaios, who was appointed by the energetic King Artaxerxes III.[102] Even though Mazday minted his coinage in Sidon and mostly kept this rebellious city under control, and even though Byblos had not participated in the revolt of ʿAbdʿaštart I of Sidon, Byblos was probably also monitored by Mazday, just as were all the other Phoenician cities.

The relatively small volume of production of ʾUrimilk's coinage (114 coins preserved) compared with that of ʿOzbaʿal (504) and the following king, ʿAynel (658), probably means that ʾUrimilk's reign was short and may have ended around 350, before the troubled period initiated by the so-called revolt of Tennes, king of Sidon. The functions of ʾUrimilk's coinage were probably the same as ʿOzbaʿal's.

8. *The Coinage of ʿAynel, Group IV.4: Approximately 350–333* B.C.E.

The successor of ʾUrimilk was ʿAynel, known from classical sources as Ἔνυλος.[103] Judging from the abundant number of coins preserved (658 instead of ʾUrimilk's 114), his reign was much longer. ʿAynel reused many of ʾUrimilk's obverse dies—first to maintain the dynastic link with his predecessor, without obliterating the abbreviation *ʾK* (that is, *ʾ*[*WRML*]*K*), then obliterating it because these dies were not yet worn and he wanted to save

100. Cf. J. Elayi, *ʿAbdʿaštart Ier/Straton de Sidon: Un roi phénicien entre Orient et Occident* (Paris, 2005) 125–38 (with bibliography).

101. Diod. XV, 90.

102. On the government of Mazday, see J. Elayi and A. G. Elayi, "Le monnayage sidonien de Mazday," *Trans* 27 (2004) 155–62; idem, *Monnayage de Sidon*, 660–64; idem, *Coinage of Tyre*, 366–71.

103. Arrian, *Anab.* II, 20.1; Quintus Curtius IV, 1.15.

money during a difficult period. At first, he had the same denominations as King ʾUrimilk: shekels (Series IV.4.1) and 16ths (Series IV.4.2). Then, around the end of his reign, new denominations were minted: quarter-shekels (Series IV.4.3), 16th-shekels with new inscriptions and anepigraphic 16ths (Series IV.4.5, IV.4.6, IV.4.7). We tentatively propose dating ʿAynel's coinage from around 350 to 333 B.C.E.

What was the political context of ʿAynel's reign? His reign during the Persian period probably corresponded to the reigns of three successive Persian kings: part of the reign of Artaxerxes III, who was murdered (around 350–338), the reign of Arses/Artaxerxes IV, who was poisoned (August–September 338–336), and part of the reign of Darius III (336–333), who was murdered in 330. This period was difficult for the Persian Empire because of dynastic crises; according to some questionable Greek accounts, Artaxerxes III did not take part in military campaigns because of his cowardice but finally decided to lead the military expedition against Egypt in 351.[104] In fact, he succeeded in putting an end to the various revolts of satraps, who were then obliged to dismiss their mercenaries, but Egypt was still independent. A second series of rebellions against the Persians was initiated by Sidon according to Diodorus, who gives a detailed but unique account of this event, so we must remain cautious.[105] In contrast to the previous period, the revolts were no longer led by Persian satraps but by local dynasts: Phoenician cities, Cypriot cities, and Egypt, and the best known was the "revolt of Tennes." Thanks to the Sidonian coinage (which was dated by the year) and all our other sources, the chronology of this revolt is now relatively well established.[106] We shall focus on the aspect of this event that was connected with Byblos.

According to Diodorus, the starting point of the revolt was a Phoenician common council in *ʾTR*/Tripolis, a city that was quite special because it was formed from three fortified cities that belonged to Sidon, Tyre and Arwad.[107] Why was Byblos, the nearest city, absent at the foundation of *ʾTR*/Tripolis? From a geographical point of view, the participation of its northern neighbor, Arwad, is easy to understand—easier at least than the southern cities of Sidon and Tyre. Perhaps the date of the founding of this

104. Diod. XVI, 40.3–5; Isocr., *Phil.* 101; Dem., *Rhod.* 11–12.

105. Diod. XVI, 40.5, 42.5, 40.33; Orose, *Histoires* III, 7.8.

106. For a detailed comment on this revolt and its date, cf. Elayi-Elayi, *Monnayage de Sidon*, 668–73.

107. Diod. XVI, 41.1–3; cf. J. Elayi, *Recherches sur les cités phéniciennes à l'époque perse* (Naples, 1987) 77–81; idem, "Tripoli (Liban) à l'époque perse," *Trans* 2 (1990) 59–71; J. Elayi and A. G. Elayi, "La première monnaie de ʾTR/Tripolis (Tripoli, Liban)?" *Trans* 5 (1992) 143–51; idem, *Monnayage de Sidon*, 668–69.

triple city corresponded to a period prior to the militarization of Byblos—that is, before the second half of the 5th century. However, even if the Byblians did not belong to the first circle ("confederation"?) of the three main Phoenician cities, they probably belonged to the greater Phoenician circle of cities and attended all the general meetings that were held in *ʾTR*/Tripoli.

In the meeting just before the revolt, the Sidonians (or only the anti-Persian Sidonian faction) took advantage of the hegemony of their city to persuade the rest of the Phoenicians to make a bid for their independence—that is, not only the Tyrians and Aradians who belonged to the first circle, but all the Phoenician cities, including Byblos. In any case, Byblos was by this time a military power and could participate in this revolt. The Cypriot kings also joined the revolt "in imitation of the Phoenicians";[108] Pharaoh Nectanebo, who had defeated the Persians in 351, made an agreement of συμμαχία with the Sidonians.[109] Diodorus then describes the important Sidonian preparations for the war, including the many war-galleys, mercenaries, weapons, and so on.[110] The Sidonians probably took advantage of the preparations that had been made for the next Persian campaign against Egypt.[111] Even though the Tyrians, Aradians, and Byblians were not mentioned, we can assume that they also participated in these preparations for fighting Egypt (even if to a lesser extent), because this was the usual case while they were in service to the Persians.

The first act of rebellion occurred in Sidon,[112] but the Tyrians, Aradians, and Byblians were probably implicated when Artaxerxes, "being apprised of the rash acts of the insurgents, issued threatening warnings to all the Phoenicians and in particular to the people of Sidon."[113] The *Philippus* of Isocrates, which was written in 347, mentions the revolts in progress in Cyprus, Phoenicia, and Cilicia: "Either they have abandoned (the Persian king) or they are overcome by such misfortunes that he could not get anything from these peoples."[114] The first reason for this revolt was, according to Diodorus, the failure of the Persian campaign against Egypt in 351:

108. Diod. XVI, 42.5.

109. Ibid., 41.3.

110. Ibid. 41.4–5; 42.2; 44.6.

111. Briant, *From Cyrus to Alexander*, 487; Elayi-Elayi, *Monnayage de Sidon*, 667–676.

112. C. Clermont-Ganneau, "Le paradeisos royal achéménide de Sidon," *RB* 30 (1921) 107–108.

113. Diod. XVI, 41.6.

114. Isocr., *Phil.* V, 102 and pp. 7–8: it was written in 347 and completed in the spring or at the beginning of the summer of 346; cf. S. Perlman, "Isocrates, Philippus: A Reinterpretation," *Hist.* 6 (1957) 306 n. 1.

"The Phoenicians and the kings of Cyprus had imitated the Egyptians."[115] Another reason for Diodorus was the unbearable presence of the Persian satraps and generals residing in Sidon.[116] However, this reason would also have been true for Tyre because the Tyrian territory was used for establishing Persian bases, such as Akko against Egypt, very close to Tyre. But it was not true for Arwad or Byblos, which were farther north. Moreover, the small city of Byblos probably feared a confrontation pitting its limited strength against the mighty army of Artaxerxes III, even if the Phoenician fleets did refuse to assist him.

We have already analyzed in detail the course of the revolt of Sidon, the role of Tennes, the role of other representative bodies, the burning of the fleet by the Sidonians themselves, and the seizure of the city after Tennes' betrayal.[117] Diodorus provides few indications about the other Phoenician cities involved in the revolt. From his presentation, it seems that Artaxerxes III decided to concentrate his forces against Sidon from the beginning, because "he encamped not far from Sidon."[118] Then "his aim was to overwhelm the Sidonians with a merciless disaster and to strike terror into the other cities by their punishment."[119] He achieved his aim: "So the disasters which had overtaken Sidon had such an ending, and the rest of the cities, panic-stricken, went over to the Persians."[120] Based on Diodorus's account, which is our only source, the other Phoenician cities, including Byblos (if it participated in this revolt), surrendered to Artaxerxes III immediately after the suppression of the Sidonian revolt. Since we know from the Sidonian coins' dates that the revolt was suppressed, and Tennes was put to death in his year 5, his last year (which was 347), we can assume that the other cities also surrendered around 347.[121] Then Artaxerxes III ordered Idrieus, satrap of Caria, to send a fleet of 40 war-galleys carrying infantry troops against the Cypriots; this contingent was led by the Athenian Phocion and by Evagoras II, the former king of Salamis. The Persian troops lined up in

115. Diod. XVI, 40.5. Cf. also C. Mossé, in Will et al., *Le monde grec et l'Orient* (Paris, 1975) 2:68.

116. Diod. XVI, 41.2.

117. Cf. Elayi-Elayi, *Monnayage de Sidon*, 670–73 (with bibliography).

118. Diod. XVI, 44.4–5.

119. Ibid., 45.2.

120. Ibid., 45.6. Artaxerxes probably also wanted to put down the Sidonian political system, which he considered responsible for the revolt (execution of the "hundred," then of the "five hundred" representative citizens). He did not intend to destroy his best naval base but to change the institutions of Sidon in order to obtain its complete submission. Cf. D. Agut-Labordère, "Les frontières intérieures de la société militaire égyptienne: L'invasion de l'Égypte par Artaxerxes III à travers Diodore XVI, 46–45," *Trans* 35 (2007) 17–27.

121. Cf. the year-dates of Tennes' coinage: Elayi-Elayi, *Monnayage de Sidon*, 667–79.

sight of Salamis in order to frighten the Cypriot kings, who probably surrendered in 347 or 346. When Tennes had been put to death, Pnytagoras of Salamis was allowed on the throne.[122] It is possible that the king who was placed on the throne of Sidon in 346 was Evagoras II, a friend of the Persian king.[123] This revolt had various consequences for the Phoenician cities: for Sidon, it was the most difficult time of the Persian domination.[124] Conversely, ʿOzmilk of Tyre (349–333/2) benefited from the failure of the Sidonian revolt.[125] The consequences for Arwad and Byblos are unknown, but they were probably not as significant, because they had been much less involved in this event.

Diodorus puts the reconquest of Egypt in his account together with the suppression of the Sidonian and Cypriot revolts. However, the Egypt campaign occurred later, although military preparations may have begun in 346. According to Diodorus, the Sidonians expelled Evagoras II in 343, probably because he was a foreign, pro-Persian king, who "misgoverned their city";[126] perhaps the Sidonians were taking advantage of the fact that the Persians were engaged in the campaign against Egypt. Evagoras II was obliged to rush off to Cyprus again, where he was "arrested and paid the penalty," probably because the anti-Persian movement had grown on the island.

It is surprising that Artaxerxes waited four years after the suppression of the Sidonian and Cypriot revolts to attack Egypt. He had probably decided to succeed this time and therefore to take the necessary time to assemble a sufficient number of troops. Even though referring to the overwhelming superiority of the number of Persian troops is a commonplace in Diodorus's account, it was probably partly true: Nectanebo had 20,000 Greek mercenaries, 20,000 Libyans, 60,000 Egyptian 'warriors' (μαχίμοι), and an incredible number of 'river-boats' (πλοῖα ποτάμια).[127] Artaxerxes had gathered 300,000 foot soldiers (among them a contingent of 4,000 soldiers commanded by Mentor, who was previously in service to Tennes), 30,000 horsemen, 300 war-galleys, and 500 additional transport ships.[128] The Tyrian, Aradian and Byblian fleets probably took part in this expedi-

122. Diod. XV, 42.6–9, 45.6; cf. Debord, *L'Asie Mineure*, 401; Elayi-Elayi, *Monnayage de Sidon*, 674–75.

123. Elayi-Elayi, ibid., 677–79.

124. Ibid., 676–85.

125. Idem, *Coinage of Tyre*, 375–89.

126. Diod. XVI, 43.3.

127. Ibid., 47.6.

128. Ibid., 40.6, 42.2, 47.4.

tion but, to a grand total of 300 war-galleys (compared with the 40 ships sent to Cyprus in 346)[129] must surely have included the Sidonian fleet.

This means that the Persian king had to wait until the Sidonians had repaired and rebuilt their fleet, which had been destroyed in 347. Even if the chronology of Diodorus is not exact, he did point out the length of the military preparations, which was true.[130] Some of them probably took place in the territory of Tyre, most likely in Akko, which was the nearest important harbor to Egypt. The last campaign against Egypt began before the end of 343, and Artaxerxes seized Memphis in the summer of 342, not in 345/4.[131] With the conquest of Egypt after several failures, Artaxerxes had attained all his objectives and had reinforced his power and prestige. According to Diodorus, there were only a few limited troubles in Asia Minor, and Mentor was appointed to suppress them—for example, the revolt of Hermeias, tyrant of Atarneus.[132] However, it is uncertain whether Phoenician fleets, in particular Byblian, were used to maintain order among local rulers. Beginning with this period, the first diplomatic and military reports between Artaxerxes and Philip II began—in particular, regarding the exile of Artabazus by Philip, then his return to Persia and the Perinthus affair.[133]

After the murder of Artaxerxes III in 338 B.C.E., the following period was difficult for the Persians because of the dynastic crises, and it seems likely that King ʿAynel encountered some difficulties, at least in the last part of his reign. The style of his coins has greatly deteriorated, as though he hired less-careful engravers or they were working in an emergency situation.[134] This hasty work could be explained by an increase in and standardization of coins produced and/or by emergency issues intended to provide the currency required for facing internal or external troubles. The monetary workshop of Byblos worked economically during this period, by

129. Ibid., 42.7.

130. Ibid., 46.7.

131. Cf. G. L. Cawkwell, "Demosthenes' Policy after Peace of Philocrates I," *CQ* 13 (1963) 136–38; E. J. Bickerman, "Notes sur la chronologie de la XXXe dynastie," in *Mélanges Maspéro* (Cairo, 1934) 1:77–82; A. B. Lloyd, "Manetho and the Thirty-First Dynasty," in *Pyramid Studies and Essays Presented to I. E. S. Edwards* (ed. J. Baines et al.; London, 1988) 154–60; contra M. Sordi, *Kokalos* 5 (1959) 107.

132. Diod. XVI, 52.3–52.8; cf. S. Ruzicka, *Politics of a Persian Dynasty: The Hecatomnids in the Fourth Century* (London, 1992) 120–22.

133. Cf. Briant, *From Cyrus to Alexander*, 688–90 (with bibliography); M. Brosius, "Why Persia Became the Enemy of Macedon," in *A Persian Perspective: Essays in Memory of Heleen Sancisi-Weerdenburg* (ed. W. Henkelman and A. Kuhrt; Leiden, 2003) 173–87.

134. For example, in Series IV.4.2.

reusing the dies of the previous king's coinage[135] and by continuing to use worn and damaged dies, which sometimes split but may have been reused anyway until they broke completely.[136] The new symbols added by ʿAynel on the reverse (lion's head and two-pronged ankhs) were possibly intended to reinforce his authority in the city; the lion's head sometimes partly obliterated the name of the city.[137] Other elements confirm that his authority had decreased and was even questioned by the Byblians. Thus, they negotiated directly with Alexander and decided by themselves to deliver their city over to him in the absence of the king.[138] Some final coin series no longer bore the usual long inscription on the reverse, 'ʿAynel, king of Byblos' (*ʿYNʾL MLK GBL*), but only *ʿG* (Series IV.4.5) and *GL* (Series IV.4.6). The name of the city alone, 'Byblos' (*G*[*B*]*L*), clearly meant that an important political change had occurred at the end of ʿAynel's reign: decrease of royal power in favor of the representative of the city's 'organism(s)'.[139] In this light, *ʿG* could be interpreted as '[assembly of the] peo[ple of] By[blos' (*ʿ*[*M*] *G*[*BL*); or at least, *ʿG* could stand for 'ʿAy[nel] By[blos' ([*ʿYNʾL*] *G*[*BL*), without his royal title.[140]

Although the sources lack information about the short reign of Arses/Artaxerxes IV (338–336), it is possible that external difficulties (since Byblos was under the Persians) had also occurred. Here we should mention the mysterious episode of Khabbabash, which is referred to in Egyptian hieroglyphs on the so-called Satrap Stela (dated 312/311). According to some authors, the mention of *Xerxes* designates Artaxerxes III or Artaxerxes IV, so Khabbabash would have reigned as a pharaoh between about 342 and 338; in other authors' works, *Xerxes* designates any of the Persian kings, so Khabbabash would have reigned between 338 and 336.[141] We are told that

135. Cf. J. Elayi and A. G. Elayi, "L'ordre de succession des derniers rois de Byblos," *Syr* 70 (1993) 112–13.

136. For example, coin nos. 931–959, 1092–1177.

137. See above, chap. 1.

138. Arrian, *Anab.* II, 15.6; cf. Elayi, *Recherches sur les cités phéniciennes*, 21–23.

139. J. Elayi and A. G. Elayi, "A Series of Coins from Byblos with the Name of the City (4th Cent. BC)," *NC* 170 (2010) 3–8.

140. Idem, "Deux séries monétaires de Byblos avec *ʿG*," *NAC* 39 (2010) 127–39; cf. Elayi, *Byblos*, 174–76.

141. Cf. A. Spalinger, "The Reign of King Chabbash: An Interpretation," *ZÄS* 105 (1978) 142–54; R. K. Ritner, "Khabbabash and the Satrap Stela: A Grammatical Rejoinder," *ZÄS* 107 (1980) 135–37; H. Goedicke, "Comments of the Satrap Stela," *BES* 6 (1985) 33–54; W. Huss, "Der Rätselhäfte Pharao Chababasch," *SEL* 11 (1994) 97–112; Briant, *From Cyrus to Alexander*, 717–18 and 1017–18 (with bibliography); D. Devauchelle, "Réflexions sur les documents égyptiens datés de la deuxième domination perse," *Trans* 10 (1995) 35–43; S. Burstein, "Prelude to Alexander: The Reign of Khababash," *AHB* 14 (2000) 149–54; E. Badian, "Darius III," *HSCP* 100 (2000) 241–68; P. Briant, *Darius dans l'ombre d'Alexandre* (Paris,

Khabbabash went to the marshes of the Delta, "inspecting all the branches of the Nile flowing into the Mediterranean in order to repel the *kbnt*-ships of Asian people out of Egypt."[142] This means a threat or attack by a Persian fleet coming from the Syro-Phoenician coast. However, we have no information about such a Persian expedition sent to Egypt to suppress the revolt of this pharaoh, who is not mentioned elsewhere. But perhaps it occurred during the reign of ʿAynel. After the participation of Byblos in the Persian conquest of Egypt in 342, the city may also have taken part in this expedition against Khabbabash.

What we do know of Byblos during the short reign of Darius III[143] is its place in the Persian military preparations against Alexander and the surrender of the city to the Macedonian king. First, in 336, the Macedonians initiated an offensive by sending an expedition to Asia Minor led by Parmenion.[144] Alexander then acceded to the throne after Philip II's murder and sent a new expedition to Asia Minor, led by Hecataeus. According to Diodorus, Darius understood how dangerous Alexander was and reacted "by fitting out a large number of ships of war and assembling numerous strong armies, choosing at the same time his best commanders, among whom was Memnon of Rhodes."[145] It is likely that the Phoenician fleets were a part of the fleet that was fitted out by Darius. At that time, Phoenician cities still occupied a unique position in the strategic Persian system as the prime location for recruiting seamen, because they had dockyards and lumber reserves in the neighboring forests of Lebanon. As Arrian wrote: "The fleet which was the best and the most powerful in the Persian fleet was that of the Phoenicians."[146] The substantial preparations of the Persian fleet by Darius III from 335 on could at least partly explain the

2003) 67–69 and 563; D. Schäfer, "Persian Foes, Ptolemaic Friends? The Persians on the Satrap Stela," in *Organisation des pouvoirs et contacts culturels dans les pays de l'empire achéménide* (ed. P. Briant and M. Chauveau; Paris, 2009) 143–52.

142. On the *kbnt*-ships, cf. A. B. Lloyd, "Triremes and the Saite Navy," *JEA* 58 (1972) 268–79; idem, "Were Necho's Triremes Phoenician?" *JHS* 95 (1975) 45–61; Spalinger, "The Reign of King Chabbash," 149 and n. 42; J. C. Darnell, "The *Kbnt.wt* Ships of the Late Period," in *Life in a Multicultural Society: Egypt from Cambyses to Constantine and Beyond* (ed. J. H. Johnson; Chicago, 1992) 67–89.

143. For the historiography of this reign, cf. Briant, *Darius dans l'ombre d'Alexandre*; cf. also R. J. van der Spek, "Darius III, Alexander the Great and Babylonian Scholarship," in *A Persian Perspective: Essays in Memory of Heleen Sancisi-Weerdenburg* (ed. W. Henkelman and A. Kuhrt; Leiden, 2003) 289–346.

144. Diod. XVI, 91.2; Justin IX.

145. Diod. XVII, 7.2.

146. Arrian, *Anab.* II, 17.3; on the value of Arrian's testimony, see, for example, P. A. Stadter, *Arrian of Nicomedia* (Chapel Hill, NC, 1980); A. B. Bosworth, *From Arrian to Alexander: Studies in Historical Interpretation* (Oxford, 1988); H. Tonnet, *Recherches sur Arrien,*

deterioration of the coinage of ʿAynel around the end of his reign.[147] At the beginning of the spring of 334, Alexander departed with his army toward the Hellespont and crossed it without the Persians trying to prevent the Macedonian landing. The reasons that they did not intervene have often been questioned.[148] The absence of the Persian fleet is not easy to understand because, a few weeks later when Alexander was in Miletus, the fleet arrived with 400 war-galleys, equipped with well-trained crews who came from Phoenicia and Cyprus particularly; this was in contrast to Alexander's fleet, which at that time consisted of only 100 triremes and transport ships.[149] The Persian defeat at the Granicus in 334 was followed by a series of impressive victories carried off by Alexander in Asia Minor.[150]

However, Darius kept the hegemony at sea by far—and all the more so because Alexander had dismissed his fleet at Miletus except for the Athenian squadron and some transport ships. In the summer of 334 B.C.E., Darius appointed Memnon as "Commander of Lower Asia (coastal area) and of the whole fleet."[151] According to Arrian, Alexander knew that he was inferior at sea, but he had no more money. However, "he considered that from then on Asia was in his power thanks to his army, that he no longer needed a fleet and that by seizing the coastal cities, he would get rid of the Persian fleet, having no further need to recruit its crews nor to carry out a landing in Asia."[152] Such a plan was very risky, and it could be countered in Asia Minor, where the Persians controlled several Lycian and Carian harbors. Alexander realized the situation in 333 and decided to assemble a new military fleet.[153] In the summer of 333, Darius left Babylon at the head of the royal army and reached Syria. In spite of some failures, the Persian fleet retained its superiority. It seems that Darius, fully conscious of how dangerous the Macedonian offensive was, had developed a double strategy—both on sea and on land. While Pharnabazus and Autophradates reconquered the coastland of Asia Minor, he himself would confront the Macedonian army. As for Alexander, he continued to move southward with

sa personnalité et ses écrits atticistes, vols. 1–2 (Amsterdam, 1988); F. Sisti, *Arriano, Anabasi di Alessandro*, vol. 1 (Florence, 2001).

147. Difficulties also occurred at that time in the Tyrian coinage: cf. Elayi-Elayi, *Coinage of Tyre*, 382.

148. Diod. XVII, 18.2, 4.

149. Arrian, *Anab.* I, 11.6, 18.5–8; II, 13.7, 18.4. Cf. E. A. Anson, "The Persian Fleet in 334," *CP* 84 (1989) 44–49.

150. Arrian, *Anab.* I, 18.3–9, 19; Diod. XVII, 22.2–4.

151. Arrian, *Anab.*, 20.3; II, 1.1; Diod. XVII, 23.5–6.

152. Arrian, *Anab.*, 20.1; cf. also I, 18.6–8; Diod. XVII, 23.1–3.

153. Quintus Curtius III, 1.19–20. For a detailed analysis of this period, cf. Elayi, *Byblos*, 176–79.

the intention of seizing the Phoenician cities before penetrating inland: he realized this goal after his victory in Issus in November 333.

The various reactions of the Phoenician cities that faced Alexander are only known from classical sources and must be analyzed with caution. Byblos is mentioned several times, although less often than Sidon and Tyre. If we can trust the sources, this would mean that this city was finally taken into consideration as a military power but was less powerful than the other cities. Tyre was the most powerful at that time, followed by Sidon which had declined, and then by Arwad. All the authors have contrasted the resistance of Tyre with the submission of the other Phoenician cities: Plutarch mentions their spontaneous submission,[154] and Diodorus speaks of their warm welcome: "As he (Alexander) came into Phoenicia, he received the submission of all the other cities, for their inhabitants accepted him willingly."[155] Arrian's account is more precise than the versions by the authors of the "vulgate." Arrian mentions the spontaneous submission of Byblos, but no more than that, and the enthusiastic welcome of Arwad and Sidon: 'Departed from Marathos, Alexander took Byblos which gave itself by an agreement, and Sidon, the Sidonians having themselves invited him as they loathed the Persians and Darius' (Ἐκ Μαράθου δὅρμηθεὶς Βύβλον τε λαμβάνει ὁμολογίᾳ ἐνδοθεῖσαν καὶ Σιδῶνα, αὐτῶν Σιδωνίων ἐπικαλεσαμένων κατὰ ἔχθος τῶν Περσῶν καὶ Δαρείου).[156] The terms used for the seizure of Byblos are not used for the other Phoenician cities: after the verb ἐνδιδόναι, which is usual for the 'surrendor' of a city, the term ὁμολογία specifies how this operation was achieved: by an agreement. This term, which literally means 'corroborating language', can designate any kind of agreement or arrangement, but also a 'war agreement', which is probably the meaning in this sentence. It is impossible to be more precise, but at any rate it was an agreement concluded between Alexander and the Byblians without their king, who was at sea. According to Curtius, Straton "had surrendered more at the desire of the people than on his own accord"; it is not known whether there was a pro-Greek faction in Sidon at that time, but the hostility of the Sidonians toward the Persians was so great that this was sufficient to explain their attitude.[157] Tyre's resistance is not presented as a hostile attitude toward Alexander but as a desire for independence: "Tyre, famous among all the cities of Syria and Phoenicia because of its extent and fame, seemed to be more prepared to consider Alexander as

154. Plut., *Alex.* XXIV, 4.

155. Diod. XVII, 40.2; Curt. IV, 2.1, whose language is not precise.

156. Arrian, *Anab.* II, 13.7; 15.6.

157. Curt. IV, 1.

an ally (*societatem*) rather than a master (*imperium*)."[158] What primarily emerges from the classical sources is the general hostility of the Phoenician cities (except Tyre) toward Darius.

The aim of Alexander was to assemble all the Phoenician fleets before penetrating farther inland, so that the Persians meanwhile could not transfer the war to Greece.[159] According to Arrian, 'At that time, Gerostratus king of Aradus and Enylus king of Byblos, when they heard that Alexander had seized their cities, left Autophradates and his fleet and joined Alexander with their fleets and the triremes of the Sidonians so that about 80 Phoenician war-galleys had sailed towards him' (Ἐν τούτῳ δὲ Γηρόστρατός τε ὁ Ἀράδου Βασιλεὺς καὶ Ἔνυλος ὁ Βύβλου ὡς ἔμαθον τὰς πόλεις σφῶν ὑπ᾽ Ἀλεξάνδρου ἐχομένας, ἀπολιπόντες Αὐτοφραδάτην τε καὶ τὰς ζὺν αὐτῷ νέας παρ᾽ Ἀλέξανδρον ζὺν τῷ ναυτικῷ τῷ σφετέρῳ ἀφίκοντο καὶ αἱ τῶν Σιδωνίων τριήρεις σὺν αὐτοῖς, ὥστε Φοινίκων μὲν νῆες ὀγδοήκοντα μάλιστα αὐτῷ παραγένοντο).[160] Alexander would have welcomed these fleets because he knew they were not serving the Persians of their own free will,[161] and in reality he needed them. There is a problem with regard to the Sidonian fleet, however: we know that only a part of the fleet joined Alexander because of the small number of ships. Where was the rest of the fleet and King ʿAbdʿaštart II? If Arrian's chronology is correct on this point, the described event took place during the siege of Tyre, after which Alexander established his naval base at Sidon: "He sailed towards Sidon taking with him the hypaspistai and Agrianes in order to assemble all the war-galleys which had already joined him."[162] Which war-galleys were these? Was the rest of the Sidonian fleet there? According to some authors, ʿAbdʿaštart had remained in Sidon with the rest of the fleet, by order of the Persians, to resist Alexander and prevent a new Sidonian revolt.[163] This hypothesis is based on a passage by Curtius, which seems to mean that the king was in his city when he surrendered.[164] This is not convincing, however, because it is unlikely that Darius did not have his main support with him—that is, the Sidonian fleet—in this difficult situation or that ʿAbdʿaštart himself

158. Ibid. IV, 2.2. On Alexander's siege of Tyre, cf. Elayi-Elayi, *Coinage of Tyre*, 384–87 (with bibliography).

159. Arrian, *Anab.* II.17.1–4.

160. Ibid., II, 20.1.

161. Ibid., 20.3.

162. Ibid., 19.6.

163. Cf. H. Hauben, "The King of the Sidonians and the Persian Imperial Fleet," *AncSoc* 1 (1970) 7 (with bibliography); followed by S. F. Bondì, "Istìtuzioni e politica a Sidone dal 351 al 332 av. Cr.," *RSF* 2 (1974) 157; Elayi, *Sidon*, 194 n. 156.

164. Curt. IV, 1.16.

was not in command of his fleet; on the other hand, Curtius's testimony arouses suspicion, since his aim was to relate how Abdalonymus was designated king.[165] We have proposed a more likely hypothesis: ʿAbdʿaštart was alongside Darius with his entire fleet; some war-galleys "of the Sidonians" deserted, following the Aradian and Byblian fleets, which perhaps can be explained by their hostility toward the Persians and their exclusion from Sidonian power. Since ʿAbdʿaštart was on the side of the Persian king, he probably remained with him until the Persian fleet no longer existed, because all the Phoenician fleets had joined Alexander. However, when Alexander reached Tyre after the surrender of Sidon, Arrian wrote that "the Persians still had supremacy over the sea."[166] This means that the Tyrian and Sidonian fleets (except for some Sidonian ships), two major fleets, remained loyal to Darius.

For the first time, Arrian provides some clear information about the war-fleet of Byblos: it was commanded by its king, ʿAynel/Enylos, following Phoenician fleet traditions. The total number of 80 galleys for Arwad, Byblos, and Sidon, if it is correct, gives an idea of the size of the Byblian fleet: if we subtract some Sidonian galleys due to dissidents, and take into consideration that the Aradian fleet was probably complete and larger than that of Byblos, we arrive at a sum of about 30 galleys for Byblos, at the most, but perhaps fewer. Byblos still had a war-fleet in 316/315 B.C.E., when Antigonus seized the Phoenician cities. According to Diodorus, "He instructed the kings (of Phoenicia) to assist him in building ships, since Ptolemy was holding in Egypt all the ships from Phoenicia together with their crews. . . . He established three shipyards in Phoenicia, at Tripoli, Byblos, and Sidon."[167] Did ʿAynel's reign continue into the beginning of the Hellenistic period? It appears that Alexander had no reason to dethrone him because Byblos had not resisted and had made an agreement with him, and because, afterward, ʿAynel surrendered immediately. The inscription *ʿY* on some Alexander tetradrachms minted in Byblos is probably an abbreviation for the name ʿAynel, which is spelled *ʿY[Nʾ L]*.[168] We cannot exclude

165. The other accounts of Diodorus, Justin, and Plutarch on this episode contain some confusing statements: cf. I. L. Merker, "Notes on Abdalonymos and the Dated Alexander Coinage of Sidon and Ake," *ANSMN* 11 (1964) 13–20; Elayi, *Recherches sur les cités phéniciennes*, 50–51.

166. Arrian, *Anab.* II, 18.2. For a more detailed analysis, cf. Elayi-Elayi, *Coinage of Tyre*, 384–88.

167. Diod. XIX, 58.1–4; cf. J. P. Brown, *The Lebanon and Phoenicia* (Beirut, 1969) 1:206–7.

168. Cf. E. T. Newell, *Alexander Hoards II: Demanhur 1905* (New York, 1923) 122–25, no. 3586; A. R. Bellinger, *Essays on the Coinage of Alexander the Great* (New York, 1963) 53; M. J. Price, *The Coinage in the Name of Alexander the Great and Philip Arrhidaeus* (Zurich,

the possibility that ʿAynel was still on the throne in 316/315, when Antigonus seized Byblos;[169] if so, he would have reigned more than 35 years, as did King Baʿalšillem II of Sidon, for example.[170] However, the civic coinage of Byblos had already been interrupted in 333 B.C.E. with the surrender of Byblos.

1991) 430–31, no. 3421; cf. Elayi, "An Updated Chronology of the Reigns of Phoenician Kings," 28.

169. Cf. J. D. Grainger, *Hellenistic Phoenicia* (Oxford, 1991) 58.

170. Cf. Elayi-Elayi, *Monnayage de Sidon*, 635–50.

Conclusion

When he excavated Byblos in 1860, E. Renan noted the large-scale plundering of the site that had already taken place: "The buildings of Beirut and Amschit have absorbed these remains. Byblos has been the vast quarry from which were extracted these precious marbles, these half-destroyed or roughly imbedded sculptures, these stones under the polishing of which it is still often possible to read an almost erased inscription."[1] He also criticized the illicit excavations that were initiated by "the absurd idea of hidden hoards." These illicit excavations never stopped and even increased, especially during the Lebanese civil war, which came after 1976, when several silver monetary hoards were discovered.[2] Byblos was excavated for a long time after E. Renan: by P. Montet from 1921 to 1924, primarily by M. Dunand from 1926 to 1965, then by J. Lauffray in 1940, and after 1970 by several underwater prospectors.[3] Publishing the Byblos excavations poses difficulties: most of the excavations have not been published, and it is difficult to publish them. Furthermore, M. Dunand's excavations are not easy to interpret, because of his method of making horizontal sections of 20 cm, which he adhered to even after the stratigraphic method came to be widely used.[4] New archaeological excavations and regional surveys in Byblos and its territory would be helpful. But, in the meantime, this book is particularly important because significant historical conclusions have been reached regarding the Persian period, based on the Byblian monetary corpus and all the other available data: Phoenician and other inscriptions, Hebrew, Greek, and Latin texts, and archaeological finds.

A chronological catalog of 1,662 coins has been created (appendix 1) that is classified by series and denominations, with descriptions and references, facsimiles of inscriptions, and photographs of the various coins. This catalog can be used equally well by scholars in search of accurate

1. E. Renan, *Mission de Phénicie* (Paris, 1864) 155.

2. N. Jidejian, *Byblos through the Ages* (Beirut, 1971) 4; Elayi-Elayi, *Trésors*, 14–16.

3. Elayi, *Byblos*, 27–29 (with bibliography).

4. P. Leriche, "La méthode de fouille de Maurice Dunand à Byblos, I: M. Dunand et l'archéologie au Proche-Orient au début du XXe siècle," *Topoi* 5 (1995) 439–52; J. Lauffray, "La méthode de fouille de Maurice Dunand à Byblos, II: Introduction à la méthode M. Dunand," ibid., 453–68.

information and by numismatists or collectors simply wishing to identify coins. It is completed by a study of the dies and classification of the coins, providing a relative chronology (appendix 3).

The monetary inscriptions complement the corpus of Byblian inscriptions, which is scanty for the Persian period. The paleographical study was more fruitful than for other inscriptions because it was based on many duplications of the letters by the same engravers or by different engravers: it was thus possible to assess the constraints on and the degree of liberty taken by each engraver, as well as the evolution of writing. We were also able to compare this evolution in Byblos with that in other Phoenician cities. We have also analyzed the techniques and tools used for engraving. Lastly, we have examined the sociocultural aspects of the monetary script of Byblos, especially the degree of alphabetizing development in Byblian society.

The Byblian monetary iconography is rich and furnishes several kinds of information. First, it provides a great deal of technical and realistic information, for example, on war-galleys, the equipment and weapons of warriors, species of animals (lions, vultures, rams, bulls, hawks, and shells), and vegetation (lotus flowers, olive twigs). It also provides information on religion: the religious protection of the city is symbolized by protective animals, real and mythic (sphinxes, seahorses, griffins). The other idea, which is connected with the preceding, was the city's sovereignty and power, expressed through the sphinx, the crook and flail on the hawk's shoulder, and the military symbols of galleys, warriors, and helmets.

The physical details of the Byblian coins inform us about the manufacturing techniques and processes. We have obtained rather precise insights into the coin-producing workshop of Byblos, which was controlled by the minting authority but probably functioned in an informal fashion. The Byblian workshop used molds with circular alveoli to produce circular flans, similar to the Tyrian and Sidonian workshops, but in Byblos it began doing this earlier: around 450 B.C.E. instead of 365 in Sidon and around 357 in Tyre. The technique of irregular flans continued simultaneously. The Byblian workshop was therefore innovative in this respect. It also used the semi-incusion technique in a unique way—different from the Tyrian and Sidonian workshops. Unlike them, it neither minted bronze coins nor year-dated coins. It preferred to write complete inscriptions rather than abbreviations; it did not adopt the Sidonian orientation of die axes at 12 h. Just like the Sidonian and Tyrian workshops, the Byblian workshop worked economically (using coins with defects, reusing coins from previous series, numerous off-centered coins), but it took these measures only during some periods and on a smaller scale. We have also tried to evaluate the volume of Byblian coins issued and show how production evolved. The problem of forged coins and intentional alterations was quite minor compared with Tyrian and Sidonian coinages.

Our metrological analysis is based on the statistical method that we developed and presented extensively in our Tyrian corpus. The first shekel standard used in Byblian coinage until the third quarter of the 5th century was 9.42 g of silver (modified standard). Afterward, Byblos used the Phoenician standard of 13.66 g in the coinage of the anonymous king, then 14.21 g under King ʾElpaʿal. Kings ʿOzbaʿal, ʾUrimilk, and ʿAynel used the same standard, and used 13.18, 13.18, and 13.12 g, respectively, for the modified standard. The silver percentage decreased slightly for the first time, from 98.6% (Group I) to 96.1% (Group II), then a second time, from 99–98% (Group III) to 91.6% (Group IV.1). It went back to the initial percentage of silver in Byblian coins from ʿOzbaʿal's coinage on (Groups IV.2, IV.3, IV.4). This analysis complements our knowledge of the metrology of Phoenician coinages and brings more coherence to this field. It confirms the common features and enlightens us regarding the distinctions for each city.

Combined with information from all the other available sources, this numismatic analysis has led to significant historical conclusions. Although it was the smallest Phoenician city, Byblos was the first to open its monetary workshop, around the end of the second quarter of the 5th century. Among the possible reasons for this initiative are the facts that Byblos was a peaceful and wealthy city, it had not suffered repeated naval defeats in Persian service, and it did not have to face substantial war expenses because it had no war fleet and no military power. Perhaps it had appraised the usefulness of Greek coins in commercial exchanges (if we presuppose that one of the functions of coins at that time was commercial). Group I of the Byblian coinage, with a shekel and five or six fractional denominations, was a flexible system that facilitated a commercial function, but it was restricted by the very limited number of coins per issue.

Group II appears to have been a transitory group between the two well-structured Groups I and III. It had retained only a few elements from Group I: the sphinx on the obverse, the first Byblian standard, and the small volume of production. However, it had no shekels and only three denominations, and the coins were less carefully made. It seems to have corresponded to a period with some unknown difficulties for the Byblian coinage. We have tentatively proposed assigning Group II to the beginning of the third quarter of the 5th century. Since Byblian coinage is not dated, unlike that of Sidon and Tyre, it is impossible to establish an absolute chronology; however, by combining several benchmarks, we are able to propose an approximate chronology.

Group III can be dated to the period stretching from the end of the third to the beginning of the last quarter of the 5th century. This anepigraphic group, minted by the so-called anonymous king, is important. It followed a new standard, Phoenician (13.66 g); it had four different denominations and new types: a war-galley with warriors and a seahorse on the obverse, a vulture and a ram on the reverse. It reflected an important event that occurred in Byblos at that time: the building of a war-fleet. The militarization of Byblos was a major political change for the city that ended a lengthy period of neutrality and marginalization. Among the negative consequences were the facts that it was obliged to put its strength at the disposal of the Persians and to participate in their military campaigns, with all the constraints and expenses that they entailed, especially in the event of defeat. However, at that time, as far as we know, there were no Persian naval battles.

From Group IV.1 on, the coins were inscribed with the name of the king and his royal title. The coinage of ʾElpaʿal is tentatively dated to the end of the 5th century. He may have belonged to the same dynasty because he retained the principal details of the preceding coinage. However, he added an inscription and replaced the vulture and ram on the reverse with a lion and bull. The modified standard was higher (14.21 g instead of 13.66 g), while the silver percentage decreased (91.6% instead of 99–98%), which could reflect some unknown difficulties during a period without any naval battles of which we are aware.

Group IV.2 was minted by King ʿOzbaʿal during the first third of the 4th century. This issue represented another major political event for Byblos known from other sources: the interruption of ʾElpaʿal's dynasty by a usurper, ʿOzbaʿal, son of Palṭibaʿal, the priest; it was a coup conducted by the clergy in order to snatch power from the legitimate dynasty. ʿOzbaʿal continued with the same iconography as ʾElpaʿal but reduced the number of denominations (to shekels and 16th-shekels). He reestablished a high percentage of silver (99%) and, at the same time, decreased the weight (13.18 g instead of 14.21 g). The volume of production of his coinage was much greater than ʾElpaʿal's (504 instead of 87 coins). During his apparently lengthy reign, we can infer logically that ʿOzbaʿal was obliged to participate in the various Persian campaigns as the other Phoenician cities did because, like them, he was militarily strong. The political context was much more troubled than in the preceding period, and Byblos was probably confronted with heavy war expenses because it was in Persian service.

Group IV.3 was minted by King ʾUrimilk shortly before 350 B.C.E. Judging from the relatively small number of coins preserved, his reign was probably much shorter. Belonging to the same illegitimate dynasty as ʿOzbaʿal, he did not introduce any change in the coinage of his predecessor, except his name. During this period, the situation in the western part of the Persian Empire was always troubled. From 355 until 333 B.C.E., Artaxerxes III appointed Mazday/Mazaios to control Transeuphratene, primarily the rebellious Sidon, but probably all the other Phoenician cities as well.

Group IV.4 was minted by King ʿAynel around 350–333 B.C.E. If we can judge from the abundant number of coins preserved (658 compared with 114 by ʾUrimilk), his reign was much longer. In the first part of his reign, he did not introduce any change to the coinage of his predecessor, except his name. He reused many obverse dies of ʾUrimilk because these dies were not yet worn, and he wanted to save money during a difficult period. The progressive and significant degradation of ʿAynel's coinage was probably connected to Byblos's difficulties during this especially troubled time on the regional level, because the city was obligated to participate in the military operations, probably inside the city as well. Indeed, some final series no longer bore the royal title of the king, or even his name, but just the name of the city. No doubt, an important political change had occurred in Byblos: decrease of royal power in favor of the city's representative body (or bodies). In the absence of its king, Byblos concluded a war agreement with Alexander and handed the city over to him; ʿAynel, when he heard about this, left the Persian fleet and joined Alexander.

Thus, this book has completed our knowledge of the history of Byblos during the 5th and 4th centuries and of the Persian policy toward Byblos. These new conclusions now need to be integrated into the history of the Persian Empire, in the same way as our previous conclusions on Sidon and Tyre, in order to provide a better understanding of the Persians' western policy. They also provide an almost comprehensive view of the history of Phoenician cities during this period, which will be complete when we publish our corpus of Aradian coinage.

In spite of several common features, each of the four principal Phoenician cities—Byblos, Tyre, Sidon, and Arwad—had its own distinctions and unique evolutions. Sidon became the first Phoenician city at the beginning of the Persian period, while its neighbor and rival Tyre, weakened by Babylonian domination, was only second in order of importance. However, Sidon lost its hegemony in 355 B.C.E., at the end of King ʿAbdʿaštart I's reign, while Tyre again became the leading city, under King ʿOzmilk's reign (ca. 349–333/2 B.C.E.). Arwad, the northern Phoenician city, was less powerful and was primarily linked with the Syrian area. In the midst of all this, the city of Byblos was completely apart from the other three main

Phoenician cities. After having been a powerful city during the 3rd and 2nd millennia B.C.E. under the protection of Egypt, during the first half of the 1st millennium it was a small, weak, quiet city. It no longer carried any military weight in the Near East but only moral influence because it was a holy city. Byblos became a military power again ca. 445–435 B.C.E., when it decided to have its own fleet and army. However, it was still a holy city, exerting a strong religious influence when ʿOzbaʿal, son of a priest, seized power in ca. 400 and founded a new dynasty, remaining on the throne until 333 B.C.E.

Appendix 1

Catalog of the Coins of Byblos

The catalog of a coin corpus must adhere to special rules, and we have therefore consulted other good catalogs in the parallel field of archaic Classical Greek coinages.[1] Those catalogs do provide precious information on the procedure to be followed, but every coinage is also unique and does not fit into a preestablished mold. In our opinion, a catalog must take into account all the special aspects of the coinage being studied. In this corpus (as in our previous publications on the Sidonian and Byblian coinages),[2] we have decided to include all the Byblian pre-Alexandrine coinage, both the large denominations and the small, including the minute coins (there were no Byblian bronze or gold coins in the Persian period). An analysis of the dies used to impress the coins was carried out, not only for large denominations but as far as possible for all sorts of small denominations. We have identified the dies only on relatively well-preserved coins or when they could be spotted by a defect or a characteristic detail. Despite these precautions, there is still an element of subjectivity in any study of dies. In the catalog, we have taken into consideration all the coins brought to our attention, whether our information is complete or not, whether the coins are illustrated or not, and whether the state of their preservation is good or poor. Far from being merely an attractive catalog of the well-preserved large denominations, our catalog includes all the coins, even the minute and poorly preserved coins. However, the coins that seemed to us to be counterfeit or doubtful have been excluded, but some of them have been presented in appendix 2.

Our aim was to present a catalog of the Byblian coinage that is as complete and as clear as possible for the reader. Therefore, we have not classified

1. For example G. Le Rider, *Antioche de Syrie sous les Séleucides: Corpus des monnaies d'or et d'argent*, vol. 1: *De Séleucos I à Antiochos V c. 300–161* (Paris, 1999); idem, *Le monnayage d'argent et d'or de Philippe II* (Paris, 1977); R. T. Williams, *The Silver Coinage of Velia* (London, 1992); U. Westermark and K. Jenkins, *The Coinage of Gela* (Berlin, 1970).

2. Elayi-Elayi, *Monnayage de Sidon*; idem, *Coinage of Tyre*. We consider it useful to provide directions for usage again in this catalog, even though directions have already been provided in our previous corpora.

the coins according to large and small denominations.[3] We have tried to classify the coins based on a relative chronology established from the die links, the overstrikings, the evolution of the defects on the dies, and any other source of information. In order to facilitate the use of this corpus, we indicate our classification proposals according to the absolute chronology that we justify in chap. 5. The catalog is presented first by groups, in chronological order—for example: "Group I: Crouched sphinx (end of the second quarter of the 5th century)"; then by decreasing denominations—for example: "I.1. Shekels AR," "I.2. Third-shekels AR," and "I.3. Sixth-shekels AR." The denominations are designated in a conventional and approximate way—for example: "I.5. F.O.T.1 AR." But refer to chap. 4 for all the necessary metrological details.

Each catalog number represents a coin: this method of numbering by coin instead of the frequently used method of numbering by die pair[4] seemed to us to be easier to refer to in the text and to list the coins for which a die analysis was impossible. The coin number is followed by the die-pair (for example, "O2–R4"), then by the weight, diameter, and die axis, when they are known. Regarding the die analysis, each series has its own numbering for the obverse and reverse dies.[5] The recut dies have not been given a new number but bear a siglum such as ′or ″ (e.g., R5, R5′, and R5″). However, it is difficult to identify recuttings due to the poor state of preservation of the coins in general. Weights can be slightly different depending on the available source of information.[6] As far as the coins from the BNF, Cabinet des Médailles of Paris, are concerned, the weights indicated in the catalog are those that we have checked personally. For the coins published in several sale catalogs, we have selected the most recent weight, reasoning that in principle weighing should become more precise because of improvements in the scales. We have presented only two digits after the decimal point, rounding up to the nearest number; the few items that still appear in grains have been converted to grams. The diameter mentioned in the catalog is the maximum diameter indicated in the publications or that we have measured ourselves directly—either the coins

3. See the remarks of L. Mildenberg, *The Coinage of the Bar Kokhba War* (Aarau, 1984) 59 n. 134 and 119 n. 314 (with bibliography).

4. Cf., for example, Le Rider, who used the two processes for two different coinages: *Le monnayage d'argent* and *De Séleucos I à Antiochos V*.

5. Die links are proposed in some publications: we have kept only those that seemed to be correct.

6. In a corpus, it is impossible to examine many of the coins, and there is no other way to proceed than by accepting the weights provided and trusting that the coins have been weighed with precision.

themselves or the casts). These indications of the die pair, weight, diameter, and die axis are followed by a description of the new obverse and reverse dies, with their possible defects, traces of overstriking, alterations, and possible technical details.

After these items, various details are presented regarding bibliographical sources, the present location of the coin, and the provenance of the coin. The location of a coin in a public collection is presented first by town, then by institution, inventory number or catalog reference number, and the present and/or previous collection to which the coin belongs/belonged; for example: "Paris, BNF, no. 3140 (ex De Luynes coll.)." A list of public and private collections is presented in the indexes (pp. 350–351).[7] The name of the collector is mentioned if permission has been granted; otherwise, the collector remains anonymous; the location of the collection is indicated wherever possible. Sometimes we mention only the "antiquities market" with the name of the country or town and the date of examination of the coin, if possible. The bibliographical references to the catalogs of collections or to the main studies are abbreviated in order to save space, and a list of abbreviations is provided in the front matter of the book. The sale catalogs are mentioned as succinctly as possible, with the name of the expert or the company where the sale took place, the number and date of the sale, and the number of the coin in the sale catalog; for example: "Berk, Chicago, 127, 25/6/2002, no. 235."[8] A list of the sale catalogs is provided in the indexes (pp. 352–357). We do not consider it useful to distinguish among the various sorts of sales (lists, catalogs, auctions, bid sales, etc.), because the number and date of a sale are enough to identify it. When a coin has been sold several times, we mention its last-known sale first, then the successive sales in reverse chronological order. Likewise, the successive transfers of coins to various collections have been mentioned. When we have seen a coin in the stock of a company, we mention the name of the company and the location, together with the date of our visit. The site of discovery is also indicated for excavation coins, and the place where the hoard was purchased when the coins were part of a hoard, for example: "Byblos excavations," "bought in Beirut," or "Byblos hoard TX," following the number of our corpus for Phoenician hoards.[9] A list of hoards containing Byblian coins appears in appendix 4.

7. We have not considered it useful to distinguish between ancient and present collections.

8. Note that dates are presented in the traditional European order of day/month/year rather than the traditional American order of month/day/year.—ed.

9. Elayi-Elayi, *Trésors*.

The order of the die pairs depends on the sequences determined by the internal chronology of the coin issues when the chronology is detectable. When it is not, the die pairs have been presented by groups, from largest to smallest. The unidentified obverse and/or reverse dies of a coin are classified at the end of the series. Group V (unclassified series) encompasses all the series that could not be classified chronologically in the present state of the documentation.

Concerning the illustrations of the coins, an asterisk placed after an obverse or reverse die (e.g., O1*–R1*) means that the die is illustrated in the plates. We have tried to illustrate, as far as possible, all the obverse and reverse dies in each different series by selecting the best illustrations. However, their quality is unequal because of their various origins: photographs of the coins, casts, and sale catalogs were often of poor quality. Since most of the photographs were taken or obtained more than 20 years ago, they have not benefited from current photographic technology. When the scale or diameter was not indicated in sale catalogs, we have been obliged to select a supposed, approximate scale. Some coins, especially the small denominations, have been illustrated by an enlarged photograph and an indication of the enlargement in cm (for example, "×3"). As we have said, our aim in this corpus is not to select only the large, beautiful coins but to take into account all the coins of Byblos. Thus, in our opinion, the scientific advantages greatly outweigh the esthetic disadvantages.

1. *Group I: Crouched Sphinx (End of the Second Quarter of the 5th Century)*

I.1. Shekels AR

1 O1*–R1*
9.61 g 19 mm
O: crouched sphinx to left, wearing the double crown of Egypt.
R: double lotus flower; border of dots; in incuse square.
Paris, BNF, no. HS 1973-1-274.

2 O2*–R1
9.52 g 20 mm
Same as 1.
New York, ANS, no. 1977.158, 753; Monnaies et Médailles, Basel, 19, 5–6/6/1959, no. 552 (found at Arwad, ca. 1950).

3 O3–R1
9.40 g 19 mm
Same as 1.
Leu, Zurich, 36, 1986, no. 186; N. Jidejian, *Lebanon and the Greek World* (Beirut, 1988) 127.

4 O3*–R2*
9.40 g 19 mm
Same as 1.
London, BM, no. 1957-12-4.1; G. K. Jenkins, "Recent Acquisitions of Greek Coins by B. M. 1939–1959," *NC* 19 (1959) 41, no. 21 and pl. 6:21; Kraay, *Greek Coins*, no. 1051; Elayi-Elayi, *Trésors*, p. 115, no. 1 and pl. 18 (North Syria hoard TXVII).

5 O4–R3 9.45 g 21 mm 12 h	Same as 1. Oval flan. *Greek Coins, Museum of Fine Arts,* Boston, 1969, no. 299.
6 O5*–R4* 9.31 g 22 mm	Same as 1. Irregular flan. New York, ANS, no. 1953.117.1; Elayi-Elayi, *Trésors*, p. 115, no. 2 and pl. 18 (North Syria hoard TXVII); Betlyon, *Coinage of Phoenicia*, pl. 8:1.
7 O?–R?	Same as 1. Rather worn and corroded. O: off-center to right. Classical Numismatic Group, Lancaster-London, 23/5/2007, no. 478.
8 O?–R? 8.80 g 12 h	Same as 1. Rather worn. E. T. Newell, *Some Unpublished Coins of Eastern Dynasts* (New York, 1926) no. 4.
9 O?–R? 8.12 g 19 mm	Same as 1. Rather worn. Private coll. LPN; Baldwin, London, 34, 13/10/2003, no. 509.
10 O ?–R ?	Same as 1. Jenkins, *NC* 19 (1959) 41; Elayi-Elayi, *Trésors*, p. 115, no. 3 (North Syria hoard TXVII).
11 O ?–R ?	Same as 1. Dunand, *Byblos II*, no. 7114 and fig. 45; Elayi-Elayi, *Trésors*, p. 88, no. 1 (Byblos hoard TX; Byblos excavations).
12–18 O ?–R ?	Same as 1. Dunand, *Byblos II*, no. 7114; Elayi-Elayi, *Trésors*, p. 88, nos. 2–9 (Byblos hoard TX; Byblos excavations).

I.2. 3rd-Shekels AR

19 O1*–R1* 3.01 g 13 mm	Same as 1. Classical Numismatic Group, Lancaster-London, 69, 8/6/2005, no. 606 = 45, 18/3/1998, no. 573.
20 O2*–R2* 2.77 g 12 mm 2 h	Same as 1. Spaer coll., Jerusalem; Poinsignon Numismatique, Strasbourg, 19–20/6/1984, no. 196.
21 O3–R3 2.47 g	Same as 1. O: off-center to left. Münzen und Medaillen, Basel, January 1968, no. 10.
22 O4*–R4* 2.88 g	Same as 1. Ponterio, San Diego, 142, 27–28/4/2007, no. 1663.
23 O?–R5* 2.75 g 11 h	Same as 1. Slightly worn. O: slightly off-center toward the top. E. T. Newell, *Some Unpublished Coins of Eastern Dynasts* (New York, 1926) no. 5.

24	O?–R? 3.28 g 14 mm	Same as 1. Rather worn. Paris, BNF, no. HS 1965-829-1 (ex Seyrig coll.).
25	O?–R? 2.74 g	Same as 1. Rather worn. London, BM, no. 1960-9-7-1; Betlyon, *Coinage of Phoenicia*, p. 112, no. 2, n. 8 and pl. 8:2.
26	O?–R? 2.70 g	Same as 1. Classical Numismatic Group, Lancaster-London, 23/5/2007, no. 479.
27	O?–R? 2.66 g 15 mm	Same as 1. Oval flan. Classical Numismatic Group, Lancaster-London, 46, 24/6/1998, no. 494.

I.3. 6th-Shekels AR

28	O1*–R1* 1.51 g 10 mm	Same as 1. Paris, BNF, no. 1965/829.3 (ex Seyrig coll.).
29	O2*–R2* 1.41 g	Same as 1. Classical Numismatic Group, Lancaster-London, 45, 18/3/1998, no. 574.
30	O3*–R3*	Same as 1. Burgan, Paris, 16/12/1989, no. 304.
31	O?–R4 1.41 g 10 mm	Same as 1. Beirut, AUB Museum, no. 765F.
32	O?–R5 1.38 g 11 mm 11 h	Same as 1. O: slightly off-center to left. Copenhagen, NatMus, no. GP 3004,1.
33	O?–R? 9 mm	Same as 1. Corroded. Paris, BNF, no. HS 5 (ex Seyrig coll.).

I.4. 12th-Shekels AR

34	O1*–R1* 0.57 g 10 mm 10 h	Same as 1. O: slightly off-center toward the bottom. Spaer coll., Jerusalem.
35	O1–R2 0.84 g 8 mm	Same as 1. R: defect on the border of dots. Classical Numismatic Group, Lancaster-London, 1/6/2009, no. 480.
36	O1–R2 0.65 g 8 mm	Same as 1. R: defect on the border of dots. Private coll.

37 O2*–R2*
0.66 g 8 mm
Same as 1.
R: defect on the border of dots.
Paris, BNF, no. 1965/829.4.

38 O3*–R2
0.62 g 10 mm
Same as 1. Oval flan.
R: defect on the border of dots.
Private coll. LPN; Baldwin, London, 34, 13/10/2003, no. 510.

39 O4–R2
0.58 g 8 mm
Same as 1.
R: defect on the border of dots.
Kovacs, San Mateo, 1988.

40 O4*–R3*
0.86 g 9 mm
Same as 1.
Paris, BNF, no. 1965/740 (ex Seyrig coll.).

41 O5*–R4*
0.79 g
Same as 1.
O: dot above the sphinx.
Peus, Frankfurt/Main, 361, 6/11/1999, no. 243.

42 O2–R?
0.61 g
12 h
Same as 1. Rather worn.
E. T. Newell, *Some Unpublished Coins of Eastern Dynasts* (New York, 1926) no. 6.

43 O6*–R?
0.60 g
11 h
Same as 1. Rather worn.
E. T. Newell, *Some Unpublished Coins of Eastern Dynasts* (New York, 1926) no. 7.

44 O?–R4
0.49 g 7 mm
Same as 1. Slightly worn.
Paris, BNF, no. 700 (ex Chandon de Briailles coll.).

45 O?–R5*
0.60 g 9 mm
12 h
Same as 1. Slightly worn.
Tel Aviv, KNM, no. K1885.

46 O?–R6*
0.57 g 8 mm
Same as 1. Slightly worn.
O: off-center toward the top.
Bartlett Well coll., Lexington, no. 4.

47 O?–R7*
0.62 g 8 mm
3 h
Same as 1. Slightly worn.
Copenhagen, NatMus, no. GP 3004,2.

48 O?–R?
0.80 g 8 mm
Same as 1. Rather worn.
Beirut, AUB Museum, no. 765D.

49 O?–R?
0.80 g 8 mm
Same as 1. Rather worn.
Paris, BNF, no. 1987/443 (ex Seyrig coll.).

50 O?–R?
0.78 g 8 mm
Same as 1. Rather worn.
Paris, BNF, no. 1987/444 (ex Seyrig coll.).

51 O?–R?
0.61 g 8 mm
Same as 1. Slightly worn and corroded.
O: off-center to left.
Private coll. LPN; Monnaies et Médailles, Stuttgart, 32, 26/5/2010, no. 428.

52	O?–R? 0.60 g 8 mm	Same as 1. Rather worn. Rouvier, *JIAN* 4 (1901) no. 628 and pl. A′3 (Rouvier coll.).
53	O?–R? 0.60 g	Same as 1. Rather worn. Poinsignon Numismatique, Strasbourg, 19–20/6/1984, no. 196.
54	O?–R? 0.50 g	Same as 1. Oxford, AM, no. 52; Münzen und Medaillen, Basel, 256, November 1965, no. 475.
55	O?–R?	Same as 1. Dunand, *Byblos II*, no. 7115 and fig. 45; Elayi-Elayi, *Trésors*, p. 88, no. 10 (Byblos hoard TX; Byblos excavations).

I.5. F.O.T. 1 AR

56	O1*–R1* 0.30 g 7 mm	Same as 1. Paris, BNF, no. 1965/829.9 (ex Seyrig coll.).
57	O1–R2* 0.38 g 8 mm 2 h	Same as 1. E. T. Newell, *Some Unpublished Coins of Eastern Dynasts* (New York, 1926) no. 8.
58	O2*–R3* 0.38 g	Same as 1. Crack on the edge. Berk, Chicago, 6, 10/1/2010, no. 244 (ex Gerson coll.) = Classical Numismatic Group, Lancaster-London, 37, 20/3/1996, no. 673.
59	O?–R3 0.30 g 6 mm	Same as 1. Slightly worn. Paris, BNF, no. 699 (ex Chandon de Briailles coll.).
60	O?–R4* 0.34 g 12 h	Same as 1. Slightly worn. E. T. Newell, *Some Unpublished Coins of Eastern Dynasts* (New York, 1926) no. 9.
61	O?–R? 0.38 g	Same as 1. Very worn. Paris, BNF, no. 1987/467 (ex Seyrig coll.).
62	O?–R? 0.35 g 6 mm	Same as 1. Rather worn. Beirut, AUB Museum, no. 765Ei.

I.6. F.O.T. 2 AR

63	O ?–R ? 0.22 g 6 mm	Same as 1. Rather worn. Paris, BNF, no. 698 (ex Chandon de Brialles coll.).

I.7. F.O.T. 3 AR

64	O1*–R? 0.10 g 4 mm	Same as 1. Slightly worn. Paris, BNF, no. 1965/829.8 (ex Seyrig coll.).

65	O2*–R? 0.02 g 5 mm	Same as 1. Slightly worn. Partly broken. Spaer coll., Jerusalem (bought in Beirut).
66	O?–R1* 0.12 g	Same as 1. Slightly worn. London, BM, no. 1960-9-7 1.

2. *Group II: Seated Sphinx (Beginning of the Third Quarter of the 5th Century)*

II.1. 3rd-Shekels AR

67	O1*–R1* 3.23 g 14 mm 12 h	O: winged sphinx seated to left, wearing the double crown of Egypt, with one wing visible. Border of dots visible on the right. R: hawk standing to left, wearing the double crown of Egypt, crook, and flail; olive twig on the right; slight incuse impression. Paris, BNF, no. 1965/829–2 (ex Seyrig coll.); Elayi, *RSF* 11 (1983) 5 and pl. 1a–b; Puech, in *ACFP* 2/1 (1991) 288; Lemaire-Elayi, *RBN* 137 (1991) 30 and pl. 1:1.
68	O2*–R2* 3.18 g 12 h	Same as 67. R: head of the hawk off the flan; shallow incuse impression. Oxford, AM, no. 47; Münzen und Medaillen, Basel, 28, 19–20/6/1964, no. 188; Lemaire-Elayi, *RBN* 137 (1991) 30 and pl. 1:2.
69	O?–R? 3.30 g 7 h	Same as 67. Beirut, NM, no. 2697; Elayi-Elayi, *Trans* 38 (2009) 67, no. 26 (Byblos hoard TLXXXIII).
70	O?–R? 3.16 g 3 h	Same as 67. Beirut, NM, no. 2696; Elayi-Elayi, *Trans* 38 (2009) 67, no. 25 (Byblos hoard TLXXXIII).
71	O?–R? 2.95 g	Same as 67. Beirut, NM, no. 2699; Elayi-Elayi, *Trans* 38 (2009) 67, no. 28 (Byblos hoard TLXXXIII).
72	O?–R? 2.37 g 6 h	Same as 67. Beirut, NM, no. 2698; Elayi-Elayi, *Trans* 38 (2009) 67, no. 27 (Byblos hoard TLXXXIII).

II.2. 12th-Shekels AR

II.2.1. Sphinx with One Wing and Anepigraphic

73	O1*–R1* 0.55 g 12 h	Same as 67, with a border of dots on the obverse and a shallow incuse impression on the reverse. Edge broken. Tel Aviv, KNM, no. K1887; Lemaire-Elayi, *RBN* 137 (1991) 31 and pl. 1:4.

74 O1–R2* 0.53 g 9 mm — Same as 73.
Vienna, KHM, no. 17; Lemaire-Elayi, *RBN* 137 (1991) 31 and pl. 1:5.

75 O2*–R3* 0.49 g 4 h — Same as 73.
Leu, Zurich, 54, 28/4/1992, no. 181.

76 O2–R4* 0.49 g 7 mm 6 h — Same as 73.
Private coll. LPN; Baldwin, London, 34, 13/10/2003, no. 511.

77 O3*–R5* 0.58 g 8 mm 6 h — Same as 73.
R: off-center to left.
Paris, BNF, no. HS 1965–753 (ex Seyrig coll.); Lemaire-Elayi, *RBN* 137 (1991) 30 and pl. 1:3.

78 O4*–R6* 0.42 g 9 mm 6 h — Same as 73.
Paris, BNF, no. HS 1987–146 (ex Seyrig coll.); Lemaire-Elayi, *RBN* 137 (1991) 30 and pl. 1:7.

79 O5*–R7* 0.49 g 8 mm 12 h — Same as 73.
R: off-center to right.
London, BM, no. 1985.5-20-5; Lemaire-Elayi, *RBN* 137 (1991) 30 and pl. 1:6; Puech, in *ACFP* 2/1 (1991) 288; Elayi-Elayi, *Trésors*, p. 94, no. 3 and pl. 5:3 (Byblos hoards TXIII, TXIV, TXV?).

80 O6*–R8* 0.66 g 9 h — Same as 73. Flaws on the obverse.
Oxford, AM, no. 48; Münzen und Medaillen, Basel, 256, November 1965, no. 492; Lemaire-Elayi, *RBN* 137 (1991) 36.

81 O7*–R9* 0.69 g 8 mm 5 h — Same as 73. Partly cut flan.
R: head of the hawk partly off the flan; traces of corrosion.
Private coll. LPN; Baldwin, London, 34, 13/10/2003, no. 512.

82 O?–R10* 0.66 g 7 mm — Same as 73. Small cracks on the edge.
O: slightly off-center to left.
R: head of the hawk partly off the flan; traces of corrosion.
Private coll. LPN; Monnaies et Médailles, Stuttgart, 32, 26/5/2010, no. 428.

83 O?–R? 0.48 g 8 mm 11 h — Same as 73. Rather worn. Scratches on the obverse.
Private coll. LPN; Baldwin, London, 34, 13/10/2003, no. 512.

II.2.2. Sphinx with Two Wings and Inscription

84 O1*–R1* 0.55 g 8 mm — O: winged sphinx seated to left, wearing the double crown of Egypt, with two wings visible; double border of dots.
R: hawk standing to left, wearing the double crown of Egypt, crook and flail; lotus flower and letters *MY/Z* on the left; ʿ]*GK* on the right; incuse impression.
Private coll.; Lemaire-Elayi, *RBN* 137 (1991) 31 and pl. 1:8.

85 O1–R2*
0.58 g 9 mm
3 h
Same as 84.
O: off-center to right.
R: off-center to left; inscription off the flan on the left and obliterated on the right.
Spaer coll., Jerusalem: Lemaire-Elayi, *RB*N 137 (1991) 31 and pl. 1:10 (bought in Beirut).

86 O2*–R3*
0.54 g
6 h
Same as 84. Slightly worn. Crack on the edge.
R: *ʿGK* on the left and inscription on the right obliterated.
New York, ANS, no. 1968.57.142; Betlyon, *Coinage of Phoenicia*, pl. 8:7; Lemaire-Elayi, *RBN* 137 (1991) 32 and pl. 1:13.

87 O2–R4
0.55 g 7 mm
7 h
Same as 84. Slightly worn.
R: *ʿG[K* on the left and *M*[on the right.
Paris, BNF, no. HS 1965-829-7 (ex Seyrig coll.); Lemaire-Elayi, *RBN* 137 (1991) 32 and pl. 1:12.

88 O3*–R4*
0.57 g 9 mm
9 h
Same as 84.
O: off-center to right.
R: *ʿGK* on the left and traces of *M*[*?* and *B ?* on the right.
Paris, BNF, no. HS 1965-829-5 (ex Seyrig coll.); Lemaire-Elayi, *RBN* 137 (1991) 32 and pl. 1:11.

89 O4*–R?
0.71 g 8 mm
5 h
Same as 84. Rather worn.
O: one border of dots visible.
R: ʿ]*GK* on the left and *M*[*?* on the right.
Paris, BNF, no. HS 1965-829-6 (ex Seyrig coll.); Lemaire-Elayi, *RBN* 137 (1991) 31 and pl. 1:9.

90 O?–R?
0.49 g 8 mm
8 h
Same as 84. Rather worn.
O : one border of dots visible.
R : off-center to left; traces of letters on the right.
Private coll. LPN; Monnaies et Médailles, Stuttgart, 32, 26/5/2010, no. 428.

91 O?–R?
0.72 g
Same as 73 or 84.
O : sphinx with one or two wings.
Beirut, NM, no. 2701; Elayi-Elayi, *Trans* 38 (2009) 67, no. 30, not illustrated (Byblos hoard TLXXXIII).

92 O?–R?
0.68 g
6 h
Same as 73 or 84.
O : sphinx with one or two wings.
Beirut, NM, no. 2700; Elayi-Elayi, *Trans* 38 (2009) 67, no. 29, not illustrated (Byblos hoard TLXXXIII).

93 O?–R?
0.63 g
6 h
Same as 73 or 84.
O : sphinx with one or two wings.
Beirut, NM, no. 2702; Elayi-Elayi, *Trans* 38 (2009) 68, no. 31, not illustrated (Byblos hoard TLXXXIII).

II.3. Sphinx with One Wing and Helmet

94	O1*–R1* 0.25 g 7 mm 9 h	O: winged sphinx seated to left, wearing the double crown of Egypt, with one wing visible; border of dots. R: helmet to left; in incuse square. BNF, Paris, no. HS 1965-829-11 (ex Seyrig coll.).
95	O2*–R2* 0.36 g 6 mm 2 h	Same as 94. O: border of dots not visible. BNF, Paris, no. HS 1965-829-10 (ex Seyrig coll.).
96	O3*–R3* 0.13 g 6 mm 5 h	Same as 94. Cracks on the edge. O: off-center to left. Private coll.
97	O4*–R? 0.20 g 6 mm 5 h	Same as 94. Slightly worn. O: off-center toward the top. Private coll.
98	O?–R4* 0.18 g 6 mm 1 h	Same as 94. Slightly worn. O: very off-center to left. Private coll.
99	O?–R? 0.13 g	Same as 94. Baldwin, London, 34, 13/10/2003, no. 513, not illustrated.

II.4. Sphinx with One Wing and Griffin's Head

100	O?–R? 0.28 g	O: winged sphinx seated to left, wearing the double crown of Egypt, with one wing visible; border of dots? Rather worn. R: griffin's head. Rather worn. BNF, Paris, no. 1987/445 (ex Seyrig coll.).

3. Group III: Galley, Vulture, and Ram (End of the 3rd–Beginning of the Last Quarter of the 5th Century)

III.1. Shekels AR

101	O1–R1 13.68 g	O: war-galley to left; prow terminating in head of a horse; inside, three warriors with shields, facing left; below, winged seahorse to left; border of dots. Defect on the warriors. Small cracks on the edge. Small holes. R: vulture, with one wing outstretched, to left, standing over an incuse ram with head looking back to right; border of dots; whole in incuse depression. Numismatica Ars Classica, Zurich, 8, 3/4/1995, no. 289.

102	O1*–R1* 13.67 g	Same as 101. O: defect on the warriors. Peus, Frankfurt/Main, 361, 6/11/1999, no. 244.
103	O1–R2* 13.94 g 30 mm 11 h	Same as 101. Oval flan. O: defect on the warriors. Paris, BNF, no. HS 1973-1-269 (ex Seyrig coll.).
104	O1–R3* 13.22 g 8 h	Same as 101. Some cracks on the edge. O: defect on the warriors. Private coll.
105	O2*–R3 13.55 g 24 mm 7 h	Same as 101. Vienna, KHM, no. 22.128.
106	O3–R3 13.90 g 27 mm	Same as 101. Beirut, NM; Chéhab, *Monnaies*, no. 821 and pl. 33:1.
107	O3*–R3 13.58 g	Same as 101. Oval flan. Hirsch, Munich, 212, 22–24/11/2000, no. 413.
108	O4–R3 13.86 g	Same as 101. Small cracks on the edge. Classical Numismatic Group, Lancaster-London, 53, 15/3/2000, no. 652.
109	O4–R3 13.03 g 25 mm 8 h	Same as 101. Small cracks on the edge. BNF, Paris, no. 1988/113 = Vinchon, Paris, 13–15/11/1986, no. 251 (ex Trampitsch coll.).
110	O4*–R3 12.89 g 24 mm 6 h	Same as 101. Small cracks on the edge. BNF, Paris, no. HS 1973-1-433 (ex Seyrig coll.)
111	O4–R4* 10.08 g	Same as 101. Partly broken. London, BM, no. 1972-6-29 1; Kraay, *Greek Coins*, no. 1052.
112	O4–R5* 13.83 g	Same as 101. Irregular flan. Freeman & Sear, New York, Triton III, 3/11–1/12/1999, no. 619 = Numismatica Ars Classica, New York, Triton II, 1–2/12/1998, no. 486.
113	O4–R6* 12.67 g 24 mm 6 h	Same as 101. BNF, Paris, no. HS 1973-1-434 (ex Seyrig coll.).
114	O5*–R5 13.89 g 28 mm 3 h	Same as 101. R: defect on the right. Athens, NomM, no. 6255a (ex De Démétrio coll.); Rouvier, *JIAN* 4 (1901) no. 630.
115	O6*–R7* 13.22 g 27 mm	Same as 101. Beirut, AUB, no. 765A.

116	O7*–R8* 13.64 g	Same as 101. Berk, Chicago, 136, 5/2/2004, no. 83 = Kovacs, San Rafael, 15, 1/10/2003, no. 146 = Berk, Chicago, 108, 12/5/1999, no. 151 = 105, 17/11/1998, no. 269.
117	O1–R? 11.52 g 26 mm 8 h	Same as 101. Slightly worn. Private coll. LPN; Baldwin, London, 34, 13/10/2003, no. 514.
118	O?–R? 14.26 g 1 h	Same as 101. Beirut, NM, no. 2693; Elayi-Elayi, *Trans* 38 (2009) 67, no. 22, not illustrated (Byblos hoard TLXXXIII).
119	O?–R? 13.93 g 10 h	Same as 101. Beirut, NM, no. 2674; Elayi-Elayi, *Trans* 38 (2009) 66, no. 3, not illustrated (Byblos hoard TLXXXIII).
120	O?–R? 13.76 g 2 h	Same as 101. Beirut, NM, no. 2677; Elayi-Elayi, *Trans* 38 (2009) 67, no. 6, not illustrated (Byblos hoard TLXXXIII).
121	O?–R? 13.69 g 5 h	Same as 101. Beirut, NM, no. 2683; Elayi-Elayi, *Trans* 38 (2009) 67, no. 12, not illustrated (Byblos hoard TLXXXIII).
122	O?–R? 13.66 g 4 h	Same as 101. Beirut, NM, no. 2678; Elayi-Elayi, *Trans* 38 (2009) 67, no. 7, not illustrated (Byblos hoard TLXXXIII).
123	O?–R? 13.65 g 11 h	Same as 101. Beirut, NM, no. 2685; Elayi-Elayi, *Trans* 38 (2009) 67, no. 14, not illustrated (Byblos hoard TLXXXIII).
124	O?–R? 13.63 g 11 h	Same as 101. Beirut, NM, no. 2694; Elayi-Elayi, *Trans* 38 (2009) 67, no. 23, not illustrated (Byblos hoard TLXXXIII).
125	O?–R? 13.54 g 11 h	Same as 101. Beirut, NM, no. 2690; Elayi-Elayi, *Trans* 38 (2009) 67, no. 19, not illustrated (Byblos hoard TLXXXIII).
126	O?–R? 13.47 g 1 h	Same as 101. Beirut, NM, no. 2695; Elayi-Elayi, *Trans* 38 (2009) 67, no. 24, not illustrated (Byblos hoard TLXXXIII).
127	O?–R? 13.46 g 11 h	Same as 101. Beirut, NM, no. 2672; Elayi-Elayi, *Trans* 38 (2009) 66, no. 1, not illustrated (Byblos hoard TLXXXIII).
128	O?–R? 13.36 g 6 h	Same as 101. Beirut, NM, no. 2691; Elayi-Elayi, *Trans* 38 (2009) 67, no. 20, not illustrated (Byblos hoard TLXXXIII).
129	O?–R? 13.34 g 7 h	Same as 101. Beirut, NM, no. 2684; Elayi-Elayi, *Trans* 38 (2009) 67, no. 13, not illustrated (Byblos hoard TLXXXIII).

130 O?–R?
13.32 g
11 h
Same as 101.
Beirut, NM, no. 2681; Elayi-Elayi, *Trans* 38 (2009) 67, no. 10, not illustrated (Byblos hoard TLXXXIII).

131 O?–R?
13.30 g
Same as 101.
R: almost obliterated.
Beirut, NM, no. 2687; Elayi-Elayi, *Trans* 38 (2009) 67, no. 16, not illustrated (Byblos hoard TLXXXIII).

132 O?–R?
13.29 g
7 h
Same as 101.
Beirut, NM, no. 2689; Elayi-Elayi, *Trans* 38 (2009) 67, no. 18, not illustrated (Byblos hoard TLXXXIII).

133 O?–R?
13.05 g
7 h
Same as 101.
Beirut, NM, no. 2686; Elayi-Elayi, *Trans* 38 (2009) 67, no. 15, not illustrated (Byblos hoard TLXXXIII).

134 O?–R?
12.82 g
5 h
Same as 101.
Beirut, NM, no. 2679; Elayi-Elayi, *Trans* 38 (2009) 67, no. 8, not illustrated (Byblos hoard TLXXXIII).

135 O?–R?
12.46 g
7 h
Same as 101.
Beirut, NM, no. 2692; Elayi-Elayi, *Trans* 38 (2009) 67, no. 21, not illustrated (Byblos hoard TLXXXIII).

136 O?–R?
12.40 g
12 h
Same as 101.
Beirut, NM, no. 2688; Elayi-Elayi, *Trans* 38 (2009) 67, no. 17, not illustrated (Byblos hoard TLXXXIII).

137 O?–R?
12.21 g
Same as 101.
R: almost obliterated.
Beirut, NM, no. 2675; Elayi-Elayi, *Trans* 38 (2009) 67, no. 4, not illustrated (Byblos hoard TLXXXIII).

138 O?–R?
11 g
9 h
Same as 101.
Beirut, NM, no. 2680; Elayi-Elayi, *Trans* 38 (2009) 67, no. 9, not illustrated (Byblos hoard TLXXXIII).

139 O?–R?
10.93 g
9 h
Same as 101.
Beirut, NM, no. 2673; Elayi-Elayi, *Trans* 38 (2009) 66, no. 2, not illustrated (Byblos hoard TLXXXIII).

140 O?–R?
10.01 g
12 h
Same as 101.
Beirut, NM, no. 2676; Elayi-Elayi, *Trans* 38 (2009) 67, no. 5, not illustrated (Byblos hoard TLXXXIII).

141 O?–R?
9.82 g
8 h
Same as 101.
Beirut, NM, no. 2682; Elayi-Elayi, *Trans* 38 (2009) 67, no. 11, not illustrated (Byblos hoard TLXXXIII).

III.2. Quarter-Shekels AR

142 O1*–R1*
3.45 g
9 h
Same as 101, but vulture with closed wings.
O: defect between the head and wing of the seahorse.
Berlin, SM, no. 322/1872.

143	O1–R1 3.17 g 16 mm 11 h	Same as 143. O: defect between the head and wing of the seahorse. Paris, BNF, no. 61 (ex De Vogüé coll.).
144	O1–R2* 3.45 g	Same as 143. O: slightly off-center toward the top. Defect between the head and wing of the seahorse R: off-center to left. London, BM, no. 1906-7-12 40.
145	O1–R3* 3.28 g 16 mm 3 h	Same as 143. O: defect between the head and wing of the seahorse. Paris, BNF, no. 62 (ex De Vogüé coll.).
146	O1–R4 2.92 g 2 h	Same as 143. Several cracks on the edge. O: defect between the head and wing of the seahorse. R: dot between vulture and ram. Spaer coll., Jerusalem.
147	O2*–R4* 3.40 g 5 h	Same as 143. Small cracks on the edge. R: dot between vulture and ram. *SNG Cambridge*, no. 6027; Hess, Lucerne, 14/4/1954, no. 187 = Serrure, Paris, 27/3/1897, no. 36 (ex Duruflé coll.).
148	O2–R4 3.29 g 16 mm 11 h	Same as 143. R: dot between vulture and ram. Naster, *Collection De Hirsch*, no. 1731.
149	O2–R4 2.85 g	Same as 143. O: off-center to left. R: off-center to right. Rouvier, *JIAN* 4 (1901) no. 631 and pl. A′5 (Rouvier coll.), found in the Byblos harbor.
150	O3*–R5* 3.08 g	Same as 143. Flan slightly irregular. Paris, BNF, no. HS 1973-1-435 (ex Seyrig coll.).
151	O4*–R6* 3.37 g 11 mm 3 h	Same as 143. BNF, Paris, no. 3133 (ex De Luynes coll.); Babelon, *Perses*, p. 192, no. 1342; idem, *Traité*, p. 535, no. 859.
152	O2–R?	Same as 143. Slightly worn. Some cracks on the edge. O and R: off-center toward the top. Ahlström, Stockholm, 54, 16–17/11/1996, no. 1765.
153	O? – R7 3.35 g 15 mm 3 h	Same as 143. Slightly worn. O: off-center to left. Paris, BNF, no. 3134 (ex De Luynes coll.); Babelon, *Perses*, no. 1343; idem, *Traité*, no. 860.
154	O? – R7* 3.28 g 14 mm 6 h	Same as 143. Slightly worn. Berlin, SM, no. 2 (ex Fox coll.).

155 O?–R? 3.24 g 15 mm 1 h — Same as 143. Rather worn.
R: off-center to left.
Private coll. LPN; Baldwin, London, 34, 13/10/2003, no. 515.

156 O?–R? 2.81 g 17 mm 3 h — Same as 143. Rather worn. Oval flan.
Paris, BNF, no. 1965/741 (ex Seyrig coll.).

157 O?–R? 1.95 g 14 mm — Same as 143. Rather worn and partly broken.
Spaer coll., Jerusalem (bought in Jerusalem).

158 O?–R? — Same as 143. Rather worn. Several cracks on the edge.
Malloy, New York, 12, 25/4/1978, no. 515.

III.3. 16th-Shekels AR

159 O1*–R1* 0.70 g — Same as 143, but with one warrior.
R: defect behind the vulture.
Private coll.

160 O1–R2* — Same as 159.
Information from L. Mildenberg, 1990.

161 O2*–R3* 0.89 g 12 mm 11 h — Same as 159.
R: Slightly off-center downward.
Spaer coll., Jerusalem (bought in Beirut).

162 O3*–R4* 0.77 g 10 mm — Same as 159.
Elsen, Brussels, 80, 12/6/2004, no. 291 = 72, 14/12/2002, no. 25 = 70, 15/6/2002, no. 109 = Freeman & Sear, New York, Triton III, 3/11–1/12/1999, no. 620.

163 O?–R2 0.79 g 4 h — Same as 159. Slightly worn.
O: off-center to left.
Oxford, AM, no. 51; Münzen und Medaillen, Basel, 256, November 1965, no. 476.

164 O?–R5* 0.84 g — Same as 159. Slightly worn
O: overstruck.
Vecchi, London, 14, 5/2/1999, no. 686.

165 O?–R? 0.91 g 10 mm 3 h — Same as 159. Rather worn.
Paris, BNF, no. 1987/446 (ex Seyrig coll.).

166 O?–R? 0.86 g 11 mm 1 h — Same as 159. Rather worn.
Private coll. LPN; Baldwin, London, 34, 13/10/2003, no. 516 (0.90 g).

167 O?–R? 0.74 g 10 mm — Same as 159. Rather worn.
Private coll. LPN; Monnaies et Médailles, Stuttgart, 32, 26/5/2010, no. 428.

168 O?–R?
0.57 g 10 mm
9 h
Same as 159. Rather worn.
O: off-center toward the top.
Paris, BNF, no. 697 (ex Chandon de Briailles coll.).

169 O?–R?
0.56 g
Same as 159. Rather worn.
O: off-center toward the top.
London, BM, no. 1960-9-7 2.

170 O?–R?
0.56 g 11 mm
6 h
Same as 159. Rather worn.
O and R: slightly off-center toward the top.
Berlin, SM, no. 11164.

171 O?–R?
0.49 g 10 mm
Same as 159. Rather worn.
O: off-center toward the top.
R: off-center downward.
Paris, BNF, no. 1987/447 (ex Seyrig coll.).

172 O?–R?
Same as 159. Rather worn.
R: off-center toward the top.
Kovacs, San Mateo, 9, February 1980, no. 27.

173 O?–R?
10 mm
Same as 159. Rather worn.
R: off-center to left.
Paris, BNF, no. HS 2 (ex Seyrig coll.).

III.4. Half-16th Shekels AR

174 O1*–R1*
0.32 g 7 mm
7 h
O: war-galley to left; prow terminating in head of a horse; inside, one warrior with shield, facing left; border of dots.
R: vulture, with closed wings, crook and flail, to left; border of dots.
Private coll. LPN; Baldwin, London, 34, 13/10/2003, no. 518 (0.33 g).

175 O2*–R2
0.32 g 8 mm
1 h
Same as 174.
O: off-center to right.
Spaer coll., Jerusalem (bought in Beirut).

176 O3–R2*
0.28 g 8 mm
3 h
Same as 174. Partly broken.
Paris, BNF, no. 678b (ex Chandon de Briailles coll.).

177 O3*–R3*
0.28 g 8 mm
6 h
Same as 174.
R: off-center to right.
Paris, BNF, no. 1965/752 (ex Seyrig coll.).

178 O2–R?
0.33 g 8 mm
11 h
Same as 174. Irregular flan. Slightly worn.
R: off-center to left.
Spaer coll., Jerusalem (bought in Jerusalem).

179 O3–R?
0.28 g 7 mm
6 h
Same as 174. Slightly worn.
Berlin, SM, no. 4.

180 O?–R?
0.30 g 7 mm
9 h
Same as 174. Rather worn.
O: very off-center to right.
R: off-center downward.
Private coll., LPN; Baldwin, London, 34, 13/10/2003, no. 517.

4. *Group IV: Galley, Lion and Bull (End of the 5th Century–333 B.C.E.)*

IV.1. ʾElpaʿal (End of the 5th Century B.C.E.)

IV.1.1. Shekels AR

181 O1*–R1*
14.85 g
O: war-galley to left; prow terminating in head of a lion; inside, three warriors with shields, facing left; below, one line of waves, winged seahorse to left and shell. Border of dots. Square flan.
R: lion to left, bringing down a bull with an incuse body to right; *ʾLPʿL / MLK GBL* on two lines above; border of dots.
Peus, Frankfurt/Main, 361, 6/11/1999, no. 245.

182 O1–R1
14.46 g 25 mm
12 h
Same as 181. Irregular flan.
R: *ʾLPʿL / MLK GB*[.
Paris, BNF, no. HS 1973-1-270 (ex Seyrig coll.).

183 O1–R2*
13.77 g 28 mm
10 h
Same as 181. Irregular flan. Chisel-cut.
R: *ʾLPʿL / MLK*[.
Private coll.

184 O1–R3*
13.21 g 29 mm
9 h
Same as 181. Oval flan. Slightly corroded.
R: *ʾLPʿL MLK GB*[on one line.
Private coll. LPN; Baldwin, London, 34, 13/10/2003, no. 521.

185 O2*–R4*
14.18 g
Same as 181.
R: *ʾLPʿL MLK GB*[.
SNG ANS, no. 1430; Empire coins, Ormond Beach, 54, 1990, no. 78 = Numismatic Art & Ancient Coins, Zurich, 3, 3/7/1982, no. 78 (ex Berry coll.).

186 O3*–R5*
14.34 g 26 mm
9 h
Same as 181. Oval flan. Slightly worn.
R: inscription off the flan.
Paris, BNF, no. 1988/114; Numismatic Fine Arts, Encino, 14–19/11/1984, no. 187 = Spink, London, 10/10/1977, no. 276; Hill, *Catalog Ward*, no. 813 (ex Ward coll.).

187 O4*–R?
12.91 g 24 mm
5 h
Same as 181. Oval flan. Slightly worn.
R: inscription off the flan.
Beirut, AUB, no. 765B; Baramki, *Coins AUB*, no. 765B and pl. 18:8.

188	O?–R6* 13.09 g 25 mm	Same as 181. Slightly worn. R: traces of inscription on one line. Beirut, NM, no. 1311; Chéhab, *Monnaies*, no. 1311 and pl. 33:2.
189	O?–R7* 14.33 g 24 mm 5 h	Same as 181. Slightly worn. O: off-center to left. R:]ʿ*L MLK GBL* on one line. Paris, BNF, no. 3142; *Catalogue De Luynes*, no. 3142; Babelon, *Perses*, no. 1344 (ex De Luynes coll.).
190	O?–R8* 14.11 g 24 mm 12 h	Same as 181. Slightly worn. O: restruck. R: traces of inscription on one line. Paris, BNF, no. 1345; Babelon, *Perses*, no. 1345.
191	O?–R? 14 g 24 mm 6 h	Same as 181. Rather worn. R: inscription off the flan. Paris, BNF, no. 3135; *Catalogue De Luynes*, no. 3135 (ex De Luynes coll.).
192	O?–R? 13.23 g 27 mm 9 h	Same as 181. Rather worn. O: off-center to left. R: inscription obliterated. Beirut, AUB, no. 2947.

IV.1.2. Quarter-Shekels AR

193	O1*–R1* 3.52 g	Same as 181. R: *ʾLPʿL / M* on two lines, partly off the flan. Leu, Zurich, 76, 27/10/1999, no. 213.
194	O1–R2* 3.41 g 16 mm 6 h	Same as 193. O: off-center to right. R: inscription obliterated. Athens, NomM, no. 8; Rouvier, *JIAN* 4 (1901) no. 635 and pl. A′8 (ex Rouvier coll.).
195	O1–R3* 3.62 g 18 mm 12 h	Same as 193. Some cracks on the edge. Split die. R: *ʾLPʿL / M* on two lines. Berlin, SM, no. 6 (ex Prokesch-Osten coll.).
196	O2–R3 3.50 g	Same as 193. Oval flan. Split die. O: dot between the prow and the first shield. R: *ʾLPʿL*[. London, BM, no. 1872-3-4 8.
197	O2–R3 3.50 g 16 mm 7 h	Same as 193. Split die. O: dot between the prow and the first shield. R: traces of inscription. Rome, VM, no. 106.

198 O2*–R3
3.49 g 19 mm
12 h
Same as 193. Irregular flan. Split die.
O: dot between the prow and the first shield.
R: *ʾLPʿL / M* on two lines.
Berlin, SM, no. 5.

199 O2–R3
3.43 g 17 mm
Same as 193. Slightly worn. Split die.
O: dot between the prow and the first shield.
R: *ʾLPʿL / M* on two lines.
Athens, NomM; Rouvier, *JIA*N 4 (1901) no. 635 and pl. A′6 (ex De Démétrio coll.).

200 O2–R3
3.31 g 18 mm
3 h
Same as 193. Irregular flan. Split die.
O: dot between the prow and the first shield.
R: *ʾLP*[.
Private coll.

201 O2–R4
2.94 g 16 mm
9 h
Same as 193.
O: two warriors visible; dot between the prow and the first shield.
R: *ʾLPʿL* / [*M*]*LK GB*[on two lines, partly off the flan.
Paris, BNF, no. HS 1973-1-271 (ex Seyrig coll.).

202 O2–R5*
3.55 g 17 mm
9 h
Same as 193.
O: dot between the prow and the first shield.
R:]*LK GB*[partly off the flan.
Berlin, SM, no. 7.

203 O3*–R6*
2.91 g 14 mm
5 h
Same as 193. Plated.
O: defect on the head of the seahorse.
R:]*LK G*[partly off the flan.
Paris, BNF, no. 64 (ex De Vogüé coll.).

204 O3–R7
3.53 g 14 mm
6 h
Same as 193.
O: defect on the head of the seahorse; two warriors visible.
R: inscription almost entirely off the flan.
Leiden, RM, no. 8024.

205 O4*–R7*
3.50 g 15 mm
7 h
Same as 193.
R: *ʾLPʿ*[on one line.
Paris, BNF, no. 3136; *Catalogue De Luynes*, no. 3136; Babelon, *Perses*, no. 1347; idem, *Traité*, no. 865 (ex De Luynes coll.).

206 O4–R7
3.45 g 18 mm
1 h
Same as 193. Irregular flan.
R: *ʾLPʿL*[on one line.
Berlin, SM, no. 8 (ex Löbbecke coll.).

207 O5*–R8*
3.60 g 15 mm
11 h
Same as 193.
O: defect of the circle on the left; two warriors visible.
R: *ʾLPʿL* on one line.
Paris, BNF, no. 1348; Babelon, *Perses*, no. 1348.

208 O5–R9*
3.43 g 15 mm
Same as 193. Small cracks on the edge.
O: off-center to right; defect in the circle on the left.
R: *ʾLP*[on one line, partly off the flan.
London, BM, no. 1858-11-25 4.

209 O6*–R10*
3.61 g
Same as 193.
O: slightly off-center toward the top.
R: *ʾLPʿL*[on one line.
Monetarium, Schweizerische Kreditanstalt Zurich, 58, Autumn 1992, no. 85 = Kovacs, San Mateo, 8, 22/4/1988, no. 90.

210 O7*–R11*
3.51 g 16 mm
Same as 193. Irregular flan.
R: *ʾLPʿL*[on one line.
Imhoof-Blumer, *Choix*, 441, no. 10 and pl. H16.

211 O?–R8*
3.50 g 16 mm
6 h
Same as 193.
O: Slightly worn; two warriors visible.
R: *ʾLPʿL*[on one line.
Paris, BNF, no. 63 (ex De Vogüé coll.).

212 O?–R12*
3.72 g 15 mm
5 h
Same as 193.
O: slightly worn; two warriors visible.
R: *ʾLPʿL* on one line.
Paris, BNF, no. 65 (ex De Vogüé coll.).

213 O?–R13*
3.57 g 17 mm
Same as 193.
O: slightly worn.
R: *ʾLPʿL* on one line.
Imhoof-Blumer, *Choix*, 441, no. 11 and pl. H17.

214 O?–R?
3.62 g 15 mm
Same as 193. Rather worn.
R: *ʾLPʿL M* on two lines.
Beirut, AUB, no. C765G; Baramki, *Coins AUB*, no. C765G and pl. 18:9.

215 O?–R?
3.55 g 16 mm
2 h
Same as 193. Rather worn.
O: two warriors visible.
R: *ʾLPʿL* on one line.
Paris, BNF, Babelon, *Perses*, no. 1349.

216 O?–R?
3.31 g 17 mm
10 h
Same as 193. Irregular flan. Rather worn. Split die.
R: *ʾLPʿL* on one line.
Private coll. LPN; Baldwin, London, 34, 13/10/2003, no. 522.

217 O?–R?
3.23 g 15 mm
4 h
Same as 193. Rather worn. Some cracks on the edge.
R: inscription off the flan.
Paris, BNF, no. 1987/448 (ex Seyrig coll.).

218 O?–R?
Same as 193. Rather worn.
R: inscription off the flan.
Malloy, New York, 24, 18/3/1988, no. 132.

219 O?–R?
16 mm
Same as 193. Rather worn. Some cracks on the edge.
R: inscription off the flan.
Paris, BNF, no. 2 (ex Seyrig coll.).

IV.1.3. 16th-Shekels AR

IV.1.3.a. With Two Warriors

220 O1*–R1*
0.80 g 10 mm
6 h
O: same as 193, but with two warriors and without line of waves.
R: same as 193, with no inscription visible.
Paris, BNF, no. 1353; Babelon, *Perses*, no. 1353.

221 O1–R2*
0.71 g
Same as 220.
Private coll.

222 O2*–R2
0.58 g 10 mm
6 h
Same as 220. Corroded.
Oxford, AM, no. 53; Münzen und Medaillen, Basel, 256, November 1965, no. 478.

223 O3*–R3*
0.73 g
Same as 220.
O: off-center to right.
Kovacs, San Mateo, 1988.

224 O8*–R?
0.65 g 10 mm
2 h
Same as 220. Slightly worn.
Oxford, AM, no. 50 (ex Osborne O'Hagan coll.).

225 O9*–R?
0.72 g 9 mm
2 h
Same as 220.
R: off-center to left; slightly worn.
Paris, BNF, no. 3137; *Catalogue De Luynes*, no. 3137 (ex De Luynes coll.).

226 O?–R9*
Same as 220. Slightly worn.
Kovacs, San Mateo, 14, 16/10/1998, no. 72.

227 O?–R?
0.52 g
Same as 220.
Baldwin, London, 34, 13/10/2003, no. 529 (not illustrated).

228 O?–R?
Same as 220.
R: countermark above the lion.
Private coll. LPN.

IV.1.3.b. With One Warrior

229 O4–R4*
0.80 g 10 mm
Same as 220, but with one warrior.
London, BM, no. 1974-4-16 1.

230 O4*–R5*
0.70 g 10 mm
5 h
Same as 229.
Paris, BNF, no. HS 2 (ex Seyrig coll.).

231	O5*–R6* 0.87 g 9 mm 11 h	Same as 229. Paris, BNF, no. 3138; *Catalogue De Luynes*, no. 3138; Babelon, *Perses*, no. 1351; idem, *Traité*, no. 867 (ex De Luynes coll.).
232	O6*–R7* 0.73 g	Same as 229. Elsen, Brussels, 62, 24/6/2000, no. 260 = Lanz, Munich, 42, 23/11/1987, no. 322.
233	O?–R8* 0.78 g	Same as 229. Irregular flan. Slightly worn. England, Quarryville-London, 12, 26/9/1990, no. 413.
234	O?–R10*	Same as 229. Slightly worn. Paris, BNF, no. HS 4 (ex Seyrig coll.).
235	O?–R? 0.91 g 10 mm 2 h	Same as 229. Rather worn. O: off-center to right. Berlin, SM, no. 9.
236	O?–R? 0.88 g 10 mm 1 h	Same as 229. Rather worn. Spaer coll., Jerusalem (bought in Jerusalem).
237	O?–R? 0.87 g	Same as 229. Rather worn. Rouvier, *JIAN* 4 (1901) no. 636 (ex Rouvier coll.).
238	O?–R? 0.72 g	Same as 229. Rather worn. Rouvier, *JIAN* 4 (1901) no. 636 and pl. A'7 (ex Rouvier coll.).
239	O?–R? 0.64 g 10 mm 9 h	Same as 229. Rather worn and corroded. R: traces of inscription? Private coll.
240	O?–R? 0.63 g 9 mm 1 h	Same as 229. Rather worn. R: traces of inscription? Spaer coll., Jerusalem (bought in Jerusalem).
241	O?–R? 0.60 g 10 mm	Same as 229. Rather worn. Private coll. LPN; Baldwin, London, 34, 13/10/2003, no. 523.

IV.1.3.c. With One or Two Warriors

242	O7*–R8*	Same as 229, but with one or two warriors. Information from L. Mildenberg.
243	O?–R4 0.86 g 10 mm 5 h	Same as 242. Slightly worn. Paris, BNF, no. 3139; *Catalogue De Luynes*, no. 3139; Babelon, *Perses*, no. 1352 (ex De Luynes coll.).
244	O?–R? 0.77 g 10 mm 1 h	Same as 242. Rather worn. Spaer coll., Jerusalem (bought in Beirut).

245 O?–R? 0.58 g — Same as 242. Rather worn.
R: off-center toward the bottom.
Kovacs, San Mateo, 1988.

246 O?–R? 0.56 g 10 mm — Same as 242. Rather worn.
Paris, BNF, no. 1987/458 (ex Seyrig coll.).

247 O?–R? 0.48 g — Same as 242. Broken and rather worn.
R: traces of inscription?
Private coll. LPN.

248 O?–R? — Same as 242. Rather worn.
Malloy, New York, 24, 18/3/1988, no. 134.

249 O?–R? — Same as 242. Rather worn.
Malloy, New York, 24, 18/3/1988, no. 162.

250 O?–R? — Same as 242. Rather worn. Small cracks on the edge.
Malloy, New York, 17/8/1995, no. 181.

IV.1.4. Half-16th Shekels AR

251 O1–R1 0.36 g 8 mm — O: war-galley to left; prow terminating in head of a lion; inside, one warrior with shield, facing left; below, one line of waves; border of dots.
R: seated lion to left, *en face*; border of dots.
Münzen und Medaillen, Basel, January 1968, no. 12.

252 O1*–R1* 0.29 g 9 mm 2 h — Same as 251.
Paris, BNF, no. 1965/829–12 (ex Seyrig coll.).

253 O1–R2* 0.33 g 8 mm 12 h — Same as 251.
Tel Aviv, KNM, no. K1888.

254 O1–R3* 0.27 g — Same as 251. Small cracks on the edge.
Rauch, Vienna, 81, 23–24/11/2007, no. 143.

255 O2–R3 0.19 g 8 mm 1 h — Same as 251. Partly broken.
Spaer coll., Jerusalem (bought in Jerusalem).

256 O2–R4 0.32 g 8 mm 3 h — Same as 251. Small cracks on the edge.
London, BM, no. 1985.5-20-6; Elayi-Elayi, *Trésors*, p. 95, no. 5 and pl. 5:5 (Byblos hoards TXIII, TXIV and TXV?).

257 O2*–R4* 0.30 g 8 mm 1 h — Same as 251.
R: off-center to left.
Paris, BNF, no. 1965/829/13 (ex Seyrig coll.).

258 O2–R5* 0.26 g — Same as 251.
Jacquier, Kehl/Rhein, 24, Spring 2000, no. 153 = 23, Autumn 1999, no. 204 = 22, Spring 1999, no. 190.

No.	Dies / Data	Description
259	O3*–R6* 0.38 g	Same as 251. Some cracks on the edge. Sternberg, Zurich, 1, 18/12/1999, no. 247.
260	O4*–R7* 0.37 g 8 mm 11 h	Same as 251. Paris, BNF, no. 1965/750 (ex Seyrig coll.).
261	O5*–R8* 0.32 g 8 mm 12 h	Same as 251. Small cracks on the edge. Private coll.
262	O?–R? 0.60 g 8 mm 4 h	Same as 251. Rather worn. London, BM, no. 1985.5–20–4; Elayi-Elayi, *Trésors*, p. 95, no. 4 and pl. 5:4 (Byblos hoards TXIII, TXIV and TXV?).
263	O?–R? 0.40 g 8 mm 9 h	Same as 251. Rather worn. Spaer coll., Jerusalem (bought in Beirut).
264	O?–R? 0.38 g 8 mm	Same as 251. Rather worn and corroded. Paris, BNF, no. 1987/462 (ex Seyrig coll.).
265	O?–R? 0.36 g 7 mm 11 h	Same as 251. Rather worn. Private coll. LPN.
266	O?–R? 0.26 g 8 mm	Same as 251. Rather worn. Small crack on the edge. Bartlett Well coll., Lexington, no. 3.
267	O?–R? 0.20 g 7 mm	Same as 251. Rather worn. Paris, BNF, no. 1987/468 (ex Seyrig coll.).

IV.2. ʿOzbaʿal (First Third of the 4th Century)

IV.2.1. Shekels AR

IV.2.1.a. Anepigraphic

No.	Dies / Data	Description
268	O1*–R1* 12.95 g 30 mm	O: war-galley to left; prow terminating in head of a lion; inside, three warriors with shields, facing left; below, one line of waves, winged seahorse to left and shell. Border of dots. Restruck. R: lion to left, bringing down a bull to left; *ʿZBʿL MLK GBL* above; border of dots. Beirut, NM, no. 2064; Chéhab, *Monnaies*, no. 2064 and pl. 34:1.
269	O1–R2 12.97 g 12 h	Same as 268. R:]*MLK GBL*. Beirut, NM; Dunand, *Byblos I*, no. 6219; Elayi-Lemaire, *Trans* 38 (2009) 78, no. 2 and pl. 9:2 (Byblos excavations; Byblos hoard TIX).

270 O2*–R3
12.92 g
5 h
Same as 268.
R: *ʿZBʿL MLK GBL.*
Beirut, NM; Dunand, *Byblos I*, no. 6218 and pl. 91:4; Elayi-Lemaire, *Trans* 38 (2009) 78, no. 3 and pl. 9:3 (Byblos excavations; Byblos hoard TIX).

271 O2–R3
12.85 g
1 h
Same as 268.
R: *ʿZBʿL MLK GBL.*
Beirut, NM; Dunand, *Byblos I*, no. 6224; Elayi-Lemaire, *Trans* 38 (2009) 78, no. 5 (Byblos excavations; Byblos hoard TIX).

272 O2–R3
12.68 g
2 h
Same as 268. Irregular flan.
R: *ʿZBʿL MLK GBL.*
Beirut, NM; Dunand, *Byblos I*, no. 6216 and pl. 91:2; Elayi-Lemaire, *Trans* 38 (2009) 78, no. 4 (Byblos excavations; Byblos hoard TIX).

273 O3–R4*
13.20 g
Same as 268.
O: defect before the head of the seahorse.
R: *ʿZBʿL MLK GBL.*
Classical Numismatic Group, Lancaster-London, 46, 24/6/1998, no. 496.

274 O3–R4
12.97 g
9 h
Same as 268.
O: defect before the head of the seahorse.
R: *ʿZBʿL MLK GBL.*
Beirut, NM; Dunand, *Byblos I*, no. 6217 and pl. 91:1; Elayi-Lemaire, *Trans* 38 (2009) 78, no. 1 and pl. 9:1 (Byblos excavations; Byblos hoard TIX).

275 O3–R5
13.23 g
Same as 268. Irregular flan.
O: defect before the head of the seahorse.
R: *ʿZBʿL MLK GBL.*
Numismatica Ars Classica, New York, Triton II, 1–2/12/1998, no. 487.

276 O3*–R5*
13.20 g
Same as 268.
O: defect before the head of the seahorse.
R: *ʿZBʿL MLK GBL.*
Elayi-Elayi, *Trésors*, p. 99, no. 214 (Byblos hoards TXIII, TXIV and TXV?).

277 O3–R5
13.16 g
Same as 268.
O: defect before the head of the seahorse.
R: *ʿZBʿL MLK GBL.*
Elayi-Elayi, *Trésors*, p. 99, no. 215, and pl. 9:215 (Byblos hoards TXIII, TXIV and TXV?).

278 O3–R5
13.12 g
Same as 268.
O: defect before the head of the seahorse.
R: slightly off-center toward the top;]ʿ*L MLK GBL*.
Monnaies et Médailles, Basel, 16, 1–2/10/1986, no. 252 = Monetarium, Schweizerische Kreditanstalt, Zurich, 47, 3/12/1985, no. 163.

279 O4–R2
13.17 g
Same as 268. Irregular flan.
R: restruck; *ʿZBʿL MLK GBL*.
London, BM, no. 1858-11-25 3.

280 O4*–R2*
13.15 g 26 mm
12 h
Same as 268. Irregular flan.
R: *ʿZBʿL MLK GBL*.
Paris, BNF, no. 3142; *Catalogue De Luynes*, no. 3142; Babelon, *Perses*, no. 1356; idem, *Traité*, no. 871 (ex De Luynes coll.).

281 O4–R3*
25 mm
Same as 268.
O: off-center to left.
R: *ʿZBʿL MLK GBL*.
Brussels, NM, no. 1738; Naster, *Collection De Hirsch*, no. 1738.

282 O4–R5
13.15 g 25 mm
2 h
Same as 268.
R: *ʿZBʿL MLK GBL*.
Paris, BNF, no. 67 (ex De Vogüé coll.).

283 O4–R5
12.93 g
11 h
Same as 268.
O: off-center to left.
R: *ʿZBʿL MLK GBL*.
Beirut, NM; Dunand, *Byblos I*, no. 6223; Elayi-Lemaire, *Trans* 38 (2009) 79, no. 8 (Byblos excavations; Byblos hoard TIX).

284 O4–R5
12.91 g
1 h
Same as 268.
O: off-center toward the top; flaw.
R: *ʿZBʿL MLK GBL*.
Beirut, NM; Dunand, *Byblos I*, no. 6221; Elayi-Lemaire, *Trans* 38 (2009) 79, no. 9 and pl. 9:9 (Byblos excavations; Byblos hoard TIX).

285 O4–R5
12.90 g
4 h
Same as 268.
O: off-center toward the top.
R:]*ZBʿL MLK GBL*.
Beirut, NM; Dunand, *Byblos I*, no. 6211; Elayi-Lemaire, *Trans* 38 (2009) 79, no. 10 (Byblos excavations; Byblos hoard TIX).

286	O4–R5 12.82 g 4 h	Same as 268. O: off-center toward the top. R: *ʿZBʿL MLK GBL* slightly indistinct. Beirut, NM; Dunand, *Byblos I*, no. 6213; Elayi-Lemaire, *Trans* 38 (2009) 79, no. 11 (Byblos excavations; Byblos hoard TIX).
287	O4–R5 12.68 g 11 h	Same as 268. R: off-center to right; *ʿZBʿL MLK GBL.* Beirut, NM; Dunand, *Byblos I*, no. 6220; Elayi-Lemaire, *Trans* 38 (2009) 79, no. 12 (Byblos excavations; Byblos hoard TIX).
288	O4–R5 12.67 g 3 h	Same as 268. R: off-center to right; *ʿZBʿL MLK GBL* slightly indistinct. Beirut, NM; Dunand, *Byblos I*, no. 6214; Elayi-Lemaire, *Trans* 38 (2009) 79, no. 13 and pl. 9:13 (Byblos excavations; Byblos hoard TIX).
289	O4–R6* 13.27 g 27 mm 6 h	Same as 268. R: *ʿZBʿL MLK GBL.* Paris, BNF, no. 3143; *Catalogue De Luynes*, no. 3143; Babelon, *Perses*, no. 1357 (ex De Luynes coll.).
290	O4–R6 13.20 g	Same as 268. R: *ʿZBʿL MLK GBL.* Vecchi, London, 5, 5/3/1997, no. 275 = Albrecht-Hoffmann, Münz Zentrum, Cologne, 74, 11–13/11/1992, no. 382 = 71, 3–5/6/1991, no. 565.
291	O4–R6 13.17 g 25 mm 9 h	Same as 268. Irregular flan. R: *ʿZBʿL MLK GBL.* Berlin, SM, no. 12 (ex Löbbecke coll.).
292	O4–R6 13.16 g	Same as 268. R: *ʿZBʿL MLK GBL.* Hirsch, Munich, 186, 10–12/5/1995, no. 555 = 162, 8–10/5/1989, no. 345.
293	O4–R6 13.10 g 25 mm 6 h	Same as 268. R: *ʿZBʿL MLK GBL.* Paris, BNF, no. 66 (ex De Vogüé coll.).
294	O4–R6 12.89 g 12 h	Same as 268. R: *ʿZBʿL MLK GBL.* Beirut, NM; Dunand, *Byblos I*, no. 6186; Elayi-Lemaire, *Trans* 38 (2009) 79, no. 15 (Byblos excavations; Byblos hoard TIX).
295	O4–R7* 13.16 g 25 mm 3 h	Same as 268. R: *ʿZBʿL MLK GBL.* Berlin, SM, no. 13.

296 O5*–R6
13.13 g

Same as 268.
O: defect on the third shield.
R: *ʿZBʿL MLK GBL.*
Classical Numismatic Group, Lancaster-London, 46, 24/6/1998, no. 495.

297 O5–R8
13.27 g

Same as 268.
O: defect on the third shield.
R: *ʿZBʿL MLK GBL.*
Berk, Chicago, 127, 25/6/2002, no. 235 = 124, 3/1/2002, no. 218 = 117, 28/11/2000, no. 260 = 107, 18/3/1999, no. 225.

298 O5–R9
13.25 g

Same as 268.
O: defect on the third shield.
R: *ʿZBʿL MLK GBL.*
Elayi-Elayi, *Trésors*, p. 100, no. 225, and pl. 10:225 (Byblos hoards TXIII, TXIV and TXV?).

299 O6*–R7

Same as 268.
R: *]Bʿ L MLK GBL.*
Numismatica Ars Classica, Zurich, 95, 26–27/10/1995, no. 247.

300 O4–R?
12.80 g
11 h

Same as 268. Slightly worn.
R: *ʿZBʿL MLK GBL.*
Beirut, NM; Dunand, *Byblos I*, no. 6212; Elayi-Lemaire, *Trans* 38 (2009) 79, no. 14 (Byblos excavations; Byblos hoard TIX).

301 O?–R1
12.71 g
7 h

Same as 268. Slightly worn.
R: *ʿZBʿL MLK GBL.*
Beirut, NM; Dunand, *Byblos I*, no. 6215; Elayi-Lemaire, *Trans* 38 (2009) 79, no. 7, and pl. 9:7 (Byblos excavations; Byblos hoard TIX).

302 O?–R3
12.63 g
11 h

Same as 268. Slightly worn. Edge broken.
R: *ʿZBʿL MLK GBL.*
Beirut, NM; Dunand, *Byblos I*, no. 6222; Elayi-Lemaire, *Trans* 38 (2009) 78, no. 6 and pl. 9:6 (Byblos excavations; Byblos hoard TIX).

303 O?–R6
12.89 g
10 h

Same as 268. Slightly worn.
R: *]Bʿ L MLK GBL.*
Beirut, NM; Dunand, *Byblos I*, no. 6147; Elayi-Lemaire, *Trans* 38 (2009) 79, no. 16 and pl. 9:16 (Byblos excavations; Byblos hoard TIX).

IV.2.1.b. With *Z* on the Obverse

304	O5′–R7 13.24 g	Same as 268 but with *Z* on the obverse, above the seahorse. R: *ʿZBʿL MLK GBL.* Classical Numismatic Group, Lancaster-London, 46, 24/6/1998, no. 497.
305	O5′–R7 13.19 g 24 mm	Same as 304. O: *Z.* R:]*L MLK GBL.* Classical Coins, 28/8/2009, no. G6011, 2731.
306	O5′–R7 13.16 g	Same as 304. O: *Z.* R: *ʿZBʿL MLK GBL.* Elayi-Elayi, *Trésors*, p. 99, no. 216, and pl. 9:216 (Byblos hoards TXIII, TXIV and TXV?).
307	O5′–R7 13.09 g 27 mm 6 h	Same as 304. O: *Z.* R:]*Bʿ L MLK GBL.* Berlin, SM, no. 14.
308	O5′*–R7	Same as 304. O: *Z.* R: *ʿZBʿL MLK GBL.* Monetarium, Schweizerische Kreditanstalt, Zurich, 57, Spring 1992, no. 108.
309	O5′–R8	Same as 304. O: *Z.* R: *ʿZBʿL MLK GBL.* Berk, Chicago, 102, 27/5/1998, no. 286.
310	O6′*–R10* 13.19 g	Same as 304. O: *Z.* R: *ʿZBʿL MLK GBL.* Elayi-Elayi, *Trésors*, p. 104, no. 408, and pl. 15:408 (Byblos hoards TXIII, TXIV and TXV?).
311	O7–R6 12.88 g	Same as 304. O: *Z.* R:]*Bʿ L MLK GBL.* Beirut, NM; Dunand, *Byblos I*, no. 6294; Elayi-Lemaire, *Trans* 38 (2009) 79, no. 17 (Byblos excavations; Byblos hoard TIX).
312	O7–R6 12.84 g	Same as 304. O: *Z.* R:]*Bʿ L MLK GB*[. Beirut, NM; Dunand, *Byblos I*, no. 6293; Elayi-Lemaire, *Trans* 38 (2009) 79, no. 18 (Byblos excavations; Byblos hoard TIX).

313 O7–R6
12.42 g
Same as 304.
O: *Z*.
R:] *MLK GBL*.
Beirut, NM; Dunand, *Byblos I*, no. 6292; Elayi-Lemaire, *Trans* 38 (2009) 79, no. 19 and pl. 9:19 (Byblos excavations; Byblos hoard TIX).

314 O7*–R7
13.03 g
Same as 304.
O: *Z*.
R: *ʿZBʿL MLK GBL*.
Monnaies et Médailles, Basel, 8, 27–28/6/1978, no. 364.

315 O7–R9*
13.32 g
Same as 304.
O: *Z*.
R: *ʿZBʿL MLK GBL*.
UBS, Zurich, 63, 6–8/9/2005, no. 217 = Monetarium, Schweizerische Kreditanstalt, 45, Spring 1986, no. 48.

316 O?–R?
Same as 304.
O: *Z*.
R:]*ʿL MLK GBL*.
Paris, BNF, moulage.

IV.2.1.c. With ʿZ on the Obverse

317 O5″–R6
12.89 g
9 h
Same as 268 but with ʿZ on the obverse, above the seahorse.
O: restruck? *ʿZ*.
R: *ʿZBʿL MLK GBL*.
Beirut, NM; Dunand, *Byblos I*, no. 6164; Elayi-Lemaire, *Trans* 38 (2009) 80, no. 24 (Byblos excavations; Byblos hoard TIX).

318 O5″*–R7
13.32 g
Same as 317.
O: *ʿZ*.
R:]*Bʿ L MLK GBL*.
Elayi-Elayi, *Trésors*, p. 99, no. 220, and pl. 10:220 (Byblos hoards TXIII, TXIV and TXV?).

319 O5″–R7
13.30 g
Same as 317.
O: *ʿZ*.
R: *ʿZBʿL MLK GBL*.
Elayi-Elayi, *Trésors*, p. 99, no. 219, and pl. 9:219 (Byblos hoards TXIII, TXIV and TXV?).

320 O5″–R7
13.25 g
Same as 317.
O: *ʿZ*.
R: *ʿZBʿL MLK GBL*.
Elayi-Elayi, *Trésors*, p. 99, no. 218, and pl. 9:218 (Byblos hoards TXIII, TXIV and TXV?).

321 O5″–R7
13.23 g
Same as 317.
O: ʿZ.
R: *ʿZBʿL MLK GBL.*
Elayi-Elayi, *Trésors*, p. 99, no. 217, and pl. 9:217 (Byblos hoards TXIII, TXIV and TXV?).

322 O5″–R7
13.22 g
Same as 317.
O: ʿZ.
R: *ʿZBʿL MLK GBL.*
Elayi-Elayi, *Trésors*, p. 99, no. 221, and pl. 10:221 (Byblos hoards TXIII, TXIV and TXV?).

323 O5″–R7
13.10 g
Same as 317.
O: ʿZ.
R: *ʿZBʿL MLK GBL.*
Elayi-Elayi, *Trésors*, p. 99, no. 222, and pl. 10:222 (Byblos hoards TXIII, TXIV and TXV?).

324 O5″–R8*
13.20 g
Same as 317.
O: traces of ʿZ.
R: *ʿZBʿL MLK GBL.*
Elsen, Brussels, 56, 18–19/12/1998, no. 248.

325 O5″–R9
13.26 g
Same as 317. Irregular flan.
O: traces of ʿZ.
R: *ʿZBʿL MLK GBL.*
Elayi-Elayi, *Trésors*, p. 100, no. 223, and pl. 10:223 (Byblos hoards TXIII, TXIV and TXV?).

326 O5″–R9
13.24 g 26 mm
Same as 317.
O: ʿZ.
R: *ʿZBʿL MLK GBL.*
Burgan, Paris, 5/11/1993, no. 136.

327 O5″–R9
13.20 g
Same as 317. Irregular flan.
O: ʿZ.
R: *ʿZBʿL MLK GB*[.
Elayi-Elayi, *Trésors*, p. 100, no. 224, and pl. 10:224 (Byblos hoards TXIII, TXIV and TXV?).

328 O5″–R9
13.17 g
Same as 317.
O: traces of ʿZ.
R: *ʿZBʿL MLK GBL.*
Berk, Chicago, 140, 27/10/2004, no. 197 = 126, 23/4/2002, no. 104.

329 O5″–R10
13.23 g
Same as 317.
O: ʿZ; flaw.
R: *ʿZBʿL MLK GBL* partly off the flan.
Elayi-Elayi, *Trésors*, p. 100, no. 226, and pl. 10:226 (Byblos hoards TXIII, TXIV and TXV?).

330 O5″–R10
13.22 g

Same as 317.
O: ʿZ.
R: *ʿZBʿL MLK GBL.*
Freeman & Sear, Chatsworth, 1, 10/3/1995, no. 220.

331 O6″–R9
13.27 g

Same as 317.
O: traces of ʿZ.
R: *ʿZBʿL MLK GBL.*
Elayi-Elayi, *Trésors*, p. 104, no. 411, and pl. 15:411 (Byblos hoards TXIII, TXIV and TXV?).

332 O6″–R9
13.22 g

Same as 317.
O: ʿZ.
R: *ʿZBʿL MLK GBL.*
Elayi-Elayi, *Trésors*, p. 104, no. 409, and pl. 15:409 (Byblos hoards TXIII, TXIV and TXV?).

333 O6″*–R9
13.27 g

Same as 317.
O: ʿZ.
R: *ʿZBʿL MLK GBL* partly off the flan. Restruck.
Elayi-Elayi, *Trésors*, p. 104, no. 410, and pl. 15:410 (Byblos hoards TXIII, TXIV and TXV?).

334 O6″–R10
13.31 g

Same as 317.
O: ʿZ.
R: *ʿZBʿL MLK GBL.*
Elayi-Elayi, *Trésors*, p. 104, no. 412, and pl. 15:412 (Byblos hoards TXIII, TXIV and TXV?).

335 O6″–R10
13.25 g

Same as 317.
O: ʿZ.
R: *ʿZBʿL MLK GBL.*
Elayi-Elayi, *Trésors*, p. 104, no. 414, and pl. 15:414 (Byblos hoards TXIII, TXIV and TXV?).

336 O6″–R10
13.20 g

Same as 317. Irregular flan.
O: ʿZ.
R: *ʿZBʿL MLK GBL.*
Elayi-Elayi, *Trésors*, p. 104, no. 413, and pl. 15:413 (Byblos hoards TXIII, TXIV and TXV?).

337 O8*–R10
13.20 g

Same as 317.
O: ʿZ.
R: *ʿZBʿL MLK GBL.*
Gorny, Munich, 101, 6/3/2000, no. 396.

338 O9*–R4
12.49 g
10 h

Same as 317.
O: traces of ʿZ.
R: *ʿZBʿL M*[.
Beirut, NM; Dunand, *Byblos I*, no. 6192; Elayi-Lemaire, *Trans* 38 (2009) 84, no. 114 (Byblos excavations; Byblos hoard TIX).

339 O9–R12 | 13.06 g 25 mm | 3 h
Same as 317.
O: traces of ʿZ.
R: *ʿZBʿL MLK GBL.*
Spaer coll., Jerusalem (bought in Jerusalem).

340 O10–R6 | 13.23 g
Same as 317.
O: ʿZ.
R: *ʿZBʿL MLK GBL*
Numismatica Ars Classica, Zurich, 2–3/3/1994, no. 1548.

341 O10–R7 | 13.13 g
Same as 317.
O: traces of ʿZ.
R: *ʿZBʿL MLK GBL*
Classical Numismatic Group, Lancaster-London, 29, 30/3/1994, no. 278.

342 O10–R7 | 13.22 g
Same as 317. Irregular flan.
O: ʿZ.
R:]*ZBʿL MLK GBL*
Künker, Osnabrück, 97, 7–8/3/2005, no. 954.

343 O10–R8 | 13.30 g
Same as 317.
O: traces of ʿZ.
R: *ʿZBʿL MLK GBL.*
Classical Numismatic Group, Lancaster-London, 53, 15/3/2000, no. 654.

344 O10–R8
Same as 317.
O: ʿZ.
R: *ʿZBʿL MLK GBL.*
Künker, Osnabrück, 158, April 2001, no. 70 = 154, August 2000, no. 46.

345 O10–R13 | 13.32 g
Same as 317.
O: ʿZ.
R: *ʿZBʿL MLK GBL.*
Münzen und Medaillen, Weil/Rhein, 5, 21–22/10/1999, no. 258.

346 O10–R13 | 13.32 g
Same as 317.
O: traces of ʿZ.
R: *ʿZBʿL MLK GBL.*
Information from H. Voegtli.

347 O10–R13 | 13.26 g
Same as 317.
O: scratch; traces of ʿZ.
R: *ʿZBʿL MLK GBL.*
Elsen, Brussels, 44, 27/4/1996, no. 241 = Noble, Sydney, 61, 4–6/8/1999, no. 2676.

348 O10–R13
Same as 317.
O: traces of ʿZ.
R: *ʿZBʿL MLK GBL*
Ahlström, Stockholm, 62, 11–12/11/2000, no. 1886.

349 O10*–R16* 13.24 g
Same as 317.
O: ʿZ.
R:]*Bʿ*L *MLK GBL*
UBS, Zurich, 55, 16–18/9/2002, no. 1746.

350 O10–R17* 13.15 g
Same as 317.
O: traces of ʿZ; scratch.
R: *ʿZBʿL MLK GBL.*
Gorny, Munich, 108, 3/4/2001, no. 1377.

351 O10–R17 13.14 g
Same as 317.
O: traces of ʿZ.
R: *ʿZBʿL MLK GBL.*
Künker, Osnabrück, 94, 27–28/9/2004, no. 1453.

352 O11–R6 12.97 g 6 h
Same as 317. Irregular flan.
O: traces of ʿZ.
R: *ʿZBʿL MLK GBL.*
Beirut, NM; Dunand, *Byblos I*, no. 6187; Elayi-Lemaire, *Trans* 38 (2009) 79, no. 20 (Byblos excavations; Byblos hoard TIX).

353 O11–R6 12.96 g 4 h
Same as 317. Irregular flan.
O: ʿZ.
R:] *MLK GBL.*
Beirut, NM; Dunand, *Byblos I*, no. 6109; Elayi-Lemaire, *Trans* 38 (2009) 79, no. 21 (Byblos excavations; Byblos hoard TIX).

354 O11–R6 12.95 g 4 h
Same as 317. Irregular flan.
O: ʿZ.
R: *ʿZBʿL MLK GBL.*
Beirut, NM; Dunand, *Byblos I*, no. 6161; Elayi-Lemaire, *Trans* 38 (2009) 79–80, no. 22 (Byblos excavations; Byblos hoard TIX).

355 O11–R6 12.90 g 10 h
Same as 317.
O: ʿZ.
R:] *MLK GBL.*
Beirut, NM; Dunand, *Byblos I*, no. 6101; Elayi-Lemaire, *Trans* 38 (2009) 80, no. 23 (Byblos excavations; Byblos hoard TIX).

356 O11–R6 12.88 g 1 h
Same as 317.
O: traces of ʿZ.
R: *ʿZBʿL MLK GBL.*
Beirut, NM; Dunand, *Byblos I*, no. 6123; Elayi-Lemaire, *Trans* 38 (2009) 80, no. 25 (Byblos excavations; Byblos hoard TIX).

357 O11–R6
12.87 g
7 h

Same as 317.
O: ʿZ.
R: *ʿZBʿL MLK GBL.*
Beirut, NM; Dunand, *Byblos I*, no. 6205; Elayi-Lemaire, *Trans* 38 (2009) 80, no. 26 (Byblos excavations; Byblos hoard TIX).

358 O11–R6
12.86 g
11 h

Same as 317.
O: restruck; ʿZ.
R: restruck; *]Bʿ L MLK GBL.*
Beirut, NM; Dunand, *Byblos I*, no. 6131; Elayi-Lemaire, *Trans* 38 (2009) 80, no. 27 (Byblos excavations; Byblos hoard TIX).

359 O11–R6
12.84 g
7 h

Same as 317.
O: ʿZ.
R: *ʿZBʿL MLK GBL.*
Beirut, NM; Dunand, *Byblos I*, no. 6150; Elayi-Lemaire, *Trans* 38 (2009) 80, no. 28 (Byblos excavations; Byblos hoard TIX).

360 O11–R6
12.82 g
10 h

Same as 317. Slightly worn.
O: ʿZ.
R: *ʿZBʿ[.*
Beirut, NM; Dunand, *Byblos I*, no. 6175; Elayi-Lemaire, *Trans* 38 (2009) 80, no. 29 (Byblos excavations; Byblos hoard TIX).

361 O11–R6
12.79 g
1 h

Same as 317.
O: traces of ʿZ.
R: restruck; *ʿZBʿL MLK GB[.*
Beirut, NM; Dunand, *Byblos I*, no. 6093; Elayi-Lemaire, *Trans* 38 (2009) 80, no. 30 (Byblos excavations; Byblos hoard TIX).

362 O11–R6
12.78 g
10 h

Same as 317.
O: ʿZ.
R: *ʿZBʿL MLK GBL.*
Beirut, NM; Dunand, *Byblos I*, no. 6152; Elayi-Lemaire, *Trans* 38 (2009) 80, no. 31 (Byblos excavations; Byblos hoard TIX).

363 O11–R6
12.71 g
9 h

Same as 317. Irregular flan.
O: ʿZ.
R:] *MLK GBL.*
Beirut, NM; Dunand, *Byblos I*, no. 6210″; Elayi-Lemaire, *Trans* 38 (2009) 80, no. 32 and pl. 9:32 (Byblos excavations; Byblos hoard TIX).

364 O11–R6 12.66 g 3 h

Same as 317.
O: traces of ʿZ.
R: *ʿZBʿL MLK GB*[.
Beirut, NM; Dunand, *Byblos I*, no. 6120; Elayi-Lemaire, *Trans* 38 (2009) 80, no. 33 (Byblos excavations; Byblos hoard TIX).

365 O11–R6 12.66 g 1 h

Same as 317.
O: traces of ʿZ.
R: *ʿZBʿL MLK GBL.*
Beirut, NM; Dunand, *Byblos I*, no. 6114; Elayi-Lemaire, *Trans* 38 (2009) 80, no. 34 (Byblos excavations; Byblos hoard TIX).

366 O11–R6 12.61 g 1 h

Same as 317.
O: ʿZ.
R: *ʿZBʿL MLK GBL.*
Beirut, NM; Dunand, *Byblos I*, no. 6112; Elayi-Lemaire, *Trans* 38 (2009) 80, no. 35 (Byblos excavations; Byblos hoard TIX).

367 O11–R6 12.61 g 11 h

Same as 317.
O: traces of ʿZ.
R: *ʿZBʿL MLK GBL.*
Beirut, NM; Dunand, *Byblos I*, no. 6191; Elayi-Lemaire, *Trans* 38 (2009) 80, no. 36 (Byblos excavations; Byblos hoard TIX).

368 O11–R6 12.61 g 1 h

Same as 317. Irregular flan.
O: ʿZ.
R:] *MLK GBL.*
Beirut, NM; Dunand, *Byblos I*, no. 6124; Elayi-Lemaire, *Trans* 38 (2009) 80, no. 37 (Byblos excavations; Byblos hoard TIX).

369 O11–R6 12.58 g 9 h

Same as 317.
O: ʿZ.
R:]*Bʿ L MLK GBL.*
Beirut, NM; Dunand, *Byblos I*, no. 6201; Elayi-Lemaire, *Trans* 38 (2009) 80, no. 38 (Byblos excavations; Byblos hoard TIX).

370 O11–R6 12.51 g 10 h

Same as 317.
O: ʿZ.
R: *ʿZBʿL MLK GB*[.
Beirut, NM; Dunand, *Byblos I*, no. 6177; Elayi-Lemaire, *Trans* 38 (2009) 80, no. 39 (Byblos excavations; Byblos hoard TIX).

371 O11–R6
12.47 g
6 h

Same as 317.
O: ʿZ.
R:]*ZBʿL MLK GBL.*
Beirut, NM; Dunand, *Byblos I*, no. 6159; Elayi-Lemaire, *Trans* 38 (2009) 80, no. 40 (Byblos excavations; Byblos hoard TIX).

372 O11–R6
12.21 g
10 h

Same as 317.
O: traces of ʿZ.
R: *ʿZBʿL MLK GBL.*
Beirut, NM; Dunand, *Byblos I*, no. 6134; Elayi-Lemaire, *Trans* 38 (2009) 80, no. 41 (Byblos excavations; Byblos hoard TIX).

373 O11*–R6

Same as 317. Irregular flan.
O: ʿZ.
R: *ʿZBʿL MLK GBL.*
Weil, Paris, 18/6/2004, no. 153.

374 O11–R7
13.28 g

Same as 317.
O: ʿZ.
R: *ʿZBʿL MLK GBL.*
Peus, Frankfurt/Main, 311, 31/10–1/11/1984, no. 341.

375 O11–R7
13.27 g

Same as 317.
O: ʿZ.
R:]*Bʿ L MLK GBL.*
Elsen, Brussels, 235, January–March 2006, no. 78 = 82, 11/12/2004, no. 230 = 226, September–December 2003, no. 108 = 223, November–December 2002, no. 81.

376 O11–R7
13.21 g

Same as 317. Irregular flan.
O: ʿZ.
R:]*ZBʿL MLK GBL.*
Classical Numismatic Group, Lancaster-London, 67, 22/9/2004, no. 910.

377 O11–R7
13.19 g

Same as 317.
O: ʿZ.
R:]*ZBʿL MLK GBL.*
Grün, Heidelberg, 28, 12–13/11/1999, no. 375.

378 O11–R9
13.38 g

Same as 317.
O: ʿZ.
R: *ʿZBʿL MLK GBL.*
Vecchi, London, 14, 5/2/1999, no. 687.

379 O11–R13
13.30 g

Same as 317. Irregular flan.
O: ʿZ.
R: *ʿZBʿL MLK GBL.*
Classical Numismatic Group, Lancaster-London, 47, 16/9/1998, no. 588.

380 O11–R13 13.05 g 5 h

Same as 317.
O: slightly damaged; scratch; *ʿZ*.
R: *ʿZBʿL MLK GBL.*
Beirut, NM; Dunand, *Byblos I*, no. 6183; Elayi-Lemaire, *Trans* 38 (2009) 80, no. 42 (Byblos excavations; Byblos hoard TIX).

381 O11–R13 13.02 g 7 h

Same as 317. Slightly irregular flan.
O: *ʿZ*.
R: *ʿZBʿL MLK GBL.*
Beirut, NM; Dunand, *Byblos I*, no. 6139; Elayi-Lemaire, *Trans* 38 (2009) 80, no. 43 and pl. 9:43 (Byblos excavations; Byblos hoard TIX).

382 O11–R13 13.02 g 11 h

Same as 317.
O: *ʿZ*.
R: *ʿZBʿL MLK GBL.*
Beirut, NM; Dunand, *Byblos I*, no. 6135; Elayi-Lemaire, *Trans* 38 (2009) 81, no. 44 (Byblos excavations; Byblos hoard TIX).

383 O11–R13 12.96 g 1 h

Same as 317.
O: slightly worn; traces of *ʿZ*.
R: *ʿZBʿL MLK G*[.
Beirut, NM; Dunand, *Byblos I*, no. 6108; Elayi-Lemaire, *Trans* 38 (2009) 81, no. 45 (Byblos excavations; Byblos hoard TIX).

384 O11–R13 12.93 g 11 h

Same as 317.
O: *ʿZ*.
R: *ʿZBʿL MLK GBL.*
Beirut, NM; Dunand, *Byblos I*, no. 6208; Elayi-Lemaire, *Trans* 38 (2009) 81, no. 46 (Byblos excavations; Byblos hoard TIX).

385 O11–R13 12.91 g 10 h

Same as 317.
O: *ʿZ*.
R: *ʿZBʿL MLK GBL.*
Beirut, NM; Dunand, *Byblos I*, no. 6132; Elayi-Lemaire, *Trans* 38 (2009) 81, no. 47 (Byblos excavations; Byblos hoard TIX).

386 O11–R13 12.88 g 5 h

Same as 317.
O: *ʿZ*.
R: *ʿZBʿL MLK G*[.
Beirut, NM; Dunand, *Byblos I*, no. 6121; Elayi-Lemaire, *Trans* 38 (2009) 81, no. 48 (Byblos excavations; Byblos hoard TIX).

387 O11–R13
12.88 g
7 h
Same as 317. Irregular flan.
O: ʿZ.
R: *ʿZBʿL MLK G*[.
Beirut, NM; Dunand, *Byblos I*, no. 6138; Elayi-Lemaire, *Trans* 38 (2009) 81, no. 49 (Byblos excavations; Byblos hoard TIX).

388 O11–R13
12.87 g
2 h
Same as 317.
O: ʿZ.
R: *ʿZBʿL MLK G*[.
Beirut, NM; Dunand, *Byblos I*, no. 6190; Elayi-Lemaire, *Trans* 38 (2009) 81, no. 50 (Byblos excavations; Byblos hoard TIX).

389 O11–R13
12.83 g
3 h
Same as 317.
O: ʿZ.
R: *ʿZBʿL MLK GBL.*
Troxell, *Davis Collection*, no. 283 (ex Davis coll.).

390 O11–R13
Same as 317.
O: ʿZ.
R: *ʿZBʿL MLK GBL.*
Berk, Chicago, 102, 27/5/1998, no. 290.

391 O11–R14
13.05 g
4 h
Same as 317.
O: split die; traces of ʿZ.
R: *ʿZBʿL MLK GBL.*
Beirut, NM; Dunand, *Byblos I*, no. 6203; Elayi-Lemaire, *Trans* 38 (2009) 81, no. 51 (Byblos excavations; Byblos hoard TIX).

392 O11–R14
12.87 g
5 h
Same as 317.
O: ʿZ.
R: *ʿZBʿL MLK G*[.
Beirut, NM; Dunand, *Byblos I*, no. 6129; Elayi-Lemaire, *Trans* 38 (2009) 81, no. 52 (Byblos excavations; Byblos hoard TIX).

393 O11–R14*
12.86 g
10 h
Same as 317.
O: ʿZ.
R:] *MLK GBL.*
Beirut, NM; Dunand, *Byblos I*, no. 6102; Elayi-Lemaire, *Trans* 38 (2009) 81, no. 53 (Byblos excavations; Byblos hoard TIX).

394 O11–R15
12.98 g
4 h
Same as 317.
O: ʿZ.
R: *ʿZBʿL MLK GBL.*
Beirut, NM; Dunand, *Byblos I*, no. 6136; Elayi-Lemaire, *Trans* 38 (2009) 81, no. 54 (Byblos excavations; Byblos hoard TIX).

395 O11–R15
12.90 g
4 h

Same as 317.
O: traces of ʿZ.
R: *ʿZBʿL MLK GBL.*
Beirut, NM; Dunand, *Byblos I*, no. 6193; Elayi-Lemaire, *Trans* 38 (2009) 84, no. 115 (Byblos excavations; Byblos hoard TIX).

396 O11–R15*
12.84 g
11 h

Same as 317.
O: traces of ʿZ.
R: *ʿZBʿL MLK GBL.*
Beirut, NM; Dunand, *Byblos I*, no. 6099; Elayi-Lemaire, *Trans* 38 (2009) 81, no. 55 and pl. 9:55 (Byblos excavations; Byblos hoard TIX).

397 O11–R15
12.72 g
10 h

Same as 317.
O: traces of ʿZ.
R: *ʿZBʿL MLK GBL.*
Beirut, NM; Dunand, *Byblos I*, no. 6189; Elayi-Lemaire, *Trans* 38 (2009) 81, no. 55 and pl. 9:56 (Byblos excavations; Byblos hoard TIX).

398 O11–R15
12.72 g
10 h

Same as 317. Irregular flan.
O: traces of ʿZ.
R:]*K GBL.*
Beirut, NM; Dunand, *Byblos I*, no. 6096; Elayi-Lemaire, *Trans* 38 (2009) 81, no. 55 and pl. 9:57 (Byblos excavations; Byblos hoard TIX).

399 O11–R15
12.64 g
8 h

Same as 317.
O: ʿZ.
R: *ʿZBʿL MLK GBL.*
Beirut, NM; Dunand, *Byblos I*, no. 6117; Elayi-Lemaire, *Trans* 38 (2009) 81, no. 58 (Byblos excavations; Byblos hoard TIX).

400 O11–R15
12.58 g
10 h

Same as 317.
O: ʿZ.
R:]*Bʿ L MLK GBL.*
Beirut, NM; Dunand, *Byblos I*, no. 6116; Elayi-Lemaire, *Trans* 38 (2009) 81, no. 59 (Byblos excavations; Byblos hoard TIX).

401 O11–R16
13.32 g

Same as 317.
O: ʿZ.
R: *ʿZBʿL MLK GBL.*
Nomisma, Tours, 11/5/1991, no. 107.

402 O11–R17
13.34 g

Same as 317.
O: ʿZ.
R: *ʿZBʿL MLK GBL* partly off the flan.
Albuquerque, Rouen, 42, 18/6/1993, no. 9.

403 O12*–R8 13.10 g 26 mm
Same as 317.
O: ʿZ.
R: *ʿZBʿL MLK GBL.*
Beirut, NM; Chéhab, *Monnaies*, no. 2308 and pl. 33:3.

404 O12–R11 12.70 g 25 mm
Same as 317.
O: ʿZ.
R:]*ZBʿL MLK GBL.*
SNG Cambridge, no. 6028; Florange-Ciani, Paris, 17–21/2/1925, no. 1047 (ex Allotte de la Füye coll.).

405 O12–R18* 13.37 g
Same as 317.
O: ʿZ.
R: *ʿZBʿL MLK GBL.*
Elsen, Brussels, 55, 19 and 21/9/1998, no. 310.

406 O12–R18 13.20 g
Same as 317. Slightly irregular flan.
O: ʿZ.
R: *ʿZBʿL MLK GBL.*
Berk, Chicago, 130, 17/12/2002, no. 169 = 128, 15/8/2002, no. 158 = 112, 13/1/2000, no. 249 = 102, 27/5/1998, no. 277 = 101, 24/3/1998, no. 189 = 99, 25/11/1997, no. 177 = 63, 29/8/1990, no. 124 = 61, 20/3/1990, no. 167.

407 O12–R18 13.02 g 6 h
Same as 317.
O: ʿZ.
R: *ʿZBʿL MLK GBL.*
Beirut, NM; Dunand, *Byblos I*, no. 6207; Elayi-Lemaire, *Trans* 38 (2009) 81, no. 60 (Byblos excavations; Byblos hoard TIX).

408 O12–R18 12.83 g 10 h
Same as 317. Oval flan.
O: ʿZ.
R: *ʿZBʿL MLK GBL.*
Beirut, NM; Dunand, *Byblos I*, no. 6127; Elayi-Lemaire, *Trans* 38 (2009) 81, no. 61 and pl. 9:61 (Byblos excavations; Byblos hoard TIX).

409 O12–R18 12.83 g 3 h
Same as 317. Slightly irregular flan.
O: ʿZ.
R: *ʿZBʿL MLK GBL.*
Beirut, NM; Dunand, *Byblos I*, no. 6210; Elayi-Lemaire, *Trans* 38 (2009) 81, no. 62 and pl. 9:62 (Byblos excavations; Byblos hoard TIX).

410 O12–R18 12.81 g 11 h
Same as 317.
O: ʿZ.
R:] *MLK GBL.*
Beirut, NM; Dunand, *Byblos I*, no. 6145; Elayi-Lemaire, *Trans* 38 (2009) 81, no. 63 (Byblos excavations; Byblos hoard TIX).

411 O12–R18
12.80 g
2 h
Same as 317.
O: ʿZ.
R: *ʿZBʿ*[.
Beirut, NM; Dunand, *Byblos I*, no. 6156; Elayi-Lemaire, *Trans* 38 (2009) 81, no. 64 (Byblos excavations; Byblos hoard TIX).

412 O12–R18
12.75 g
10 h
Same as 317.
O: slightly off-center to right; ʿZ.
R: *ʿZBʿL MLK GBL.*
Beirut, NM; Dunand, *Byblos I*, no. 6195; Elayi-Lemaire, *Trans* 38 (2009) 82, no. 65 (Byblos excavations; Byblos hoard TIX).

413 O12–R18
12.71 g
10 h
Same as 317.
O: ʿZ.
R: *ʿZBʿL MLK GBL.*
Beirut, NM; Dunand, *Byblos I*, no. 6141; Elayi-Lemaire, *Trans* 38 (2009) 82, no. 66 (Byblos excavations; Byblos hoard TIX).

414 O12–R18
12.70 g
10 h
Same as 317.
O: ʿZ.
R:] *MLK GBL.*
Beirut, NM; Dunand, *Byblos I*, no. 6169; Elayi-Lemaire, *Trans* 38 (2009) 82, no. 67 (Byblos excavations; Byblos hoard TIX).

415 O12–R18
12.69 g
11 h
Same as 317.
O: ʿZ.
R: *ʿZBʿL MLK GBL.*
Beirut, NM; Dunand, *Byblos I*, no. 6137; Elayi-Lemaire, *Trans* 38 (2009) 82, no. 68 (Byblos excavations; Byblos hoard TIX).

416 O12–R18
12.61 g
2 h
Same as 317. Irregular flan.
O: chisel-cut; traces of ʿZ.
R:] *GBL.*
Beirut, NM; Dunand, *Byblos I*, no. 6125; Elayi-Lemaire, *Trans* 38 (2009) 82, no. 69 (Byblos excavations; Byblos hoard TIX).

417 O12–R18
12.60 g
7 h
Same as 317.
O: ʿZ.
R: *ʿZBʿL MLK GBL.*
Beirut, NM; Dunand, *Byblos I*, no. 6144; Elayi-Lemaire, *Trans* 38 (2009) 82, no. 70 (Byblos excavations; Byblos hoard TIX).

418 O12–R19 | 13.07 g | 5 h
Same as 317.
O: chisel-cut; ʿ[.
R: *ʿZBʿL MLK GBL.*
Beirut, NM; Dunand, *Byblos I*, no. 6128; Elayi-Lemaire, *Trans* 38 (2009) 82, no. 71 and pl. 9:71 (Byblos excavations; Byblos hoard TIX).

419 O12–R19 | 12.88 g | 5 h
Same as 317.
O: off-center toward the bottom; *ʿZ.*
R:] *MLK GBL.*
Beirut, NM; Dunand, *Byblos I*, no. 6204; Elayi-Lemaire, *Trans* 38 (2009) 82, no. 72 (Byblos excavations; Byblos hoard TIX).

420 O12–R19 | 12.82 g | 11 h
Same as 317.
O: off-center to left; ʿ[.
R: slightly worn;] *MLK GB*[.
Beirut, NM; Dunand, *Byblos I*, no. 6122; Elayi-Lemaire, *Trans* 38 (2009) 82, no. 73 (Byblos excavations; Byblos hoard TIX).

421 O12–R19 | 12.74 g | 5 h
Same as 317.
O: *ʿZ.*
R:]*Bʿ L MLK GBL.*
Beirut, NM; Dunand, *Byblos I*, no. 6154; Elayi-Lemaire, *Trans* 38 (2009) 82, no. 74 (Byblos excavations; Byblos hoard TIX).

422 O12–R19 | 12.52 g | 10 h
Same as 317. Slightly irregular flan. Slightly worn.
O: *ʿZ.*
R:] *MLK GBL.*
Beirut, NM; Dunand, *Byblos I*, no. 6091; Elayi-Lemaire, *Trans* 38 (2009) 82, no. 75 (Byblos excavations; Byblos hoard TIX).

423 O12–R19 | 12.24 g | 7 h
Same as 317. Slightly irregular flan.
O: *ʿZ.*
R:]*ZBʿL MLK GBL.*
Beirut, NM; Dunand, *Byblos I*, no. 6113; Elayi-Lemaire, *Trans* 38 (2009) 82, no. 76 (Byblos excavations; Byblos hoard TIX).

424 O12–R20* | 13.25 g
Same as 317.
O: *ʿZ.*
R: *ʿZBʿL MLK GBL* partly off the flan.
Coin Galleries, New York, 10/2/1993, no. 137.

425 O12–R20 | 12.68 g | 3 h
Same as 317. Slightly irregular flan.
O: *ʿZ.*
R: *ʿZBʿL MLK GBL.*
Beirut, NM; Dunand, *Byblos I*, no. 6162; Elayi-Lemaire, *Trans* 38 (2009) 82, no. 77 and pl. 9:77 (Byblos excavations; Byblos hoard TIX).

426 O12–R21 12.97 g 5 h

Same as 317. Slightly irregular flan.
O: ʿZ.
R: *ʿZBʿL MLK GBL.*
Beirut, NM; Dunand, *Byblos I*, no. 6170; Elayi-Lemaire, *Trans* 38 (2009) 82, no. 78 (Byblos excavations; Byblos hoard TIX).

427 O12–R21 12.96 g 2 h

Same as 317. Slightly irregular flan.
O: off-center toward the bottom; traces of ʿZ.
R: *ʿZBʿL MLK GBL.*
Beirut, NM; Dunand, *Byblos I*, no. 6199; Elayi-Lemaire, *Trans* 38 (2009) 82, no. 79 (Byblos excavations; Byblos hoard TIX).

428 O12–R21 12.92 g 11 h

Same as 317. Slightly irregular flan.
O: ʿZ.
R:]*Bʿl MLK GBL.*
Beirut, NM; Dunand, *Byblos I*, no. 6097; Elayi-Lemaire, *Trans* 38 (2009) 82, no. 80 (Byblos excavations; Byblos hoard TIX).

429 O12–R21 12.87 g 4 h

Same as 317. Slightly irregular flan.
O: traces of ʿZ.
R:]*MLK GBL.*
Beirut, NM; Dunand, *Byblos I*, no. 6106; Elayi-Lemaire, *Trans* 38 (2009) 82, no. 81 (Byblos excavations; Byblos hoard TIX).

430 O12–R21 12.87 g 4 h

Same as 317.
O: ʿZ.
R: *ʿZBʿL MLK GBL.*
Beirut, NM; Dunand, *Byblos I*, no. 6118; Elayi-Lemaire, *Trans* 38 (2009) 82, no. 82 and pl. 9:82 (Byblos excavations; Byblos hoard TIX).

431 O12–R21 12.86 g 6 h

Same as 317.
O: ʿZ.
R: inscription obliterated.
Beirut, NM; Dunand, *Byblos I*, no. 6171; Elayi-Lemaire, *Trans* 38 (2009) 82, no. 83 (Byblos excavations; Byblos hoard TIX).

432 O12–R21 12.86 g 11 h

Same as 317.
O: ʿZ.
R: *ʿZBʿL MLK GBL.*
Beirut, NM; Dunand, *Byblos I*, no. 6188; Elayi-Lemaire, *Trans* 38 (2009) 82, no. 84 (Byblos excavations; Byblos hoard TIX).

433 O12–R21
12.86 g
3 h

Same as 317.
O: ʿZ.
R: *ʿZBʿL MLK GBL.*
Beirut, NM; Dunand, *Byblos I*, no. 6181; Elayi-Lemaire, *Trans* 38 (2009) 82, no. 85 (Byblos excavations; Byblos hoard TIX).

434 O12–R21
12.82 g
4 h

Same as 317.
O: ʿZ.
R:]*ʿL MLK GBL.*
Beirut, NM; Dunand, *Byblos I*, no. 6149; Elayi-Lemaire, *Trans* 38 (2009) 83, no. 86 (Byblos excavations; Byblos hoard TIX).

435 O12–R21
12.80 g
10 h

Same as 317.
O: ʿZ.
R: *ʿZBʿL MLK GBL.*
Beirut, NM; Dunand, *Byblos I*, no. 6142; Elayi-Lemaire, *Trans* 38 (2009) 83, no. 87 (Byblos excavations; Byblos hoard TIX).

436 O12–R21
12.74 g
3 h

Same as 317. Slightly irregular flan.
O: ʿZ.
R: *ʿZBʿL MLK GBL.*
Beirut, NM; Dunand, *Byblos I*, no. 6173; Elayi-Lemaire, *Trans* 38 (2009) 83, no. 88 (Byblos excavations; Byblos hoard TIX).

437 O12–R21
12.73 g
4 h

Same as 317. Slightly irregular flan.
O: ʿZ.
R: *ʿZBʿL MLK GBL.*
Beirut, NM; Dunand, *Byblos I*, no. 6200; Elayi-Lemaire, *Trans* 38 (2009) 83, no. 89 (Byblos excavations; Byblos hoard TIX).

438 O12–R21
12.70 g
11 h

Same as 317. Slightly worn.
O: ʿZ.
R: *ʿZBʿL MLK GBL.*
Beirut, NM; Dunand, *Byblos I*, no. 6210′; Elayi-Lemaire, *Trans* 38 (2009) 83, no. 90 (Byblos excavations; Byblos hoard TIX).

439 O12–R21
12.70 g
11 h

Same as 317. Slightly worn.
O: ʿZ.
R: *ʿZB*[.
Beirut, NM; Dunand, *Byblos I*, no. 6111; Elayi-Lemaire, *Trans* 38 (2009) 83, no. 91 (Byblos excavations; Byblos hoard TIX).

440 O12–R21
12.52 g
7 h

Same as 317. Slightly worn.
O: ʿZ.
R:]*Bʿ L MLK GBL.*
Beirut, NM; Dunand, *Byblos I*, no. 6202; Elayi-Lemaire, *Trans* 38 (2009) 83, no. 92 (Byblos excavations; Byblos hoard TIX).

441 O12–R22
13.22 g

Same as 317. Slightly irregular flan.
O: ʿZ.
R: *ʿZBʿL MLK GBL.*
Elayi-Elayi, *Trésors*, p. 100, no. 237 and pl. 11:237 (Byblos hoards TXIII, TXIV and TXV?).

442 O12–R22
12.94 g
7 h

Same as 317. Slightly irregular flan.
O: ʿZ.
R:]*Bʿ L MLK GBL.*
Beirut, NM; Dunand, *Byblos I*, no. 6209; Elayi-Lemaire, *Trans* 38 (2009) 83, no. 93 (Byblos excavations; Byblos hoard TIX).

443 O12–R22
12.61 g
11 h

Same as 317. Slightly worn.
O: ʿZ.
R:]*L MLK GBL.*
Beirut, NM; Dunand, *Byblos I*, no. 6105; Elayi-Lemaire, *Trans* 38 (2009) 83, no. 94 and pl. 10:94 (Byblos excavations; Byblos hoard TIX).

444 O12–R23
13.15 g

Same as 317.
O: slightly off-center to right; ʿZ.
R:]*Bʿ L MLK GBL.*
Elayi-Elayi, *Trésors*, p. 100, no. 236, and pl. 11:236 (Byblos hoards TXIII, TXIV and TXV?).

445 O12–R23
13.01 g
1 h

Same as 317.
O: ʿZ.
R: *ʿZBʿL MLK GBL.*
Beirut, NM; Dunand, *Byblos I*, no. 6197; Elayi-Lemaire, *Trans* 38 (2009) 83, no. 95 (Byblos excavations; Byblos hoard TIX).

446 O12–R23
12.86 g
4 h

Same as 317.
O: ʿZ.
R: restruck;]*ʿL MLK GBL.*
Beirut, NM; Dunand, *Byblos I*, no. 6098; Elayi-Lemaire, *Trans* 38 (2009) 83, no. 96 and pl. 10:96 (Byblos excavations; Byblos hoard TIX).

447 O12–R23
12.84 g
6 h
Same as 317.
O: ʿZ.
R: *ʿZBʿL MLK GBL.*
Beirut, NM; Dunand, *Byblos I*, no. 6110; Elayi-Lemaire, *Trans* 38 (2009) 83, no. 97 (Byblos excavations; Byblos hoard TIX).

448 O12–R23
12.84 g
10 h
Same as 317.
O: ʿZ.
R: *ʿZBʿL MLK GBL.*
Beirut, NM; Dunand, *Byblos I*, no. 6165; Elayi-Lemaire, *Trans* 38 (2009) 83, no. 98 (Byblos excavations; Byblos hoard TIX).

449 O12–R23
12.82 g
1 h
Same as 317.
O: ʿZ.
R: *ʿZBʿL MLK GBL.*
Beirut, NM; Dunand, *Byblos I*, no. 6160; Elayi-Lemaire, *Trans* 38 (2009) 83, no. 99 (Byblos excavations; Byblos hoard TIX).

450 O12–R23
12.82 g
9 h
Same as 317. Slightly irregular flan.
O: ʿZ.
R: *ʿZBʿL MLK GBL.*
Beirut, NM; Dunand, *Byblos I*, no. 6180; Elayi-Lemaire, *Trans* 38 (2009) 83, no. 100 (Byblos excavations; Byblos hoard TIX).

451 O12–R23
12.73 g
11 h
Same as 317.
O: ʿZ.
R: *]Bʿ L MLK GBL.*
Beirut, NM; Dunand, *Byblos I*, no. 6151; Elayi-Lemaire, *Trans* 38 (2009) 83, no. 101 (Byblos excavations; Byblos hoard TIX).

452 O12–R23
12.73 g
5 h
Same as 317. Slightly irregular flan.
O: ʿZ.
R: *]BʿL MLK GBL.*
Beirut, NM; Dunand, *Byblos I*, no. 6179; Elayi-Lemaire, *Trans* 38 (2009) 83, no. 102 (Byblos excavations; Byblos hoard TIX).

453 O12–R23
12.70 g
5 h
Same as 317.
O: ʿZ.
R: *ʿZBʿL MLK GBL.*
Beirut, NM; Dunand, *Byblos I*, no. 6172; Elayi-Lemaire, *Trans* 38 (2009) 83, no. 103 (Byblos excavations; Byblos hoard TIX).

454 O12–R23
12.67 g
8 h

Same as 317.
O: ʿZ.
R: *ʿZBʿL MLK GBL.*
Beirut, NM; Dunand, *Byblos I*, no. 6167; Elayi-Lemaire, *Trans* 38 (2009) 83, no. 104 (Byblos excavations; Byblos hoard TIX).

455 O12–R23
12.45 g
12 h

Same as 317. Slightly worn.
O: ʿZ.
R: *ʿZBʿL MLK GBL.*
Beirut, NM; Dunand, *Byblos I*, no. 6176; Elayi-Lemaire, *Trans* 38 (2009) 83, no. 105 (Byblos excavations; Byblos hoard TIX).

456 O12–R24*
13.27 g

Same as 317. Slightly worn.
O: off-center toward the bottom; ʿZ.
R: *ʿZBʿL MLK GBL.*
Hirsch, Munich, 159, 21–24/9/1988, no. 457.

457 O12–R24
12.92 g
4 h

Same as 317.
O: ʿZ.
R: restruck; *ʿZBʿL MLK GBL.*
Beirut, NM; Dunand, *Byblos I*, no. 6104; Elayi-Lemaire, *Trans* 38 (2009) 83, no. 106 (Byblos excavations; Byblos hoard TIX).

458 O12–R24
12.90 g
4 h

Same as 317.
O: ʿZ.
R: *ʿZBʿL MLK GBL.*
Beirut, NM; Dunand, *Byblos I*, no. 6119; Elayi-Lemaire, *Trans* 38 (2009) 84, no. 107 and pl. 10:107 (Byblos excavations; Byblos hoard TIX).

459 O12–R24
12.79 g
9 h

Same as 317.
O: ʿZ.
R: traces of overstrike; *ʿZBʿL MLK GB*[.
Beirut, NM; Dunand, *Byblos I*, no. 6157; Elayi-Lemaire, *Trans* 38 (2009) 84, no. 108 (Byblos excavations; Byblos hoard TIX).

460 O12–R24
12.66 g
7 h

Same as 317. slightly worn.
O: restruck; traces of ʿZ.
R: *ʿZBʿL MLK GBL.*
Beirut, NM; Dunand, *Byblos I*, no. 6194; Elayi-Lemaire, *Trans* 38 (2009) 84, no. 109 (Byblos excavations; Byblos hoard TIX).

461 O12–R25
13.27 g

Same as 317.
O: ʿZ.
R: *ʿZBʿL MLK GBL.*
Védrines, Paris, 7/7/1984, no. 73.

462 O12–R25
13.25 g

Same as 317.
O: ʿZ.
R: *ʿZBʿL MLK GBL.*
Burgan, Paris, 45, 26/6/2004, no. 145.

463 O12–R25
13.21 g

Same as 317. Irregular flan.
O: ʿZ.
R: *ʿZBʿL MLK GBL.*
Rubinger, Antiqua, Woodland Hills, 19, 2007, no. 65 = Lanz, Munich, 72, 29/5/1995, no. 299 = 60, 11/6/1992, no. 260.

464 O12–R25
12.99 g
4 h

Same as 317. Slightly worn.
O: ʿZ.
R:]*ʿL MLK GBL.*
Beirut, NM; Dunand, *Byblos I*, no. 6126; Elayi-Lemaire, *Trans* 38 (2009) 84, no. 110 and pl. 10:110 (Byblos excavations; Byblos hoard TIX).

465 O12–R25
12.96 g
2 h

Same as 317. Slightly irregular flan.
O: ʿZ.
R: *ʿZBʿL MLK GBL.*
Beirut, NM; Dunand, *Byblos I*, no. 6100; Elayi-Lemaire, *Trans* 38 (2009) 84, no. 111 (Byblos excavations; Byblos hoard TIX).

466 O12–R25
12.96 g
5 h

Same as 317. Slightly irregular flan.
O: off-center toward the bottom; ʿZ.
R:] *MLK GBL.*
Beirut, NM; Dunand, *Byblos I*, no. 6148; Elayi-Lemaire, *Trans* 38 (2009) 84, no. 112 (Byblos excavations; Byblos hoard TIX).

467 O12–R25*
12.77 g

Same as 317.
O: ʿZ.
R: *ʿZBʿL MLK GBL.*
Berk, Chicago, 108, 12/5/1999, no. 152.

468 O12–R25
12.58 g
3 h

Same as 317.
O: ʿZ.
R: *ʿZBʿL MLK GBL.*
Beirut, NM; Dunand, *Byblos I*, no. 6146; Elayi-Lemaire, *Trans* 38 (2009) 84, no. 113 (Byblos excavations; Byblos hoard TIX).

469 O12–R25

Same as 317.
O: off-center to right; ʿZ.
R: *ʿZBʿL MLK GBL.*
Berk, Chicago, 65, 26/2/1991, no. 375.

470 O12–R26 13.28 g
Same as 317.
O: ʿZ.
R: *ʿZBʿL MLK GBL.*
Elayi-Elayi, *Trésors*, p. 100, no. 238 and pl. 11:238 (Byblos hoards TXIII, TXIV, and TXV?).

471 O12–R27 13.19 g
Same as 317. Slightly irregular flan.
O: ʿZ.
R: *ʿZBʿL MLK GBL.*
Elayi-Elayi, *Trésors*, p. 100, no. 233 and pl. 10:233 (Byblos hoards TXIII, TXIV, and TXV?).

472 O13–R8 13.24 g
Same as 317. Slightly irregular flan.
O: off-center toward the bottom; ʿZ.
R: *ʿZBʿL MLK GBL.*
Classical Numismatic Group, Lancaster-London, 29, 30/3/1994, no. 280.

473 O13–R12 13.27 g
Same as 317.
O: ʿZ.
R: *ʿZBʿL MLK GBL.*
Elayi-Elayi, *Trésors*, p. 100, no. 228, and pl. 10:228 (Byblos hoards TXIII, TXIV, and TXV?).

474 O13*–R12 13.27 g
Same as 317.
O: ʿZ.
R: *ʿZBʿL MLK GBL.*
Elayi-Elayi, *Trésors*, p. 104, no. 415, and pl. 15:415 (Byblos hoards TXIII, TXIV, and TXV?).

475 O13–R12* 13.22 g
Same as 317.
O: ʿZ.
R: *ʿZBʿL MLK GBL.*
Elayi-Elayi, *Trésors*, p. 100, no. 229, and pl. 10:229 (Byblos hoards TXIII, TXIV, and TXV?).

476 O13–R12 13.19 g
Same as 317.
O: ʿZ.
R: *ʿZBʿL MLK GBL.*
Elayi-Elayi, *Trésors*, p. 100, no. 230, and pl. 10:230 (Byblos hoards TXIII, TXIV, and TXV?).

477 O13–R13* 25 mm
Same as 317. Slightly irregular flan.
O: ʿZ.
R: *ʿZBʿL MLK GBL.*
Boston, Museum of Fine Arts, no. 2341.

478 O13–R18 13.24 g
Same as 317. Slightly irregular flan.
O: ʿZ.
R: *ʿZBʿL MLK GBL.*
Parsy, Paris, 12–13/10/2004, no. 98.

479 O13–R19* Same as 317.
13.15 g
O: ʿZ.
R: *ʿZBʿL MLK GBL.*
Vinchon, Paris, 27/10/2000, no. 253 = Numismatic Fine Arts, Beverly Hills, 20, 9–10/3/1988, no. 809.

480 O13–R20 Same as 317.
13.11 g
3 h
O: ʿZ.
R: *ʿZBʿL MLǨ GBL.*
Leu, Zurich, 72, 12/5/1998, no. 312.

481 O13–R21 Same as 317.
13.28 g
O: off-center toward the bottom; ʿZ.
R: *ʿZBʿL MLK GBL.*
Berk, Chicago, 122, 6/9/2001, no. 248 = 119, 15/3/2001, no. 284 = 106, 20/1/1999, no. 325 = 103, 28/7/1998, no. 213.

482 O13–R22* Same as 317.
O: off-center to right; ʿZ.
R: *ʿZBʿL MLK GBL.*
Weil, Paris, 30/3/2004, no. 264.

483 O13–R23 Same as 317.
13.25 g 25 mm
6 h
O: ʿZ.
R: *ʿZBʿL MLK GBL.*
Comptoir Général Financier, Paris, 16/6/2000, no. 91 = 26/6/1998, no. 123.

484 O13–R24 Same as 317.
13.28 g
O: ʿZ.
R: *ʿZBʿL MLK* [.
Elayi-Elayi, *Trésors*, p. 101, no. 232, and pl. 10:232 (Byblos hoards TXIII, TXIV, and TXV?).

485 O13–R24 Same as 317.
13.27 g
O: ʿZ.
R: *ʿZBʿL MLK GBL.*
Elayi-Elayi, *Trésors*, p. 100, no. 231, and pl. 10:231 (Byblos hoards TXIII, TXIV, and TXV?).

486 O13–R24 Same as 317.
13.26 g
O: off-center to left; ʿZ.
R:]*ZBʿL MLK GBL.*
Elayi-Elayi, *Trésors*, p. 105, no. 416, and pl. 15:416 (Byblos hoards TXIII, TXIV and TXV?).

487 O13–R24 Same as 317.
13.26 g
O: slightly off-center toward the bottom;ʿZ.
R: *ʿZBʿL MLK GBL.*
Hirsch, Munich, 161, 22–24/2/1989, no. 346.

488 O13–R24 13.26 g
Same as 317.
O: ʿZ.
R: *ʿZBʿL MLK GBL* partly off the flan.
Elsen, Brussels, 61, 18–19/3/2000, no. 170 = Leu, Zurich, Autumn 1998, no. 97 = Peus, Frankfurt/Main, 332, 23–25 and 28/10/1991, no. 284.

489 O13–R24 13.25 g
Same as 317.
O: ʿZ.
R: *ʿZBʿL MLK GBL*.
Numismatica Ars Classica, Zurich, 40, 4/12/1996, no. 1081.

490 O13–R24 13.24 g
Same as 317.
O: ʿZ.
R: *ʿZBʿL MLK GBL*.
Ponterio, San Diego, 1/8/1995, no. 337.

491 O13–R25 13.30 g
Same as 317.
O: ʿZ.
R:]*Bʿ L MLK GBL*.
Noble, Sydney, 60, 21–23/4/1999, no. 1961.

492 O13–R25 13.28 g
Same as 317.
O: slightly off-center toward the bottom; restruck; ʿZ.
R: *ʿZBʿL MLK GBL*.
Gorny, Munich, 108, 3/4/2001, no. 1376.

493 O13–R25 12.84 g
Same as 317.
O: ʿZ.
R: *ʿZBʿL MLK GBL*.
SNG Cambridge, no. 6029.

494 O13–R25
Same as 317.
O: off-center toward the bottom; ʿZ.
R: *ʿZBʿL MLK GBL*.
Weil, Paris, 18/6/2004, no. 155.

495 O13–R28* 13.22 g
Same as 317.
O: ʿZ.
R: *ʿZBʿL MLK GBL*.
Elayi-Elayi, *Trésors*, p. 105, no. 418 and pl. 15:418 (Byblos hoards TXIII, TXIV, and TXV?).

496 O13–R29* 13.25 g
Same as 317.
O: ʿZ.
R:]*Bʿ L MLK GBL* partly off the flan.
Elayi-Elayi, *Trésors*, p. 105, no. 417, and pl. 15:417 (Byblos hoards TXIII, TXIV, and TXV?).

497 O14–R8 13.25 g
Same as 317.
O: defect above the tail of the seahorse; ʿZ.
R: *ʿZBʿL MLK GBL*.
Gorny, Munich, 90, 12–13/10/1998, no. 479.

498 O14–R11
13.26 g

Same as 317.
O: defect above the tail of the seahorse; ʿZ.
R: *ʿZBʿL MLK GBL.*
Classical Numismatic Group, Lancaster-London, 53, 15/3/2000, no. 653 = England, Quarryville-London, 4, 21/9/1986, no. 125.

499 O14*–R11
13.23 g 25 mm

Same as 317.
O: defect above the tail of the seahorse; ʿZ.
R: *ʿZBʿL MLK GBL;* dot before the inscription.
Hanover, Kestner Museum, no. 1958.11.

500 O14–R11

Same as 317.
O: defect above the tail of the seahorse; ʿZ.
R: *ʿZBʿL MLK GBL.*
Ritter, Dusseldorf, 32, December 1991, no. 328.

501 O14–R12
13.19 g 27 mm
3 h

Same as 317.
O: ʿZ.
R: *ʿZBʿL MLK GBL.*
Paris, BNF, no. HS 1973-1-272 (ex Seyrig coll.).

502 O14–R12
13.17 g

Same as 317. Slightly irregular flan.
O: defect above the tail of the seahorse; ʿZ.
R: *ʿZBʿL MLK GBL.*
England, Quarryville-London, 9, 7/12/1989, no. 115.

503 O14–R12
13.16 g

Same as 317.
O: defect above the tail of the seahorse; ʿZ.
R: *ʿZBʿL MLK GBL.*
England, Quarryville-London, 1, 1/5/1987, no. 87.

504 O14–R12
13.13 g

Same as 317. Irregular flan.
O: defect above the tail of the seahorse; ʿZ.
R: *ʿZBʿL MLK GBL.*
Berk, Chicago, 121, 10/7/2001, no. 231 = 118, 17/1/2001, no. 250.

505 O14–R18
13.34 g

Same as 317. Irregular flan.
O: defect above the tail of the seahorse; ʿZ.
R: *ʿZBʿL MLK GBL* partly off the flan.
Elayi-Elayi, *Trésors*, p. 105, no. 422 and pl. 16:422 (Byblos hoards TXIII, TXIV, and TXV?).

506 O14–R18
13.28 g

Same as 317.
O: defect above the tail of the seahorse; ʿZ.
R: *ʿZBʿL MLK GBL.*
Ponterio, San Diego, 104, 4/11/1999, no. 493.

507 O14–R18

Same as 317.
O: defect above the tail of the seahorse; ʿZ.
R: *ʿZBʿL MLK GBL.*
Numismatica Ars Classica, Zurich, N, 26/6/2003, no. 1388.

508	O14–R20 13.14 g	Same as 317. Slightly irregular flan. O: defect above the tail of the seahorse; ʿZ. R: *ʿZBʿL MLK GBL.* England, Quarryville-London, 26, 11/6/1993, no. 362.
509	O14–R21 13.14 g 3 h	Same as 317. O: defect above the tail of the seahorse; ʿZ. R: *ʿZBʿL MLK GBL.* Numismatic Fine Arts, Beverly Hills, 30, 8/12/1992, no. 128.
510	O14–R22 13.23 g	Same as 317. O: defect above the tail of the seahorse; ʿZ. R: *ʿZBʿL MLK GBL.* England, Quarryville-London, 18, 3/12/1991, no. 198.
511	O14–R22	Same as 317. Slightly irregular. O: defect above the tail of the seahorse; ʿZ. R: *ʿZBʿL MLK GBL.* Berk, Chicago, 103, 28/7/1998, no. 215.
512	O14–R23* 13.24 g	Same as 317. O: defect above the tail of the seahorse; ʿZ. R: *ʿZBʿL MLK GBL.* Elayi-Elayi, *Trésors*, p. 105, no. 421, and pl. 16:421 (Byblos hoards TXIII, TXIV and TXV?).
513	O14–R23 12.55 g	Same as 317. O: defect above the tail of the seahorse; ʿZ. R: off-center toward the top; *]LK GBL.* Stack's, New York, 19–20/6/1969, no. 206.
514	O14–R24 13.20 g	Same as 317. Irregular flan. O: defect above the tail of the seahorse; ʿZ. R: restruck; *ʿZBʿL MLK GBL.* Richelieu Numismatique, Paris, May 1995, no. 69.
515	O14–R24 13.19 g	Same as 317. O: defect above the tail of the seahorse; ʿZ. R: *ʿZBʿL MLK GBL.* Gorny, Munich, 76, 22/4/1993, no. 219 = 64, 11/10/1995, no. 223.
516	O14–R25	Same as 317. O: defect above the tail of the seahorse; ʿZ. R: *ʿZBʿL MLK GBL.* Berk, Chicago, 59, 1/11/1989, no. 321.
517	O14–R26* 13.17 g	Same as 317. Slightly irregular flan. O: defect above the tail of the seahorse; ʿZ. R: *ʿZBʿL MLK GBL.* Elayi-Elayi, *Trésors*, p. 105, no. 419, and pl. 15:419 (Byblos hoards TXIII, TXIV, and TXV?).

518 O14–R27* 13.26 g
Same as 317.
O: defect above the tail of the seahorse; ʿZ.
R: *ʿZBʿL MLK GBL.*
Gorny-Mosch, Giessener Münzhandlung, Munich, 126, 13–14/10/2003, no. 1450.

519 O14–R27
Same as 317.
O: defect above the tail of the seahorse; ʿZ.
R: *ʿZBʿL MLK GBL.*
Berk, Chicago, 64, 20/11/1990, no. 123.

520 O14–R30 13.33 g
Same as 317. Irregular flan.
O: defect above the tail of the seahorse; ʿZ.
R: *ʿZBʿL MLK GBL* partly off the flan.
Elayi-Elayi, *Trésors*, p. 100, no. 241, and pl. 11:241 (Byblos hoards TXIII, TXIV, and TXV?).

521 O14–R30 13.24 g 6 h
Same as 317.
O: defect above the tail of the seahorse; ʿZ.
R: *ʿZBʿL MLK GBL.*
Sotheby's, Zurich, 27–28/10/1993, no. 872 = Numismatic Fine Arts, Beverly Hills, 26, 14/8/1991, no. 116.

522 O14–R30 13.23 g
Same as 317.
O: defect above the tail of the seahorse; ʿZ.
R: *ʿZBʿL MLK GB*[.
UBS, Zurich, 78, 9–10/9/2008, no. 1059.

523 O14–R30 13.18 g
Same as 317. Irregular flan.
O: defect above the tail of the seahorse; ʿZ.
R: *ʿZBʿL MLK GBL.*
Berk, Chicago, 6, 10/1/2010, no. 245.

524 O14–R30* 13.18 g
Same as 317.
O: off-center toward the top; defect above the tail of the seahorse; ʿZ.
R: slightly off-center to left; *ʿZBʿL MLK GBL* partly off the flan.
Elayi-Elayi, *Trésors*, p. 105, no. 420, and pl. 16:420 (Byblos hoards TXIII, TXIV and TXV?).

525 O14–R30
Same as 317.
O: slightly off-center toward the top; defect above the tail of the seahorse; ʿZ.
R: slightly off-center toward the top; *ʿZBʿL MLK GBL* partly off the flan.
Weil, Paris, 30/3/2004, no. 263.

526 O14–R31* 13.19 g
Same as 317.
O: defect above the tail of the seahorse; ʿZ.
R: scratch; *ʿZBʿL MLK GBL.*
Elayi-Elayi, *Trésors*, p. 105, no. 423, and pl. 16:423 (Byblos hoards TXIII, TXIV, and TXV?).

527 O14–R32 13.38 g
Same as 317.
O: off-center toward the top; defect above the tail of the seahorse; ʿZ.
R: *ʿZBʿL MLK GBL.*
Ponterio, San Diego, 145, 11–12/1/2008, no. 187.

528 O14–R32* 13.26 g
Same as 317.
O: defect above the tail of the seahorse; ʿZ.
R: *ʿZBʿL MLK GBL.*
Ponterio, San Diego, 145, 11–12/1/2008, no. 186.

529 O14–R32 13.29 g
Same as 317.
O: defect above the tail of the seahorse; ʿZ.
R: *ʿZBʿL MLK GBL.*
Henzen, Amerongen, 163, September 2005, no. 287 = 159, May 2005, no. 247 = 151, August 2004, no. 165 = 146, March 2004, no. 175.

530 O14–R32 13.23 g
Same as 317.
O: defect above the tail of the seahorse; ʿZ.
R: *ʿZBʿL MLK GBL.*
Brandt, Stuttgart, 1, Autumn 1999, no. 96.

531 O14–R32 13.21 g
Same as 317. Slightly worn.
O: defect above the tail of the seahorse; ʿZ.
R: *ʿZBʿL MLK GBL.*
Classical Numismatic Group, Lancaster-London, 67, 22/9/2004, no. 911.

532 O14–R32 13.21 g
Same as 317.
O: defect above the tail of the seahorse; ʿZ.
R: *ʿZBʿL MLK GBL.*
Henzen, Amerongen, 165, December 2005, no. 251 = Classical Numismatic Group, Lancaster-London, 29, March 1994, no. 128.

533 O14–R32 13.21 g
Same as 317.
O: off-center to left; defect above the tail of the seahorse; ʿZ.
R: *ʿZBʿL MLK GBL.*
Numismatica Ars Classica, Zurich, 11, 29/4/1998, no. 116.

534 O14–R32
Same as 317. Slightly irregular flan.
O: defect above the tail of the seahorse; ʿZ.
R: *ʿZBʿL MLK GBL.*
Ponterio, San Diego, 47, 8–9/3/1991, no. 1337.

535 O14–R32
Same as 317.
O: defect above the tail of the seahorse; ʿZ.
R: off-center to right; *ʿZBʿL MLK GBL*.
Poinsignon Numismatique, Strasbourg, 44, October 1999, no. 703.

536 O14–R33*
13.18 g
Same as 317.
O: defect above the tail of the seahorse; ʿZ.
R: *ʿZBʿL MLK GBL*.
Vecchi, London, 5, 5/3/1997, no. 274.

537 O14–R34
13.35 g
Same as 317.
O: defect above the tail of the seahorse; ʿZ.
R: *ʿZBʿL MLK GBL*.
UBS, Zurich, 63, 6–8/9/2005, no. 218.

538 O14–R34*
13.22 g
Same as 317.
O: defect above the tail of the seahorse; ʿZ.
R: *ʿZBʿL MLK GBL*.
Gorny, Munich, 101, 6/3/2000, no. 395.

539 O14–R34
13.22 g
Same as 317.
O: off-center toward the top; defect above the tail of the seahorse; ʿZ.
R: *ʿZBʿL MLK GBL*.
Platt, Paris, November 1998, no. 145.

540 O14–R34
13.07 g
Same as 317.
O: off-center toward the bottom; defect above the tail of the seahorse; ʿZ.
R: *ʿZBʿL MLK GBL* partly off the flan and worn.
Bourgey, Paris, 8/3/1999, no. 11.

541 O14–R35
13.28 g
Same as 317.
O: off-center toward the bottom; defect above the tail of the seahorse; ʿZ.
R: off-center toward the top;]*L MLK GBL*.
Berk, Chicago, 146, 29/11/2005, no. 139 = 144, 13/7/2005, no. 172.

542 O14–R35*
13.19 g
Same as 317. Irregular flan.
O: defect above the tail of the seahorse; ʿZ.
R: *ʿZBʿL MLK GBL*.
Noble, Sydney, 60, 21–23/4/1999, no. 1960.

543 O14–R36*
13.31 g
Same as 317.
O: defect above the tail of the seahorse; ʿZ.
R:]*ZBʿL MLK GBL*.
Gorny, Munich, 90, 12–13/10/1998, no. 478.

544 O14–R36
13.28 g
Same as 317.
O: off-center toward the bottom; defect above the tail of the seahorse; ʿZ.
R: *ʿZBʿL MLK GBL.*
Sotheby's, London, 6–7/11/1997, no. 113.

545 O14–R36
13.25 g
Same as 317. Slightly worn.
O: defect above the tail of the seahorse; ʿZ.
R: *ʿZBʿL MLK GBL.*
Spink, London, 60, 7/10/1987, no. 161.

546 O14–R36
13.23 g
Same as 317.
O: off-center to left; defect above the tail of the seahorse; ʿZ.
R: *ʿZBʿL MLK GBL.*
Lanz, Munich, 125, 1/11/2005, no. 494.

547 O14–R36
13.22 g
Same as 317. Slightly irregular flan.
O: defect above the tail of the seahorse; ʿZ.
R: *ʿZBʿL MLK GBL.*
Lanz, Munich, 66, 22/11/1993, no. 330.

548 O14–R36*
13.21 g
Same as 317.
O: defect above the tail of the seahorse; ʿZ.
R: *ʿZBʿL MLK GBL.*
Gorny, Munich, 87, 2/3/1998, no. 288.

549 O14–R36
13.20 g
Same as 317. Slightly irregular flan.
O: off-center toward the bottom; defect above the tail of the seahorse; ʿZ.
R: *ʿZBʿL MLK GBL.*
Peus, Frankfurt/Main, 357, 28–30/10/1998, no. 338.

550 O15–R12
13.12 g
Same as 317. Slightly irregular flan.
O: off-center to right; traces of overstrike; ʿZ.
R: *ʿZBʿL MLK GBL.*
Noble, Sydney, 61, 4–6/8/1999, no. 2675.

551 O15–R18
Same as 317.
O: slightly off-center toward the top; ʿZ. Flaw.
R: *ʿZBʿL MLK GBL.*
Kovacs, San Mateo, 9, 21/11/1988, no. 127.

552 O15*–R24
13.20 g
Same as 317.
O: off-center to left; ʿZ.
R:]*ZBʿL MLK GBL.*
Müller, Münz Zentrum-Rheinland, Solingen, 121, 12–14/5/2004, no. 429 = Künker, Osnabrück, 43, 2–3/9/1998, no. 181.

553 O16–R9 14.04 g
Same as 317.
O: defect under the line of waves; ʿZ.
R: *ʿZBʿL MLK GB*[.
Gorny-Mosch, Giessener Münzhandlung, Munich, 134, 11–12/10/2004, no. 76.

554 O16–R9 13.78 g
Same as 317.
O: defect under the line of waves; ʿZ.
R: *ʿZBʿL MLK GBL.*
Classical Numismatic Group, Lancaster-London, 37, 20/3/1996, no. 674.

555 O16–R9 13.34 g
Same as 317.
O: defect under the line of waves; ʿZ.
R: *ʿZBʿL MLK GB*[.
Gorny-Mosch, Giessener Münzhandlung, Munich, 134, 11–12/10/2004, no. 75.

556 O16*–R9 13.32 g
Same as 317.
O: defect under the line of waves; ʿZ.
R: *ʿZBʿL MLK GBL.*
Monetarium, Schweizerische Kreditanstalt, Zurich, Spring 1996, no. 78.

557 O16–R11 13.05 g
Same as 317.
O: defect under the line of waves; ʿZ.
R: *ʿZBʿL MLK GBL.*
Hirsch, Munich, 169, 20–22/2/1991, no. 548.

558 O17*–R8 13.27 g
Same as 317.
O: off-center to right; defect on the foreleg of the bull; ʿZ.
R: *ʿZBʿL MLK GBL* slightly worn.
Spink, London, 135, 6/10/1999, no. 179.

559 O17–R8 13.26 g
Same as 317. Slightly worn.
O: ʿZ.
R: defect on the foreleg of the bull; *ʿZBʿL MLK GBL.*
Ponterio, San Diego, 142, 27–28/4/2007, no. 1664.

560 O17–R8 13.25 g
Same as 317.
O: ʿZ.
R: defect on the foreleg of the bull; *ʿZBʿL MLK GBL.*
Markov, New York, 11, 2–3/9/2003, no. 94.

561 O17–R8 13.21 g
Same as 317. Slightly worn.
O: ʿZ.
R: defect on the foreleg of the bull; *ʿZBʿL MLK GBL* partly obliterated.
Classical Numismatic Group, Lancaster-London, 45, 18/3/1998, no. 575.

562 O17–R19 | Same as 317. Slightly worn.
O: off-center toward the bottom; ʿZ.
R: *ʿZBʿL MLK GBL*.
Berk, Chicago, 57, 29/3/1989, no. 161.

563 O17–R22
13.23 g | Same as 317. Slightly worn.
O: slightly off-center to right; ʿZ.
R: *ʿZBʿL MLK GBL* partly obliterated.
Elayi-Elayi, *Trésors*, p. 100, no. 240, and pl. 11:240 (Byblos hoards TXIII, TXIV, and TXV?).

564 O17–R24
13.19 g | Same as 317. Slightly irregular flan.
O: off-center to right; ʿZ.
R: off-center toward the bottom; restruck; *ʿZBʿL MLK GBL*.
Numismatica Ars Classica, Zurich, L, 18/5/2001, no. 1415.

565 O17–R24
13.17 g
3 h | Same as 317. Slightly irregular flan.
O: ʿZ.
R: *ʿZBʿL MLK GBL*.
Ars Antiqua, London, 2, 4/10/2001, no. 127 = Leu, Zurich, 79, 31/10/2000, no. 765.

566 O17–R25
12.85 g
11 h | Same as 317. Slightly worn.
O: ʿZ.
R: *ʿZBʿL MLK GBL*.
Hess, Lucerne, 14/4/1954, no. 188.

567 O6″–R?
13.14 g | Same as 317. Rather worn.
O: ʿZ.
R: restruck;]*ZBʿL MLK GBL*.
Hirsch, Munich, 204, 5–7/5/1999, no. 493.

568 O9–R?
11.83 g | Same as 317. Rather worn.
O: ʿZ.
R: inscription illegible.
Baldwin, London, 37, 4–5/5/2004, no. 744 = 34, 13/10/2003, no. 524 = Bourgey, Paris, 24–25/2/1983, no. 122 = Myers, New York, March 1974, no. 100.

569 O10–R?
13.32 g | Same as 317. Slightly worn.
O: ʿZ.
R: inscription illegible.
Gorny, Munich, 95, 9/3/1999, no. 393.

570 O10–R?
13.25 g | Same as 317. Slightly worn.
O: ʿZ.
R: inscription illegible.
Elayi-Elayi, *Trésors*, p. 100, no. 227, and pl. 10:227 (Byblos hoards TXIII, TXIV, and TXV?).

571 O10–R?
13.22 g
Same as 317. Slightly worn.
O: ʿZ.
R: ʿ*ZB*ʿ[partly off the flan.
Hirsch, Munich, 175, 21–26/9/1992, no. 527.

572 O10–R?
13.17 g
Same as 317. Slightly worn.
O: ʿZ.
R: inscription illegible.
Elsen, Brussels, 12, 18/2/1989, no. 71.

573 O10–R?
13.01 g
12 h
Same as 317. Slightly worn.
O: ʿZ.
R: restruck; inscription illegible.
Private coll.

574 O10–R?
12.93 g 24 mm
9 h
Same as 317. Slightly worn.
O: ʿZ.
R: inscription illegible.
Copenhagen, NatMus, no. 132; *SNG Copenhagen*, no. 132.

575 O11–R?
12.77 g
4 h
Same as 317. Slightly worn.
O: traces of ʿZ.
R: restruck; ʿ*ZB*ʿ*L* [ ] *GBL*.
Beirut, NM; Dunand, *Byblos I*, no. 6193; Elayi-Lemaire, *Trans* 38 (2009) 84, no. 115 (Byblos excavations; Byblos hoard TIX).

576 O11–R?
12.71 g
5 h
Same as 317. Slightly worn.
O: traces of ʿZ.
R: restruck; inscription illegible
Beirut, NM; Dunand, *Byblos I*, no. 6130; Elayi-Lemaire, *Trans* 38 (2009) 84, no. 116 (Byblos excavations; Byblos hoard TIX).

577 O12–R?
13.21 g
Same as 317. Slightly worn.
O: off-center to right; ʿZ.
R:]*B*ʿ[partly obliterated.
Elayi-Elayi, *Trésors*, p. 100, no. 239, and pl. 11:239 (Byblos hoards TXIII, TXIV, and TXV?).

578 O12–R?
13.16 g
Same as 317. Slightly worn.
O: off-center toward the top; ʿZ.
R: traces of ʿ*ZB*ʿ*L MLK GBL*.
Kricheldorf, Stuttgart, 39, 6–7/2/1987, no. 103.

579 O12–R?
13 g
10 h
Same as 317. Slightly worn.
O: ʿZ.
R: traces of ʿ*ZB*ʿ*L MLK GBL*.
Beirut, NM; Dunand, *Byblos I*, no. 6166; Elayi-Lemaire, *Trans* 38 (2009) 84, no. 117 (Byblos excavations; Byblos hoard TIX).

580 O12–R?
12.99 g
4 h

Same as 317. Slightly worn.
O: ʿZ.
R: traces of *ʿZBʿL MLK GBL*.
Beirut, NM; Dunand, *Byblos I*, no. 6178; Elayi-Lemaire, *Trans* 38 (2009) 84, no. 117 (Byblos excavations; Byblos hoard TIX).

581 O12–R?
12.90 g
4 h

Same as 317. Slightly worn.
O: ʿZ.
R: inscription illegible.
Beirut, NM; Dunand, *Byblos I*, no. 6103; Elayi-Lemaire, *Trans* 38 (2009) 84, no. 119 (Byblos excavations; Byblos hoard TIX).

582 O12–R?
12.83 g
3 h

Same as 317. Slightly worn.
O: ʿZ.
R: traces of *ʿZBʿL MLK GBL*.
Beirut, NM; Dunand, *Byblos I*, no. 6182; Elayi-Lemaire, *Trans* 38 (2009) 84, no. 120 (Byblos excavations; Byblos hoard TIX).

583 O12–R?

Same as 317. Slightly worn.
O: ʿZ.
R: traces of *ʿZBʿL MLK GBL*.
Buckland, London, 1/6/1994, no. 603.

584 O13–R?
13.27 g

Same as 317. Slightly worn.
O: off-center toward the bottom; ʿZ.
R: traces of *ʿZBʿL MLK GBL*.
Classical Numismatic Group, Lancaster-London, 60, 22/5/2002, no. 933 = Berk, Chicago, 106, 20/1/1999, no. 324.

585 O13–R?
13.26 g

Same as 317. Slightly worn.
O: slightly off-center toward the bottom; ʿZ.
R: *ʿZBʿL MLK* [.
Spink, Zurich, 41, 30/4/1992, no. 35.

586 O13–R?
13.24 g

Same as 317. Slightly worn.
O: ʿZ.
R: *ʿZBʿL M*[.
Argenor Numismatique, Paris, 22/4/2004, no. 65.

587 O13–R?
13.23 g

Same as 317. Slightly worn.
O: slightly off-center toward the bottom; ʿZ.
R: traces of *ʿZBʿL MLK GBL*.
Kovacs, San Mateo, 10, 18/5/1990, no. 167.

588 O13–R?
13.22 g

Same as 317. Slightly worn.
O: off-center toward the bottom; ʿZ.
R: traces of *ʿZBʿL MLK GBL*.
Elayi-Elayi, *Trésors*, p. 100, no. 235, and pl. 11:235 (Byblos hoards TXIII, TXIV, and TXV?).

589 O14–R?
13.33 g
Same as 317. Slightly worn.
O: off-center toward the bottom; defect above the tail of the seahorse; ʿZ.
R: traces of *ʿZBʿL MLK GBL.*
Lanz, Munich, 40, 25/5/1987, no. 396.

590 O14–R?
13.28 g
Same as 317. Slightly worn. Irregular flan.
O: off-center toward the top; defect above the tail of the seahorse; ʿZ.
R: traces of *ʿZBʿL MLK GBL.*
Freeman & Sear, Chatsworth, 12, 28/10/2005, no. 211.

591 O14–R?
13.27 g
Same as 317. Slightly worn.
O: defect above the tail of the seahorse; ʿZ.
R: inscription illegible.
Vecchi, London, 13, 4/9/1998, no. 454.

592 O14–R?
13.25 g
Same as 317. Slightly worn.
O: defect above the tail of the seahorse; ʿZ.
R: traces of *ʿZBʿL MLK GBL.*
Elayi-Elayi, *Trésors*, p. 100, no. 242, and pl. 11:242 (Byblos hoards TXIII, TXIV, and TXV?).

593 O14–R?
13.25 g
Same as 317. Slightly worn.
O: off-center to right; defect above the tail of the seahorse; ʿZ.
R: traces of *ʿZBʿL MLK GBL.*
Classical Numismatic Group, Lancaster-London, 46, 24/6/1998, no. 498.

594 O14–R?
13.23 g
Same as 317. Slightly worn.
O: defect above the tail of the seahorse; ʿZ.
R: inscription illegible.
Gorny, Munich, 97, 11/10/1999, no. 520.

595 O14–R?
13.20 g
Same as 317. Slightly worn. Irregular flan.
O: defect above the tail of the seahorse; ʿZ.
R: traces of *ʿZBʿL MLK GBL.*
Berk, Chicago, 117, 28/11/2000, no. 261 = 112, 13/1/2000, no. 251 = 107, 18/3/1999, no. 227.

596 O14–R?
13.19 g
Same as 317. Slightly worn.
O: defect above the tail of the seahorse; ʿZ.
R: traces of *ʿZBʿL MLK GBL.*
Numismatica Ars Classica, New York, Triton II, 1–2/12/1998, no. 488.

597 O14–R?
13.12 g
Same as 317. Slightly worn.
O: defect above the tail of the seahorse; ʿZ.
R: restruck; traces of] *MLK GBL.*
Richelieu Numismatique, Paris, November 1993, no. 23.

598 O14–R? 13.12 g
Same as 317. Rather worn.
O: off-center toward the top; defect above the tail of the seahorse; ʿZ.
R: traces of *ʿZBʿL MLK GBL.*
Hirsch, Munich, 204, 5–7/5/1999, no. 492.

599 O14–R? 12.98 g
Same as 317. Slightly worn. Irregular flan.
O: defect above the tail of the seahorse; ʿZ.
R: traces of *ʿZBʿL MLK GBL.*
Berk, Chicago, 116, 17/10/2000, no. 361 = 105, 17/11/1998, no. 271.

600 O14–R?
Same as 317. Slightly worn. Irregular flan.
O: defect above the tail of the seahorse; ʿZ.
R: traces of *ʿZBʿL MLK GBL.*
Berk, Chicago, 102, 27/5/1998, no. 284.

601 O14–R?
Same as 317. Slightly worn.
O: defect above the tail of the seahorse; ʿZ.
R: traces of *ʿZBʿL MLK GBL.*
Berk, Chicago, 102, 27/5/1998, no. 281.

602 O14–R?
Same as 317. Slightly worn.
O: defect above the tail of the seahorse; ʿZ.
R: traces of *ʿZBʿL MLK GBL.*
Martin, London, 17/2, G46.

603 O15–R? 13.21 g
Same as 317. Slightly worn.
O: ʿZ.
R: traces of *ʿZBʿL MLK GBL.*
Vecchi, London, 16, 9/10/1999, no. 291.

604 O15–R? 12.93 g 3 h
Same as 317. Slightly worn.
O: ʿZ.
R: off-center to left; traces of *ʿZBʿL MLK GBL.*
Kricheldorf, Stuttgart, 39, 6–7/2/1987, no. 102; *SNG ANS*, no. 1431 (ex Berry coll.).

605 O15–R?
Same as 317. Slightly worn.
O: ʿZ.
R: traces of *ʿZBʿL MLK GBL.*
Berk, Chicago, 57, 29/3/1989, no. 162.

606 O17–R? 13.25 g
Same as 317. Slightly worn.
O: off-center toward the bottom; ʿZ.
R: traces of *ʿZBʿL MLK GBL.*
Gorny, Munich, 89, 5/5/1998, no. 275 = 71, 3/5/1995, no. 419.

607 O17–R? 13.18 g
Same as 317. Slightly worn.
O: ʿZ.
R: traces of *ʿZBʿL MLK GBL.*
Berk, Chicago, 114, 23/5/2000, no. 242.

608 O17–R?
Same as 317. Slightly worn.
O: slightly off-center toward the bottom; ʿZ.
R: traces of *ʿZBʿL MLK GBL*.
Berk, Chicago, 103, 28/7/1998, no. 218.

609 O18*–R? 13.18 g
Same as 317. Slightly worn. Oval flan.
O: off-center toward the top; ʿZ.
R: traces of *ʿZBʿL MLK GBL*.
Spink, Zurich, 20, 6/10/1986, no. 374.

610 O18–R?
Same as 317. Slightly worn. Split die.
O: ʿZ.
R: traces of *ʿZBʿL MLK GBL*.
Berk, Chicago, 102, 27/5/1998, no. 280.

611 O?–R6 12.85 g
Same as 317. Slightly worn. Irregular flan.
O: restruck; ʿZ.
R: traces of *ʿZBʿL MLK GBL*.
Beirut, NM; Dunand, *Byblos I*, no. 6196; Elayi-Lemaire, *Trans* 38 (2009) 84, no. 122 (Byblos excavations; Byblos hoard TIX).

612 O?–R6 12.76 g
Same as 317. Slightly worn.
O: traces of ʿZ.
R: *ʿZBʿL MLK GBL*.
Beirut, NM; Dunand, *Byblos I*, no. 6184; Elayi-Lemaire, *Trans* 38 (2009) 84, no. 123 (Byblos excavations; Byblos hoard TIX).

613 O?–R8 13.33 g
Same as 317. Slightly worn. Irregular flan.
O: traces of ʿZ.
R: traces of *ʿZBʿL MLK GBL*.
Elsen, Brussels, 242, October–December 2007, no. 136 = 89, 9/9/2006, no. 845 = 77, 13/12/2003, no. 154 = 71, 20–21/9/2002, no. 313 = 63, 16/9/2000, no. 569.

614 O?–R8 13.25 g
Same as 317. Slightly worn.
O: traces of ʿZ.
R: *ʿZBʿL MLK GBL* partly off the flan.
Berk, Chicago, 105, 17/11/1998, no. 273 = 102, 27/5/1998, no. 278.

615 O?–R8 13.23 g
Same as 317. Slightly worn.
O: traces of ʿZ.
R: *ʿZBʿL MLK GBL*.
Gorny, Munich, 92, 20–21/11/1998, no. 278.

616 O?–R8 13.23 g
Same as 317. Slightly worn.
O: ʿZ.
R: traces of *ʿZBʿL MLK GBL*.
Coin Galleries, New York, 14/4/1993, no. 721.

617 O?–R8
13.20 g
Same as 317. Slightly worn.
O: traces of ʿZ.
R: *ʿZBʿL MLK GBL.*
Künker, Osnabrück, 46, 9–11/3/1999, no. 138.

618 O?–R8
Same as 317. Slightly worn.
O: traces of ʿZ.
R:]*BʿL MLK GBL.*
Berk, Chicago, 102, 27/5/1998, no. 283.

619 O?–R8
Same as 317. Slightly worn.
O: traces of ʿZ.
R:]*ZBʿL MLK GBL.*
Berk, Chicago, 103, 28/7/1998, no. 217.

620 O?–R8
Same as 317. Slightly worn.
O: traces of ʿZ.
R: *ʿZBʿL MLK GBL.*
Berk, Chicago, 102, 27/5/1998, no. 285.

621 O?–R11
13.14 g
Same as 317. Slightly worn.
O: traces of ʿZ.
R:]*ZBʿL MLK GBL.*
Hirsch, Munich, 212, 22–24/11/2000, no. 414.

622 O?–R11
13.14 g
Same as 317. Slightly worn.
O: off-center toward the bottom; traces of ʿZ.
R: *ʿZBʿL MLK GBL.*
Berk, Chicago, 135, 10/12/2003, no. 118 = 129, 16/10/2002, no. 119 = 119, 15/3/2001, no. 283.

623 O?–R11
13 g
Same as 317. Slightly worn. Irregular flan.
O: traces of ʿZ.
R:]*BʿL MLK GBL.*
Empire Coins, Ormond Beach, 4, 9–10/11/1985, no. 125.

624 O?–R12
13.22 g
Same as 317. Slightly worn. Slightly irregular flan.
O: ʿZ.
R: *ʿZBʿL MLK GB*[.
Freeman & Sear, Chatsworth, 3, 10/12/1996, no. 290.

625 O?–R12
13.22 g
Same as 317. Slightly worn.
O: traces of ʿZ.
R: *ʿZBʿL MLK GBL.*
Superior Galleries, Beverly Hills, 11–12/6/1986, no. 1406 = Monnaies et Médailles/Münzen und Medaillen, Basel, 23–24/6/1983, no. 380.

626 O?–R12
13.22 g
Same as 317. Slightly worn.
O: traces of ʿZ.
R: *ʿZBʿL MLK GBL.*
Classical Numismatic Group, Lancaster-London, 53, 15/3/2000, no. 655.

627	O?–R12 13.14 g	Same as 317. Slightly worn. Slightly irregular flan. O: traces of ʿZ. R: *ʿZBʿL MLK GBL.* UBS, Zurich, 55, 16–18/9/2002, no. 1748.
628	O?–R15 12.80 g 1 h	Same as 317. Slightly worn. O: traces of ʿZ. R:]*Bʿl MLK GBL.* Beirut, NM; Dunand, *Byblos I*, no. 6174; Elayi-Lemaire, *Trans* 38 (2009) 84, no. 124 (Byblos excavations; Byblos hoard TIX).
629	O?–R15 12.61 g	Same as 317. Slightly worn. O: traces of ʿZ. R: *ʿZBʿL MLK GB*[. Beirut, NM; Dunand, *Byblos I*, no. 6163; Elayi-Lemaire, *Trans* 38 (2009) 84, no. 125 (Byblos excavations; Byblos hoard TIX).
630	O?–R17 13.32 g	Same as 317. Slightly worn. O: traces of ʿZ. R: *ʿZBʿL MLK GBL.* Spink, London, 36, 30–31/5/1986, no. 43.
631	O?–R17 13.29 g 3 h	Same as 317. Slightly worn. Irregular flan. O: traces of ʿZ. R: traces of *ʿZBʿL MLK GBL.* Argenor Numismatique, Paris, October 2002, no. 362.
632	O?–R17 13.26 g 26 mm 12 h	Same as 317. Slightly worn. O: restruck; traces of ʿZ. R: *ʿZBʿL MLK GB*[. Private coll.
633	O?–R17 13.23 g	Same as 317. Slightly worn. Slightly irregular flan. O: traces of ʿZ. R: traces of *ʿZBʿL MLK GB*[. Henzen, Amerongen, 162, August 2005, no. 212 = 145, 2004, no. 165.
634	O?–R17 13.22 g	Same as 317. Slightly worn. O: scratches; traces of ʿZ. R: traces of *ʿZBʿL MLK GB*[. Künker, Osnabrück, 59, 26–28/9/2000, no. 296 = 145, January 1999, no. 39.
635	O?–R17 13.20 g	Same as 317. Slightly worn. Slightly irregular flan. O: traces of ʿZ. R: traces of *ʿZBʿL MLK GBL.* Glendining, London, 43, December 1992, no. 176 = 4/6/1992, no. 99 = Müller, Münz Zentrum-Rheinland, Solingen, 60, 20–21/1/1989, no. 122.

636	O?–R17 13.20 g	Same as 317. Slightly worn. O: traces of ʿZ. R: *ʿZBʿL MLK GB*[. Ponterio, San Diego, 61, 26–27/2/1993, no. 303.
637	O?–R17 13.18 g	Same as 317. Slightly worn. O: flaw; traces of ʿZ. R: *ʿZBʿL MLK GB*[. Künker, Osnabrück, 67, 9/10/2001, no. 467.
638	O?–R17 13.17 g	Same as 317. Slightly worn. O: traces of ʿZ. R: *ʿZBʿL MLK GBL.* Berk, Chicago, 108, 12/5/1999, no. 153.
639	O?–R17 13.13 g	Same as 317. Slightly worn. Irregular flan. O: traces of ʿZ. R: *ʿZBʿL MLK GBL.* Hirsch, Munich, 201, 24–26/9/1998, no. 381 = Gorny, Munich, 78, 13/6/1996, no. 288.
640	O?–R17	Same as 317. Slightly worn. O: traces of ʿZ. R: *ʿZBʿL MLK GBL.* Berk, Chicago, 62, 13/6/1990, no. 192.
641	O?–R17	Same as 317. Slightly worn. O: traces of ʿZ. R: *ʿZBʿL MLK GBL.* Berk, Chicago, 59, 1/11/1989, no. 322.
642	O?–R18 13.29 g	Same as 317. Slightly worn. O: off-center toward the bottom; traces of ʿZ. R: *ʿZBʿL MLK GBL* partly off the flan. Elsen, Brussels, 70, 15/6/2002, no. 110 = 69, 16/3/2002, no. 257.
643	O?–R18 13.22 g	Same as 317. Slightly worn. O: scratch; slightly off-center to left; traces of ʿZ. R: *ʿZBʿL MLK GBL.* Berk, Chicago, 138, 1/6/2004, no. 158.
644	O?–R18 13.20 g	Same as 317. Slightly worn. O: slightly off-center toward the bottom; traces of ʿZ. R: *ʿZBʿL MLK GBL.* Berk, Chicago, 117, 28/11/2000, no. 261 = 112, 13/1/2000, no. 250 = 107, 18/3/1999, no. 227.
645	O?–R18 13.17 g	Same as 317. Slightly worn. O: slightly off-center toward the bottom; traces of ʿZ. R: *ʿZBʿL MLK GBL.* Berk, Chicago, 133, 22/7/2003, no. 171 = 131, 2/4/2003, no. 105 = 126, 23/4/2002, no. 103 = 111, 28/10/1999, no. 177 = 106, 20/1/1999, no. 326.

646 O?–R18
13.10 g
Same as 317. Slightly worn.
O: slightly off-center toward the bottom; traces of ʿZ.
R: *ʿZBʿL MLK GBL.*
Berk, Chicago, 107, 18/3/1999, no. 226.

647 O?–R18
12.49 g
12 h
Same as 317. Slightly worn.
O: traces of ʿZ.
R: *ʿZBʿL MLK GBL.*
Beirut, NM; Dunand, *Byblos I*, no. 6094; Elayi-Lemaire, *Trans* 38 (2009) 84, no. 126 (Byblos excavations; Byblos hoard TIX).

648 O?–R18
Same as 317. Slightly worn.
O: ʿZ.
R: *ʿZBʿL MLK GB*[.
Berk, 102, 27/5/1998, no. 282.

649 O?–R18
Same as 317. Slightly worn.
O: traces of ʿZ.
R: *ʿZBʿL MLK GBL.*
Berk, Chicago, 58, 28/6/1981, no. 183.

650 O?–R21
13.15 g
Same as 317. Slightly worn. Irregular flan.
O: ʿZ.
R:] *MLK GBL.*
Berk, Chicago, 111, 28/10/1999, no. 178 = 105, 17/11/1998, no. 272.

651 O?–R23
12.89 g
Same as 317. Slightly worn.
O: traces of ʿZ.
R: *ʿZBʿL MLK GBL.*
Berk, Chicago, 107, 18/3/1999, no. 228.

652 O?–R22
11.92 g
10 h
Same as 317. Slightly worn.
O: off-center to left; traces of ʿZ.
R: *ʿZBʿL MLK GBL.*
Beirut, NM; Dunand, *Byblos I*, no. 6133; Elayi-Lemaire, *Trans* 38 (2009) 84, no. 127 (Byblos excavations; Byblos hoard TIX).

653 O?–R24
13.21 g
Same as 317. Slightly worn.
O: slightly off-center toward the bottom; traces of ʿZ.
R: *ʿZBʿL MLK GBL.*
Berk, Chicago, 116, 17/10/2000, no. 360 = 77, 16/6/1993, no. 167.

654 O?–R24
13.21 g
Same as 317. Slightly worn.
O: traces of ʿZ.
R: *ʿZBʿL MLK GBL.*
Classical Numismatic Group, Lancaster-London, 41, 19/3/1997, no. 696.

655 O?–R24
12.96 g
Same as 317. Slightly worn.
O: traces of ʿZ.
R: *ʿZBʿL MLK GBL.*
Forrer, *Weber Collection*, no. 8039 (Weber coll.).

656 O?–R24
10.80 g
Same as 317. Slightly worn.
O: off-center toward the bottom; traces of ʿZ.
R: *ʿZBʿL MLK GBL* partly off the flan.
Argenor Numismatique, Paris, October 2001, no. 450.

657 O?–R24
Same as 317. Slightly worn.
O: slightly off-center toward the top; traces of ʿZ.
R: *ʿZBʿL MLK GBL.*
Berk, Chicago, 102, 27/5/1998, no. 279.

658 O?–R24
Same as 317. Slightly worn.
O: traces of ʿZ.
R: *ʿZBʿL MLK GBL.*
Berk, Chicago, 100, 29/1/1998, no. 287 = 96, 18/6/1997, no. 156 = 94, 16/1/1997, no. 207 = 90, 17/4/1996, no. 177.

659 O?–R24
Same as 317. Slightly worn.
O: off-center toward the bottom; traces of ʿZ.
R: *ʿZBʿL MLK GBL.*
Berk, Chicago, 84, 19/1/1995, no. 331.

660 O?–R24
Same as 317. Slightly worn. Slightly irregular flan.
O: traces of ʿZ.
R: *ʿZBʿL MLK GBL.*
Weil, Paris, 18/6/2004, no. 154.

661 O?–R25
12.66 g
11 h
Same as 317. Slightly worn. Irregular flan.
O: off-center toward the bottom; traces of ʿZ.
R:]*ʿL MLK GBL.*
Beirut, NM; Dunand, *Byblos I*, no. 6115; Elayi-Lemaire, *Trans* 38 (2009) 85, no. 128 (Byblos excavations; Byblos hoard TIX).

662 O?–R32
13.21 g
Same as 317. Slightly worn.
O: off-center toward the bottom; traces of ʿZ.
R: *ʿZBʿL MLK GBL* partly off the flan.
Vecchi, London, 17, 15/12/1999, no. 379.

663 O?–R32
13.24 g
Same as 317. Slightly worn.
O: slightly off-center to left; traces of ʿZ.
R: *ʿZBʿL MLK* [.
Freeman & Sear, Chatsworth, 3, 10/12/1996, no. 291 = 1, 10/3/1995, no. 221.

664 O?–R32
13.13 g
Same as 317. Slightly worn. Slightly irregular flan.
O: traces of ʿZ.
R: *ʿZBʿL MLK GBL.*
Berk, Chicago, 105, 17/11/1998, no. 274.

665 O?–R35 13.24 g

Same as 317. Slightly worn.
O: traces of ʿZ.
R: *ʿZBʿL MLK GBL.*
UBS, Zurich, 55, 16–18/9/2002, no. 1747.

666 O?–R35 13.20 g

Same as 317. Slightly worn.
O: off-center toward the top; traces of ʿZ.
R: *ʿZBʿL MLK GBL.*
Hirsch, Munich, 162, 8–10/5/1989, no. 344 = 159, 21–24/9/1988, no. 456.

667 O?–R35 13.20 g

Same as 317. Slightly worn.
O: slightly off-center toward the bottom; traces of ʿZ.
R: slightly off-center to left; *ʿZBʿL MLK GBL.*
Berk, Chicago, 74, 4/11/1992, no. 157 = 72, 4/8/1992, no. 168.

668 O?–R35 13.16 g

Same as 317. Slightly worn.
O: slightly off-center toward the bottom; traces of ʿZ.
R: *ʿZBʿL MLK GBL.*
Richelieu Numismatique, Paris, 1994, no. 35.

669 O?–R35

Same as 317. Slightly worn.
O: off-center toward the top; ʿZ.
R: traces of *ʿZBʿL MLK GBL.*
Berk, Chicago, 103, 28/7/1998, no. 214.

670 O?–R36 13.29 g

Same as 317. Slightly worn.
O: slightly off-center toward the bottom; traces of ʿZ.
R: traces of *ʿZBʿL MLK GBL.*
Berk, Chicago, 139, 4/8/2004, no. 202 = 133, 22/7/2003, no. 170.

671 O?–R36 13.26 g

Same as 317. Slightly worn.
O: slightly off-center to left; traces of ʿZ.
R: *ʿZBʿL MLK GBL.*
Gorny, Munich, 79, 14/10/1996, no. 292.

672 O?–R36 13.11 g

Same as 317. Slightly worn.
O: slightly off-center to left; traces of ʿZ.
R: *ʿZBʿL MLK GBL.*
Gorny, Munich, 32, 12–13/11/1985, no. 127.

673 O?–R36 13.09 g

Same as 317. Slightly worn. Irregular flan.
O: slightly off-center to left; traces of ʿZ.
R:]*BʿL MLK GBL.*
Berk, Chicago, 125, 27/2/2002, no. 199 = 103, 28/7/1998, no. 212.

674 O?–R36

Same as 317. Slightly worn.
O: slightly off-center to right; traces of ʿZ.
R: *ʿZBʿL MLK GBL.*
Martin, London, January 1990, no. G40.

675 O?–R37
13.24 g
Same as 317. Slightly worn. Slightly irregular flan.
O: traces of ʿZ.
R: *ʿZBʿL MLK GBL.*
Poindessault-Védrines, Paris, 31/3/1997, no. 112.

676 O?–R37
13.20 g
Same as 317. Slightly worn.
O: traces of ʿZ.
R: slightly off-center to left; *ʿZBʿL MLK GB*[.
Berk, Chicago, 97, 12/8/1997, no. 211 = 88, 28/11/1995, no. 228 = 66, 11/6/1991, no. 159.

677 O?–R37*
Same as 317. Slightly worn.
O: traces of ʿZ.
R: *ʿZBʿL MLK GB*[.
Berk, Chicago, 87, 13/9/1995, no. 184.

678 O?–R38
13.26 g
Same as 317. Slightly worn.
O: slightly off-center toward the top; traces of ʿZ.
R: *ʿZBʿL MLK GBL.*
Hess-Divo, Zurich, 299, 27/10/2004, no. 110.

679 O?–R38
13.25 g
Same as 317. Slightly worn.
O: traces of ʿZ.
R: *ʿZBʿL MLK GBL* partly off the flan.
Künker, Osnabrück, 52, 29–30/9/1999, no. 3184 = 46, 9–11/3/1999, no. 139.

680 O?–R38*
13.05 g 25 mm
6 h
Same as 317. Slightly worn.
O: traces of ʿZ.
R: *ʿZBʿL MLK GBL.*
Copenhagen, NatMus, no. KP 2239,1.

681 O?–R38
Same as 317. Slightly worn.
O: traces of ʿZ.
R: *ʿZBʿL MLK GBL.*
Berk, Chicago, 102, 27/5/1998, no. 287.

682 O?–R39*
13.25 g
Same as 317. Slightly worn. Irregular flan.
O: traces of ʿZ.
R: traces of *ʿZBʿL MLK GBL.*
Monetarium, Schweizerische Kreditanstalt, Zurich, 50, Autumn 1988, no. 80 = 47, Spring 1987, no. 53.

683 O?–R40*
13.22 g
Same as 317. Slightly worn.
O: slightly off-center to left; traces of ʿZ.
R: *ʿZBʿL MLK GBL.*
Freeman & Sear, Chatsworth, 1, 10/3/1995, no. 219.

684 O?–R40
13.21 g
Same as 317. Slightly worn. Slightly irregular flan.
O: slightly off-center toward the top; traces of ʿZ.
R: *ʿZBʿL MLK GBL.*
Berk, Chicago, 156, 23/10/2007, no. 163 = 132, 14/5/2003, no. 163 = 89, 14/2/1996, no. 191 = 71, 28/5/1992, no. 180 = 70, 16/3/1992, no. 219 = 58, 28/6/1981, no. 184.

685 O?–R40
13.10 g
Same as 317. Slightly worn.
O: traces of ʿZ.
R: *ʿZBʿL MLK GBL*.
Freeman & Sear, Chatsworth, 4, 14/1/1998, no. 192.

686 O?–R?
13.40 g 25 mm
Same as 317. Rather worn.
O: traces of ʿZ.
R: traces of *ʿZBʿL MLK GBL*.
Beirut, AUB Museum, no. 2947D.

687 O?–R?
13.30 g 25 mm
Same as 317. Rather worn.
O: traces of ʿZ.
R: traces of *ʿZBʿL MLK GBL*.
Platt, Paris, November 1998, no. 144.

688 O?–R?
13.27 g
Same as 317. Rather worn.
O: traces of ʿZ.
R: *ʿZB*[.
Kölner Münzkabinett, Cologne, 37, 22–23/11/1984, no. 34.

689 O?–R?
13.26 g
Same as 317. Rather worn.
O: off-center toward the bottom; traces of ʿZ.
R: *ʿZBʿL MLK GBL* partly off the flan.
Classical Numismatic Group, Lancaster-London, 63, 21/5/2003, no. 670.

690 O?–R?
13.23 g
Same as 317. Rather worn.
O: traces of ʿZ.
R: traces of *ʿZBʿL MLK GBL*.
Gorny, Munich, 92, 20–21/11/1998, no. 279.

691 O?–R?
13.22 g 25 mm
9 h
Same as 317. Rather worn.
O: traces of ʿZ.
R: *ʿZBʿL MLK GBL*.
Private coll. LPN.

692 O?–R?
13.22 g 25 mm
Same as 317. Rather worn. Slightly irregular flan.
O: traces of ʿZ.
R: *ʿZBʿL MLK G*[.
Beirut, AUB Museum, no. 2946.

693 O?–R?
13.22 g
Same as 317. Rather worn.
O: flaw; traces of ʿZ.
R: traces of *ʿZBʿL MLK GBL*.
Gorny, Munich, 78, 13/6/1996, no. 287.

694 O?–R?
13.21 g
Same as 317. Rather worn.
O: off-center to left; traces of ʿZ.
R: traces of *ʿZBʿL MLK GBL*.
Classical Numismatic Group, Lancaster-London, 29, 30/3/1994, no. 279.

695 O?–R?
13.20 g
7 h

Same as 317. Rather worn.
O: traces of *ʿZ*.
R: traces of *ʿZBʿL MLK GBL*.
Classical Numismatic Group, Lancaster-London, 13/9/2006, no. 463.

696 O?–R?
13.17 g

Same as 317. Rather worn. Slightly irregular flan.
O: traces of *ʿZ*.
R: traces of *ʿZBʿL MLK GBL*.
Monnaies et Médailles/Münzen und Medaillen, Basel, 198, 11–13/2/1998, no. 377.

697 O?–R?
13.17 g

Same as 317. Rather worn.
O: traces of *ʿZ*.
R: overstruck; traces of *ʿZBʿL MLK GBL*.
Ponterio, San Diego, 102, 29/7/1999, no. 210.

698 O?–R?
13.17 g

Same as 317. Rather worn.
O: traces of *ʿZ*.
R: traces of *ʿZBʿL MLK GBL*.
Gorny, Munich, 31, 24–26/4/1985, no. 218.

699 O?–R?
13.16 g

Same as 317. Rather worn.
O: off-center to right; traces of *ʿZ*.
R:]*GBL*.
Berk, Chicago, 136, 5/2/2004, no. 84 = 123, 23/10/2001, no. 180 = 118, 17/1/2001, no. 251 = 105, 17/11/1998, no. 270.

700 O?–R?
13.15 g

Same as 317. Rather worn. Slightly irregular flan.
O: traces of *ʿZ*.
R: traces of *ʿZBʿL MLK GBL*.
Elayi-Elayi, *Trésors*, p. 100, no. 243, and pl. 11:243 (Byblos hoards TXIII, TXIV, and TXV?).

701 O?–R?
13.12 g

Same as 317. Rather worn. Slightly irregular flan.
O: traces of *ʿZ*.
R: traces of *ʿZBʿL MLK GBL*.
Hirsch, Munich, 170, 22–25/5/1991, no. 690 = 166, 16–19/5/1990, no. 541 = 162, 8–10/5/1989, no. 346 = 157, 24–26/2/1988, no. 200.

702 O?–R?
13.04 g
4 h

Same as 317. Rather worn.
O: traces of *ʿZ*.
R: *ʿZBʿL MLK GB*[.
Beirut, NM; Dunand, *Byblos I*, no. 6092; Elayi-Lemaire, *Trans* 38 (2009) 85, no. 129 (Byblos excavations; Byblos hoard TIX).

703 O?–R?
13.02 g
5 h
Same as 317. Rather worn.
O: off-center toward the top; traces of ʿZ.
R: inscription off the flan.
Mildenberg-Hurter, *Dewing Collection*, no. 2662 (Dewing coll.).

704 O?–R?
13.02 g
Same as 317. Rather worn.
O: off-center to right; traces of ʿZ.
R: traces of *ʿZBʿL MLK GBL*.
Berk, Chicago, 141, 5/1/2005, no. 149 = 125, 27/2/2002, no. 200.

705 O?–R?
12.98 g
5 h
Same as 317. Rather worn.
O: traces of ʿZ.
R: *ʿZBʿL MLK GBL*.
Beirut, NM; Dunand, *Byblos I*, no. 6140; Elayi-Lemaire, *Trans* 38 (2009) 85, no. 130 (Byblos excavations; Byblos hoard TIX).

706 O?–R?
12.97 g
4 h
Same as 317. Rather worn.
O: traces of ʿZ.
R: *ʿZBʿL M*[.
Beirut, NM; Dunand, *Byblos I*, no. 6107; Elayi-Lemaire, *Trans* 38 (2009) 85, no. 131 (Byblos excavations; Byblos hoard TIX).

707 O?–R?
12.93 g
Same as 317. Rather worn. Slightly irregular flan.
O: traces of ʿZ.
R: traces of *ʿZBʿL MLK GBL*.
SNG ANS, no. 1431 (ex Berry coll.).

708 O?–R?
12.91 g
7 h
Same as 317. Rather worn.
O: slightly off-center toward the top; ʿZ.
R: traces of *ʿZBʿL MLK GBL*.
Beirut, NM; Dunand, *Byblos I*, no. 6168; Elayi-Lemaire, *Trans* 38 (2009) 85, no. 132 (Byblos excavations; Byblos hoard TIX).

709 O?–R?
12.88 g
5 h
Same as 317. Rather worn.
O: traces of ʿZ.
R: traces of *ʿZBʿL MLK GBL*.
Beirut, NM; Dunand, *Byblos I*, no. 6143; Elayi-Lemaire, *Trans* 38 (2009) 85, no. 133 (Byblos excavations; Byblos hoard TIX).

710 O?–R?
12.85 g 25 mm
Same as 317. Rather worn.
O: slightly off-center toward the top; traces of ʿZ.
R: traces of *ʿZBʿL MLK GBL*.
Beirut, AUB Museum, no. 2947B.

711 O?–R? 12.78 g 4 h
Same as 317. Rather worn. Irregular flan.
O: slightly off-center toward the top; traces of ʿZ.
R:]*ZBʿL* [.
Beirut, NM; Dunand, *Byblos I*, no. 6153; Elayi-Lemaire, *Trans* 38 (2009) 85, no. 134 (Byblos excavations; Byblos hoard TIX).

712 O?–R? 12.76 g 10 h
Same as 317. Rather worn.
O: traces of ʿZ.
R: *ʿZBʿL MLK GBL* partly off the flan.
Beirut, NM; Dunand, *Byblos I*, no. 6198; Elayi-Lemaire, *Trans* 38 (2009) 85, no. 135 (Byblos excavations; Byblos hoard TIX).

713 O?–R? 12.71 g
Same as 317. Rather worn.
O: traces of ʿZ.
R:]*ZBʿL MLK GBL*.
Glendining, London, 21–23/2/1961, no. 2665.

714 O?–R? 12.68 g 4 h
Same as 317. Rather worn.
O: off-center toward the bottom; ʿZ.
R: traces of *ʿZBʿL MLK GBL*.
Beirut, NM; Dunand, *Byblos I*, no. 6185; Elayi-Lemaire, *Trans* 38 (2009) 85, no. 136 (Byblos excavations; Byblos hoard TIX).

715 O?–R? 12.65 g 10 h
Same as 317. Rather worn.
O: traces of ʿZ.
R:]*L MLK GBL*.
Beirut, NM; Dunand, *Byblos I*, no. 6155; Elayi-Lemaire, *Trans* 38 (2009) 85, no. 137 (Byblos excavations; Byblos hoard TIX).

716 O?–R? 12.65 g 6 h
Same as 317. Rather worn.
O: traces of ʿZ.
R:] *MLK GBL*.
Beirut, NM; Dunand, *Byblos I*, no. 6095; Elayi-Lemaire, *Trans* 38 (2009) 85, no. 139 (Byblos excavations; Byblos hoard TIX).

717 O?–R? 12.55 g 25 mm 2 h
Same as 317. Rather worn.
O: off-center toward the top; traces of ʿZ.
R: traces of ʿ[ ]*B*ʿ[.
Paris, BNF, no. 2994 (ex Delepierre coll.).

718 O?–R? 12.47 g 27 mm
Same as 317. Rather worn. Slightly irregular flan.
O: traces of ʿZ.
R: traces of *ʿZBʿL MLK GBL*.
Boston, MFA, no. 2341; Brett, *Greek Coins*, no. 2341.

719 O?–R? 12.02 g 3 h — Same as 317. Rather worn.
O: ʿZ.
R:]*ZBʿL M*[.
Beirut, NM; Dunand, *Byblos I*, no. 6158; Elayi-Lemaire, *Trans* 38 (2009) 85, no. 138 (Byblos excavations; Byblos hoard TIX).

720 O?–R? — Same as 317. Rather worn.
O: slightly off-center toward the bottom; ʿZ.
R: traces of *ʿZBʿL MLK GBL*.
Ponterio, San Diego, 47, 8–9/3/1991, no. 1336.

721 O?–R? — Same as 317. Rather worn. Slightly irregular flan.
O: off-center to left; traces of ʿZ.
R: *ʿZBʿ*[.
Bourgey, Paris, 14–15/4/1910, no. 209 (ex Norman coll.).

722 O?–R? — Same as 317. Rather worn.
O: slightly off-center toward the bottom; traces of ʿZ.
R: *ʿZBʿL MLK GBL* partly off the flan.
Berk, Chicago, 92, 11/9/1996, no. 174 = 85, 9/3/1995, no. 128.

723 O?–R? — Same as 317. Rather worn.
O: slightly off-center toward the top; ʿZ.
R: traces of *ʿZBʿL MLK GBL*.
Berk, Chicago, 102, 27/5/1998, no. 288.

724 O?–R? — Same as 317. Rather worn. Slightly irregular flan.
O: slightly off-center to left; ʿZ.
R: inscription obliterated.
Berk, Chicago, 102, 27/5/1998, no. 289.

725 O?–R? 13.32 g — Same as 317. Rather worn.
O: inscription obliterated.
R: traces of *ʿZBʿL MLK GBL*.
Elayi-Elayi, *Trésors*, p. 107, no. 487 (Byblos hoards TXIII, TXIV, and TXV?).

726 O?–R? — Same as 317. Rather worn.
R: *ʿZBʿL MLK GBL* (not illustrated).
Monnaies et Médailles/Münzen und Medaillen, Basel, January 1968, no. 11 (erroneous weight: 15.58 g).

IV.2.2. 16th-Shekels AR

727 O1–R1 0.80 g — O: war-galley to left; prow terminating in head of a lion; inside, two warriors represented by helmets and shields; below, ʿZ and winged seahorse to left. Border of dots. Off-center to right.
R: same as 317.
Elsen, Brussels, 83, 12/3/2005, no. 259 = 226, September–December 2003, no. 109.

728 O1*–R1
0.68 g
Same as 727. Small cracks on the edge.
O: ‘Z.
R: *‘ZB‘L MLK GBL.*
Gorny, Munich, 48, 2/4/1990, no. 592.

729 O2–R1*
0.68 g
Same as 727.
O: split die; off-center toward the top; ‘Z.
R: *‘ZB‘L MLK GBL.*
Classical Numismatic Group, Lancaster-London, 41, 19/3/1997, no. 697.

730 O2–R1
0.67 g
Same as 727.
O: split die; ‘Z.
R: *‘ZB‘L MLK GBL.*
Henzen, Amerongen, 161, July 2005, no. 246 = 154, October 2004, no. 173.

731 O2*–R2*
0.82 g 11 mm
9 h
Same as 727.
O: split die; ‘Z.
R: *‘ZB‘L MLK GBL.*
Paris, BNF, no. 68 (ex De Vogüé coll.).

732 O2–R2
0.74 g
Same as 727. Pierced.
O: split die; ‘Z.
R: *‘ZB‘L MLK GBL.*
London, BM, no. 1840–12–26 156.

733 O3*–R2
0.62 g 10 mm
3 h
Same as 727.
O: ‘Z.
R: *‘ZB‘L MLK GBL.*
Paris, BNF, no. 3145; *Catalogue De Luynes*, no. 3145 (ex De Luynes coll.).

734 O3–R3*
Same as 727.
O: off-center toward the bottom; ‘Z.
R: *‘ZB‘L MLK GB*[.
Elayi-Elayi, *Trésors*, p. 95, no. 15, and pl. 6:15 (Byblos hoards TXIII, TXIV, and TXV?).

735 O3*–R4*
0.74 g
Same as 727.
O: off-center to right; traces of ‘Z.
R: *‘ZB‘L MLK GBL.*
London, BM, no. 1849–7-10 21.

736 O4*–R2
0.65 g
Same as 727.
O: ‘Z.
R: *‘ZB‘L MLK GBL.*
Private coll.

737 O5–R3 0.75 g
Same as 727.
O: traces of ʿZ.
R: *ʿZBʿL MLK GB*[.
Elayi-Elayi, *Trésors*, p. 102, no. 292, and pl. 12:292 (Byblos hoards TXIII, TXIV, and TXV?).

738 O6–R5* 0.82 g 10 mm 6 h
Same as 727.
O: slightly off-center toward the bottom; ʿZ.
R: *ʿZBʿL MLK G*[.
Paris, BNF, no. 3144; *Catalogue De Luynes*, no. 3144; Babelon, *Perses*, no. 1358; idem, *Traité*, no. 872 (ex De Luynes coll.).

739 O6–R6 0.73 g 11 mm 12 h
Same as 727.
O: ʿZ.
R:]*Bʿ L MLK G*[.
Berlin, SM, no. 15 (ex Löbbecke coll.).

740 O7–R3 0.68 g
Same as 727.
O: ʿZ.
R: *ʿZBʿL MLK G*[.
Monnaies et Médailles/Münzen und Medaillen, Basel, 505, November–December 1987, no. 99.

741 O7–R3
Same as 727.
O: ʿZ.
R: *ʿZBʿL M*[.
Elayi-Elayi, *Trésors*, p. 95, no. 17, and pl. 6:17 (Byblos hoards TXIII, TXIV, and TXV?).

742 O7*–R6* 0.75 g
Same as 727.
O: slightly off-center toward the top; ʿZ.
R:]*Bʿ L MLK GB*[.
Baldwin, London, 34, 13/10/2003, no. 526.

743 O7–R7* 0.72 g 11 mm
Same as 727.
O: ʿZ.
R:]*ZBʿL MLK G*[.
Beirut, AUB Museum, no. 765.

744 O7–R8* 0.61 g
Same as 727.
O: off-center toward the bottom; ʿZ off the flan.
R: *ʿZBʿL M*[.
Elayi-Elayi, *Trésors*, p. 95, no. 15, and pl. 6:15 (Byblos hoards TXIII, TXIV, and TXV?).

745 O8–R8 0.79 g
Same as 727.
O: ʿZ.
R: *ʿZBʿL MLK GBL*.
Elayi-Elayi, *Trésors*, p. 100, no. 244, and pl. 7:244 (Byblos hoards TXIII, TXIV, and TXV?).

746 O9*–R9*
Same as 727.
O: off-center to right; ʿZ.
R: *ʿZBʿL MLK G*[.
Ritter, Dusseldorf, 35, December 1993, no. 376.

747 O9–R10*
0.77 g
Same as 727.
O: ʿZ.
R:]*Bʿ L MLK G*[.
Elayi-Elayi, *Trésors*, p. 102, no. 291, and pl. 7:291 (Byblos hoards TXIII, TXIV, and TXV?).

748 O9–R11
0.65 g 10 mm
3 h
Same as 727.
O: off-center toward the top; ʿZ.
R: *ʿZBʿL MLK* [.
Berlin, SM, no. 16.

749 O10*–R11*
0.74 g
Same as 727. Slightly irregular flan.
O: off-center to left; defect between the shields; ʿZ.
R: *ʿZBʿL MLK* [.
England, Quarryville-London, 18, 3/12/1991, no. 199.

750 O10–R11
0.60 g 10 mm
6 h
Same as 727.
O: off-center to right; defect between the shields; ʿZ.
R: *ʿZBʿL ML*[.
Paris, BNF, no. 1359a.

751 O11–R11
0.76 g
Same as 727.
O: off-center to right; ʿZ.
R: *ʿZBʿL MLK* [.
Elayi-Elayi, *Trésors*, p. 98, no. 184, and pl. 9:184 (Byblos hoards TXIII, TXIV, and TXV?).

752 O11–R12*
0.73 g
Same as 727. Oval flan.
O: ʿZ.
R: *ʿZBʿL MLK GB*[.
Monnaies et Médailles/Münzen und Medaillen, Basel, 480, August 1985, no. 22.

753 O11*–R13*
0.64 g
Same as 727.
O: slightly off-center toward the bottom; ʿZ.
R: *ʿZBʿL MLK GBL.*
Forrer, *Weber Collection*, no. 8040 (Weber coll.).

754 O11–R14*
0.66 g
3 h
Same as 727.
O: ʿZ.
R: *ʿZBʿL MLK G*[.
Elayi-Elayi, *Trésors*, p. 102, no. 293 and pl. 12:293 (Byblos hoards TXIII, TXIV and TXV?).

755 O11–R15 0.74 g
Same as 727.
O: slightly off-center to right; ʿZ.
R:]*BʿL MLK GBL*.
Elayi-Elayi, *Trésors*, p. 105, no. 426 and pl. 16:426 (Byblos hoards TXIII, TXIV and TXV?).

756 O12*–R15* 0.75 g
Same as 727.
O: off-center to left; ʿZ.
R: *ʿZBʿL MLK G*[.
Elayi-Elayi, *Trésors*, p. 105, no. 425 and pl. 16:425 (Byblos hoards TXIII, TXIV and TXV?).

757 O13–R16* 0.82 g
Same as 727.
O: off-center to right; dot under the seahorse; ʿZ.
R: *ʿZBʿL M*[.
Elayi-Elayi, *Trésors*, p. 105, no. 424 and pl. 16:424 (Byblos hoards TXIII, TXIV and TXV?).

758 O13–R17*
Same as 727.
O: dot under the seahorse; ʿZ.
R: *ʿZBʿL MLK GBL*.
Elayi-Elayi, *Trésors*, p. 95, no. 16 and pl. 7:16 (Byblos hoards TXIII, TXIV and TXV?).

759 O13*–R18* 0.65 g
Same as 727.
O: dot under the seahorse; ʿZ.
R: *ʿZBʿL MLK G*[.
Elayi-Elayi, *Trésors*, p. 101, no. 253 and pl. 7:253 (Byblos hoards TXIII, TXIV and TXV?).

760 O14–R19*
Same as 727.
O: ʿZ.
R: *ʿZBʿL MLK G*[.
Berk, Chicago, 84, 19/1/1995, no. 329.

761 O14*–R20* 0.68 g
Same as 727.
O: ʿZ.
R: *ʿZBʿL MLK G*[.
Elsen, Brussels, 239, 2008, no. 114 = 235, January–March 2006, no. 79 = 230, October–December 2004, no. 74.

762 O1–R? 0.67 g 11 mm 12 h
Same as 727. Slightly worn.
O: ʿZ.
R:]*BʿL M*[.
Spaer coll., Jerusalem (bought in Beth-Shean).

763 O7–R? 0.70 g 11 mm 6 h
Same as 727. Slightly worn.
O: off-center to left;ʿZ.
R: traces of *ʿZBʿL MLK GBL*.
Spaer coll., Jerusalem (bought in Jerusalem).

764	O8–R? 0.78 g	Same as 727. Slightly worn. O: off-center to right; ʿZ. R: traces of *ʿZBʿL MLK GBL.* Müller, Münz Zentrum-Rheinland, Solingen, 60, 20–21/1/1989, no. 123.
765	O8–R?	Same as 727. Slightly worn. Oval flan. O: off-center to left; ʿZ. R: traces of *ʿZBʿL MLK GBL.* Kovacs, San Mateo, 5, 31/8/1984, no. 149.
766	O15*–R? 0.65 g	Same as 727. Slightly worn. O: off-center to left; ʿZ. R: traces of *ʿZBʿL MLK GBL.* Superior Galleries, Beverly Hills, 11–12/6/1986, no. 1407.
767	O?–R? 0.56 g 10 mm 12 h	Same as 727. Rather worn. Slightly broken edge. O: traces of ʿZ. R: traces of *ʿZBʿL MLK GBL.* Spaer coll., Jerusalem (bought in Beirut).
768	O?–R? 0.81 g	Same as 727. Rather worn. O: traces of ʿZ. R: traces of *ʿZBʿL MLK GBL.* Nomisma, Tours, 30/5/1992, no. 53.
769	O?–R?	Same as 727. Rather worn. O: split die; traces of ʿZ. R: traces of *ʿZBʿL MLK GBL.* Elayi-Elayi, *Trésors*, p. 95, no. 14 and pl. 5:14 (Byblos hoards TXIII, TXIV and TXV?).
770	O?–R? 0.62 g 5 h	Same as 727. Rather worn. Broken in two pieces. O: traces of ʿZ. R: traces of *ʿZBʿL MLK GBL.* Elayi-Elayi, *Trésors*, p. 102, no. 294 (Byblos hoards TXIII, TXIV and TXV?).
771	O?–R?	Same as 727. Rather worn. Broken. O: traces of ʿZ. R: traces of *ʿZBʿL MLK GBL.* Private coll. LPN.

IV.3. ʾUrimilk (Shortly before 350 B.C.E.)

IV.3.1. Shekels AR

772	O16 of ʿOzbaʿal–R1* 13.44 g	O: same as 317. R: lion to left, bringing down a bull to left; *ʾWRMLK MLK GBL* above; border of dots. Comptoir Général Financier, Paris, 12/12/1998, no. 104.

773 O1–R2
13.86 g

O: war-galley to left; prow terminating in head of a lion; inside, three warriors with shields, facing left; below, one line of waves, letters *ʾK*, winged seahorse with one leg to left and shell. Border of dots.
R: lion to left, bringing down a bull to left; *ʾWRMLK MLK GBL* above; border of dots.
Elsen, Brussels, 9, 6/2/1988, no. 89.

774 O1–R2
13.63 g

Same as 773.
O: *ʾK*.
R: defect under the tail of the lion; *ʾWRMLK MLK GBL* partly off the flan.
Platt, Paris, December 1994, no. 126.

775 O2–R2
13.32 g

Same as 773.
O: *ʾK*.
R: defect under the tail of the lion; *ʾWRMLK MLK GBL* partly off the flan.
Numismatica Ars Classica, New York, Triton II, 1–2/12/1998, no. 489.

776 O2–R2
13.31 g

Same as 773.
O: traces of *ʾK*.
R: defect under the tail of the lion; *ʾWRMLK MLK GBL*.
Gorny, Munich, 36, 8/4/1987, no. 296.

777 O2–R2
13.29 g

Same as 773.
O: slightly off-center to left; *ʾK*.
R: defect under the tail of the lion; *ʾWRMLK MLK GBL*.
Elayi-Elayi, *Trésors*, p. 100, no. 246 and pl. 11:246 (Byblos hoards TXIII, TXIV and TXV?).

778 O2–R2
13.27 g
3 h

Same as 773.
O: overstruck; slightly off-center toward the bottom; *ʾK*.
R: defect under the tail of the lion; *ʾWRMLK MLK GBL*.
Leu, Zurich, 38, 13/5/1986, no. 154.

779 O2–R2
13.29 g
6 h

Same as 773.
O: *ʾK*.
R: defect under the tail of the lion; *ʾWRMLK MLK GBL*.
Numismatic Fine Arts, Beverly Hills, 30, 8/12/1992, no. 129.

780 O2–R2
13.26 g

Same as 773. Slightly irregular flan.
O: *ʾK*.
R: off-center to right;]*MLK MLK GBL*.
Classical Numismatic Group, Lancaster-London, 46, 24/6/1998, no. 499.

781 O2–R2
13.24 g

Same as 773.
O: *ʾK*.
R: defect under the tail of the lion; *ʾWRMLK MLK GBL*.
Lanz, Munich, 44, 16/5/1988, no. 285.

782 O2–R2 | 13.23 g | 9 h

Same as 773.
O: slightly off-center to right; *ʾK*.
R: defect under the tail of the lion; *ʾWRMLK MLK GBL*.
Sotheby's, Zurich, 27–28/10/1993, no. 873 = Numismatic Fine Arts, Encino, 27, 4–5/12/1991, no. 82 = 22, 1/6/1989, no. 340.

783 O2–R2 | 13.23 g

Same as 773.
O: scratch; *ʾK*.
R: restruck; defect under the tail of the lion; *ʾWRMLK MLK GBL*.
Hirsch, Munich, 176, 19–20/11/1992, no. 383.

784 O2–R2 | 13.23 g

Same as 773.
O: *ʾK*.
R: defect under the tail of the lion; *ʾWRMLK MLK GBL*.
Gorny, Munich, 64, 11/10/1993, no. 222.

785 O2–R2 | 13.22 g

Same as 773.
O: slightly off-center to left; *ʾK*.
R: defect under the tail of the lion; *ʾWRMLK MLK GBL*.
Peus, Frankfurt/Main, 334, 4/11/1992, no. 524 = 333, 6–11/5/1992, no. 351.

786 O2–R2 | 13.22 g

Same as 773.
O: overstruck; *ʾK*.
R: restruck; defect under the tail of the lion; *ʾWRMLK MLK GBL*.
Tkalec, Zurich, 22/4/2007, no. 103.

787 O2–R2 | 13.21 g

Same as 773.
O: traces of overstrike; slightly off-center to left; *ʾK*.
R: defect under the tail of the lion; *ʾWRMLK MLK GBL*.
Tkalec, Zurich, 23/10/1992, no. 167.

788 O2–R2 | 13.21 g

Same as 773.
O: traces of overstrike; slightly off-center to left; *ʾK*.
R: defect under the tail of the lion; *ʾWRMLK MLK GBL*.
Numismatica Ars Classica, Zurich, 2, February 1990, no. 229.

789 O2–R2 | 13.21 g

Same as 773.
O: slightly off-center to right; *ʾK*.
R: defect under the tail of the lion; *ʾWRMLK MLK GBL*.
Stack's, New York, 14/1/2008, no. 2263 (ex Stack coll.).

790 O2–R2 | 13.21 g

Same as 773. Slightly irregular flan.
O: slightly off-center to left; *ʾK*.
R: overstruck; defect under the tail of the lion; *ʾWRMLK M[*.
Malter, Encino, 39, 2/4/1989, no. 498.

791 O2–R2 13.21 g
Same as 773. Slightly irregular flan.
O: slightly off-center to left; ʾ*K*.
R: defect under the tail of the lion; ʾ*WRMLK MLK GBL*.
Elsen, Brussels, 32, 11/12/1993, no. 138 = Leu, Zurich, 53, 21–22/10/1991, no. 157 = Superior Galleries, Beverly Hills, 12–14/12/1987, no. 543.

792 O2–R2 13.20 g
Same as 773.
O: scratch; slightly off-center to left; ʾ*K*.
R: defect under the tail of the lion; ʾ*WRMLK MLK GBL*.
Martin, London, 21/3, July 1994, no. G57 = Hariga, Brussels, June-July 1992, no. 23 = 29/10/1988, no. 38.

793 O2*–R2* 13.19 g
Same as 773. Slightly irregular flan.
O: slightly off-center toward the top; ʾ*K*.
R: defect under the tail of the lion; ʾ*WRMLK MLK GBL*.
London, BM, 1948–3-6 1; Jenkins, *Greek Coins*, no. 220; Kraay-Hirmer, *Greek Coins*, no. 685; Head, *A Guide*, no. 7.

794 O2–R2 13.19 g
Same as 773.
O: ʾ*K*.
R: defect under the tail of the lion; ʾ*WRMLK MLK GBL*.
Peus, Frankfurt/Main, 274, 29/10/1970, no. 1654.

795 O2–R2 13.19 g
Same as 773.
O: slightly off-center toward the bottom; ʾ*K*.
R: defect under the tail of the lion; ʾ*WRMLK MLK GBL* partly off the flan.
Rauch, Vienna, 42, 16–18/6/1989, no. 3108 = Gorny, Munich, 42, 11/10/1988, no. 423 = Kunst und Münzen, Lugano (Asta), 26, 13–15/5/1988, no. 109.

796 O2–R2 13.15 g
Same as 773.
O: slightly off-center toward the top; ʾ*K*.
R: defect under the tail of the lion; ʾ*WRMLK MLK GBL*.
Monnaies et Médailles/Münzen und Medaillen, Basel, 95, 25/10/2005, no. 720 = Gorny, Munich, 69, 18/11/1994, no. 434 = 67, 2/5/1994, no. 343 = Bourgey, Paris, 5–6/12/1977, no. 124 = Hess-Leu, Lucerne, 49, 27–28/4/1971, no. 264.

797 O2–R2 13.14 g
Same as 773.
O: ʾ*K*.
R: defect under the tail of the lion; ʾ*WRMLK MLK GBL*.
Monnaies et Médailles/Münzen und Medaillen, Basel, 32, 20/10/1966, no. 151.

798 O2–R2 13.13 g
Same as 773.
O: slightly off-center toward the bottom; ʾ*K*.
R: defect under the tail of the lion;]*MLK MLK GBL*.
Tkalec-Rauch, Zurich, 14–15/4/1986, no. 160.

799 O2–R2 | 13.11 g | 12 h

Same as 773.
O: ʾK.
R: defect under the tail of the lion; *ʾWRMLK MLK GBL.*
Sotheby's, London, 5/7/1995, no. 86 = Glendining, London, 10/12/1986, no. 336 = Leu, Münzen und Medaillen, Basel, 3–4/12/1965, no. 482 (ex Niggeler coll.).

800 O2–R2 | 13.06 g

Same as 773.
O: ʾK.
R: defect under the tail of the lion; *ʾWRMLK MLK GBL.*
Hirsch, Munich, 167, 26–29/9/1990, no. 567.

801 O2–R2 | 13.05 g 26 mm | 12 h

Same as 773.
O: off-center toward the top; ʾK.
R: defect under the tail of the lion; *ʾWRMLK MLK GBL.*
Paris, BNF, no. HS 1973-1-273 (ex Seyrig coll.).

802 O2–R2 | 13.01 g

Same as 773.
O: ʾK.
R: defect under the tail of the lion; *ʾWRMLK MLK GBL.*
Numismatic Fine Arts, Beverly Hills, 16, 2/12/1985, no. 265; Jidejian, *Lebanon, Its Gods*, 29, 32.

803 O2–R2 | 13.01 g

Same as 773.
O: ʾK.
R: defect under the tail of the lion; *ʾWRMLK MLK GBL* partly off the flan.
Leu, Zurich, 76, 27/10/1999, no. 214 = Hess-Leu, Lucerne, 31, 6–7/12/1966, no. 526.

804 O2–R2 | 12.85 g | 11 h

Same as 773. Irregular flan.
O: ʾK.
R: defect under the tail of the lion; *ʾWRMLK MLK G*[.
Leu, Zurich, 13, 29–30/4/1975, no. 312.

805 O2–R2 | 12.82 g | 1 h

Same as 773.
O: ʾK.
R: defect under the tail of the lion; *ʾWRMLK MLK GBL.*
Beirut, NM; Dunand, *Byblos I*, no. 6235; Elayi-Lemaire, *Trans* 38 (2009) 86, no. 148 (Byblos excavations; Byblos hoard TIX).

806 O2–R2 | 11.99 g

Same as 773.
O: off-center toward the top; ʾK.
R: defect under the tail of the lion; *ʾWRMLK MLK GBL.*
Monnaies et Médailles/Münzen und Medaillen, Basel, 30/9–1/10/1976, no. 302 = Myers, New York, 6/12/1973, no. 74.

807 O2–R2 11.45 g 11 h	Same as 773. O: slightly off-center toward the top; ʾ*K*. R: defect under the tail of the lion; traces of ʾ*WRMLK MLK GBL*. *SNG Cambridge*, no. 6031.
808 O2–R2 10.77 g 24 mm 9 h	Same as 773. O: off-center to left; ʾ*K*. R: defect under the tail of the lion; ʾ*WRMLK MLK GBL*. Private coll.
809 O2–R2 10.08 g 9 h	Same as 773. Clipped edge. O: off-center toward the top; ʾ*K*. R: defect under the tail of the lion; ʾ*WRMLK MLK GBL*. Private coll.
810 O2–R2	Same as 773. Slightly worn. O: ʾ*K*. R: defect under the tail of the lion; ʾ*WRMLK MLK GBL*. Beirut, NM; Elayi-Lemaire, *Trans* 38 (2009) 86, no. 155 (cast IDAM) (Byblos excavations; Byblos hoard TIX).
811 O2–R2	Same as 773. Slightly worn. O: ʾ*K*. R: defect under the tail of the lion; ʾ*WRMLK MLK GBL*. Beirut, NM; Elayi-Lemaire, *Trans* 38 (2009) 86, no. 157 (cast IDAM) (Byblos excavations; Byblos hoard TIX).
812 O2–R2	Same as 773. Slightly worn. O: ʾ*K*. R: defect under the tail of the lion; ʾ*WRMLK MLK GBL*. Beirut, NM; Elayi-Lemaire, *Trans* 38 (2009) 86, no. 158 and pl. 10:158 (cast IDAM) (Byblos excavations; Byblos hoard TIX).
813 O2–R2	Same as 773. O: off-center toward the top; ʾ*K*. R: defect under the tail of the lion; ʾ*WRMLK MLK GBL*. Weil, Paris, 18/6/2004, no. 156.
814 O2–R2	Same as 773. O: off-center to right; ʾ*K*. R: defect under the tail of the lion; ʾ*WRMLK MLK GBL*. Stockholm, RCC, no. 100566.
815 O2–R3* 12.67 g 4 h	Same as 773. Slightly irregular flan. O: traces of ʾ*K*. R: ʾ*WRMLK MLK GBL*. Beirut, NM; Dunand, *Byblos I*, no. 6227; Elayi-Lemaire, *Trans* 38 (2009) 85, no. 141 and pl. 10:141 (Byblos excavations; Byblos hoard TIX).

816	O2–R4* 12.73 g 9 h	Same as 773. Slightly irregular flan. O: ʾK. R: ʾ*WRMLK MLK GBL.* Beirut, NM; Dunand, *Byblos I*, no. 6230; Elayi-Lemaire, *Trans* 38 (2009) 85, no. 142 and pl. 10:142 (Byblos excavations; Byblos hoard TIX).
817	O2–R5 12.84 g 6 h	Same as 773. Slightly irregular flan. O: ʾK. R: ʾ*WRMLK MLK GBL.* Beirut, NM; Dunand, *Byblos I*, no. 6231; Elayi-Lemaire, *Trans* 38 (2009) 85, no. 143 (Byblos excavations; Byblos hoard TIX).
818	O2–R5*	Same as 773. Slightly irregular flan. O: ʾK. R: ʾ*WRMLK MLK GBL.* Beirut, NM; Elayi-Lemaire, *Trans* 38 (2009) 85, no. 144 and pl. 10:144 (cast IDAM) (Byblos excavations; Byblos hoard TIX).
819	O2–R6* 12.77 g 4 h	Same as 773. Slightly irregular flan. O: scratch; ʾK. R: ʾ*WRMLK MLK GBL.* Beirut, NM; Dunand, *Byblos I*, no. 6232; Elayi-Lemaire, *Trans* 38 (2009) 85, no. 145 and pl. 10:145 (Byblos excavations; Byblos hoard TIX).
820	O2–R7 12.96 g 10 h	Same as 773. Slightly worn. O: slightly off-center toward the top; ʾK. R: ʾ*WRMLK MLK GBL.* Beirut, NM; Dunand, *Byblos I*, no. 6236; Elayi-Lemaire, *Trans* 38 (2009) 86, no. 146 (Byblos excavations; Byblos hoard TIX).
821	O2–R7* 12.85 g 7 h	Same as 773. O: off-center to left; ʾK. R: ʾ*WRMLK MLK GBL.* Beirut, NM; Dunand, *Byblos I*, no. 6238; Elayi-Lemaire, *Trans* 38 (2009) 86, no. 147 and pl. 10:147 (Byblos excavations; Byblos hoard TIX).
822	O2–R7 12.76 g 1 h	Same as 773. Slightly worn. O: flaw; ʾK. R: ʾ*WRMLK MLK GBL.* Beirut, NM; Dunand, *Byblos I*, no. 6233; Elayi-Lemaire, *Trans* 38 (2009) 86, no. 149 (Byblos excavations; Byblos hoard TIX).

823 O2–R7 12.62 g 2 h — Same as 773. Slightly worn.
O: *ʾK.*
R: *ʾWRMLK MLK GBL.*
Beirut, NM; Dunand, *Byblos I*, no. 6237; Elayi-Lemaire, *Trans* 38 (2009) 86, no. 150 (Byblos excavations; Byblos hoard TIX).

824 O2–R8 12.37 g 3 h — Same as 773. Slightly worn.
O: traces of *ʾK.*
R: *ʾWRMLK MLK GBL.*
Beirut, NM; Dunand, *Byblos I*, no. 6234; Elayi-Lemaire, *Trans* 38 (2009) 86, no. 151 (Byblos excavations; Byblos hoard TIX).

825 O2–R8* — Same as 773. Slightly worn.
O: *ʾK.*
R: *ʾWRMLK MLK GBL.*
Beirut, NM; Elayi-Lemaire, *Trans* 38 (2009) 86, no. 152 and pl. 10:152 (cast IDAM) (Byblos excavations; Byblos hoard TIX).

826 O2–R8 — Same as 773. Slightly worn.
O: *ʾK.*
R: *ʾWRMLK MLK GB*[.; Byblos hoard TIX
Beirut, NM; Elayi-Lemaire, *Trans* 38 (2009) 86, no. 153 (cast IDAM) (Byblos excavations; Byblos hoard TIX).

827 O2–R9 — Same as 773. Slightly worn.
O: *ʾK.*
R: *ʾWRMLK MLK GBL.*
Beirut, NM; Elayi-Lemaire, *Trans* 38 (2009) 86, no. 154 (cast IDAM) (Byblos excavations; Byblos hoard TIX).

828 O2–R9* — Same as 773. Slightly worn.
O: *ʾK.*
R: *ʾWRMLK MLK GBL.*
Beirut, NM; Elayi-Lemaire, *Trans* 38 (2009) 86, no. 156 and pl. 10:156 (cast IDAM) (Byblos excavations; Byblos hoard TIX).

829 O2–R10* 13.06 g 7 h — Same as 773. Slightly worn.
O: traces of *ʾK.*
R: *ʾWRMLK MLK GBL.*
Beirut, NM; Dunand, *Byblos I*, no. 6226; Elayi-Lemaire, *Trans* 38 (2009) 85, no. 140 and pl. 10:140 (Byblos excavations; Byblos hoard TIX).

830	O2–R11*	Same as 773. Slightly worn. O: traces of *ʾK*. R: *ʾWRMLK MLK GBL*. Beirut, NM; Elayi-Lemaire, *Trans* 38 (2009) 86, no. 159 and pl. 10:159 (cast IDAM) (Byblos excavations; Byblos hoard TIX).
831	O2–R12* 12.10 g 26 mm	Same as 773. Slightly worn. O: *ʾK*. R: *ʾWRMLK MLK GBL*. Spaer coll., Jerusalem.
832	O2–R12	Same as 773. Slightly worn. O: off-center toward the bottom; *ʾK*. R: *ʾWRMLK MLK GB*[. Beirut, NM; Elayi-Lemaire, *Trans* 38 (2009) 86, no. 160 and pl. 10:160 (cast IDAM) (Byblos excavations; Byblos hoard TIX).
833	O2–R13*	Same as 773. O: off-center to left; *ʾK*. R: *ʾWRMLK MLK GBL*. Beirut, NM; Elayi-Lemaire, *Trans* 38 (2009) 86, no. 161 and pl. 10:161 (cast IDAM) (Byblos excavations; Byblos hoard TIX).
834	o2–R14* 13.01 g	Same as 773. O: overtruck;*ʾK*. R:]*MLK MLK GBL*. Classical Numismatic Group, Lancaster-London, 70, 21/9/2005, no. 391 = Elsen, Brussels, 28, 20/2/1993, no. 293; Elayi-Elayi, *Trésors*, p. 100, no. 248, and pl. 11:248 (Byblos hoards TXIII, TXIV, and TXV?).
835	O2–R? 13.25 g 9 h	Same as 773. Slightly worn. O: *ʾK*. R: restruck; *ʾWRMLK MLK GBL*. Leu, Zurich, 72, 12/5/1998, no. 311.
836	O2–R? 12.80 g 25 mm 9 h	Same as 773. Slightly worn. O: off-center to right; *ʾK*. R: traces of *ʾWRMLK MLK GBL*. Beirut, AUB Museum, no. 2328; Baramki, *Coins AUB*, no. 2328 and pl. 28:11.
837	O2–R? 12.54 g 7 h	Same as 773. Slightly worn. O: *ʾK*. R: traces of *ʾWRMLK MLK GBL*. Beirut, NM; Dunand, *Byblos I*, no. 6229; Elayi-Lemaire, *Trans* 38 (2009) 86, no. 162 and pl. 10:162 (Byblos excavations; Byblos hoard TIX).

838 O2–R?
12.51 g
7 h
Same as 773. Slightly worn.
O: ʾK.
R: traces of *ʾWRMLK MLK GBL.*
Beirut, NM; Dunand, *Byblos I*, no. 6228; Elayi-Lemaire, *Trans* 38 (2009) 86, no. 163 and pl. 10:163 (Byblos excavations; Byblos hoard TIX).

839 O2–R?
Same as 773. Slightly worn.
O: ʾK.
R: traces of *ʾWRMLK MLK GBL.*
Beirut, NM; Elayi-Lemaire, *Trans* 38 (2009) 86, no. 164 (cast IDAM) (Byblos excavations; Byblos hoard TIX).

840 O2–R?
Same as 773. Slightly worn.
O: ʾK.
R: traces of *ʾWRMLK MLK GBL.*
Beirut, NM; Elayi-Lemaire, *Trans* 38 (2009) 86, no. 165 (cast IDAM) (Byblos excavations; Byblos hoard TIX).

841 O2–R?
Same as 773. Slightly irregular flan. Slightly worn.
O: ʾK.
R: traces of *ʾWRMLK MLK GBL.*
Beirut, NM; Elayi-Lemaire, *Trans* 38 (2009) 86, no. 166 (cast IDAM) (Byblos excavations; Byblos hoard TIX).

842 O2–R?
Same as 773. Slightly worn.
O: ʾK.
R: traces of inscription.
Beirut, NM; Elayi-Lemaire, *Trans* 38 (2009) 87, no. 167 (cast IDAM) (Byblos excavations; Byblos hoard TIX).

843 O2–R?
Same as 773. Slightly worn.
O: ʾK.
R: traces of *ʾWRMLK MLK GBL.*
Beirut, NM; Elayi-Lemaire, *Trans* 38 (2009) 87, no. 168 (cast IDAM) (Byblos excavations; Byblos hoard TIX).

844 O2–R?
Same as 773. Slightly worn.
O: ʾK.
R: traces of *ʾWRMLK MLK GBL.*
Beirut, NM; Elayi-Lemaire, *Trans* 38 (2009) 87, no. 169 (cast IDAM) (Byblos excavations; Byblos hoard TIX).

845 O2–R?
Same as 773. Slightly worn.
O: ʾK.
R: not illustrated.
Beirut, NM; Jidejian, *Lebanon, Its Gods*, p. 31.

IV.3.2. 16th-Shekels AR

846 O11 of ʿOzbaʿal–R1
0.78 g 10 mm
6 h
O: same as 727; off-center to left; ʿZ.
R: same as 773;]*WRMLK MLK GBL.*
Elayi-Elayi, *RBN* 139 (1993) 17, no. 1 and pl. 1:1 (hoard from Near East TLXXX).

847 O11 of ʿOzbaʿal–R2*
0.84 g
O: same as 727; off-center toward the top; ʿZ.
R: same as 773; *ʾWRMLK MLK GBL.*
Elayi-Elayi, *Trésors*, p. 98, no. 185, and pl. 9:185 (Byblos hoards TXIII, TXIV, and TXV?).

848 O11 of ʿOzbaʿal–R3*
0.74 g
Some cracks on the edge.
O: same as 727; ʿZ.
R: same as 773; *ʾWRMLK MLK GBL*
Gorny, Munich, 95, 9/3/1999, no. 394.

849 O16 of ʿOzbaʿal–R6*
O: same as 727; off-center to left; ʿZ.
R: same as 773; *ʾWRM*[ ]*LK GB*[.
Elayi-Elayi, *Trésors*, p. 95, no. 25, and pl. 6:25 (Byblos hoards TXIII, TXIV, and TXV?).

850 O16 of ʿOzbaʿal–R7*
O: same as 727; ʿZ.
R: same as 773; *ʾWRMLK MLK GB*[.
Elayi-Elayi, *Trésors*, p. 95, no. 26, and pl. 6:26 (Byblos hoards TXIII, TXIV, and TXV?).

851 O1*–R1*
0.82 g
O: war-galley to left; prow terminating in head of a lion; inside, two warriors represented by helmets and shields; below, *ʾK* and winged seahorse to left. Border of dots.
R: same as 773; traces of *ʾWRMLK MLK GBL.*
Elayi-Elayi, *Trésors*, p. 105, no. 430 and pl. 16:430 (Byblos hoards TXIII, TXIV, and TXV?).

852 O1–R4*
Same as 851. Small cracks on the edge.
O: *ʾK.*
R: *ʾWRMLK MLK GBL.*
Elayi-Elayi, *Trésors*, p. 105, no. 430, and pl. 16:430 (Byblos hoards TXIII, TXIV, and TXV?).

853 O1–R5
0.66 g 10 mm
11 h
Same as 851.
O: off-center to left; *ʾK.*
R: *ʾWRMLK MLK* [.
Private coll.

854 O2*–R5*
0.70 g
Same as 851. Slightly worn.
O: off-center to right;*ʾK.*
R: *ʾWRMLK MLK GBL.*
Müller, Cologne, 58, 23–25/4/1986, no. 1475.

855 O3–R7
Same as 851. Slightly worn.
O: off-center toward the bottom; inscription obliterated.
R: *ʾWRMLK MLK GBL.*
Elayi-Elayi, *Trésors*, p. 95, no. 24, and pl. 6:24 (Byblos hoards TXIII, TXIV, and TXV?).

856 O3–R8*
0.73 g
Same as 851. Slightly worn.
O: off-center to left; *ʾK.*
R:]*RMLK MLK GBL.*
Burgan, Paris, 25/6/1993, no. 113 = 25/3/1993, no. 85.

857 O3–R9*
0.80 g
Same as 851.
O: off-center toward the top; *ʾK.*
R: *ʾWRMLK MLK GBL* partly off the flan.
Elayi-Elayi, *Trésors*, p. 105, no. 428, and pl. 16:428 (Byblos hoards TXIII, TXIV, and TXV?).

858 O3–R9
0.79 g
Same as 851.
O: very off-center toward the top;*ʾK.*
R: *ʾWRMLK MLK G*[.
Elayi-Elayi, *Trésors*, p. 105, no. 429, and pl. 16:429 (Byblos hoards TXIII, TXIV, and TXV?).

859 O3*–R10*
0.76 g 11 mm
7 h
Same as 851.
O: *ʾK.*
R: *ʾWRMLK MLK GBL* partly off the flan.
Paris, BNF, no. 3141; *Catalogue De Luynes*, no. 3141; Babelon, *Perses*, no. 1355; idem, *Traité*, no. 869 (ex De Luynes coll.).

860 O3–R10
0.73 g
Same as 851.
O: very off-center toward the bottom; *ʾK.*
R:]*WRMLK MLK GBL.*
Elayi-Elayi, *Trésors*, p. 98, no. 187, and pl. 9:187 (Byblos hoards TXIII, TXIV, and TXV?).

861 O4–R10
0.74 g
Same as 851.
O: off-center to left; *ʾK.*
R: *ʾWRMLK MLK GBL.*
Elsen, Brussels, 94, 27/11/2007, no. 402.

862 O4*–R11
0.60 g 10 mm
12 h
Same as 851. Slightly worn.
O: *ʾK.*
R: traces of *ʾWRMLK MLK GBL.*
Berlin, SM, no. 9962.

863 O4–R11*
Same as 851.
O: off-center toward the bottom; traces of *ʾK.*
R: *ʾWRMLK MLK GBL.*
Berk, Chicago, 63, 29/8/1990, no. 125.

864 O5*–R12* 0.75 g
Same as 851.
O: ʾ*K.*
R: ʾ*WRMLK MLK G*[.
Elayi-Elayi, *Trésors*, p. 98, no. 186, and pl. 9:186 (Byblos hoards TXIII, TXIV, and TXV?).

865 O5–R13* 0.71 g 11 mm 6 h
Same as 851.
O: off-center toward the bottom; traces of ʾ*K.*
R: ʾ*WRMLK*[.
Elayi-Elayi, *RBN* 139 (1993) 17, no. 3 and pl. 1:3 (hoard from Near East TLXXX).

866 O6*–R14* 0.61 g 9 mm 9 h
Same as 851.
O: off-center to left; ʾ*K.*
R:]*MLK MLK GBL.*
Berlin, SM, no. 10.

867 O7*–R14 0.74 g
Same as 851.
O: ʾ*K.*
R: ʾ*WRMLK MLK G*[.
England, Quarryville-London, 25, 24/3/1993, no. 397.

868 O8*–R15* 0.68 g 11 mm 6 h
Same as 851.
O: ʾ*K.*
R: ʾ*WRMLK MLK G*[.
Paris, BNF, no. 3140; *Catalogue De Luynes*, no. 3140; Babelon, *Perses*, no. 1354; idem, *Traité*, no. 868 (ex De Luynes coll.).

869 O11 of ʿOzbaʿal–R? 0.72 g
Same as 851. Slightly worn.
O: off-center toward the bottom; ʾ*K.*
R:]*MLK M*[ ]*K G*[.
Elayi-Elayi, *Trésors*, p. 101, no. 255, and pl. 12:255 (Byblos hoards TXIII, TXIV, and TXV?).

870 O2–R? 0.67 g
Same as 851. Slightly worn.
O: traces of ʾ*K.*
R: ʾ*WRMLK M*[.
Elayi-Elayi, *Trésors*, p. 101, no. 257, and pl. 12:257 (Byblos hoards TXIII, TXIV, and TXV?).

871 O3–R? 0.64 g
Same as 851. Slightly worn.
O: ʾ*K.*
R:]*MLK MLK*[.
London, BM, no. 1896-3-4 4.

872 O3–R? 0.61 g 11 mm 5 h
Same as 851. Slightly worn.
O: ʾ*K.*
R: ʾ*W*[.
Elayi-Elayi, *RBN* 139 (1993) 18, no. 4 and pl. 1:4 (hoard from Near East TLXXX).

873 O4–R? 0.73 g
Same as 851. Slightly worn. Edge slightly broken.
O: traces of ʾ*K*.
R:]*MLK MLK*[.
Elayi-Elayi, *Trésors*, p. 95, no. 22, and pl. 6:22 (Byblos hoards TXIII, TXIV, and TXV?).

874 O4–R? 0.63 g
Same as 851. Slightly worn.
O: ʾ*K*.
R: ʾ*W*[ ]*MLK ML*[.
Elayi-Elayi, *Trésors*, p. 100, no. 250, and pl. 11:250 (Byblos hoards TXIII, TXIV, and TXV?).

875 O7–R? 0.79 g
Same as 851. Slightly worn.
O: off-center to left; ʾ*K*.
R:]*WRMLK MLK GBL*.
Elayi-Elayi, *Trésors*, p. 101, no. 256, and pl. 12:256 (Byblos hoards TXIII, TXIV, and TXV?).

876 O7–R? 0.73 g 11 mm 11 h
Same as 851. Slightly worn.
O: ʾ*K*.
R:]*MLK M*[.
Elayi-Elayi, *RBN* 139 (1993) 17, no. 2 and pl. 1:2.

877 O?–R8 0.77 g
Same as 851. Slightly worn.
O: off-center toward the bottom; ʾ*K*.
R: ʾ*WRMLK MLK GB*[.
Künker, Osnabrück, 67, 9/10/2001, no. 468.

878 O?–R16*
Same as 851. Some cracks on the edge. Slightly worn.
O: traces of ʾ*K*.
R: ʾ*WRMLK MLK G*[.
Elayi-Elayi, *Trésors*, p. 95, no. 20, and pl. 6:20 (Byblos hoards TXIII, TXIV, and TXV?).

879 O?–R? 0.76 g 6 h
Same as 851. Rather worn.
O: off-center to left; traces of ʾ*K*.
R: traces of ʾ*WRMLK MLK GBL*.
SNG Copenhagen, no. 134; Forrer, *Weber Collection*, no. 8041 (ex Weber coll.).

880 O?–R? 0.76 g 11 mm 6 h
Same as 851. Rather worn.
O: ʾ*K*.
R: traces of ʾ*WRMLK MLK GBL*.
Private coll. LPN.

881 O?–R? 0.74 g 11 mm 6 h
Same as 851. Rather worn.
O: off-center toward the top; traces of ʾ*K*.
R: ʾ*WRMLK MLK G*[.
Berlin, SM, no. 21 (ex Fox coll.).

882 O?–R? 0.67 g

Same as 851. Rather worn.
O: off-center to right; inscription off the flan.
R: *ʾWRMLK MLK*[.
Elayi-Elayi, *Trésors*, p. 95, no. 18, and pl. 6:18 (Byblos hoards TXIII, TXIV, and TXV?).

883 O?–R? 0.66 g

Same as 851. Rather worn.
O: traces of *ʾK*.
R: traces of *ʾWRMLK MLK GBL*.
Müller, Münz Zentrum-Rheinland, Solingen, 63, 29–30/9/1989, no. 79.

884 O?–R? 0.60 g

Same as 851. Rather worn.
O: traces of *ʾK*.
R:]*MLK MLK GB*[.
Elayi-Elayi, *Trésors*, p. 95, no. 23, and pl. 6:23 (Byblos hoards TXIII, TXIV, and TXV?).

885 O?–R?

Same as 851. Rather worn.
O: traces of *ʾK*.
R: traces of *ʾWRMLK MLK GBL*.
Monetarium, Schweizerische Kreditanstalt, Zurich, 47, December 1989, no. 63 = 41, November 1983, no. 93.

IV.4.1. ʿAynel (Around 350–333 B.C.E.)

IV.4.1 Shekels AR

886 O1*–R1* 13,27 g 25 mm 3 h

O: war-galley to left; prow terminating in head of a lion; inside, three warriors with shields, facing left; below, one line of waves, winged seahorse with two legs to left and shell. Border of dots.
R: lion to left, bringing down a bull to left; *ʿYNʾL MLK GBL* above; head of lion at the end of the inscription; border of dots.
Paris, BNF, no. HS 1973-1-439 (ex Seyrig coll.).

887 O1–R1 12.42 g

Same as 886.
R: slightly off-center toward the bottom; *ʿYNʾL MLK GBL* ; head of lion at the end of the inscription.
Beirut, NM; Dunand, *Byblos I*, no. 6259; Elayi-Lemaire, *Trans* 38 (2009) 87, no. 170 and pl. 10:170 (Byblos excavations; Byblos hoard TIX).

888 O1–R2* 11.10 g

Same as 886.
O: slightly off-center to left.
R: traces of *ʿYNʾL MLK G*[; head of lion on the last two letters.
Schulman, Amsterdam, 234, March 1987, no. 2115.

889 O1–R2 10.91 g
Same as 886.
R: *ʿYNʾL MLK G*[; head of lion on the last two letters.
Beirut, NM; Dunand, *Byblos I*, no. 6277; Elayi-Lemaire, *Trans* 38 (2009) 87, no. 171 and pl. 10:171 (Byblos excavations; Byblos hoard TIX).

890 O1–R3 12.86 g
Same as 886.
R: *ʿYNʾL MLK GBL*; head of lion at the end of the inscription.
Beirut, NM; Dunand, *Byblos I*, no. 6274; Elayi-Lemaire, *Trans* 38 (2009) 87, no. 172 (Byblos excavations; Byblos hoard TIX).

891 O1–R3 12.82 g
Same as 886.
R: *ʿYNʾL MLK GB*[; head of lion at the end of the inscription.
Beirut, NM; Dunand, *Byblos I*, no. 6275; Elayi-Lemaire, *Trans* 38 (2009) 87, no. 173 (Byblos excavations; Byblos hoard TIX).

892 O1–R3 12.74 g
Same as 886.
R: *ʿYNʾL MLK GBL*; head of lion at the end of the inscription.
Beirut, NM; Dunand, *Byblos I*, no. 6276; Elayi-Lemaire, *Trans* 38 (2009) 87, no. 174 (Byblos excavations; Byblos hoard TIX).

893 O1–R3* 12.71 g
Same as 886.
R: *ʿYNʾL MLK GBL*; head of lion at the end of the inscription.
Beirut, NM; Dunand, *Byblos I*, no. 6272; Elayi-Lemaire, *Trans* 38 (2009) 87, no. 175 and pl. 11:175 (Byblos excavations; Byblos hoard TIX).

894 O1–R3 12.63 g 8 h
Same as 886.
O: slightly off-center toward the top.
R:]*K GB*[; head of lion at the end of the inscription.
Beirut, NM, no. 13; Elayi-Lemaire, *Trans* 38 (2009) 87, no. 176 (Byblos excavations; Byblos hoard TIX).

895 O1–R3 12.56 g 11 h
Same as 886.
R: traces of inscription and of head of lion.
Beirut, NM, no. 3; Elayi-Lemaire, *Trans* 38 (2009) 87, no. 177 (Byblos excavations; Byblos hoard TIX).

896 O1–R3 12.49 g
Same as 886. Slightly irregular flan.
O: off-center toward the bottom.
R: *ʿYNʾL MLK GB*[; head of lion at the end of the inscription.
Beirut, NM; Dunand, *Byblos I*, no. 6273; Elayi-Lemaire, *Trans* 38 (2009) 87, no. 178 (Byblos excavations; Byblos hoard TIX).

897 O1–R4* 12.57 g

Same as 886.
R: *ʿYNʾL MLK GBL*; head of lion at the end of the inscription.
Beirut, NM; Dunand, *Byblos I*, no. 6261; Elayi-Lemaire, *Trans* 38 (2009) 87, no. 179 and pl. 11:179 (Byblos excavations; Byblos hoard TIX).

898 O1–R5 12.97 g

Same as 886. Slightly worn.
O: off-center to left.
R:] *MLK GB*[; head of lion on the last letter.
Beirut, NM; Dunand, *Byblos I*, no. 6281; Elayi-Lemaire, *Trans* 38 (2009) 87, no. 180 (Byblos excavations; Byblos hoard TIX).

899 O1–R5 12.71 g

Same as 886.
R:]*Nʾ L MLK GB*[; head of lion on the last letter.
Beirut, NM; Dunand, *Byblos I*, no. 6280; Elayi-Lemaire, *Trans* 38 (2009) 87, no. 181 (Byblos excavations; Byblos hoard TIX).

900 O1–R5 12.64 g

Same as 886. Irregular flan.
R: *ʿYNʾL MLK GB*[; head of lion on the last letter.
Beirut, NM; Dunand, *Byblos I*, no. 6279; Elayi-Lemaire, *Trans* 38 (2009) 87, no. 182 (Byblos excavations; Byblos hoard TIX).

901 O1–R5* 12.50 g

Same as 886.
O: off-center to left.
R:]*ʾL MLK GB*[; head of lion on the last letter.
Beirut, NM; Dunand, *Byblos I*, no. 6278; Elayi-Lemaire, *Trans* 38 (2009) 87, no. 183 and pl. 11:183 (Byblos excavations; Byblos hoard TIX).

902 O1–R6 12.93 g

Same as 886, but without head of lion. Slightly irregular flan.
R: *ʿYNʾL MLK GBL*.
Beirut, NM; Dunand, *Byblos I*, no. 6262; Elayi-Lemaire, *Trans* 38 (2009) 87, no. 184 (Byblos excavations; Byblos hoard TIX).

903 O1–R6* 12.70 g

Same as 886, but without head of lion.
R: *ʿYNʾL MLK GBL*.
Beirut, NM; Dunand, *Byblos I*, no. 6258; Elayi-Lemaire, *Trans* 38 (2009) 87–88, no. 185 (Byblos excavations; Byblos hoard TIX).

904 O1–R7* 13.11 g

Same as 886, but without head of lion.
O: off-center to left.
R: *ʿYNʾL MLK GBL*.
London, BM, no. 1946-10-4 2337.

905 O1–R7
12.60 g
Same as 886, but without head of lion.
R: *ʿYNʾL MLK GB*[.
Beirut, NM; Dunand, *Byblos I*, no. 6270; Elayi-Lemaire, *Trans* 38 (2009) 88, no. 186 (Byblos excavations; Byblos hoard TIX).

906 O1–R7
12.52 g
Same as 886, but without head of lion.
O: restruck.
R: *ʿYNʾL MLK GBL.*
Beirut, NM; Dunand, *Byblos I*, no. 6268; Elayi-Lemaire, *Trans* 38 (2009) 88, no. 187 and pl. 11:187 (Byblos excavations; Byblos hoard TIX).

907 O1–R7
12.51 g
Same as 886, but without head of lion. Slightly worn.
R:] *MLK GBL.*
Beirut, NM; Dunand, *Byblos I*, no. 6257; Elayi-Lemaire, *Trans* 38 (2009) 88, no. 188 (Byblos excavations; Byblos hoard TIX).

908 O1–R7
12.22 g
Same as 886, but without head of lion. Slightly worn.
O: off-center toward the bottom.
R:]*YNʾL MLK GB*[.
Beirut, NM; Dunand, *Byblos I*, no. 6271; Elayi-Lemaire, *Trans* 38 (2009) 88, no. 189 (Byblos excavations; Byblos hoard TIX).

909 O1–R8
13.18 g
9 h
Same as 886, but without head of lion.
R: *ʿYNʾL MLK GBL.*
Leu, Zurich, 103, 5/5/2009, no. 146 = 20, 25–26/4/1978, no. 167.

910 O1–R8*
13.15 g 20 mm
Same as 886, but without head of lion.
R: *ʿYNʾL MLK GBL.*
Beirut, NM, no. 2635; Chéhab, *Monnaies*, no. 2635 and pl. 34:2.

911 O1–R8
12.97 g
Same as 886, but without head of lion. Some cracks on the edge.
O: off-center toward the bottom.
R:]*Nʾ L MLK GBL.*
Beirut, NM; Dunand, *Byblos I*, no. 6269; Elayi-Lemaire, *Trans* 38 (2009) 88, no. 190 (Byblos excavations; Byblos hoard TIX).

912 O1–R8
12.94 g
Same as 886, but without head of lion.
R: *ʿYNʾL MLK GBL.*
Beirut, NM; Dunand, *Byblos I*, no. 6267; Elayi-Lemaire, *Trans* 38 (2009) 88, no. 191 and pl. 11:191 (Byblos excavations; Byblos hoard TIX).

913 O1–R8
12.86 g
Same as 886, but without head of lion. Irregular flan.
R: *ʿYNʾL MLK GBL.*
Beirut, NM; Dunand, *Byblos I*, no. 6263; Elayi-Lemaire, *Trans* 38 (2009) 88, no. 192 (Byblos excavations; Byblos hoard TIX).

914 O1–R8
12.85 g
Same as 886, but without head of lion. Slightly irregular flan.
R: *ʿYNʾL MLK GBL.*
Beirut, NM; Dunand, *Byblos I*, no. 6265; Elayi-Lemaire, *Trans* 38 (2009) 88, no. 193 (Byblos excavations; Byblos hoard TIX).

915 O1–R8
12.84 g
7 h
Same as 886, but without head of lion. Oval flan.
R:]*YNʾL MLK GBL.*
Leu, Lucerne, 2/4/1958, no. 254.

916 O1–R8
12.76 g
Same as 886, but without head of lion. Small crack on the edge.
R: *ʿYNʾL MLK GB*[.
Beirut, NM; Dunand, *Byblos I*, no. 6260; Elayi-Lemaire, *Trans* 38 (2009) 88, no. 194 (Byblos excavations; Byblos hoard TIX).

917 O1–R8
12.71 g
2 h
Same as 886, but without head of lion.
O: off-center to left.
R:]*Nʾ L MLK GBL.*
Beirut, NM; Dunand, *Byblos I*, no. 6266; Elayi-Lemaire, *Trans* 38 (2009) 88, no. 195 (Byblos excavations; Byblos hoard TIX).

918 O1–R8
12.62 g
11 h
Same as 886, but without head of lion.
R: *ʿYNʾL MLK GBL.*
Beirut, NM; Dunand, *Byblos I*, no. 6264; Elayi-Lemaire, *Trans* 38 (2009) 88, no. 196 (Byblos excavations; Byblos hoard TIX).

919 O1–R9*
13.01 g
2 h
Same as 886, but without head of lion. Slightly irregular flan.
R: inscription off the flan.
Beirut, NM, no. 4; Elayi-Lemaire, *Trans* 38 (2009) 88, no. 197 and pl. 11:197 (Byblos excavations; Byblos hoard TIX).

920 O1–R9
12.83 g
11 h
Same as 886, but without head of lion. Irregular flan.
R: traces of *ʿYNʾL MLK GBL.*
Beirut, NM, no. 2; Elayi-Lemaire, *Trans* 38 (2009) 88, no. 198 (Byblos excavations; Byblos hoard TIX).

921	O1–R9 12.13 g 4 h	Same as 886, but without head of lion. Slightly worn. R: traces of *ʿYNʾL MLK GBL.* Beirut, NM, no. 7; Elayi-Lemaire, *Trans* 38 (2009) 89, no. 217 (Byblos excavations; Byblos hoard TIX).
922	O1–R10 12.79 g 10 h	Same as 886, but without head of lion. Slightly worn. R: off-center toward the top; inscription off the flan. Beirut, NM, no. 10; Elayi-Lemaire, *Trans* 38 (2009) 88, no. 199 (Byblos excavations; Byblos hoard TIX).
923	O1–R10* 12.47 g	Same as 886. R: two-pronged ankh under the lion; head of lion at the end of the inscription (?); *ʿYNʾL MLK GBL.* Beirut, NM, no. 6; Elayi-Lemaire, *Trans* 38 (2009) 88, no. 200 and pl. 11:200 (Byblos excavations; Byblos hoard TIX).
924	O1–R11* 12.89 g 1 h	Same as 886, but without head of lion. R: off-center toward the top; inscription off the flan. Beirut, NM, no. 8; Elayi-Lemaire, *Trans* 38 (2009) 88, no. 201 and pl. 11:201 (Byblos excavations; Byblos hoard TIX).
925	O1–R12* 12.62 g 8 h	Same as 886. Slightly worn. R: head of lion on the last letter (?). Beirut, NM, no. 15; Elayi-Lemaire, *Trans* 38 (2009) 88, no. 202 and pl. 11:202 (Byblos excavations; Byblos hoard TIX).
926	O1–R13* 12.56 g 4 h	Same as 886, but without head of lion. Slightly worn. R:]*L MLK GBL.* Beirut, NM, no. 11; Elayi-Lemaire, *Trans* 38 (2009) 89, no. 218 (Byblos excavations; Byblos hoard TIX).
927	O1–R14 13.23 g 5 h	Same as 886, but without head of lion. R: *ʿYNʾL MLK GBL.* *SNG Cambridge*, no. 6030.
928	O1–R14 13.18 g	Same as 886, but without head of lion. R: *ʿYNʾL MLK GBL.* Ritter, Dusseldorf, 74, August 2005, no. 104 = Künker, Osnabrück, 97, 7–8/3/2005, no. 955 = Münzen und Medaillen, Weil/Rhein, 8, 10/5/2001, no. 208.
929	O1–R14* 13.18 g	Same as 886, but without head of lion. O: off-center toward the top. R: *ʿYNʾL MLK GBL.* Peus, Frankfurt/Main, 321, 27–29/4 and 2/5/1988, no. 227 = 300, 3–4 and 9/11/1987, no. 1214 = Tradart, New York, 3, 1/12/1985, no. 163.

930	O1–R14 13.12 g	Same as 886, but without head of lion. O: overstruck. R:]*N'L MLK GBL.* Numismatic Fine Arts, Encino, 12/10/1988, no. 560.
931	O2*–R15* 13.70 g 25 mm 7 h	Same as 886, but without head of lion. O: split die. R: *'YN'L MLK GBL.* Vienna, KHM, no. 22.125.
932	O2–R15 12.94 g 2 h	Same as 886, but without head of lion. Slightly worn. O: split die. R: two dots under the stomach of the lion; *'YN*[ ] *GBL.* Beirut, NM, no. 1; Elayi-Lemaire, *Trans* 38 (2009) 88, no. 204 (Byblos excavations; Byblos hoard TIX).
933	O2–R15 12.75 g 3 h	Same as 886, but without head of lion. Slightly worn. O: split die. R: two dots under the stomach of the lion; *'YN'L MLK GB*[. Beirut, NM, no. 12; Elayi-Lemaire, *Trans* 38 (2009) 88, no. 205 (Byblos excavations; Byblos hoard TIX).
934	O2*–R16 13.20 g 26 mm 10 h	Same as 886, but without head of lion. Partly worn. O: split die. R: three two-pronged ankhs under the stomachs of the lion and bull, and on the crupper of the bull; *'YN'*[. Paris, BNF, no. 3147; *Catalogue De Luynes*, no. 3147; Babelon, *Perses*, no. 1362; idem, *Traité*, no. 874 (ex De Luynes coll.).
935	O2–R16* 13.04 g	Same as 886, but without head of lion. Slightly worn. O: split die. R: three two-pronged ankhs under the stomachs of the lion and bull; inscription off the flan. Berk, Chicago, 114, 23/5/2000, no. 243 = Classical Numismatic Group, Lancaster-London, 29, 30/3/1994, no. 281.
936	O2–R16 13.38 g	Same as 886, but without head of lion. Slightly worn. O: split die. R: three two-pronged ankhs under the stomachs of the lion and bull, and on the crupper of the bull; *'YN'L MLK GB*[. Classical Numismatic Group, Lancaster-London, 46, 24/6/1998, no. 500.
937	O2–R17 13.26 g	Same as 886, but without head of lion. Slightly worn. O: split die. R: one two-pronged ankh under the stomach of the lion; inscription off the flan. Berk, Chicago, 143, 18/5/2005, no. 130 = 140, 27/10/2004, no. 196.

938 O2–R17
12.75 g
Same as 886, but without head of lion. Slightly worn.
O: split die.
R: one two-pronged ankh under the stomach of the lion;] *N'L MLK GB*[.
Beirut, NM; Dunand, *Byblos I*, no. 6282; Elayi-Lemaire, *Trans* 38 (2009) 88, no. 203 and pl. 11:203 (Byblos excavations; Byblos hoard TIX).

939 O2–R17*
12.52 g
Same as 886, but without head of lion. Slightly worn.
O: split die.
R: *'YN'L MLK GB*[.
Beirut, NM; Dunand, *Byblos I*, no. 6283; Elayi-Lemaire, *Trans* 38 (2009) 89, no. 206 and pl. 11:206 (Byblos excavations; Byblos hoard TIX).

940 O2–R18*
12.59 g
Same as 886, but without head of lion. Slightly worn.
O: split die.
R: off-center toward the top; one two-pronged ankh under the stomach of the lion; inscription off the flan.
Beirut, NM; Dunand, *Byblos I*, no. 6286; Elayi-Lemaire, *Trans* 38 (2009) 89, no. 209 and pl. 11:209 (Byblos excavations; Byblos hoard TIX).

941 O2–R19*
12.77 g
Same as 886, but without head of lion. Slightly worn.
O: split die.
R: one two-pronged ankh under the stomach of the lion; *'YN'L MLK GB*[.
Beirut, NM; Dunand, *Byblos I*, no. 6284; Elayi-Lemaire, *Trans* 38 (2009) 89, no. 207 and pl. 11:207 (Byblos excavations; Byblos hoard TIX).

942 O2–R20*
12.79 g
Same as 886, but without head of lion. Slightly worn.
O: split die.
R: one two-pronged ankh under the stomach of the lion; *'YN'L MLK* [.
Beirut, NM; Dunand, *Byblos I*, no. 6285; Elayi-Lemaire, *Trans* 38 (2009) 89, no. 208 and pl. 11:208 (Byblos excavations; Byblos hoard TIX).

943 O2–R21*
13.20 g
Same as 886, but without head of lion. Slightly worn.
O: split die.
R: one two-pronged ankh under the stomach of the lion; *'YN'L MLK GBL*.
Ritter, Dusseldorf, 31, April 1991, no. 219 = 29, July 1990, no. 259 = Müller, Münz Zentrum-Rheinland, Solingen, 62, 19–20/5/1989, no. 121.

944 O2–R21
12.58 g

Same as 886, but without head of lion. Slightly worn.
O: split die.
R: one two-pronged ankh under the stomach of the lion; *ʿYNʾL MLK GB*[.
Beirut, NM; Dunand, *Byblos I*, no. 6287; Elayi-Lemaire, *Trans* 38 (2009) 89, no. 210 and pl. 11:210 (Byblos excavations; Byblos hoard TIX).

945 O2–R22*
13.10 g
11 h

Same as 886, but without head of lion. Slightly worn.
O: split die.
R: two two-pronged ankhs under the stomachs of the lion and bull; *ʿYNʾL MLK GB*[.
London, BM, no. 1951-10-7-9; Kraay, *Greek Coins*, no. 1053.

946 O2–R22
12.58 g

Same as 886, but without head of lion. Slightly worn.
O: split die.
R: two two-pronged ankhs under the stomachs of the lion and bull;]*YNʾL MLK GB*[.
Beirut, NM; Dunand, *Byblos I*, no. 6288; Elayi-Lemaire, *Trans* 38 (2009) 89, no. 211 and pl. 11:211 (Byblos excavations; Byblos hoard TIX).

947 O2–R23
12.73 g

Same as 886, but without head of lion. Slightly worn.
O: split die.
R: two two-pronged ankhs under the stomachs of the lion and bull;]*ʾL MLK GBL*.
Beirut, NM; Dunand, *Byblos I*, no. 6290; Elayi-Lemaire, *Trans* 38 (2009) 89, no. 212 and pl. 11:212 (Byblos excavations; Byblos hoard TIX).

948 O2–R23
12.56 g

Same as 886, but without head of lion. Slightly worn.
O: split die.
R: two two-pronged ankhs under the stomachs of the lion and bull; *ʿYNʾL MLK GBL*.
Beirut, NM; Dunand, *Byblos I*, no. 6289; Elayi-Lemaire, *Trans* 38 (2009) 89, no. 213 (Byblos excavations; Byblos hoard TIX).

949 O2–R23
12.45 g

Same as 886, but without head of lion. Slightly worn.
O: split die.
R: two two-pronged ankhs under the stomachs of the lion and bull;] *MLK GB*[.
Beirut, NM, no. 5; Elayi-Lemaire, *Trans* 38 (2009) 89, no. 214 (Byblos excavations; Byblos hoard TIX).

950 O2–R24*
12.79 g
11 h

Same as 886, but without head of lion. Slightly worn.
O: split die.
R: dots under the stomachs of the lion and bull; inscription off the flan.
Beirut, NM, no. 9; Elayi-Lemaire, *Trans* 38 (2009) 89, no. 215 (Byblos excavations; Byblos hoard TIX).

951 O2–R25
13 g 23 mm
9 h
Same as 886, but without head of lion. Slightly worn.
O: off-center toward the top; split die.
R: one two-pronged ankh under the stomach of the lion;]ʾL MLK GBL.
Rome, VM, no. 105.

952 O2–R25
12.44 g 25 mm
8 h
Same as 886, but without head of lion. Partly worn.
O: split die.
R: one two-pronged ankh under the stomach of the lion;]YNʾL *MLK GBL*.
Berlin, SM, no. 17.

953 O2–R25*
Same as 886, but without head of lion. Partly worn.
O: split die.
R: one two-pronged ankh under the stomach of the lion; *ʿYNʾL MLK GBL*.
Elayi-Elayi, *Trésors*, p. 107, no. 486 and pl. 17:486 (hoards of Byblos TXIII, TXIV, TXV?).

954 O2–R26
13.05 g
Same as 886, but without head of lion. Slightly worn.
O: off-center to left; split die.
R: two two-pronged ankhs under the stomachs of the lion and bull;]*YNʾL MLK GBL*.
Empire Coins, Ormond Beach, 4, 9–10/11/1985, no. 126.

955 O2–R26*
13 g
Same as 886, but without head of lion. Square flan.
O: split die.
R: two two-pronged ankhs under the stomachs of the lion and bull;]*NʾL MLK GBL*.
Classical Numismatic Group, Lancaster-London, 46, 24/6/1998, no. 502.

956 O2–R27*
13.12 g
Same as 886, but without head of lion. Slightly worn.
O: off-center to left; split die.
R: three two-pronged ankhs under the stomachs of the lion and bull, and one on the crupper of the bull; dot behind the bull; traces of *ʿYNʾL MLK GBL*.
Classical Numismatic Group, Lancaster-London, 46, 24/6/1998, no. 501.

957 O2–R27
13.05 g 26 mm
Same as 886, but without head of lion. Rather worn.
O: split die.
R: three two-pronged ankhs under the stomachs of the lion and bull, and one on the crupper of the bull (?); dot behind the bull; traces of *ʿYNʾL MLK GBL*.
Hirsch, Munich, 31, 6/5/1912, no. 488 (ex Niess and Barron coll.).

958	O2–R28* 13.06 g 28 mm 6 h	Same as 886, but without head of lion. Partly worn. O: off-center to right; split die. R: one two-pronged ankh under the stomach of the lion; circle behind the bull; *ʿYNʾL MLK GB*[. Paris, BNF, no. 3148; *Catalogue De Luynes*, no. 3148; Babelon, *Perses*, no. 1363; idem, *Traité*, no. 875 (ex De Luynes coll.).
959	O2–R28 13.05 g 26 mm 3 h	Same as 886, but without head of lion. Partly worn. O: split die. R: one two-pronged ankh under the stomach of the lion; circle behind the bull; *ʿYNʾL MLK GB*[. Paris, BNF, no. 69 (ex De Vogüé coll.).
960	O2–R29* 13.15 g 25 mm 7 h	Same as 886, but without head of lion. Partly worn. O: split die. R: two two-pronged ankhs under the stomachs of the lion and the bull; dot behind the bull; *ʿYNʾL MLK GB*[. Paris, BNF, no. 70 (ex De Vogüé coll.).
961	O3*–R30* 13.56 g 26 mm 2 h	Same as 886, but without head of lion. Partly worn. R:]*ʾL MLK G*[. Paris, BNF, no. 3146; *Catalogue De Luynes*, no. 3146; Babelon, *Perses*, no. 1361; idem, *Traité*, no. 873 (ex De Luynes coll.).
962	O4*–R30 12.98 g	Same as 886, but without head of lion. Slightly worn. R: traces of *ʿYNʾL MLK GBL*. Baldwin, London, 34, 13/10/2003, no. 530.
963	O2–R? 13.07 g 4 h	Same as 886, but without head of lion. Slightly worn. O: split die. R: traces of *ʿYNʾL MLK GB*[. Leiden, RM, no. 8026.
964	O2–R? 12.70 g 25 mm	Same as 886, but without head of lion. Irregular flan. Slightly worn. O: split die. R: traces of *ʿYNʾL MLK GBL*. Beirut, AUB Museum, no. 2947C.
965	O?–R3 12.84 g 11 h	Same as 886, but without head of lion. Slightly worn. O: off-center to left. R:]*K GB*[. Beirut, NM, no. 14; Elayi-Lemaire, *Trans* 38 (2009) 89, no. 216 (Byblos excavations; Byblos hoard TIX).

IV.4.2. 16th-Shekels AR

No.	Die / Weight	Description
966	O9 of ʾUrimilk–R1 0.73 g 11 mm 6 h	Slightly worn. O: same as 851; *ʾK.* R: same as 886; *ʿYNʾL MLK GBL.* Elayi-Elayi, *Trésors*, p. 102, no. 297, and pl. 12:297 (Byblos hoards TXIII, TXIV, and TXV?).
967	O10 of ʾUrimilk–R2* 0.80 g	O: same as 851; off-center toward the bottom; *ʾK.* R: same as 886; *ʿYNʾL MLK G*[. Elsen, Brussels, 241, July–September 2007, no. 95.
968	O10 of ʾUrimilk–R3 0.82 g 11 mm 2 h	O: same as 851; off-center toward the bottom; traces of *ʾK.* R: same as 886; *ʿYNʾL MLK G*[. Elayi-Elayi, *Trésors*, p. 103, no. 362, and pl. 14:362 (Byblos hoards TXIII, TXIV, and TXV?).
969	O10 of ʾUrimilk–R4 0.88 g	O: same as 851; off-center toward the bottom; traces of *ʾK.* R: same as 886; *ʿYNʾL MLK* [. Elayi-Elayi, *Trésors*, p. 101, no. 268, and pl. 14:268 (Byblos hoards TXIII, TXIV, and TXV?).
970	O11 of ʾUrimilk–R4* 0.66 g	O: same as 851; *ʾK.* R: same as 886; *ʿYNʾL MLK* [. Hirsch, Munich, 175, 21–26/9/1992, no. 528.
971	O11 of ʾUrimilk–R5 0.64 g	O: same as 851; traces of *ʾK.* R: same as 886; *ʿYNʾL MLK GB*[. Elayi-Elayi, *Trésors*, p. 105, no. 443, and pl. 16:443 (Byblos hoards TXIII, TXIV, and TXV?).
972	O11 of ʾUrimilk–R6 0.76 g	O: same as 851; off-center toward the top; traces of *ʾK.* R: same as 886; *ʿYNʾL MLK GB*[. Elsen, Brussels, July–September, 2009, no. 97.
973	O11 of ʾUrimilk–R7* 0.67 g	O: same as 851; off-center to left; traces of *ʾK.* R: same as 886; *ʿYNʾL MLK* [. Elayi-Elayi, *Trésors*, p. 96, no. 53, and pl. 7:53 (Byblos hoards TXIII, TXIV, and TXV?).
974	O12 of ʾUrimilk–R6 0.73 g 12 mm 7 h	Two cracks on the edge. O: same as 851; off-center to right; *ʾK.* R: same as 886; *ʿYNʾL ML*[ ] *GB*[. Elayi-Elayi, *RBN* 139 (1993) 18, no. 5 and pl. 1:5 (hoard from Near East TLXXX).
975	O12 of ʾUrimilk–R7 0.76 g 11 mm 7 h	O: same as 851; *ʾK.* R: same as 886; *ʿYNʾL MLK GB*[. Elayi-Elayi, *Trésors*, p. 102, no. 295 (Byblos hoards TXIII, TXIV, and TXV?).
976	O12 of ʾUrimilk–R8 0.83 g	O: same as 851; off-center to left; *ʾK.* R: same as 886; *ʿYNʾL MLK* [. Elayi-Elayi, *Trésors*, p. 95, no. 27, and pl. 6:27 (Byblos hoards TXIII, TXIV, and TXV?).

977 O12 of ʾUrimilk–R9 0.83 g
O: same as 851; *ʾK.*
R: same as 886; traces of *ʿYNʾL MLK GBL.*
Elayi-Elayi, *Trésors*, p. 98, no. 188, and pl. 9:188 (Byblos hoards TXIII, TXIV, and TXV?).

978 O12 of ʾUrimilk–R9 0.70 g 11 mm 5 h
O: same as 851; off-center to left; *ʾK.*
R: same as 886; inscription obliterated.
Elayi-Elayi, *RBN* 139 (1993) 18, no. 13 and pl. 2:13.

979 O12 of ʾUrimilk–R10 0.77 g 11 mm 3 h
O: same as 851; off-center to left; *ʾK.*
R: same as 886; *ʿYNʾL MLK* [.
Elayi-Elayi, *Trésors*, p. 102, no. 296, and pl. 7:296 (Byblos hoards TXIII, TXIV, and TXV?).

980 O12 of ʾUrimilk–R11 0.79 g
O: same as 851; *ʾK.*
R: same as 886; traces of *ʿYNʾL MLK* [.
Elayi-Elayi, *Trésors*, p. 98, no. 189, and pl. 9:189 (Byblos hoards TXIII, TXIV, and TXV?).

981 O13 of ʾUrimilk–R5 0.68 g
O: same as 851; off-center to left; traces of *ʾK.*
R: same as 886; *ʿYNʾL MLK GB*[.
Elayi-Elayi, *Trésors*, p. 98, no. 190, and pl. 9:190 (Byblos hoards TXIII, TXIV, and TXV?).

982 O13 of ʾUrimilk–R5 0.68 g
O: same as 851; off-center to left; *ʾK.*
R: same as 886;]*Nʾ L MLK G*[.
Elayi-Elayi, *Trésors*, p. 101, no. 258, and pl. 12:258 (Byblos hoards TXIII, TXIV, and TXV?).

983 O13 of ʾUrimilk–R6 0.77 g 11 mm 4 h
O: same as 851; off-center to right; *ʾK.*
R: same as 886; *ʿYNʾL MLK G*[.
Elayi-Elayi, *Trésors*, p. 102, no. 298, and pl. 12:298 (Byblos hoards TXIII, TXIV, and TXV?).

984 O13 of ʾUrimilk–R6 0.69 g
O: same as 851; traces of *ʾK.*
R: same as 886; *ʿYNʾL ML*[.
Elayi-Elayi, *Trésors*, p. 102, no. 299, and pl. 13:299 (Byblos hoards TXIII, TXIV, and TXV?).

985 O13 of ʾUrimilk–R6 0.67 g
Small cracks on the edge.
O: same as 851; off-center to left; traces of *ʾK.*
R: same as 886;]*YNʾL* [ ] *GB*[.
Elayi-Elayi, *Trésors*, p. 101, no. 259, and pl. 12:259 (Byblos hoards TXIII, TXIV, and TXV?).

986 O13 of ʾUrimilk–R12 0.70 g
O: same as 851; off-center toward the top; traces of *ʾK.*
R: same as 886; *ʿYNʾL MLK GB*[.
Elayi-Elayi, *Trésors*, p. 105, no. 431, and pl. 16:431 (Byblos hoards TXIII, TXIV, and TXV?).

987	O13 of ʾUrimilk–R13 0.70 g	O: same as 851; traces of *ʾK*. R: same as 886; *ʿYNʾL MLK GB*[. Elayi-Elayi, *Trésors*, p. 98, no. 191, and pl. 9:191 (Byblos hoards TXIII, TXIV, and TXV?).
988	O13 of ʾUrimilk–R14 0.70 g 9 mm 9 h	O: same as 851; off-center to right; traces of *ʾK*. R: same as 886; *ʿYNʾL MLK GB*[. Spaer coll., Jerusalem (bought in Jerusalem).
989	O13 of ʾUrimilk–R15 0.74 g	O: same as 851; off-center toward the top; traces of *ʾK*. R: same as 886; *ʿYNʾL MLK GB*[. Elayi-Elayi, *Trésors*, p. 105, no. 433 and pl. 16:433 (Byblos hoards TXIII, TXIV and TXV?).
990	O13 of ʾUrimilk–R16 0.73 g	O: same as 851; off-center to right; traces of *ʾK*. R: same as 886; *ʿYNʾL ML*[. Elayi-Elayi, *Trésors*, p. 95, no. 29, and pl. 3:29 (Byblos hoards TXIII, TXIV and TXV?).
991	O14 of ʾUrimilk–R2 0.82 g 11 mm 12 h	O: same as 851; traces of *ʾK*. R: same as 886; *ʿYNʾL MLK G*[. Elayi-Elayi, *RBN* 139 (1993) 18, no. 9 and pl. 1:9 (hoard from Near East TLXXX).
992	O14 of ʾUrimilk–R6 0.86 g 11 mm 5 h	O: same as 851; traces of *ʾK*. R: same as 886; *ʿYNʾL MLK GB*[. Elayi-Elayi, *RBN* 139 (1993) 18, no. 8 and pl. 1:8 (hoard from Near East TLXXX).
993	O14 of ʾUrimilk–R6 0.70 g	O: same as 851; off-center toward the bottom; traces of *ʾK*. R: same as 886; *ʿYNʾL MLK GB*[. Elayi-Elayi, *Trésors*, p. 102, no. 314, and pl. 13:314 (Byblos hoards TXIII, TXIV, and TXV?).
994	O14 of ʾUrimilk–R8 0.83 g	O: same as 851; off-center to right; *ʾK*. R: same as 886; *ʿYNʾL MLK GB*[. Monnaies et Médailles/Münzen und Medaillen, Basel, 27, 10–11/12/1996, no. 405.
995	O14 of ʾUrimilk–R8 0.74 g 10 mm 11 h	O: same as 851; traces of *ʾK*. R: same as 886;]*Nʾ L MLK* [. Elayi-Elayi, *Trésors*, p. 102, no. 309, and pl. 13:309 (Byblos hoards TXIII, TXIV, and TXV?).
996	O14 of ʾUrimilk–R8 0.70 g 11 mm 7 h	Small crack on the edge. O: same as 851; off-center to left; traces of *ʾK*. R: same as 886; *ʿYNʾL M*[. Elayi-Elayi, *Trésors*, p. 102, no. 310, and pl. 13:310 (Byblos hoards TXIII, TXIV, and TXV?).

997 O14 of ʾUrimilk–R9 0.80 g 11 mm 7 h
O: same as 851; traces of *ʾK*.
R: same as 886; traces of *ʿYNʾL MLK GBL*.
Elayi-Elayi, *RBN* 139 (1993) 18, no. 11 and pl. 1:11 (hoard from Near East TLXXX).

998 O14 of ʾUrimilk–R9 0.76 g 11 mm 3 h
O: same as 851; off-center to left; traces of *ʾK*.
R: same as 886;]*Nʾ L MLK* [.
Elayi-Elayi, *Trésors*, p. 102, no. 311, and pl. 13:311 (Byblos hoards TXIII, TXIV, and TXV?).

999 O14 of ʾUrimilk–R9 0.75 g
O: same as 851; off-center toward the top; traces of *ʾK*.
R: same as 886;]*ʾL MLK* [.
Elayi-Elayi, *Trésors*, p. 105, no. 444, and pl. 16:444 (Byblos hoards TXIII, TXIV, and TXV?).

1000 O14 of ʾUrimilk–R9 0.68 g 11 mm 7 h
O: same as 851; traces of *ʾK*.
R: same as 886; traces of *ʿYNʾL MLK GBL*.
Elayi-Elayi, *RBN* 139 (1993) 18, no. 14 and pl. 2:14 (hoard from Near East TLXXX).

1001 O14 of ʾUrimilk–R12 0.71 g 11 mm 6 h
O: same as 851; off-center to right; traces of *ʾK*.
R: same as 886;]*YNʾL MLK GB*[.
Elayi-Elayi, *Trésors*, p. 102, no. 312, and pl. 13:312 (Byblos hoards TXIII, TXIV, and TXV?).

1002 O14 of ʾUrimilk–R17 0.69 g
Small cracks on the edge.
O: same as 851; off-center to right; traces of *ʾK*.
R: same as 886; *ʿYNʾL ML*[.
Monnaies et Médailles/Münzen und Medaillen, Basel, 22, 16–17/6/1992, no. 382.

1003 O14 of ʾUrimilk–R18* 0.80 g
O: same as 851; off-center to right; traces of *ʾK*.
R: same as 886; *ʿYNʾL MLK GBL*.
Monnaies et Médailles/Münzen und Medaillen, Basel, 505, November–December 1987, no. 100.

1004 O14 of ʾUrimilk–R18 0.69 g
O: same as 851; off-center to right; traces of *ʾK*.
R: same as 886; *ʿYNʾL ML*[ ] *GBL*.
Elayi-Elayi, *Trésors*, p. 107, no. 491, and pl. 16:491 (Byblos hoards TXIII, TXIV, and TXV?).

1005 O14 of ʾUrimilk–R19 0.69 g 11 mm 1 h
O: same as 851; off-center to left; traces of *ʾK*.
R: same as 886; *ʿYNʾL MLK GB*[.
Elayi-Elayi, *Trésors*, p. 102, no. 313, and pl. 13:313 (Byblos hoards TXIII, TXIV, and TXV?).

1006 O15 of ʾUrimilk–R2 0.78 g
O: same as 851; off-center to left; traces of *ʾK*.
R: same as 886;]*YNʾL ML*[ ] *GB*[.
Elayi-Elayi, *Trésors*, p. 96, no. 39, and pl. 6:39 (Byblos hoards TXIII, TXIV, and TXV?).

1007 O15 of ʾUrimilk–R2 0.70 g
O: same as 851; traces of *ʾK*.
R: same as 886; *ʿYNʾL MLK GB*[.
Monnaies et Médailles/Münzen und Medaillen, Basel, 472, November–December 1984, no. 82.

1008 O15 of ʾUrimilk–R2 0.70 g
O: same as 851; traces of *ʾK*.
R: same as 886; *ʿYNʾL MLK GB*[.
Müller, Münz Zentrum-Rheinland, Solingen, 52, 26–27/6/1986, no. 82.

1009 O15 of ʾUrimilk–R2
O: same as 851; traces of *ʾK*.
R: same as 886; *ʿYNʾL MLK G*[.
Berk, Chicago, 84, 19/1/1995, no. 330.

1010 O15 of ʾUrimilk–R3 0.77 g
O: same as 851; traces of *ʾK*.
R: same as 886; *ʿYNʾL MLK G*[.
Elayi-Elayi, *Trésors*, p. 96, no. 42, and pl. 6:42 (Byblos hoards TXIII, TXIV, and TXV?).

1011 O15 of ʾUrimilk–R3* 0.73 g
O: same as 851; off-center to left; *ʾK*.
R: same as 886;] *MLK GBL*.
Gorny, Munich, 32, 12–13/11/1985, no. 128.

1012 O15 of ʾUrimilk–R5 0.83 g
O: same as 851; traces of *ʾK*.
R: same as 886;]*Nʾ L MLK GBL*.
Elayi-Elayi, *Trésors*, p. 96, no. 37, and pl. 6:37 (Byblos hoards TXIII, TXIV, and TXV?).

1013 O15 of ʾUrimilk–R5 0.80 g
O: same as 851; off-center toward the top; traces of *ʾK*.
R: same as 886; *ʿYNʾL MLK GBL*.
Elayi-Elayi, *Trésors*, p. 96, no. 38, and pl. 6:38 (Byblos hoards TXIII, TXIV, and TXV?).

1014 O15 of ʾUrimilk–R6 0.72 g 10 mm 3 h
O: same as 851; off-center to left; traces of *ʾK*.
R: same as 886; *ʿYNʾL M*[ ] *G*[ ].
Elayi-Elayi, *Trésors*, p. 102, no. 307, and pl. 13:307 (Byblos hoards TXIII, TXIV, and TXV?).

1015 O15 of ʾUrimilk–R8 0.69 g
O: same as 851; traces of *ʾK*.
R: same as 886; *ʿYNʾL MLK GB*[.
Elayi-Elayi, *Trésors*, p. 96, no. 30, and pl. 6:30 (Byblos hoards TXIII, TXIV, and TXV?).

1016 O15 of ʾUrimilk–R9 0.86 g
O: same as 851; traces of *ʾK*.
R: same as 886;]*Nʾ L* [.
Elayi-Elayi, *Trésors*, p. 105, no. 434, and pl. 16:434 (Byblos hoards TXIII, TXIV, and TXV?).

1017 O15 of ʾUrimilk–R9 0.85 g
O: same as 851; traces of *ʾK*.
R: same as 886;]*Nʾ L ML*[.
Elayi-Elayi, *Trésors*, p. 105, no. 435, and pl. 16:435 (Byblos hoards TXIII, TXIV, and TXV?).

1018 O15 of ʾUrimilk–R9 0.83 g
O: same as 851; off-center to right; traces of *ʾK*.
R: same as 886; *ʿYNʾL MLK* [.
Elayi-Elayi, *Trésors*, p. 96, no. 32, and pl. 6:32 (Byblos hoards TXIII, TXIV, and TXV?).

1019 O15 of ʾUrimilk–R9 0.78 g
O: same as 851; traces of *ʾK*.
R: same as 886; split die; traces of *ʿYNʾL MLK GBL*.
Elayi-Elayi, *Trésors*, p. 105, no. 436, and pl. 16:436 (Byblos hoards TXIII, TXIV, and TXV?).

1020 O15 of ʾUrimilk–R9* 0.78 g
O: same as 851; off-center toward the bottom; traces of *ʾK*.
R: same as 886; split die; traces of *ʿYNʾL MLK GBL*.
Rauch, Vienna, 42, 16–18/1/1989, no. 3109.

1021 O15 of ʾUrimilk–R9 0.77 g
O: same as 851; off-center to left; traces of *ʾK*.
R: same as 886; split die; traces of]*NʾL ML*[.
Rauch, Vienna, 42, 16–18/1/1989, no. 3108.

1022 O15 of ʾUrimilk–R9 0.76 g
O: same as 851; off-center to left; traces of *ʾK*.
R: same as 886; split die;]*ʾL MLK G*[.
Elayi-Elayi, *Trésors*, p. 105, no. 437, and pl. 16:437 (Byblos hoards TXIII, TXIV, and TXV?).

1023 O15 of ʾUrimilk–R9 0.74 g 10 mm 1 h
O: same as 851; traces of *ʾK*.
R: same as 886; split die; *ʿYNʾL* [.
Elayi-Elayi, *RBN* 139 (1993) 18, no. 12, and pl. 2:12 (hoard from Near East TLXXX).

1024 O15 of ʾUrimilk–R11 0.54 g
O: same as 851; traces of *ʾK*.
R: same as 886; *ʿYNʾL M*[.
Elayi-Elayi, *Trésors*, p. 105, no. 442, and pl. 16:442 (Byblos hoards TXIII, TXIV, and TXV?).

1025 O15 of ʾUrimilk–R12 0.80 g
O: same as 851; off-center toward the top; traces of *ʾK*.
R: same as 886;]*YNʾL MLK G*[.
Elayi-Elayi, *Trésors*, p. 105, no. 438, and pl. 16:438 (Byblos hoards TXIII, TXIV, and TXV?).

1026 O15 of ʾUrimilk–R12 0.71 g
O: same as 851; traces of *ʾK*.
R: same as 886; *ʿYNʾL MLK GB*[.
Elayi-Elayi, *Trésors*, p. 95, no. 33, and pl. 6:33 (Byblos hoards TXIII, TXIV, and TXV?).

1027 O15 of ʾUrimilk–R12* 0.71 g
O: same as 851; traces of *ʾK*.
R: same as 886; *ʿYNʾL MLK GB*[.
Peus, Frankfurt/Main, 369, 31/10/2001, no. 252.

1028 O15 of ʾUrimilk–R12 0.69 g
Small cracks on the edge.
O: same as 851; traces of *ʾK*.
R: same as 886; *ʿYNʾL MLK GB*[.
Elayi-Elayi, *Trésors*, p. 95, no. 34, and pl. 6:34 (Byblos hoards TXIII, TXIV, and TXV?).

1029	O15 of ʾUrimilk–R12 0.68 g 11 mm 3 h	O: same as 851; traces of *ʾK*. R: same as 886; inscription off the flan. Elayi-Elayi, *Trésors*, p. 102, no. 302, and pl. 13:302 (Byblos hoards TXIII, TXIV, and TXV?).
1030	O15 of ʾUrimilk–R13 0.72 g	O: same as 851; off-center topwards; *ʾK*. R: same as 886; *ʿYNʾL MLK GB*[. Hirsch, Munich, 157, 24–26/2/1988, no. 201.
1031	O15 of ʾUrimilk–R14* 0.69 g	O: same as 851; off-center toward the top; *ʾK*. R: same as 886; *ʿYNʾL MLK GBL*. Monetarium, Schweizerische Kreditanstalt, Zurich, 48, Autumn 1987, no. 35.
1032	O15 of ʾUrimilk–R16 0.71 g	O: same as 851; traces of *ʾK*. R: same as 886; *ʿYNʾL MLK GBL*. Elayi-Elayi, *Trésors*, p. 95, no. 31, and pl. 6:31 (Byblos hoards TXIII, TXIV, and TXV?).
1033	O15 of ʾUrimilk–R16 0.68 g	O: same as 851; *ʾK*. R: same as 886; *ʿYNʾL MLK GBL*. Schulten, Cologne, 20–21/10/1988, no. 459.
1034	O15 of ʾUrimilk–R17 0.76 g	O: same as 851; traces of *ʾK*. R: same as 886; *ʿYNʾL* [. Classical Numismatic Group, Lancaster-London, 43, 24/9/1997, no. 750.
1035	O15 of ʾUrimilk–R17 0.75 g	O: same as 851; traces of *ʾK*. R: same as 886; *ʿYNʾL M*[. Münzen und Medaillen, Weil/Rhein, 10, 22/3/2002, no. 233.
1036	O15 of ʾUrimilk–R17 0.65 g	O: same as 851; traces of *ʾK*. R: same as 886; *ʿYNʾL M*[. Elayi-Elayi, *Trésors*, p. 96, no. 43, and pl. 6:43 (Byblos hoards TXIII, TXIV, and TXV?).
1037	O15 of ʾUrimilk–R18 0.77 g 10 mm	O: same as 851; off-center toward the top; traces of *ʾK*. R: same as 886; *ʿYNʾL MLK GB*[. Burgan, Paris, 25/11/1991, no. 300.
1038	O15 of ʾUrimilk–R18 0.61 g 11 mm 12 h	O: same as 851; traces of *ʾK*. R: same as 886;]*YNʾL M*[. Elayi-Elayi, *Trésors*, p. 102, no. 304, and pl. 13:304 (Byblos hoards TXIII, TXIV, and TXV?).
1039	O15 of ʾUrimilk–R20 0.83 g	O: same as 851; traces of *ʾK*. R: same as 886;]*Nʾ L MLK GB*[. Elayi-Elayi, *Trésors*, p. 105, no. 439, and pl. 16:439 (Byblos hoards TXIII, TXIV, and TXV?).

1040	O15 of ʾUrimilk–R20* 0.72 g	O: same as 851; off-center to right; traces of *ʾK*. R: same as 886; *ʿYNʾL MLK G*[. Elayi-Elayi, *Trésors*, p. 95, no. 35, and pl. 6:35 (Byblos hoards TXIII, TXIV, and TXV?).
1041	O15 of ʾUrimilk–R20 0.72 g	O: same as 851; off-center to left; traces of *ʾK*. R: same as 886; *ʿYNʾL MLK G*[. Elayi-Elayi, *Trésors*, p. 95, no. 36, and pl. 6:36 (Byblos hoards TXIII, TXIV, and TXV?).
1042	O15 of ʾUrimilk–R21 0.82 g	O: same as 851; traces of *ʾK*. R: same as 886; *ʿYNʾL M*[. Elayi-Elayi, *Trésors*, p. 96, no. 40, and pl. 6:40 (Byblos hoards TXIII, TXIV, and TXV?).
1043	O15 of ʾUrimilk–R21* 0.72 g	O: same as 851; traces of *ʾK*. R: same as 886; *ʿYNʾL M*[. Elayi-Elayi, *Trésors*, p. 96, no. 41, and pl. 6:41 (Byblos hoards TXIII, TXIV, and TXV?).
1044	O15 of ʾUrimilk–R21 0.72 g 11 mm 5 h	O: same as 851; traces of *ʾK*. R: same as 886; *ʿYNʾL* [. Elayi-Elayi, *Trésors*, p. 102, no. 303, and pl. 13:303 (Byblos hoards TXIII, TXIV, and TXV?).
1045	O15 of ʾUrimilk–R22 0.80 g	O: same as 851; off-center toward the top; traces of *ʾK*. R: same as 886; *ʿYNʾL M*[. Elayi-Elayi, *Trésors*, p. 105, no. 440, and pl. 16:440 (Byblos hoards TXIII, TXIV, and TXV?).
1046	O15 of ʾUrimilk–R23 0.73 g	O: same as 851; off-center toward the top; traces of *ʾK*. R: same as 886; *ʿYNʾL MLK GB*[. Elayi-Elayi, *Trésors*, p. 105, no. 441, and pl. 16:441 (Byblos hoards TXIII, TXIV, and TXV?).
1047	O15 of ʾUrimilk–R24* 0.78 g	O: same as 851; traces of *ʾK*. R: same as 886; *ʿYNʾL MLK GB*[. Gorny, Munich, 101, 6/3/2000, no. 397.
1048	O15 of ʾUrimilk–R24 0.57 g 10 mm 6 h	O: same as 851; off-center to right; traces of *ʾK*. R: same as 886;]*ʾL MLK G*[. Elayi-Elayi, *Trésors*, p. 102, no. 305, and pl. 13:305 (Byblos hoards TXIII, TXIV, and TXV?).
1049	O15 of ʾUrimilk–R25* 0.73 g 11 mm 7 h	O: same as 851; off-center toward the bottom; traces of *ʾK*. R: same as 886; *ʿYNʾL M*[. Elayi-Elayi, *Trésors*, p. 102, no. 306, and pl. 13:306 (Byblos hoards TXIII, TXIV, and TXV?).
1050	O15 of ʾUrimilk–R26 0.73 g	O: same as 851; off-center to right; traces of *ʾK*. R: same as 886; *ʿYNʾL MLK GBL*. Elayi-Elayi, *Trésors*, p. 99, no. 192, and pl. 9:192 (Byblos hoards TXIII, TXIV, and TXV?).

1051	O15 of ʾUrimilk–R27* 0.35 g	O: same as 851; traces of *ʾK.* R: same as 886; *ʿYNʾL MLK GBL.* Schulten, Cologne, 21–23/10/1986, no. 125.
1052	O15 of ʾUrimilk–R28* 0.49 g	O: same as 851; traces of *ʾK.* R: same as 886; *ʿYNʾL MLK GBL.* Private coll.
1053	O15 of ʾUrimilk–R29* 0.80 g 10 mm 8 h	O: same as 851; *ʾK.* R: same as 886; *ʿYNʾL MLK GB*[. Moussaieff coll., London.
1054	O15 of ʾUrimilk–R30* 0.64 g	O: same as 851; traces of *ʾK.* R: same as 886; *ʿYNʾL MLK GB*[. Sternberg, Zurich, 20–21/11/1989, no. 134.
1055	O15 of ʾUrimilk–R31* 0.83 g	O: same as 851; off-center to right; *ʾK.* R: same as 886; *ʿYNʾL MLK GBL.* Elayi-Elayi, *Trésors*, p. 107, no. 488, and pl. 17:488 (Byblos hoards TXIII, TXIV, and TXV?).
1056	O15 of ʾUrimilk–R32* 0.72 g 9 h	O: same as 851; off-center to right; traces of *ʾK.* R: same as 886; split coin; *ʿYNʾL M*[. Klein, *Sammlung*, no. 711 (Klein coll.).
1057	O9 of ʾUrimilk–R?	Slightly worn. O: same as 851; off-center to left; traces of *ʾK.* R: same as 886; traces of *ʿYNʾL MLK GBL.* Berk, Chicago, 57, 29/3/1989, no. 160.
1058	O10 of ʾUrimilk–R? 0.69 g 10 mm 6 h	Slightly worn. O: same as 851; traces of *ʾK.* R: same as 886;]*ʾL M*[. Elayi-Elayi, *Trésors*, p. 103, no. 363, and pl. 14:363 (Byblos hoards TXIII, TXIV, and TXV?).
1059	O12 of ʾUrimilk–R? 0.81 g	Slightly worn. O: same as 851; off-center to left; traces of *ʾK.* R: same as 886; *ʿYNʾL ML*[ ]*B*[. Elayi-Elayi, *Trésors*, p. 95, no. 28, and pl. 6:28 (Byblos hoards TXIII, TXIV, and TXV?).
1060	O13 of ʾUrimilk–R? 0.76 g 11 mm 6 h	Slightly worn. O: same as 851; traces of *ʾK.* R: same as 886;]*Y*[ ]*ʾL MLK* [. Elayi-Elayi, *Trésors*, p. 102, no. 301, and pl. 13:301 (Byblos hoards TXIII, TXIV, and TXV?).

1061 O13 of ʾUrimilk–R? 0.71 g 11 mm 10 h
Slightly worn.
O: same as 851; off-center to left; traces of *ʾK*.
R: same as 886;]*ʾL* [.
Elayi-Elayi, *Trésors*, p. 102, no. 300, and pl. 13:300 (Byblos hoards TXIII, TXIV, and TXV?).

1062 O14 of ʾUrimilk–R? 0.81 g
Slightly worn.
O: same as 851; off-center to left; traces of *ʾK*.
R: same as 886;]*NʾL MLK G*[.
Elayi-Elayi, *Trésors*, p. 105, no. 445 (Byblos hoards TXIII, TXIV, and TXV?).

1063 O14 of ʾUrimilk–R? 0.75 g
Slightly worn.
O: same as 851; off-center toward the top; traces of *ʾK*.
R: same as 886;]*YNʾL MLK GB*[.
Elayi-Elayi, *Trésors*, p. 105, no. 446 (Byblos hoards TXIII, TXIV, and TXV?).

1064 O14 of ʾUrimilk–R? 0.72 g
Slightly worn.
O: same as 851; traces of *ʾK*.
R: same as 886; *ʿYNʾL MLK G*[.
Elayi-Elayi, *Trésors*, p. 105, no. 447, and pl. 16:447 (Byblos hoards TXIII, TXIV, and TXV?).

1065 O14 of ʾUrimilk–R? 0.70 g
Slightly worn. Small cracks on the edge.
O: same as 851; traces of *ʾK*.
R: same as 886;] *MLK G*[.
Elayi-Elayi, *Trésors*, p. 105, no. 447, and pl. 16:447 (Byblos hoards TXIII, TXIV, and TXV?).

1066 O14 of ʾUrimilk–R? 0.68 g 11 mm 12 h
Slightly worn. Oval flan.
O: same as 851; traces of *ʾK*.
R: same as 886; *ʿ*[.
Elayi-Elayi, *RBN* 139 (1993) 18, no. 15 and pl. 2:15 (hoard from Near East TLXXX).

1067 O14 of ʾUrimilk–R?
Slightly worn. Small cracks on the edge.
O: same as 851; traces of *ʾK*.
R: same as 886; *ʿYNʾL MLK* [.
Stockholm, RCC, no. 101345.

1068 O15 of ʾUrimilk–R? 0.80 g 11 mm 3 h
Slightly worn.
O: same as 851; very off-center to left; *ʾK*.
R: same as 886;] *G*[.
Elayi-Elayi, *RBN* 139 (1993) 18, no. 10 and pl. 1:10 (hoard from Near East TLXXX).

1069 O15 of ʾUrimilk–R? 0.75 g
Slightly worn.
O: same as 851; traces of *ʾK*.
R: same as 886; *ʿYN*[ ]*K G*[.
Elayi-Elayi, *Trésors*, p. 107, no. 490, and pl. 17:490 (Byblos hoards TXIII, TXIV, and TXV?).

1070	O15 of ʾUrimilk–R? 0.74 g	Slightly worn. O: same as 851; off-center to right; traces of *ʾK*. R: same as 886; *ʿYNʾL M*[. Elayi-Elayi, *Trésors*, p. 96, no. 44, and pl. 6:44 (Byblos hoards TXIII, TXIV, and TXV?).
1071	O15 of ʾUrimilk–R? 0.72 g	Slightly worn. O: same as 851; traces of *ʾK*. R: same as 886;]*YNʾL M*[. Elayi-Elayi, *Trésors*, p. 96, no. 45, and pl. 6:45 (Byblos hoards TXIII, TXIV, and TXV?).
1072	O15 of ʾUrimilk–R? 0.69 g 11 mm 7 h	Slightly worn. O: same as 851; traces of *ʾK*. R: same as 886; *ʿYNʾ*[. Elayi-Elayi, *Trésors*, p. 102, no. 308, and pl. 13:308 (Byblos hoards TXIII, TXIV, and TXV?).
1073	O15 of ʾUrimilk–R? 0.69 g	Slightly worn. O: same as 851; *ʾK*. R: same as 886; *ʿYNʾL M*[. Albrecht-Hoffmann, Münz Zentrum, Cologne, 59, 29–31/10/1986, no. 1214.
1074	O15 of ʾUrimilk–R? 0.67 g	Slightly worn. O: same as 851; traces of *ʾK*. R: same as 886;] *GB*[. Elayi-Elayi, *Trésors*, p. 96, no. 46, and pl. 6:46 (Byblos hoards TXIII, TXIV, and TXV?).
1075	O15 of ʾUrimilk–R? 0.64 g	Slightly worn. O: same as 851; traces of *ʾK*. R: same as 886;]*ʾL MLK* [. Elayi-Elayi, *Trésors*, p. 96, no. 47, and pl. 6:47 (Byblos hoards TXIII, TXIV, and TXV?).
1076	O15 of ʾUrimilk–R?	Slightly worn. O: same as 851; traces of *ʾK*. R: same as 886. Elayi-Elayi, *Trésors*, p. 106, no. 481 (Byblos hoards TXIII, TXIV, and TXV?).
1077	O? of ʾUrimilk–R2 0.73 g	Slightly worn. O: same as 851; overstruck; traces of *ʾK*. R: same as 886; *ʿYNʾL M*[. Elayi-Elayi, *Trésors*, p. 97, no. 122, and pl. 8:122 (Byblos hoards TXIII, TXIV and TXV?).

1078	O? of ʾUrimilk-R2 0.61 g 11 mm 6 h	Slightly worn. O: same as 851; off-center to left; traces of *ʾK*. R: same as 886; *ʿYNʾL MLK G*[. Elayi-Elayi, *RBN* 139 (1993) 22, no. 74, and pl. 5:74 (hoard from Near East TLXXX).
1079	O? of ʾUrimilk-R11*	Slightly worn. O: same as 851; off-center toward the top; traces of *ʾK*. R: same as 886; *ʿYNʾL MLK G*[. Silberstein, Paris, 1989.
1080	O? of ʾUrimilk-R17 0.73 g	Slightly worn. Some cracks on the edge. O: same as 851; off-center to left; traces of *ʾK*. R: same as 886; *ʿYNʾL M*[. Elsen, Brussels, 231, January–March 2005, no. 103 = 227, January–March 2004, no. 109 = 222, September–October 2002, no. 86 = 218, October–November 2001, no. 212 = 216, June–July 2001, no. 145 = 204, May–July 1999, no. 102 = 56, 18–19/12/1998, no. 249.
1081	O? of ʾUrimilk-R17 0.68 g 11 mm 4 h	Slightly worn. O: same as 851; very off-center to left; *ʾK*. R: same as 886; *ʿYNʾL M*[. Elayi-Elayi, *RBN* 139 (1993) 18, no. 7 and pl. 1:7 (hoard from Near East TLXXX).
1082	O? of ʾUrimilk-R23* 0.72 g	Slightly worn. O: same as 851; off-center toward the bottom; *ʾK*. R: same as 886;]*YNʾL MLK GBL*. Elayi-Elayi, *Trésors*, p. 107, no. 489, and pl. 17:489 (Byblos hoards TXIII, TXIV, and TXV?).
1083	O? of ʾUrimilk-R39* 0.77 g	Slightly worn. O: same as 851; traces of *ʾK*. R: same as 886;]*NʾL M*[. Elsen, Brussels, 238, October–December 2006, no. 81.
1084	O? of ʾUrimilk-R? 0.83 g	Worn. O: same as 851; *ʾK*. R: same as 886; *ʿYNʾL ML*[. Vecchi, London, July–August 1986, no. 71.
1085	O? of ʾUrimilk-R? 0.73 g	Worn. O: same as 851; traces of *ʾK*. R: same as 886; traces of *ʿYNʾL MLK GBL*. Schulten, Cologne, 1–3/4/1987, no. 229.
1086	O? of ʾUrimilk-R? 0.63 g	Worn. O: same as 851; *ʾK*. R: same as 886; *ʿYNʾL M*[. Albrecht-Hoffmann, Münz Zentrum, Cologne, 63, 13–14/4/1988, no. 1445.

1087	O? of 'Urimilk–R?	Worn. O: same as 851; off-center to right; traces of *'K*. R: same as 886; *'YN'L M*[. Lanz, Munich, 34, 25/11/1985, no. 289.
1088	O? of 'Urimilk–R?	Worn. O: same as 851; *'K*. R: same as 886; *'YN'L ML*[. Brandt, Stuttgart, 4, Autumn 1986, no. 89.
1089	O1*–R5 0.73 g 8 h	O: war-galley to left; prow terminating in head of a lion; inside, two warriors represented by helmets and shields; below, winged seahorse to left. Border of dots. R: same as 886; *]N'L MLK GBL*. Elayi-Elayi, *Trésors*, p. 103, no. 367, and pl. 14:367 (Byblos hoards TXIII, TXIV, and TXV?).
1090	O2*–R10* 0.78 g	O: same as 1089. R: same as 886; *'YN'L ML*[ ] *G*[. Elayi-Elayi, *Trésors*, p. 107, no. 493, and pl. 17:493 (Byblos hoards TXIII, TXIV, and TXV?).
1091	O2–R13 0.67 g 11 mm 12 h	O: same as 1089. R: same as 886; *'YN'L MLK* [. Elayi-Elayi, *RBN* 139 (1993) 21, no. 62, and pl. 4:62 (hoard from Near East TLXXX).
1092	O3–R1* 0.75 g 10 mm 2 h	O: same as 1089; split die. R: same as 886; *'YN'L MLK* [. Paris, BNF, no. 3150; Babelon, *Perses*, no. 365; idem, *Traité*, no. 876 (ex De Luynes coll.).
1093	O3–R2 0.84 g	O: same as 1089; split die. R: same as 886; *'YN'L MLK* [. Elayi-Elayi, *Trésors*, p. 106, no. 458, and pl. 17:458 (Byblos hoards TXIII, TXIV, and TXV?).
1094	O3–R2 0.62 g 11 mm 6 h	Some cracks on the edge. O: same as 1089; split die. R: same as 886; *'YN'L MLK G*[. Elayi-Elayi, *Trésors*, p. 103, no. 328, and pl. 13:328 (Byblos hoards TXIII, TXIV, and TXV?).
1095	O3–R6* 0.70 g	O: same as 1089; split die. R: same as 886; *'YN'L ML*[. Elayi-Elayi, *Trésors*, p. 101, no. 263, and pl. 12:263 (Byblos hoards TXIII, TXIV, and TXV?).
1096	O3–R8* 0.76 g	O: same as 1089; split die. R: same as 886; *'YN'L MLK G*[. Lanz, Munich, 78, 25/11/1996, no. 356.

1097 O3–R9 0.86 g
O: same as 1089; split die; off-center toward the top.
R: same as 886;]*N'L MLK* [.
Elayi-Elayi, *Trésors*, p. 105, no. 449, and pl. 16:449 (Byblos hoards TXIII, TXIV, and TXV?).

1098 O3–R9 0.85 g
O: same as 1089; split die.
R: same as 886; *'YN'L MLK* [.
Elayi-Elayi, *Trésors*, p. 103, no. 195, and pl. 9:195 (Byblos hoards TXIII, TXIV, and TXV?).

1099 O3–R9 0.84 g
O: same as 1089; split die.
R: same as 886;]*N'L MLK* [.
Elayi-Elayi, *Trésors*, p. 105, no. 450, and pl. 16:450 (Byblos hoards TXIII, TXIV, and TXV?).

1100 O3–R9 0.82 g
O: same as 1089; off-center to left; split die.
R: same as 886; *'YN'L MLK G*[.
Elayi-Elayi, *Trésors*, p. 96, no. 55, and pl. 6:55 (Byblos hoards TXIII, TXIV, and TXV?).

1101 O3–R9 0.82 g
O: same as 1089; split die.
R: same as 886;]*N'L M*[.
Elayi-Elayi, *Trésors*, p. 105, no. 451, and pl. 16:451 (Byblos hoards TXIII, TXIV, and TXV?).

1102 O3–R9 0.82 g 10 h
Edge broken.
O: same as 1089; off-center to left; split die.
R: same as 886;]*YN'L* [.
Elayi-Elayi, *RBN* 139 (1993) 19, no. 20, and pl. 2:20 (hoard from Near East TLXXX).

1103 O3–R9 0.78 g
Edge broken.
O: same as 1089; split die.
R: same as 886; *'YN'L MLK G*[ ]*L*.
Elayi-Elayi, *Trésors*, p. 96, no. 56, and pl. 6:56 (Byblos hoards TXIII, TXIV, and TXV?).

1104 O3–R9 0.77 g
O: same as 1089; split die.
R: same as 886;]*YN'L MLK* [.
Elayi-Elayi, *Trésors*, p. 96, no. 57, and pl. 6:57 (Byblos hoards TXIII, TXIV, and TXV?).

1105 O3–R9 0.75 g
O: same as 1089; split die; off-center to left.
R: same as 886; *'YN'L M*[.
Elayi-Elayi, *Trésors*, p. 105, no. 452, and pl. 16:452 (Byblos hoards TXIII, TXIV, and TXV?).

1106 O3–R9 0.74 g
O: same as 1089; split die.
R: same as 886; traces of *'YN'L MLK GBL*.
Elayi-Elayi, *Trésors*, p. 96, no. 58, and pl. 6:58 (Byblos hoards TXIII, TXIV, and TXV?).

1107 O3–R9
0.74 g 11 mm
9 h
O: same as 1089; split die.
R: same as 886;]*N'L ML*[.
Elayi-Elayi, *Trésors*, p. 103, no. 321, and pl. 13:321 (Byblos hoards TXIII, TXIV, and TXV?).

1108 O3–R9
0.73 g 11 mm
6 h
O: same as 1089; split die; off-center to left.
R: same as 886; *'YN'L MLK GBL*.
Elayi-Elayi, *Trésors*, p. 96, no. 59, and pl. 6:59 (Byblos hoards TXIII, TXIV, and TXV?).

1109 O3–R9
0.73 g 11 mm
6 h
O: same as 1089; split die; off-center toward the bottom.
R: same as 886; traces of *'YN'L MLK GBL*.
Elayi-Elayi, *RBN* 139 (1993) 20, no. 44 and pl. 2:44 (hoard from Near East TLXXX).

1110 O3–R9
0.72 g 10 mm
7 h
O: same as 1089; split die; very off-center toward the top.
R: same as 886; *'YN'L MLK* [.
Elayi-Elayi, *Trésors*, p. 103, no. 322, and pl. 13:322 (Byblos hoards TXIII, TXIV, and TXV?).

1111 O3–R9
0.71 g
O: same as 1089; split die; off-center to left.
R: same as 886; *'YN'L M*[.
Elayi-Elayi, *Trésors*, p. 96, no. 60, and pl. 6:60 (Byblos hoards TXIII, TXIV, and TXV?).

1112 O3–R9
0.71 g
O: same as 1089; split die.
R: same as 886;]*N'L M*[.
Elayi-Elayi, *Trésors*, p. 105, no. 453, and pl. 16:453 (Byblos hoards TXIII, TXIV, and TXV?).

1113 O3–R9
0.70 g 11 mm
5 h
O: same as 1089; split die; off-center to left.
R: same as 886;]*L MLK G*[.
Elayi-Elayi, *Trésors*, p. 103, no. 323, and pl. 13:323 (Byblos hoards TXIII, TXIV, and TXV?).

1114 O3–R9
0.70 g
1 h
O: same as 1089; split die.
R: same as 886;]*Y*[ ]*L*[.
Elayi-Elayi, *Trésors*, p. 103, no. 324, and pl. 13:324 (Byblos hoards TXIII, TXIV, and TXV?).

1115 O3–R9
0.70 g 11 mm
5 h
O: same as 1089; split die; off-center toward the bottom.
R: same as 886; *'YN'L MLK G*[.
Elayi-Elayi, *Trésors*, p. 103, no. 329, and pl. 13:329 (Byblos hoards TXIII, TXIV, and TXV?).

1116 O3–R9
0.69 g
O: same as 1089; split die.
R: same as 886; inscription obliterated.
Elayi-Elayi, *Trésors*, p. 96, no. 61 ,and pl. 6:61 (Byblos hoards TXIII, TXIV, and TXV?).

1117 O3–R9
0.65 g 11 mm
11 h
O: same as 1089; split die; off-center toward the bottom.
R: same as 886; *'YN'L MLK G*[.
Elayi-Elayi, *Trésors*, p. 102, no. 315, and pl. 13:315 (Byblos hoards TXIII, TXIV, and TXV?).

1118	O3–R9 0.65 g	O: same as 1089; split die. R: same as 886; *ʿYNʾL* [. Hirsch, Munich, 169, 20–22/2/1991, no. 549.
1119	O3–R9 0.64 g	Small crack on the edge. O: same as 1089; split die. R: same as 886; inscription obliterated. Elayi-Elayi, *Trésors*, p. 96, no. 62, and pl. 6:62 (Byblos hoards TXIII, TXIV, and TXV?).
1120	O3–R9 0.63 g	O: same as 1089; split die; off-center toward the top. R: same as 886;]*YNʾL ML*[. Elayi-Elayi, *Trésors*, p. 96, no. 63, and pl. 6:63 (Byblos hoards TXIII, TXIV, and TXV?).
1121	O3–R9 0.61 g	O: same as 1089; split die; off-center toward the top. R: same as 886;]*LK* [. Elayi-Elayi, *Trésors*, p. 96, no. 64, and pl. 6:64 (Byblos hoards TXIII, TXIV, and TXV?).
1122	O3–R9	O: same as 1089; split die. R: same as 886; *ʿYNʾL MLK G*[. Vecchi, London, 15, 15/6/1999, no. 428.
1123	O3–R11 0.79 g 11 mm 12 h	O: same as 1089; split die; very off-center toward the bottom. R: same as 886; *ʿYNʾL M*[. Elayi-Elayi, *Trésors*, p. 103, no. 334, and pl. 13:334 (Byblos hoards TXIII, TXIV, and TXV?).
1124	O3–R11 0.78 g 11 mm 7 h	O: same as 1089; split die; off-center to left. R: same as 886; *ʿYNʾL M*[. Elayi-Elayi, *RBN* 139 (1993) 19, no. 25 and pl. 2:25 (hoard from Near East TLXXX).
1125	O3–R11 0.74 g 11 mm 5 h	Small crack on the edge. O: same as 1089; split die; off-center to left. R: same as 886;]*Nʾ L M*[. Elayi-Elayi, *Trésors*, p. 103, no. 335, and pl. 13:335 (Byblos hoards TXIII, TXIV, and TXV?).
1126	O3–R11 0.73 g	O: same as 1089; split die; off-center to right. R: same as 886; *ʿYNʾL M*[. Elayi-Elayi, *Trésors*, p. 99, no. 197, and pl. 9:197 (Byblos hoards TXIII, TXIV, and TXV?).
1127	O3–R12 0.86 g	O: same as 1089; split die; off-center to right. R: same as 886;]*ʾL MLK GB*[. Elayi-Elayi, *Trésors*, p. 106, no. 454 ,and pl. 16:454 (Byblos hoards TXIII, TXIV, and TXV?).

1128 O3–R12
0.81 g
O: same as 1089; split die; off-center to left.
R: same as 886; *ʿYNʾL M*[.
Elayi-Elayi, *Trésors*, p. 106, no. 455, and pl. 16:455 (Byblos hoards TXIII, TXIV, and TXV?).

1129 O3–R12
0.79 g
O: same as 1089; split die.
R: same as 886;]*L MLK* [.
Elayi-Elayi, *Trésors*, p. 96, no. 65, and pl. 7:65 (Byblos hoards TXIII, TXIV, and TXV?).

1130 O3–R12
0.79 g
O: same as 1089; split die.
R: same as 886; *ʿYNʾL MLK GB*[.
Elayi-Elayi, *Trésors*, p. 106, no. 456, and pl. 16:456 (Byblos hoards TXIII, TXIV, and TXV?).

1131 O3–R12
0.76 g 11 mm
6 h
O: same as 1089; split die.
R: same as 886; *ʿYNʾL MLK GB*[.
Paris, BNF, no. 71 (ex De Vogüé coll.).

1132 O3–R12
0.74 g 11 mm
5 h
O: same as 1089; split die.
R: same as 886;]*L MLK G*[.
Elayi-Elayi, *Trésors*, p. 103, no. 325, and pl. 13:325 (Byblos hoards TXIII, TXIV, and TXV?).

1133 O3–R12
0.73 g
O: same as 1089; split die.
R: same as 886;]*Nʾ L M*[.
Elayi-Elayi, *Trésors*, p. 106, no. 457, and pl. 17:457 (Byblos hoards TXIII, TXIV, and TXV?).

1134 O3–R13
0.76 g
Edge broken.
O: same as 1089; split die.
R: same as 886; *ʿYNʾL MLK G*[.
Elayi-Elayi, *Trésors*, p. 96, no. 70, and pl. 7:70 (Byblos hoards TXIII, TXIV and TXV?).

1135 O3–R13
0.75 g
O: same as 1089; split die; off-center toward the bottom.
R: same as 886; *ʿYNʾL ML*[.
Elayi-Elayi, *Trésors*, p. 106, no. 460, and pl. 17:460 (Byblos hoards TXIII, TXIV, and TXV?).

1136 O3–R14
0.77 g
O: same as 1089; split die; very off-center toward the top.
R: same as 886; *ʿYNʾL MLK GBL*.
Elayi-Elayi, *Trésors*, p. 106, no. 461, and pl. 17:461 (Byblos hoards TXIII, TXIV, and TXV?).

1137 O3–R14
0.72 g
O: same as 1089; split die; off-center to right.
R: same as 886; *ʿYNʾL MLK G*[.
Elayi-Elayi, *Trésors*, p. 101, no. 260, and pl. 12:260 (Byblos hoards TXIII, TXIV, and TXV?).

1138 O3–R14
0.71 g
O: same as 1089; split die.
R: same as 886; *ʿYNʾL* [.
Elayi-Elayi, *Trésors*, p. 101, no. 269, and pl. 12:269 (Byblos hoards TXIII, TXIV, and TXV?).

1139	O3–R14 0.68 g	O: same as 1089; split die. R: same as 886; *ʿYNʾL MLK GBL.* Private coll.
1140	O3–R14 0.63 g	O: same as 1089; split die. R: same as 886; *ʿYNʾL M*[. Elayi-Elayi, *Trésors*, p. 101, no. 262, and pl. 12:262 (Byblos hoards TXIII, TXIV, and TXV?).
1141	O3–R15 0.74 g	O: same as 1089; split die. R: same as 886;]*ʾL MLK G*[. Elayi-Elayi, *Trésors*, p. 106, no. 464, and pl. 17:464 (Byblos hoards TXIII, TXIV, and TXV?).
1142	O3–R16* 0.76 g	O: same as 1089; split die. R: same as 886; *ʿYNʾL MLK GB*[. Elsen, Brussels, 26, 12/9/1992, no. 417.
1143	O3–R16 0.68 g	O: same as 1089; split die. R: same as 886;]*YNʾL ML*[. Elayi-Elayi, *Trésors*, p. 96, no. 54, and pl. 6:54 (Byblos hoards TXIII, TXIV, and TXV?).
1144	O3–R16	O: same as 1089; split die. R: same as 886; *ʿYNʾL M*[. Hirsch, Munich, 211, 21–23/9/2000, no. 1404.
1145	O3–R17 0.71 g	O: same as 1089; split die. R: same as 886; *ʿYNʾL M*[ ]*G*[. Elayi-Elayi, *Trésors*, p. 96, no. 67, and pl. 7:67 (Byblos hoards TXIII, TXIV, and TXV?).
1146	O3–R17 0.71 g	O: same as 1089; split die. R: same as 886; *ʿYNʾL M*[. Elayi-Elayi, *Trésors*, p. 96, no. 68, and pl. 7:68 (Byblos hoards TXIII, TXIV, and TXV?).
1147	O3–R18 0.78 g	O: same as 1089; split die. R: same as 886; *ʿYNʾL MLK* [. Elayi-Elayi, *Trésors*, p. 96, no. 72, and pl. 7:72 (Byblos hoards TXIII, TXIV, and TXV?).
1148	O3–R20 0.80 g	O: same as 1089; split die. R: same as 886; *ʿYNʾL MLK GB*[. Elayi-Elayi, *Trésors*, p. 99, no. 196, and pl. 9:196 (Byblos hoards TXIII, TXIV, and TXV?).
1149	O3–R20 0.66 g	O: same as 1089; split die. R: same as 886; *ʿYNʾL MLK* [. Elayi-Elayi, *Trésors*, p. 96, no. 66, and pl. 7:66 (Byblos hoards TXIII, TXIV, and TXV?).

1150 O3–R20 0.61 g 10 mm 3 h
O: same as 1089; split die.
R: same as 886; *ʿYNʾL MLK* [.
Elayi-Elayi, *Trésors*, p. 103, no. 327, and pl. 13:327 (Byblos hoards TXIII, TXIV, and TXV?).

1151 O3–R22 0.68 g 11 mm 5 h
O: same as 1089; split die.
R: same as 886;]*Nʾ L MLK G*[.
Elayi-Elayi, *RBN* 139 (1993) 21, no. 59 and pl. 4:59 (hoard from Near East TLXXX).

1152 O3–R23 0.70 g 11 mm 1 h
Oval flan. Small crack on the edge.
O: same as 1089; split die.
R: same as 886; *ʿYNʾL MLK G*[.
Elayi-Elayi, *RBN* 139 (1993) 18, no. 6 and pl. 1:6 (hoard from Near East TLXXX).

1153 O3–R23 0.69 g
O: same as 1089; split die.
R: same as 886;]*Nʾ L MLK GB*[.
Elayi-Elayi, *Trésors*, p. 96, no. 71, and pl. 7:71 (Byblos hoards TXIII, TXIV, and TXV?).

1154 O3–R25 0.79 g
O: same as 1089; split die.
R: same as 886; *ʿYNʾL MLK GBL.*
Elayi-Elayi, *Trésors*, p. 106, no. 463, and pl. 17:463 (Byblos hoards TXIII, TXIV, and TXV?).

1155 O3–R25 0.75 g
O: same as 1089; split die; off-center to left.
R: same as 886; *ʿYNʾL MLK GBL.*
Elayi-Elayi, *Trésors*, p. 101, no. 270, and pl. 12:270 (Byblos hoards TXIII, TXIV, and TXV?).

1156 O3–R26 0.78 g
O: same as 1089; split die; off-center toward the top.
R: same as 886; *ʿYNʾL MLK GB*[.
Elayi-Elayi, *Trésors*, p. 101, no. 271, and pl. 12:271 (Byblos hoards TXIII, TXIV, and TXV?).

1157 O3–R26* 0.66 g 11 mm 4 h
O: same as 1089; split die; off-center to left.
R: same as 886;]*ʾL MLK* [.
Elayi-Elayi, *Trésors*, p. 103, no. 336, and pl. 13:336 (Byblos hoards TXIII, TXIV, and TXV?).

1158 O3–R33* 0.75 g
O: same as 1089; split die; off-center toward the top.
R: same as 886; *ʿYNʾL MLK* [.
Künker, Osnabrück, 83, 17/6/2003, no. 424.

1159 O3–R34* 0.77 g
O: same as 1089; split die.
R: same as 886; *ʿYNʾL M*[.
Gorny, Munich, 42, 11/10/1988, no. 424.

1160 O3–R35 0.85 g
O: same as 1089; split die.
R: same as 886;]*YNʾL MLK GBL.*
Elayi-Elayi, *Trésors*, p. 100, no. 251, and pl. 11:251 (Byblos hoards TXIII, TXIV, and TXV?).

1161 O3–R35
0.78 g 11 mm
12 h
O: same as 1089; split die.
R: same as 886; *ʿYNʾL MLK* [.
Elayi-Elayi, *Trésors*, p. 103, no. 330, and pl. 13:330 (Byblos hoards TXIII, TXIV, and TXV?).

1162 O3–R35
0.77 g
Oval flan.
O: same as 1089; split die.
R: same as 886; *ʿYNʾL MLK G*[.
Elayi-Elayi, *Trésors*, p. 106, no. 459, and pl. 17:459 (Byblos hoards TXIII, TXIV, and TXV?).

1163 O3–R35
0.69 g 11 mm
12 h
Small cracks on the edge.
O: same as 1089; split die.
R: same as 886; *ʿYNʾL MLK* [.
Elayi-Elayi, *Trésors*, p. 103, no. 331, and pl. 13:331 (Byblos hoards TXIII, TXIV, and TXV?).

1164 O3–R36*
0.74 g
O: same as 1089; split die.
R: same as 886; *ʿYNʾL M* [.
Elayi-Elayi, *Trésors*, p. 96, no. 69, and pl. 7:69 (Byblos hoards TXIII, TXIV, and TXV?).

1165 O3–R37*
0.75 g
O: same as 1089; split die.
R: same as 886; *ʿYNʾL MLK GBL.*
Elayi-Elayi, *Trésors*, p. 96, no. 73, and pl. 7:73 (Byblos hoards TXIII, TXIV, and TXV?).

1166 O3–R38
0.80 g 10 mm
5 h
O: same as 1089; split die; off-center toward the bottom.
R: same as 886; off-center to left; *ʿYNʾL* [.
Elayi-Elayi, *Trésors*, p. 103, no. 332, and pl. 13:332 (Byblos hoards TXIII, TXIV, and TXV?).

1167 O3–R38
0.80 g 11 mm
6 h
Oval flan.
O: same as 1089; split die.
R: same as 886; *ʿYNʾL M*[.
Elayi-Elayi, *Trésors*, p. 103, no. 333, and pl. 13:333 (Byblos hoards TXIII, TXIV, and TXV?).

1168 O3–R38
0.72 g 11 mm
3 h
Oval flan.
O: same as 1089; split die.
R: same as 886; *ʿYNʾL MLK G*[.
Private coll.

1169 O3–R38*
0.70 g
O: same as 1089; split die.
R: same as 886; *ʿYNʾL M*[.
Elsen, Brussels, 26, 12/9/1992, no. 415.

1170 O3–R39
0.81 g 10 mm
12 h
O: same as 1089; split die.
R: same as 886; *ʿYNʾL MLK G*[.
Elayi-Elayi, *Trésors*, p. 101, no. 272, and pl. 12:272 (Byblos hoards TXIII, TXIV, and TXV?).

1171	O3–R40 0.74 g 11 mm 5 h	O: same as 1089; split die; off-center to left. R: same as 886;] *YN'L MLK* [. Elayi-Elayi, *Trésors*, p. 103, no. 337, and pl. 13:337 (Byblos hoards TXIII, TXIV, and TXV?).
1172	O3–R40 0.73 g 11 mm 3 h	O: same as 1089; split die. R: same as 886;]*N'L MLK* [. Elayi-Elayi, *Trésors*, p. 103, no. 338, and pl. 13:338 (Byblos hoards TXIII, TXIV, and TXV?).
1173	O3–R41 0.82 g	O: same as 1089; split die. R: same as 886; *'YN'L MLK GBL*. Elayi-Elayi, *Trésors*, p. 106, no. 465, and pl. 17:465 (Byblos hoards TXIII, TXIV, and TXV?).
1174	O3–R41* 0.75 g	O: same as 1089; split die. R: same as 886; *'YN'L MLK GBL* partly off the flan. Hirsch, Munich, 211, 21–23/9/2000, no. 1403 = 208, 17–19/2/2000, no. 1861.
1175	O3*–R42* 0.74 g	Small crack on the edge. O: same as 1089; split die. R: same as 886; off-center to right; traces of *'YN'L MLK GBL*. Hirsch, Munich, 155, 23–26/9/1987, no. 196.
1176	O3–R42 0.53 g 11 mm 6 h	O: same as 1089; split die. R: same as 886; *'YN'*[. Elayi-Elayi, *RBN* 139 (1993) 22, no. 77 and pl. 5:77 (hoard from Near East TLXXX).
1177	O3–R51* 0.70 g	O: same as 1089; split die. R: same as 886; *'YN'L MLK* [. Hirsch, Munich, 209, 3–5/5/2000, no. 241.
1178	O4*–R15* 0.80 g	Oval flan. O: same as 1089; off-center to left. R: same as 886; *'YN'L MLK G*[. Berk, Chicago, 66, 11/6/1991, no. 160.
1179	O4–R20 0.80 g	O: same as 1089; off-center to left. R: same as 886; *'YN'L M*[. Elayi-Elayi, *Trésors*, p. 106, no. 469, and pl. 17:469 (Byblos hoards TXIII, TXIV, and TXV?).
1180	O5*–R9 0.74 g 11 mm 3 h	O: same as 1089; off-center to right; defect on the prow. R: same as 886;] *YN'L* [. Elayi-Elayi, *RBN* 139 (1993) 20, no. 38 and pl. 3:38 (hoard from Near East TLXXX).
1181	O5–R43* 0.72 g 11 mm 7 h	O: same as 1089; off-center to left; defect on the prow. R: same as 886; *'YN'L M*[. Elayi-Elayi, *RBN* 139 (1993) 20, no. 45 and pl. 3:45 (hoard from Near East TLXXX).

1182	O6*–R35* 0.68 g 10 mm 4 h	O: same as 1089. R: same as 886; *ʿYNʾL MLK* [. Paris, BNF, no. 72 (ex De Vogüé coll.).
1183	O7*–R22* 0.89 g	O: same as 1089. R: same as 886; *ʿYNʾL MLK GBL* partly off the flan. Gorny, Munich, 90, 12–13/10/1998, no. 481.
1184	O7–R27 0.67 g	O: same as 1089. R: same as 886; *ʿYNʾL MLK GBL.* Elayi-Elayi, *Trésors*, p. 99, no. 203, and pl. 9:203 (Byblos hoards TXIII, TXIV, and TXV?).
1185	O8*–R27 0.78 g	Small crack on the edge. O: same as 1089; off-center to left. R: same as 886;]*YNʾL MLK GBL.* Gorny, Munich, 92, 20–21/11/1998, no. 280.
1186	O9*–R24 0.76 g	O: same as 1089; off-center toward the top. R: same as 886; *ʿYNʾL MLK* [. Elayi-Elayi, *Trésors*, p. 97, no. 107, and pl. 7:107 (Byblos hoards TXIII, TXIV, and TXV?).
1187	O9–R24 0.70 g	O: same as 1089; off-center toward the top. R: same as 886; *ʿYNʾL MLK G*[ ]*L.* Elayi-Elayi, *Trésors*, p. 97, no. 108, and pl. 7:108 (Byblos hoards TXIII, TXIV, and TXV?).
1188	O10*–R32 0.67 g 11 mm 9 h	O: same as 1089; very off-center to left. R: same as 886; *ʿYNʾL MLK G*[. Elayi-Elayi, *RBN* 139 (1993) 20, no. 45 and pl. 4:45 (hoard from Near East TLXXX).
1189	O11–R2 0.65 g 11 mm 5 h	Small crack on the edge. O: same as 1089; split die. R: same as 886; *ʿYNʾL MLK GB*[. Elayi-Elayi, *RBN* 139 (1993) 22, no. 71 and pl. 4:71 (hoard from Near East TLXXX).
1190	O11–R5 0.87 g 10 mm 3 h	O: same as 1089; split die. R: same as 886;]*Nʾ L ML*[. Elayi-Elayi, *Trésors*, p. 102, no. 316, and pl. 13:316 (Byblos hoards TXIII, TXIV, and TXV?).
1191	O11*–R5* 0.81 g	O: same as 1089; split die. R: same as 886; *ʿYNʾL MLK GBL.* Sternberg, Zurich, 15, 11–12/4/1985, no. 148.
1192	O11–R5 0.75 g 11 mm 5 h	O: same as 1089; split die. R: same as 886;]*YNʾL MLK G*[. Elayi-Elayi, *Trésors*, p. 102, no. 317, and pl. 13:317 (Byblos hoards TXIII, TXIV, and TXV?).

1193 O11–R9
0.71 g
O: same as 1089; off-center toward the top; split die.
R: same as 886;] *MLK* [.
Elayi-Elayi, *Trésors*, p. 106, no. 470, and pl. 17:470 (Byblos hoards TXIII, TXIV, and TXV?).

1194 O11–R9
0.66 g
O: same as 1089; off-center to right; split die.
R: same as 886; *ʿYNʾL MLK* [.
Elayi-Elayi, *Trésors*, p. 96, no. 49, and pl. 6:49 (Byblos hoards TXIII, TXIV, and TXV?).

1195 O11–R11
0.62 g
O: same as 1089; split die.
R: same as 886; *ʿYNʾL M*[.
Elayi-Elayi, *Trésors*, p. 99, no. 193, and pl. 9:193 (Byblos hoards TXIII, TXIV, and TXV?).

1196 O11–R12
0.76 g 10 mm
11 h
O: same as 1089; split die.
R: same as 886; *ʿYNʾL M*[.
Elayi-Elayi, *RBN* 139 (1993) 20, no. 32 and pl. 2:32 (hoard from Near East TLXXX).

1197 O11–R15
0.92 g
O: same as 1089; off-center toward the top; split die.
R: same as 886; *ʿYNʾL MLK* [.
Elayi-Elayi, *Trésors*, p. 105, no. 448, and pl. 16:448 (Byblos hoards TXIII, TXIV, and TXV?).

1198 O11–R22
0.76 g
O: same as 1089; split die.
R: same as 886; *ʿYNʾL MLK* [.
Elayi-Elayi, *Trésors*, p. 96, no. 50, and pl. 6:50 (Byblos hoards TXIII, TXIV, and TXV?).

1199 O11–R23
0.64 g 11 mm
3 h
O: same as 1089; split die.
R: same as 886;]*Nʾ L MLK G*[.
Elayi-Elayi, *Trésors*, p. 102, no. 318, and pl. 13:318 (Byblos hoards TXIII, TXIV, and TXV?).

1200 O11–R35
0.74 g
O: same as 1089; split die.
R: same as 886; five dots before the bull;]*ʾL MLK* [.
Elayi-Elayi, *Trésors*, p. 101, no. 261, and pl. 12:261 (Byblos hoards TXIII, TXIV, and TXV?).

1201 O11–R35
0.70 g
Small crack on the edge.
O: same as 1089; split die.
R: same as 886; off-center to left; *ʿYNʾL MLK* [.
Elayi-Elayi, *Trésors*, p. 96, no. 51, and pl. 6:51 (Byblos hoards TXIII, TXIV, and TXV?).

1202 O11–R35
0.66 g 11 mm
7 h
Slightly irregular flan.
O: same as 1089; split die.
R: same as 886;]*YNʾL MLK* [.
Elayi-Elayi, *RBN* 139 (1993) 22, no. 69, and pl. 4:69 (hoard from Near East TLXXX).

1203 O11–R44* 0.71 g 11 mm 9 h
Small cracks on the edge.
O: same as 1089; split die; off-center toward the top.
R: same as 886; *ʿYNʾL MLK* [ ]*BL.*
Elayi-Elayi, *Trésors*, p. 103, no. 319, and pl. 13:319 (Byblos hoards TXIII, TXIV, and TXV?).

1204 O12–R4 0.73 g
O: same as 1089; off-center toward the top.
R: same as 886; *ʿYNʾL M*[.
Elayi-Elayi, *Trésors*, p. 99, no. 201, and pl. 9:201 (Byblos hoards TXIII, TXIV, and TXV?).

1205 O12–R12 0.79 g
O: same as 1089; off-center toward the top.
R: same as 886; *ʿYNʾL MLK* [.
Elayi-Elayi, *Trésors*, p. 101, no. 265, and pl. 12:265 (Byblos hoards TXIII, TXIV, and TXV?).

1206 O12*–R12 0.78 g
O: same as 1089; off-center to left; restruck.
R: same as 886; *ʿYNʾL MLK GBL.*
Elayi-Elayi, *Trésors*, p. 101, no. 96, and pl. 7:86 (Byblos hoards TXIII, TXIV, and TXV?).

1207 O12–R12 0.68 g
O: same as 1089; off-center to left; restruck.
R: same as 886; *ʿYNʾL MLK G*[.
Elayi-Elayi, *Trésors*, p. 96, no. 87, and pl. 7:87 (Byblos hoards TXIII, TXIV, and TXV?).

1208 O12–R20 0.79 g
O: same as 1089; off-center to left.
R: same as 886;]*Nʾ L MLK* [.
Elayi-Elayi, *Trésors*, p. 99, no. 200, and pl. 9:200 (Byblos hoards TXIII, TXIV, and TXV?).

1209 O12–R39 0.71 g 10 mm 7 h
O: same as 1089.
R: same as 886;]*YNʾL MLK GBL.*
Elayi-Elayi, *Trésors*, p. 103, no. 350, and pl. 14:350 (Byblos hoards TXIII, TXIV, and TXV?).

1210 O12–R45 0.73 g
O: same as 1089.
R: same as 886; *ʿYNʾL MLK* [.
Elayi-Elayi, *Trésors*, p. 97, no. 88, and pl. 7:88 (Byblos hoards TXIII, TXIV, and TXV?).

1211 O12–R45 0.72 g
Small crack on the edge.
O: same as 1089.
R: same as 886;]*YNʾL MLK GBL.*
Elayi-Elayi, *Trésors*, p. 97, no. 89, and pl. 7:89 (Byblos hoards TXIII, TXIV, and TXV?).

1212 O12–R45 0.70 g
O: same as 1089.
R: same as 886; *ʿYNʾL MLK GBL.*
Elayi-Elayi, *Trésors*, p. 97, no. 90, and pl. 7:90 (Byblos hoards TXIII, TXIV, and TXV?).

1213 O12–R46
0.76 g
O: same as 1089.
R: same as 886; *ʿYNʾL MLK GB*[.
Elayi-Elayi, *Trésors*, p. 97, no. 91, and pl. 7:91 (Byblos hoards TXIII, TXIV, and TXV?).

1214 O12–R46*
0.76 g
O: same as 1089.
R: same as 886;]*YNʾL MLK GBL*.
Elayi-Elayi, *Trésors*, p. 97, no. 92, and pl. 7:92 (Byblos hoards TXIII, TXIV, and TXV?).

1215 O12–R47*
0.74 g
O: same as 1089.
R: same as 886; *ʿYNʾL ML*[.
Elayi-Elayi, *Trésors*, p. 97, no. 93, and pl. 7:93 (Byblos hoards TXIII, TXIV, and TXV?).

1216 O12–R48*
0.71 g 11 mm
4 h
O: same as 1089.
R: same as 886;]*Nʾ L MLK* [.
Elayi-Elayi, *Trésors*, p. 103, no. 348, and pl. 14:348 (Byblos hoards TXIII, TXIV, and TXV?).

1217 O12–R49
0.60 g 10 mm
7 h
O: same as 1089; off-center toward the top.
R: same as 886;]*YNʾL MLK GBL*.
Elayi-Elayi, *Trésors*, p. 103, no. 349, and pl. 14:349 (Byblos hoards TXIII, TXIV, and TXV?).

1218 O12–R50
0.74 g
O: same as 1089.
R: same as 886;]*YNʾL MLK G*[.
Elayi-Elayi, *Trésors*, p. 101, no. 266, and pl. 12:266 (Byblos hoards TXIII, TXIV, and TXV?).

1219 O13–R6
0.76 g 11 mm
4 h
O: same as 1089.
R: same as 886; *ʿYNʾL M*[.
Elayi-Elayi, *Trésors*, p. 103, no. 360, and pl. 14:360 (Byblos hoards TXIII, TXIV, and TXV?).

1220 O13–R12
0.82 g
O: same as 1089; off-center to right.
R: same as 886; *ʿYNʾL MLK* [.
Elayi-Elayi, *Trésors*, p. 97, no. 100, and pl. 7:100 (Byblos hoards TXIII, TXIV, and TXV?).

1221 O13*–R16
0.78 g
O: same as 1089.
R: same as 886; *ʿYNʾL MLK G*[.
England, Quarryville-London, 18, 3/12/1991, no. 200.

1222 O13–R18
0.80 g
O: same as 1089; very off-center toward the top.
R: same as 886; *ʿYNʾL M*[ ]*B*[.
Elayi-Elayi, *Trésors*, p. 97, no. 101, and pl. 7:101 (Byblos hoards TXIII, TXIV, and TXV?).

1223 O13–R18
0.77 g
O: same as 1089; off-center to left.
R: same as 886; *ʿYNʾL ML*[.
Elayi-Elayi, *Trésors*, p. 97, no. 102, and pl. 7:102 (Byblos hoards TXIII, TXIV, and TXV?).

1224 O13–R18
0.67 g

Small cracks on the edge.
O: same as 1089; off-center toward the top.
R: same as 886; *ʿYNʾL M*[.
Elayi-Elayi, *Trésors*, p. 97, no. 103, and pl. 7:103 (Byblos hoards TXIII, TXIV, and TXV?).

1225 O13–R49
0.83 g 11 mm
12 h

O: same as 1089; very off-center to left.
R: same as 886; *ʿYNʾL MLK GBL.*
Elayi-Elayi, *RBN* 139 (1993) 19, no. 19 and pl. 2:19 (hoard from Near East TLXXX).

1226 O14–R8
0.66 g

O: same as 1089; off-center toward the top.
R: same as 886; *ʿYNʾL MLK* [.
Elsen, Brussels, 50, 14/6/1997, no. 296.

1227 O14–R12
0.78 g 11 mm
7 h

O: same as 1089; off-center to left.
R: same as 886; *ʿYNʾL ML*[.
Elayi-Elayi, *RBN* 139 (1993) 19, no. 26, and pl. 2:26 (hoard from Near East TLXXX).

1228 O14*–R13*
0.83 g
12 h

O: same as 1089; off-center to left.
R: same as 886; *ʿYNʾL MLK* [.
England, Quarryville-London, 14, 20/3/1991, no. 200.

1229 O14–R13
0.80 g

O: same as 1089.
R: same as 886; *ʿYNʾL MLK GB*[.
Vecchi, London, 15, 15/6/1999, no. 428 = 6, 9–10/6/1997, no. 512.

1230 O14–R21
0.75 g 10 mm
4 h

O: same as 1089.
R: same as 886; *ʿYNʾL MLK G*[.
Elayi-Elayi, *RBN* 139 (1993) 20, no. 34 and pl. 3:34 (hoard from Near East TLXXX).

1231 O14–R49*
0.70 g

O: same as 1089.
R: same as 886; off-center to right;]*Nʾl MLK G*[.
Hirsch, Munich, 166, 16–19/5/1990, no. 543.

1232 O15–R6
0.80 g 10 mm
2 h

O: same as 1089; very off-center to right.
R: same as 886; *ʿYNʾL M*[.
Elayi-Elayi, *Trésors*, p. 103, no. 351, and pl. 14:351 (Byblos hoards TXIII, TXIV, and TXV?).

1233 O15–R6
0.68 g

O: same as 1089.
R: same as 886; *ʿYNʾL ML*[.
Elayi-Elayi, *Trésors*, p. 101, no. 267, and pl. 12:267 (Byblos hoards TXIII, TXIV, and TXV?).

1234 O15–R9
0.88 g 10 mm
12 h

O: same as 1089.
R: same as 886;]*Nʾl MLK G*[.
Elayi-Elayi, *RBN* 139 (1993) 19, no. 17 and pl. 2:17 (hoard from Near East TLXXX).

1235 O15*–R12
0.86 g — O: same as 1089.
R: same as 886; *ʿYNʾL MLK* [.
Elayi-Elayi, *Trésors*, p. 97, no. 94, and pl. 7:94 (Byblos hoards TXIII, TXIV, and TXV?).

1236 O15–R12
0.79 g — O: same as 1089.
R: same as 886;]*ʾL MLK* [.
Elayi-Elayi, *Trésors*, p. 97, no. 95, and pl. 7:95 (Byblos hoards TXIII, TXIV, and TXV?).

1237 O16–R9
0.79 g — O: same as 1089; defect above the warriors.
R: same as 886; *ʿYNʾL ML*[.
Elayi-Elayi, *Trésors*, p. 107, no. 492, and pl. 17:492 (Byblos hoards TXIII, TXIV, and TXV?).

1238 O16*–R9
0.69 g — Irregular flan.
O: same as 1089; defect above the warriors; off-center toward the bottom.
R: same as 886; *ʿYNʾL MLK GBL* partly off the flan.
Berk, Chicago, 87, 13/9/1995, no. 183 = 70, 16/3/1992, no. 220 = 65, 26/2/1991, no. 375B.

1239 O16–R18
0.70 g — O: same as 1089; defect above the warriors; off-center toward the bottom.
R: same as 886; *ʿYNʾL ML*[.
Elayi-Elayi, *Trésors*, p. 97, no. 106, and pl. 7:106 (Byblos hoards TXIII, TXIV, and TXV?).

1240 O16–R18
0.68 g 10 mm
11 h — O: same as 1089; defect above the warriors; off-center to right.
R: same as 886; *ʿYNʾL ML*[.
Elayi-Elayi, *RBN* 139 (1993) 21, no. 61 and pl. 4:61 (hoard from Near East TLXXX).

1241 O17–R16
0.71 g 11 mm
3 h — O: same as 1089.
R: same as 886; *ʿYNʾL M*[.
Elayi-Elayi, *RBN* 139 (1993) 20, no. 47 and pl. 3:47 (hoard from Near East TLXXX).

1242 O17–R17
0.68 g 10 mm
10 h — O: same as 1089.
R: same as 886; *ʿYNʾL M*[.
Elayi-Elayi, *RBN* 139 (1993) 21, no. 56 and pl. 4:56 (hoard from Near East TLXXX).

1243 O17*–R17 — O: same as 1089.
R: same as 886; *ʿYNʾL MLK GB*[.
Berk, Chicago, 65, 26/2/1991, no. 375A.

1244 O17–R20
0.79 g 11 mm
9 h — O: same as 1089; off-center to right.
R: same as 886; *ʿYNʾL MLK* [.
Elayi-Elayi, *Trésors*, p. 103, no. 326, and pl. 13:326 (Byblos hoards TXIII, TXIV, and TXV?).

1245 O17–R28 0.66 g 11 mm 6 h
O: same as 1089.
R: same as 886; *ʿYNʾL MLK G*[.
Elayi-Elayi, *RBN* 139 (1993) 21, no. 67 and pl. 4:67 (hoard from Near East TLXXX).

1246 O17–R38
O: same as 1089.
R: same as 886; *ʿYNʾL MLK G*[.
Private coll.

1247 O18*–R17* 0.76 g
O: same as 1089.
R: same as 886; *ʿYNʾL M*[.
Münzen Auktion, Essen, 69, 31/5–2/6/1995, no. 121.

1248 O18–R17
O: same as 1089; off-center to right.
R: same as 886; *ʿYNʾL ML*[.
Munich, SMS, no. 26.

1249 O19–R38 0.70 g
O: same as 1089; off-center to left.
R: same as 886;]*Nʾ L M*[ ]*K G*[.
Elayi-Elayi, *Trésors*, p. 97, no. 109, and pl. 7:109 (Byblos hoards TXIII, TXIV, and TXV?).

1250 O20–R8 0.70 g
O: same as 1089; off-center toward the top.
R: same as 886; *ʿYNʾL MLK* [.
Elsen, Brussels, 44, 27/4/1996, no. 242.

1251 O20–R11 0.77 g
O: same as 1089; off-center toward the bottom.
R: same as 886; *ʿYNʾ*[.
Elsen, Brussels, 246, October-December 2008, no. 74.

1252 O20*–R12 0.75 g
O: same as 1089; off-center toward the bottom.
R: same as 886;]*YNʾL MLK G*[.
Elsen, Brussels, 210, June-July 2000, no. 144.

1253 O21–R5 0.77 g
O: same as 1089.
R: same as 886; *ʿYNʾL MLK GB*[.
Ponterio, San Diego, 1/8/1995, no. 338.

1254 O21–R9 0.75 g 11 mm 9 h
O: same as 1089; off-center toward the top.
R: same as 886;]*YNʾL M*[.
Elayi-Elayi, *RBN* 139 (1993) 20, no. 35 and pl. 3:35 (hoard from Near East TLXXX).

1255 O21–R9 0.75 g 11 mm 2 h
O: same as 1089; off-center to left.
R: same as 886; *ʿYNʾL ML*[.
Elayi-Elayi, *Trésors*, p. 103, no. 353, and pl. 14:353 (Byblos hoards TXIII, TXIV, and TXV?).

1256 O21–R38 0.77 g 10 mm 6 h
O: same as 1089; off-center to left.
R: same as 886; *ʿYNʾ*[.
Elayi-Elayi, *RBN* 139 (1993) 19, no. 28 and pl. 2:28 (hoard from Near East TLXXX).

1257 O21–R45 0.69 g
O: same as 1089; off-center to left.
R: same as 886;]*N'L MLK* [.
Elayi-Elayi, *Trésors*, p. 97, no. 98, and pl. 7:98 (Byblos hoards TXIII, TXIV, and TXV?).

1258 O22–R11 0.64 g 11 mm 5 h
O: same as 1089; off-center toward the top.
R: same as 886; *'YN'L M*[.
Elayi-Elayi, *RBN* 139 (1993) 22, no. 72 and pl. 4:72 (hoard from Near East TLXXX).

1259 O22–R12 0.78 g 11 mm 12 h
O: same as 1089; defect on the seahorse; off-center toward the bottom.
R: same as 886; off-center to left; *'YN'L MLK* [.
Bartlett Well coll., Lexington, no. 5.

1260 O22*–R13 0.73 g 10 mm 4 h
O: same as 1089; defect on the seahorse; off-center to left.
R: same as 886; *'YN'L MLK* [.
Elsen, Brussels, 32, 11/12/1993, no. 139.

1261 O22–R17 0.69 g 11 mm 5 h
O: same as 1089; defect on the seahorse; off-center toward the top.
R: same as 886; *'YN'L ML*[.
Elayi-Elayi, *RBN* 139 (1993) 21, no. 52 and pl. 3:52 (hoard from Near East TLXXX).

1262 O23–R2 0.82 g 11 mm 5 h
O: same as 1089; off-center toward the bottom.
R: same as 886; *'YN'L MLK GB*[.
Elsen, Brussels, 237, July–September 2006, no. 66.

1263 O23–R2 0.70 g
O: same as 1089.
R: same as 886; *'YN'L MLK GB*[.
Elayi-Elayi, *Trésors*, p. 97, no. 99, and pl. 7:99 (Byblos hoards TXIII, TXIV, and TXV?).

1264 O23–R9 0.74 g 11 mm 6 h
O: same as 1089; off-center to left.
R: same as 886; *'YN'L MLK* [.
Elayi-Elayi, *Trésors*, p. 103, no. 355, and pl. 14:355 (Byblos hoards TXIII, TXIV, and TXV?).

1265 O23–R9 0.63 g 10 mm 1 h
O: same as 1089.
R: same as 886; inscription obliterated.
Elayi-Elayi, *RBN* 139 (1993) 22, no. 73 and pl. 5:73 (hoard from Near East TLXXX).

1266 O23–R19 0.72 g 11 mm 2 h
O: same as 1089; off-center toward the bottom.
R: same as 886; *'YN'L MLK GB*[.
Elayi-Elayi, *Trésors*, p. 103, no. 357, and pl. 14:357 (Byblos hoards TXIII, TXIV, and TXV?).

1267 O23*–R42 0.86 g
O: same as 1089; off-center toward the top.
R: same as 886; *'YN'L M*[.
England, Quarryville-London, 12, 26/9/1990, no. 412.

1268 O23–R46
0.69 g 11 mm
4 h
O: same as 1089.
R: same as 886; *ʿYNʾL MLK GB*[.
Elayi-Elayi, *Trésors*, p. 103, no. 356, and pl. 14:356 (Byblos hoards TXIII, TXIV, and TXV?).

1269 O23–R50*
0.68 g 11 mm
7 h
O: same as 1089; off-center toward the bottom.
R: same as 886; *ʿYNʾL MLK G*[.
Elayi-Elayi, *Trésors*, p. 103, no. 358, and pl. 14:358 (Byblos hoards TXIII, TXIV, and TXV?).

1270 O24–R13
0.76 g
O: same as 1089; off-center toward the bottom; split die.
R: same as 886; *ʿYNʾL MLK GBL.*
Elsen, Brussels, 248, April-June 2009, no. 113.

1271 O24–R51
0.81 g
O: same as 1089; split die.
R: same as 886; *ʿYNʾL MLK G*[.
Elsen, Brussels, 247, January-March 2009, no. 91.

1272 O24*–R52*
0.74 g
O: same as 1089; split die.
R: same as 886; *ʿYNʾL MLK* [ ]*B*[.
Elayi-Elayi, *Trésors*, p. 107, no. 495, and pl. 17:495 (Byblos hoards TXIII, TXIV, and TXV?).

1273 O25–R53*
0.76 g
O: same as 1089; off-center toward the top.
R: same as 886;]*Nʾ L MLK GBL.*
Elayi-Elayi, *Trésors*, p. 107, no. 494, and pl. 17:494 (Byblos hoards TXIII, TXIV, and TXV?).

1274 O25*–R54*
0.70 g
O: same as 1089.
R: same as 886; *ʿYNʾL MLK GBL.*
Schulten, Cologne, 11–12/4/1988, no. 196.

1275 O26*–R55*
O: same as 1089; off-center toward the top.
R: same as 886; *ʿYNʾL MLK* [.
Berk, Chicago, 50, 18/11/1987, no. 254.

1276 O2–R?
0.67 g 11 mm
6 h
Oval flan. Slightly worn.
O: same as 1089; off-center to right.
R: same as 886; *ʿYNʾ*[.
Elayi-Elayi, *RBN* 139 (1993) 21, no. 65 and pl. 4:65 (hoard from Near East TLXXX).

1277 O3–R?
0.87 g 11 mm
10 h
Slightly worn.
O: same as 1089; off-center toward the bottom; split die.
R: same as 886;]*ʾL MLK* [.
Elayi-Elayi, *Trésors*, p. 103, no. 339, and pl. 13:339 (Byblos hoards TXIII, TXIV, and TXV?).

1278 O3–R?
0.84 g
Oval flan. Slightly worn.
O: same as 1089; split die.
R: same as 886;]*YNʾL ML*[.
Elayi-Elayi, *Trésors*, p. 96, no. 74, and pl. 7:74 (Byblos hoards TXIII, TXIV, and TXV?).

1279 O3–R? 0.83 g
Slightly worn.
O: same as 1089; split die.
R: same as 886; *ʿYNʾL MLK G*[.
Elayi-Elayi, *Trésors*, p. 106, no. 466 (Byblos hoards TXIII, TXIV, and TXV?).

1280 O3–R? 0.82 g
Slightly worn.
O: same as 1089; split die.
R: same as 886;]*ʾL MLK G*[.
Elayi-Elayi, *Trésors*, p. 96, no. 75, and pl. 7:75 (Byblos hoards TXIII, TXIV, and TXV?).

1281 O3–R? 0.81 g 11 mm 12 h
Slightly worn.
O: same as 1089; split die.
R: same as 886;]*ʾL*[.
Elayi-Elayi, *Trésors*, p. 103, no. 340, and pl. 13:340 (Byblos hoards TXIII, TXIV, and TXV?).

1282 O3–R? 0.81 g
Oval flan. Slightly worn.
O: same as 1089; split die.
R: same as 886; *ʿYNʾL ML*[.
Elayi-Elayi, *Trésors*, p. 106, no. 467, and pl. 17:467 (Byblos hoards TXIII, TXIV, and TXV?).

1283 O3–R? 0.80 g
Oval flan. Slightly worn.
O: same as 1089; split die.
R: same as 886;] *MLK G*[.
Elayi-Elayi, *Trésors*, p. 96, no. 76, and pl. 7:76 (Byblos hoards TXIII, TXIV, and TXV?).

1284 O3–R? 0.80 g
Slightly worn.
O: same as 1089; off-center to left; split die.
R: same as 886; traces of *ʿYNʾL MLK GBL.*
Elayi-Elayi, *Trésors*, p. 106, no. 468 (Byblos hoards TXIII, TXIV, and TXV?).

1285 O3–R? 0.77 g 11 mm 5 h
Oval flan. Slightly worn.
O: same as 1089; very off-center to left; split die.
R: same as 886; ʿ[ ]*LK* [.
Elayi-Elayi, *Trésors*, p. 103, no. 341, and pl. 13:341 (Byblos hoards TXIII, TXIV, and TXV?).

1286 O3–R? 0.75 g
Slightly worn.
O: same as 1089; split die.
R: same as 886;]*YNʾL*[ ]*G*[.
Elayi-Elayi, *Trésors*, p. 96, no. 77, and pl. 7:77 (Byblos hoards TXIII, TXIV, and TXV?).

1287 O3–R?
0.75 g

Slightly worn.
O: same as 1089; split die.
R: same as 886;]*YNʾL MLK* [.
Elayi-Elayi, *Trésors*, p. 99, no. 198, and pl. 9:198 (Byblos hoards TXIII, TXIV, and TXV?).

1288 O3–R?
0.75 g 11 mm
6 h

Slightly worn.
O: same as 1089; split die.
R: same as 886; traces of *ʿYNʾL MLK GBL.*
Elayi-Elayi, *Trésors*, p. 103, no. 342, and pl. 13:342 (Byblos hoards TXIII, TXIV, and TXV?).

1289 O3–R?
0.73 g

Slightly worn.
O: same as 1089; split die.
R: same as 886; *ʿYNʾL MLK G*[.
Elayi-Elayi, *Trésors*, p. 96, no. 78, and pl. 7:78 (Byblos hoards TXIII, TXIV, and TXV?).

1290 O3–R?
0.73 g

Slightly worn.
O: same as 1089; split die.
R: same as 886;]*YNʾL* [.
Elayi-Elayi, *Trésors*, p. 101, no. 264, and pl. 12:264 (Byblos hoards TXIII, TXIV, and TXV?).

1291 O3–R?
0.73 g 11 mm
11 h

Slightly worn.
O: same as 1089; split die.
R: same as 886; *ʿYNʾL MLK* [.
Elayi-Elayi, *Trésors*, p. 103, no. 343, and pl. 13:343 (Byblos hoards TXIII, TXIV, and TXV?).

1292 O3–R?
0.73 g 11 mm
6 h

Slightly worn.
O: same as 1089; split die.
R: same as 886; *ʿYNʾ*[ ] *MLK* [.
Elayi-Elayi, *Trésors*, p. 103, no. 364, and pl. 14:364 (Byblos hoards TXIII, TXIV, and TXV?).

1293 O3–R?
0.72 g

Slightly worn.
O: same as 1089; off-center to left; split die.
R: same as 886; inscription off the flan.
Elayi-Elayi, *Trésors*, p. 96, no. 79, and pl. 7:79 (Byblos hoards TXIII, TXIV, and TXV?).

1294 O3–R?
0.71 g

Slightly worn.
O: same as 1089; off-center to left; split die.
R: same as 886; inscription off the flan.
Elayi-Elayi, *Trésors*, p. 96, no. 80, and pl. 7:80 (Byblos hoards TXIII, TXIV, and TXV?).

1295	O3–R? 0.71 g	Slightly worn. O: same as 1089; off-center to left; split die. R: same as 886; *ʿYNʾL MLK* [. Elayi-Elayi, *Trésors*, p. 101, no. 273, and pl. 12:273 (Byblos hoards TXIII, TXIV, and TXV?).
1296	O3–R? 0.71 g 11 mm 7 h	Slightly worn. O: same as 1089; very off-center to left; split die. R: same as 886;]*Nʾ L MLK* [. Elayi-Elayi, *Trésors*, p. 103, no. 344, and pl. 13:344 (Byblos hoards TXIII, TXIV, and TXV?).
1297	O3–R? 0.71 g 11 mm 5 h	Slightly worn. O: same as 1089; off-center to left; split die. R: same as 886;]*LK GB*[. Elayi-Elayi, *RBN* 139 (1993) 21, no. 50 and pl. 3:50 (hoard from Near East TLXXX).
1298	O3–R? 0.71 g	Slightly worn. O: same as 1089; off-center toward the top; split die. R: same as 886; *ʿYNʾ*[. Superior Stamp and Coin, Beverly Hills, 24/5, Winter 1988/89, no. C42.
1299	O3–R? 0.70 g	Slightly worn. O: same as 1089; off-center toward the top; split die. R: same as 886; *ʿYNʾL M*[. Elayi-Elayi, *Trésors*, p. 96, no. 81, and pl. 7:81 (Byblos hoards TXIII, TXIV, and TXV?).
1300	O3–R? 0.70 g	Oval flan. Slightly worn. O: same as 1089; off-center to left; split die. R: same as 886;] *MLK* [. Elayi-Elayi, *Trésors*, p. 96, no. 82, and pl. 7:82 (Byblos hoards TXIII, TXIV, and TXV?).
1301	O3–R? 0.69 g 10 mm 7 h	Slightly worn. O: same as 1089; split die. R: same as 886;]*Y*[ ] *MLK* [. Elayi-Elayi, *Trésors*, p. 103, no. 345, and pl. 13:345 (Byblos hoards TXIII, TXIV, and TXV?).
1302	O3–R? 0.66 g	Slightly worn. O: same as 1089; split die. R: same as 886;]*L MLK G*[. Elayi-Elayi, *Trésors*, p. 96, no. 83, and pl. 7:83 (Byblos hoards TXIII, TXIV, and TXV?).

1303 O3–R?
0.64 g

Slightly worn.
O: same as 1089; off-center toward the top; split die.
R: same as 886; inscription obliterated.
Elayi-Elayi, *Trésors*, p. 96, no. 84, and pl. 7:84 (Byblos hoards TXIII, TXIV, and TXV?).

1304 O3–R?
0.64 g

Slightly worn.
O: same as 1089; split die.
R: same as 886; *ʿYNʾL MLK G*[.
Elayi-Elayi, *Trésors*, p. 99, no. 199, and pl. 9:199 (Byblos hoards TXIII, TXIV, and TXV?).

1305 O3–R?
0.64 g 10 mm
4 h

Slightly worn.
O: same as 1089; split die.
R: same as 886; traces of *ʿYNʾL MLK GBL.*
Elayi-Elayi, *Trésors*, p. 103, no. 346, and pl. 13:346 (Byblos hoards TXIII, TXIV, and TXV?).

1306 O3–R?
0.60 g

Slightly worn.
O: same as 1089; off-center toward the bottom; split die.
R: same as 886; off-center to left; inscription off the flan.
Elayi-Elayi, *Trésors*, p. 103, no. 347, and pl. 13:347 (Byblos hoards TXIII, TXIV, and TXV?).

1307 O3–R?
0.54 g

Slightly worn.
O: same as 1089; off-center toward the bottom; split die.
R: same as 886; traces of *ʿYNʾL MLK GBL.*
Elayi-Elayi, *Trésors*, p. 96, no. 85, and pl. 7:85 (Byblos hoards TXIII, TXIV, and TXV?).

1308 O3–R?

Slightly worn.
O: same as 1089; off-center to right; split die.
R: same as 886; traces of *ʿYNʾL MLK GBL.*
Jacquier, Kehl/Rhein, 5, Autumn 1986, no. 83.

1309 O11–R?
0.81 g 11 mm
7 h

Slightly worn.
O: same as 1089; off-center to left.
R: same as 886; traces of]*K G*[.
Elayi-Elayi, *RBN* 139 (1993) 23, no. 85 and pl. 5:85 (hoard from Near East TLXXX).

1310 O11–R?
0.69 g

Slightly worn.
O: same as 1089.
R: same as 886; *ʿYNʾL* [.
Elayi-Elayi, *Trésors*, p. 99, no. 194, and pl. 9:194 (Byblos hoards TXIII, TXIV, and TXV?).

1311 O11–R?
0.69 g 11 mm
7 h

Slightly worn.
O: same as 1089.
R: same as 886; *ʿYN*[.
Elayi-Elayi, *Trésors*, p. 103, no. 320, and pl. 13:320 (Byblos hoards TXIII, TXIV, and TXV?).

1312 O11–R? 0.69 g 11 mm 5 h
Slightly worn.
O: same as 1089.
R: same as 886; ʿYN[.
Elayi-Elayi, *RBN* 139 (1993) 23, no. 89 and pl. 5:89 (hoard from Near East TLXXX).

1313 O11–R? 0.65 g
Slightly worn. Irregular flan.
O: same as 1089.
R: same as 886; restruck;]ʾ*L ML*[.
Elayi-Elayi, *Trésors*, p. 96, no. 52, and pl. 6:52 (Byblos hoards TXIII, TXIV, and TXV?).

1314 O11–R? 0.61 g 10 mm 5 h
Slightly worn.
O: same as 1089; off-center to right.
R: same as 886;]*N*ʾ*L ML*[.
Elayi-Elayi, *Trésors*, p. 103, no. 365, and pl. 7:365 (Byblos hoards TXIII, TXIV, and TXV?).

1315 O12–R? 0.77 g
Slightly worn.
O: same as 1089; off-center to left.
R: same as 886; ʿ*YN*ʾ*L* [.
Elayi-Elayi, *Trésors*, p. 99, no. 202, and pl. 9:202 (Byblos hoards TXIII, TXIV, and TXV?).

1316 O13–R? 0.84 g 10 mm 8 h
Slightly worn.
O: same as 1089.
R: same as 886;]*N*ʾ*L MLK* [.
Elayi-Elayi, *RBN* 139 (1993) 19, no. 18 and pl. 2:18 (hoard from Near East TLXXX).

1317 O13–R? 0.80 g 11 mm 3 h
Slightly worn.
O: same as 1089.
R: same as 886; ʿ*YN*ʾ*L MLK* [.
Elayi-Elayi, *RBN* 139 (1993) 19, no. 22 and pl. 2:22 (hoard from Near East TLXXX).

1318 O13–R? 0.63 g
Slightly worn.
O: same as 1089.
R: same as 886;]ʾ*L* [ ]*K* [.
Elayi-Elayi, *Trésors*, p. 97, no. 104, and pl. 7:104 (Byblos hoards TXIII, TXIV, and TXV?).

1319 O14–R? 0.80 g
Slightly worn.
O: same as 1089.
R: same as 886; ʿ*YN*ʾ*L M*[.
Classical Numismatic Group, Lancaster-London, 29, 30/3/1994, no. 129.

1320 O14–R? 0.78 g
Slightly worn.
O: same as 1089; off-center toward the top.
R: same as 886; traces of ʿ*YN*ʾ*L MLK GBL*.
Spink, London, 36, 30–31/5/1986, no. 45.

1321 O14–R? 0.71 g 11 mm 3 h
Slightly worn.
O: same as 1089.
R: same as 886; *ʿYNʾL M*[.
Elayi-Elayi, *RBN* 139 (1993) 20, no. 48 and pl. 3:48 (hoard from Near East TLXXX).

1322 O14–R? 0.70 g
Slightly worn. Small crack on the edge.
O: same as 1089; off-center to left.
R: same as 886; traces of *ʿYNʾL MLK GBL*.
Elayi-Elayi, *Trésors*, p. 107, no. 496, and pl. 17:496 (Byblos hoards TXIII, TXIV, and TXV?).

1323 O15–R? 0.88 g
Slightly worn.
O: same as 1089; defect before the seahorse; off-center to right.
R: same as 886; *ʿYNʾL MLK* [.
Elayi-Elayi, *Trésors*, p. 97, no. 96, and pl. 7:96 (Byblos hoards TXIII, TXIV, and TXV?).

1324 O15–R? 0.79 g
Worn.
O: same as 1089; defect before the seahorse; off-center to right.
R: same as 886; traces of *ʿYNʾL MLK GBL*.
Elsen, Brussels, 94, 27/11/2007, no. 122.

1325 O15–R? 0.75 g 11 mm 4 h
Slightly worn. Irregular flan.
O: same as 1089.
R: same as 886;]*L MLK* [.
Elayi-Elayi, *RBN* 139 (1993) 20, no. 36 and pl. 3:36 (hoard from Near East TLXXX).

1326 O15–R? 0.74 g 11 mm 4 h
Slightly worn.
O: same as 1089; very off-center to right.
R: same as 886;]*YNʾL MLK* [.
Elayi-Elayi, *RBN* 139 (1993) 20, no. 37 and pl. 3:37 (hoard from Near East TLXXX).

1327 O15–R? 0.68 g
Slightly worn.
O: same as 1089.
R: same as 886; *ʿYNʾL ML*[.
Elayi-Elayi, *Trésors*, p. 97, no. 97, and pl. 7:97 (Byblos hoards TXIII, TXIV, and TXV?).

1328 O15–R? 0.67 g 11 mm 6 h
Slightly worn.
O: same as 1089; off-center to right.
R: same as 886;]*YNʾL MLK G*[.
Elayi-Elayi, *Trésors*, p. 103, no. 352, and pl. 14:352 (Byblos hoards TXIII, TXIV, and TXV?).

1329 O16–R?
0.85 g

Slightly worn.
O: same as 1089; off-center toward the bottom.
R: same as 886; traces of *ʿYNʾL MLK GBL.*
Hirsch, Munich, 171, 25–28/9/1991, no. 445.

1330 O16–R?
0.80 g 10 mm
11 h

Slightly worn.
O: same as 1089; off-center toward the bottom.
R: same as 886; *ʿYNʾL* [.
Elayi-Elayi, *RBN* 139 (1993) 19, no. 23 and pl. 2:23 (hoard from Near East TLXXX).

1331 O16–R?
0.69 g 11 mm
3 h

Slightly worn.
O: same as 1089; off-center toward the bottom.
R: same as 886; *ʿY*[ ]*ʾL MLK G*[.
Elayi-Elayi, *RBN* 139 (1993) 21, no. 53 and pl. 4:53 (hoard from Near East TLXXX).

1332 O21–R?
0.79 g

Slightly worn.
O: same as 1089; off-center toward the bottom.
R: same as 886; *ʿYNʾL MLK G*[.
Kroha, Kölner Münzkabinett, Cologne, 37, 22–23/11/1984, no. 35.

1333 O21–R?
0.73 g 11 mm
6 h

Slightly worn.
O: same as 1089.
R: same as 886; *ʿYNʾ*[.
Elayi-Elayi, *RBN* 139 (1993) 20, no. 41 and pl. 3:41 (hoard from Near East TLXXX).

1334 O21*–R?
0.71 g

Slightly worn.
O: same as 1089; off-center toward the bottom.
R: same as 886; *ʿYNʾL* [.
Müller, Münz Zentrum-Rheinland, Solingen, 72, 23/10/1992, no. 126.

1335 O21–R?
0.62 g 11 mm
6 h

Slightly worn.
O: same as 1089; off-center to left.
R: same as 886; *ʿYNʾL* [.
Elayi-Elayi, *Trésors*, p. 103, no. 354, and pl. 14:354 (Byblos hoards TXIII, TXIV, and TXV?).

1336 O22–R?
0.92 g 11 mm
12 h

Slightly worn.
O: same as 1089; off-center to left; defect above the tail of the seahorse.
R: same as 886; *ʿYNʾL* [.
Elayi-Elayi, *RBN* 139 (1993) 19, no. 16 and pl. 2:16 (hoard from Near East TLXXX).

1337	O22–R? 0.79 g	Slightly worn. O: same as 1089; overstruck; defect above the tail of the seahorse. R: same as 886; *ʿY*[. Elayi-Elayi, *Trésors*, p. 95, no. 19, and pl. 6:19 (Byblos hoards TXIII, TXIV, and TXV?).
1338	O22–R? 0.73 g 11 mm 5 h	Slightly worn. O: same as 1089; off-center to left; defect above the tail of the seahorse. R: same as 886; *ʿYNʾL* [ ] *G*[. Elayi-Elayi, *RBN* 139 (1993) 20, no. 42 and pl. 3:42 (hoard from Near East TLXXX).
1339	O22–R? 0.70 g 10 mm 5 h	Slightly worn. O: same as 1089; off-center to left; defect above the tail of the seahorse. R: same as 886;]*YNʾL* [. Elayi-Elayi, *RBN* 139 (1993) 21, no. 51 and pl. 3:51 (hoard from Near East TLXXX).
1340	O23–R? 0.65 g 11 mm 1 h	Slightly worn. O: same as 1089; off-center toward the bottom. R: same as 886;]*YNʾ*[. Elayi-Elayi, *Trésors*, p. 103, no. 359, and pl. 14:359 (Byblos hoards TXIII, TXIV, and TXV?).
1341	O26–R? 0.70 g 11 mm 6 h	Slightly worn. O: same as 1089. R: same as 886;]*ʾL* [. Elayi-Elayi, *Trésors*, p. 103, no. 366, and pl. 14:366 (Byblos hoards TXIII, TXIV, and TXV?).
1342	O27*–R? 0.81 g	Slightly worn. O: same as 1089; off-center toward the top. R: same as 886;]*YNʾL MLK G*[. Elayi-Elayi, *Trésors*, p. 97, no. 105, and pl. 7:105 (Byblos hoards TXIII, TXIV, and TXV?).
1343	O27–R? 0.66 g 11 mm 5 h	Slightly worn. Small cracks on the edge. O: same as 1089. R: same as 886; *ʿYNʾL M*[. Elayi-Elayi, *Trésors*, p. 103, no. 361, and pl. 14:361 (Byblos hoards TXIII, TXIV, and TXV?).
1344	O28*–R? 0.71 g 11 mm 6 h	Slightly worn. O: same as 1089. R: same as 886;]*Nʾ L* [. Elayi-Elayi, *RBN* 139 (1993) 20, no. 49 and pl. 3:49 (hoard from Near East TLXXX).

1345 O29*–R?
0.57 g 11 mm
9 h
Slightly worn.
O: same as 1089.
R: same as 886;]*YN'L M*[.
Spaer coll., Jerusalem (bought in Beirut).

1346 O?–R4
0.76 g
Slightly worn.
O: same as 1089.
R: same as 886; *ʿYN'L M*[.
Elayi-Elayi, *Trésors*, p. 99, no. 208, and pl. 9:208 (Byblos hoards TXIII, TXIV, and TXV?).

1347 O?–R6
0.63 g
Slightly worn.
O: same as 1089; off-center to right.
R: same as 886; *ʿYN'L M*[.
Elayi-Elayi, *Trésors*, p. 101, no. 276, and pl. 12:276 (Byblos hoards TXIII, TXIV, and TXV?).

1348 O?–R6
0.63 g
Slightly worn. Edge broken.
O: same as 1089.
R: same as 886; *ʿYN'L MLK GB*[.
Elayi-Elayi, *Trésors*, p. 101, no. 277, and pl. 12:277 (Byblos hoards TXIII, TXIV, and TXV?).

1349 O?–R6
0.63 g
Slightly worn.
O: same as 1089.
R: same as 886; *ʿYN'L M*[.
Elayi-Elayi, *Trésors*, p. 104, no. 375, and pl. 14:375 (Byblos hoards TXIII, TXIV, and TXV?).

1350 O?–R7
0.78 g
Slightly worn.
O: same as 1089.
R: same as 886;]*N'L MLK GB*[.
Elayi-Elayi, *Trésors*, p. 97, no. 124, and pl. 8:124 (Byblos hoards TXIII, TXIV, and TXV?).

1351 O?–R8
0.71 g 11 mm
12 h
Slightly worn.
O: motif almost entirely off the flan; same as 1089?
R: same as 886; *ʿYN'L MLK* [.
Elayi-Elayi, *RBN* 139 (1993) 20, no. 46 and pl. 3:46 (hoard from Near East TLXXX).

1352 O?–R9
0.81 g
Slightly worn.
O: same as 1089.
R: same as 886; split die; traces of *ʿYN'L MLK GBL*.
Vecchi, London, July–August 1986, no. 72.

1353 O?–R9
0.80 g
Slightly worn. Oval flan. Small crack on the edge.
O: same as 1089.
R: same as 886; split die; traces of *ʿYN'L MLK GBL*.
Elayi-Elayi, *Trésors*, p. 97, no. 112, and pl. 8:112 (Byblos hoards TXIII, TXIV, and TXV?).

1354 O?–R9
0.78 g

Slightly worn.
O: same as 1089; off-center toward the top.
R: same as 886; split die; traces of *ʿYNʾL MLK GBL*.
Elayi-Elayi, *Trésors*, p. 97, no. 113, and pl. 8:113 (Byblos hoards TXIII, TXIV, and TXV?).

1355 O?–R9
0.78 g

Slightly worn.
O: same as 1089.
R: same as 886; split die; *ʿYNʾL MLK GBL* partly off the flan.
Elayi-Elayi, *Trésors*, p. 97, no. 114, and pl. 8:114 (Byblos hoards TXIII, TXIV, and TXV?).

1356 O?–R9
0.78 g 10 mm
8 h

Slightly worn.
O: same as 1089.
R: same as 886; split die;]*K G*[.
Elayi-Elayi, *RBN* 139 (1993) 19, no. 27 and pl. 2:27 (hoard from Near East TLXXX).

1357 O?–R9
0.77 11 mm
6 h

Slightly worn.
O: same as 1089; off-center toward the bottom.
R: same as 886; split die; traces of *ʿYNʾL MLK GBL*.
Elayi-Elayi, *RBN* 139 (1993) 19, no. 29 and pl. 2:29 (hoard from Near East TLXXX).

1358 O?–R9
0.75 g

Slightly worn.
O: same as 1089; off-center toward the top.
R: same as 886; split die;]*Y*[ ] *MLK* [.
Elayi-Elayi, *Trésors*, p. 97, no. 115, and pl. 8:115 (Byblos hoards TXIII, TXIV, and TXV?).

1359 O?–R9
0.73 11 mm
7 h

Slightly worn. Partly broken.
O: same as 1089.
R: same as 886; split die; *ʿYNʾL M*[.
Elayi-Elayi, *RBN* 139 (1993) 20, no. 43 and pl. 3:43 (hoard from Near East TLXXX).

1360 O?–R9
0.72 g 11 mm
7 h

Slightly worn.
O: same as 1089.
R: same as 886; split die;]*YNʾ*[.
Elayi-Elayi, *Trésors*, p. 104, no. 368, and pl. 14:368 (Byblos hoards TXIII, TXIV, and TXV?).

1361 O?–R9
0.72 g 11 mm
7 h

Slightly worn. Small crack on the edge.
O: same as 1089.
R: same as 886; split die; traces of *ʿYNʾL MLK GBL*.
Elayi-Elayi, *Trésors*, p. 104, no. 369, and pl. 14:369 (Byblos hoards TXIII, TXIV, and TXV?).

1362 O?–R9
0.71 g 11 mm
6 h
Slightly worn.
O: same as 1089; off-center to right.
R: same as 886; split die;]ʾ*L MLK* [.
Elayi-Elayi, *Trésors*, p. 104, no. 370, and pl. 14:370 (Byblos hoards TXIII, TXIV, and TXV?).

1363 O?–R9
0.71 g
Oval flan. Slightly worn.
O: same as 1089.
R: same as 886; split die; traces of *ʿYNʾL MLK GBL* partly off the flan.
Elayi-Elayi, *Trésors*, p. 97, no. 116, and pl. 8:116 (Byblos hoards TXIII, TXIV, and TXV?).

1364 O?–R9
0.70 g
Slightly worn. Small crack on the edge.
O: same as 1089.
R: same as 886; split die;]*YNʾL MLK* [.
Elayi-Elayi, *Trésors*, p. 97, no. 117, and pl. 8:117 (Byblos hoards TXIII, TXIV, and TXV?).

1365 O?–R9
0.68 g 10 mm
6 h
Slightly worn.
O: same as 1089; off-center toward the bottom.
R: same as 886; split die;]*YNʾL M*[.
Elayi-Elayi, *RBN* 139 (1993) 21, no. 60 and pl. 4:60 (hoard from Near East TLXXX).

1366 O?–R9
0.67 g
Slightly worn.
O: same as 1089; off-center to left.
R: same as 886; split die;]ʾ*L MLK G*[.
Elayi-Elayi, *Trésors*, p. 97, no. 118, and pl. 8:118 (Byblos hoards TXIII, TXIV, and TXV?).

1367 O?–R9
0.66 g
Slightly worn. Irregular flan.
O: same as 1089; off-center to left.
R: same as 886; split die; restruck; inscription off the flan.
Elayi-Elayi, *Trésors*, p. 97, no. 119, and pl. 8:119 (Byblos hoards TXIII, TXIV, and TXV?).

1368 O?–R9
0.64 g 11 mm
6 h
Slightly worn.
O: same as 1089; off-center to right.
R: same as 886; split die; inscription obliterated.
Elayi-Elayi, *Trésors*, p. 104, no. 371, and pl. 14:371 (Byblos hoards TXIII, TXIV, and TXV?).

1369 O?–R9
0.63 g 11 mm
7 h
Slightly worn and corroded.
O: same as 1089.
R: same as 886; split die;]*L ML*[.
Elayi-Elayi, *Trésors*, p. 104, no. 372, and pl. 14:372 (Byblos hoards TXIII, TXIV, and TXV?).

1370 O?–R10 Slightly worn.
0.76 g O: same as 1089.
R: same as 886; *ʿYNʾL ML*[.
Elayi-Elayi, *Trésors*, p. 97, no. 129, and pl. 8:129 (Byblos hoards TXIII, TXIV, and TXV?).

1371 O?–R10 Slightly worn.
0.67 g O: same as 1089.
R: same as 886; *ʿYNʾL M*[.
Elayi-Elayi, *Trésors*, p. 97, no. 130, and pl. 8:130 (Byblos hoards TXIII, TXIV, and TXV?).

1372 O?–R11 Slightly worn. Small chisel-cut.
0.76 g 10 mm O: same as 1089.
1 h R: same as 886; *ʿYNʾL M*[.
Elayi-Elayi, *RBN* 139 (1993) 21, no. 54 and pl. 4:54 (hoard from Near East TLXXX).

1373 O?–R12 Slightly worn.
0.82 g O: same as 1089.
R: same as 886;]*ʾL MLK GB*[.
Elayi-Elayi, *Trésors*, p. 106, no. 471, and pl. 17:471 (Byblos hoards TXIII, TXIV, and TXV?).

1374 O?–R12 Slightly worn.
0.81 g 11 mm O: same as 1089.
12 h R: same as 886; *ʿYNʾL ML*[.
Elayi-Elayi, *RBN* 139 (1993) 19, no. 21 and pl. 2:21 (hoard from Near East TLXXX).

1375 O?–R12 Slightly worn.
0.78 g O: same as 1089.
R: same as 886; *ʿYNʾL MLK GB*[.
Elayi-Elayi, *Trésors*, p. 97, no. 120, and pl. 8:120 (Byblos hoards TXIII, TXIV, and TXV?).

1376 O?–R12 Slightly worn.
0.72 g 11 mm O: same as 1089.
12 h R: same as 886; *ʿYNʾL MLK*[.
Elayi-Elayi, *Trésors*, p. 104, no. 373, and pl. 14:373 (Byblos hoards TXIII, TXIV, and TXV?).

1377 O?–R12 Slightly worn.
0.64 g 12 mm O: same as 1089; very off-center to left.
3 h R: same as 886; *ʿYNʾL MLK* [.
Bartlett Well coll., Lexington, no. 6.

1378 O?–R12 Slightly worn. Small cracks on the edge.
O: same as 1089; off-center toward the bottom.
R: same as 886; *ʿYNʾL ML*[.
Ritter, Dusseldorf, 63, August 2003, no. 671.

1379 O?–R14
0.73 g
Slightly worn.
O: same as 1089.
R: same as 886; *ʿYNʾL MLK G*[.
Elayi-Elayi, *Trésors*, p. 97, no. 127, and pl. 8:127 (Byblos hoards TXIII, TXIV, and TXV?).

1380 O?–R16
0.76 g 11 mm
6 h
Slightly worn.
O: same as 1089; restruck.
R: same as 886; *ʿYNʾL MLK GBL.*
Private coll.

1381 O?–R16
0.67 g
Slightly worn.
O: same as 1089.
R: same as 886;]*YNʾL* [ ] *GB*[.
Elayi-Elayi, *Trésors*, p. 97, no. 110, and pl. 7:110 (Byblos hoards TXIII, TXIV, and TXV?).

1382 O?–R16
0.65 g
Slightly worn.
O: same as 1089.
R: same as 886;]*YNʾL MLK GBL.*
Elayi-Elayi, *Trésors*, p. 97, no. 111, and pl. 7:111 (Byblos hoards TXIII, TXIV, and TXV?).

1383 O?–R18
0.63 g
Slightly worn.
O: same as 1089.
R: same as 886;]*NʾL ML*[.
Elayi-Elayi, *Trésors*, p. 97, no. 125, and pl. 8:125 (Byblos hoards TXIII, TXIV, and TXV?).

1384 O?–R18
0.55 g
Slightly worn.
O: same as 1089.
R: same as 886; *ʿYNʾL M*[.
Elayi-Elayi, *Trésors*, p. 97, no. 126, and pl. 8:126 (Byblos hoards TXIII, TXIV, and TXV?).

1385 O?–R18
0.55 g
Slightly worn.
O: same as 1089; motif almost off the flan.
R: same as 886; *ʿYNʾL* [.
Elayi-Elayi, *Trésors*, p. 101, no. 275, and pl. 12:275 (Byblos hoards TXIII, TXIV, and TXV?).

1386 O?–R19
0.67 g
Slightly worn.
O: same as 1089; off-center to left.
R: same as 886; *ʿYNʾL MLK GB*[.
Elayi-Elayi, *Trésors*, p. 97, no. 131, and pl. 8:131 (Byblos hoards TXIII, TXIV, and TXV?).

1387 O?–R20
0.73 g
Slightly worn.
O: same as 1089; off-center to right.
R: same as 886;]*NʾL ML*[.
Elayi-Elayi, *Trésors*, p. 97, no. 121, and pl. 8:121 (Byblos hoards TXIII, TXIV, and TXV?).

1388 O?–R23 — 0.72 g 10 mm — 9 h
Slightly worn.
O: same as 1089; off-center toward the top.
R: same as 886;]*N'L MLK G*[.
Berlin, SM, no. 11 (ex Löbbecke coll.).

1389 O?–R25 — 0.72 g
Slightly worn.
O: same as 1089; scratches.
R: same as 886; *'YN'L MLK* [.
Elayi-Elayi, *Trésors*, p. 97, no. 128, and pl. 8:128 (Byblos hoards TXIII, TXIV, and TXV?).

1390 O?–R29 — 0.74 g 10 mm — 3 h
Slightly worn.
O: same as 1089.
R: same as 886; *'YN*[.
Elayi-Elayi, *RBN* 139 (1993) 19, no. 39 and pl. 3:39 (hoard from Near East TLXXX).

1391 O?–R35 — 0.87 g
Slightly worn. Corroded.
O: same as 1089.
R: same as 886; *'YN'L MLK* [.
Elayi-Elayi, *Trésors*, p. 99, no. 204 (Byblos hoards TXIII, TXIV, and TXV?).

1392 O?–R35 — 0.87 g
Slightly worn.
O: same as 1089.
R: same as 886;]*YN'L MLK* [.
Elayi-Elayi, *Trésors*, p. 99, no. 205, and pl. 9:205 (Byblos hoards TXIII, TXIV, and TXV?).

1393 O?–R35 — 0.83 g
Slightly worn.
O: same as 1089; off-center toward the bottom.
R: same as 886; *'YN'L MLK* [.
Elayi-Elayi, *Trésors*, p. 99, no. 206, and pl. 9:206 (Byblos hoards TXIII, TXIV, and TXV?).

1394 O?–R35 — 0.78 g 11 mm — 2 h
Slightly worn.
O: same as 1089; off-center toward the bottom.
R: same as 886;]*YN'L MLK* [.
Elayi-Elayi, *RBN* 139 (1993) 19, no. 24 and pl. 2:24 (hoard from Near East TLXXX).

1395 O?–R35 — 0.69 g
Slightly worn. Small crack on the edge.
O: same as 1089.
R: same as 886;]*YN'L MLK* [.
Elayi-Elayi, *Trésors*, p. 101, no. 274, and pl. 12:274 (Byblos hoards TXIII, TXIV, and TXV?).

1396 O?–R35 — 0.66 g
Slightly worn.
O: same as 1089; off-center to left.
R: same as 886; off-center toward the top; *'YN'L MLK* [.
London, BM, no. 1877-4-6 6.

1397 O?–R35
0.66 g
Slightly worn. Corroded.
O: same as 1089.
R: same as 886; *ʿYNʾL MLK* [.
Elayi-Elayi, *Trésors*, p. 99, no. 207, and pl. 9:207 (Byblos hoards TXIII, TXIV, and TXV?).

1398 O?–R35
0.65 g
Slightly worn. Small crack on the edge.
O: same as 1089; off-center to left.
R: same as 886;] *YNʾL MLK* [.
Elayi-Elayi, *Trésors*, p. 97, no. 123, and pl. 8:123 (Byblos hoards TXIII, TXIV, and TXV?).

1399 O?–R37
0.75 g 11 mm
7 h
Slightly worn.
O: same as 1089.
R: same as 886; *ʿYNʾL MLK G*[.
Elayi-Elayi, *Trésors*, p. 104, no. 376, and pl. 14:376 (Byblos hoards TXIII, TXIV, and TXV?).

1400 O?–R38
0.74 g
Slightly worn. Edge slightly broken.
O: same as 1089.
R: same as 886; traces of *ʿYNʾL MLK GBL*.
Lanz, Munich, 42, 23/11/1987, no. 323.

1401 O?–R39
0.67 g 11 mm
3 h
Slightly worn.
O: same as 1089.
R: same as 886; *ʿYNʾL MLK* [.
Paris, BNF, no. 3149; *Catalogue De Luynes*, no. 3149; Babelon, *Perses*, no. 1364 (ex De Luynes coll.).

1402 O?–R40*
0.81 g
Slightly worn.
O: same as 1089.
R: same as 886;] *YNʾL MLK* [.
Elsen, Brussels, 76, 13/9/2003, no. 187.

1403 O?–R40
0.58 g
Slightly worn.
O: same as 1089.
R: same as 886; off-center to left; *ʿYNʾL ML*[.
London, BM, no. 1906–11–3 64.

1404 O?–R45*
0.90 g
Oval flan. Slightly worn.
O: same as 1089; off-center toward the bottom.
R: same as 886; *ʿYNʾL MLK* [.
Berk, Chicago, 66, 11/6/1991, no. 161.

1405 O?–R48
0.77 g
Slightly worn.
O: same as 1089.
R: same as 886; *ʿYNʾL MLK* [.
Elayi-Elayi, *Trésors*, p. 99, no. 209, and pl. 9:209 (Byblos hoards TXIII, TXIV, and TXV?).

1406 O?–R48 0.68 g 10 mm 6 h
Slightly worn.
O: same as 1089.
R: same as 886; *ʿYNʾL MLK GB*[.
Elayi-Elayi, *Trésors*, p. 104, no. 374, and pl. 14:374 (Byblos hoards TXIII, TXIV, and TXV?).

1407 O?–R49 0.77 g
Slightly worn.
O: same as 1089; off-center toward the bottom.
R: same as 886; *ʿYNʾL MLK* [.
Elayi-Elayi, *Trésors*, p. 99, no. 210, and pl. 9:210 (Byblos hoards TXIII, TXIV, and TXV?).

1408 O?–R? 0.90 g
Rather worn. Small crack on the edge.
O: same as 1089.
R: same as 886;]*ʾL MLK GB*[.
Elayi-Elayi, *Trésors*, p. 97, no. 132, and pl. 8:132 (Byblos hoards TXIII, TXIV, and TXV?).

1409 O?–R? 0.89 g 10 mm 6 h
Rather worn.
O: same as 1089.
R: same as 886; *ʿYNʾL MLK GB*[.
Elayi-Elayi, *Trésors*, p. 97, no. 133, and pl. 8:133 (Byblos hoards TXIII, TXIV, and TXV?).

1410 O?–R? 0.89 g
Rather worn.
O: same as 1089.
R: same as 886; *ʿYNʾL M*[.
Gradl, Nürnberg, 9, 9/12/1989, no. 16 = 5, 12/12/1987, no. 15.

1411 O?–R? 0.86 g
Worn.
O: same as 1089.
R: same as 886; *ʿY*[.
Hoffmann, Münz Zentrum, Cologne, 59, 29–31/10/1986, no. 1209.

1412 O?–R? 0.83 g 11 mm 11 h
Rather worn.
O: same as 1089; off-center toward the top.
R: same as 886; *ʿYNʾL* [.
Elayi-Elayi, *Trésors*, p. 97, no. 134, and pl. 8:134 (Byblos hoards TXIII, TXIV, and TXV?).

1413 O?–R? 0.82 g 11 mm 11 h
Rather worn. Oval flan.
O: same as 1089.
R: same as 886;]*YNʾL MLK G*[.
Elayi-Elayi, *Trésors*, p. 104, no. 377, and pl. 14:377 (Byblos hoards TXIII, TXIV, and TXV?).

1414 O?–R? 0.81 g
Rather worn.
O: same as 1089.
R: same as 886; *ʿYNʾL ML*[.
Tkalec-Rauch, Zurich, 14–15/4/1986, no. 161.

1415 O?–R? 0.78 g
Rather worn.
O: same as 1089; off-center toward the top.
R: same as 886; *ʿYNʾL MLK* [.
Elayi-Elayi, *Trésors*, p. 97, no. 135, and pl. 8:135 (Byblos hoards TXIII, TXIV, and TXV?).

1416 O?–R? 0.78 g
Rather worn. Oval flan.
O: same as 1089.
R: same as 886; *ʿYNʾ*[.
Elayi-Elayi, *Trésors*, p. 97, no. 136, and pl. 8:136 (Byblos hoards TXIII, TXIV, and TXV?).

1417 O?–R? 0.78 g
Rather worn.
O: same as 1089.
R: same as 886; *ʿYNʾL ML*[.
Elayi-Elayi, *Trésors*, p. 101, no. 278, and pl. 12:278 (Byblos hoards TXIII, TXIV, and TXV?).

1418 O?–R? 0.76 g
Rather worn.
O: same as 1089; off-center toward the top.
R: same as 886;]*YNʾL M*[.
Elayi-Elayi, *Trésors*, p. 97, no. 137, and pl. 8:137 (Byblos hoards TXIII, TXIV, and TXV?).

1419 O?–R? 0.76 g 11 mm 3 h
Rather worn.
O: same as 1089; off-center toward the bottom.
R: same as 886; *ʿYNʾL M*[.
Elayi-Elayi, *RBN* 139 (1993) 19, no. 30 and pl. 2:30 (hoard from Near East TLXXX).

1420 O?–R? 0.76 g 11 mm 9 h
Rather worn. Small crack on the edge.
O: same as 1089.
R: same as 886; *ʿYNʾL M*[.
Elayi-Elayi, *RBN* 139 (1993) 19, no. 31 and pl. 2:31 (hoard from Near East TLXXX).

1421 O?–R? 0.75 g 10 mm 4 h
Rather worn.
O: same as 1089; off-center to left.
R: same as 886;]*YNʾL M*[.
Elayi-Elayi, *RBN* 139 (1993) 20, no. 33 and pl. 3:33 (hoard from Near East TLXXX).

1422 O?–R? 0.74 g
Rather worn.
O: same as 1089.
R: same as 886;]*ʾL MLK G*[.
Elayi-Elayi, *Trésors*, p. 97, no. 138, and pl. 8:138 (Byblos hoards TXIII, TXIV, and TXV?).

1423 O?–R? 0.74 g
Rather worn.
O: same as 1089; off-center to right.
R: same as 886;]*YN*ʾ *L ML*[.
Elayi-Elayi, *Trésors*, p. 101, no. 279, and pl. 12:279 (Byblos hoards TXIII, TXIV, and TXV?).

1424 O?–R? 0.74 g
Rather worn.
O: same as 1089.
R: same as 886; ʿ*YN*ʾ *L* [.
Elayi-Elayi, *Trésors*, p. 101, no. 279, and pl. 12:279 (Byblos hoards TXIII, TXIV, and TXV?).

1425 O?–R? 0.74 g 11 mm 1 h
Rather worn.
O: same as 1089; off-center to right.
R: same as 886; ʿ*YN*[.
Elayi-Elayi, *Trésors*, p. 104, no. 378, and pl. 14:378 (Byblos hoards TXIII, TXIV, and TXV?).

1426 O?–R? 0.73 g 11 mm 11 h
Rather worn.
O: same as 1089.
R: same as 886; ʿ*YN*ʾ*L M*[.
Elayi-Elayi, *RBN* 139 (1993) 20, no. 40 and pl. 3:40 (hoard from Near East TLXXX).

1427 O?–R? 0.73 g
Oval flan. Rather worn.
O: same as 1089; off-center to right.
R: same as 886;]*N*ʾ*L MLK* [.
Elayi-Elayi, *Trésors*, p. 97, no. 139, and pl. 8:139 (Byblos hoards TXIII, TXIV, and TXV?).

1428 O?–R? 0.73 g
Rather worn.
O: same as 1089.
R: same as 886;]ʾ*L M*[.
Elayi-Elayi, *Trésors*, p. 97, no. 140, and pl. 8:140 (Byblos hoards TXIII, TXIV, and TXV?).

1429 O?–R? 0.73 g 10 mm 7 h
Rather worn.
O: same as 1089; off-center toward the bottom.
R: same as 886; ʿ*YN*ʾ*L* [.
Elayi-Elayi, *Trésors*, p. 104, no. 379, and pl. 14:379 (Byblos hoards TXIII, TXIV, and TXV?).

1430 O?–R? 0.73 g 10 mm 6 h
Rather worn.
O: same as 1089.
R: same as 886;]ʾ*L MLK* [.
Elayi-Elayi, *Trésors*, p. 104, no. 380, and pl. 14:380 (Byblos hoards TXIII, TXIV, and TXV?).

1431 O?–R? 0.72 g
Rather worn.
O: same as 1089.
R: same as 886;]ʾ*L ML*[.
Elayi-Elayi, *Trésors*, p. 97, no. 141, and pl. 8:141 (Byblos hoards TXIII, TXIV, and TXV?).

1432 O?–R? 0.72 g
Rather worn.
O: same as 1089.
R: same as 886;]*Y*[ ] *MLK* [.
Elayi-Elayi, *Trésors*, p. 97, no. 142, and pl. 8:142 (Byblos hoards TXIII, TXIV, and TXV?).

1433 O?–R? 0.71 g
Rather worn.
O: same as 1089.
R: same as 886;]ʾ*L MLK* [.
Elayi-Elayi, *Trésors*, p. 97, no. 143, and pl. 8:143 (Byblos hoards TXIII, TXIV, and TXV?).

1434 O?–R? 0.71 g 10 mm 4 h
Rather worn.
O: same as 1089.
R: same as 886;]*YN*ʾ*L ML*[.
Elayi-Elayi, *Trésors*, p. 104, no. 381, and pl. 14:381 (Byblos hoards TXIII, TXIV, and TXV?).

1435 O?–R? 0.70 g 11 mm 5 h
Rather worn.
O: same as 1089; off-center to left.
R: same as 886;]ʾ*L M*[.
Paris, BNF, no. 3151; *Catalogue De Luynes*, no. 3151; Babelon, *Perses*, no. 1366 (ex De Luynes coll.).

1436 O?–R? 0.70 g
Rather worn.
O: same as 1089.
R: same as 886.
Or Gestion Numismatique, Paris, Autumn 1992, no. 30 (not illustrated).

1437 O?–R? 0.69 g 11 mm 7 h
Rather worn.
O: same as 1089.
R: same as 886; ʿ*YN*ʾ*L MLK* [.
Elayi-Elayi, *Trésors*, p. 97, no. 144, and pl. 8:144 (Byblos hoards TXIII, TXIV, and TXV?).

1438 O?–R? 0.69 g
Rather worn. Small crack on the edge.
O: same as 1089.
R: same as 886; ʿ*YN*ʾ*L MLK* [.
Elayi-Elayi, *Trésors*, p. 97, no. 145, and pl. 8:145 (Byblos hoards TXIII, TXIV, and TXV?).

1439 O?–R? 0.69 g 11 mm 1 h
Rather worn. Oval flan.
O: same as 1089.
R: same as 886; *ʿYNʾL* [.
Elayi-Elayi, *Trésors*, p. 104, no. 382, and pl. 14:382 (Byblos hoards TXIII, TXIV, and TXV?).

1440 O?–R? 0.69 g 11 mm 12 h
Rather worn.
O: same as 1089.
R: same as 886; *ʿYNʾL M*[.
Elayi-Elayi, *RBN* 139 (1993) 21, no. 55 and pl. 4:55 (hoard from Near East TLXXX).

1441 O?–R? 0.69 g
Rather worn.
O: same as 1089.
R: same as 886; *ʿYNʾL M*[.
Berk, Chicago, 61, 20/3/1990, no. 166.

1442 O?–R? 0.68 g 11 mm 5 h
Rather worn.
O: same as 1089.
R: same as 886; *ʿYNʾL M*[.
Elayi-Elayi, *RBN* 139 (1993) 21, no. 57 and pl. 4:57 (hoard from Near East TLXXX).

1443 O?–R? 0.68 g 11 mm 6 h
Rather worn.
O: same as 1089; off-center to left.
R: same as 886; *ʿYNʾL MLK* [.
Elayi-Elayi, *RBN* 139 (1993) 21, no. 58 and pl. 4:58 (hoard from Near East TLXXX).

1444 O?–R? 0.68 g
Rather worn.
O: same as 1089; overstruck.
R: same as 886; *ʿY*[ ]*ʾL M*[.
Elayi-Elayi, *Trésors*, p. 97, no. 146, and pl. 8:146 (Byblos hoards TXIII, TXIV, and TXV?).

1445 O?–R? 0.68 g
Rather worn.
O: same as 1089; off-center to left.
R: same as 886;]*YNʾL ML*[.
Elayi-Elayi, *Trésors*, p. 100, no. 281, and pl. 12:281 (Byblos hoards TXIII, TXIV, and TXV?).

1446 O?–R? 0.68 g 10 mm 5 h
Rather worn.
O: same as 1089; off-center toward the top.
R: same as 886; *ʿYNʾL* [.
Elayi-Elayi, *Trésors*, p. 104, no. 383, and pl. 14:383 (Byblos hoards TXIII, TXIV, and TXV?).

1447 O?–R? 0.68 g 11 mm 10 h
Rather worn.
O: same as 1089; off-center to right.
R: same as 886; *ʿY*[.
Elayi-Elayi, *Trésors*, p. 104, no. 384, and pl. 14:384 (Byblos hoards TXIII, TXIV, and TXV?).

1448 O?–R? 0.67 g

Rather worn.
O: same as 1089; off-center toward the top.
R: same as 886; *ʿYNʾL M*[.
Monnaies et Médailles/Münzen und Medaillen, Basel, 461, November–December 1983, no. 31.

1449 O?–R? 0.67 g 11 mm 6 h

Rather worn.
O: same as 1089.
R: same as 886; ʿ[ ]*Nʾl ML*[.
Elayi-Elayi, *RBN* 139 (1993) 21, no. 63 and pl. 4:63 (hoard from Near East TLXXX).

1450 O?–R? 0.67 g 11 mm 5 h

Rather worn.
O: same as 1089.
R: same as 886;]*L ML*[.
Elayi-Elayi, *RBN* 139 (1993) 21, no. 64 and pl. 4:64 (hoard from Near East TLXXX).

1451 O?–R? 0.67 g

Rather worn.
O: same as 1089.
R: same as 886; *ʿYN*[ ]*L* [.
Elayi-Elayi, *Trésors*, p. 97, no. 147, and pl. 8:147 (Byblos hoards TXIII, TXIV, and TXV?).

1452 O?–R? 0.66 g

Rather worn.
O: same as 1089.
R: same as 886;]*YNʾL MLK GB*[.
Elayi-Elayi, *Trésors*, p. 97, no. 148, and pl. 8:148 (Byblos hoards TXIII, TXIV, and TXV?).

1453 O?–R? 0.66 g

Rather worn.
O: same as 1089; off-center to right.
R: same as 886; *ʿYN*[.
Elayi-Elayi, *Trésors*, p. 97, no. 149, and pl. 8:149 (Byblos hoards TXIII, TXIV, and TXV?).

1454 O?–R? 0.66 g

Rather worn.
O: same as 1089.
R: same as 886;]*Nʾl MLK* [.
Elayi-Elayi, *Trésors*, p. 97, no. 150, and pl. 8:150 (Byblos hoards TXIII, TXIV, and TXV?).

1455 O?–R? 0.66 g

Irregular flan. Rather worn.
O: same as 1089.
R: same as 886; *ʿYNʾL* [ ] *G*[.
Elayi-Elayi, *Trésors*, p. 101, no. 282, and pl. 12:282 (Byblos hoards TXIII, TXIV, and TXV?).

1456 O?–R? Rather worn.
0.66 g 11 mm O: same as 1089.
3 h R: same as 886; ʿ*YN*ʾ*L M*[.
Elayi-Elayi, *RBN* 139 (1993) 22, no. 68 and pl. 4:68 (hoard from Near East TLXXX).

1457 O?–R? Rather worn.
0.66 g 11 mm O: same as 1089; off-center to left.
12 h R: same as 886;]*N*[ ]*L MLK G*[.
Elayi-Elayi, *RBN* 139 (1993) 22, no. 70 and pl. 4:70 (hoard from Near East TLXXX).

1458 O?–R? Rather worn.
0.65 g O: same as 1089.
R: same as 886;]*YN*ʾ*L MLK* [.
Elayi-Elayi, *Trésors*, p. 97, no. 151, and pl. 8:151 (Byblos hoards TXIII, TXIV, and TXV?).

1459 O?–R? Rather worn. Small cracks on the edge.
0.64 g O: same as 1089.
R: same as 886;]ʾ*L MLK GB*[.
Elayi-Elayi, *Trésors*, p. 97, no. 152, and pl. 8:152 (Byblos hoards TXIII, TXIV, and TXV?).

1460 O?–R? Rather worn.
0.64 g O: same as 1089.
R: same as 886.
Baldwin, London, 34, 13/10/2003, no. 531 (not illustrated).

1461 O?–R? Rather worn.
0.63 g O: same as 1089.
R: same as 886;]*N*ʾ*L MLK* [.
Elayi-Elayi, *Trésors*, p. 97, no. 153, and pl. 8:153 (Byblos hoards TXIII, TXIV, and TXV?).

1462 O?–R? Rather worn. Small crack on the edge.
0.63 g 11 mm O: same as 1089.
3 h R: same as 886;]*Y*[ ]*L ML*[.
Elayi-Elayi, *Trésors*, p. 104, no. 385, and pl. 14:385 (Byblos hoards TXIII, TXIV, and TXV?).

1463 O?–R? Rather worn.
0.62 g 11 mm O: same as 1089; very off-center to right.
6 h R: same as 886;]ʾ*L MLK* [.
Elayi-Elayi, *Trésors*, p. 104, no. 386, and pl. 14:386 (Byblos hoards TXIII, TXIV, and TXV?).

1464 O?–R? Rather worn.
0.62 g 10 mm O: same as 1089.
5 h R: same as 886;]*L M*[.
Elayi-Elayi, *Trésors*, p. 104, no. 387, and pl. 14:387 (Byblos hoards TXIII, TXIV, and TXV?).

1465 O?–R? 0.60 g 11 mm 4 h
Rather worn.
O: same as 1089.
R: same as 886; *ʿYNʾL MLK G*[.
Berlin, SM, no. 18.

1466 O?–R? 0.60 g 11 mm 12 h
Rather worn.
O: same as 1089.
R: same as 886;]*Nʾ L M*[.
Elayi-Elayi, *RBN* 139 (1993) 22, no. 75 and pl. 5:75 (hoard from Near East TLXXX).

1467 O?–R? 0.59 g 11 mm 4 h
Rather worn. Small cracks on the edge.
O: same as 1089.
R: same as 886;]*L ML*[.
Elayi-Elayi, *RBN* 139 (1993) 22, no. 76 and pl. 5:76 (hoard from Near East TLXXX).

1468 O?–R? 0.59 g 11 mm 11 h
Irregular flan. Rather worn.
O: same as 1089.
R: same as 886;]*Nʾ L MLK G*[.
Elayi-Elayi, *Trésors*, p. 104, no. 388, and pl. 14:388 (Byblos hoards TXIII, TXIV, and TXV?).

1469 O?–R? 0.57 g
Rather worn.
O: same as 1089; off-center to right.
R: same as 886; *ʿYNʾL MLK* [.
Elayi-Elayi, *Trésors*, p. 97, no. 154, and pl. 8:154 (Byblos hoards TXIII, TXIV, and TXV?).

1470 O?–R? 0.56 g
Partly broken. Rather worn.
O: same as 1089.
R: same as 886; *ʿYNʾ*[.
Elayi-Elayi, *Trésors*, p. 101, no. 283, and pl. 12:283 (Byblos hoards TXIII, TXIV, and TXV?).

1471 O?–R? 0.54 g
Partly broken. Rather worn.
O: same as 1089.
R: same as 886;]*YNʾL ML*[ ] *GBL*.
Elayi-Elayi, *Trésors*, p. 97, no. 155, and pl. 8:155 (Byblos hoards TXIII, TXIV, and TXV?).

1472 O?–R?
Partly broken. Rather worn.
O: same as 1089.
R: same as 886; *ʿYNʾL MLK* [.
Elayi-Elayi, *Trésors*, p. 101, no. 284, and pl. 12:284 (Byblos hoards TXIII, TXIV, and TXV?).

1473 O?–R?
O: same as 1089.
R: same as 886.
Poinsignon Numismatique, Strasbourg, 34, October 1992, no. 402.

IV.4.3. Quarter-Shekels AR with ʿG

1474 O1*–R1*
3.65 g 15 mm
6 h
O: same as 1089.
R: lion to left, bringing down a bull to left; *ʿG* above; border of dots.
Paris, BNF, no. 1363a; Babelon, *Perses*, no. 1363a.

1475 O2*–R2*
3.19 g
3 h
O: same as 1089.
R: same as 1474; *ʿG*.
SNG Copenhagen, no. 133; Glendining, London, 4, 1955, no. 606.

1476 O3*–R3*
3.32 g
O: same as 1089.
R: same as 1474; *ʿG*.
Peus, Frankfurt/Main, 321, 27–29/4 and 2/5/1988, no. 228.

1477 O4*–R?
2.97 g
Slightly worn.
O: same as 1089.
R: same as 1474;]*G*.
Private coll.

IV.4.4. 16th-Shekel AR with ʿMG?

1478 O?–R?
0.67 g 10 mm
9 h
Rather worn.
O: same as 1089.
R: lion to left, bringing down a bull to left; *ʿMG?* above; border of dots.
Paris, BNF, no. 3152; *Catalogue De Luynes*, no. 3152; Babelon, *Perses*, no. 1367; idem, *Traité*, no. 877 (ex De Luynes coll.).

IV.4.5. 16th-Shekels AR with ʿG

1479 O1–R1*
0.65 g 11 mm
1 h
Slightly worn. Small crack on the edge.
O: same as 1089.
R: lion to left, bringing down a bull to left; *ʿG* above; one two-pronged ankh under the stomach of the lion; border of dots.
Elayi-Elayi, *RBN* 139 (1993) 22, no. 80 and pl. 5:80 (hoard from Near East TLXXX).

1480 O1*–R2*
0.72 g 11 mm
6 h
Slightly worn.
O: same as 1089.
R: same as 1479; off-center toward the bottom; *ʿG*.
Elayi-Elayi, *Trésors*, p. 104, no. 392, and pl. 14:392 (Byblos hoards TXIII, TXIV, and TXV?).

1481 O2–R3
0.72 g
O: same as 1089.
R: same as 1479; overstruck; *ʿG*.
Hirsch, Munich, 150, 5–7/5/1986, no. 245.

1482	O2–R3 0.71 g 11 mm 11 h	O: same as 1089. R: same as 1479; overstruck; one two-pronged ankh under the stomach of the lion (?); ʿG. Spaer coll., Jerusalem (bought in Jerusalem).
1483	O3–R3 0.72 g 11 mm	O: same as 1089. R: same as 1479; one two-pronged ankh under the stomach of the lion (?); ʿG. Elayi-Elayi, *Trésors*, p. 99, no. 211, and pl. 9:211 (Byblos hoards TXIII, TXIV, and TXV?).
1484	O3*–R4 0.74 g 11 mm 1 h	O: same as 1089; off-center to right. R: same as 1479; ʿG. Spaer coll., Jerusalem (bought in Beirut).
1485	O4*–R4* 11 mm	O: same as 1089. Small dies. R: same as 1479; ʿG. Winterthur, Münzkabinett, no. 5209.
1486	O5*–R5* 0.63 g 11 mm 12 h	O: same as 1089; countermark between the galley and the seahorse. R: same as 1479; ʿG. Oxford, AM, no. 49.
1487	O5–R6* 0.72 g 11 mm 12 h	O: same as 1089; off-center toward the top; defect under the seahorse; traces of overstrike. R: same as 1479; traces of overstrike; ʿG. Elayi-Elayi, *RBN* 139 (1993) 22, no. 78 and pl. 5:78 (hoard from Near East TLXXX).
1488	O6*–R7* 0.81 g	O: same as 1089; off-center toward the top. R: same as 1479; defect above the lion; ʿG. London, BM, no. 1989, 119.
1489	O7*–R8* 0.74 g 10 mm 3 h	Irregular flan. O: same as 1089; off-center toward the top. R: same as 1479; ʿG. Paris, BNF, no. 696 (ex Chandon de Briailles coll.).
1490	O8*–R9* 0.77 g	O: same as 1089; defect at the stern. R: same as 1479; ʿG. Elayi-Elayi, *Trésors*, p. 100, no. 252, and pl. 11:252 (Byblos hoards TXIII, TXIV, and TXV?).
1491	O9*–R10* 0.73 g 16 mm	O: same as 1089; off-center toward the bottom; traces of overstrike. R: same as 1479; defect above the inscription; ʿG. Florange-Ciani, Paris, 17–21/2/1925, no. 1047 (ex Allotte de la Füye coll.).
1492	O10*–R11* 0.65 g	O: same as 1089; off-center toward the bottom. R: same as 1479; ʿG. Hirsch, Munich, 208, 17–19/2/2000, no. 1862.

1493	O11*–R12* 0.68 g	O: same as 1089. R: same as 1479; ʿG. Private coll.
1494	O12*–R13* 0.69 g 10 mm	O: same as 1089. R: same as 1479; small die; ʿG. Private coll. LPN; Monnaies et Médailles, Stuttgart, 32, 26/5/2010, no. 428.
1495	O13–R14 0.81 g	O: same as 1089. R: same as 1479; small die; ʿG. Hirsch, Munich, 260, 12–14/2/2009, no. 1821.
1496	O14*–R? 0.69 g	Slightly worn. O: same as 1089. R: same as 1479; traces of ʿG. Myers, New York, November 1977, no. 124.
1497	O15*–R? 0.70 g 10 mm 1 h	Slightly worn. O: same as 1089; restruck. R: same as 1479; off-center toward the top; traces of ʿG. Elayi-Elayi, *Trésors*, p. 106, no. 472, and pl. 17:472 (Byblos hoards TXIII, TXIV, and TXV?).
1498	O?–R2 0.57 g 11 mm 6 h	Slightly worn. O: same as 1089; off-center toward the top. R: same as 1479; one two-pronged ankh under the stomach of the lion (?); ʿG. Elayi-Elayi, *RBN* 139 (1993) 22, no. 81 and pl. 5:81 (hoard from Near East TLXXX).
1499	O?–R3 0.75 g 10 mm 9 h	Slightly worn. O: same as 1089; off-center toward the bottom. R: same as 1479; one two-pronged ankh under the stomach of the lion (?) ; ʿG. Paris, BNF, no. 73 (ex De Vogüé coll.).
1500	O?–R11 0.69 g 11 mm 12 h	Slightly worn. O: same as 1089; off-center toward the top. R: same as 1479; off-center to right; ʿG. Elayi-Elayi, *RBN* 139 (1993) 22, no. 79 and pl. 5:79 (hoard from Near East TLXXX).
1501	O?–R15* 0.75 g 11 mm 1 h	Slightly worn. O: same as 1089; off-center to left. R: same as 1479; ʿG. Elayi-Elayi, *Trésors*, p. 104, no. 390, and pl. 14:390 (Byblos hoards TXIII, TXIV, and TXV?).
1502	O?–R16*	Slightly worn. Oval flan. O: same as 1089. R: same as 1479; ʿG. Shahaf coll., Haifa, no. 11.

1503 O?–R17*
0.69 g 11 mm
1 h
Slightly worn.
O: same as 1089.
R: same as 1479; ʿG.
Elayi-Elayi, *Trésors*, p. 104, no. 393, and pl. 14:393 (Byblos hoards TXIII, TXIV, and TXV?).

1504 O?–R18*
0.77 g 10 mm
5 h
Slightly worn.
O: same as 1089.
R: same as 1479; small die; ʿG.
Paris, BNF, no. 3153; *Catalogue De Luynes*, no. 3153; Babelon, *Perses*, no. 1368; idem, *Traité*, no. 878 (ex De Luynes coll.).

1505 O?–R19*
0.70 g 10 mm
12 h
Slightly worn.
O: same as 1089.
R: same as 1479; ʿG.
New York, ANS, no. 1944.100.70814.

1506 O?–R20*
0.74 g
Slightly worn. Small dies.
O: same as 1089.
R: same as 1479; ʿG.
Baldwin, London, 34, 13/10/2003, no. 527.

1507 O?–R?
0.87 g
9 h
Rather worn. Small dies.
O: same as 1089.
R: same as 1479; ʿG.
Classical Numismatic Group, Lancaster-London, 14/6/2006, no. 960.

1508 O?–R?
0.77 g 10 mm
4 h
Rather worn.
O: same as 1089.
R: same as 1479; ʿG partly off the flan.
Elayi-Elayi, *Trésors*, p. 104, no. 389, and pl. 14:389 (Byblos hoards TXIII, TXIV, and TXV?).

1509 O?–R?
0.77 g
O: same as 1089.
R: same as 1479; ʿG.
Blau, *NZ* 8 (1876) 229 (facsimile).

1510 O?–R?
0.75 g 9 mm
Rather worn.
O: same as 1089.
R: same as 1479; small die; ʿG.
Beirut, AUB Museum, no. C768; Baramki, *Coins AUB*, no. C768 and pl. 18:10.

1511 O?–R?
0.74 g 10 mm
11 h
Rather worn.
O: same as 1089.
R: same as 1479; ʿG.
Elayi-Elayi, *Trésors*, p. 104, no. 391, and pl. 14:391 (Byblos hoards TXIII, TXIV, and TXV?).

1512	O?–R? 0.72 g 9 mm	Rather worn. O: same as 1089. R: same as 1479; ʿ*G*. Beirut, AUB Museum, no. C773.
1513	O?–R? 0.70 g 10 mm	O: same as 1089. R: same as 1479; ʿ*G*. Rouvier, *JIAN* 4 (1901) 42, no. 647, not illustrated (Rouvier coll.).
1514	O?–R? 0.61 g 9 mm	Rather worn. Small crack on the edge. O: same as 1089. R: same as 1479; small die; ʿ*G*. Private coll. LPN; Monnaies et Médailles, Stuttgart, 32, 26/5/2010, no. 428.
1515	O?–R? 0.54 g	O: same as 1089. R: same as 1479; ʿ*G*. Baldwin, London, 34, 13/10/2003, no. 528, not illustrated.
1516	O?–R? 0.53 g 10 mm 1 h	Rather worn. Irregular flan. Edge broken. O: same as 1089; off-center toward the bottom. R: same as 1479; off-center to left; small die; ʿ*G*. Spaer coll., Jerusalem (bought in Jerusalem).
1517	O?–R? 0.50 g 10 mm 8 h	Rather worn. Irregular flan. O: same as 1089; scratches; letter *B* (?) between the galley and the seahorse. R: same as 1479; off-center to left; small die; traces of ʿ*G*. Tel Aviv, KNM, no. 1884.
1518	O?–R? 0.49 g 10 mm 2 h	Rather worn. O: same as 1089. R: same as 1479; traces of ʿ*G*. Spaer coll., Jerusalem (bought in Beirut).
1519	O?–R?	O: same as 1089. R: same as 1479; ʿ*G*. Rouvier, *RN* 6 (1902) 258–59; Elayi-Elayi, *Trésors*, p. 134, no. 1, not illustrated (Qasr Naba hoard TXXIII).
1520	O?–R?	O: same as 1089. R: same as 1479; ʿ*G*. Rouvier, *RN* 6 (1902) 258–59; Elayi-Elayi, *Trésors*, p. 134, no. 2, not illustrated (Qasr Naba hoard TXXIII).
1521	O?–R?	O: same as 1089. R: same as 1479; ʿ*G*. Elayi-Elayi, *Trésors*, p. 137, no. 1, not illustrated (Qasr Naba hoard TXXIV).

IV.4.6. 16th-Shekels AR with GL

1522 O1*–R1* 0.82 g 10 mm 9 h
Small dies.
O: same as 1089; defect above the tail of the seahorse.
R: lion to left, bringing down a bull to left; *GL* above; border of dots; defect above the lion.
Paris, BNF, no. 3154; *Catalogue De Luynes*, no. 3154; Babelon, *Perses*, no. 1369; idem, *Traité*, no. 879 (ex De Luynes coll.).

1523 O1–R1 0.68 g 10 mm 1 h
Broken.
O: same as 1089; defect above the tail of the seahorse.
R: same as 1522; defect above the lion; *GL*.
Paris, BNF, no. 1965/829.17 (ex Seyrig coll.).

1524 O1–R1
Small dies.
O: same as 1089; off-center toward the bottom; defect above the tail of the seahorse.
R: same as 1522; defect above the lion; *GL*.
Sternberg, Zurich, 4, July-August 1992, no. 78.

1525 O1–R2* 0.73 g 10 mm 6 h
Small dies.
O: same as 1089; defect above the tail of the seahorse.
R: same as 1522; *GL*.
Elayi-Elayi, *Trésors*, p. 104, no. 394, and pl. 14:394 (Byblos hoards TXIII, TXIV, and TXV?).

1526 O1–R3* 0.77 g 10 mm 10 h
O: same as 1089; defect above the tail of the seahorse.
R: same as 1522; defect on the head of the bull; *GL* partly obliterated.
London, BM, no. 1985.5–20–1; Elayi-Elayi, *Trésors*, p. 98, no. 156, and pl. 8:156 (Byblos hoards TXIII, TXIV, and TXV?).

1527 O1–R3 0.62 g 10 mm 11 h
Small dies.
O: same as 1089; off-center toward the bottom; defect above the tail of the seahorse.
R: same as 1522; defect on the head of the bull; *GL*.
Paris, BNF, no. 1360; Babelon, *Perses*, no. 1360; Rouvier, *JIAN* 4 (1901) no. 641 (ex Rouvier coll.).

1528 O1–R3 10 mm
O: same as 1089; defect above the tail of the seahorse.
R: same as 1522; defect on the head of the bull; *GL* partly obliterated.
Elayi-Elayi, *Trésors*, p. 98, no. 159, and pl. 8:159 (Byblos hoards TXIII, TXIV, and TXV?).

1529 O1–R4* 0.77 g 9 mm 9 h
O: same as 1089; defect above the tail of the seahorse.
R: same as 1522; one two-pronged ankh under the stomach of the lion; *GL* partly obliterated.
Paris, BNF, no. 74 (ex De Vogüé coll.).

1530 O1–R4
0.63 g 10 mm
4 h
O: same as 1089; off-center to left; defect above the tail of the seahorse.
R: same as 1522; one two-pronged ankh under the stomach of the lion; *GL* partly obliterated.
Elayi-Elayi, *RBN* 139 (1993) 22, no. 82 and pl. 5:82 (hoard from Near East TLXXX).

1531 O?–R1
0.77 g 10 mm
Slightly worn.
O: same as 1089.
R: same as 1522; defect above the lion; *GL*.
London, BM, no. 1840-12-26 157.

1532 O?–R2
0.71 g 11 mm
Slightly worn.
O: same as 1089; very off-center toward the bottom.
R: same as 1522; *GL*.
Elayi-Elayi, *Trésors*, p. 98, no. 157, and pl. 8:157 (Byblos hoards TXIII, TXIV, and TXV?).

1533 O?–R3
0.80 g 10 mm
12 h
Slightly worn.
O: same as 1089; very off-center to left.
R: same as 1522; defect on the head of the bull; *GL* partly obliterated.
Berlin, SM, no. 9961.

1534 O?–R?
0.67 g
Rather worn.
O: same as 1089.
R: same as 1522; *GL* partly obliterated.
New York, ANS, no. 1944.100.70800; Betlyon, *Coinage of Phoenicia*, p. 118, no. 16, and pl. 9, 1.

1535 O?–R?
10 mm
Rather worn.
O: same as 1089; very off-center toward the top.
R: same as 1522; off-center to left;]*L*.
Elayi-Elayi, *Trésors*, p. 98, no. 158, and pl. 8:158 (Byblos hoards TXIII, TXIV, and TXV?).

1536 O?–R?
0.78 g
O: same as 1089.
R: same as 1522; *GL*.
Rouvier, *JIAN* 4 (1901) 42, no. 648; Babelon, *Perses*, no. 1370, not illustrated.

IV.4.7. Anepigraphic 16th-Shekels AR

1537 O1–R1
0.76 g 10 mm
7 h
O: same as 1089.
R: lion to left, bringing down a bull to left; border of dots.
Split die.
Elayi-Elayi, *RBN* 139 (1993) 22, no. 83 and pl. 5:83 (hoard from Near East TLXXX).

1538 O1*–R1*
0.74 g 10 mm
3 h
O: same as 1089; off-center to left.
R: same as 1537. Split die.
Paris, BNF, no. 75 (ex De Vogüé coll.).

1539 O1–R2*
0.74 g 10 mm
12 h
O: same as 1089; off-center toward the bottom.
R: same as 1537. Split die.
Elayi-Elayi, *RBN* 139 (1993) 22, no. 84 and pl. 5:84 (hoard from Near East TLXXX).

1540 O?–R?
0.74 g 10 mm
11 h
Rather worn.
O: same as 1089.
R: same as 1537.
Elayi-Elayi, *Trésors*, p. 98, no. 166, and pl. 9:166 (Byblos hoards TXIII, TXIV, and TXV?).

1541 O?–R?
0.69 g 11 mm
1 h
Rather worn.
O: same as 1089.
R: same as 1537.
Elayi-Elayi, *Trésors*, p. 104, no. 395, and pl. 14:395 (Byblos hoards TXIII, TXIV, and TXV?).

1542 O?–R?
0.68 g
Oval flan. Rather worn.
O: same as 1089; off-center to right.
R: same as 1537.
Elayi-Elayi, *Trésors*, p. 98, no. 171, and pl. 8:171 (Byblos hoards TXIII, TXIV, and TXV?).

1543 O?–R?
Rather worn.
O: same as 1089; off-center to left.
R: same as 1537.
Elayi-Elayi, *Trésors*, p. 98, no. 182, and pl. 8:182 (Byblos hoards TXIII, TXIV, and TXV?).

5. *Group V: Unclassified Series*

V.1. Half-16th Shekels AR with Griffin

1544 O1*–R1*
0.36 g 8 mm
3 h
O: same as 1089.
R: winged griffin, seated left, raising forepaw; border of dots. Split die.
Private coll. LPN.

1545 O1–R1
0.29 g 8 mm
12 h
O: same as 1089.
R: same as 1544. Split die.
Spaer coll., Jerusalem (bought in Beirut).

1546 O2–R1
0.30 g 7 mm
11 h
O: same as 1089.
R: same as 1544. Split die.
Paris, BNF, no. 1965/829/15 (ex Seyrig coll.).

1547	O2–R2* 0.34 g 9 h	O: same as 1089. R: same as 1544. Oxford, AM, no. 54; Monnaies et Médailles/Münzen und Medaillen, Basel, 256, November 1965, no. 483.
1548	O2–R3 0.37 g 7 mm 9 h	Small crack on the edge. O: same as 1089; very off-center to right. R: same as 1544. Elayi-Elayi, *Trésors*, p. 95, no. 6, and pl. 5:6 (Byblos hoards TXIII, TXIV, and TXV?).
1549	O2*–R3* 0.24 g 8 mm 5 h	Oval flan. O: same as 1089. R: same as 1544. Paris, BNF, no. 1987/147 (ex Seyrig coll.).
1550	O3*–R1 0.36 g 7 mm 9 h	O: same as 1089; very off-center to right. R: same as 1544. Split die. Private coll.; Baldwin, London, 34, 13/10/2003, no. 520.
1551	O3–R1 0.28 g 7 mm 7 h	O: same as 1089; off-center toward the top. R: same as 1544. Elayi-Elayi, *Trésors*, p. 95, no. 9, and pl. 5:9 (Byblos hoards TXIII, TXIV, and TXV?).
1552	O3–R2 0.35 g	O: same as 1089. R: same as 1544. Peus, Frankfurt/Rhein, 294, 15/3/1978, no. 299.
1553	O4*–R3* 0.39 g 8 mm 5 h	O: same as 1089. R: same as 1544; off-center to left. Paris, BNF, no. 3155; *Catalogue De Luynes*, no. 3155; Babelon, *Perses*, no. 1371; idem, *Traité*, no. 881 (ex De Luynes coll.).
1554	O4–R4 0.32 g 7 mm 10 h	O: same as 1089. R: same as 1544; off-center to right. London, BM, no. 1985.5-20-14; Elayi-Elayi, *Trésors*, p. 95, no. 7, and pl. 5:7 (Byblos hoards TXIII, TXIV, and TXV?).
1555	O5*–R5* 0.28 g 7 mm 11 h	O: same as 1089. R: same as 1544; defect behind the griffin. London, BM, no. 1985.5-20-10; Elayi-Elayi, *Trésors*, p. 95, no. 10, and pl. 5:10 (Byblos hoards TXIII, TXIV, and TXV?).
1556	O1–R? 0.31 g 8 mm 6 h	Slightly worn. O: same as 1089. R: same as 1544. Paris, BNF, no. 1965/829/16 (ex Seyrig coll.).

1557 O1–R?
0.25 g
11 h
Slightly worn.
O: same as 1089.
R: same as 1544.
Klein, *Sammlung*, no. 712 (Klein coll.).

1558 O1–R?
0.24 g 7 mm
6 h
Slightly worn. Edge broken.
O: same as 1089.
R: same as 1544.
London, BM, no. 1985.5-20-7; Elayi-Elayi, *Trésors*, p. 95, no. 7, and pl. 5:7 (Byblos hoards TXIII, TXIV, and TXV?).

1559 O3–R?
0.32 g 7 mm
6 h
Slightly worn.
O: same as 1089.
R: same as 1544.
London, BM, no. 1985.5-20-12; Elayi-Elayi, *Trésors*, p. 95, no. 8, and pl. 5:8 (Byblos hoards TXIII, TXIV, and TXV?).

1560 O?–R6
0.33 g 7 mm
6 h
Slightly worn.
O: same as 1089; off-center toward the top.
R: same as 1544.
London, BM, no. 1985.5-20-9; Elayi-Elayi, *Trésors*, p. 95, no. 13, and pl. 5:13 (Byblos hoards TXIII, TXIV, and TXV?).

1561 O?–R?
0.36 g
Rather worn.
O: same as 1089.
R: same as 1544.
Baldwin, London, 34, 13/10/2003, no. 519, not illustrated.

1562 O?–R?
0.28 g 8 mm
3 h
Rather worn.
O: same as 1089; off-center toward the bottom.
R: same as 1544.
London, BM, no. 1985.5-20-11; Elayi-Elayi, *Trésors*, p. 95, no. 11, and pl. 5:11 (Byblos hoards TXIII, TXIV, and TXV?).

1563 O?–R?
0.26 g 8 mm
Rather worn.
O: same as 1089.
R: same as 1544.
Paris, BNF, no. 1987/463 (ex Seyrig coll.).

V.2. Small Fractions AR with Griffin's Head

1564 O1*–R1*
0.07 g 5 mm
2 h
O: war-galley to left; prow terminating in head of animal; inside, one warrior represented by helmet and shield. Border of dots.
R: head of griffin, to right; border of dots.
Paris, BNF, no. 1965/829/14 (ex Seyrig coll.).

1565 O2*–R2*
0.05 g 5 mm
Edge broken.
O: same as 1564.
R: same as 1564, to left; off-center toward the top.
Paris, BNF, no. 1968/135 (ex Seyrig coll.).

V.3. Small Fractions AR with Bearded Head

1566 O1*–R1* 0.06 g 5 mm
O: bearded head to right.
R: bearded head, with *kausia*, to right.
Paris, BNF, no. 3047; *Catalogue De Luynes*, no. 3047; Babelon, *Traité*, no. 868 (ex De Luynes coll.).

1567 O2*–R2* 0.05 g 4 mm
O and R: same as 1566.
Paris, BNF, no. 1968/139 (ex Seyrig coll.).

1568 O1–R? 0.04 g 5 mm
Slightly worn. Edge broken.
O and R: same as 1566.
Paris, BNF, no. 3049; *Catalogue De Luynes*, no. 3049; Babelon, *Traité*, no. 870 (ex De Luynes coll.).

1569 O?–R3* 0.06 g
Slightly worn. Edge broken.
O and R: same as 1566.
Paris, BNF, no. 3048; *Catalogue De Luynes*, no. 3048; Babelon, *Traité*, no. 869 (ex De Luynes coll.).

1570 O?–R? 0.08 g
O and R: same as 1566.
Paris, BNF, no. 1968/142 (ex Seyrig coll.).

V.4. Shekels AR of ʿOzbaʿal, ʾUrimilk, or ʿAynel

1571 14.16 g 25 mm
Rather worn.
O: war-galley to left; inside, three warriors with shields, facing left; below, one line of waves, winged seahorse to left and shell. Border of dots.
R: lion to left, bringing down a bull to left; inscription illegible; border of dots.
Beirut, AUB, no. C765C.

1572 12.91 g 23 mm
Rather worn.
O and R: same as 1571.
Beirut, AUB, no. C2947A.

V.5. 16th-Shekels AR of ʾUrimilk or ʿAynel

1573 0.77 g
Rather worn.
O: war-galley to left; prow terminating in head of a lion; inside, two warriors represented by helmets and shields; below, *ʾK* and winged seahorse to left. Border of dots.
R: lion to left, bringing down a bull to left; inscription illegible; border of dots.
Elayi-Elayi, *Trésors*, p. 99, no. 212 (Byblos hoards TXIII, TXIV, and TXV?).

1574 0.76 g
11 h

Rather worn.
O: same as 1573; very off-center toward the top; traces of ʾK.
R: same as 1573; inscription illegible.
Elayi-Elayi, *Trésors*, p. 104, no. 396, and pl. 14:396 (Byblos hoards TXIII, TXIV and TXV?).

1575 0.74 g
11 h

Rather worn.
O: same as 1573; traces of ʾK.
R: same as 1573; inscription illegible.
Elayi-Elayi, *Trésors*, p. 98, no. 161 (Byblos hoards TXIII, TXIV, and TXV?).

1576 0.74 g

Rather worn.
O: same as 1573; off-center to left; traces of ʾK.
R: same as 1573; inscription illegible.
Elayi-Elayi, *Trésors*, p. 99, no. 213 (Byblos hoards TXIII, TXIV, and TXV?).

1577 0.73 g

Rather worn.
O: same as 1573; off-center toward the top; traces of ʾK.
R: same as 1573; inscription illegible.
Burgan, Paris, 3/7/1992, no. 506.

1578 0.72 g

Rather worn.
O: same as 1573; off-center toward the bottom; traces of ʾK.
R: same as 1573; inscription illegible.
Münzen und Medaillen, information of H. Voegtli, 1991.

1579 0.70 g

Rather worn.
O: same as 1573; traces of ʾK.
R: same as 1573; inscription illegible.
Baldwin, London, 34, 13/10/2003, no. 532.

1580 0.63 g
12 h

Rather worn.
O: same as 1573; traces of ʾK.
R: same as 1573; inscription illegible.
Elayi-Elayi, *Trésors*, p. 104, no. 397 (Byblos hoards TXIII, TXIV, and TXV?).

V.6. 16th-Shekels AR of ʿOzbaʿal, ʾUrimilk, or ʿAynel

No.	Weight	Diam.	Description
1581	0.85 g		Rather worn. O: war-galley to left; prow terminating in head of a lion; inside, two warriors represented by helmets and shields; below, winged seahorse to left. No inscription visible. Border of dots. R: lion to left, bringing down a bull to left; inscription illegible; border of dots. Elayi-Elayi, *Trésors*, p. 104, no. 162 (Byblos hoards TXIII, TXIV, and TXV?).
1582	0.81 g		Rather worn. O and R: same as 1581. No inscriptions visible. Elayi-Elayi, *Trésors*, p. 104, no. 163 (Byblos hoards TXIII, TXIV, and TXV?).
1583	0.81 g 4 h	11 mm	Rather worn. O and R: same as 1581. No inscriptions visible. Berlin, SM, no. 22 (ex Prokesch-Osten coll.).
1584	0.78 g		Rather worn. O and R: same as 1581. No inscriptions visible. Berlin, SM, no. 20 (ex Fox coll.).
1585	0.77 g		Rather worn. O and R: same as 1581. No inscriptions visible. Elayi-Elayi, *Trésors*, p. 104, no. 165 (Byblos hoards TXIII, TXIV, and TXV?).
1586	0.77 g 12 h	11 mm	Rather worn. O and R: same as 1581. No inscriptions visible. Elayi-Elayi, *RBN* 139 (1993) 23, no. 86 and pl. 5:86 (hoard from Near East TLXXX).
1587	0.77 g 12 h	12 mm	Rather worn. O and R: same as 1581. No inscriptions visible. Paris, BNF, no. 1987/452 (ex Seyrig coll.).
1588	0.76 g		Rather worn. Hoffmann, Münz Zentrum, Cologne, 74, 11–13/11/1992, no. 381.
1589	0.76 g		Rather worn. O and R: same as 1581. No inscriptions visible. Berk, Chicago, 60, 16/1/1990, no. 157.
1590	0.76 g 4 h	11 mm	Rather worn. O and R: same as 1581. No inscriptions visible. Elayi-Elayi, *RBN* 139 (1993) 23, no. 87 and pl. 5:87 (hoard from Near East TLXXX).

1591 0.76 g 11 mm 3 h
Rather worn.
O and R: same as 1581. No inscriptions visible.
Elayi-Elayi, *RBN* 139 (1993) 23, no. 88 and pl. 5:88 (hoard from Near East TLXXX).

1592 0.75 g 4 h
Rather worn.
O and R: same as 1581. No inscriptions visible.
Elayi-Elayi, *Trésors*, p. 104, no. 398 (Byblos hoards TXIII, TXIV, and TXV?).

1593 0.75 g 10 mm
Rather worn.
O and R: same as 1581. No inscriptions visible.
Beirut, AUB Museum, no. 769.

1594 0.75 g 9 mm
Rather worn.
O and R: same as 1581. No inscriptions visible.
Bologna, ArchM, no. 7.

1595 0.74 g 5 h
Rather worn.
O and R: same as 1581. No inscriptions visible.
Elayi-Elayi, *Trésors*, p. 104, no. 399 (Byblos hoards TXIII, TXIV, and TXV?).

1596 0.74 g 5 h
Rather worn.
O and R: same as 1581. No inscriptions visible.
Elayi-Elayi, *Trésors*, p. 104, no. 400 (Byblos hoards TXIII, TXIV, and TXV?).

1597 0.74 g 11 mm 9 h
Rather worn.
O and R: same as 1581. No inscriptions visible.
Paris, BNF, no. 1987/453 (ex Seyrig coll.).

1598 0.73 g
Rather worn. Edge broken.
O and R: same as 1581. No inscriptions visible.
Elayi-Elayi, *Trésors*, p. 98, no. 167 (Byblos hoards TXIII, TXIV, and TXV?).

1599 0.73 g
Rather worn.
O and R: same as 1581. No inscriptions visible.
Elayi-Elayi, *Trésors*, p. 98, no. 168 (Byblos hoards TXIII, TXIV, and TXV?).

1600 0.73 g
Rather worn.
O and R: same as 1581. No inscriptions visible.
Elayi-Elayi, *Trésors*, p. 98, no. 169 (Byblos hoards TXIII, TXIV, and TXV?).

1601 0.72 g
Rather worn.
O and R: same as 1581. No inscriptions visible.
Elayi-Elayi, *Trésors*, p. 101, no. 285, and pl. 12:285 (Byblos hoards TXIII, TXIV, and TXV?).

1602 0.72 g 11 mm
Rather worn.
O and R: same as 1581. No inscriptions visible.
Beirut, AUB Museum, no. 766.

1603 0.71 g 2 h
Rather worn.
O and R: same as 1581. No inscriptions visible.
Elayi-Elayi, *Trésors*, p. 104, no. 401 (Byblos hoards TXIII, TXIV, and TXV?).

1604 0.71 g 1 h
Rather worn.
O and R: same as 1581. No inscriptions visible.
Elayi-Elayi, *Trésors*, p. 104, no. 402 (Byblos hoards TXIII, TXIV, and TXV?).

1605 0.69 g 5 h
Rather worn.
O and R: same as 1581. No inscriptions visible.
Elayi-Elayi, *Trésors*, p. 104, no. 403 (Byblos hoards TXIII, TXIV, and TXV?).

1606 0.69 g
Rather worn.
O and R: same as 1581. No inscriptions visible.
Elayi-Elayi, *Trésors*, p. 101, no. 287, and pl. 12:287 (Byblos hoards TXIII, TXIV, and TXV?).

1607 0.68 g
Rather worn.
O and R: same as 1581. No inscriptions visible.
Elayi-Elayi, *Trésors*, p. 98, no. 170 (Byblos hoards TXIII, TXIV, and TXV?).

1608 0.68 g
Rather worn.
O and R: same as 1581. No inscriptions visible.
Elayi-Elayi, *Trésors*, p. 98, no. 172 (Byblos hoards TXIII, TXIV, and TXV?).

1609 0.68 g 8 h
Rather worn.
O and R: same as 1581. No inscriptions visible.
Elayi-Elayi, *Trésors*, p. 104, no. 404 (Byblos hoards TXIII, TXIV, and TXV?).

1610 0.67 g
Rather worn.
O and R: same as 1581. No inscriptions visible.
Elayi-Elayi, *Trésors*, p. 98, no. 173 (Byblos hoards TXIII, TXIV, and TXV?).

1611 0.67 g
Rather worn. Some cracks on the edge.
O and R: same as 1581. No inscriptions visible.
Elayi-Elayi, *Trésors*, p. 98, no. 174 (Byblos hoards TXIII, TXIV, and TXV?).

1612 0.67 g 11 mm
Rather worn.
O and R: same as 1581. No inscriptions visible.
Paris, BNF, no. 1987/456 (ex Seyrig coll.).

1613 0.66 g — Rather worn.
O and R: same as 1581. No inscriptions visible.
Elayi-Elayi, *Trésors*, p. 98, no. 175 (Byblos hoards TXIII, TXIV, and TXV?).

1614 0.66 g — Rather worn. Small crack on the edge.
O and R: same as 1581. No inscriptions visible.
Elayi-Elayi, *Trésors*, p. 98, no. 176 (Byblos hoards TXIII, TXIV, and TXV?).

1615 0.66 g — Rather worn. Some cracks on the edge.
O and R: same as 1581. No inscriptions visible.
Paris, BNF, no. 1987/460 (ex Seyrig coll.).

1616 0.65 g 11 h — Rather worn. Oval flan.
O and R: same as 1581. No inscriptions visible.
Elayi-Elayi, *Trésors*, p. 104, no. 405 (Byblos hoards TXIII, TXIV, and TXV?).

1617 0.65 g 12 h — Rather worn. Irregular flan.
O and R: same as 1581. No inscriptions visible.
Elayi-Elayi, *RBN* 139 (1993) 22, no. 90 and pl. 5:90 (hoard from Near East TLXXX).

1618 0.65 g 11 mm — Rather worn.
O and R: same as 1581. No inscriptions visible.
Paris, BNF, no. 1987/450 (ex Seyrig coll.).

1619 0.64 g — Rather worn.
O and R: same as 1581. No inscriptions visible.
Elayi-Elayi, *Trésors*, p. 101, no. 286, and pl. 12:286 (Byblos hoards TXIII, TXIV, and TXV?).

1620 0.64 g 11 mm 4 h — Rather worn. Small crack on the edge.
O and R: same as 1581. No inscriptions visible.
Elayi-Elayi, *RBN* 139 (1993) 22, no. 91 and pl. 5:91 (hoard from Near East TLXXX).

1621 0.64 g 10 mm — Rather worn.
O and R: same as 1581. No inscriptions visible.
Beirut, AUB Museum, no. 767.

1622 0.63 g — Rather worn.
O and R: same as 1581. No inscriptions visible.
Elayi-Elayi, *Trésors*, p. 98, no. 177 (Byblos hoards TXIII, TXIV, and TXV?).

1623 0.63 g — Rather worn. Broken in two pieces.
O and R: same as 1581. No inscriptions visible.
Elayi-Elayi, *Trésors*, p. 98, no. 178 (Byblos hoards TXIII, TXIV, and TXV?).

1624 0.62 g — Rather worn.
O and R: same as 1581. No inscriptions visible.
Elayi-Elayi, *Trésors*, p. 98, no. 179 (Byblos hoards TXIII, TXIV, and TXV?).

1625 0.61 g, 6 h — Rather worn.
O and R: same as 1581. No inscriptions visible.
Elayi-Elayi, *Trésors*, p. 104, no. 406 (Byblos hoards TXIII, TXIV, and TXV?).

1626 0.61 g 11 mm — Rather worn.
O and R: same as 1581. No inscriptions visible.
Paris, BNF, no. 1987/457 (ex Seyrig coll.).

1627 0.60 g, 9 h — Rather worn.
O and R: same as 1581. No inscriptions visible.
Elayi-Elayi, *Trésors*, p. 104, no. 407 (Byblos hoards TXIII, TXIV, and TXV?).

1628 0.60 g, 2 h — Rather worn. Broken.
O and R: same as 1581. No inscriptions visible.
Tel Aviv, KNM, no. 9051.

1629 0.58 g 11 mm, 1 h — Rather worn. Small crack on the edge.
O and R: same as 1581. No inscriptions visible.
Elayi-Elayi, *RBN* 139 (1993) 22, no. 92 and pl. 5:92 (hoard from Near East TLXXX).

1630 0.57 g — Rather worn. Broken.
O and R: same as 1581. No inscriptions visible.
Elayi-Elayi, *Trésors*, p. 98, no. 180 (Byblos hoards TXIII, TXIV, and TXV?).

1631 0.55 g — Rather worn. Broken.
O and R: same as 1581. No inscriptions visible.
Elayi-Elayi, *Trésors*, p. 98, no. 181 (Byblos hoards TXIII, TXIV, and TXV?).

1632 0.52 g — Rather worn. Broken.
O and R: same as 1581. No inscriptions visible.
Elayi-Elayi, *Trésors*, p. 202, no. 3 (Beirut area hoard TXLIII).

1633 0.46 g — Rather worn.
O and R: same as 1581. No inscriptions visible.
Paris, BNF, no. 1987/451 (ex Seyrig coll.).

1634 0.43 g — Rather worn. Broken.
O and R: same as 1581. No inscriptions visible.
Paris, BNF, no. 1987/459 (ex Seyrig coll.).

1635 0.41 g — Rather worn. Broken.
O and R: same as 1581. No inscriptions visible.
Paris, BNF, no. 1987/461 (ex Seyrig coll.).

1636 Rather worn.
O and R: same as 1581. No inscriptions visible.
Poinsignon Numismatique, Strasbourg, 32, March 1991, no. 291.

1637 Rather worn.
O and R: same as 1581. No inscriptions visible.
Classical Numismatic Group, Lancaster-London, 29, 30/3/1994, no. 131.

1638 Rather worn.
O and R: same as 1581. No inscriptions visible.
Malloy, New York, 24, 18/3/1988, no. 135.

1639 Rather worn.
O and R: same as 1581. No inscriptions visible.
Copenhagen, NatMus, no. 134.

1640 Rather worn. Broken.
O and R: same as 1581. No inscriptions visible.
Elayi-Elayi, *Trésors*, p. 101, no. 288 (Byblos hoards TXIII, TXIV, and TXV?).

1641 Rather worn. Broken.
O and R: same as 1581. No inscriptions visible.
Elayi-Elayi, *Trésors*, p. 101, no. 289 (Byblos hoards TXIII, TXIV, and TXV?).

1642 Rather worn.
O and R: same as 1581. No inscriptions visible.
Elayi-Elayi, *Trésors*, p. 106, no. 482 (Byblos hoards TXIII, TXIV, and TXV?).

1643–1645 O and R: same as 1581. No inscriptions visible.
Elayi-Elayi, *Trésors*, p. 106, nos. 483–85, not illustrated (Byblos hoards TXIII, TXIV, and TXV?).

1646 Rather worn.
O and R: same as 1581. No inscriptions visible.
Paris, BNF, no. H.S. 23 (ex Seyrig coll.).

1647–1661 Rather worn.
O and R: same as 1581. No inscriptions visible.
Superior Galleries, New York, 31/5/1989, no. 6102.

1662 O and R: same as 1581.
Elayi-Elayi, *Trésors*, p. 271, some coins not illustrated (Tigris hoard TLXIV).

Appendix 2

Counterfeit or Dubious Byblian Coins

1* 13.22 g Irregular flan.
O: war-galley to left; prow terminating in head of a lion; inside, three warriors with shields, facing left; below, one line of waves, ʿZ, winged seahorse to left and shell. Border of dots.
R: lion to left, bringing down a bull to left; *ʿZBʿL MLK GBL* above; border of dots.
Monnaies et Médailles/Münzen und Medaillen, Basel, 457, July 1983, no. 14.; cf. *Bulletin of Counterfeits* 9/1 (1984) 6–7.

2* 12.55 g O: same as 1*, but ʿZ are on one horizontal line.
R: same as 1*.
Berk, Chicago, 103, 28/7/1998, no. 216.

3* 1.19 g O: war-galley to left; prow terminating in head of a lion; inside, one warrior with shield, facing left; below, one line of waves and winged seahorse to left. Border of dots.
R: lion to left, bringing down a bull with an incuse body to right; no inscription visible. Wrong weight for a 16th-shekel.
Private coll. LPN.

4* 0.69 g O: war-galley to left; prow terminating in head of a lion; inside, two warriors represented by helmets and shields; below, *Z* instead of ʿZ, and winged seahorse to left. Border of dots.
R: lion to left, bringing down a bull to left; inscription obliterated; border of dots.
Elayi-Elayi, *Trésors*, 98, no. 160 (Byblos hoards TXIII, TXIV, and TXV?).

5* 0.59 g O: war-galley to left; prow terminating in head of a lion; inside, three warriors instead of two; below, winged seahorse to left. Border of dots.
R: lion to left, bringing down a bull to left; inscription without any meaning; border of dots.
Leiden, RM, no. 8025.

Appendix 3

Study of Dies and Relative Chronology

This chapter is a numismatic analysis of the catalog in appendix 1. We shall comment on the dies, including die pairs and die links, and explain the arrangement proposed for this corpus based on a relative chronology, by groups and series.

1. *Group I: Crouched Sphinx*

The whole of Group I is characterized, whatever the denomination may be, by the obverse motif, which is always a crouched sphinx facing left, wearing the double crown of Egypt; and by the reverse motif, which is always a double lotus flower with a dotted border, in an incuse square. The choice of iconography was probably intended to keep the unity of the group by using the same motifs on the obverse and reverse. In the first group of Tyrian coins, the obverse motif was always a dolphin above lines of waves, but there were differences among the five denominations of this group related to the number of lines of waves and the inscription on the reverse.[1] This differentiation was necessary for the very small denominations, which have similar weights.[2] In the first Byblian group, it was difficult to differentiate the series simply by weight and diameter for the smallest denominations. We have clearly distinguished Series I.1 (shekels), I.2 (3rd-shekels), I.3 (6th-shekels) and I.4 (12th-shekels). Then we have tentatively proposed distinguishing three more series: Series I.5, Series I.6, and Series I.7. Even if the last two series constitute only one series, note that Group I comprised a complete system of denominations, as did the first groups of Tyrian coins.

In order to form a corpus, a die sequence must be established first, because it is the sole valid principle of organization. The die sequence is determined by the die comparison method, developed by numismatists

1. Elayi-Elayi, *Coinage of Tyre*, 201–2.

2. Except for Series I.1.4 and I.1.5, which had the same motifs but different weights and different diameters.

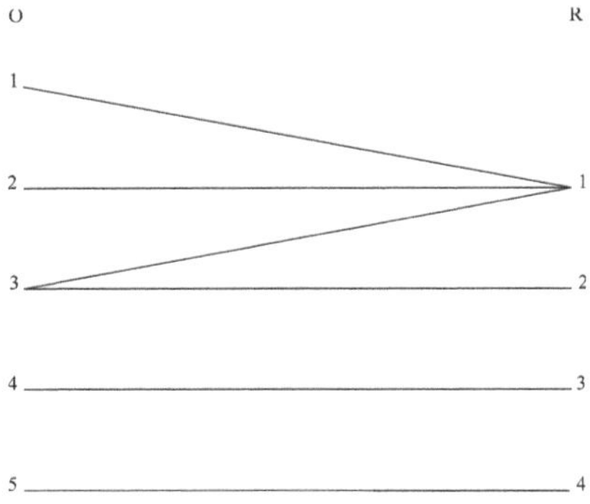

Fig. A3.1. *Dies of shekels (I.1).*

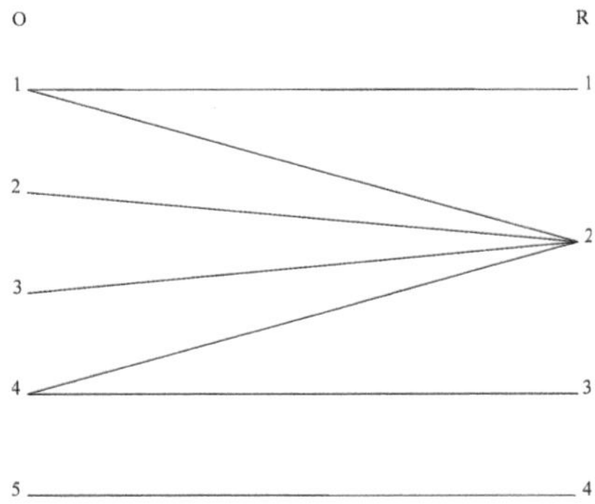

Fig. A3.2. *Dies of 12th-shekels (I.4).*

since the end of the 19th century.[3] The die analysis is limited for Group I because the seven (?) series contain only 1 to 21 coins each. The shekel series (I.1) is only represented by 6 coins (out of a total of 18),[4] and we have identified 6 die pairs and 5 obverse dies. R1 is linked with O1, O2, and O3; R2 is linked with O3 (fig. A3.1). The ratio of n:o = 1.20:1, which means that this series is insufficiently known because it is insufficiently represented.[5] The 3rd-shekel series (I.2) is only represented by 4 coins (out of a total of 9): 4 obverse dies and 4 die pairs, O1–R1, O2–R2, O3–R3, and O4–R4; there is no link.[6] The 6th-shekel series (I.3) is represented by 3 coins (out of 6): 3 die pairs and 3 obverses, O1–R1, O2–R2, and O3–R3; there is no link. The 12th-shekel series (I.4) is represented by 8 coins (out of 22), and we have identified 7 die pairs and 5 obverse dies (fig. A3.2). O1 is linked with R1 and R2; R2 is also linked with O2, O3, and O4, which is linked with R3. There is one isolated pair of dies: O5–R4; and 3 isolated dies: R5, R6, and R7. The ratio of n:o in this series, which is insufficiently known, is 1.60:1. Series I.5 is only represented by 3 coins out of 7, with 3 die pairs and 2 obverse dies. O1 is linked with R1 and R2; O2 with R3; R4 is isolated. The ratio of n:o = 1.50:1, which means that this series is insufficiently known/represented. Series I.6 is only represented by 1 coin, and Series I.7 by 3 coins, with 3 isolated dies (O1, O2, R1). The quantity of Group I coins is relatively small: only 66 coins

3. For the first die study, see F. Imhoof-Blumer, "Die Münzen Akarnaniens," *NZ* (1878) 1–186.

4. Number of coins considered by the die analysis out of all the coins preserved.

5. n = number of coins studied, o = number of obverse dies. For determining the number of coins manufactured from the number of coins preserved, see, §3.6 above.

6. R5 is isolated because the obverse is indistinct. We do not take into account the isolated coins.

(total number) for seven (?) series—that is, 23 die pairs and 19 obverse dies (not including isolated dies).

We now must explain why we have classified Group I at the beginning of Byblian coinage. Several authors do not mention it in their catalogs of Byblian coins.[7] Others considered it to be the first Byblian group: J. Rouvier was the first in 1901; then G. F. Hill, who mistakenly interpreted the reverse motif as a lion (?); J. W. Betlyon, who wrongly believed that the standard was Attic; and L. Solé.[8] We have shown that Group I was at the beginning of the Byblian coinage for several reasons.[9] The coins of this group are different from the iconography and standard of later coins. Their manufacture is similar to that of a Tyrian shekel in Series I.1.1 found in the Jordan hoard TLIII.[10] Another reason is that the Group I Byblian coins were found together with one coin from Group I of Tyre in the Byblos hoard TX.[11] However, they are older because they did not yet conform to the Phoenician standard. There is no information either on the coins or in the avaible documentation for identifying the first king of Byblos to begin minting coins.

2. *Group II: Seated Sphinx*

The whole of Group II is characterized by the obverse motif, which is always, whatever the denomination may be, a winged sphinx that is seated facing left and wearing the double crown of Egypt. However, there are some variations on the denominations, and there are several reverse motifs. The reverse motif of the 3rd-shekels (Series II.1) is a hawk facing left, wearing the double crown of Egypt, crook and flail, having an olive twig, and placed in an incuse impression; on the obverse, the sphinx has one wing visible. The 12th-shekels of Series II.2.1 have exactly the same iconography, but those of Series II.2.2 are different: the sphinx has two wings, and the reverse bears a lotus flower and the letters *MY/Z* on the left of the hawk and the letters *ʿGK* on the right. Series II.2.3 contains the coins on which it is uncertain whether the sphinx has one or two wings. The minute coins of Series II.3 bear the same sphinx with one wing on the obverse; and a helmet

7. Head, *Historia Numorum*, 791; Babelon, *Perses*, 192; *Catalogue De Luynes*, 142.

8. J. Rouvier, "Numismatique des villes de la Phénicie: Gebal-Byblos," *JIAN* 4 (1901) 39–42; *BMC Phoenicia*, lxv; Betlyon, *Coinage of Phoenicia*, 111–12; L. Solé, "Nuove considerazioni sull'unità ponderale della prima serie monetale di Biblo," *Trans* 20 (2000) 61–72.

9. Elayi, "Phénomène monétaire," 22–23; idem, "L'ouverture du premier atelier monétaire phénicien," *BCEN* 32 (1995) 73–78.

10. Elayi-Elayi, *Trésors*, 240–41; idem, *Coinage of Tyre*, 328–31.

11. Elayi-Elayi, *Trésors*, 87–90.

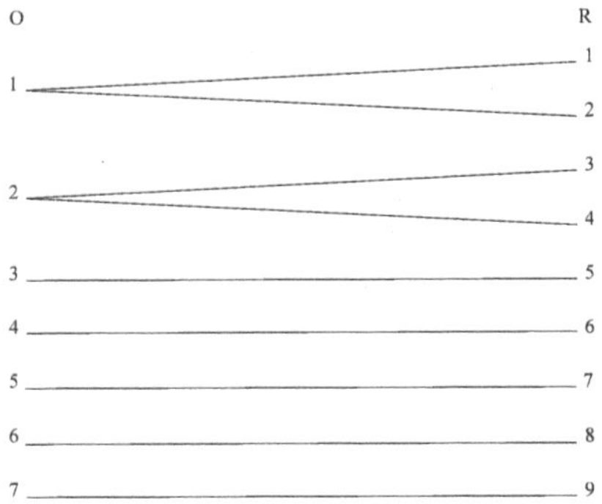

Fig. A3.3. *Dies of 12th-shekels (II.2.1).*

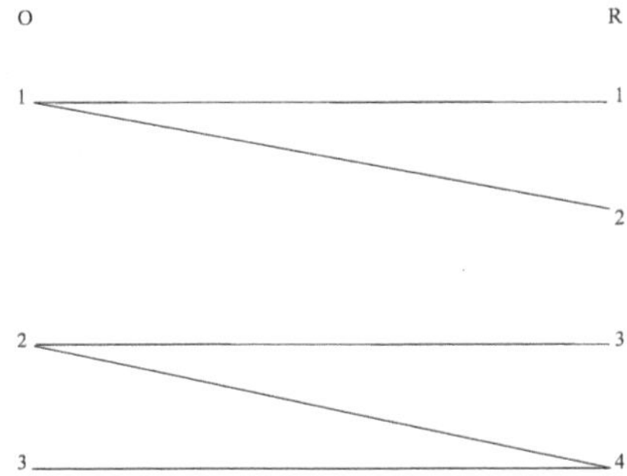

Fig. A3.4. *Dies of 12th-shekels (II.2.2).*

to the left and in an incuse square on the reverse. Series II.4 has the same obverse type and a griffin's head on the reverse.

Series II.1 is only represented by 2 coins (out of 6): 2 obverse and 2 die pairs (O1–R1, O2–R2). Series II.2.1 is represented by 9 coins (out of 11), and we have identified 9 die pairs and 7 obverse dies (fig. A3.3). O1 is linked with R1 and R2; O2 with R3 and R4; O3 with R5, O4 with R6, O5 with R7, O6 with R8, and O7 with R9; R10 is isolated. The ratio of n:o = 1.29:1, which means that this series is insufficiently known. Series II.2.2 is only represented by 5 coins (out of 10), and we have identified 5 die pairs and 3 obverse dies (fig. A3.4). O1 is linked with R1 and R2, O2 with R3 and R4, which is linked with O3; O4 is isolated. The ratio of n:o is also small (1.67:1). Series II.3 is only represented by 3 coins (out of 6): 3 die pairs, with O1–R1, O2–R2, O3–R3, and 3 obverse dies; O4 is isolated. There is no link. The volume of Group II is even smaller than that of Group I: 34 coins (total number) for five series, 18 die pairs and 17 obverse dies (for identified dies).

Group II is a somewhat confusing group compared with Group I. The quantity in the issues has decreased (34 coins instead of 66), as has the number of die pairs (18 instead of 24), and obverse dies (17 instead of 22). It contains fewer denominations, a smaller number of coins, and a system that is less organized. However, it must be placed between Groups I and III for several reasons: its standard is the same as in Group I; its iconography links it to both the preceding and the following groups. On the one hand, the obverse motif is always a sphinx, but it no longer has the Egyptian style; the lotus flower is still represented on the reverse. On the other hand, the crook and flail, helmet, and griffin motifs portend the series to come. We consider the context of Group II in chap. 5.

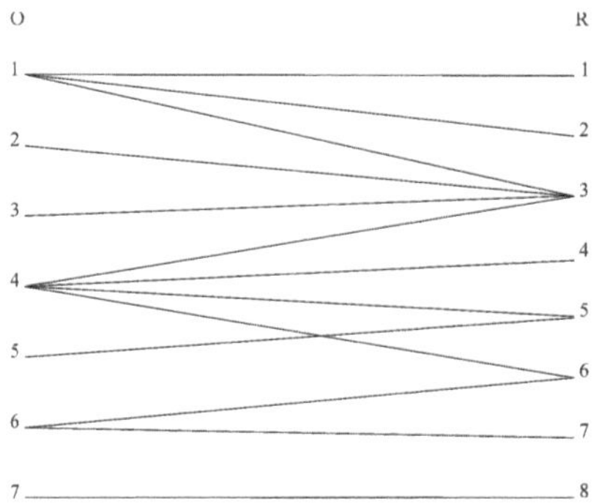

Fig. A3.5. *Dies of shekels (III.1).*

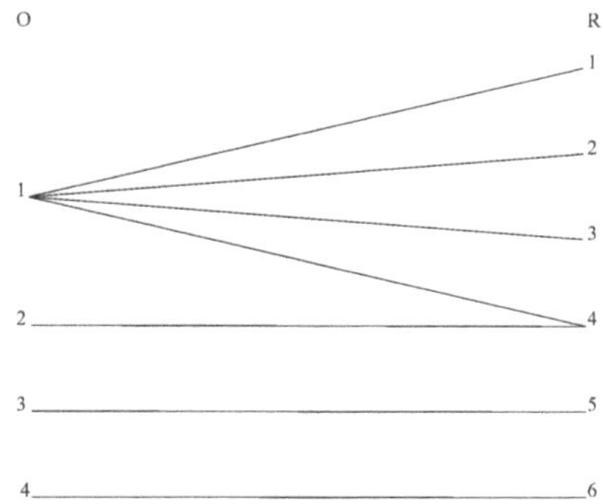

Fig. A3.6. *Dies of quarter-shekels (III.2).*

3. *Group III: Galley, Vulture, and Ram*

An important change occurred in the obverse and reverse types of Group III: instead of the sphinx as the obverse motif, there was a war-galley, with its prow terminating in the head of a horse; three warriors with shields on the deck; and a winged seahorse below. The various reverse motifs of Group II were replaced with a vulture standing over an incuse ram. The standard was also changed—from the first Byblian standard to the so-called Phoenician standard. We have classified four denominations in Group III: shekels, quarter-shekels, 16ths, and half-16ths. These denominations were identified by some differences in the types: the vulture of the quarters does not have one wing outstretched but both wings closed; the 16ths have one warrior on the deck instead of three; the half-16ths also have one warrior and a vulture without ram on the reverse, but with crook and flail. These small differences probably provided additional help to the differentiation by weights. The crook and flail, symbols of kingship, link with the hawk in the preceding Group II. Moreover, in hoard TLXXXIII, the Byblian coins were exclusively coins from Groups II and III.[12] The attribution of Series III.4 to Group III is based on the iconography and confirmed by the metallic composition of its coins.[13]

Because they did not know our Group II or, in some cases, our Group I, most authors have not classified our Group II and sometimes have not classified our Group I. Most authors classified our Group III as Group II—for

12. J. Elayi and A. G. Elayi, "Nouveau trésor de Byblos d'après les archives de H. Seyrig (TLXXXIII)," *Trans* 38 (2009) 66–68, nos. 1–31.

13. Cf. A. G. Elayi, M. Blet-Lemarquand, and J. Elayi, "Silver Coinage Fluctuations at Byblos (5th–4th Cent. BCE) as Determined by LA-ICP-MS and FNAA," *AJN* (2012) 1–10.

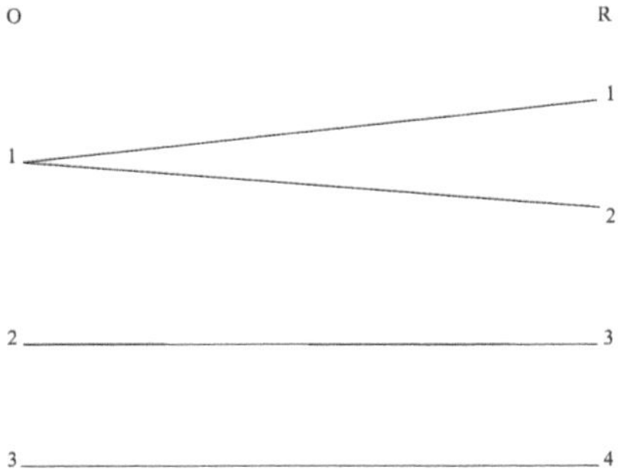

Fig. A3.7. *Dies of 16th-shekels (III.3).*

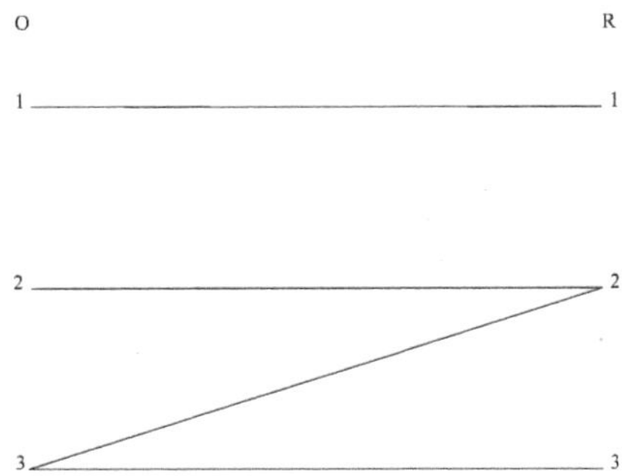

Fig. A3.8. *Dies of half-16th-shekels (III.4).*

example, J. Rouvier, G. F. Hill, and J. W. Betlyon; or as Group I, for example, E. Babelon and J. Babelon.[14] The series in Group III were even attributed to the satrap Aryandes by H. De Luynes and C. Lenormant, who read APYAN in the lines of the body of the ram, but J. Rouvier rightly rejected this reading and attribution.[15]

The III.1 shekel series is represented by 16 coins (out of a total number of 41; see fig. A3.5). We have identified 13 die pairs and 7 obverse dies. O1 is linked with R1, R2, and R3, which is also linked with O2, O3, and O4. O4 is also linked with R4, R5, and R6; O5 with R5 and O6 with R6 and R7. Therefore, O1–O6 are linked together, and it is the same for R1–R7. O7 is linked with R8. The ratio of n:o = 2.29:1, which means that this series is insufficiently known. The series of quarter-shekels (III.2) is represented by 10 coins (out of 17), with 7 pairs and 4 obverse dies (fig. A3.6). O1 is linked with R1, R2, R3, and R4, which is linked with O2; therefore, O1 and O2 are linked together and also R1–R4. O3 is linked with R5 and O4 with R6. The ratio of n:o = 2.50:1, which means that this series is not well known but is better-known than the preceding series. Series III.3 is only represented by 4 coins (out of 15), with 4 pairs and 3 obverse dies (fig. A3.7). O1 is linked with R1 and R2, which are therefore linked together. O2 is linked with R3 and O3 with R4. The ratio of n:o = 1.33:1. Series III.4 is only represented by

14. Rouvier, "Numismatique des villes," 39; *BMC Phoenicia*, lxv; Betlyon, *Coinage of Phoenicia*, 113–14; Babelon, *Perses*, 192; *Catalogue De Luynes*, 142.

15. Rouvier, "Numismatique des villes," 38–39, nos. 630–31 (with bibliography).

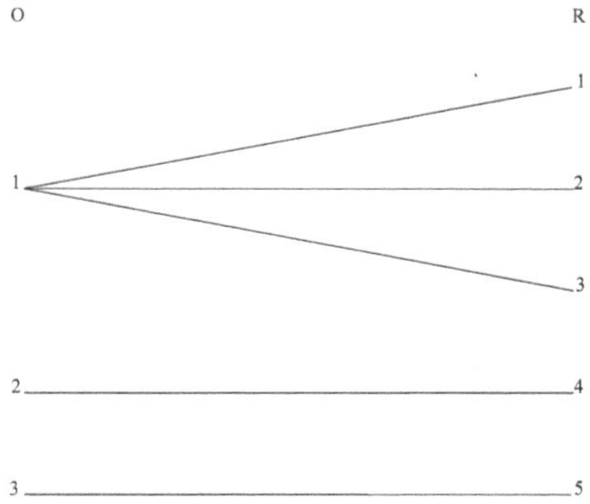

Fig. A3.9. *Dies of ʾElpaʿal's shekels (IV.1.1).*

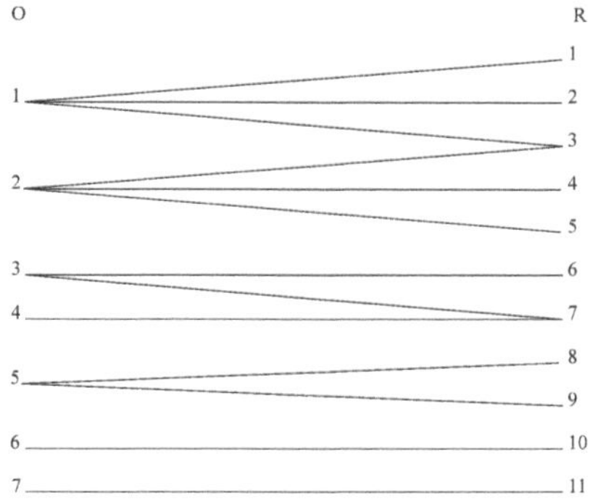

Fig. A3.10. *Dies of ʾElpaʿal's quarter-shekels (IV.1.2).*

4 coins (out of 7), with 4 pairs and 3 obverse dies (fig. A3.8). The ratio n:o = 1.33:1 is also very low.

The volume of issues has increased (80 coins instead of 34), similarly the number of die pairs (28 instead of 19), and of obverse dies (17 instead of 15).

4. *Group IV.1: ʾElpaʿal*

Two changes occurred in the reverse types of Group IV.1: instead of the vulture standing over an incuse ram, there was a lion standing over a bull with an incuse body; the name of the king was inscribed above the lion: 'ʾElpaʿal'; in the following series, three other kings' names were inscribed on the coins. The difficulty consisted in establishing the relative chronology of these four kings. All authors concur in the belief that King ʾElpaʿal was the first. As a matter of fact, in his coinage the incuse method was used, partly in relief and partly in hollow, as in the preceding Group III; then this method was no longer used. We have classified four denominations in Group IV.1—the same denominations as in Group III: shekels, quarter-shekels, 16ths and half-16ths. There are some differences in the types of these four denominations, probably in order to distinguish them somehow other than by their weight. The shekels (IV.1.1) have three warriors and a complete inscription on the reverse: *ʾLPʿL/MLK GBL*, on two lines. The quarter-shekels (IV.1.2), in most cases, have *ʾLPʿL M*[and the end of the inscription missing (off the flan?). The 16ths (IV.1.3) have one or two

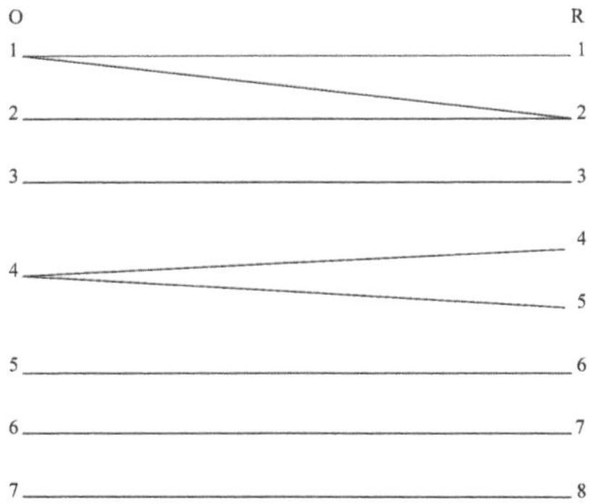

Fig. A3.11. *Dies of ʾElpaʿal's 16th-shekels (IV.1.3).*

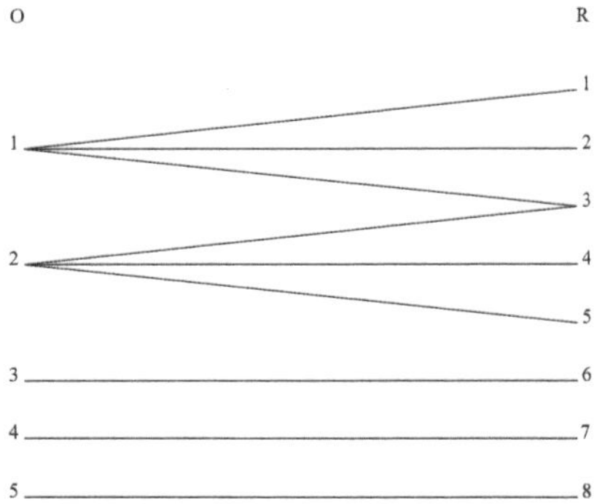

Fig. A3.12. *Dies of ʾElpaʿal's half-16th-shekels (IV.1.4).*

warriors, and apparently no line of waves and no shell on the obverse, and no inscription on the reverse. The half-16ths (IV.1.4), on the obverse, have one warrior, one line of waves, and neither seahorse nor shell; they have a seated lion on the reverse. The attribution of Series IV.1.4 to ʾElpaʿal's coinage is based on the iconography and is confirmed by the metallic composition of its coins.[16]

The IV.1.1 series of shekels is only represented by 6 coins (out of 12; fig. A3.9). We have identified 5 die pairs and 3 obverse dies. O1 is linked with R1, R2, and R3, which are therefore linked together; O2 is linked with R4 and O3 with R5; O4, R6, R7, and R8 are isolated. The ratio of n:o is low (2:1). The IV.1.2 series of quarter-shekels is represented by 18 coins (out of 27), with 13 pairs and 7 obverse dies (fig. A3.10). O1 is linked with R1, R2, and R3, and O2 with R3, R4, and R5: this means that O1 is linked with O2, and R1 to R5 are linked together. O3 is linked with R6 and R7, which is linked with O4: therefore O3 and O4, and R6 and R7 are linked together. O5 is linked with R8 and R9, which are linked together. O6 is linked with R10 and O7 with R11; R12 and R13 are isolated. The ratio of n:o = 2.57:1, which means that this series is insufficiently known. Series IV.1.3 (16th-shekels) is represented by 9 coins (out of 31), with 9 die pairs and 7 obverse dies (fig. A3.11). O1 is linked with R1 and R2, which is linked with O2; R1 and R2 are therefore linked together. O3 is linked with R3, O4 with R4 and R5 (linked together), O5 with R6, O6 with R7, and O7 with R8. The ratio of n:o = 1.29:1. Series IV.1.4 (half-16ths) is represented by 11 coins (out of 17), with 9 die pairs and 5 obverse dies (fig. A3.12). O1 is linked with R1, R2,

16. Cf. Elayi, Blet-Lemarquand, and Elayi, "Silver Coinage Fluctuations at Byblos."

and R3; O2 with R3, R4, and R5: therefore, O1 and O2 are linked together, and R–R5 as well. O3 is linked with R6, O4 with R7, and O5 with R8. The ratio of n:o = 2.20:1, which means that this series is insufficiently known.

The volume of issues has slightly increased (87 coins instead of 80); similarly, the number of die pairs (36 instead of 28) and of obverse dies (22 instead of 17).

5. *Group IV.2: ʿOzbaʿal*

In Group IV.2, the incuse method was no longer used and the name of the king was changed, but the types remained the same. The chronology of the last three kings of Byblos has been much debated because there has been no way to distinguish the order of their coinages based on the typology. Four classifications have been proposed, successively, without conclusive evidence:

ʿAynel – ʿOzbaʿal – ʾUrimilk,[17]
ʿOzbaʿal – ʿAynel – ʾUrimilk,[18]
ʾUrimilk – ʿOzbaʿal – ʿAynel,[19]
ʿOzbaʿal – ʾUrimilk – ʿAynel,[20]

We had already chosen the last hypothesis because of the following arguments: ʿAynel seemed to correspond to King Enylos in classical sources, on the throne in 333 B.C.E., and ʿOzbaʿal seemed to correspond to the usurper king mentioned in the Batnoʿam inscription *KAI* 11;[21] moreover, some

17. J. P. Six, "Observations sur les monnaies phéniciennes," *NC* 17 (1877) 180–182. The correct reading is now ʾUrimilk and not ʾAddirmilk: see chap. 3.

18. Head, *Historia Numorum*, 791; *BMC Phoenicia*, lxvi-lxviii; *SNG Copenhagen*, 37 (1961) nos. 132–34; D. Baramki, *Phoenicia and the Phoenicians* (Beirut, 1961) 81.

19. Babelon, *Perses*, clxvi–clxvii; Rouvier, "Numismatique des villes," 40–42; Babelon, *Traité*, part 2/2, col. 534; *Catalogue De Luynes*, 143–45; P. R. Franke and M. Hirmer, *Die Griechische Münzen* (Munich, 1964) pl. 195; Kraay, *Greek Coins*, 290; P. Naster, "L'ordre de succession des rois de Byblos d'après leurs monnaies," *BSFN* 20 (1965) 478; idem, "Trésors de monnaies de Byblos du IVe siècle av. J.-C. trouvées à Byblos," in *Numismatique et histoire économique phéniciennes et puniques* (ed. T. Hackens and G. Moucharte; Studia Phoenicia 9; Louvain-la-Neuve, 1992) 41–49.

20. Dunand, *Byblos I*, 407–9 and pl. 91 (however, in *Byblos, Son histoire, ses ruines, ses légendes* [Paris, 1963] 35, he put a king 'Urimilk' between ʾAddirmilk and ʿAynel); J. B. Peckham, *The Development of the Late Phoenician Scripts* (Cambridge, 1968) 47–50, proposes without any argument, to add a fifth unknown king *ZKR* (?) before or after Addirmilk; Betlyon, *Coinage of Phoenicia*, 118–22, followed by É. Puech in *RB* 92 (1985) 288.

21. J. Elayi, "Les monnaies phéniciennes de Byblos," *BFSN* 41 (1986) 13–16; idem, "Le monnayage de Byblos," *BSFN* 41 (1986) 13–16; idem, "Le monnayage de Byblos avant Alexandre: problèmes et perspectives," *Trans* 1 (1989) 17–18; Elayi-Elayi, *Trésors*, 92–115.

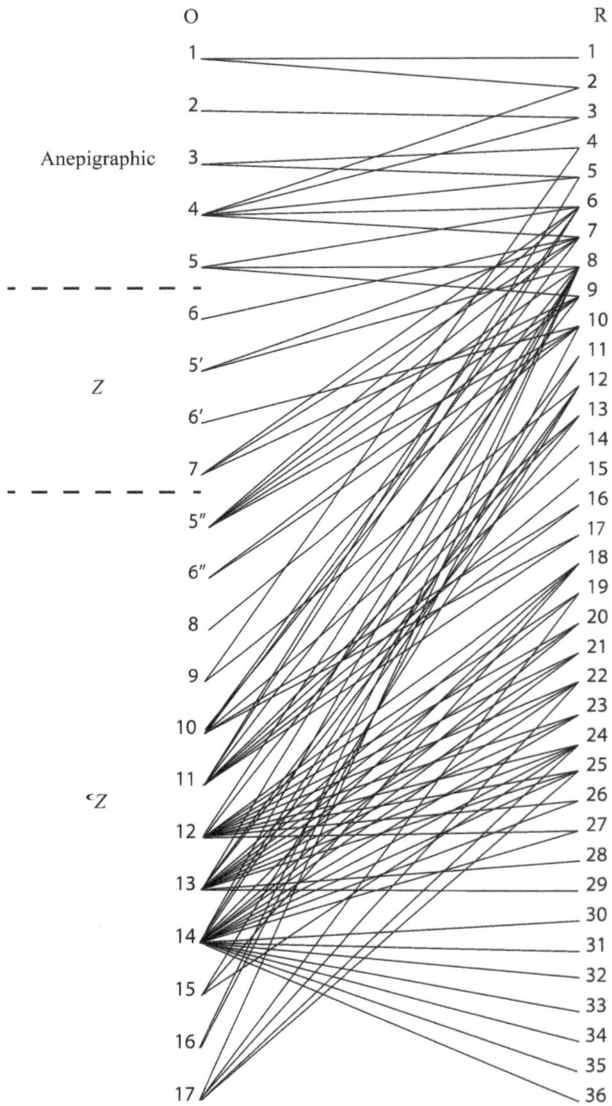

Fig. A3.13. *Dies of ʿOzbaʿal's shekels (IV.2.1).*

tetradrachms of Alexander issued by the mint of Byblos bear the letters *ʿY*, probably the first two letters of *ʿYNʾL*, who was therefore the last king of the Persian period.[22] These arguments were interesting but the order ʿOzbaʿal –

22. E. T. Newell, *Alexander Hoards II. Demanhur 1905* (New York, 1923) 3586; Arr., *An.* II, 20.1.

ʾUrimilk – ʿAynel remained a hypothesis. By chance, new elements appeared which were conclusive. In the abundant hoards, found during the 1980s (TXIII, TXIV, TXV?) that we have published, we have demonstrated that ʾUrimilk had reused ʿOzbaʿal's obverse dies and that ʿAynel had reused ʾUrimilk's obverse dies.[23] The order of the last three kings of Byblos was definitively established. Moreover, this order was further confirmed by some die links as we shall see.

Two changes occurred in ʿOzbaʿal's coinage. The incuse method of the reverse was no longer used, and the inscription changed: letters on some obverse series, and the name of the king and his title on the reverse. There were only two denominations in Group IV.2: shekels and 16th-shekels, but some of the unclassified coins (Group V) may belong to this group. The only difference between the two denominations is the number of warriors: there are three on the shekels and two on the 16ths. These could be a means of differentiation, even though the size difference was easy to distinguish. The obverse of the 16th-shekels bears only the letters ʿ and *Z*. We propose that the obverse of the shekels be categorized in three series: (1) anepigraphic (IV.2.1.a), (2) with the letter *Z* (IV.2.1.b), and (3) with the letters ʿ*Z* (IV.2.1.c). The reasoning behind this proposal is this: some of the first Phoenician series are anepigraphic; the inscription on the reverse is a horizontal line on part of Series IV.2.1.a, as in the preceding Series III.1.1; there are die links among the three series, as we shall see.

There is an abundant supply of ʿOzbaʿal shekels: 459 coins (in contrast to 12 ʾElpaʿal shekels), that is: 36 coins with an anepigraphic obverse, 13 coins with a *Z*, and 410 coins with ʿ*Z* (by far the most abundant). The series of ʿOzbaʿal's shekels (IV.2.1) is represented by 294 coins (out of 459). We have identified 97 die pairs and 17 obverse dies (fig. A3.13). O1 is linked with R1 and R2; O2 with R3; O3 with R4 and R5; O4 with R2, R3, R5, R6, and R7; O5 with R6, R8, and R9; and O6 with R7. Therefore, O1–O6 and R1–R9 are linked together. O5 and O6 were recut with the addition of *Z*. O5′ is linked with R7–R8; O6′ with R10; and O7 with R6, R7, and R9. Therefore, O1–O7 and R1–R10 are linked together. O5′ and O6′ were recut with the addition of ʿ to *Z*. O5″ is linked with R6–R10, and O6″ with R9–R10. O8 is linked with R10; O9 with R4 and R12; O10 with R6–R8, R13, R16, and R17. O11 is linked with R6, R7, R9, and R13–R17. O12 is linked with R8, R11, and R18–R27. O13 is linked with R8, R12, R13, R18–R25, and R28–R29. O14 is linked with R8, R11, R12, R18, R20–R27, and R30–R36. O15 is linked with R12, R18, and R24; O16 with R9 and R11; O17 with R8, R19, R22, and

23. J. Elayi and A. G. Elayi, "L'ordre de succession des derniers rois de Byblos," *Syr* 70 (1993) 109–115.

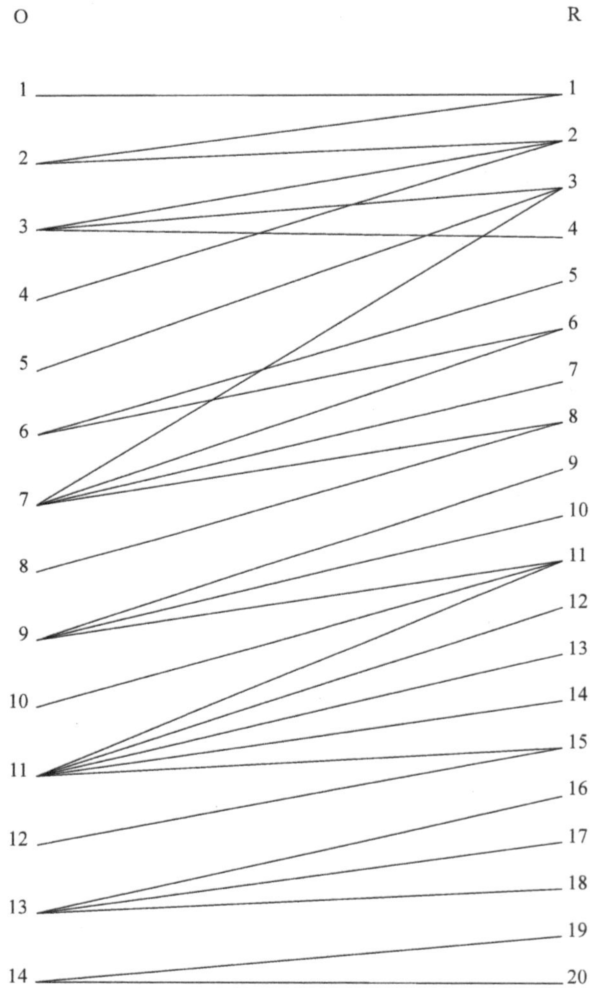

Fig. A3.14. *Dies of ʿOzbaʿal's 16th-shekels (IV.2.2).*

R24–R25. Therefore, O1–O17 are linked together, just as are R1–R36. There are also one isolated obverse (O18) and four isolated reverses (R37–R40).

We must point out that two obverse dies in this series were recut twice (O5′, O5″, O6′, O6″); that O13 has been used with 13 obverse dies; and O14 and O12 with 12 obverse dies. The ratio of n:o = 17.29:1, which means that this series is very well known.

The series of 16th-shekels (IV.2.2) is much less abundant than the series of shekels: 35 coins (out of 45). We have identified 30 pairs and 14 obverse dies (fig. A3.14). In the first two groups of dies, O1 is linked with R1, O2 with R1–R2, O3 with R2–R4, O4 with R2, O5 with R3, and O6 with

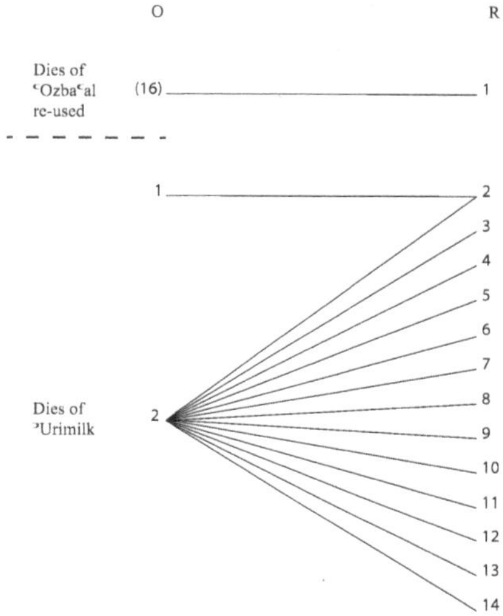

Fig. A3.15. *Dies of ʾUrimilk's shekels (IV.3.1).*

R5–R6. O7 is linked with R3 and R6–R8; O8 is linked with R8, O9 with R9–R11, O10 with R11, O11 with R11–R15, and O12 with R15. Therefore, O1–O8 and O9 to O12 are linked together, just as are R1–R8 and R9–R15. In a third group of dies, O13 is linked with R16–R18, thus linked together. In a fourth group of dies, O14 is linked with R19–R20, thus linked together. Two obverse dies are isolated: O15 and O16. O16 was reused by ʾUrimilk, as we shall see. The ratio of n:o = 2.50:1, which means that this series is not well known/represented.

On the whole, the number of coins issued has increased considerably (504 coins instead of 87); so has the number of die pairs (127 instead of 36) and obverse dies (34 instead of 25). We explain the reasons for this spectacular increase in chap. 5.

6. *Group IV.3: ʾUrimilk*

The only change in ʾUrimilk's coinage was the change of inscription: the letters *ʾK* on the obverse; the name of the new king and his title on the reverse. As in the preceding group, there are only two denominations in Group IV.3: shekels and 16th-shekels, but some of the unclassified denominations (Group V) may belong to this group. The only difference between the two denominations is again the number of warriors: three on the shekels, two on the 16ths.

The series of ʾUrimilk's shekels (IV.3.1) is represented by 63 coins (out of 74). We have identified 15 die pairs and 3 obverse dies, one of them being O16 of ʿOzbaʿal, which was reused by his successor (fig. A3.15). O16 of

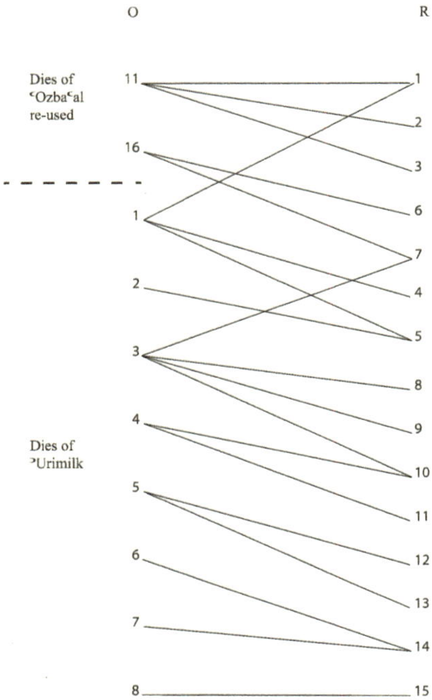

Fig. A3.16. *Dies of ʾUrimilk's 16th-shekels (IV.3.2).*

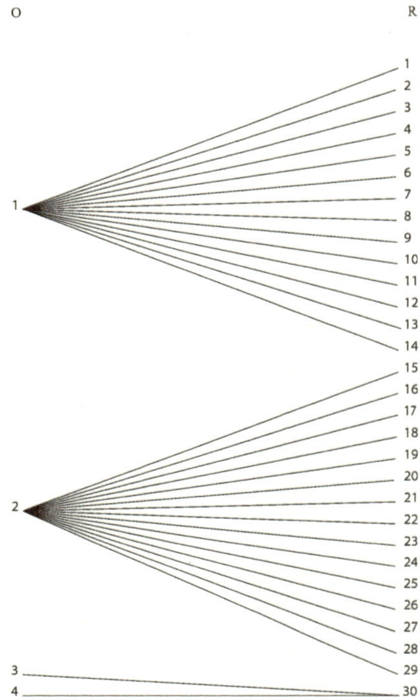

Fig. A3.17. *Dies of ʿAynel's shekels (IV.4.1).*

ʿOzbaʿal is linked with R1. O1 is linked with R2. O2 is linked with 13 different reverses: R2–R14. Therefore, O16 of ʿOzbaʿal and O1–O2 of ʾUrimilk are linked together, just as are R1–R14. What is important is that Series IV.2.1 of ʿOzbaʿal and Series IV.3.1 of ʾUrimilk are linked together. The ratio of n:o = 21:1, which means that this series is the best known of all the Byblian series.

The series of 16th-shekels (IV.3.2) is represented by 23 coins (out of 40). We have identified 20 die pairs and 10 obverse dies. Two of them (O11 and O16) belong to ʿOzbaʿal, ʾUrimilk's predecessor (fig. A3.16). In a first group of dies, O11 of ʿOzbaʿal is linked with R1, R2, and R3; O16 of ʿOzbaʿal is linked with R6 and R7. Then O1 of ʾUrimilk is linked with R1, R4, and R5; O2 with R5; O3 with R7, R8, R9, and R10; O4 with R10 and R11. Therefore, O11 and O16 of ʿOzbaʿal and O1–O4 of ʾUrimilk are linked together, just as are R1–R11. In a second group of dies, O5 is linked with R12 and R13, which are thus linked together. In a third group, O6 and O7 are linked with R14, and thus linked together. There is an isolated pair: O8–R15 and an isolated reverse (R16). What is important is that Series IV.2.2 of ʿOzbaʿal and Series IV.3.2 of ʾUrimilk are linked together. The ratio of n:o = 2.30:1, which means that this series is much less well-known than the preceding series.

The volume of issues has considerably decreased (114 coins in contrast to 504); similarly, the number of die pairs (35 instead of 127) and of obverse dies (13 instead of 31) has decreased. We explain the reasons for this important decrease in chap. 5.

7. *Group IV.4: ʿAynel*

There was no change in the iconography of ʿAynel's coins—only changes in the inscriptions: no more inscription on the obverse, name of the new king and title on the reverse, or various abbreviations. As in the preceding group, there were the same two denominations: shekels and 16th-shekels, with 3 and 2 warriors, respectively, on the deck of the galley. Besides these two series, there were five other series of small denominations: quarter-shekels with *ʿG* (IV.4.3), possibly 16th-shekels with *ʿMG*? (IV.4.4), 16ths with *ʿG* (IV.4.5), 16ths with *GL* (IV.4.6), and anepigraphic 16ths (IV.4.7).

The series of ʿAynel's shekels (IV.4.1) is represented by 77 coins (out of 80). We have identified 31 die pairs with 4 obverse dies (fig. A3.17). O1 is linked with 14 reverse dies: R1–R14, which are thus linked together. O2 is linked with 15 reverse dies: R15–R29, which are thus linked together. O3 and O4 are linked with R30 and thus linked together. The ratio of n:o = 19.25:1, which means that this series is very well known.

The series of 16th-shekels (IV.4.2) is the most abundant of Byblian coinage. It is represented by 310 coins (out of 508). We have identified 166 die pairs and 33 obverse dies, 7 of them being ʾUrimilk's obverse dies (O9–O15; fig. A3.18a).[24] None of these 7 obverse dies has been encountered in Series IV.3.2 of ʾUrimilk. First, we examine 7 obverses: O9 is linked with R1. O10 is linked with R2–R4; O11 with R4–R7; O12 with R6–R11; O13 with R5, R6, and R12–R16; O14 with R2, R6, R8, R9, R12, R17, R18, and R19. O15 is linked with 26 reverse dies: R2, R3, R5, R6, R8, R9, R10, R12, R13, R14, R16, R17, R18, and R20–R32. Therefore, O9–O15 are linked together, just as are R2–R32.

Then we examine ʿAynel's obverse dies: O1 is linked with R5; O2 with R10 and R13. O3 was the most frequently used obverse die, because it is linked with 30 reverse dies: R1–R3, R6, R8, R9, R11–R18, R20, R22, R23, R25,

24. It was difficult to represent such a large number of dies and links in fig. A3.18a–c: to make it easier, the reverse dies are repeated as often as necessary. The repeated numbers are in italics.

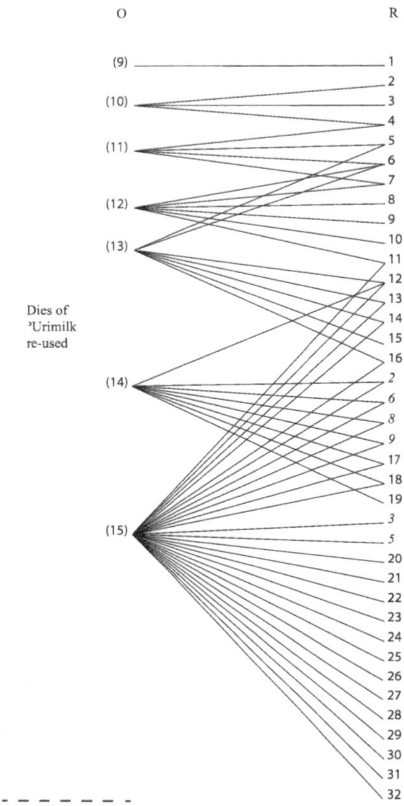

Fig. A3.18a. *Dies of ʿAynel's 16th-shekels (IV.4.1), part 1.*

R26, R33–R42, and R51. O4 is linked with R15 and R20; O5 with R9 and R43; O6 with R35; O7 with R22 and R27; O8 with R27; O9 with R24; O10 with R32. O11 is linked with 11 reverse dies: R2, R3, R5, R9, R11, R12, R15, R22, R23, R35, and R44. O12 is also linked with 10 obverse dies: R4, R12, R20, R39, and R45–R50. O13 is linked with R6, R12, R16, R18, and R49. O14 is linked with R8, R12, R13, R21, and R49. O15 is linked with R6, R9, and R12; O16 with R9 and R18; O17 with R9, R16, R17, R20, R28, and R38; O18 with R17; O19 with R38; O20 with R8, R11, and R12; O21 with R5, R9, R20, R38, and R45; O22 with R11–R13 and R17. R23 is linked with R2, R9, R19, R42, R46, and R50; O24 with R13, R51, and R52. Therefore, O1–O24 are linked together and to the 7 obverse dies of ʾUrimilk; R1–R52 are linked together. O25 is linked with R53 and R54, which are thus linked together. The pair O26–R55 is isolated. There are 3 isolated obverse dies (O27–O29). What is important is that Series IV.4.2 of ʿAynel and Series IV.3.2 of ʾUrimilk are linked together. The ratio of n:o = 9.39:1, which means that Series IV.4.2 is well known, however not as well as Series IV.4.1 of ʿAynel's shekels.

The series of quarter-shekels (IV.4.3) and the series of 16ths (IV.4.5) do not bear the name of ʿAynel explicitly, as the two preceding series did, but only the letters ʿ and *G*. E. Babelon and J. Babelon hesitated to attribute these two series to either ʿOzbaʿal or ʿAynel without providing a basis for their decision.[25] The attribution to ʿAynel is based on several arguments.[26]

25. E. Babelon, *Perses*, 196, no. 1368, followed by J. Babelon, *Catalogue De Luynes*, 145, no. 3153. Cf. Betlyon, *Coinage of Phoenicia*, 121 (ʿAynel, with no argumentation provided).

26. J. Elayi and A. G. Elayi, "Deux séries monétaires de Byblos avec ʿG," *NAC* 39 (2010) 127–39.

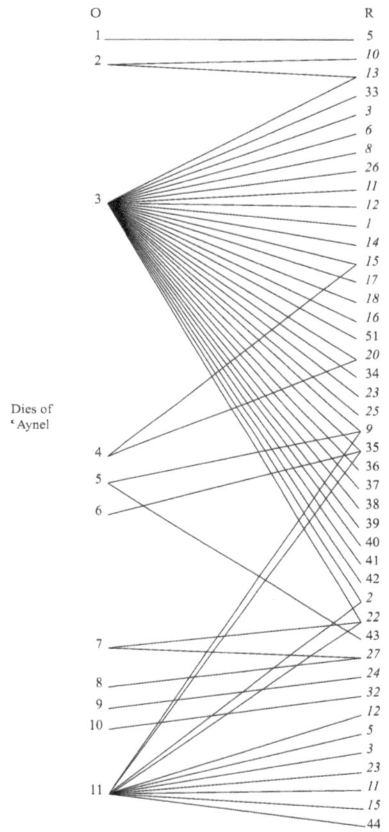

Fig. A3.18b. *Dies of ʿAynel's 16th-shekels (IV.4.1), part 2.*

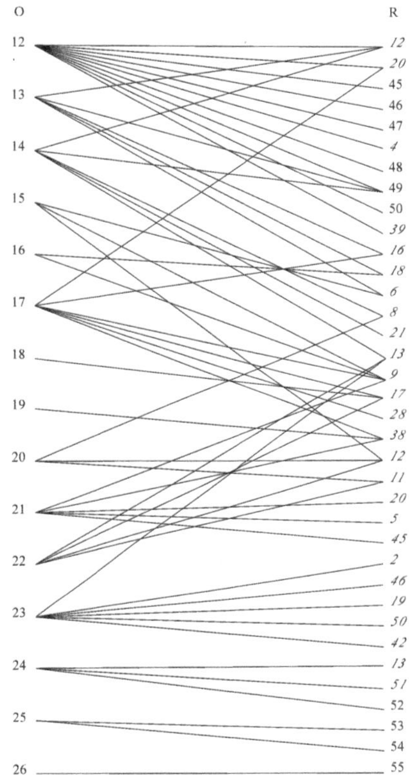

Fig. A3.18c. *Dies of ʿAynel's 16th-shekels (IV.4.1), part 3.*

Some coins of these series (nos. 1479, 1482, 1483, 1498, and 1499) bear the two-pronged ankh on the reverse, under the stomach of the lion, as on some ʿAynel's shekels. As we have seen in chap. 3, the first engraver of Series IV.4.5 also worked on Series IV.4.1. of ʿAynel. Similar defects occurred in these two series. Some 16ths with *ʿG* were overstruck, probably on 16th-shekels from Series IV.4.2, with the complete inscription of ʿAynel. In the Byblos hoard TLXXX, Series IV.4.5 16th-shekels are associated with ʿAynel's Series IV.4.2 16th-shekels;[27] in this hoard, there were only 4 of ʾUrimilk's 16ths and none of ʿOzbaʿal's.

27. J. Elayi and A. G. Elayi, "Nouveau trésor de monnaies de Byblos (1992)," *RBN* 139 (1993) 17–30.

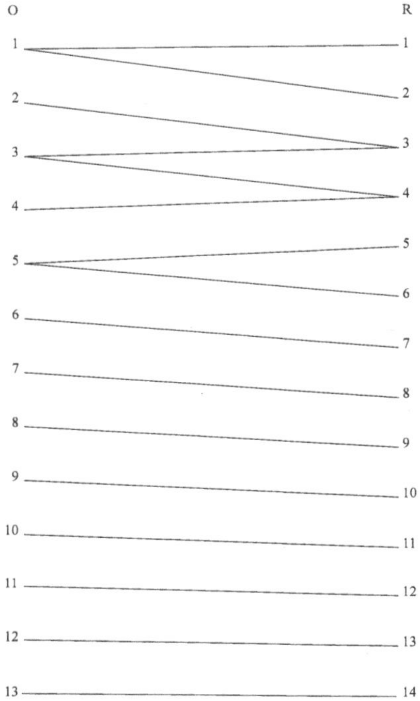

Fig. A3.19. *Dies of 16th-shekels with ʿG (IV.4.4).*

Our first die analysis of Byblian Series IV.4.3 and IV.4.5[28] can now be updated with new specimens, new observations, and a reexamination of dies. Series IV.4.3 is only represented by 3 coins (out of 4), with 3 coins and 3 isolated die pairs (O1–R1, O2–R2, O3–R3) and one isolated obverse die (O4). It is not quite clear whether coin no. 1478 bears the inscription ʿ*MG* (Series IV.4.4). Series IV.4.5 is represented by 17 coins (out of 43). We have identified 16 die pairs with 13 obverse dies (fig. A3.19). O1 is linked with R1 and R2, which are thus linked together. O2 is linked with R3; O3 with R3 and R4; O4 with R4: therefore, O2, O3, and O4 are linked together, just as are R3 and R4. O5 is linked with R5 and R6, which are thus linked together. There are also 8 isolated die pairs: O6–R7, O7–R8, O8–R9, O9–R10, O10–R11, O11–R12, O12–R13, and O13–R14; 2 isolated obverse dies (O14, O15); and 6 isolated reverse dies (R15–R20). The ratio of n:o = 1.31:1.

Another series of 16th-shekels (IV.4.6) does not bear the name of ʿAynel but only the letters *G* and *L*. Without any supporting argument, this series was attributed to King ʿOzbaʿal by J. Rouvier, E. Babelon, and J. W. Betlyon.[29] It must be attributed to ʿAynel instead, for the following reasons. First, coin nos. 1529 and 1530 bear a two-pronged ankh on the reverse, as on some shekels issued by ʿAynel. Second, the engraver of the dies of this series also worked on the series of ʿAynel's shekels with the two-pronged ankh. Moreover, die flaws also characterized this series of shekels. The presence of coin no. 1530 in the Byblian hoard TLXXX[30] is also significant because this hoard comprises 73 16th-shekels of ʿAynel bearing the inscription " ʿAynel, King of Byblos" and only four fractional coin denominations

28. Cf. Elayi and Elayi, "Deux séries monétaires."

29. Rouvier, "Numismatique des villes de la Phénicie," 42; Babelon, *Perses*, no. 1369; Betlyon, *Coinage of Phoenicia*, 118.

30. Elayi-Elayi, "Nouveau trésor de monnaies de Byblos," 17–30.

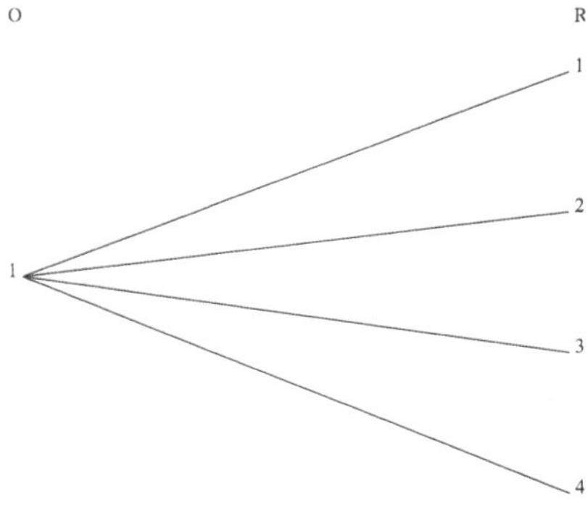

Fig. A3.20. *Dies of 16th-shekels with GL (IV.4.5).*

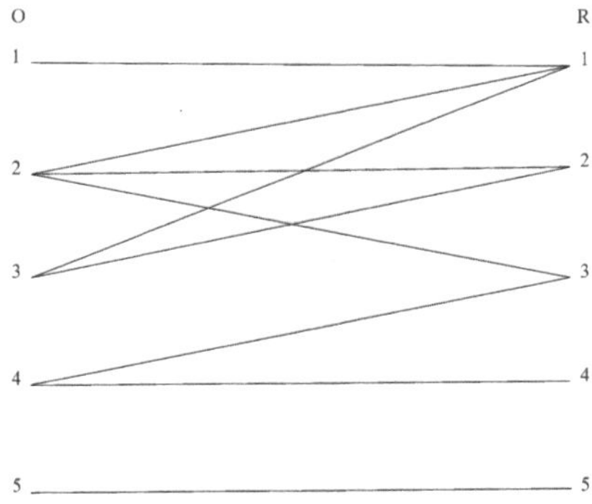

Fig. A3.21. *Dies of half-16th shekels (V.1).*

of ʾUrimilk. It is also associated with four 16ths in this hoard that bear the inscription *ʿG* and with two anepigraphic 16ths.[31]

Our first die analysis of Series IV.4.6[32] can now be updated with new observations and a reexamination of the dies. This series is only represented by 9 coins (out of 15), with 4 die pairs and 1 obverse die (fig. A3.20). O1 is linked with R1, R2, R3, and R4, which are thus linked together. This series is well known (n:o = 9:1), but what is important is that the obverse die O1 of Series IV.4.6 is the same as O1 in Series IV.4.5: therefore, the two series are linked together. Another series of 16th-shekels (IV.4.7), which is anepigraphic, seems to have the same style of engraving as Series IV.4.6, and we propose therefore to classify it at the end of ʿAynel's coinage as well. It is only represented by 3 coins (out of 7), with 2 die pairs and 1 obverse die. O1 is linked with R1 and R2, which are thus linked together. This series is not well known (n:o = 3:1).

The volume of issues has again increased considerably (658 coins instead of 114), just as has the number of die pairs (222 instead of 35) and obverse dies (61 instead of 13). We explain the reasons for this important increase in chap. 5.

8. *Group V: Unclassified Series*

A few series of denominations remain unclassified. On the obverse, the half-16ths of Series V.1 bear the same Byblian war-galley with two warriors

31. Idem, "A Series of Coins from Byblos with the Name of the City (4th Cent. BC)," *NC* (2010) 3–8.

32. Ibid.

and a winged seahorse and, on the reverse, a winged griffin, seated facing left, with a raised forepaw. This series is represented by 12 coins (out of 20), with 9 die pairs and 5 obverse dies (fig. A3.21). O1 is linked with R1; O2 with R1, R2, and R3; O3 with R1 and R2; O4 with R3 and R4: therefore, O1–O4 are linked together, just as are R1–R4. There is an isolated couple of dies (O5–R5) and an isolated reverse die (R6). This series is insufficiently known (of n:o = 2.40:1). We have collected only 2 coins for Series V.2, representing the war-galley, with one warrior on the obverse, and a stylized griffin's head on the reverse. The attribution of this series to the Byblos mint is not certain and is only based on H. Seyrig's discovery of some of them on the beach of Byblos.[33] Two die pairs were identified (O1–R1, O2–R2). We have collected only 5 coins for Series V.3, representing a bearded head on the obverse and a bearded head with *kausia* on the reverse. There are 2 pairs of dies (O1–R1, O2–R2) and 1 isolated reverse coin (R3).

9. *False or Dubious Byblian Coins*

In general (and unlike Sidonian and Tyrian coins), the problem of false attributions of coins to the Byblos mint or false attributions of Byblian coins to other mints has not been raised because the name *Byblos* is written explicitly on the coins, except for a few series. The question cannot be solved for some of the minute coins with uncertain motifs, which are at least partly Phoenician, but these could be Byblian or Aradian.[34] We hesitate regarding some coins that appear to be the usual Byblian types but are dubious or false (appendix 2). Coin no. 1* was published as false in the *Bulletin of Counterfeits*. Coin no. 2* has the two letters ʿZ on one horizontal line instead of being written vertically. Coin no. 3* has the wrong weight for a 16th-shekel. Coin no. 4* has *Z* instead of ʿZ on the obverse, and coin no. 5* has an incomprehensible legend on the reverse.

33. J. Elayi, "Une monnaie phénicienne de 0.05g," *RSF* 13 (1985) 1–4.
34. Ibid.

Appendix 4

Hoards Containing Coins from Byblos

In appendix 4, we list hoards that are mostly composed of coins from Byblos or that contain some coins from Byblos. The numbering system of the hoards is the same as in the corpus of Phoenician hoards that we published in 1993.[1] That corpus is herewith being updated to include the new discoveries and publications. Where necessary, we have corrected the burial dates based on the updated chronologies of Sidonian, Tyrian, and Byblian coinages.

- TII: hoard from the area of Arwad, end of 1983.[2]
- TIX: Byblos hoard, 1931.[3] This hoard was published in full in 2009 by J. Elayi and A. Lemaire[4] with the authorization of P. Naster and R. Doncel, thanks to the photographs and notes made by R. Doncel in the National Museum of Beirut in 1964. This documentation was completed by photographs of casts from the Israel Department of Antiquities and Museums, and by the archives of H. Seyrig in the BNF, Cabinet des Médailles. It contained 218 coins from Kings ʿOzbaʿal (139), ʾUrimilk (30), and ʿAynel (49) that are dated to the 4th century B.C.E., but it was probably buried during the Diadochi Wars. It may have been a reserve used by several individuals, perhaps in a family, for example.
- TX: Byblos hoard, 1933–38.[5]
- TXI: Byblos hoard, 1933–38.[6]

---

1. Elayi-Elayi, *Trésors*; for each hoard, we also mention the location and date of discovery.

2. Ibid., 35–43 = *CH* VIII, no. 123 = *CH* IX, no. 386; idem, "Nouveaux trésors de monnaies phéniciennes (*CH* VIII)," *Trans* 11 (1996) 99; idem, "Nouveaux trésors de monnaies phéniciennes (*CH* IX)," *Trans* 26 (2003) 109.

3. Elayi-Elayi, *Trésors*, 83–87 = *CH* IX, no. 435; idem, "Nouveaux trésors de monnaies phéniciennes (*CH* IX)," 112.

4. J. Elayi and A. Lemaire, "Le trésor de Byblos TIX," *Trans* 38 (2009) 77–98.

5. Elayi-Elayi, *Trésors*, 87–90 = *CH* IX, no. 356; idem, "Nouveaux trésors de monnaies phéniciennes (*CH* IX)," 106.

6. Idem, *Trésors*, 90–97 = *CH* IX, no. 437; idem, "Nouveaux trésors de monnaies phéniciennes (*CH* IX)," 113.

- TXII: Byblos hoard, 1957.[7]
- TXIII, TXIV, TXV (?): Byblos hoards, beginning of March 1983, end of 1984/beginning of 1985, 1988 (?).[8] These three hoards were all found in Byblos in illegal excavations during the Lebanese civil war. We have presented them together because we were unable to assemble any clear information on them individually, because they were scattered throughout the antiquities market. We were able to study 496 coins, which only represent some of the coins in these hoards. The hoard of 400 shekels from Byblos reported to have been found in Beirut in around 1983 probably corresponds to our hoard TXIII.[9] The hoard of the 12 so-called Byblian fractions (one of them being Tyrian) is also probably from our hoards TXIII–TXV (?).[10]
- TXVI: Phoenician hoard, 1947.[11]
- TXVII: hoard from North Syria, 1953.[12] This small hoard contained at least 4 coins: 3 Byblian shekels and 1 Persian shekel. Because the Phoenician coins were only represented by Byblian coins from Group I, we have considered this hoard, which was buried slightly before 450 B.C.E., to be the oldest hoard containing Phoenician coins.
- TXXIII: Qasr Naba hoard, beginning of 1902.[13]
- TXXIV: Qasr Naba hoard, 1929–67.[14]
- TXLII: Byblos hoard, 1931.[15] We studied the relationship between hoards TIX and TXLII because they were found together by M. Dunand.[16]

---

7. Idem, *Trésors*, 91–92 = *CH* IX, no. 438; idem, "Nouveaux trésors de monnaies phéniciennes (*CH* IX)," 113.

8. Idem, *Trésors*, 92–114.

9. *CH* VIII, no. 118; idem, "Nouveaux trésors de monnaies phéniciennes (*CH* VIII)," 98–99.

10. *CH* VIII, no. 120; ibid., 99; *CH* IX, nos. 373, 374, and 439; idem, "Nouveaux trésors de monnaies phéniciennes (*CH* IX)," 108.

11. Idem, *Trésors*, 114–15 = *CH* IX, no. 443; idem, "Nouveaux trésors de monnaies phéniciennes (*CH* IX)," 113.

12. Idem, *Trésors*, 115–16 = *CH* IX, no. 357; idem, "Nouveaux trésors de monnaies phéniciennes (*CH* IX)," 106.

13. Idem, *Trésors*, 133–37 = *CH* IX, no. 445; idem, "Nouveaux trésors de monnaies phéniciennes (*CH* IX)," 113.

14. Idem, *Trésors*, 137–39 = *CH* IX, no. 425; idem, "Nouveaux trésors de monnaies phéniciennes (*CH* IX)," 111.

15. Idem, *Trésors*, 201 = *CH* IX, no. 436; idem, "Nouveaux trésors de monnaies phéniciennes (*CH* IX)," 112.

16. Cf. also Dunand, *Byblos I*, 407–9; A. R. Bellinger, "An Alexander Hoard from Byblos," *Berytus* 10 (1950–51) 37–49; P. Naster, "Trésors de monnaies de Byblos du IVe s. av. J.-C. trouvés à Byblos," in *Numismatique et histoire économiques dans le monde phénico-*

- TXLIII: hoard from the area of Beirut, autumn 1966.[17] This hoard contained, among other things, one small denomination from Arwad, 3 from Byblos, 7 from Sidon, and 12 from Tyre (of which 6 are bronze).
- TLI: Naplouse hoard, 1968.[18] This hoard is erroneously called the "first Naplouse hoard," whereas hoard TL was found much earlier (about 1891) in Naplouse or in the area of Naplouse.[19]
- TLXIV: Tigris hoard, 1810–August 1816.[20] The Phoenician coins of this hoard consisted of several Sidonian coins, some Byblian coins, one Aradian small denomination, and 7 Tyrian shekels of Series II.1.2 (around 393–358 B.C.E.). The date of burial proposed, 330 B.C.E., is not disputed.[21]
- TLXXX: hoard from the Middle East, 1990–92.[22] This hoard contained 393 coins; among them at least 302 were 16th-shekels from Byblos, and we have published 92 of them, which had been cleaned. Four 16th-shekels out of a lot of 75 were published by A. Ronde:[23] after having examined this lot, we have concluded that they belonged to the same hoard. It was probably buried between ca. 339 and 335 B.C.E.
- TLXXXIII: Byblos hoard, around 1960.[24] This new hoard, which we have studied by using the archives of H. Seyrig, consists of 54 silver coins (staters and small denominations) and 3 silver fragments. Most of the coins (24) are Byblian coins; the hoard also contains 8 Tyrian coins, 5 Sidonian, 1 Athenian, 1 Lycian, and 5 uncertain fractions. The hoard was buried during the last quarter of the 5th century B.C.E.

---

punique (ed. T. Hackens and G. Moucharte; Studia Phoenicia 9; Louvain-la-Neuve, 1992) 41–49.

17. Elayi-Elayi, *Trésors*, 201–6 = *CH* VIII, no. 90; idem, "Nouveaux trésors de monnaies phéniciennes (*CH* VIII)," 98 = *CH* IX, no. 404; idem, "Nouveaux trésors de monnaies phéniciennes (*CH* IX)," 110.

18. Idem, *Trésors*, 231–39 = *CH* IX, no. 440; idem, "Nouveaux trésors de monnaies phéniciennes (*CH* IX)," 113.

19. Idem, *Trésors*, 231.

20. Ibid., 270–73.

21. *CH* IX, no. 450; idem, "Nouveaux trésors de monnaies phéniciennes (*CH* IX)," 114.

22. J. Elayi and A. G. Elayi, "Nouveau trésor de monnaies de Byblos (1992)," *RBN* 139 (1993) 17–30 = *CH* IX, no. 432; idem, "Nouveaux trésors de monnaies phéniciennes (*CH* IX)," 112, 116.

23. A. Ronde, "Étude sommaire de trois 'trésors' proches-orientaux de provenance incertaine," *BSFN* 57/4 (2002) 57–62.

24. J. Elayi and A. G. Elayi, "Nouveau trésor de Byblos d'après les archives de H. Seyrig (TLXXXIII)," *Trans* 38 (2009) 65–76.

In total, 16 out of the 84 hoards containing Phoenician coins include coins from Byblos. This is considerably fewer than Sidonian coins, which are represented in 47 hoards,[25] and Tyrian coins, which appear in 40 hoards.[26]

25. Idem, *Monnayage de Sidon*, 695–99. The last published hoard (TLXXXIII) contains 78 Aradian coins and 2 Sidonian double shekels: idem, "Un nouveau trésor d'Arwad du 4e s. av. J.-C.," *RN* 167 (2011) 403–21.

26. Idem, *Coinage of Tyre*, 397–402.

Bibliography

Agut-Labordère, D. "Les frontières intérieures de la société militaire égyptienne: l'Invasion de l'Égypte par Artaxerxès III à travers Diodore XVI, 46–45." *Trans* 35 (2007) 17–27.

Anson, E. A. "The Persian Fleet in 334." *CP* 84 (1989) 44–49.

Avigad, N., and Sass, B. *Corpus of West Semitic Stamp Seals*. Jerusalem, 1997.

Badian, E. "Darius III." *HSCP* 100 (2000) 241–68.

________. "The King's Peace." Pp. 25–48 in *Georgica: Greek Studies in Honor of G. Cawkwell*. BICSSup 58. London, 1991.

________. "The Peace of Callias." *JHS* 107 (1987) 1–39.

Barrandon, J.-N., and Guerra, M. F. "Méthodes d'analyse appliquées à la numismatique." Pp. 825–30 in *A Survey of Numismatic Research 1990–1995*, ed. C. Morrisson and B. Kluge. Berlin, 1997.

Basch, L. "Phoenician Oared Ship. Part II." *The Mariner's Mirror* 55 (1969) 139–162.

Bellinger, A. R. "An Alexander Hoard from Byblos." *Ber* 10 (1950–51) 37–49.

Bérend, D. "Réflexions sur les fractions du monnayage grec." Pp. 7–30 in *Studies in Honor of Leo Mildenberg*, ed. A. Houghton et al. Wetteren, 1984.

Bickerman, E. J. "Notes sur la chronologie de la XXXe dynastie." Pp. 77–82 in *Mélanges Maspéro*, vol. 1. Cairo, 1934.

Bisi, A. M. *Il grifone*. Rome, 1965.

Bivar, A. D. H. "A Persian Monument at Athens and Its Connections with the Achaemenid State Seals." Pp. 43–61 in *W. B. Henning: Memorial Volume*. London, 1970.

Blanco Freijeiro, A., et al. *Ancient Mining and Metallurgy in South-West Spain*. London, 1982.

Blau, O. "Azubal König von Byblos." *NZ* 8 (1876) 229–32.

Bloedow, E. "The Peace of Callias." *SO* 67 (1992) 41–68.

Bogaert, P.-M. "Le Chérub de Tyr (Ez 28, 14.16) et l'hippocampe de ses monnaies." Pp. 29–38 in *Prophetie und geschichtliche Wirklichkeit in alter Israel: Festschrift für S. Herrmann*, ed. R. Liwak and S. Wagner. Stuttgart, 1991.

Bonnet, C. *Astarté: Dossier documentaire et perspectives historiques*. Rome, 1996.

________. *Melqart: Cultes et mythes de l'Héraclès tyrien en Méditerranée*. Leuven, 1988.

Bordreuil, P. "Astarté, la dame de Byblos." *CRAIBL* (1998) 1153–64.

Bosworth, A. B. *From Arrian to Alexander: Studies in Historical Interpretation*. Oxford, 1988.

________. "Plutarch, Callisthenes and the Peace of Callias." *JHS* 110 (1990) 1–13.

Bouyon, B., et al., *Systèmes et technologie des monnaies de bronze (4e s. avant J.-C.–3e s. après J.-C.)*. Wetteren, 2000.

Brandis, J. *Das Münz-, Mass- und Gewichtswesen in Vorderasien bis aus Alexander den Grossen*. Berlin, 1866.

Briant, P. *Darius dans l'ombre d'Alexandre*. Paris, 2003.

________. *From Cyrus to Alexander: A History of the Persian Empire*. Winona Lake, IN, 2002.

________. "Histoire et idéologie: les Grecs et la 'décadence perse.'" Pp. 33–47 in *Mélanges P. Lévêque*, vol. 2. Paris, 1989.

Briant, P., and Descat, R. "Un registre douanier de la satrapie d'Égypte à l'époque achéménide (*TAD* C3, 7)." Pp. 59–104 in *Le commerce en Égypte ancienne*, ed. N. Grimal and B. Menu. Cairo, 1996.

Brosius, M. "Why Persia Became the Enemy of Macedon." Pp. 173–187 in *A Persian Perspective: Essays in Memory of Heleen Sancisi-Weerdenburg*, ed. W. Henkelman and A. Kuhrt. Leiden, 2003.

Brown, J. P. *The Lebanon and Phoenicia*, vol. 1. Beirut, 1969.

Burstein, S. "Prelude to Alexander: The Reign of Khababash." *AHB* 14 (2000) 149–54.

Buttrey, S., and Buttrey, T. V. "Calculating Ancient Coin Production, Again." *AJN* 9 (1997) 113–35.

Buttrey, T. V. "Calculating Ancient Coin Production: Facts and Fantasies." *NC* 153 (1993) 335–51.

Callataÿ, F. de. "À propos du volume des émissions monétaires dans l'Antiquité." *RBN* 130 (1984) 37–48.

________. "Calculating Ancient Coin Production: Seeking a Balance." *NC* 155 (1995) 289–311.

________. "La dimension des coins monétaires de tétradrachmes hellénistiques d'après l'étude des monnaies décentrées." Pp. 244–51 in *XII. Internationaler Numismatischer Kongress: Berlin, 1997, Akten I*, ed. B. Kluge and B. Weisser. Berlin, 2000.

________. "L'estimation du nombre originel de coins: En augmentant l'échantillon." *Acta Numismatica* 21–23 (*Homenatge al Dr. Leandre Villaronga*; 1991–93) 31–48.

________. "Étude de technique monétaire: Le Rapport 'nombre de coins de revers/nombre de coins de droit' à l'époque hellénistique." *RAHAL* 32 (1999) 91–102.

________. "Les taux de survie des émissions monétaires antiques, médiévales et modernes: Essai de mise en perspective et conséquences quant à la productivité des coins dans l'Antiquité." *RN* (2000) 87–109.

________. "Le volume des émissions monétaires dans l'antiquité." *AIIN* 44 (1997) 53–62.

Callataÿ, F. de, et al. *L'argent monnayé d'Alexandre le Grand à Auguste*. Brussels, 1993.

Carrez-Maratray, J.-Y. "Psammétique le tyran: Pouvoir, usurpation et alliances en Méditerranée orientale au IVe s. av. J.-C." *Trans* 30 (2005) 37–63.

Carter, G. F. "Simplified Method for Calculating the Original Number of Dies from Die-Link Statistics." *ANSMN* 28 (1983) 195–206.

Casabonne, O. "Notes ciliciennes." *Anatolia Antiqua* 5 (1997) 35–38.

Casson, L. *Ships and Seamanship in the Ancient World*. Princeton, 1971.

Cau, N. "La classificacione delle monetazioni licie in età achemenide: Storia e problemi." *Annali* 44 (1997) 241–79.

Cawkwell, G. L. "Demosthenes' Policy after Peace of Philocrates I." *CQ* 13 (1963) 120–38.

Clermont-Ganneau, C. "Le paradeisos royal achéménide de Sidon." *RB* 30 (1921) 176–82.

Cooper, D. R. *The Art and Craft of Coinmaking: A History of Minting Technology*. London, 1988.

Cornelius, I. "The Lion in the Art of the Ancient Near East: A Study of Selected Motifs." *JNSL* 15 (1989) 53–79.

Cour-Marty, M.-A. "Les poids égyptiens, de précieux jalons archéologiques." *CRIPEL* 12 (1990) 17–55.

________. "Une norme pondérale dominante en Égypte pharaonique." *GöMisz* 69 (1983) 27–30.

Crowfoot, J. W., and Crowfoot, G. M. *Early Ivories*. London, 1938.

Dandamayev, M. "A Governor of Byblos in Sippar." Pp. 29–31 in *Immigration and Emigration within the Ancient Near East: Festschrift E. Lipiński*, ed. K. van Lerberghe and A. Schoors. Leuven, 1995.

Darnell, J. C. "The *Kbnt.wt* Ships of the Late Period." Pp. 67–89 in *Life in a Multicultural Society: Egypt from Cambyses to Constantine and Beyond*, ed. J. H. Johnson. Chicago, 1992.

Debord, P. *L'Asie Mineure au IVᵉ siècle (412–323 a.c.): Pouvoirs et jeux politiques*. Bordeaux, 1999.

Delplace, C. *Le griffon de l'archaïsme à l'époque impériale*. Brussels, 1980.

Dessenne, A. *Le Sphinx, étude iconographique*. Paris, 1957.

Destrooper-Georgiades, A. "Chypre et l'Égypte à l'époque achéménide à la lumière des témoignages numismatiques." *Trans* 9 (1995) 149–60.

Devauchelle, D. "Réflexions sur les documents égyptiens datés de la deuxième domination perse." *Trans* 10 (1995) 35–43.

Dhénin, M. "Quelques remarques sur le travail des graveurs de coins." Pp. 453–57 in *Rythmes de la production monétaire, de l'Antiquité à nos jours*, ed. G. Depeyrot et al. Louvain-la-Neuve, 1987.

Domergue, C. *Les mines de la Péninsule Ibérique dans l'Antiquité romaine*. Rome, 1989.

Dunand, M. "L'architecture à Byblos au temps des Achéménides." *BMB* 22 (1969) 93–99.

________. "La défense du front méditerranéen de l'Empire achéménide." Pp. 43–52 in *The Role of the Phoenicians in the Interaction of Mediterranean Civilizations: Archaeological Symposium at the American University of Beirut*, ed. W. A. Ward. Beirut, 1968.

________. "Rapport préliminaire sur les fouilles de Byblos en 1964." *BMB* 19 (1966) 95–101.

________. "Rapport préliminaire sur les fouilles de Byblos en 1965." *BMB* 20 (1967) 21–26.

Dunand, M., and Saliby, N. *Le Temple d'Amrit dans la pérée d'Aradus*. Paris, 1985.

Duyrat, F. *Arados hellénistique: Étude historique et monétaire*. Beirut, 2005.

Elayi, A. G.; Barrandon, J.-N.; and Elayi, J. "The Change of Standard of Tyrian Silver Coinage about 357 BCE as Determined by Fast Neutron Activation Analysis." *NC* (2008) 15–20.

________. "The Devaluation of Sidonian Coins in 365 B.C.E. as Determined by Fast Neutron Activation Analysis and First Bronze Issues." *AJN* 17 (2007) 1–8.

Elayi, A. G.; Blet-Lemarquand, M.; and Elayi, J. "Silver Coinage Fluctuations at Byblos (5th–4th cent. BCE) as Determined by LA-ICP-MS and FNAA," *AJN* (2012) 1–10.

Elayi, J. *ʿAbdʿaštart Ier/Straton de Sidon: Un Roi phénicien entre Orient et Occident.* Paris, 2005.

________. *Byblos, cité sacrée (8e–4e s. av. J.-C.).* Paris, 2009.

________. "Byblos et Sidon, deux modèles de cités phéniciennes à l'époque perse." *Trans* 35 (2008) 100–114.

________. "Les cités phéniciennes entre liberté et sujétion." *DHA* 16 (1990) 93–113.

________. "Étude paléographique des légendes monétaires phéniciennes d'époque perse." *Trans* 5 (1992) 21–43.

________. "Les monnaies de Byblos au sphinx et au faucon." *RSF* 11 (1983) 5–17.

________. "Le monnayage de Byblos avant Alexandre: Problèmes et perspectives." *Trans* 1 (1989) 9–20.

________. "L'ouverture du premier atelier monétaire phénicien." *BCEN* 32 (1995) 73–78.

________. *Pénétration grecque en Phénicie sous l'Empire perse.* Nancy, 1988.

________. "Remarques méthodologiques sur l'étude paléographique des légendes monétaires phéniciennes." Pp. 187–200 in *Phoinikeia Grammata: Lire et écrire en Méditerranée*, ed. C. Baurain et al. Namur, 1991.

________. "The Role of the Phoenician Kings at the Battle of Salamis (480 B.C.E.)." *JAOS* 126 (2006) 411–18.

________. "Les symboles de la puissance militaire sur les monnaies de Byblos." *RN* 26 (1984) 40–47.

________. "Tripoli (Liban) à l'époque perse." *Trans* 2 (1990) 59–71.

________. "Une monnaie phénicienne de 0,05 g." *RSF* 13 (1985) 1–4.

________. "An Updated Chronology of the Reigns of Phoenician Kings during the Persian Period (539–333 BCE)." *Trans* 32 (2006) 11–43.

Elayi, J., and Elayi, A. G. "Deux séries monétaires de Byblos avec ʿ*G*." *NAC* 39 (2010) 127–39.

________. "Nouveau trésor de Byblos d'après les archives de H. Seyrig (TLXXXIII)." *Trans* 38 (2009) 65–76.

________. "Nouveau trésor de monnaies de Byblos (1992)." *RBN* 139 (1993) 17–30.

________. "Nouveaux trésors de monnaies phéniciennes (*CH* VIII)." *Trans* 11 (1996) 95–114.

________. "Nouveaux trésors de monnaies phéniciennes (*CH* IX)." *Trans* 26 (2003) 105–17.

________. "L'ordre de succession des derniers rois de Byblos." *Syr* 70 (1993) 109–15.

________. "A Series of Coins from Byblos with the Name of the City (4th Cent. BC)." *NC* 170 (2010) 3–8.

________. "Systems of Abbreviations Used by Byblos, Tyre and Arados in Their Pre-Alexandrine Coinages." *JNG* 37–38 (1987–88) 11–22.

Elayi, J., and Haykal, M. R. *Nouvelles découvertes sur les usages funéraires des Phéniciens d'Arwad.* Paris, 1996.

Elayi, J., and Lemaire, A. *Graffiti et contremarques ouest-sémitiques sur les monnaies grecques et proche-orientales.* Milan, 1998.

________. "Le trésor de Byblos TIX." *Trans* 38 (2009) 77–98.

Elayi, J., and Planas Palau, A. *Les pointes de flèches en bronze d'Ibiza dans le cadre de la colonisation phénico-punique.* Paris, 1995.

Elayi, J., and Sapin, J. *Nouveaux regards sur la Transeuphratène.* Brepols, 1991. [*Beyond the River: New Perspectives on Transeuphratene.* JSOTSup 250. Sheffield, 1998.]

________. *Quinze ans de recherches (1985–2000) sur la Transeuphratène à l'époque perse*. Paris, 2000.
Esty, W. W. "Estimation of the Size of a Coinage: A Survey and Comparison of Methods." *NC* 146 (1986) 185–215.
Farkas, A. *Achaemenid Sculpture*. Istanbul, 1974.
Goedicke, H. "Comments of the Satrap Stela." *BES* 6 (1985) 33–54.
Griffiths, J. G. *The Conflict of Horus and Seth*. Liverpool, 1960.
Gubel, É. *Art phénicien: La sculpture de tradition phénicienne*. Paris, 2002.
________. "La glyptique et la genèse de l'iconographie monétaire phénicienne." Pp. 1–11 in *Numismatique et histoire économique phéniciennes et puniques*, ed. T. Hackens and G. Moucharte. Studia Phoenicia 9. Louvain-la-Neuve, 1992.
________. *Phoenician Furniture*. Studia Phoenicia 7. Leuven, 1987.
Hackens, T. "Terminologie et techniques de fabrication." Pp. 10–12 in *Numismatique antique: Problèmes et méthodes*. Annales de l'Est. Nancy, 1975.
Hassan, S. *The Sphinx: Its History in the Light of Recent Excavations*. Cairo, 1949.
Hauben, H. "The King of the Sidonians and the Persian imperial Fleet." *AncSoc* 1 (1970) 1–8.
Heltzer, M. "The Persian Invasion of Cyprus and the Date of the Submission of Evagoras." Pp. 717–19 in *Acts of the Third International Congress of Cypriot Studies*. Nicosia, 2000.
Henige, D. "Josephus and the Tyrian King List." *Trans* 38 (2009) 35–64.
Huss, W. "Der Rätselhäfte Pharao Chababasch." *SEL* 11 (1994) 97–112.
Jenkins, G. K. "Recent Acquisitions of Greek Coins by the British Museum." *NC* 19 (1959) 41–42.
Jidejian, N. *Byblos through the Ages*. Beirut, 1971.
Joannès, F. "Métaux précieux et moyens de paiement en Babylonie achéménide et hellénistique." *Trans* 8 (1994) 137–44.
Klimorvsky, E. W. *On Ancient Palestinian and Other Coins: Their Symbolism and Metrology*. Tel Aviv, 1974.
Kraay, C. M. "Hoards, Small Change and the Origin of Coinage." *JHS* 84 (1964) 76–91.
Kraay, C. M., and Moorey, P. R. S. "Two Fifth Century Hoards from the Near East." *RN* 10 (1968) 181–235.
Kukahn, E. *Anthropoide Sarkophage in Beyrouth*. Berlin, 1955.
Lauffray, J. "La méthode de fouilles de Maurice Dunand à Byblos, II: Introduction à la méthode M. Dunand." *Topoi* 5 (1995) 453–68.
Le Rider, G. *La naissance de la monnaie: Pratiques monétaires de l'Orient ancien*. Paris, 2001.
Leclant, J. "Les Phéniciens et l'Égypte." Pp. 7–17 in *ACFP* 2/1. Rome, 1991.
Lemaire, A., and Elayi, J. "Les monnaies de Byblos au sphinx et au faucon: Nouveaux documents et essai de classement." *RBN* 137 (1991) 29–36.
Leriche, P. "La méthode de fouille de Maurice Dunand à Byblos, I: M. Dunand et l'archéologie au Proche-Orient au début du XXe siècle." *Topoi* 5 (1995) 439–52.
Lewis, D. M. "The Phoenician Fleet in 411." *Historia* 7 (1958) 392–97.
Lipiński, E. *Itineraria Phoenicia*. Leuven, 2004.
Lloyd, A. B. "Were Necho's Triremes Phoenician?" *JHS* 95 (1975) 45–61.
Lockyear, K. "Hoard Structure and Coin Production in Antiquity: An Empirical Investigation." *NC* 159 (1999) 215–43.
Luynes, H. de. *Essai sur la numismatique des Satrapes de la Phénicie*. Paris, 1846.

Mattingly, H. B. "The Jordan Hoard (IGCH 1482) and Kimon's Last Expedition." Pp. 59–64 in *Proceedings of the 10th International Congress of Numismatics*. London, 1986.

Mercer, S. *Horus: Royal God of Egypt*. Grafton, 1942.

Merker, I. L. "Notes on Abdalonymos and the Dated Alexander Coinage of Sidon and Ake." *ANSMN* 11 (1964) 13–20.

Montet, P. *Byblos et l'Égypte: Quatre campagnes de fouilles à Gebeil 1921, 1922, 1923, 1924*. Paris, 1928.

Moysey, R. A. "Diodorus, the Satraps and the Decline of the Persian Empire." *AHB* 5 (1991) 113–22.

________. *Greek Relations with the Persian Satraps: 371–343* B.C. Princeton, 1974.

________. "IG II² and the Great Satrap's Revolt." *ZPE* 67 (1987) 93–100.

________. "Observations on the Numismatic Evidence relating to the Great Satrapal Revolt of 362/1 B.C." *REA* 91 (1989) 107–139.

________. "Plutarch, Nepos and the Satrapal Revolt of 362/1 B.C." *Historia* 41 (1992) 158–66.

Naster, P. "Le chien et le murex des monnaies impériales de Tyr." *NAC* 14 (1985) 257–60.

________. "Le développement des monnayages phéniciens avant Alexandre, d'après les trésors." Pp. 3–24 in *The Patterns of the Monetary Development in Phoenicia and Palestine in Antiquity—International Numismatic Convention: Jerusalem 1963*, ed. A. Kindler. Jerusalem, 1967.

________. "L'ordre de succession des rois de Byblos d'après leurs monnaies." *BSFN* 20 (1965) 478.

________. *Scripta Nummaria: Contributions à la méthodologie numismatique*. Louvain-la-Neuve, 1983.

________. "La technique des revers partiellement incus des monnaies phéniciennes." Pp. 503–11 in *Centennial Publications of the American Numismatic Society*. New York, 1958.

________. "Trésors de monnaies de Byblos du IVᵉ s. av. J.-C. trouvés à Byblos." Pp. 17–49 in *Numismatique et histoire économique phéniciennes et puniques*, ed. T. Hackens and G. Moucharte. Studia Phoenicia 9. Louvain-la-Neuve, 1992.

Newell, E. T. *Some Unpublished Coins of Eastern Dynasts*. *NNM* 30. New York, 1926.

Peckham, J. B. *The Development of the Late Phoenician Scripts*. Cambridge, MA, 1968.

Porada, E. "Notes on the Sarcophagus of Ahiram." *JANES* 5 (1973) 355–72.

Psoma, S. "Le nombre de chalques dans l'obole dans le monde grec." *RN* 154 (1998) 12–24.

Puech, É. "Les premières émissions byblites et les rois de Byblos à la fin du Vᵉ siècle av. J.-C." Pp. 287–98 in *ACFP*, vol. 2. Rome, 1991.

________. 'Remarques sur quelques inscriptions phéniciennes de Byblos." *RSF* 9 (1981) 153–68.

Renan, E. *Mission de Phénicie*. Paris, 1864.

Ronde, A. "Étude sommaire de trois 'trésors' proche-orientaux de provenance incertaine." *BSFN* 57/4 (2002) 57–62.

Root, M. C. *The King and Kingship in Achaemenid Art*. Leiden, 1979.

Rouvier, J. "Numismatique des villes de la Phénicie: Gebal-Byblos." *JIAN* 4 (1901) 39–42.

Salles, J.-F. "La mort à Byblos: Les Nécropoles." Pp. 49–72 in *Biblo: Una città e la sua cultura*, ed. E. Acquaro et al. Rome, 1994.

Scandone, G. "Testimonianze egiziane in Fenicia dal XII al IV sec. a.c." *RSF* 12 (1984) 133–63.

Servet, J.-M. *Nomismata: État et origines de la monnaie*. Lyon, 1984.

Sheridan, W. W. "From Cyzicus to Tyre: Numismatic Evidence of an Ancient Ship's Trip, circa 400 B.C." *Numismatist* 8 (1971) 1127–33.

Sisti, F. *Arriano, Anabasi di Alessandro*, vol. 1. Florence, 2001.

Six, J. P. "Observations sur les monnaies phéniciennes." *NC* n.s. 17 (1877) 127–241.

Solé, L. "Le emissioni monetali della Fenicia prima di Alessandro-I." *SEAP* 16 (1997) 75–125.

________. "Le emissioni monetali della Fenicia prima di Alessandro-II." *SEAP* 18 (1998) 81–147.

________. "Nuove considerazioni sull'unità ponderale della prima serie monetale di Biblo." *Trans* 20 (2000) 61–72.

Spalinger, A. "The Reign of King Chabbash: An Interpretation." *ZÄS* 105 (1978) 142–54.

Stadter, P. A. *Arrian of Nicomedia*. Chapel Hill, NC, 1980.

Svoronos, J. N. "Stylides, ancres, hierae, aphlasta, stoloi, akrostolia, embola, proembola et totems marins." *JIAN* 16 (1914) 81–152.

Thurneyssen, J. "Le gouvernail antique." *DArch* 29 (1978) 74–80.

Tonnet, H. *Recherches sur Arrien, sa personnalité et ses écrits atticistes*, vols. 1–2. Amsterdam, 1988.

Valbelle, D. "Le faucon et le roi." Pp. 205–20 in *L'imperio ramesside*. Rome, 1997.

Vargyas, P. "Silver and Money in Achaemenid and Hellenistic Babylonia." Pp. 513–21 in *Assyrologia et Semitica: Festschrift für J. Oelsner*. AOAT 252. Neukirchen-Vluyn, 2000.

Villaronga, L. "De nuevo la estimaciòn del número original de cuños de una emisión monetaria." *Gacetta Numismática* 85 (1987) 31–36.

Virolleaud, C. "Découverte à Byblos d'un hypogée de la douzième dynastie égyptienne." *Syr* 3 (1922) 273–90.

Vismara, N. *Monetazione arcaica della Licia III*. Milan, 1996.

________. "Monetazione arcaica della Lycia: Prime rilevanze circa l'approvvigionamento metallico." *REA* 103 (2001) 343–67.

________. "Un particolare nell'iconografia del cavallo nelle terre di confine nell'Asia Minore: Elemento decorativo diffuso od indizio culturale? Alcuni spunti per una riflessione." *Trans* 37 (2009) 155–67.

Wallinga, H. "The Ancient Persian Navy and Its Predecessors." Pp. 47–78 in *Achaemenid History*, vol. 1: *Sources, Structures and Synthesis*, ed. H. Sancisi-Weerdenburg. Leiden, 1987.

________. *Ships and Sea-Power before the Great Persian War: The Ancestry of the Ancient Trireme*. Leiden, 1993.

Watanabe, C. E. "Symbolism of the Royal Lion Hunt in Assyria." Pp. 439–50 in *Intellectual Life of the Ancient Near East*, ed. J. Prosecky. Prague, 1998.

Weiskopf, M. *The So-Called "Great Satraps' Revolt," 366–360 B.C.* Wiesbaden, 1989.

Zivie-Coche, C. *Sphinx! Le Père de la terreur: Histoire d'une statue*. Paris, 1977.

Index of Geographical Names

Note to reader: Byblos has not been indexed because it appears so frequently in the text.

Index of Public and Private Collections

Note to reader: The numbers represent the coin numbers in the catalog of appendix 1.

Index of Sale Catalogs

Note to reader: The numbers are coin numbers in the catalog of appendix 1.

Index of Hoards

Note to reader: The numbers are the coin numbers in the catalog of appendix 1.

Plates

Plate 1

I.1

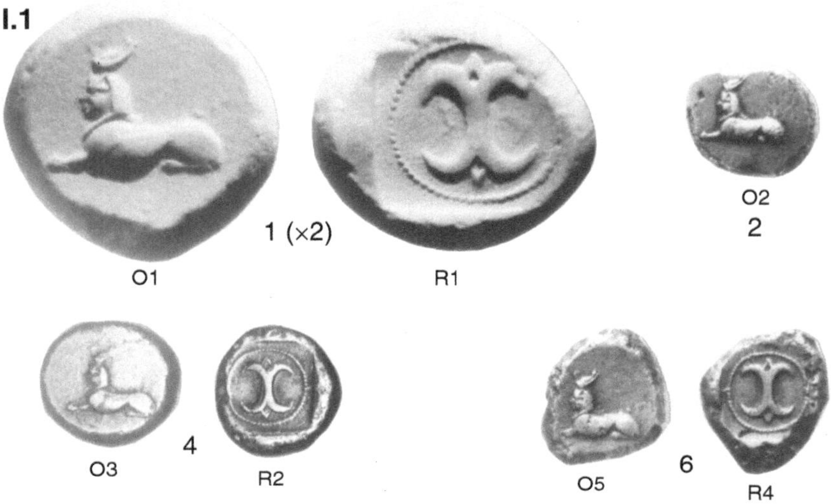

O1 1 (×2) R1 O2 2

O3 4 R2 O5 6 R4

I.2

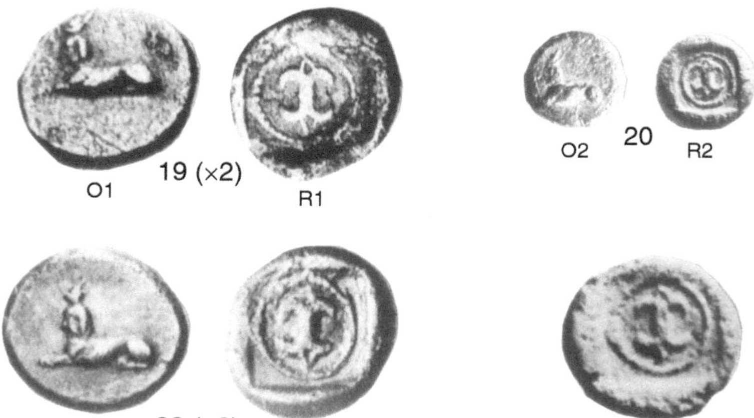

O1 19 (×2) R1 O2 20 R2

O4 22 (×2) R4 R5 23 (×2)

I.3

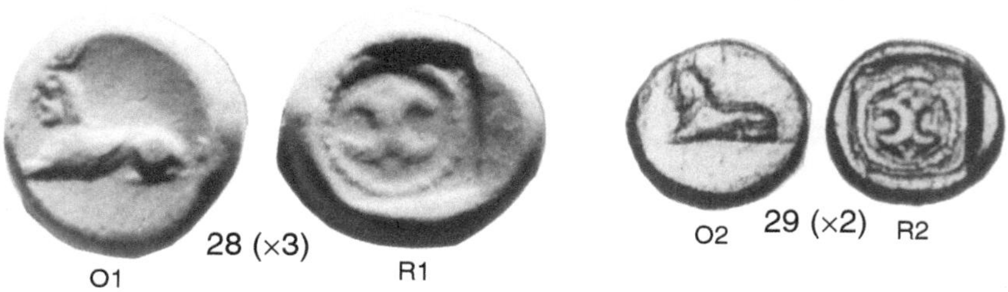

O1 28 (×3) R1 O2 29 (×2) R2

Plate 2

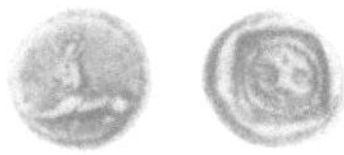
O3 R3
30

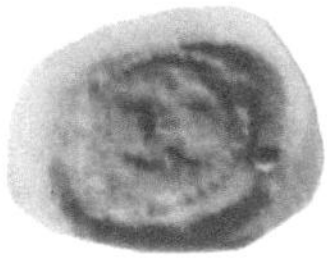
R4
31 (×2)

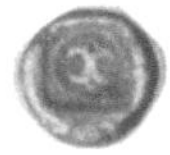
R5
32

I.4

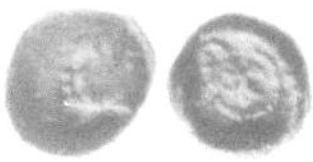
O1 R1
34

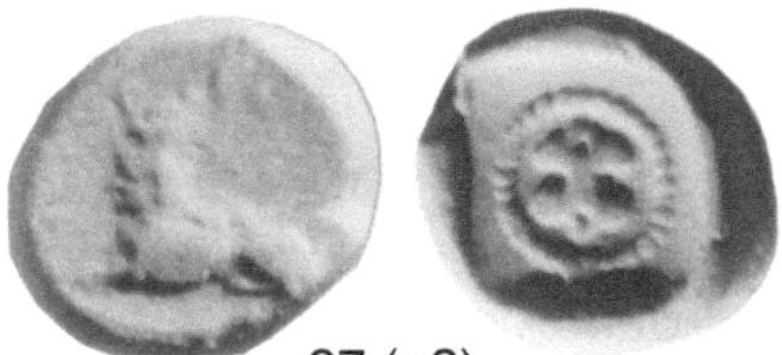
O2 37 (×2) R2

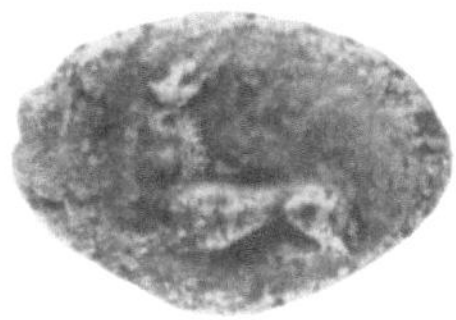
O3
38 (×3)

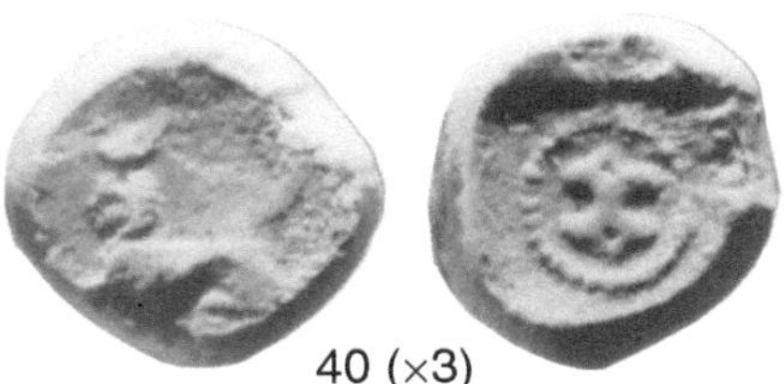
O4 40 (×3) R3

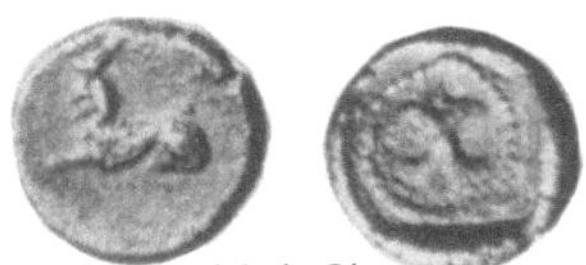
O5 41 (×2) R4

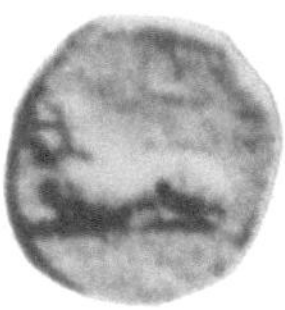
O6
43 (×2)

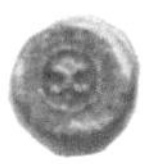
R5
45

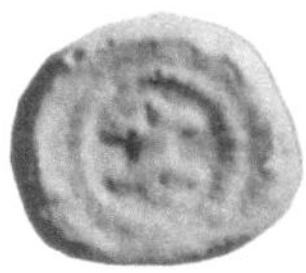
R6
46 (×2)

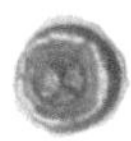
R7
47

I.5

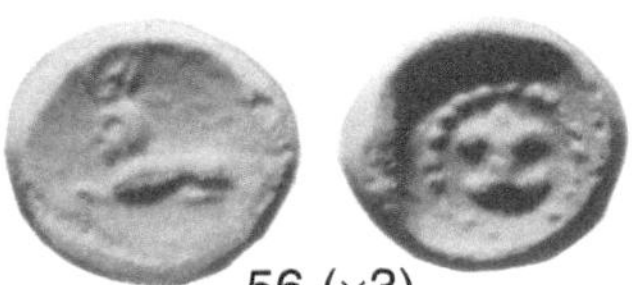
O1 56 (×3) R1

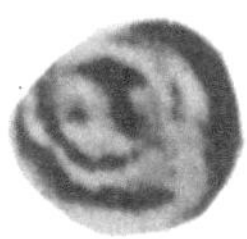
R2
57 (×2)

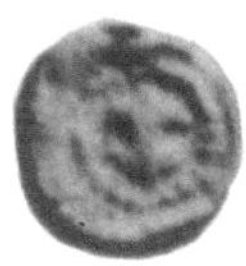
R4
60 (×2)

Plate 3

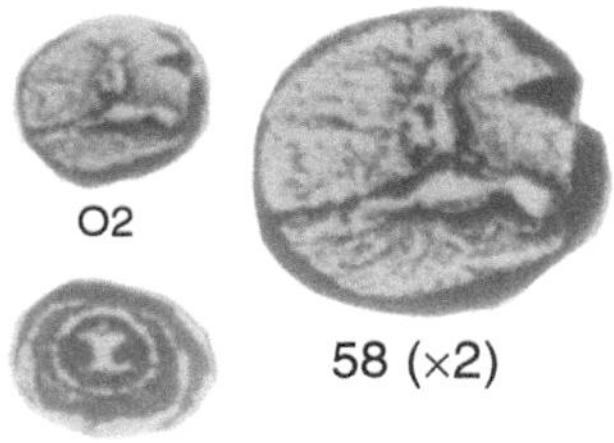

O2

R3

58 (×2)

I.7

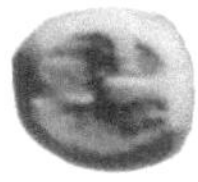

O1

64 (×3)

O2

65

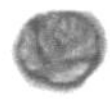

R1

66

II.1

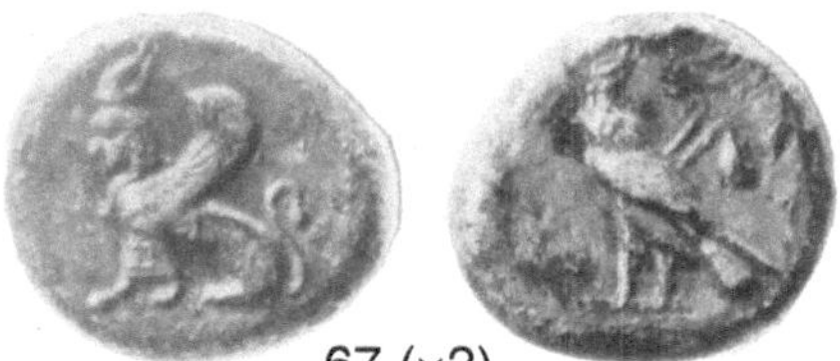

O1 67 (×2) R1

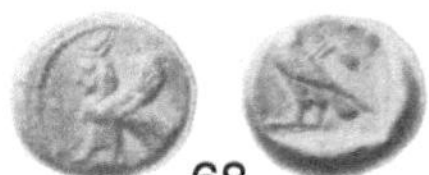

O2 68 R2

II.2

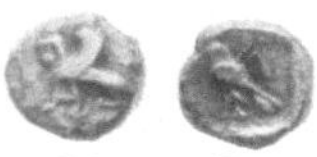

O1 R1

73

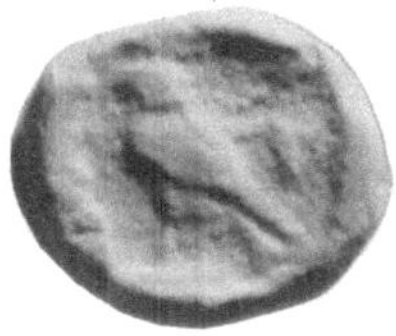

R2

74 (×3)

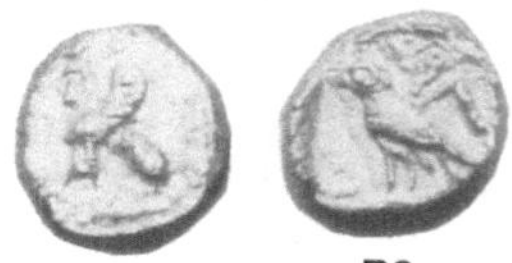

O2 R3

75 (×2)

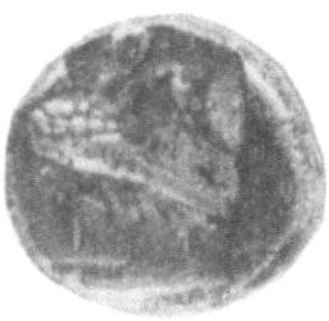

R4

76 (×3)

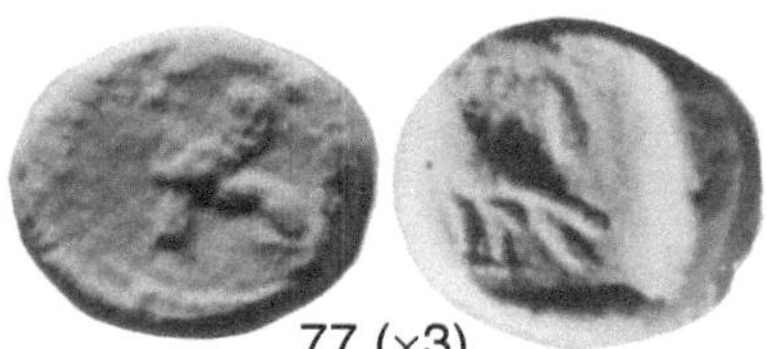

O3 77 (×3) R5

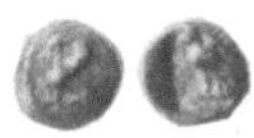

O5 R7

79

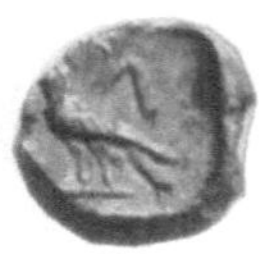

R10

82 (×2)

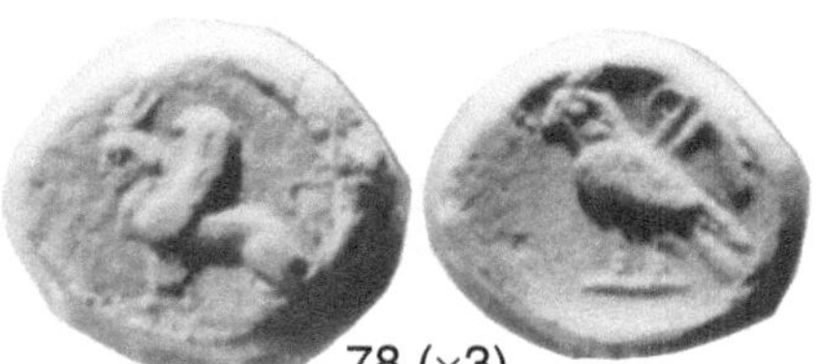

O4 78 (×3) R6

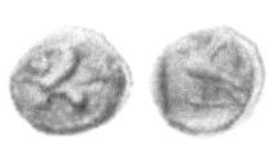

O6 R8

80

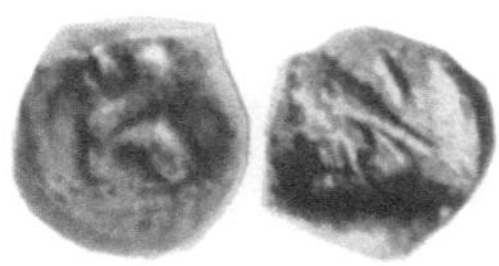

O7 R9

81 (×2)

Plate 4

II.2.2

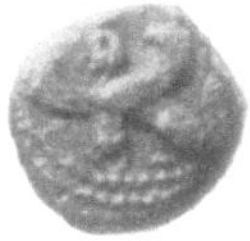
O1
84 (×2)

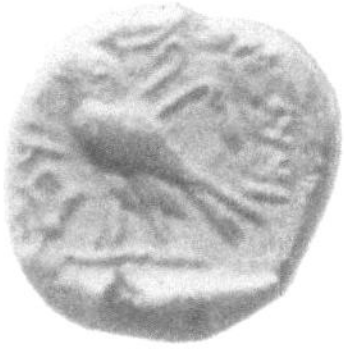
R1
84 (×3)

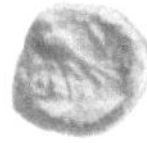
R2
85

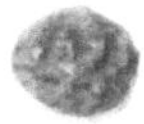
O2

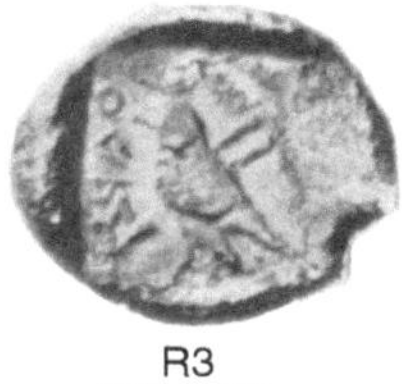
R3
86 (×3)

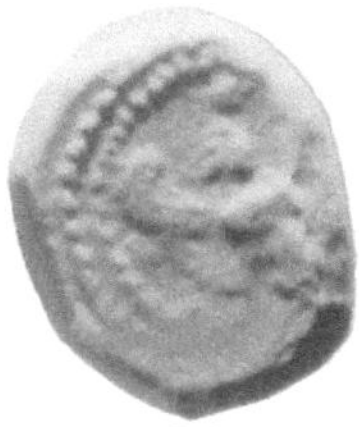
O3
88 (×3)

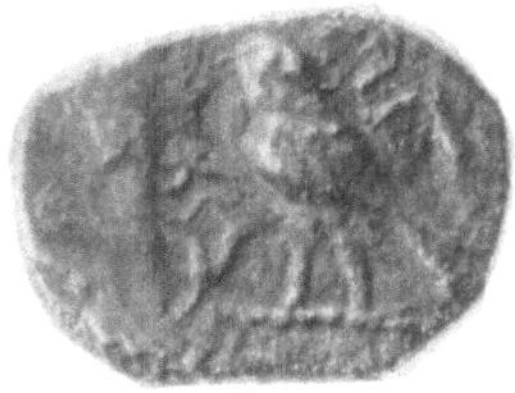
R4
88 (×4)

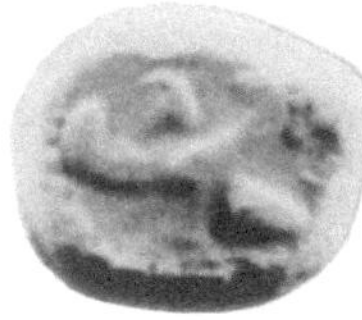
O4
89 (×3)

II.3

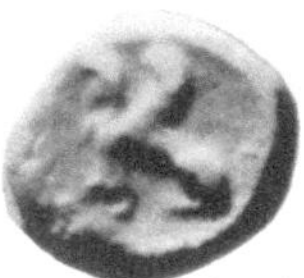
O1

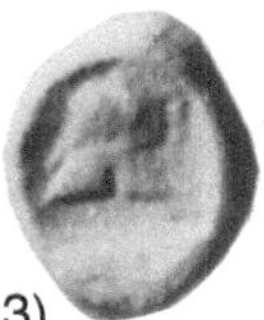
94 (×3)
R1

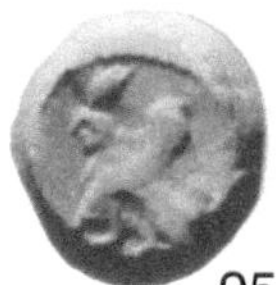
O2

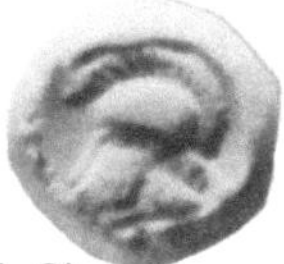
95 (×3)
R2

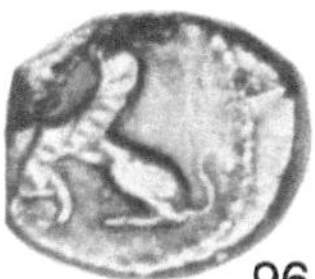
O3

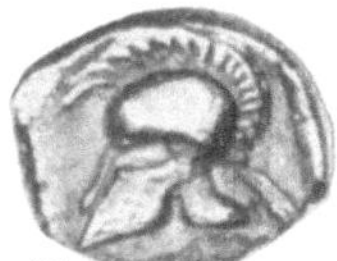
96 (×3)
R3

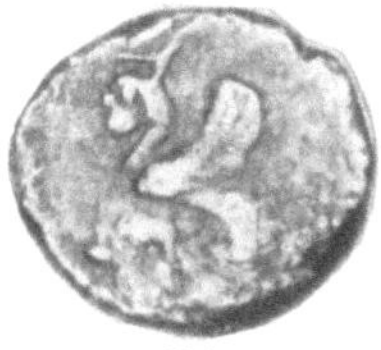
O4
97 (×3)

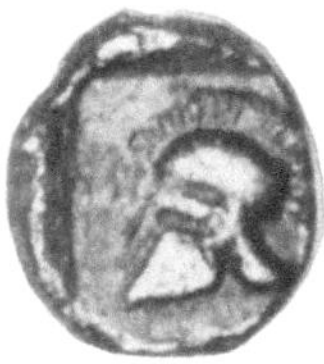
R4
98 (×3)

III.1

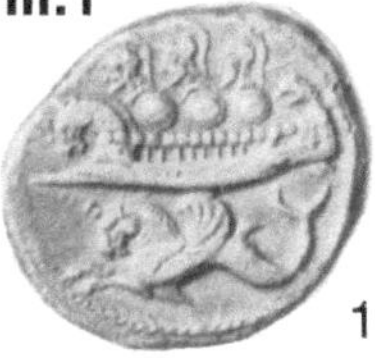
O1

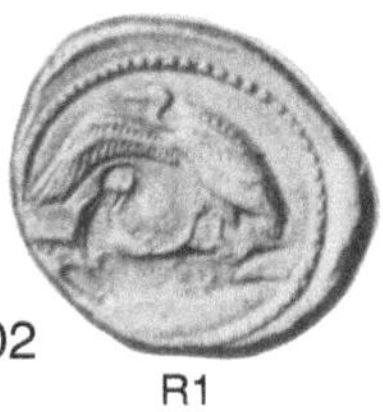
102
R1

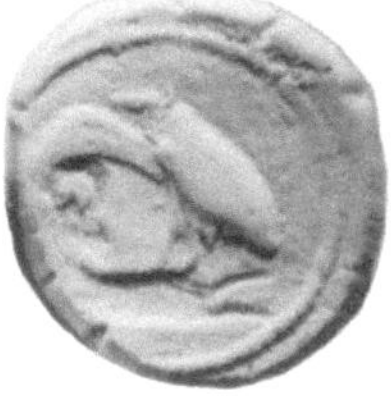
O2
103

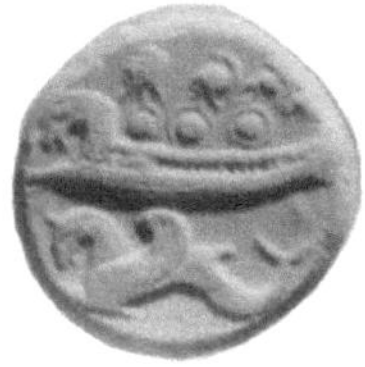
R2
105

Plate 5

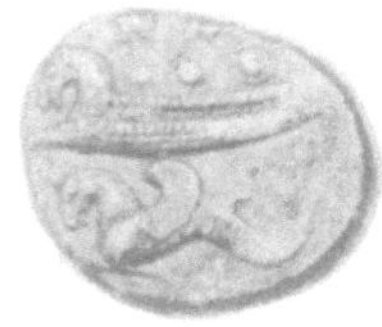
O3
107

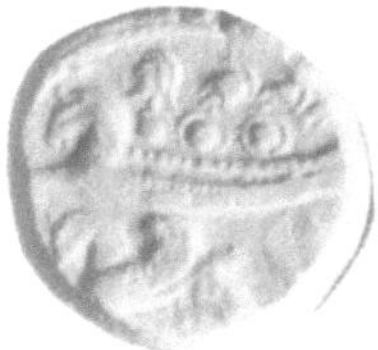
O4
110

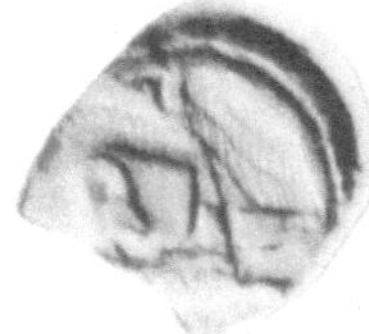
R4
111

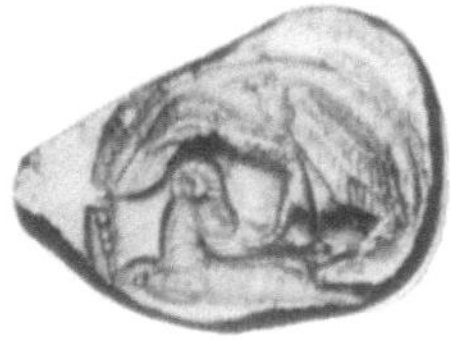
R5
112

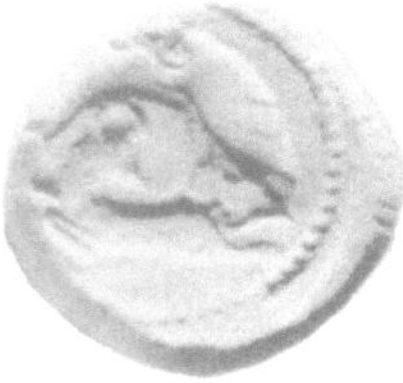
R6
113

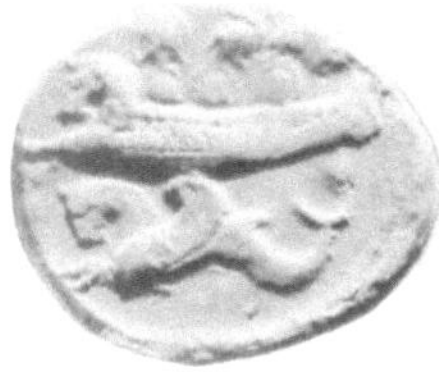
O5
114

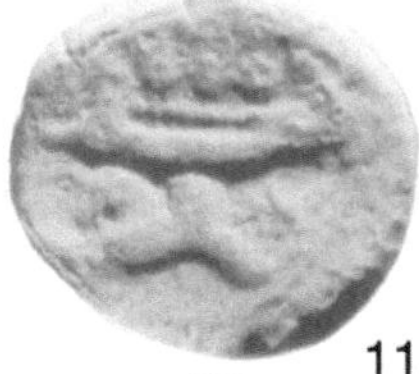
O6
115

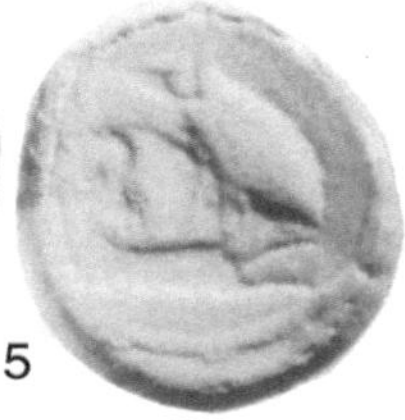
R7

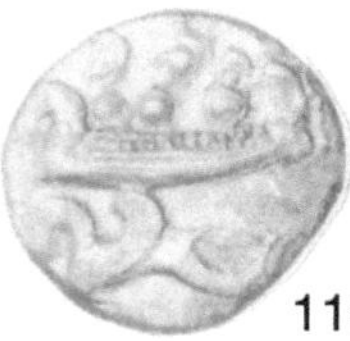
O7
116

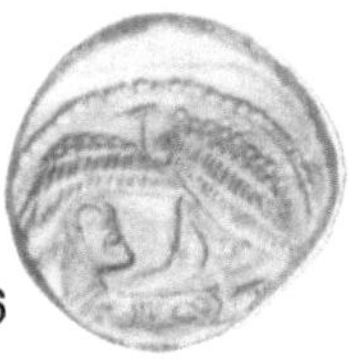
R8

III.2

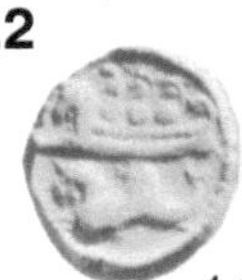
O1
142

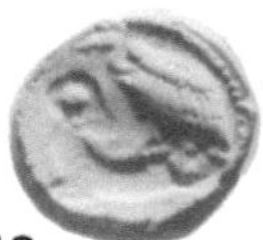
R1

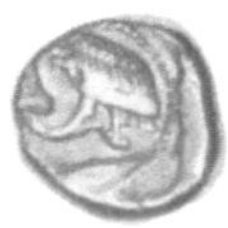
R2
144

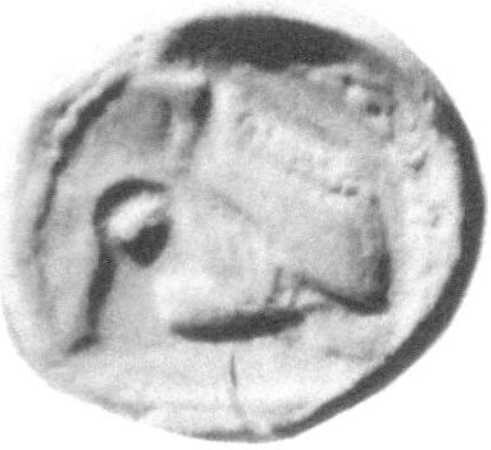
R3
145 (×2)

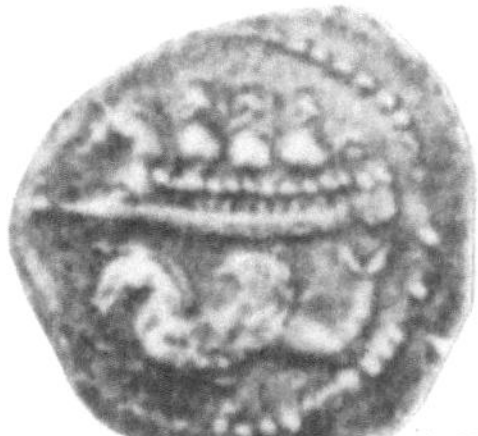
O2
147 (×2)

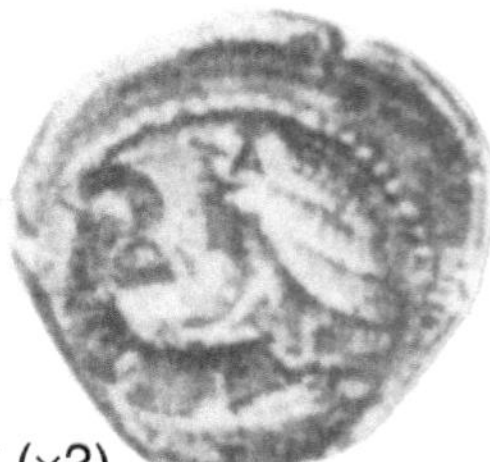
R4

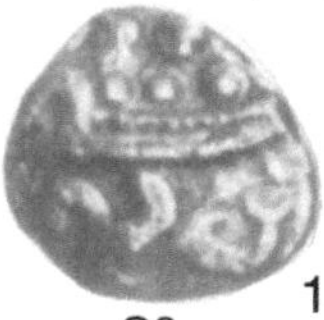
O3
150

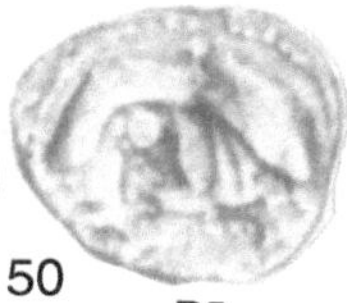
R5

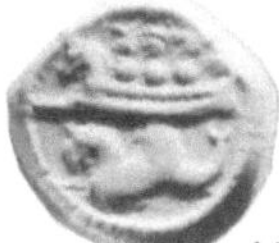
O4
151

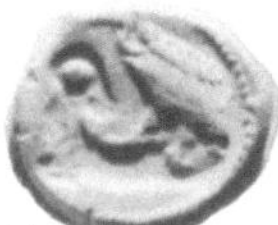
R6

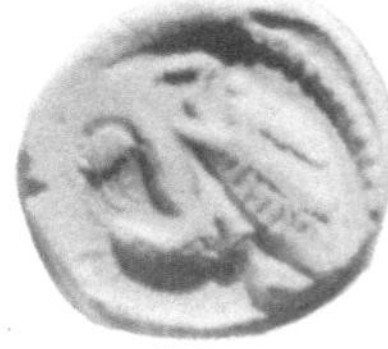
R7
154 (×2)

Plate 6

III.3

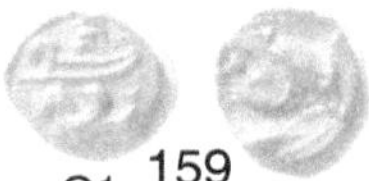

O1 159 R1

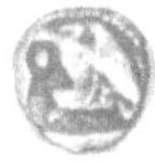

R2
160

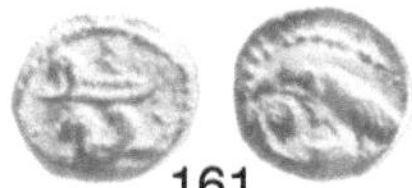

O2 161 R3

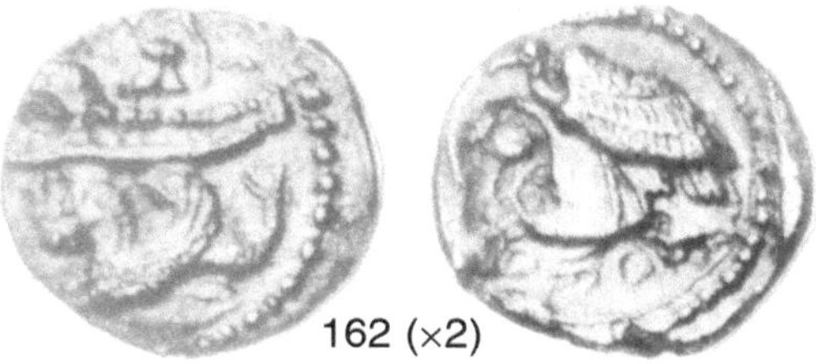

O3 162 (×2) R4

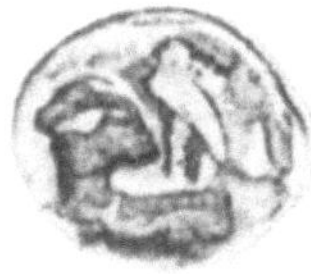

R5
164 (×2)

III.4

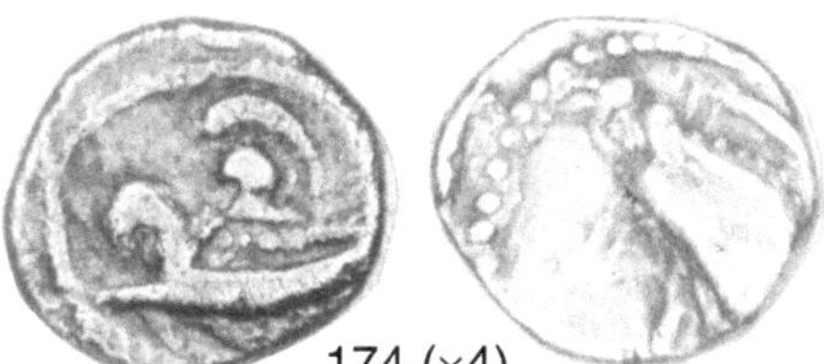

O1 174 (×4) R1

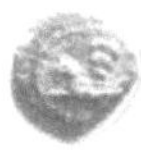

O2
175

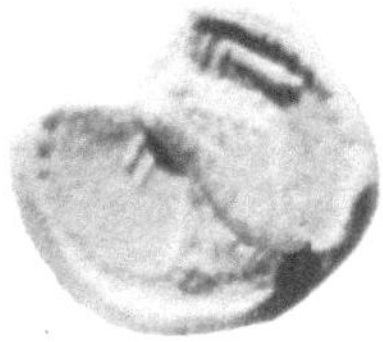

R2
176 (×3)

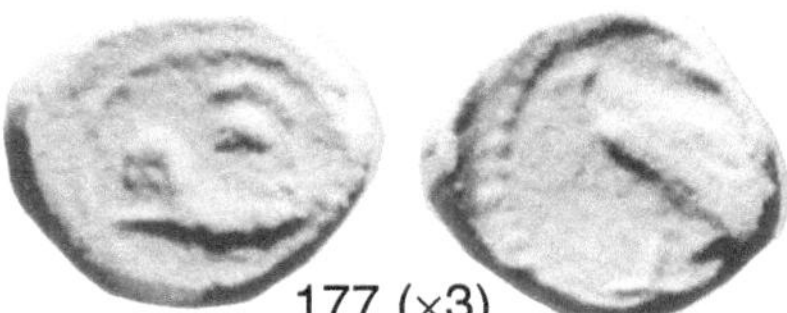

O3 177 (×3) R3

IV.1.1

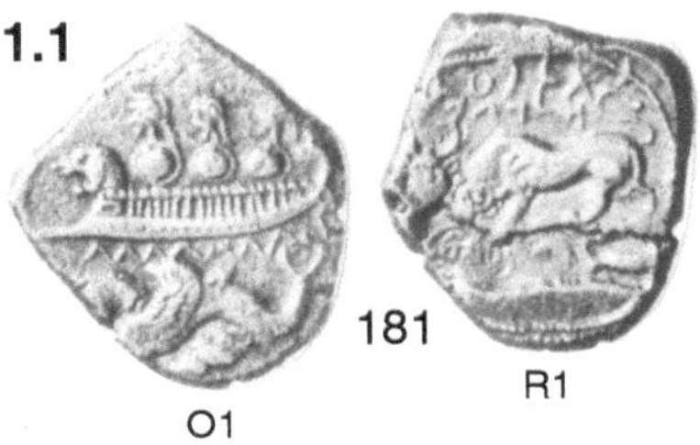

O1 181 R1

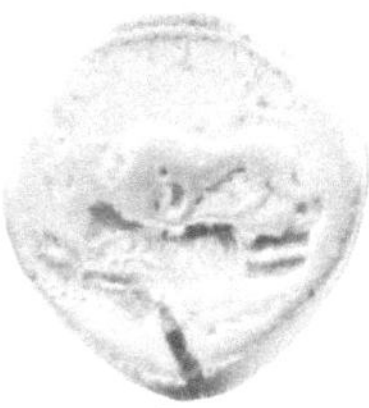

R2
183

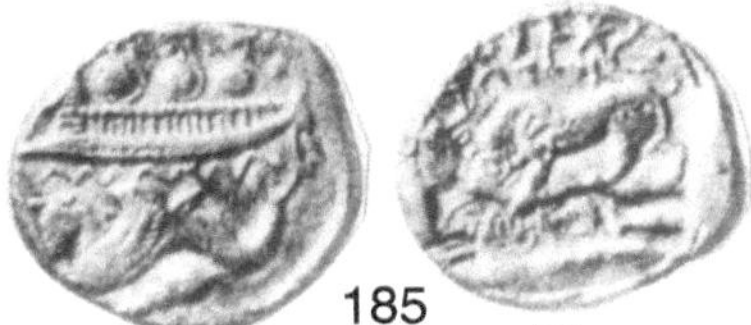

O2 185 R4

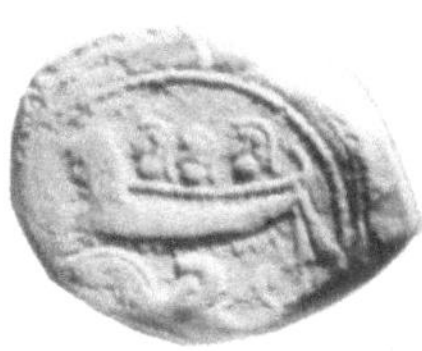

O4
187

Plate 7

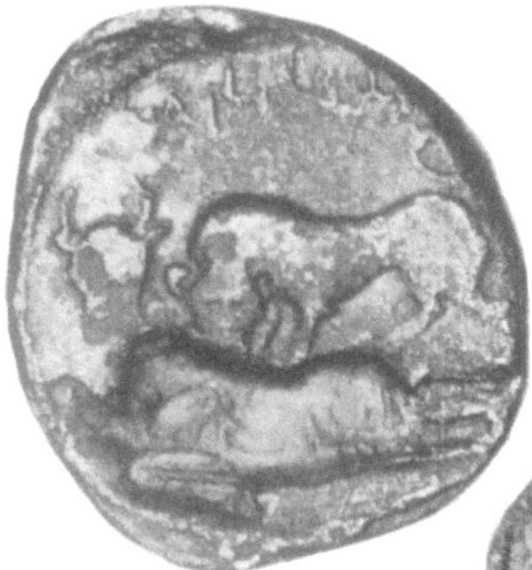

R3
184 (×2)

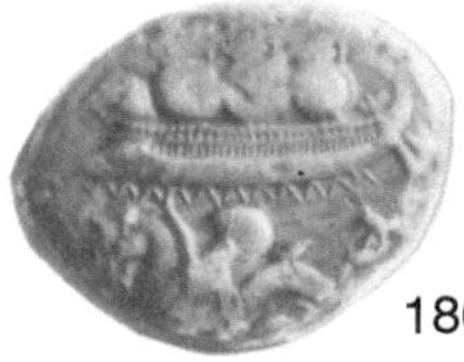

O3

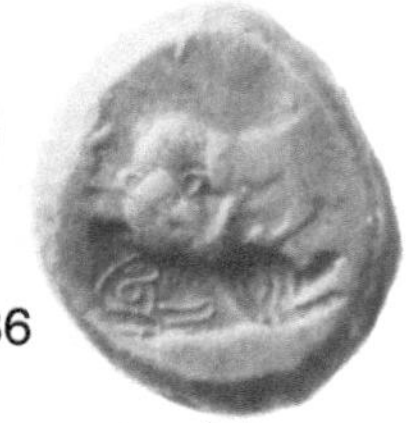

186
R5

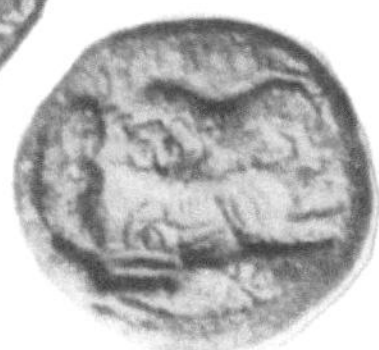

R6
188

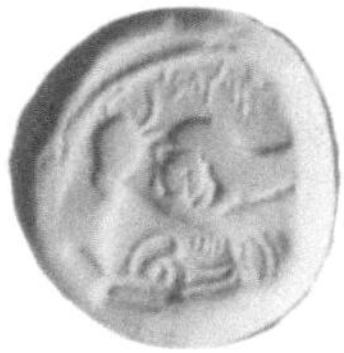

R7
189

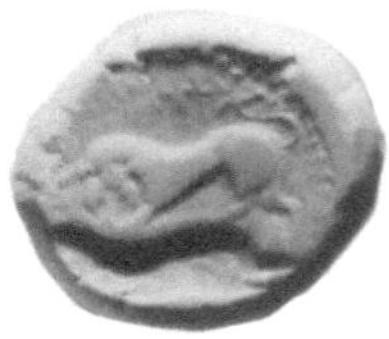

R8
190

IV.1.2

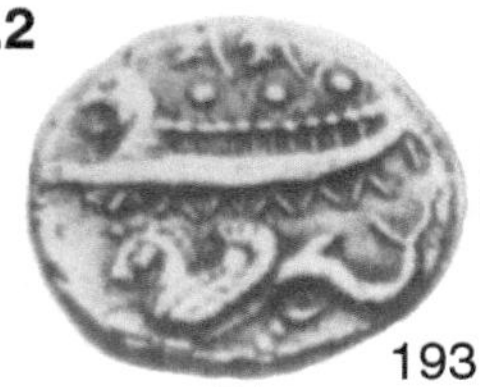

O1

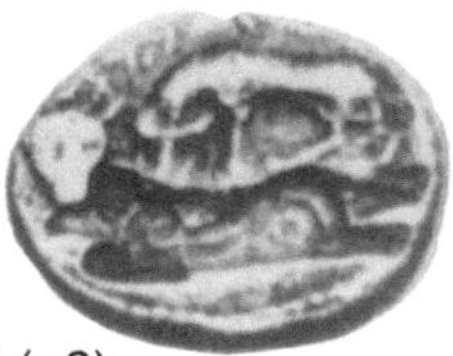

193 (×2) R1

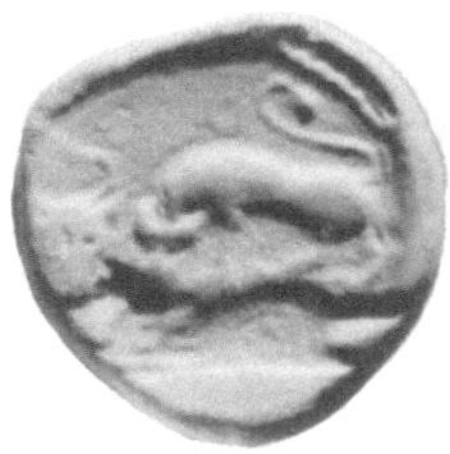

R2
194 (×2)

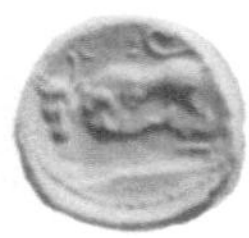

R5
202

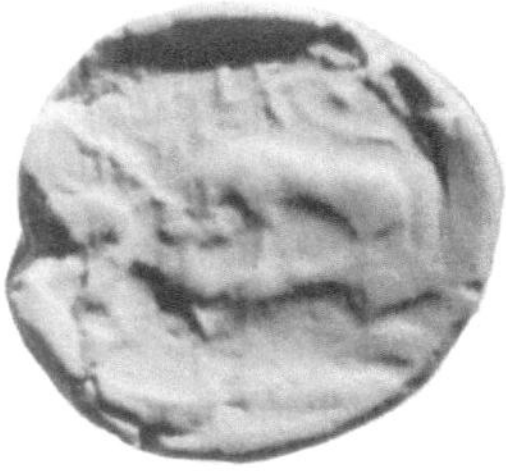

R3
195
(×2)

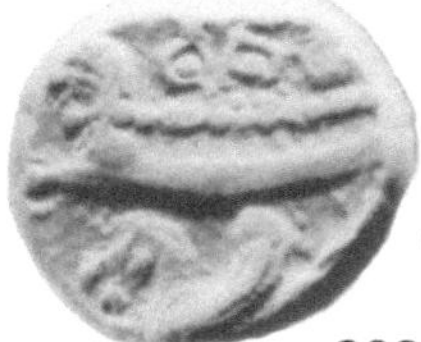

O3

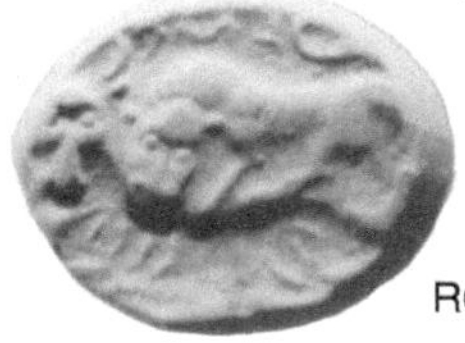

R6
203 (×2)

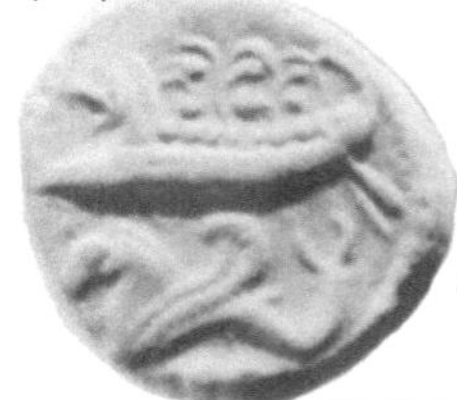

O4

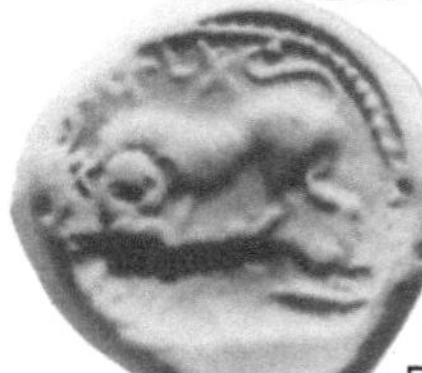

R7
205 (×2)

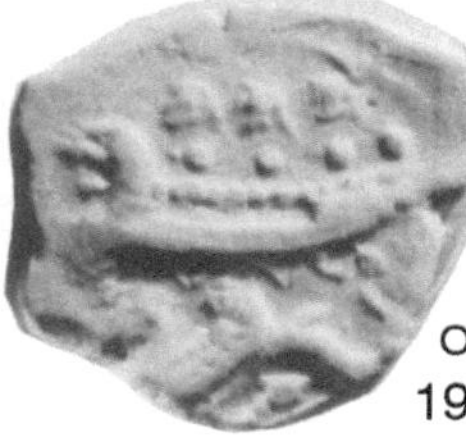

O2
198 (×2)

Plate 8

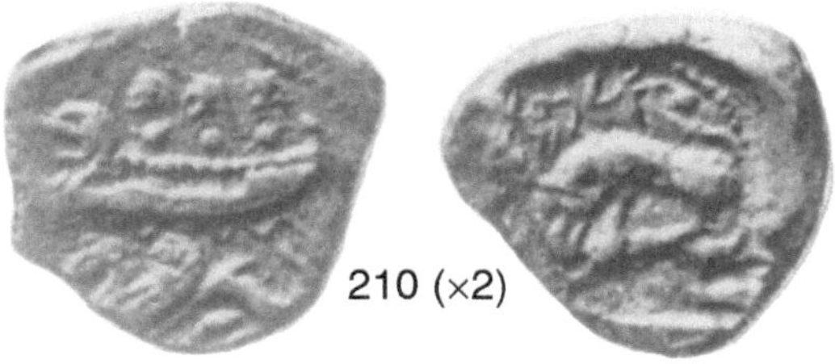

O7 R11

210 (×2)

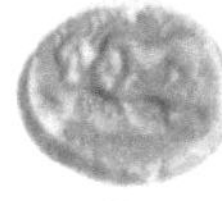

R9

208

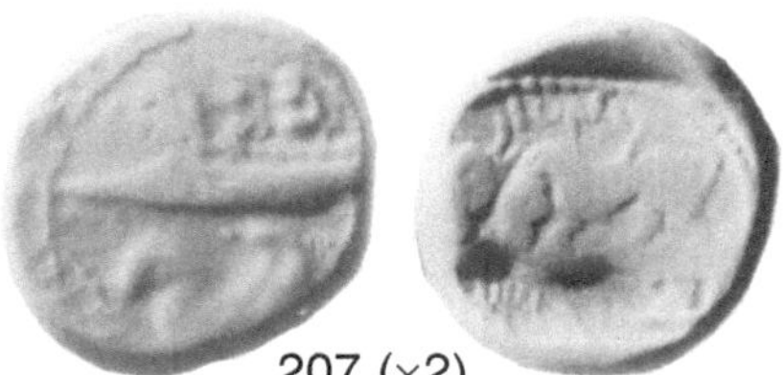

O5 R8

207 (×2)

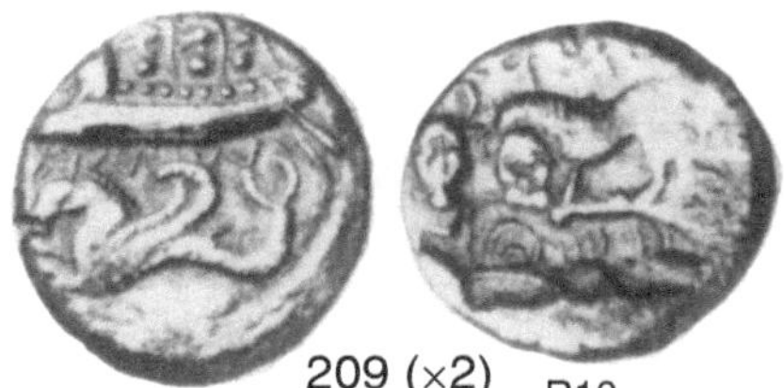

O6 R10

209 (×2)

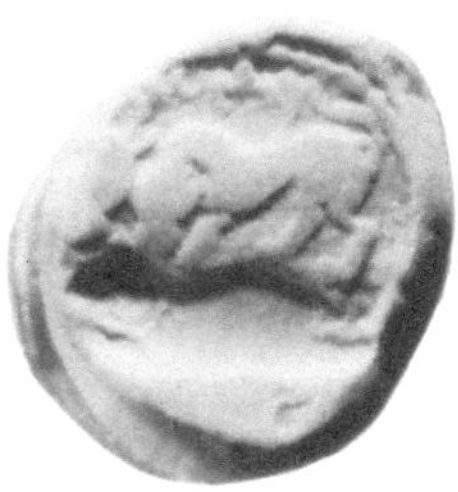

R8

211 (×2)

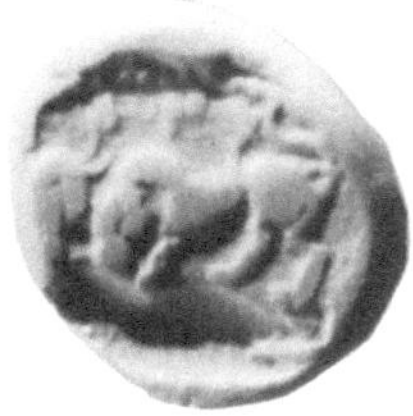

R12

212 (×2)

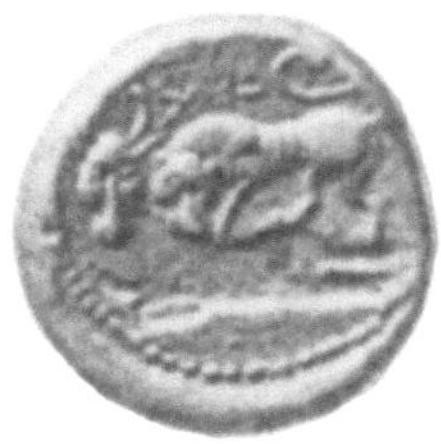

R13

213 (×2)

IV.1.3.a

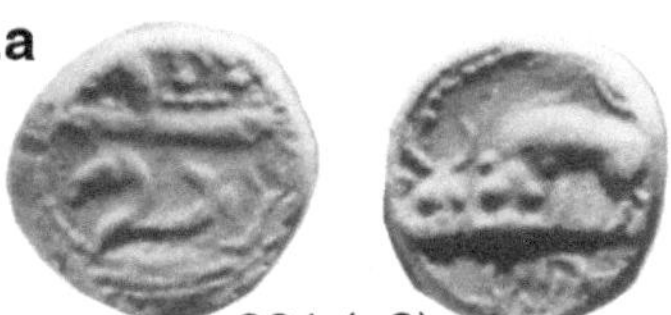

O1 R1

221 (×2)

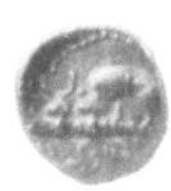

R2

221

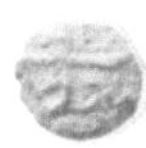

O2

222

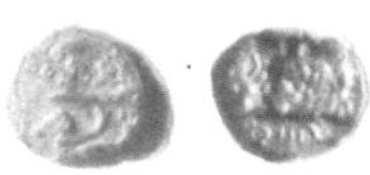

O3 R3

223

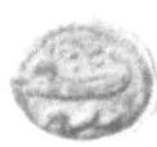

O8

224

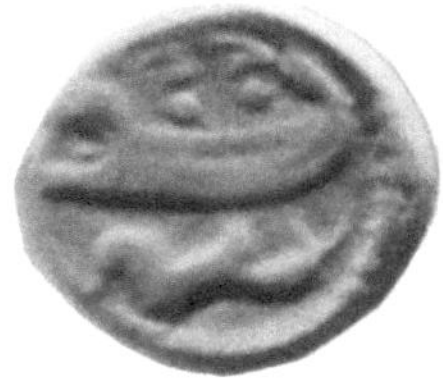

O9

225 (×3)

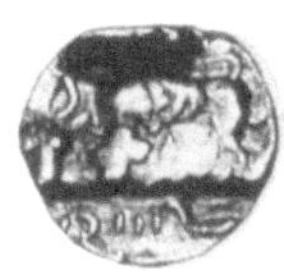

R9

226 (×2)

Plate 9

IV.1.3.b

R4
229

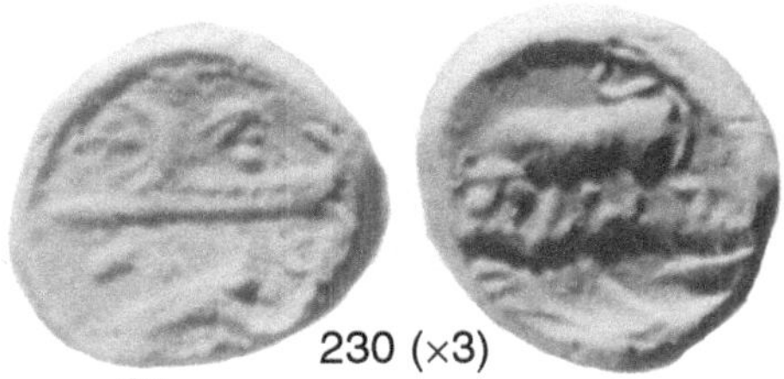
O4 230 (×3) R5

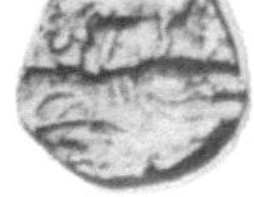
R8
233 (×2)

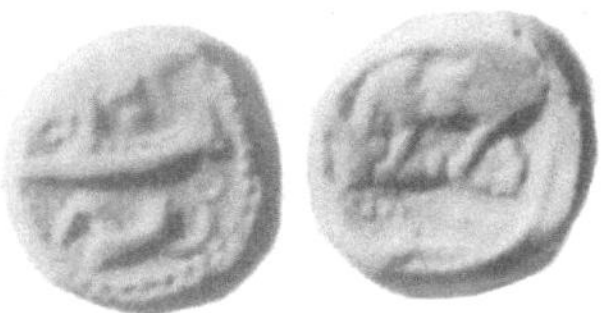
O5 R6
231 (×2)

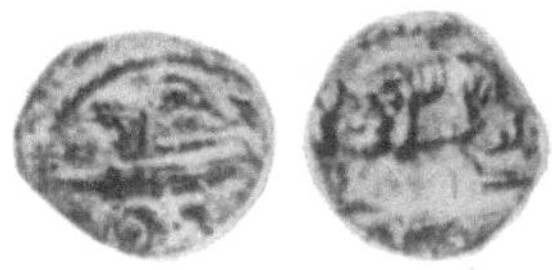
O6 R7
232 (×2)

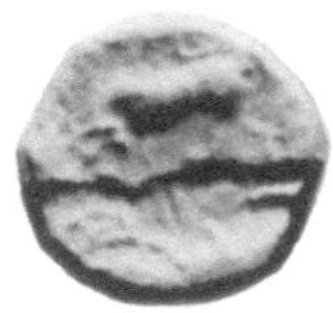
R10
234 (×2)

IV.1.3.c

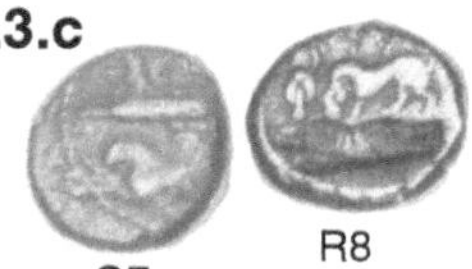
O7 R8
242 (×1.5)

IV.1.4

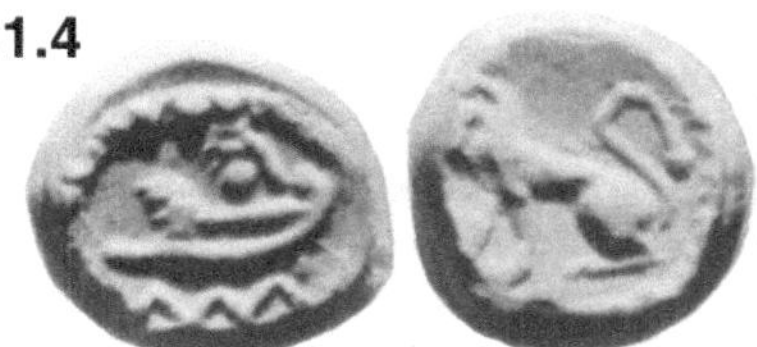
O1 252 (×3) R1

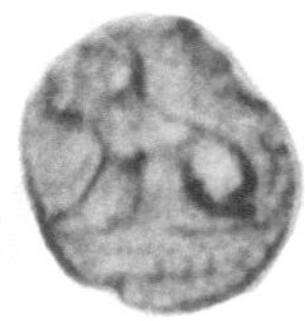
R3
254 (×3)

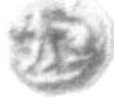
R2
253

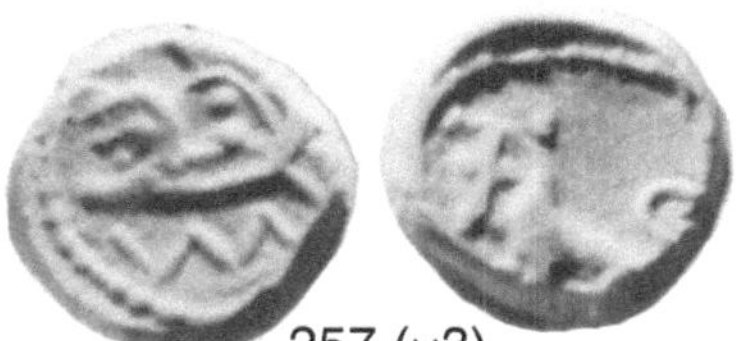
O2 257 (×3) R4

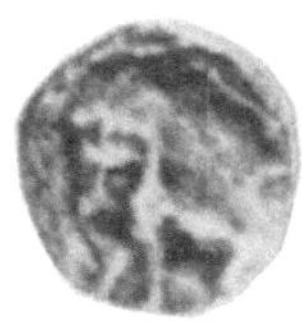
R5
258 (×3)

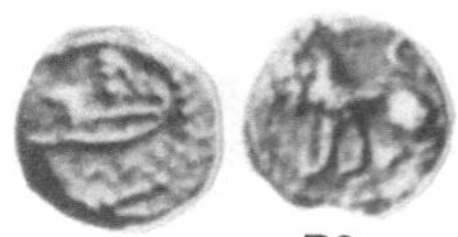
O3 R6
259 (×2)

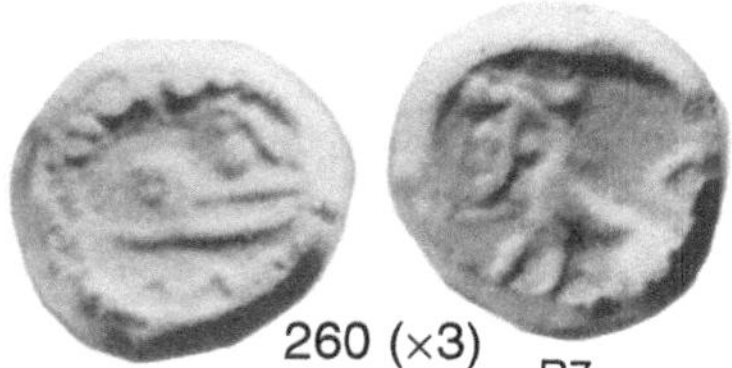
O4 260 (×3) R7

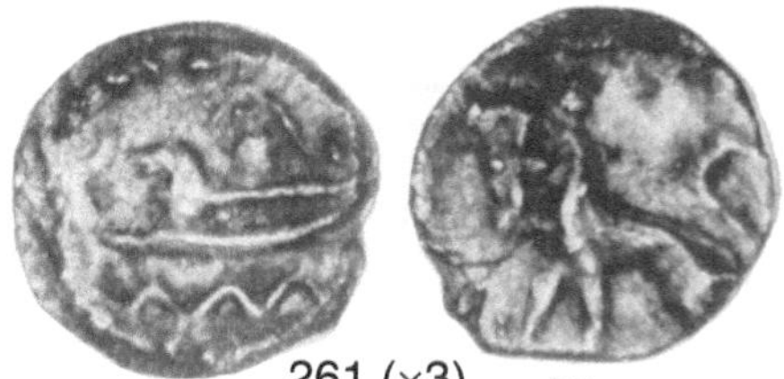
O5 261 (×3) R8

Plate 10

IV.2.1.a

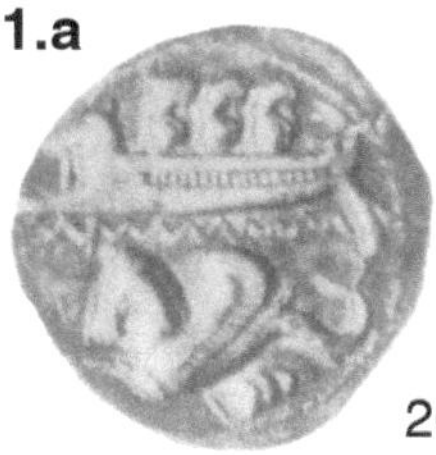
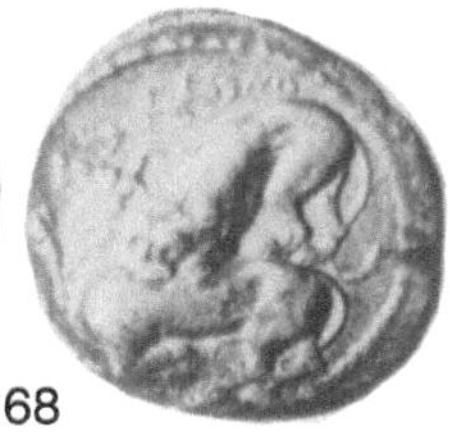

268

O1 R1

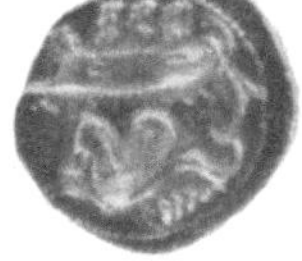

O2
270

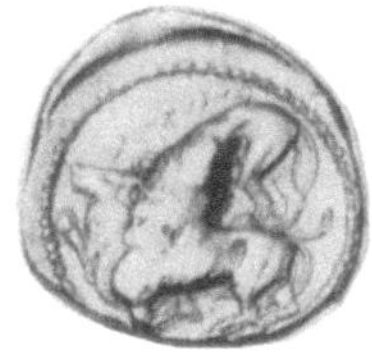

R4
273

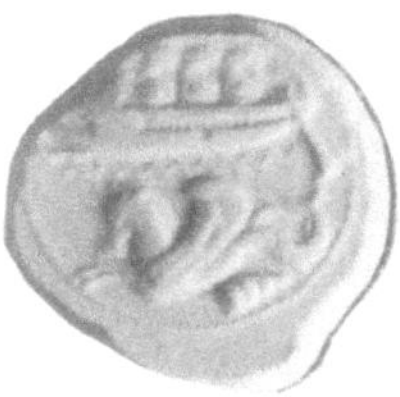

O4
280

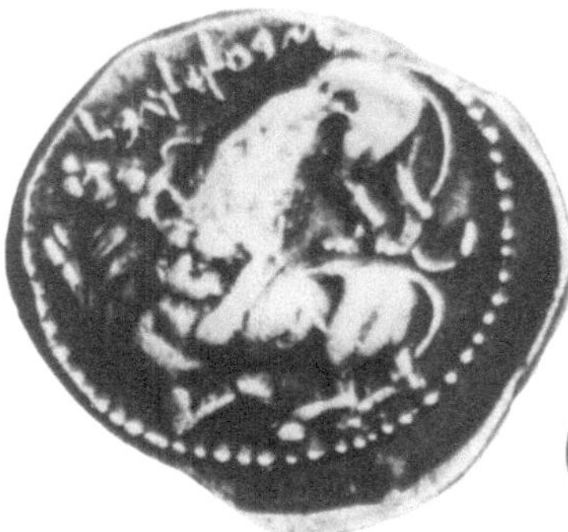

R2
280 (×2)

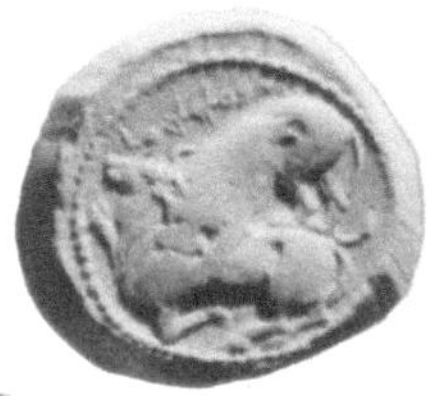

R3
281

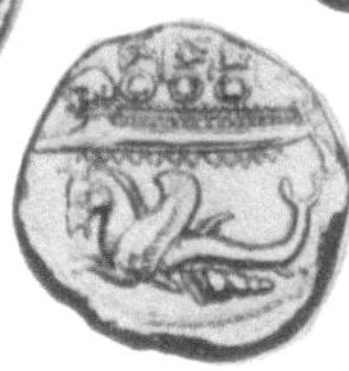

O5
296

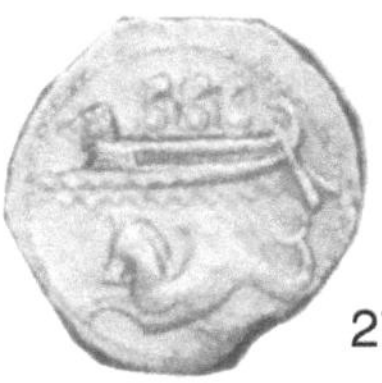
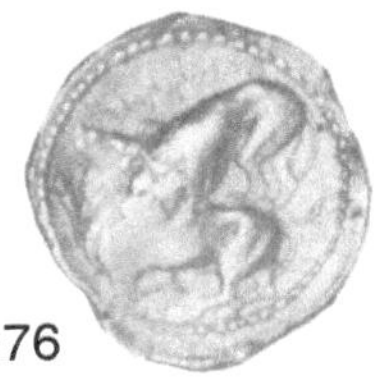

276

O3 R5

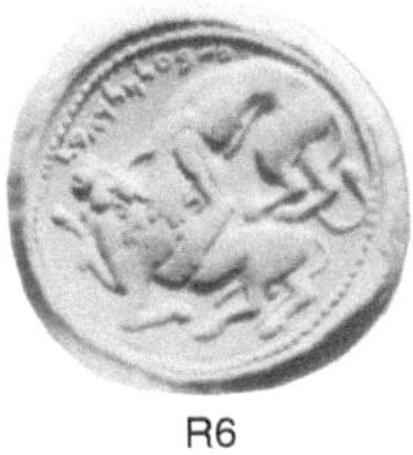

R6
289

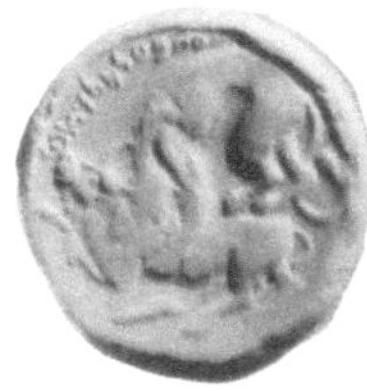

R7
295

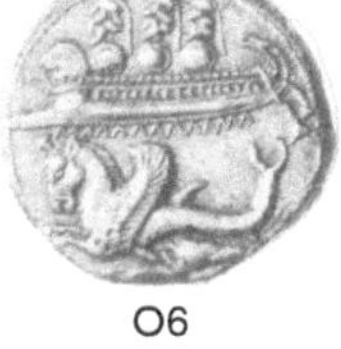

O6
299

IV.2.1.b

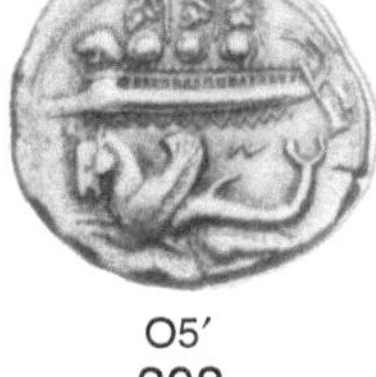

O5′
308

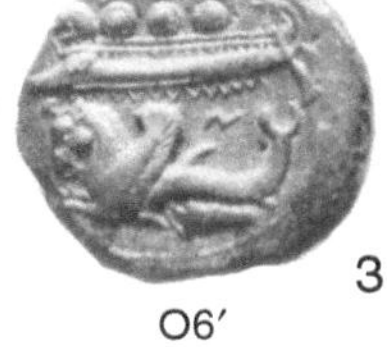
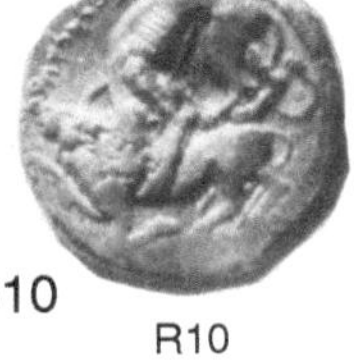

310

O6′ R10

Plate 11

IV.2.1.c

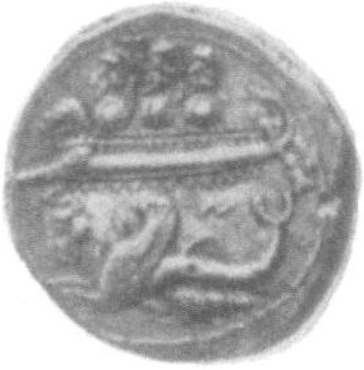

O7
314

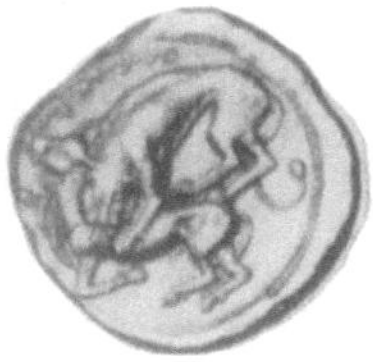

R9
315

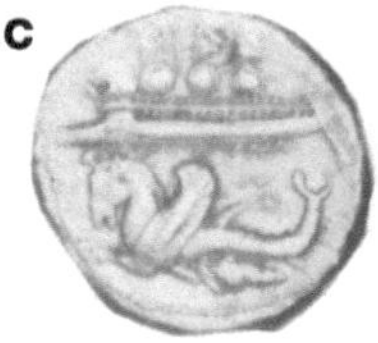

O5″
318

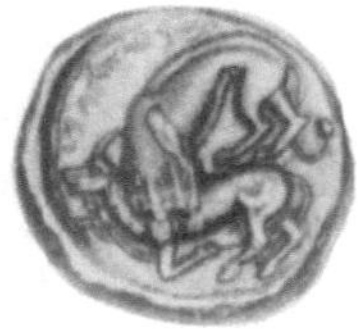

R8
324

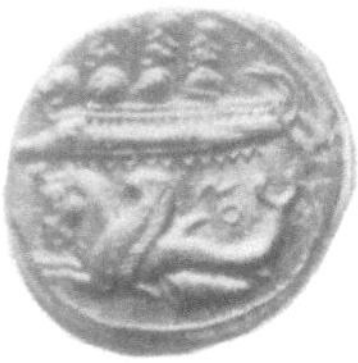

O6″
333

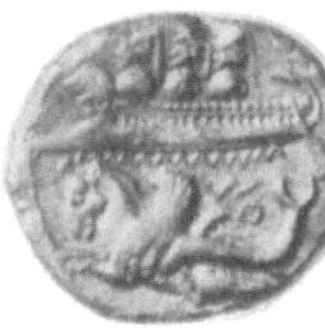

O8
337

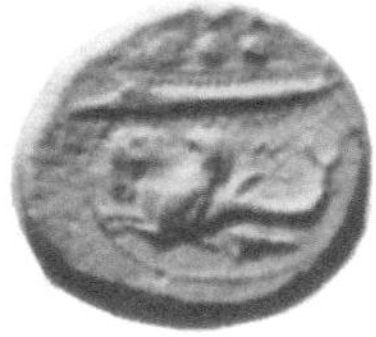

O9
338

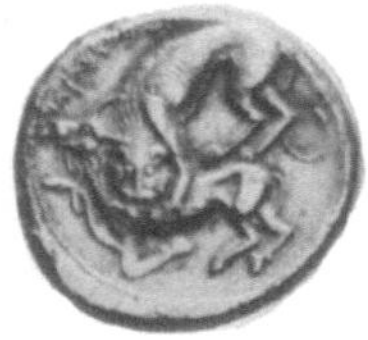

R17
350

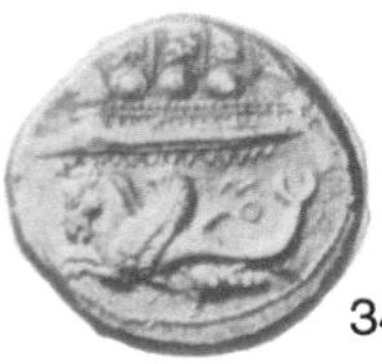

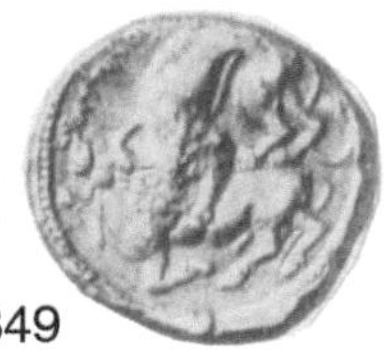

349

O10

R16

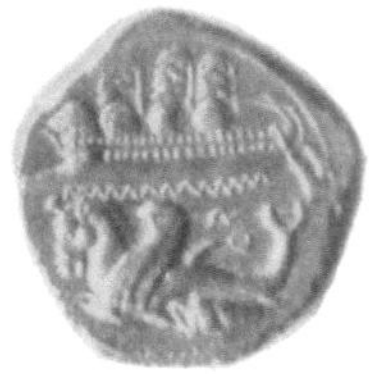

O11
373

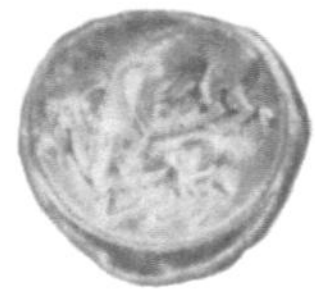

R14
393

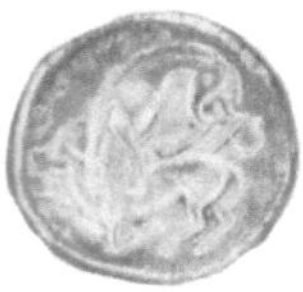

R15
396

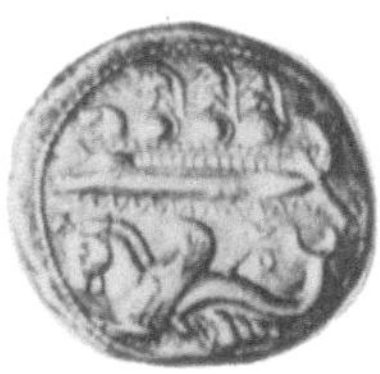

O12
403

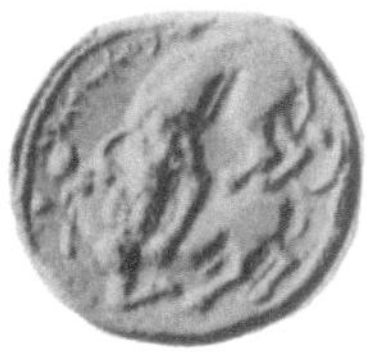

R11
404

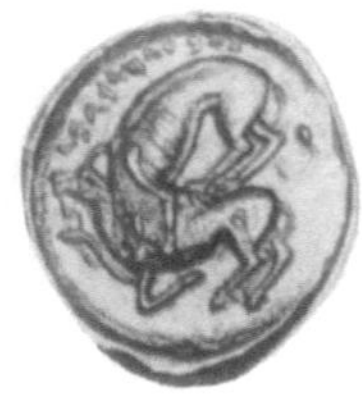

R18
405

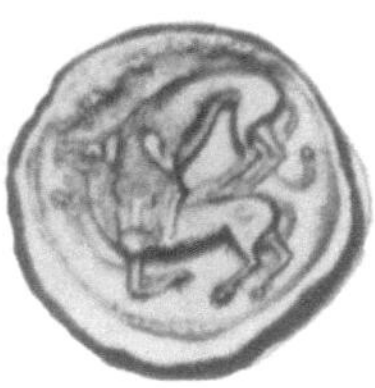

R20
424

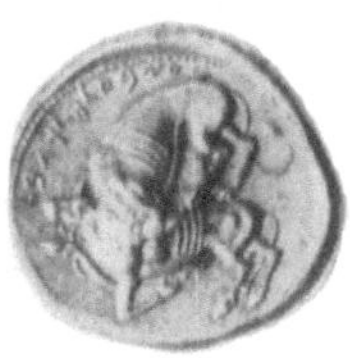

R24
456

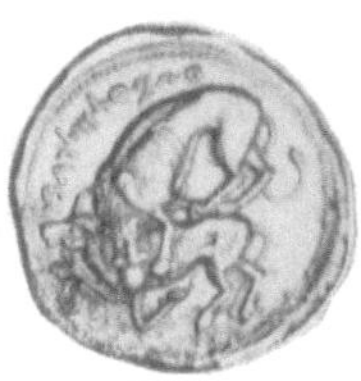

R25
467

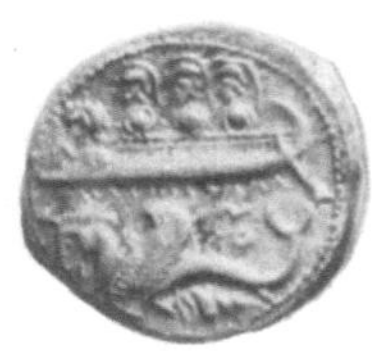

O13
474

Plate 12

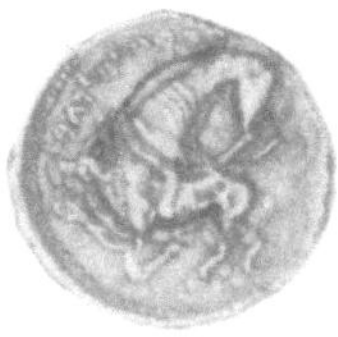
R12
475

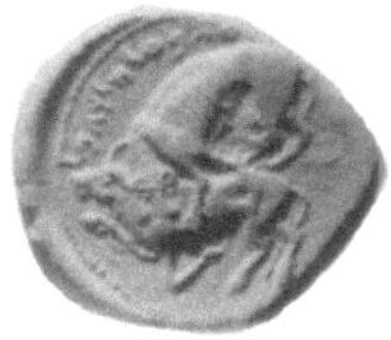
R13
477

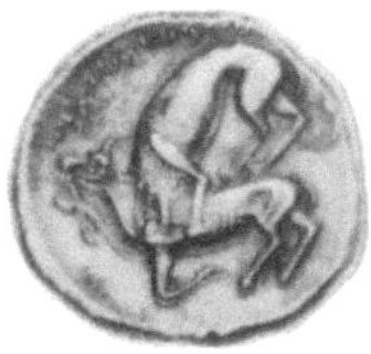
R19
479

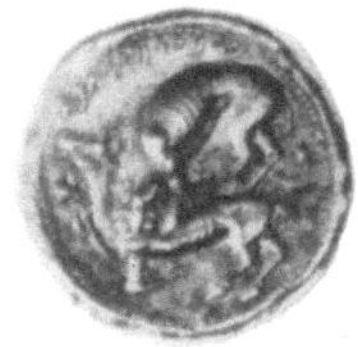
R22
482

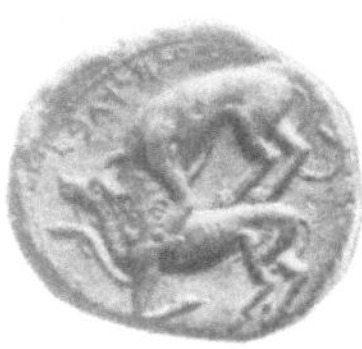
R28
495

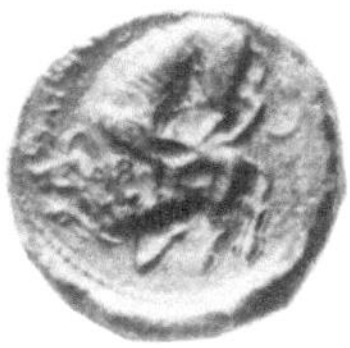
R29
496

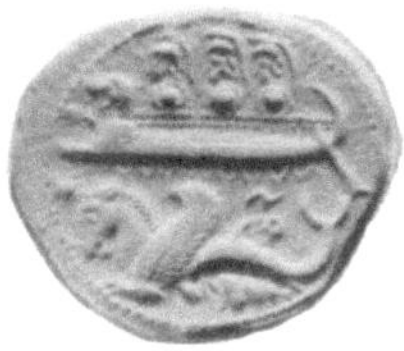
O14
499

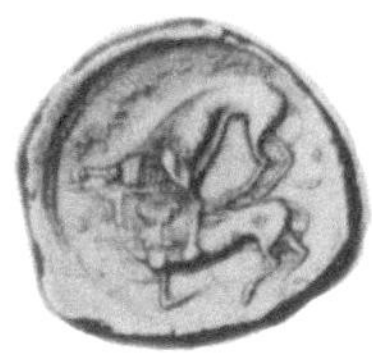
R21
509

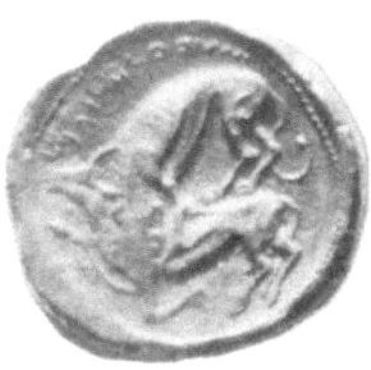
R23
512

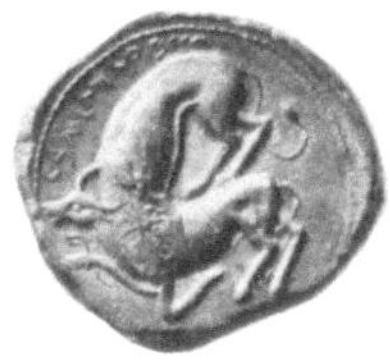
R26
517

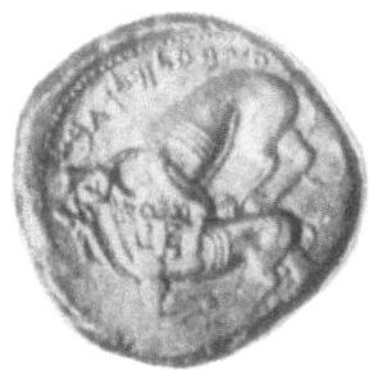
R27
518

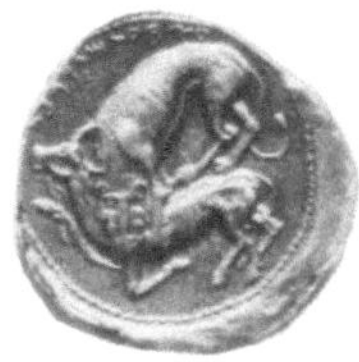
R30
524

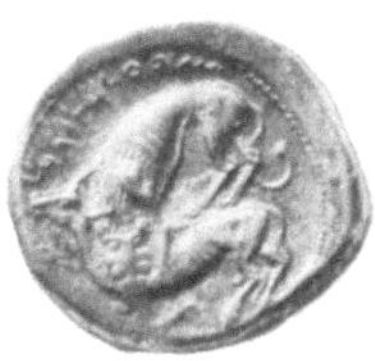
R31
526

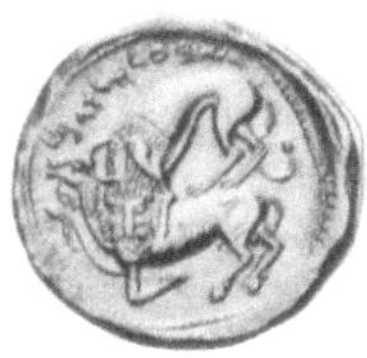
R32
528

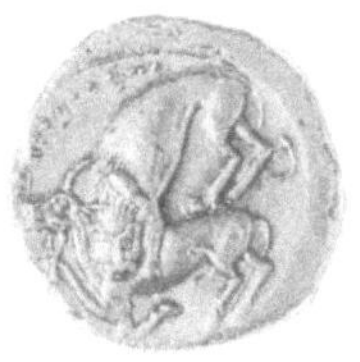
R33
536

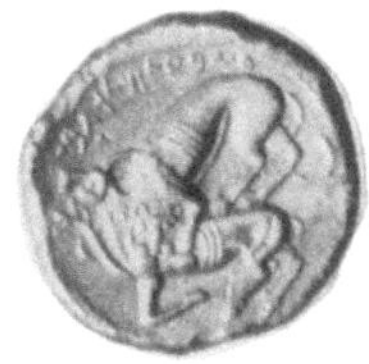
R34
538

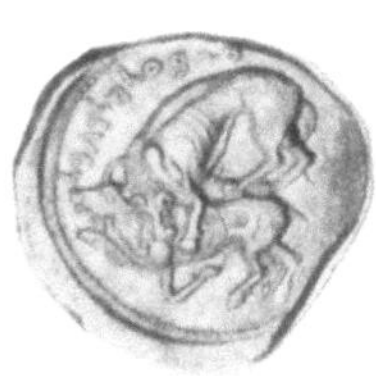
R35
542

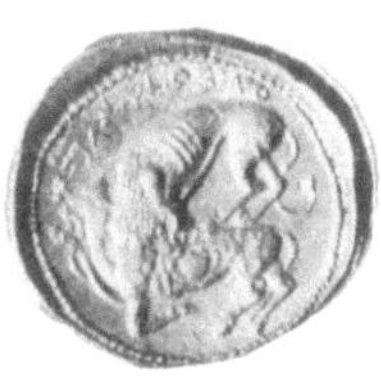
R36
548

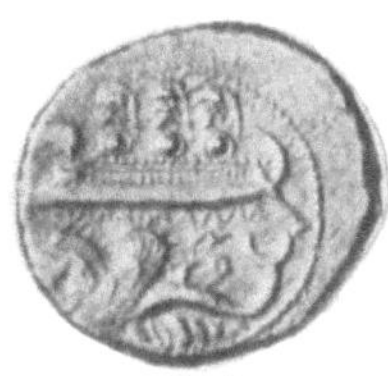
O15
552

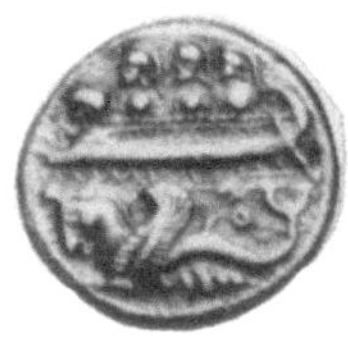
O16
556

Plate 13

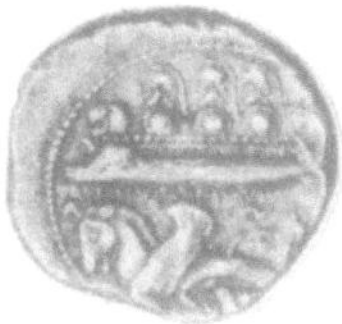
O17
558

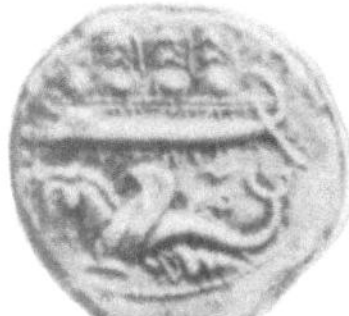
O18
609

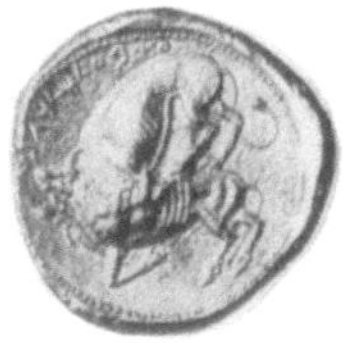
R37
677

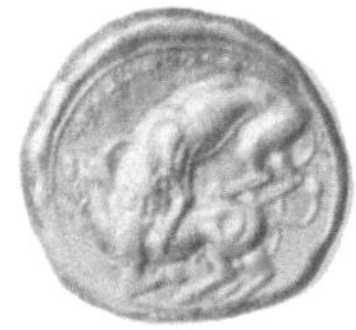
R38
680

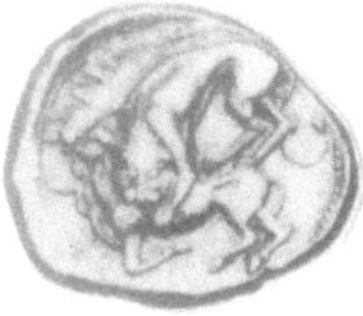
R39
682

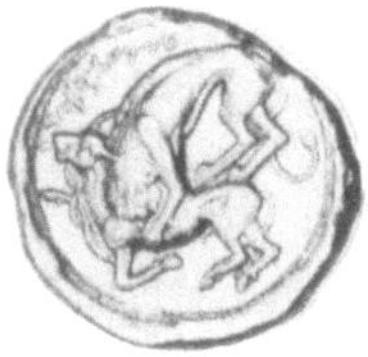
R40
683

IV.2.2

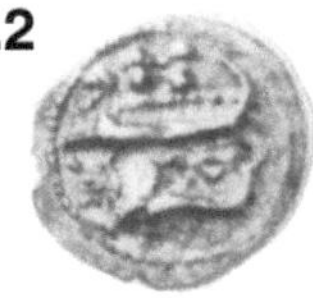
O1
728 (×2)

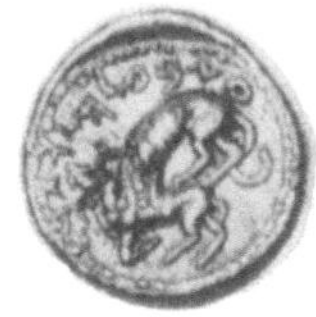
R1
729 (×2)

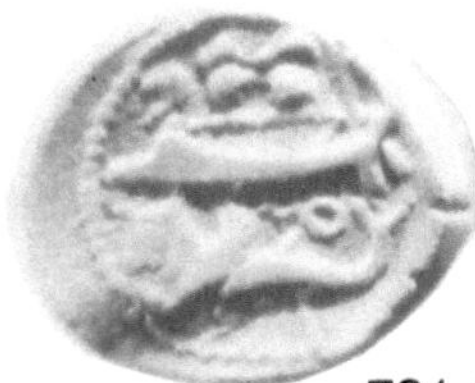
O2

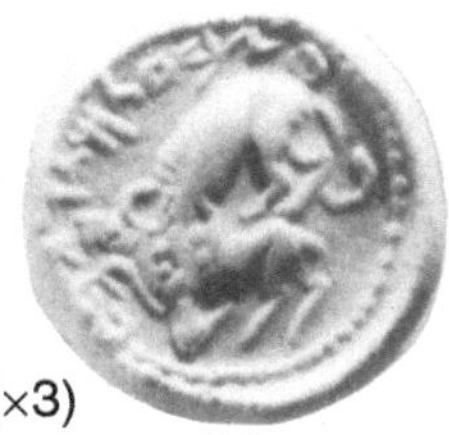
R2

731 (×3)

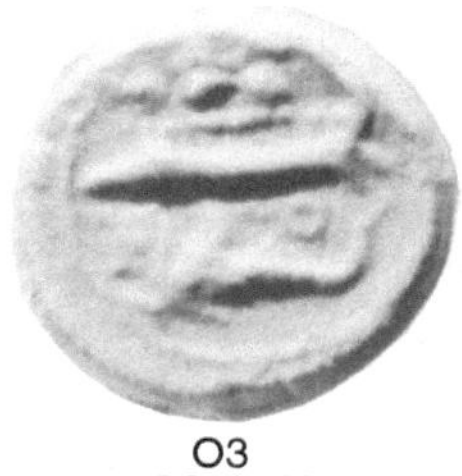
O3
733 (×3)

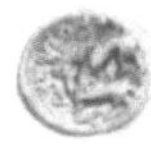
R3
734

O3

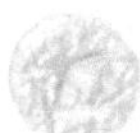
R4

735

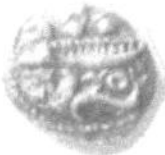
O4
736

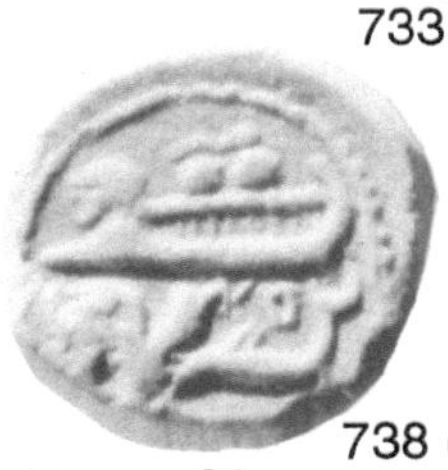
O6

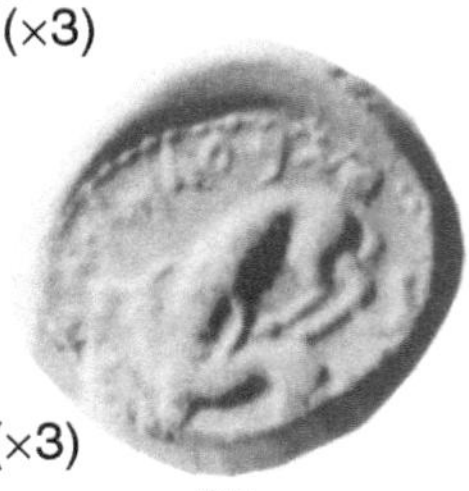
R5

738 (×3)

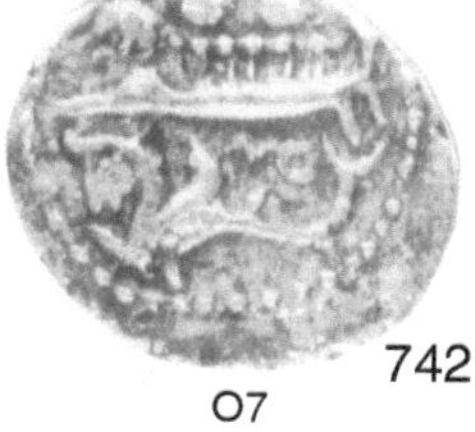
O7

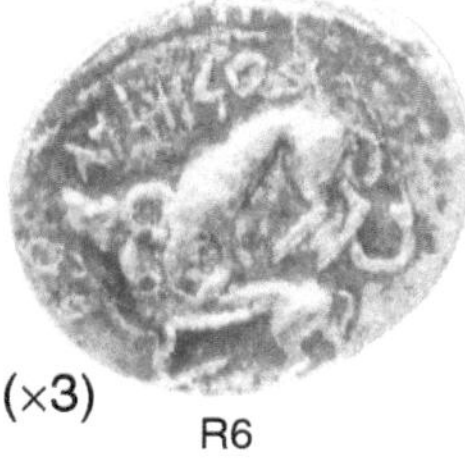
R6

742 (×3)

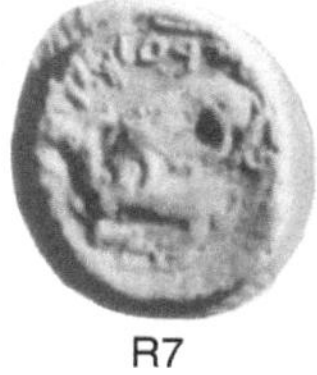
R7
743 (×2)

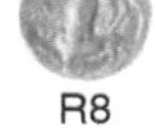
R8
744

Plate 14

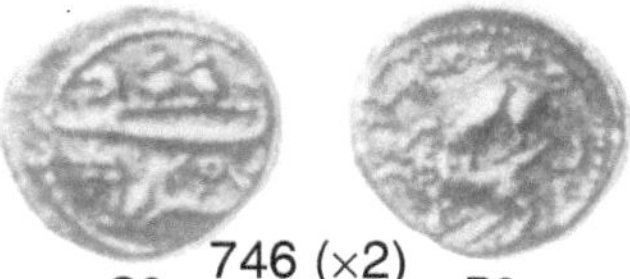

O9 746 (×2) R9

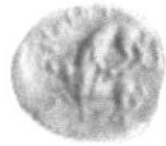

R10
747

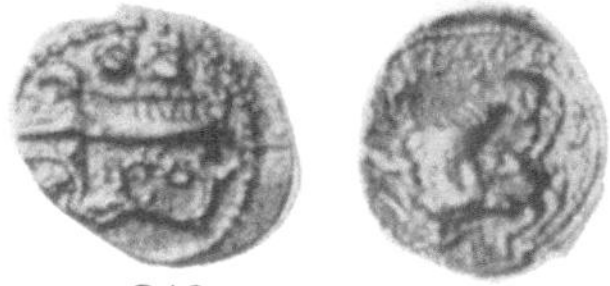

O10 749 (×2) R11

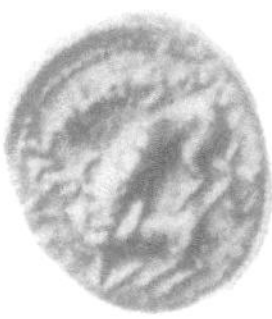

R12
752 (×2)

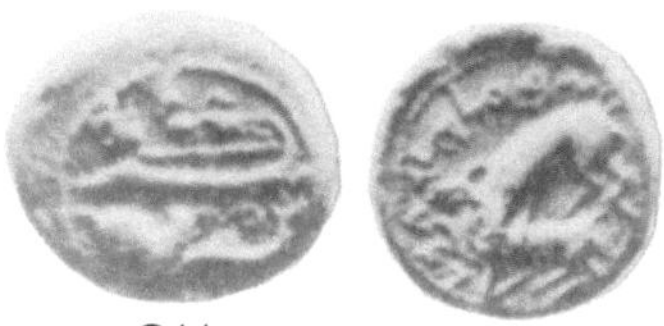

O11 753 (×2) R13

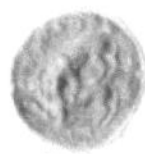

R14
754

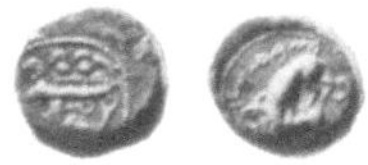

O12 756 R15

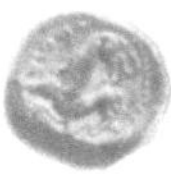

R16
757

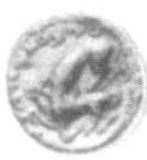

R17
758

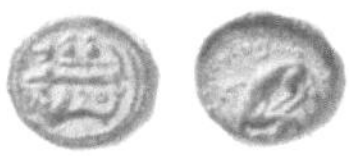

O13 759 R18

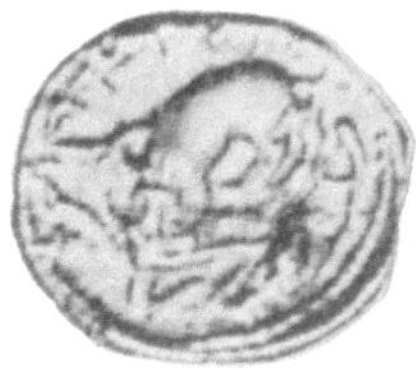

O14
760 (×3)

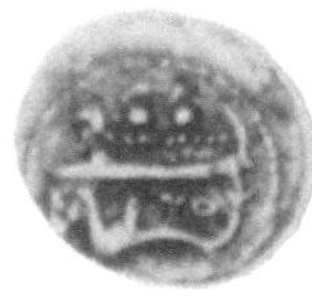

O15
766 (×2)

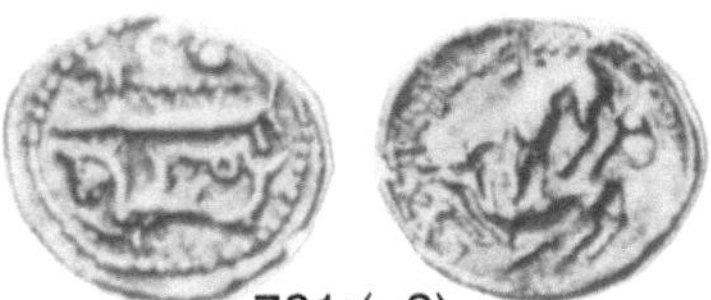

O14 761 (×2) R20

IV.3.1

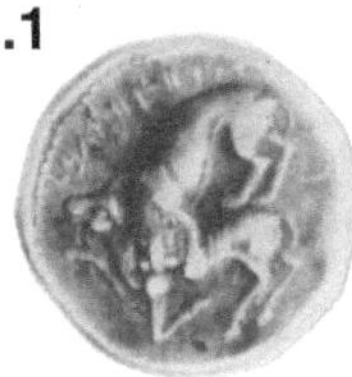

R1
772

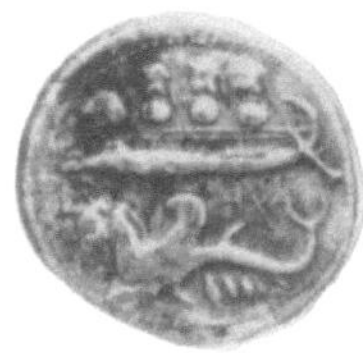

O1
773

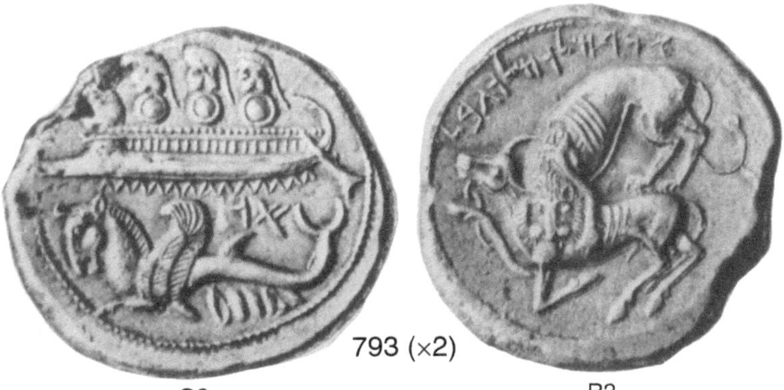

O2 793 (×2) R2

Plate 15

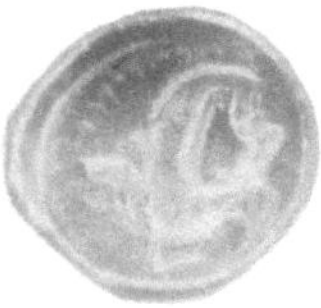
R3
815

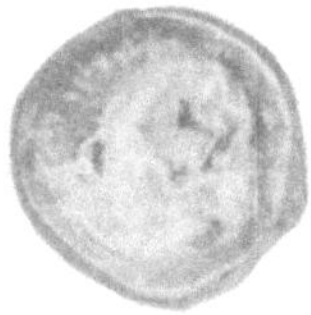
R4
816

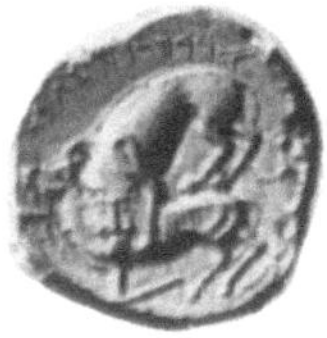
R5
818

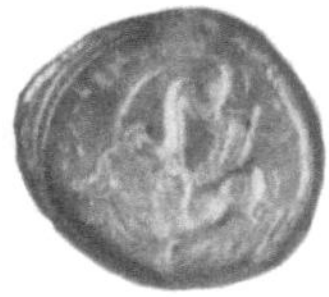
R6
819

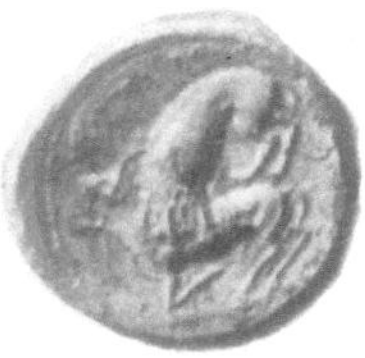
R7
821

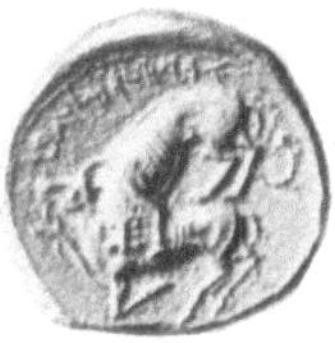
R8
825

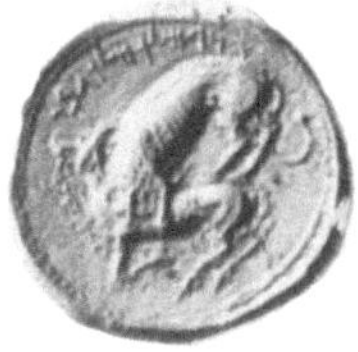
R9
828

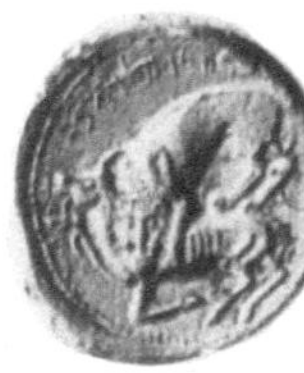
R10
829

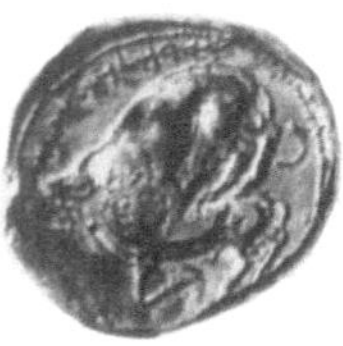
R11
830

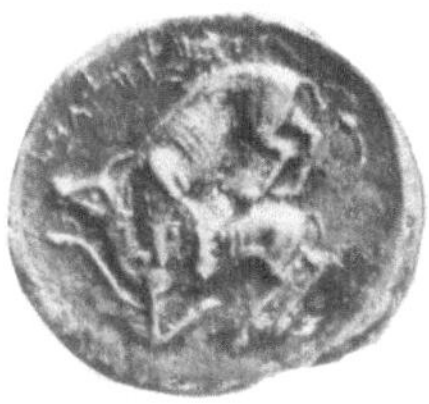
R12
831

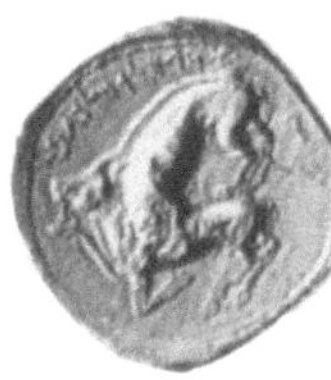
R13
833

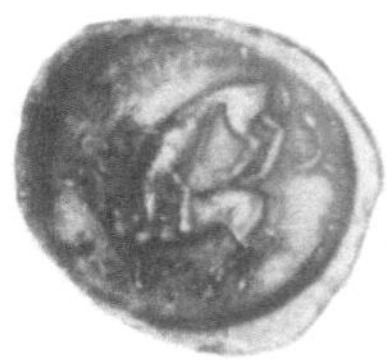
R14
834

IV.3.2

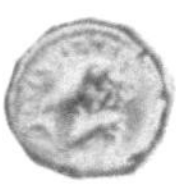
R2
847

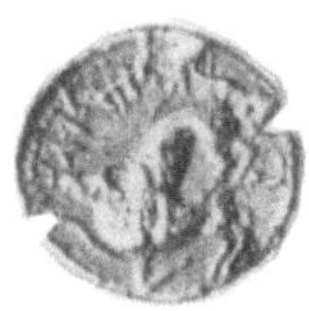
R3
848 (×2)

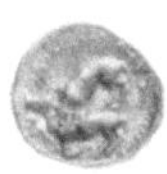
R6
849

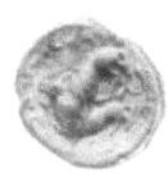
R7
850

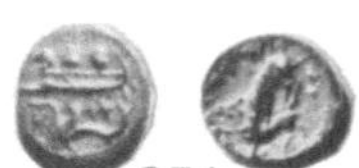
01 851 R1

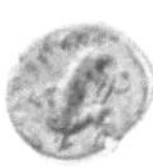
R4
852

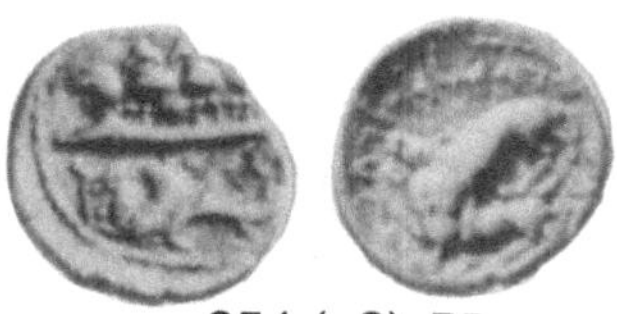
O2 854 (×2) R5

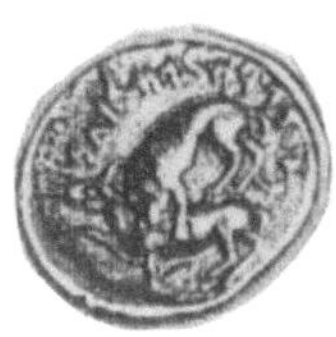
R8
856 (×2)

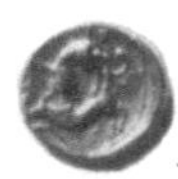
R9
857

Plate 16

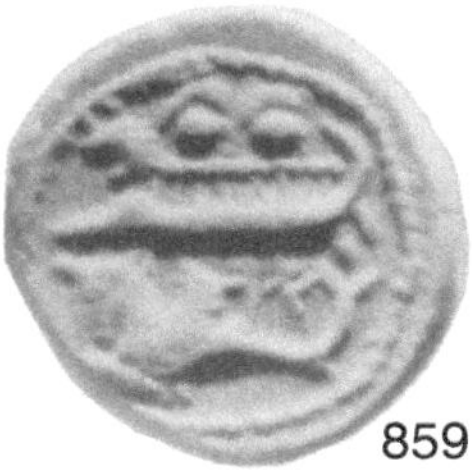
O3

859 (×3)

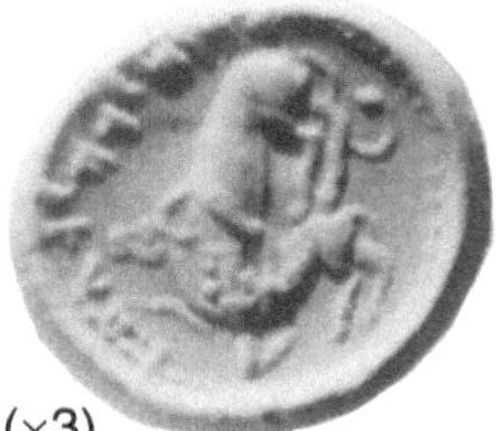
R10

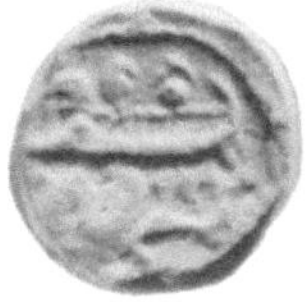
O4
862 (×2)

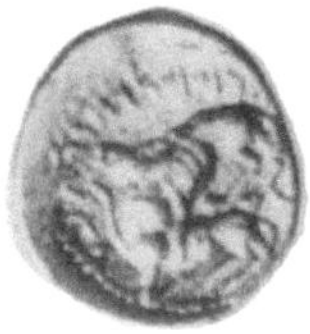
R11
863 (×2)

05

864

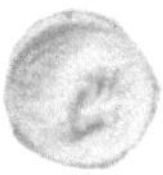
R12

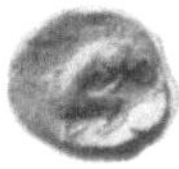
R13
865

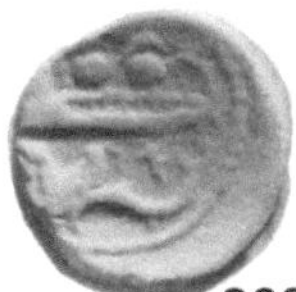
O6

866 (×2)

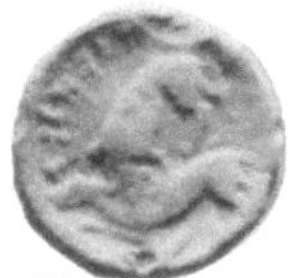
R14

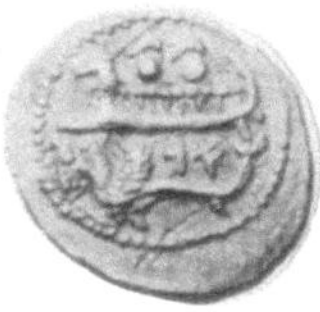
O7
867 (×2)

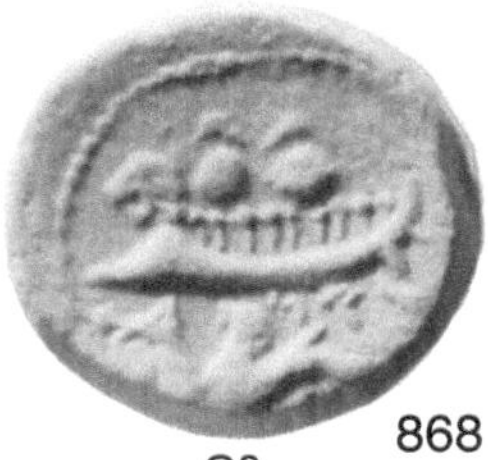
O8

868 (×3)

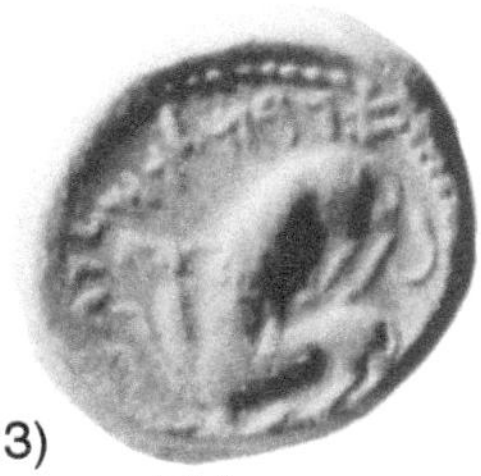
R15

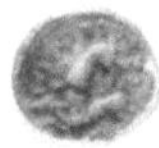
R16
878

IV.4.1

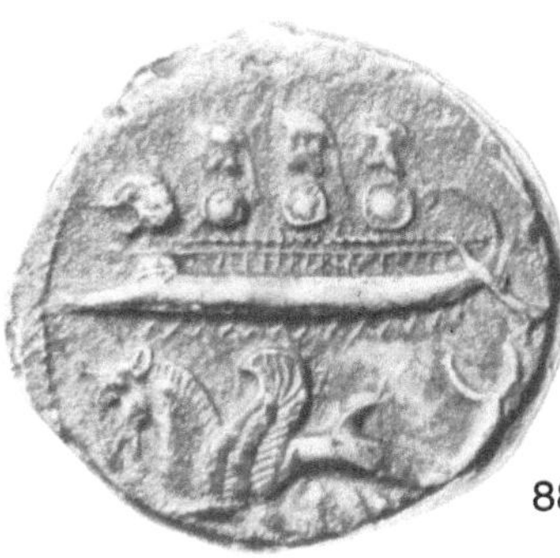
O1

886 (×2)

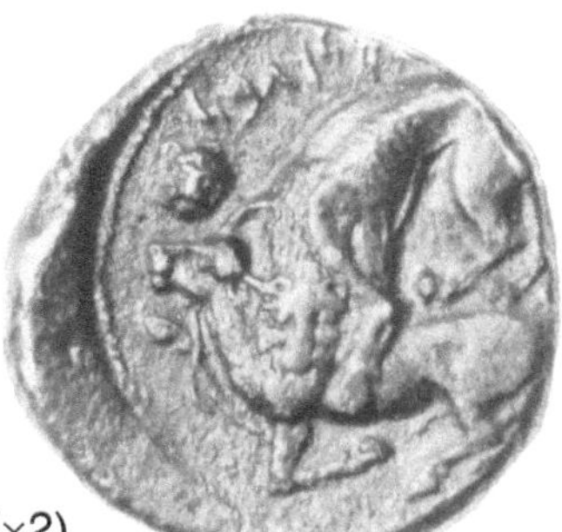
R1

Plate 17

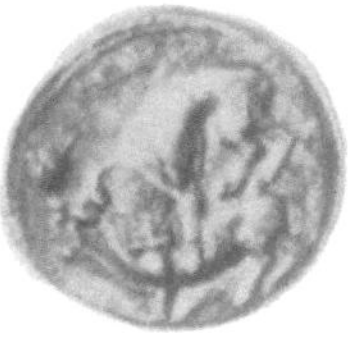
R2
888

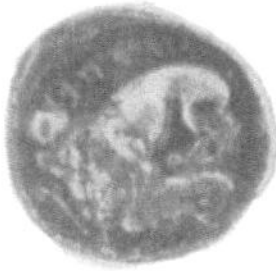
R3
893

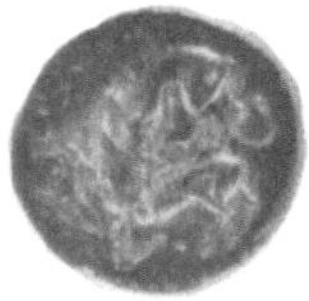
R4
897

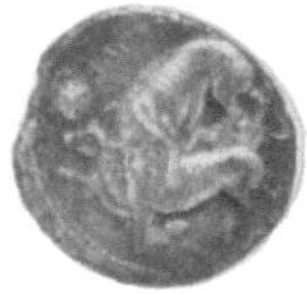
R5
901

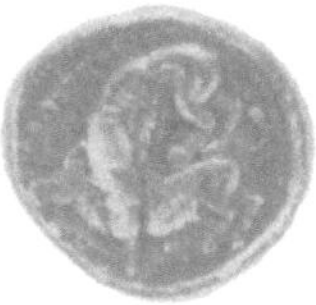
R6
903

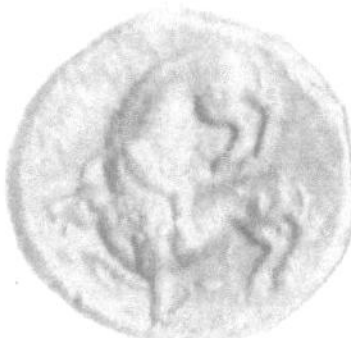
R7
904

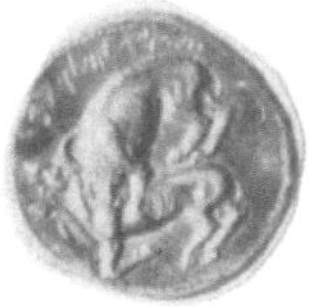
R8
910

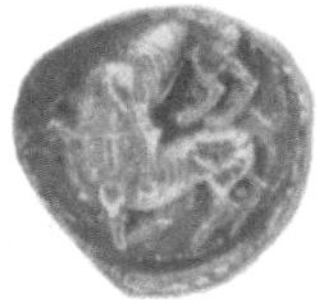
R9
919

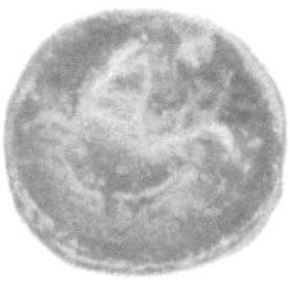
R10
923

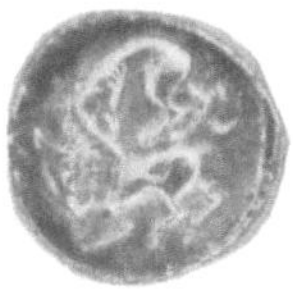
R11
924

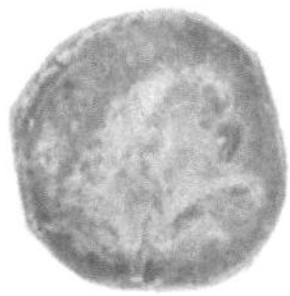
R12
925

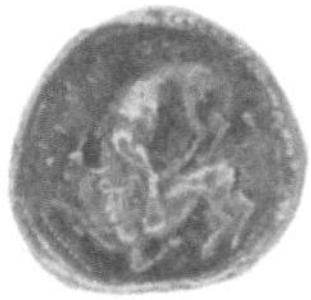
R13
926

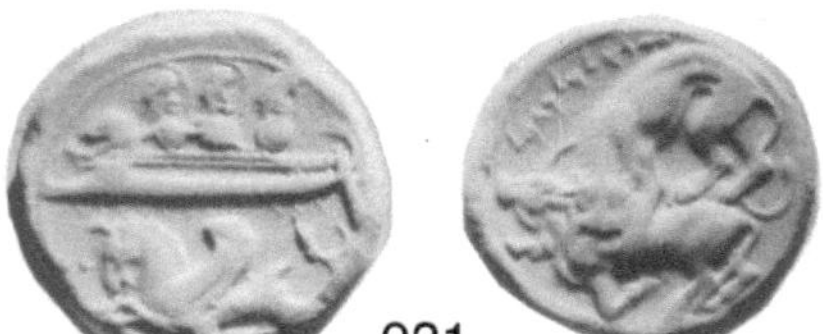
O2 931 R15

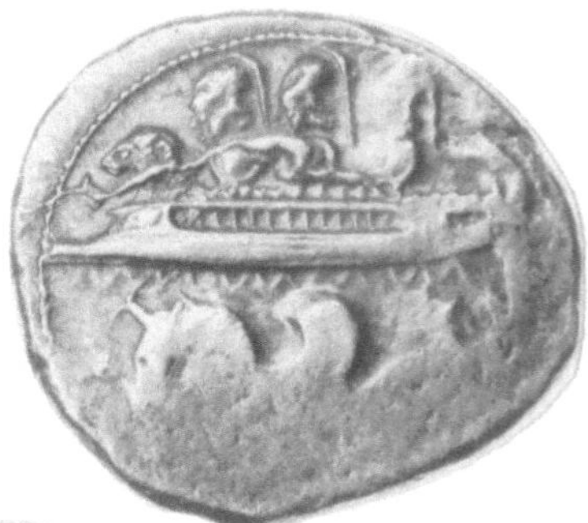
O2
934 (×2)

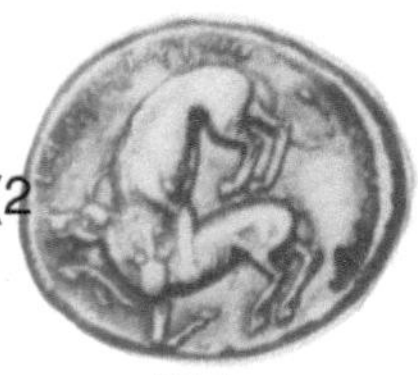
R14
929

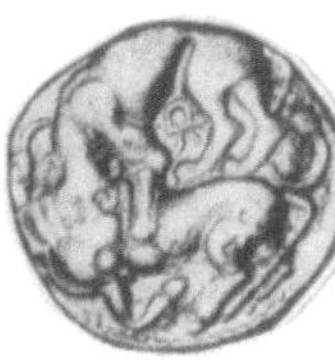
R16
935

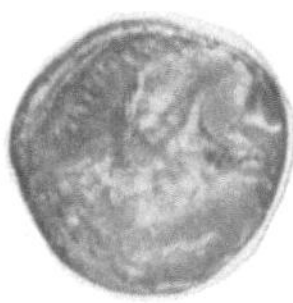
R17
939

Plate 18

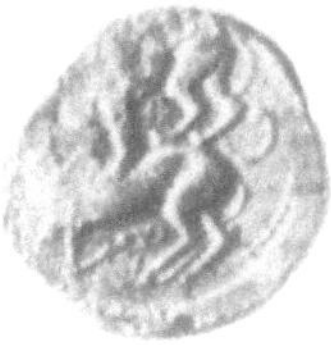

R18
940

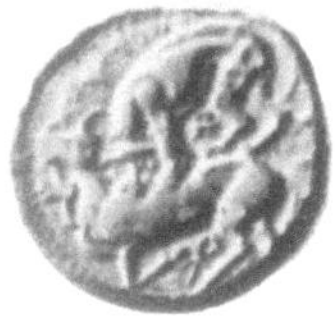

R19
941

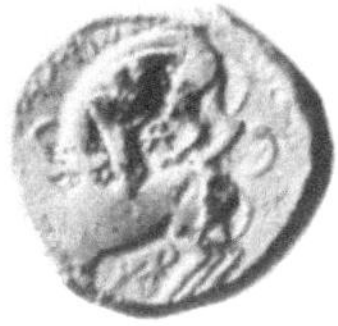

R20
942

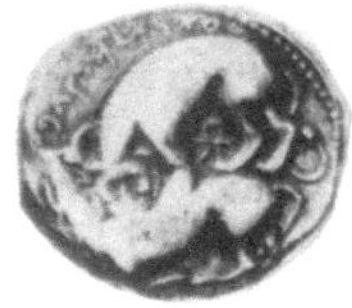

R21
943

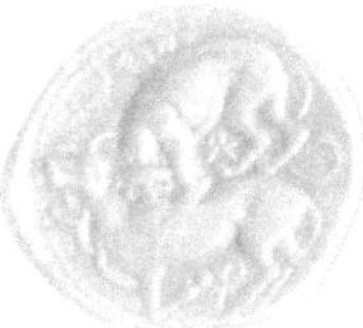

R22
945

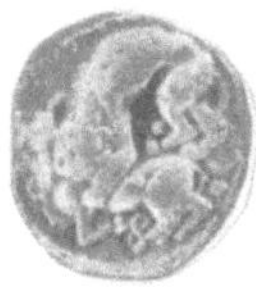

R23
947

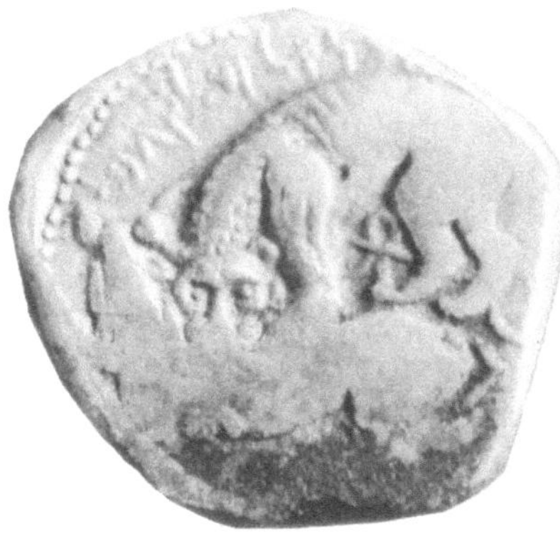

R25
953 (×3)

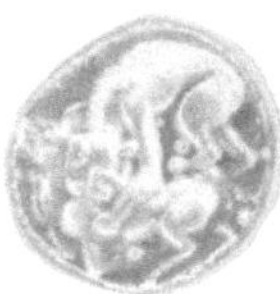

R24
950

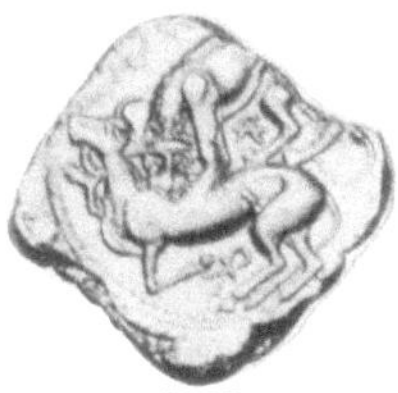

R26
955

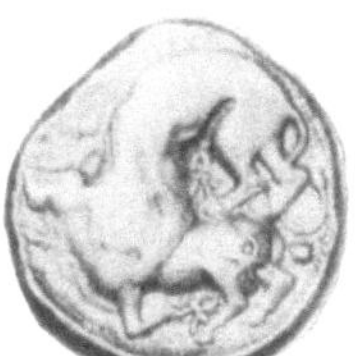

R27
956

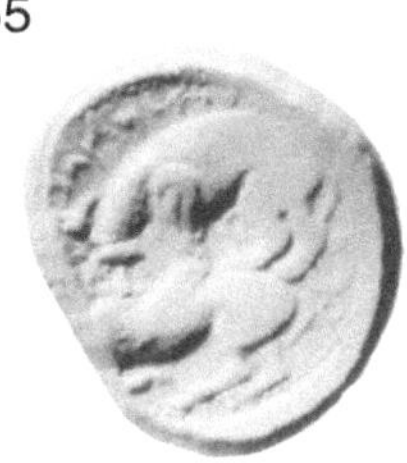

R28
958

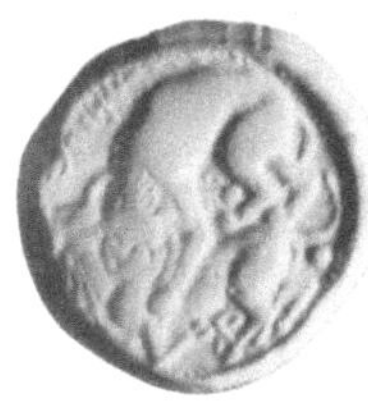

R29
960

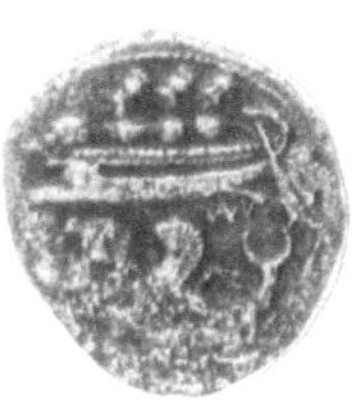

04
962

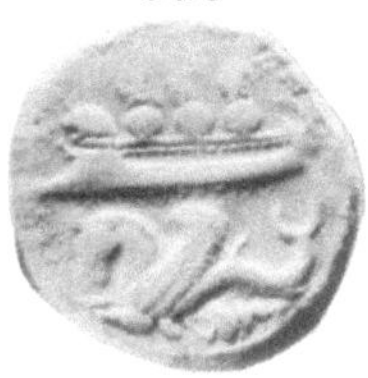

O3

961

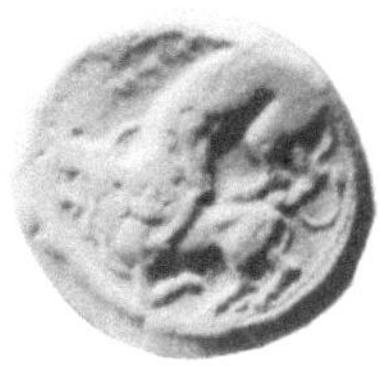

R30

Plate 19

IV.4.2

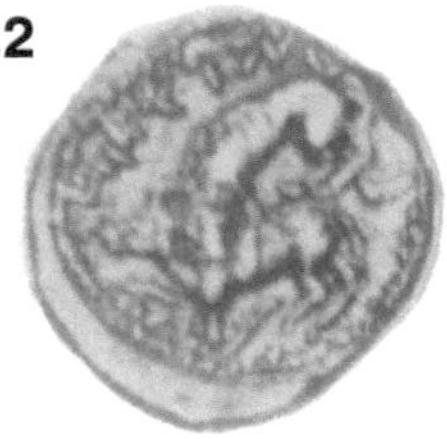
R2
967 (×3)

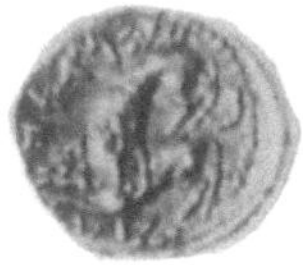
R4
970 (×2)

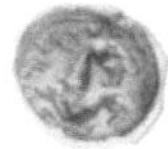
R7
973

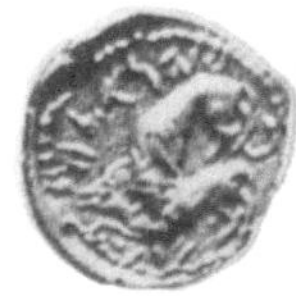
R18
1003 (×2)

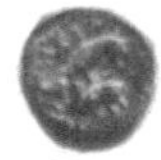
R19
1005

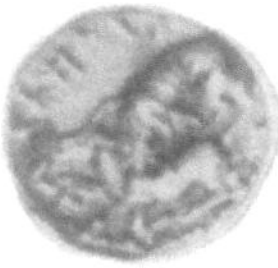
R3
1011 (x2)

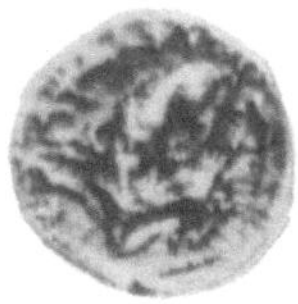
R9
1020 (x2)

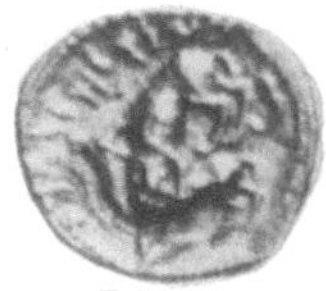
R12
1027 (x2)

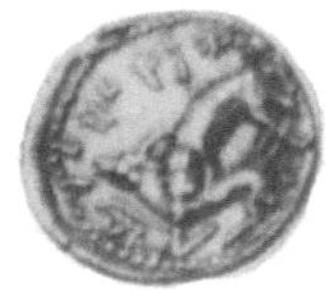
R14
1031 (x2)

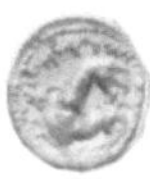
R20
1040

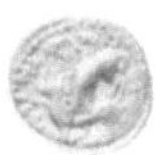
R21
1043

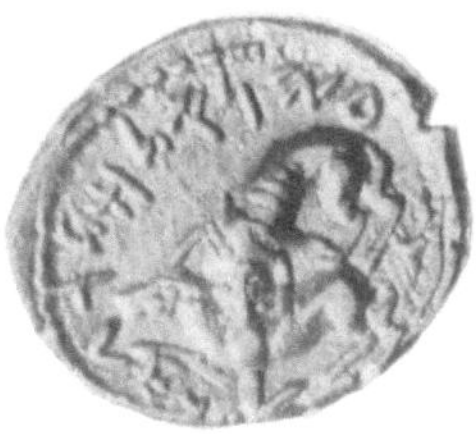
R24
1047 (×3)

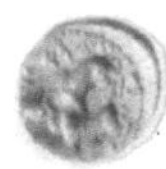
R25
1049

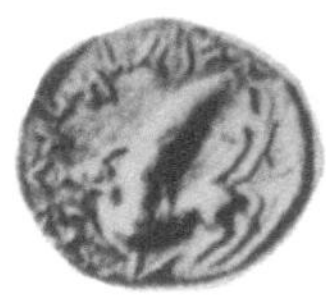
R27
1051 (×2)

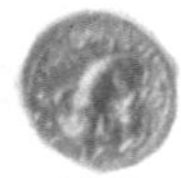
R28
1052

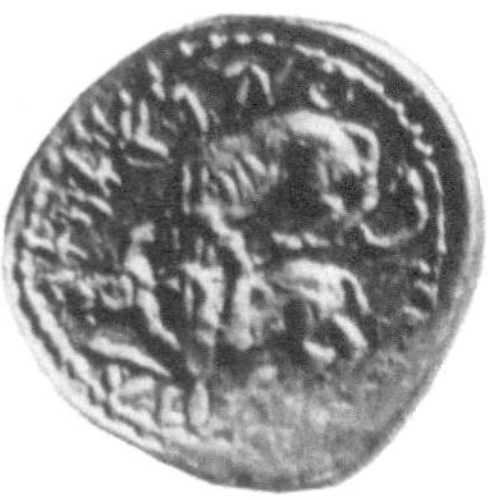
R29
1053 (×3)

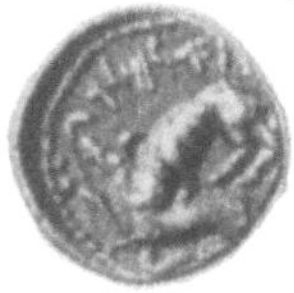
R30
1054 (×2)

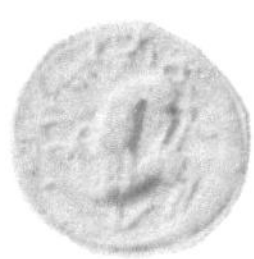
R31
1055 (×1.5)

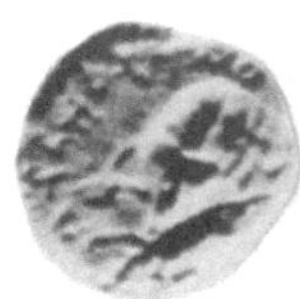
R32
1056 (×2)

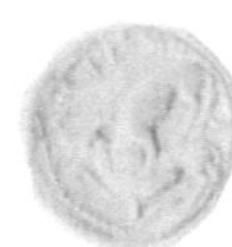
R23
1082 (×1.5)

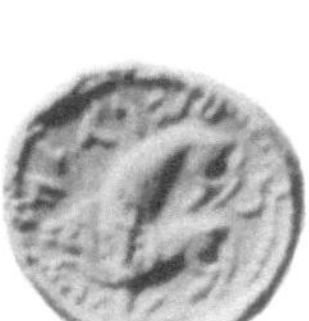
R11
1079 (×2)

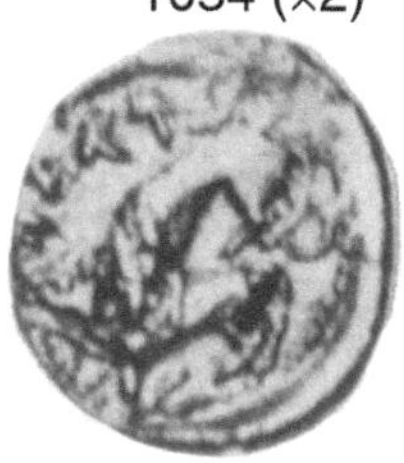
R39
1083 (×3)

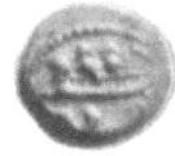
O1
1089

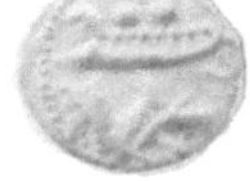
O2

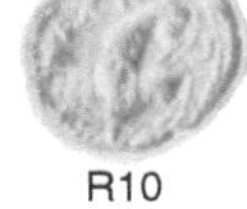
R10
1090 (×1.5)

Plate 20

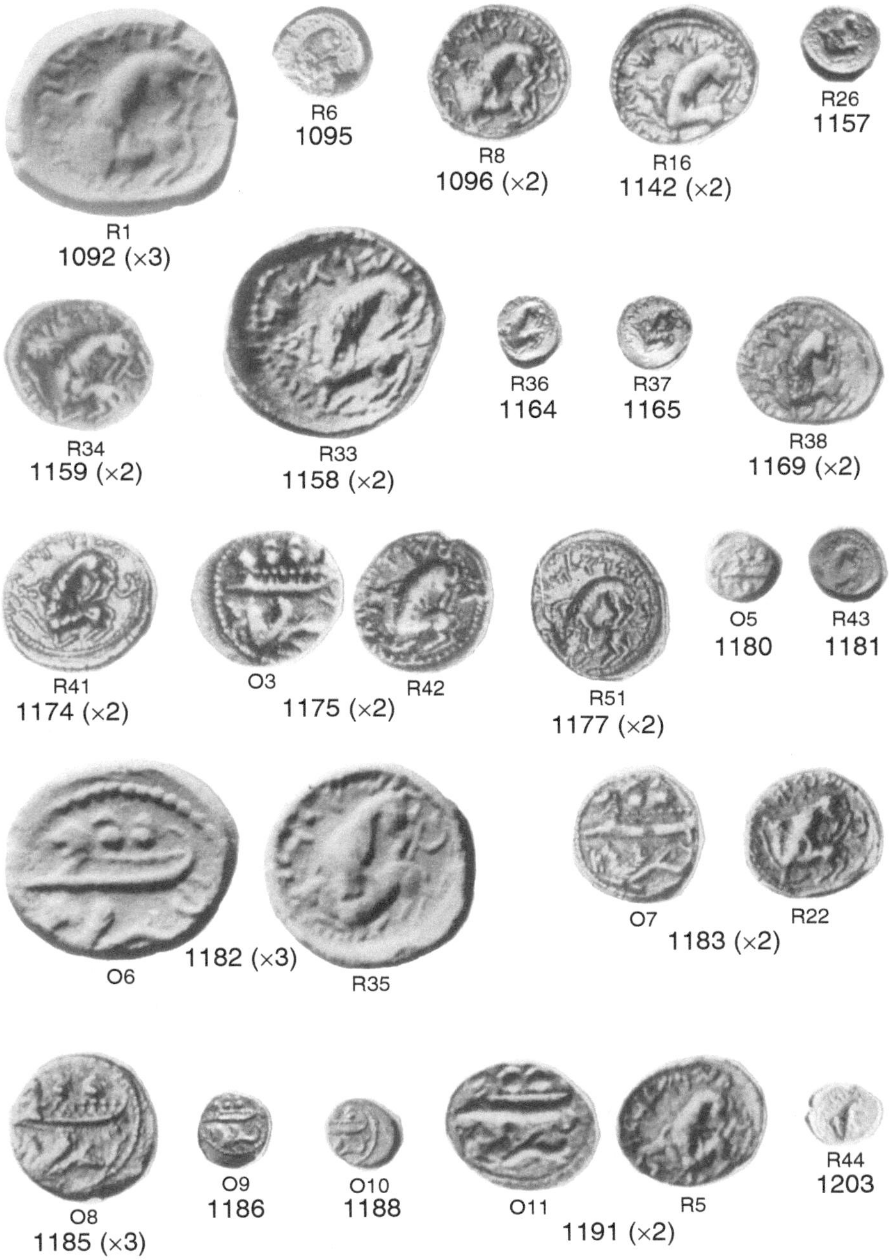

R1 1092 (×3)
R6 1095
R8 1096 (×2)
R16 1142 (×2)
R26 1157
R34 1159 (×2)
R33 1158 (×2)
R36 1164
R37 1165
R38 1169 (×2)
R41 1174 (×2)
O3 1175 (×2) R42
R51 1177 (×2)
O5 1180
R43 1181
O6 1182 (×3) R35
O7 1183 (×2) R22
O8 1185 (×3)
O9 1186
O10 1188
O11 1191 (×2) R5
R44 1203

Plate 21

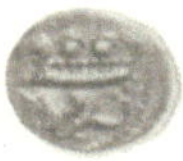
O12
1206

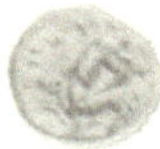
R46
1214

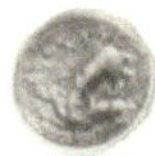
R47
1215

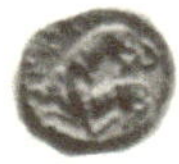
R48
1216

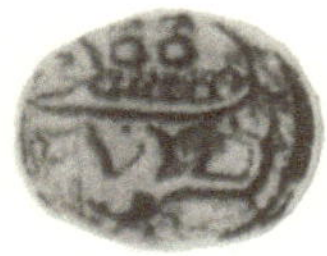
O13
1221 (×2)

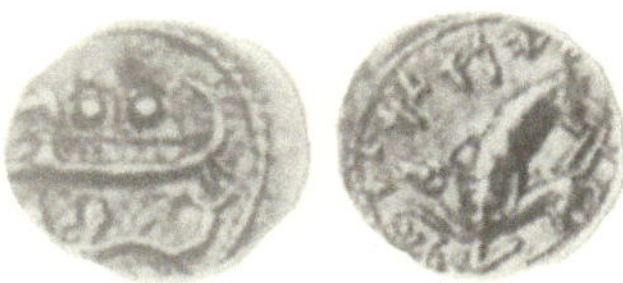
O14 R13
1228 (×2)

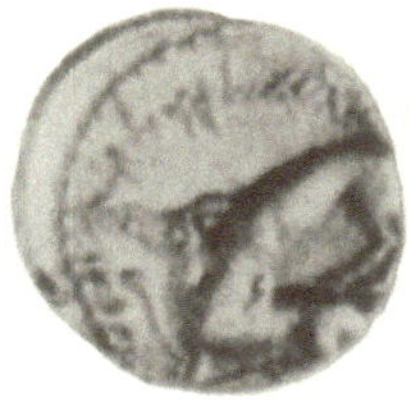
R49
1231 (×3)

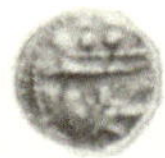
O15
1235

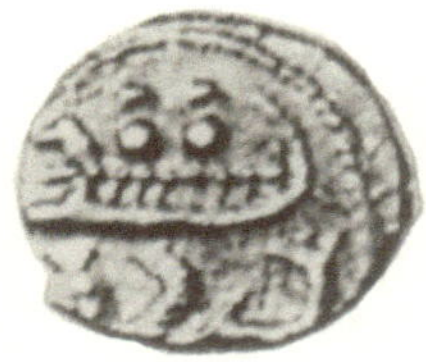
O16
1238 (×3)

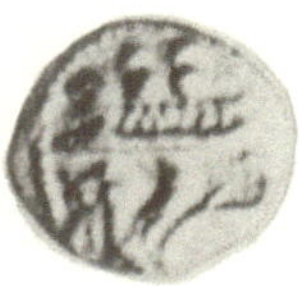
O17
1243 (×2)

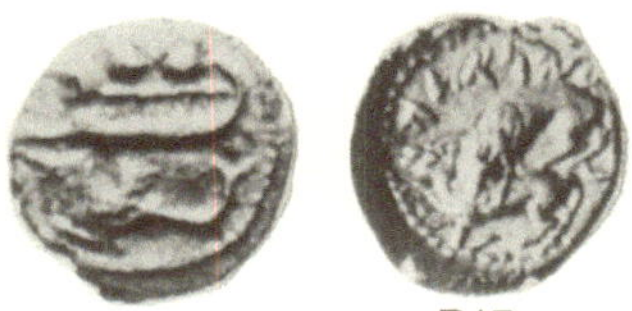
O18 R17
1247 (×2)

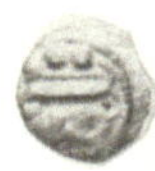
O19
1249

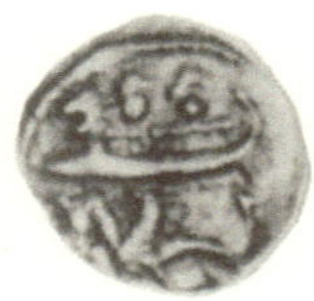
O20
1252 (×2)

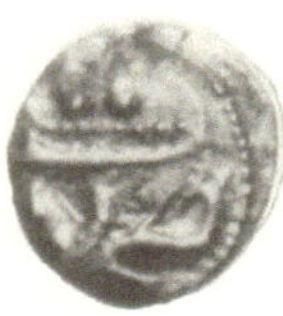
O22
1260 (×2)

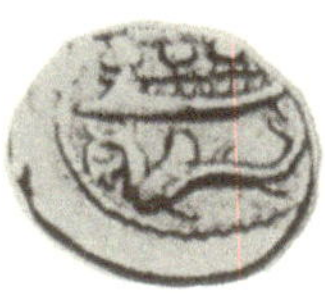
O23
1267 (×2)

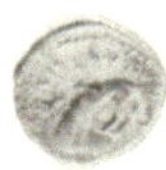
R50
1269

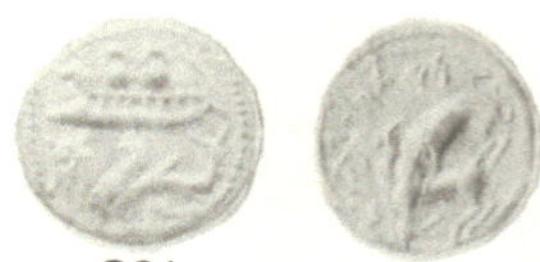
O24 R52
1272 (×1.5)

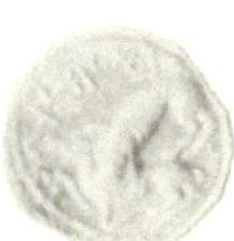
R53
1273 (×1.5)

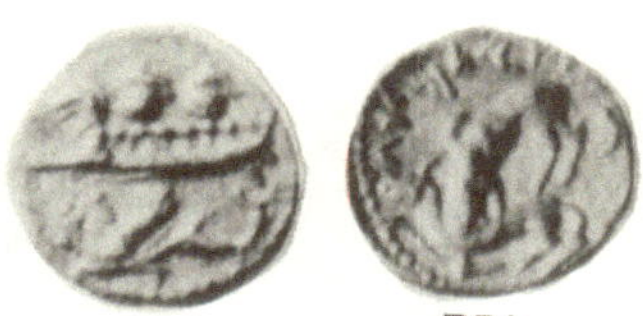
O25 R54
1274 (×2)

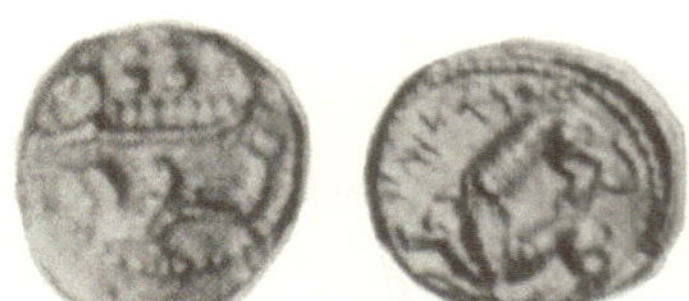
O26 R55
1275 (×2)

Plate 22

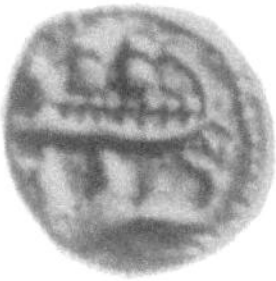

O21
1334 (×2)

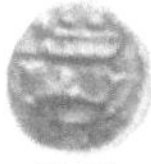

O27
1342

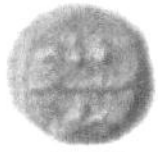

O28
1344

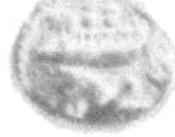

O29
1345

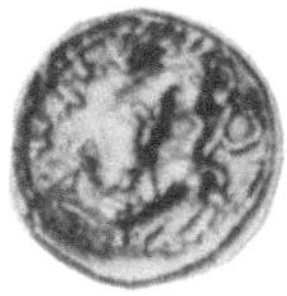

R40
1402 (×2)

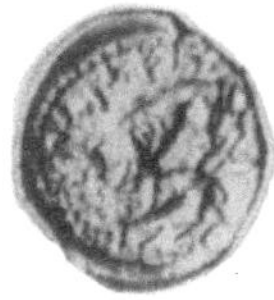

R45
1404 (×2)

IV.4.3

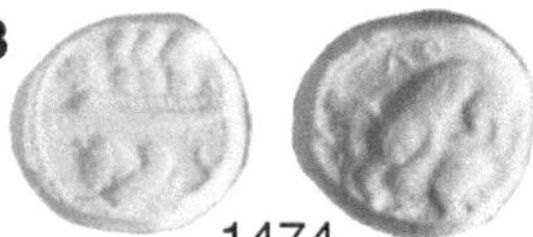

O1 1474 R1

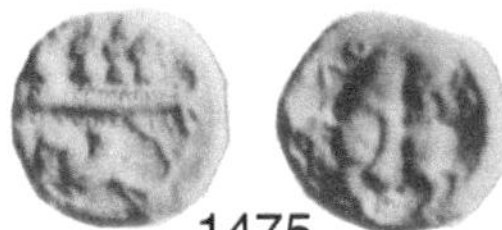

O2 1475 R2

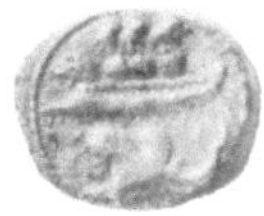

O4
1477

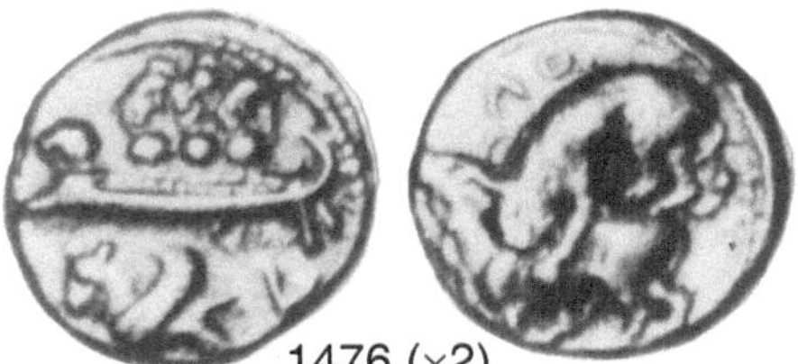

O3 1476 (×2) R3

IV.4.5

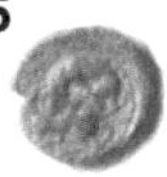

R1
1479

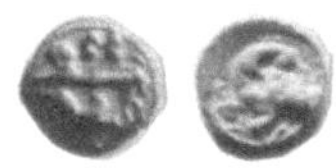

O1 R2
1480

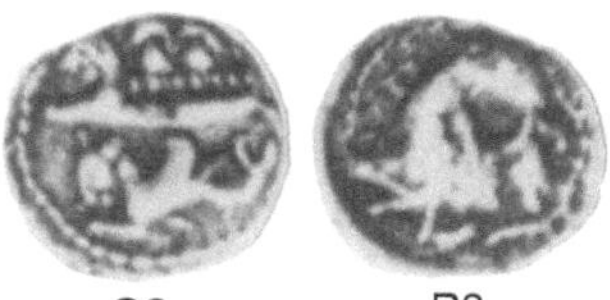

O2 R3
1481 (×2)

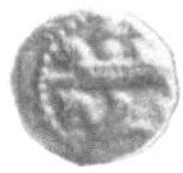

O3
1484

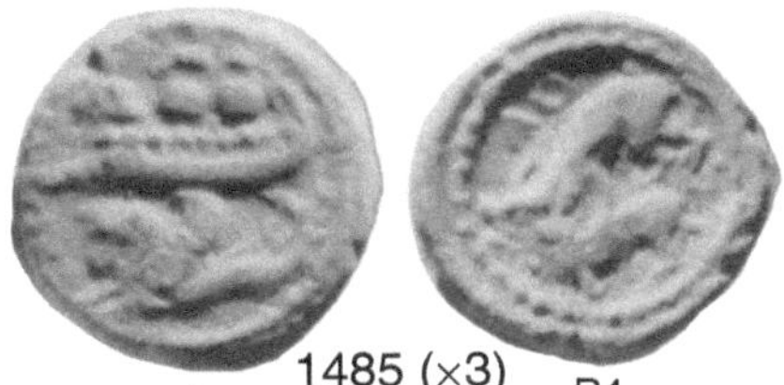

O4 1485 (×3) R4

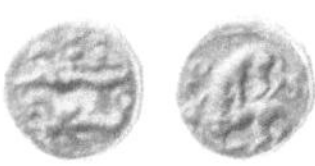

O5 R5
1486

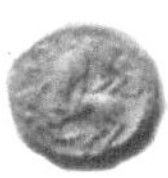

R6
1487

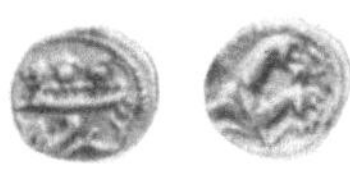

O6 R7
1488

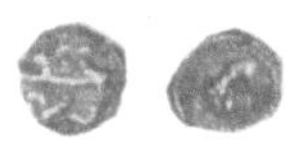

O8 R9
1490

Plate 23

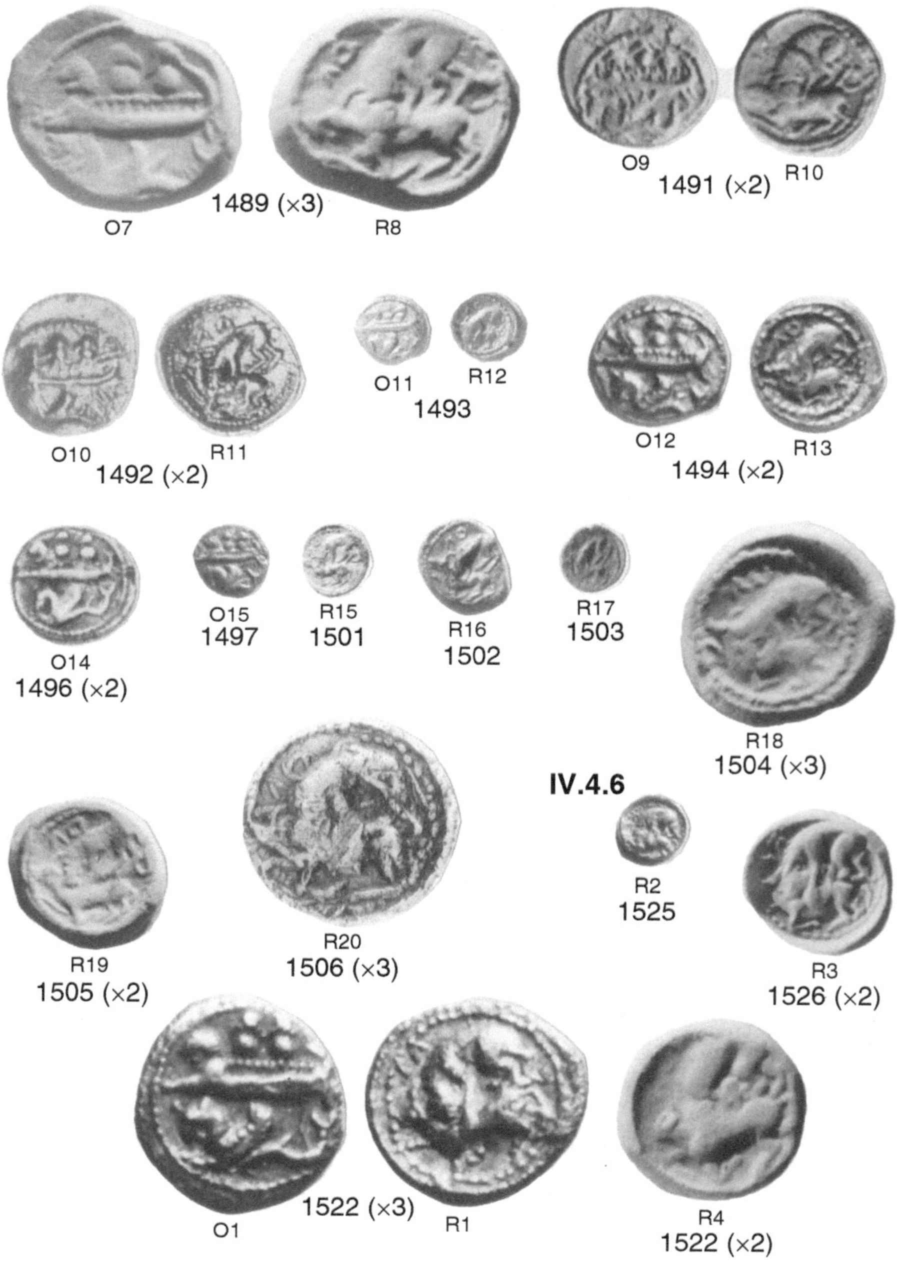
O7
1489 (×3)
R8
O9
1491 (×2)
R10
O10
1492 (×2)
R11
O11
R12
1493
O12
1494 (×2)
R13
O14
1496 (×2)
O15
1497
R15
1501
R16
1502
R17
1503
R18
1504 (×3)
IV.4.6
R2
1525
R19
1505 (×2)
R20
1506 (×3)
R3
1526 (×2)
O1
1522 (×3)
R1
R4
1522 (×2)

Plate 24

IV.4.7

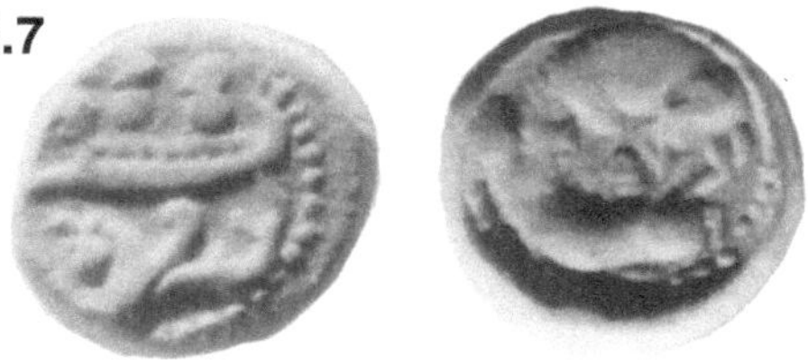

O1 1538 (x3) R1

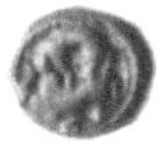

R2
1539

V.1

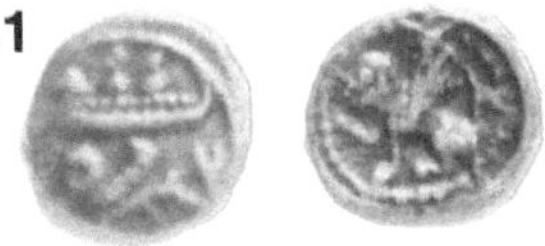

O1 1544 (x2) R1

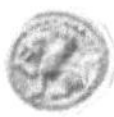

R2
1541

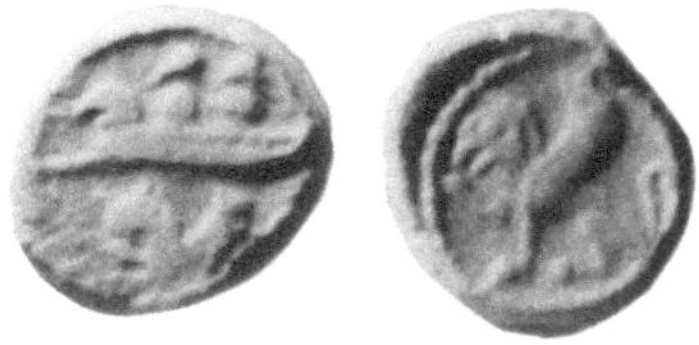

O2 1549 (x3) R3

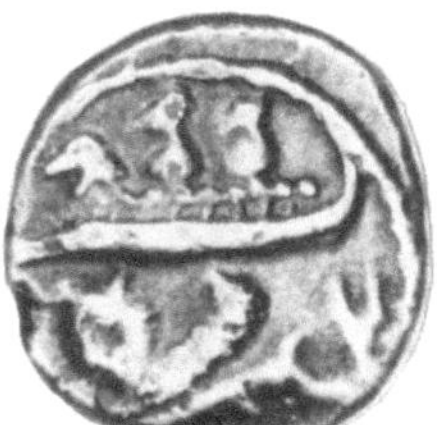

O3
1550 (x4)

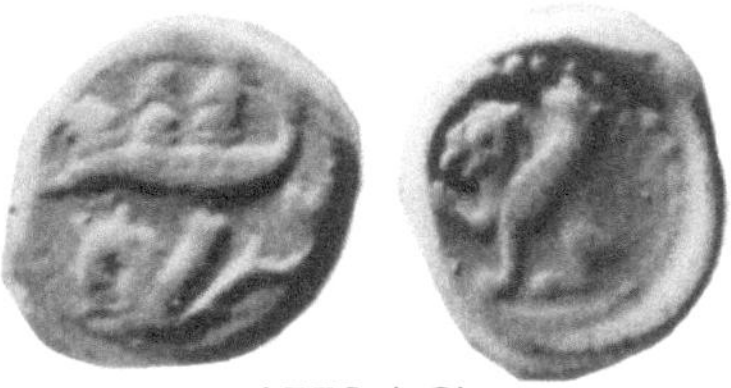

O4 1553 (x3) R3

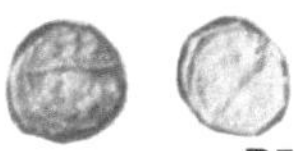

O5 1555 R5

V.2

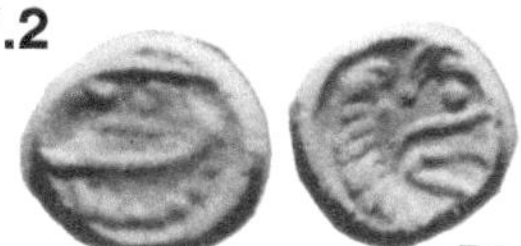

O1 1564 (x3) R1

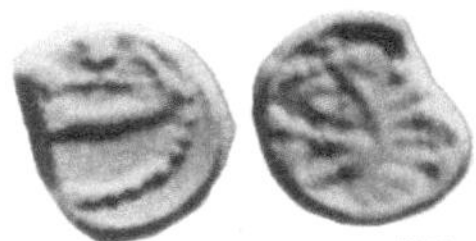

O2 1565 (x3) R2

V.3

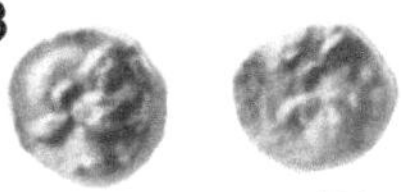

O1 1566 (x2) R1

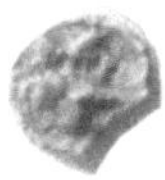

R3 1569 (x2)

Plate 25

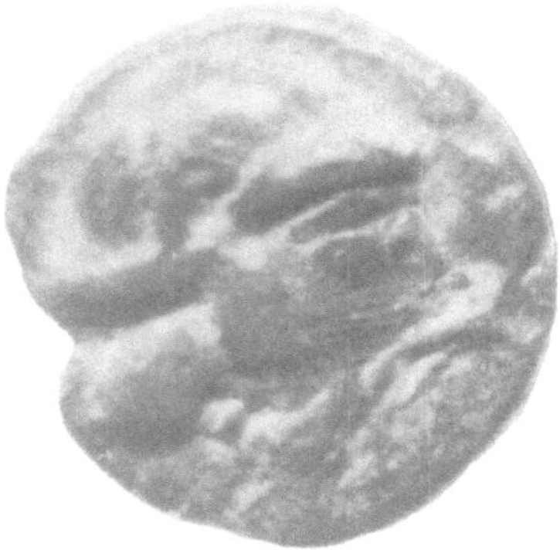

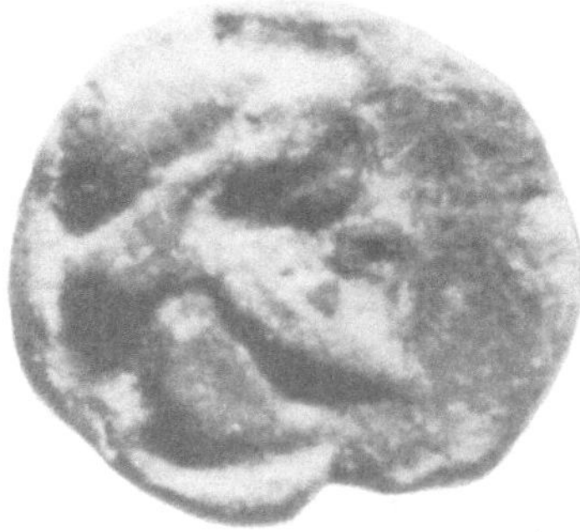

R2

O2

1567 (x12)

Counterfeit or Dubious Coins

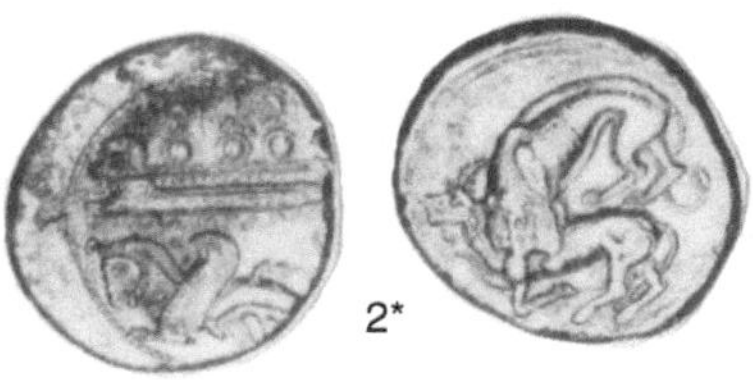

2*

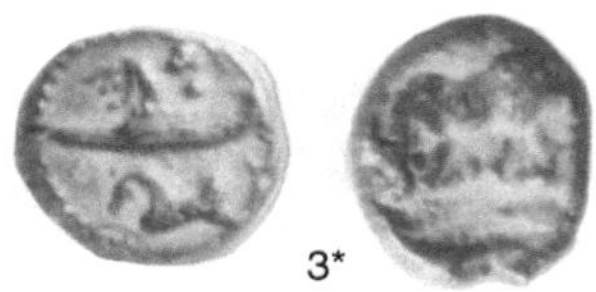

3*

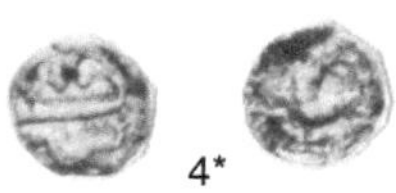

4*

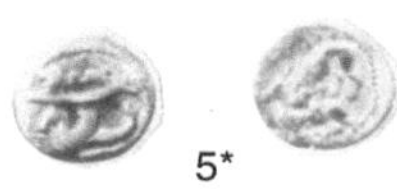

5*

www.ingramcontent.com/pod-product-compliance
Lightning Source LLC
LaVergne TN
LVHW101455200926
848483LV00001B/137

* 9 7 8 1 5 7 5 0 6 3 0 4 1 *